Literary Non

D0462067

Literary
Nonfiction

Learning by Example

Edited by
PATSY SIMS

New York ⁓ Oxford
OXFORD UNIVERSITY PRESS
2002

Oxford University Press

Oxford   New York
Athens   Auckland   Bangkok   Bogotá   Buenos Aires   Cape Town
Chennai   Dar es Salaam   Delhi   Florence   Hong Kong   Istanbul   Karachi
Kolkata   Kuala Lumpur   Madrid   Melbourne   Mexico City   Mumbai   Nairobi
Paris   São Paulo   Shanghai   Singapore   Taipei   Tokyo   Toronto   Warsaw

and associated companies in
Berlin   Ibadan

Published by Oxford University Press, Inc.
198 Madison Avenue, New York, New York, 10016
http://www.oup-usa.org

Oxford is a registered trademark of Oxford University Press

Library of Congress Cataloging-in-Publication Data

Literary nonfiction : learning by example / edited by Patsy Sims.
      p. cm.
   Includes index.
   ISBN-13 978-0-19-513844-3

    1. College readers. 2. Prose literature. 3. English language—Rhetoric—Problems,
exercises, etc. 4. Report writing—Problems, exercises, etc. I. Sims, Patsy.

PE1417 .L625 2001
808'.0427—dc21   2001018506

For Robert Cashdollar

Contents

Introduction
Learning by Example

*A*s a developing young writer, Joan Didion looked to Ernest Hemingway, Joseph Conrad, and Henry James as models. From Hemingway and Conrad, she learned about sentences—how short sentences worked in a paragraph, the effect of longer ones, where the commas went, how every word had to matter. From James, she learned about keeping your options open.

"It made me excited about words," she once told an interviewer. "The sentences sounded wonderful. I remember being so excited once, when I discovered that the key lines in *Heart of Darkness* were in parentheses. James, whom I didn't read until I was in college, was important to me in trying to come to terms with the impossibility of getting it right. James's sentences, with all those clauses, had to do with keeping the options open, letting the sentence cover as much as it could. That impressed me a great deal."

For Susan Sheehan, it was *New Yorker* writers E. B. White and Joseph Mitchell whose works she turned to as she was starting out. "White's *Here Is New York* is still, to me, the best book ever written about the city," she says. "It's hard to forget lines like 'I heard the Queen Mary blow one midnight . . . and the sound carried the whole history of departure and longing and loss.' The Queen Mary is no longer (well, maybe it's parked in the waters off Long Beach, California), but the prose endures. Probably because I'm a writer my favorite lines by E. B. White are the closing lines of *Charlotte's Web*. 'It is not often that someone comes along who is a true friend and a good writer. Charlotte was both.' I try to be a true friend and a good writer."

Even now, before writing a long article or beginning a book, Sheehan takes down her paperback copy of *McSorley's Wonderful Saloon*. "Mitchell made so many of us realize that simplicity was a virtue, not a crime," she says. "I turn to 'Mazie' and reread the opening sentence: 'A bossy, yellow-haired blonde named Mazie P. Gordon is a celebrity on the Bowery.' That and other opening lines of Joe's made it possible for me to begin *A Welfare Mother* with the simple line 'Carmen Santana is a welfare mother.'"

If you ask most writers how they learned to write, as I have the ones who appear in this anthology, they will tell you it was by reading the works of men and women who were doing the kind of writing they wanted to do and by trying to figure out how they did it. Today, even as *their* own work is being studied by younger writers who hope to emulate them, they often return to the models who first inspired them, as Sheehan does to Mitchell and White. If you were to enter their studies, you would see copies of the books they repeatedly look to for inspiration and for help in solving an occasional technical problem or achieving a particular mood.

For some, the list is long and varied and has changed over time. Names like James Agee, Truman Capote, Ernest Hemingway, A. J. Liebling, John McPhee, Mark Twain, and Tom Wolfe occur again and again—especially Wolfe. Mike Sager calls Wolfe's *The New Journalism* "a literal epiphany" that changed his life. For Tim Cahill, it was Wolfe's *The Kandy-Kolored Tangerine-Flake Streamline Baby* that showed him you could write journalism in a stylish and insightful manner. About the same time, he also came across Edward Abbey's *Desert Solitaire,* particularly the short story "The Dead Man at Grandview Point." From there, the list of writers who influenced him grows.

"I don't underline, though I find myself memorizing great lines and analyzing techniques," he says. "I find it difficult to read an author I admire, then write the next morning without, inadvertently, sounding like that writer."

While Tracy Kidder doesn't recall ever turning to stories or books to learn particular techniques and, in fact, thinks such a practice is a bad idea, he firmly believes in the importance of reading.

"Technique, I think, is something one absorbs from other writers, reinventing along the way," he says. "I do believe in reading for that purpose and also for inspiration. There are various authors who have made me want to try my own hand. The lists have changed over the years. Hemingway and Fitzgerald when I was in school; Conrad in my early twenties; Orwell (his nonfiction) and A. J. Liebling and Tom Wolfe (some of his nonfiction) and John McPhee and Norman Mailer when I first discovered nonfiction narrative. Right now I'm reading and rereading Graham Greene, my current favorite writer. A few years ago it was Nabokov and the great Italian poet Eugenio Montale. Reading is a part of writing and vice versa. I choose to think that there's mystery involved in both."

As Kidder has observed, reading is an integral, and I would say critical, part of writing. In fact, I would venture to say that you are only as good a writer as you are a good reader. Trying to write without reading is like attempting to play an instrument without ever listening to music or resorting to a Betty Crocker yellow cake mix when there are thousands of possibilities for baking a cake.

I am not talking here about reading for entertainment, the way you approach, say, a murder mystery or a romance novel. I mean the kind of close reading that was required to annotate the fifteen stories that appear in this book. I mean analytically studying the work of a writer you admire, taking it apart like a clock and examining the parts to see what makes it work. We can all appreciate a good piece of writing, but we don't always understand *why* it is good until we examine it more closely.

It is looking at Susan Sheehan's lead for "Ain't No Middle Class" and discovering the power in its simplicity. It is examining Jane Kramer's use of voice and details like the purple satin canopy and the titanium hip pin to bring the eccentric vintner Armande to life. It is getting a feel for the way Mike Sager uses long sentences to recreate a morning's tranquility, and David Finkel's short ones heighten drama. It is trying to figure out the reason for Madeleine Blais's sustained shrine metaphor, and how, in "True Detective," Walt Harrington knew how many times the detective knocked and how long he waited before knocking again, how he knew that the stream of blood at a crime scene was running in a southwesterly direction. It is paying attention to Jon Franklin's use of pacing devices, Joan Didion's accumulation of status details, James Conaway's poetically turned phrases, and Tim Cahill's colorful scenes that cause the more run-of-the-mill travel writers' sunsets to pale.

So where to start? First, assemble a list of your own, and I can think of no better place to start than the writers who appear in this anthology. Together they have published scores of articles and books that you can turn to when you have finished here. Turn also to the writers who inspired them, and to some of the other fine writers I was unable to include, writers like Truman Capote, Ted Conover, Tom French, John Hersey, Mark Kramer, Susan Orlean, David Quammen, Richard Rhodes, Mark Singer, Brent Staples, Gay Talese, Alec Wilkinson.

Strive for a list that will educate, not just entertain (though a good writer will certainly do both). In creating that list, choose widely. Include both the classics and the best of what is being published today, and don't limit yourself only to nonfiction—the writers in this collection haven't. The list of writers who have influenced Jon Franklin, for example, runs the gamut, from Russian short story writer Anton Chekhov to Tom Wolfe; to poets Edgar Allan Poe, A. E. Housman, and Robert Frost; even to William Shakespeare and the French playwright Moliere.

At the end of most selections in this anthology you will find the writer's comments about the works that influenced him or her. From those, you should find more than enough reading to last you for a long time to come. If you can afford to, I would suggest you buy your own copies because surely many will become old friends that you will return to again and again as you develop as a writer.

If you are in the habit of reading at bedtime to ease yourself to sleep, that is not the time for the kind of reading I am suggesting. To learn from other writers, you need to be alert. Turn off the television and, I'd say, even the radio. Focus solely on the pages before you.

Read with a pencil or pen at hand, highlighting those paragraphs and passages you want to return to for closer scrutiny. Some people, including some of the writers included here, may consider it heresy to take a pen to a good book, but my own feeling is that you will read more closely if you are engaged. (Some of the writers who don't share my penchant for underlining have their own approach. For example, when Sheehan was younger and had more time, she transcribed favorite lines into a chapbook, a practice she regrets having less time to do now.)

Read first for the overall structure and tone and mood. Then go back and study the piece more closely, concentrating on the paragraphs and passages you highlighted (the "keepers," the ones you may find yourself returning to twenty years from now), the sentences you want to take apart to see what makes them work. Mark the transitions (especially unusually smooth ones, like John McPhee's use of a crane operator to move us in and out of a long digression on stream channelization), vivid word choices (like Michael Paterniti's "caroom," "peckled," and "blowsy"), metaphors that are both fresh and appropriate to the subject matter (like Tom Hallman's comparison of lost memory to a computer that needs rebooting).

Keep a dictionary and thesaurus at hand, and use them. Look up words that are unfamiliar (like Wolfe's "peckerwood" or "antediluvian") and work at refining your own vocabulary, at learning the subtle differences between words like "say," "mutter," "mumble," "utter."

To truly get a feel for how a sentence or a paragraph or a passage is put together, sit down at your computer or take a legal pad in hand and copy that sentence or paragraph or passage. Sometimes this act of actually typing an example of fine writing can help you understand what makes it work more clearly than merely reading it. To do so is not to mimic them, but rather it can give you a sense of how, in a good paragraph or passage, everything has its function, its place, its order. It will show you possibilities.

In this anthology, I have tried to give you a head start by pointing out the various techniques that make these fifteen stories good. Once you have finished them try your own hand at annotating stories, perhaps other works by the writers included here, or even other anthologies, to get a feel for what I mean. You may not always annotate so fully, but by doing so a few times you will cultivate the habit of slowing down and reading more closely and analytically.

When you embark on a new article of your own, go back and find a work that helps put you in the right frame of mind, and when you find yourself faced with a particular puzzle, look for another writer who has successfully solved that puzzle and see how he or she did it. As I was writing a book about Louisiana sugarcane workers, I often returned to favorite passages of James Agee's *Let Us Now Praise Famous Men* to see how he captured the poetry of the tenant farm families' everyday lives. When it came time to re-create a trial, I looked to, among others, the one in Truman Capote's *In Cold Blood*. You don't necessarily need to limit yourself to literary nonfiction. Before Walt Harrington began his research for "True Detective," he read a half-dozen detective novels to see what gave them their gritty, tactile texture. The answer, he found, was in the extraordinary amount of detail, and so the already meticulous reporter doubled his efforts as he followed detective V.I. Smith to Washington, D.C., crime scenes.

Once you begin reading in this careful manner, you will wonder how you ever breezed through Wolfe's *The Right Stuff* without noticing the way he uses the unflappable voice of airline pilots to draw us into the story of Chuck Yeager, or Capote's *In Cold Blood* without realizing he shifts to the present tense when he finally discloses how the murders occurred. And, yes, once you begin reading so attentively, I think you will see your own writing gaining strength. Then some day down the line, a young aspiring writer will be turning to your work for guidance and inspiration, to learn by example.

Madeleine Blais

When Madeleine Blais set out to profile homeless activist Carol Fennelly, she wanted to avoid the all too familiar interview in which the reformer is intent on offering up the same well-rehearsed lines she's delivered at countless press conferences and demonstrations. But how to do it? Fennelly is an articulate, talkative woman who was used to talking to the press, but after several interview sessions Blais found herself with the usual platitudes and propaganda. Then the two women visited Fennelly's room at a Washington, D.C., shelter, and Blais knew immediately she had what she needed to give her profile the kind of texture and heft she was aiming for.

"What captivated me," she says, "was how fiercely personal and even materialistic (though not in a bad sense) her room was, as compared to the overall facility, which had the bureaucratic sheen of impersonality. Here was an oasis that was totally alive and passionate. I like to orient the reader to place, to latitude and longitude, and this room more than amply helped me in that regard. Further, it occurred to me that each object was lovingly displayed and there must be a story behind it all. And there was. Suddenly in talking about these things that meant so much to her, this zealot, who had abdicated wealth but not hominess, came alive. Of course some of her treasured objects might give the rest of us pause—the guys in the urn, the killer gallstone, the mash note from Mitch with its peculiarly crusading overtones. Profiles really are portraits in words: to say that is to speak the obvious, but as writers we forget that sometimes. She was willing to sit for a picture. It was up to me to find the right lighting, the right pose, the right frame."

When it came time to write, Blais used the room and its furnishings to structure the profile—an approach that was both fresh and fitting for a story about a woman whose life evolved around shelters and the homeless. The strategy was similar to the way she used the contents of a "care" barrel destined for Jamaica in an earlier profile she wrote while working on the staff of the Miami Herald's Tropic Magazine.

"Abstractions are meaningless unless they are embedded in reality," she says. "This observation is, to my way of thinking, the basic building block of good writing. There are others, such as 'cut to the energy,' 'juxto is all' and, the old Hollywood screenwriting credo, 'get in every scene as late as possible, and out as early as possible.' What is most striking about high-quality literary journalism is that it obeys, embodies and encapsulates the rules that govern all great writing, no matter what the genre, and that is what distinguishes it, when it is distinguished, from run of the mill journalism."

Blais has been described as a writer of infinite range, who can be poignant, whimsical, and tough. While she most often writes about ordinary people, her treatment of the famous has been marked by equal sensitivity. She was awarded a Pulitzer Prize in feature writing while on staff at the Herald. Her work has appeared in numerous publications, including the Boston Globe, the Washington Post, the New York Times Magazine, and Newsday. She is the author of The Heart Is an Instrument: Portraits in

Journalism *and* In These Girls, Hope Is a Muscle, *which was a finalist for the 1995 National Book Critics Circle nonfiction book award. Her newest book,* Uphill Walkers: Memoir of a Family, *was published last spring by Grove/Atlantic. She is a professor of journalism at the University of Massachusetts.*

A Room of Her Own[*][1]

AT FIRST IT WAS IMPOSSIBLE TO sleep; every time she closed her eyes she saw his face. So sometimes late at night Carol Fennelly would put on the nightgown her dead lover had given her as an engagement present.[1] It is pastel and long and silky, not secondhand like most of her clothes, but purchased brand-new from a real store, Victoria's Secret.[2] Then she would light one of the candles next to her bed,[3] illuminating a room unlike any other at the shelter for the homeless where she lives.[4] It is a small space (she estimates the dimensions as 12 by 10 by 18), and while the walls are typical government issue, bland and civic and institutional, almost zealously nondescript,[5] she has domesticated them with a vengeance, turning them into a beckoning tumble of color and icons and artifacts.[6] In her pink slippers she would move about in a soft glide,[7] almost ghostly, and she would light another candle and another and another.[8] Their glow would join the flickers from a comic bulbish appliance called a plasma ball that she sometimes leaves on all night. It belonged to her companion of 13 years, and it produces jets of color, reckless ricochets of pink and purple. She would put on music, especially a tape of love songs he had put together for her.[9] The peace of this moment would be a consoling contrast to the tumult of his final days: the fights, the screams and the harangues, the slamming of doors, the threats to throw her furniture out the window, the calling of terrible names:[10]

"A Room of Her Own" first appeared in the *Washington Post Magazine* in 1991. Reprinted by permission of the author.

* The title comes from the Virginia Woolf essay.

1. The opening scene of Fennelly attempting to conjure up her dead lover (Mitch Snyder) both sets the scene and draws readers into the story. The pull begins with the first sentence: Why was it difficult to sleep? Who is this woman and the man whose face she sees? The next sentence continues to strengthen Blais's hold on us with the introduction of the nightgown and the fact it was a gift from the dead lover. The impact of that sentence has as much to do with structure as it does content. It begins softly with an introductory phrase, then builds, placing the fact that the gown was an engagement present at the end of the sentence, where it gains added emphasis and lingers in the reader's mind.

2. The description of the gown conveys the sense of it being both feminine and pretty, without being specific. The latter effect is achieved through the use of soft-sounding words and of "and" rather than commas in constructing the list. Commas would cause readers to pause; "and" lets the words fall in a gentle cascade. The fact that the gown is not secondhand conveys information about Fennelly's lifestyle. Note how Blais again withholds the most important detail ("Victoria's Secret") until the end of the sentence.

3. The lighting of the candle begins the metaphor of the room as a shrine.

4. This establishes where Fennelly lives and places the reader.

5. The spare description of the room provides an empty stage on which Fennelly's story will unfold. Blais's choice of words and the specific dimensions give readers a picture of the room. For most of us, "typical government issue" conjures up a definite image that is reinforced by the phrase "bland and civic and institutional." The use of "and" rather than commas creates a cumulative effect that underscores the bureaucratic blandness.

6. The description conveys the feeling of a warm, inviting room. "Icons and artifacts" continues the metaphor of the room as shrine. The tumble of colors is replicated in a cascade of words combined with "and."

7. "Pink" reveals a femininity we might not expect of an activist. "Glides" lets us "see" her movements.

8. The lighting of candles further develops the shrine metaphor. It also carries connotations of a séance.

9. In the course of this paragraph, notice how much we learn about Fennelly and Snyder through the accumulation of facts and details. The Victoria's Secret nightgown and the tape of love songs show us a side of the somewhat brash Snyder the public never knew.

10. The list is an economical way to sum up the storminess of the couple's final days.

Lady in red
Is dancing with me
Cheek to cheek
Nobody here
Just you and me
It's where I want to be.[11]

And so while the music played and the shadows throughout the room pulsated and contorted, she would try to get Mitch Snyder to pay a visit.[12]

But of course he never did.

* * *

She hesitates to call this room at the Community for Creative Non-Violence a shrine[13] and prefers to think of it instead as a refuge, a place for restoration after her long public days as a spokesperson-by-default at the shelter,[14] where all the unpaid workers are equal but some are more prominent in their equalness.[15] The days begin at 5 in the morning, grueling whirlwinds of glad-handing and politicking and working the phones for favors in a kind of upper-class panhandling (her goal is not spare change so much as free rides on jets for visiting celebrities who will create goodwill for the shelter at media events) and cajoling her contacts at assignment desks throughout the city[16] ("How about a cold weather story? We have 50 volunteer nurses in our health clinic right now giving free flu shots to our residents!") and smiling a lot, smiling all the time, telling everyone yes, yes; she's fine, just fine.[17]

He killed himself in the room next door. The last time anyone spoke to him was at about 5 in the afternoon on Tuesday, July 3. After that he stopped answering his pages, and he was discovered, with his cat, by a fellow worker at the community on Thursday, July 5.[18] He left a note addressed to Carol: "I loved you an awful lot. All I ever wanted was for you to love me more than anyone else in the world. Sorry for all the pain I caused you in the last 13 years."[19] He also mentioned where he had hidden $8,000 in cash that belonged to the shelter. It fell to his unofficial widow[20] to make the public announcement. Those who saw her that day say that she looked ravaged. Normally a pretty woman who is all circles and softness, with curly brown hair and two somewhat protuberant front teeth that make her look younger, more eager than her 41 years, she stood puffy-faced and dark-eyed outside that now-famous building

---

11. The lyrics show Snyder's more romantic side.

12. A return to the notion of a séance, and Fennelly's attempt to conjure up her dead lover.

13. "Hesitates" implies that for Fennelly the room is indeed a shrine to Snyder and their life together.

14. A concise description of her role at the shelter.

15. A diplomatic way to describe the celebrity status Fennelly and Snyder achieved.

16. Word choices ("glad-handing," "politicking," "upper-class panhandling") capture the tenor of their work with the homeless, without the writer becoming heavy-handed.

17. Writer uses brief, direct quotes to let readers "hear" Fennelly coaxing the press. Throughout the story, however, direct quotes are used sparingly, and yet readers get the sense they are hearing her voice via indirect quotes such as "telling everyone yes, yes; she's fine, just fine."

18. Details of Snyder's death, gleaned from interviews and newspaper clippings. The cat is a "telling" detail that helps further characterize Snyder.

19. The suicide note provides insight into Snyder and the couple's relationship. It also illustrates the range of materials Blais drew on to profile Fennelly.

20. "Unofficial widow" conveys the closeness of the couple's relationship.

at Second and D NW and spoke very quietly.[21] The words she used were simple, spare, plain and true. In her distinctive speaking voice—it is both soft and forceful—she told the crowd of about 50 reporters and photographers that Mitch Snyder, famous activist, government gadfly, street angel,[22] always said good things happened when it rained.

"Well, today," she said, "he was wrong."[23]

* * *

Before he died she had sequestered herself with friends "to get some space, I never wanted to leave the center; it was for personal survival that I did." A week later she moved back in.[24]

The day was thick with heat, humid and motionless, but at the shelter the air conditioning mercifully was on.[25] She could not imagine sleeping ever again in the room they had shared, so she turned it into the archives, the official repository of the boxes and papers and important records of the community, including what Carol Fennelly likes to call "the guys." "The guys," she says, "are actually a coed crowd," consisting of the ashes of 30 men and women who froze to death in the District and who, Mitch vowed, would never again be homeless. Often it was she or Mitch who was called by the morgue to come and claim them.[26]

Slowly, she lugged their bed and their dining room table and their dressers into an adjoining room, and, standing amid the cartons and the dust, she felt invigorated by the disarray.[27] Grief transformed itself into activity. Her plan was simple. She would set about making sense of her life by making sense of her things.[28] She put the big tapestry on the wall above her bed; it is filled with blues and magentas, and the pattern consists of two mandalas, the wheel of life. She bought it on layaway 21 years ago when she was unwed and pregnant and living under her parents' roof in her home state of California; it was a symbol of her hope that someday she would have her own place.[29] On the bed near the pillows she placed the collection of about a dozen teddy bears she had given to Mitch over the years.[30]

---

21. Blais has chosen those features and details that quickly convey Fennelly's personality and what she looks like in much the way a caricature artist zeroes in on the features that make an individual immediately recognizable. "All circles and softness" implies both that she is feminine and, diplomatically, overweight. The author's characterization of the death announcement is equally vivid yet brief, so that it doesn't interrupt the narrative.

22. The description of Snyder has the ring both of an obituary and the public's view of him.

23. The quote shows a somewhat macabre sense of humor on Fennelly's part. It also provides a dramatic note on which to end the section.

24. Transition into digression, moving us from Snyder's death to Fennelly's return to the shelter.

25. Blais captures the feel of the July day and thus brings the readers into the scene.

26. The quote about "the guys" reflects Fennelly's offbeat sense of humor. The ashes and trips to the morgue provide background into her and Snyder's work with the homeless.

27. The sentence structure here replicates Fennelly's actions. The verb "lugged" and the list of furniture linked by "and" convey both Fennelly's physical effort and her compulsion to keep going until every piece had been moved. With that accomplished, Fennelly stands among the cartons and dust and takes stock. Suddenly, she and her grief are transformed into action.

28. A statement of the article's focus: The profile will use the room's furnishings to reconstruct Fennelly's life. The focus also provides a structure for the story. Blais, too, will make sense of Fennelly's life by making sense of her belongings. She sets out to describe each item and to give its history.

29. Blais uses the tapestry to fill in some of Fennelly's past. The word "layaway" provides information about her financial status, as does the fact she is living at home with her parents.

30. The teddy bears show both a gentler side to Snyder and, since they were gifts from Fennelly, the warm, playful nature of their relationship.

In the days and weeks and months that followed[31] she concentrated on making her room as cheerful and as aesthetically pleasing as possible.

In the room's single window[32] she arranged her greenery, mostly tough, can't-lose plants such as ivy and philodendron, cousins to the weed in their tenacity.[33] All her photos she put up on the wall opposite her bed above the old wobbly desk; pictures that provide an instant history of her life. There's a picture of her dressed as a clown back when she was into amateur clowning as one of the ways to attract crowds at CCNV events; she had made the headdress herself by gluing red fringe to some pantyhose. There are several pictures of Mitch, one with his friend Cher, who is part of a group of celebrities who have supported the shelter, most of them inspired by the made-for-TV movie called "Samaritan" in which Martin Sheen played Mitch. A photo of Mitch and an elderly woman everyone called Granny shows him leaning over with his head touching hers so that their joint silhouette is that of a heart.[34] It is the image being used on a new line of T-shirts being sold to raise money for the shelter. By the last year of his life, Mitch's lectures all over the country were raising about $100,000 a year.[35]

She devoted two bookshelves to books, many of them inspirational in nature, such as *Mahatma Gandhi and His Apostles, The Wycliffe Bible Commentary* and *The Autobiography of St. Therese of Lisieux.* She likes to cook and there are several recipe books, including what counts as her one indisputably yuppie possession, *The Silver Palate Cookbook.*[36]

She decided to use a third shelf for her dishes—plates and bowls and pots and pottery she had accumulated over the years, some of it broken, all of it treasured.[37]

Throughout[38] she placed her several potpourris, a category of gift she receives with enough frequency to prompt her to think there's some kind of etiquette book that recommends these tasteful little baskets filled with scented petals as perfect for the lady activist.[39]

On top of her bureau[40] she placed a glass jar containing the gallstone that killed her friend Big John: a small brown thing like a marble that never should have had that much power. It was given to her by Mitch; she doesn't quite count it as a present.[41] She also placed there an old juice bottle that she and Mitch had filled with

---

31. Transition shows passage of time, or what is sometimes referred to as "compressed time." In one sentence we get a sense of what Fennelly did over the course of months.

32. Place transition. Note throughout the story how Blais uses introductory prepositional phrases to situate the items before she elaborates on them. These help orient readers so they can move about the room with her.

33. The tough, "can't-lose" plants reflect Fennelly's own tenacity.

34. Blais uses the photographs to piece together the couple's history. Note that she does not describe *every* photo, but rather selects those that enable her to tell the couple's story. The clown photo shows a playful, yet practical, make-do side (the use of pantyhose for a headband) of Fennelly. The picture of Mitch and Cher provides an opportunity to talk about the movie of Snyder's life and the celebrities the two collected. The one of him and Granny posed like a Valentine hints at a schmaltzy side.

35. Information on the couple's fundraising.

36. Books reflect Fennelly's personality and interests. The Gandhi book is in keeping with her belief in nonviolent protests; the Bible commentary and St. Therese autobiography reveal a religious side that will be further developed. The cookbooks reveal a more traditional, domestic side.

37. The broken dishes "show" a sentimental streak.

38. Place transition.

39. "The lady activist" sounds like the words of Fennelly's more loyal admirers rather than Blais and conveys their view of her as feminine. The gifts of potpourri support that view.

40. Place transition.

41. "Like a marble" helps reader see what the gallstone looks like.

water from the Sacramento River in California. They wanted to have a baby together, and the water was for its baptismal ceremony.[42]

"Sacramento," she says softly, "means blessed."

Mitch had two children from a previous marriage, whom he abandoned when they were very young.[43] Now they are in their twenties; the last Carol heard,[44] Rick was looking for work as an accountant and Dean was in the military. "It was a painful subject for him," she says. His absences as a father echoed the absence of his own father during childhood. He did not send his former wife any support money. "No one at the shelter has private money," says Carol. "He had none to send." He used to believe children should be little radicals, and tried to get Carol to feed hers on the soup line.[45] As time went on, his ideas about how to rear children became more tolerant.

On the wall[46] she hung up her artwork, message-laden reminders of the existence of ghettos and of pain, of moons and Madonnas.[47]

She put up the crucifix that was made by a homeless man while he was in detox.

She put up the crucifix that was made by her son, Shamus, when he was 7.

She hung two small rosaries that were left by anonymous mourners on Mitch's coffin during the service. Next to her bed is a wooden rosary from Italy, about five feet long. It is near an icon of a birthing scene that she bought during a trip to the Soviet Union last spring.[48]

In one corner[49] she placed a life-size papier-maché statue of a homeless woman dressed in rags, donated to the community by an art student. Carol calls the statue Frances, after a homeless woman whom she once knew and who was very dear and who has since disappeared.

By the side of her bed[50] she placed a box left on Mitch's coffin by a Vietnam veteran. It contains the vet's Bronze Star[51] and a typewritten note.[52] By the side of her bed she also keeps one of her favorite books, a collection of poetry that includes the poem by Edna St. Vincent Millay that she read at his funeral:[53]

My candle burns at both ends;
It will not last the night;
But, ah, my foes, and, oh, my friends—
It gives a lovely light.

Pinned to a board above her desk[54] like an old corsage is a nostalgic cluster of plastic identification bands from the times their political actions led them to the hos-

---

42. The baptismal water and their plans to have a child reveal both a more traditional and religious side to the couple. The detail of "the old juice bottle" creates a visual image.

43. The fact that Snyder abandoned his own children when they were *very* young implies that he was selfish, without the writer having to say so directly.

44. Implies an estrangement from Snyder's children.

45. Supports the view that for Snyder activism came before family.

46. Place transition.

47. Note again the sentence structure, how it starts slowly and builds to the more important point. Note, too, the juxtaposition of the more earthly ghettos and pain and the more ethereal moons and Madonnas. The alliteration gives a somewhat whimsical feel to the latter.

48. The crucifixes and rosaries are used to reveal Fennelly's past and her preoccupation with religion.

49. Place transition.

50. Place transition.

51. Bronze Star demonstrates the esteem for Snyder.

52. Note how Blais withholds the contents of the note for use later, where it will carry more weight.

53. The book of poetry and the reading of the St. Vincent Millay poem reveal a sensitive side to Fennelly.

54. Place transition.

pital or jail.[55] On her desk is a wedding album that will remain empty. There is also the bill from the funeral home that charged $275 for the oak urn with a cross that contains his ashes.[56]

Carol Fennelly believes in the corporal works of mercy, in feeding the hungry, clothing the naked. She also believes in the mortification of the flesh[57] and at times gives up food and drink, except for sips of water. She converted to Catholicism a few years back, and in her room next to her bed there is even a kneeler, a dark imposing railing where she sometimes bows her head and prays for inner peace.

But she is not a nun.[58]

In the closet[59] she hung her pretty clothes, almost all secondhand, the swankiest from her friend Suzie Goldman.[60] Mitch disapproved of abundance; he always wore the same jeans and the same boots and the same army jacket to the point that when it began to disintegrate she would steal it in his sleep and replace it with another for him to also wear into oblivion. "Excess is theft," he always used to say, but she could never quite match the depth of his material abnegation. He was a true ascetic; he felt rich in proportion to what he could do without: "You only need one pair of shoes."[61]

Her attitude has always been that there is no reason to add to the drabness of an already too drab world. Carol Fennelly even has a jewelry box, though it does not contain precious gems so much as fanciful engaging baubles. She has her hair done in a stylish bob about once a month at the upscale Okyo salon by Bernard Portelli, a fan of the shelter who donates his services to her. She likes pretty things, and one of the most common adjectives used by friends to describe her is feminine.[62]

Maneuvering in the small space, flushed with exertion, relieved to be so busy, gladly auditioning the placement of the large dining table that she likes to point out is solid oak,[63] and the TV, and the trunk she inherited from her grandmother, placing on the high bureau some old political pins that Mitch had kept as well as a little tray with his toiletries,[64] she kept reciting like a mantra her favorite saying.[65] "I think

---

55. Simile ("like an old corsage") implies that the two viewed their activism with a kind of sentimentality, not unlike the way high school students look back on proms.

56. The $275 bill for the urn speaks volumes about a woman who wears secondhand clothes and, for the most part, has spurned material possessions to live in a homeless shelter. It reflects her love for Snyder and, to some extent, her preoccupation with appearances.

57. The rhythm and content of these first two sentences echo the Apostles' Creed, conveying a sense that, for Fennelly, her work with the homeless has become almost a religious mission. It also reflects her fervor for Catholicism. The kneeler and the image of her praying suggest a nun.

58. This sentence brings us abruptly back to reality: The room may be a shrine and Fennelly may be deeply religious, but she is, in the end, human.

59. Place transition.

60. "Pretty" and "swankiest" imply that while Fennelly may wear jeans in the trenches, she likes nice clothes, even if they are secondhand. Suzie Goldman is a sometime benefactor of the shelter.

61. In contrast, Blais shows us by example that Snyder shunned material possession. The repetition of "same" reinforces that point.

62. The "baubles" and "stylish bob" reinforce Fennelly's love of "pretty things." It is a more feminine—and materialistic—side than that which the public saw. In light of the earlier reference to her "upper-class panhandling," the suggestion here is that Fennelly may have prevailed on Portelli to volunteer his services.

63. "Likes to point out" implies boasting, a certain pride in the solid oak table—it is not cheap veneer.

64. The fact that Fennelly still keeps Snyder's political pins and his toiletries on her bureau, along with the baptismal water, reinforces the metaphor of the room as shrine and the bureau as an altar.

65. The "mantra" becomes a self-justification for her worldly possessions.

it's from Dostoevsky, who I think was a famous Russian philosopher,"[66] she says. "Anyway what he supposedly said was:

"'Beauty will save the world.'"

* * *

For a long time,[67] of course, she thought the burden of universal redemption belonged not to beauty but to her and Mitch Snyder. "We were," she says, "addicted to changing the world."[68]

They had been a movement couple[69] since the second time she saw him, leafleting at a rally on January 7, 1977. She'd been in town for four months, living at a left-wing community called Sojourners, running a free day-care center for inner-city children. By then her own children were in public school. At the time, Mitch had been with CCNV since 1973; he had heard about the community from an antiwar activist he had met in prison.[70]

She bummed a cigarette even though she did not smoke.[71] In their faded jeans and shirts embroidered with flowers, they embodied an old-fashioned '60s idealism, a power-to-the-people sense of the world that today seems quaint.[72]

"We courted," she says, "by going out to the heat grates to pick up people."[73]

Sometimes when sleep comes dropping slow, she pores through a little basket on her bureau filled with Mitch's old political pins: "John Wayne Needs Sensitivity Training . . . Dump Watt . . . Jesse . . . 300 More Today . . . Free the 99th Congress . . . Vote for 17 . . . If the People Lead Eventually the Leaders Will Follow."

Her favorite novel is in this room, James Carroll's *Mortal Friends,* which is about the fictional lives of people who are just like her and Mitch. She has only to glance at the title to feel that it is her story, their story, about not just the hardship of a life dedicated to sweeping social change, but also about the intoxication, the romance.[74] Oh,[75] how their struggles changed, from the fight against the war in Vietnam to the fight for the ERA to the more recent triumph of actually getting the government to fork over[76] a huge empty building on Second Street to shelter the homeless, but their ardor did not. Together they adored the highs and lows of a life filled with political action. She giggles sometimes, just remembering the kinds of ideas Mitch came up with. He would plan what he called happenings, or events. Her personal favorite, the one that serves as the absolute model of peaceful yet antic disruption,[77] was back in,

---

66. Dostoevsky was a Russian novelist. Note how Blais uses the quote to "show" something about Fennelly: She is not well read.

67. Time transition begins a loop, or digression, into her background.

68. "Telling" quote. "Addicted" implies that changing the world provided a "high" not unlike drugs.

69. "Movement couple" conveys an element of radical chic.

70. Background information.

71. The anecdote hints at a kind of girlish crush or flirtation.

72. The uniform of the 1960s flower children. Succinct characterization of the couple as both idealists and romantics.

73. Quote is a more interesting way of saying they worked with the homeless while dating.

74. Blais uses the book as a springboard for "showing" the romantic giddiness of Fennelly and Snyder's activism.

75. "Oh" reinforces that sense of giddiness.

76. "Fork over" sounds like Fennelly's voice. It implies the government did so only under duress.

77. "Ardor," "adored the highs and lows," and "antic disruption" suggest intoxication as much as commitment. They had fun.

when was it, '84? Yes, '84.[78] Mitch found out that a group called the American Conservative Union had baked the world's largest pie, 17 feet of crust and fruit, and as a demonstration of the "trickledown" theory it was going to give out slices: Under Republicanism, everyone can have a piece of the pie. Mitch Snyder served as chauffeur to Carol and others who dressed up as businessmen and jumped into the pie, splattering apples everywhere.[79]

"We were charged," she says, her face shining with merriment, "with unlawful trespass of a pie."[80]

"Don't you see?" she says, trying to sum up what made them different from other people.

"We always did what we dreamed."[81]

It took genius to be that daring, that nettlesome. In her eyes, Mitch was a brilliant maverick.[82]

The former Maytag appliance salesman from Brooklyn who passed bad checks and did time in the Danbury, Conn., federal prison, which is where he met the Berrigan brothers[83] and found his true path, was more than mere mortal; he was spellbinder, hero, saint.[84] She never expects to meet a man like him again. He was an original; except for the nightgown and a garish three-dimensional plaster of Paris rendition of the Last Supper that hangs on a fake gold chain next to the shelf with the dishes and, well, Big John's gallstone, he did not shower her with the gifts that might be expected from a normal suitor. His finest offering was in fact abstract, the wonderful edgy, almost contagious passion of someone who insists on leading life to a feverish hilt.[85] It is only now, looking back, that she realizes with a shiver of fear the kind of hold he had on her. It was not mere influence; it was, she says, "absolute power."[86]

* * *

They also courted by courting death.[87]

"All right now," he would sometimes say, especially right before he was about to embark on a fast that might kill him, "what do I want!"[88]

---

78. While this is not a direct quote, it sounds like Fennelly's voice. We hear her recalling their antics.

79. Anecdote illustrates the couple's "antic disruption."

80. The quote reveals something about Fennelly beyond what it actually says: It shows both her sense of humor and the enjoyment she derives from her activism.

81. Quote sums up their approach to activism. It also reinforces the notion of the couple as romantic dreamers.

82. Word choices ("daring," "nettlesome," "brilliant maverick") conjure up Fennelly's image of Snyder as a hero.

83. Philip and Daniel Berrigan, former priests-turned-antiwar protestors. They served time for destroying draft records during the Vietnam War.

84. The reference to Snyder being "more than a mere mortal" and a spellbinder, hero, and saint further characterizes Fennelly's romantic view of him and carries inferences to him being god-like.

85. A continuation of Fennelly's view of Snyder. While it is not a direct quote, it again sounds as though she, not Blais, is speaking. This notion of it being her voice begins with "She never expects to meet a man like him again," a statement we can imagine her making. The hesitation when she comes to the gallstone ("and, well, Big John's gallstone") and the word choices ("finest offering," "wonderful," "feverish hilt") again sound as if Fennelly is speaking. The gifts support her view that Snyder is unique.

86. Up to now, the tone of Fennelly's reflection has been buoyant, hero-worshipping. In the final two sentences of the paragraph, the mood darkens. Note how Blais once more withholds the most important point ("absolute power") for the end of the sentence and paragraph, the position of greatest emphasis.

87. A poetic way of saying they lived dangerously.

88. The scene of them playfully planning Snyder's funeral reveals their interests and views.

She would flash her trademark smile, a large lopsided grin,[89] and then the list of specifications would begin:

"You want gospel music.

"And the song 'Vincent.'[90]

"Dick Gregory.[91]

"Both Berrigans."

And then, in more recent years: "Martin Sheen."[92]

Always, he wanted:

"Lots of people.

"It should be outdoors in a public place.[93]

"And civil disobedience."

When she said it right his face would light up with pleasure, and it was always his face that drew her to him, that long bony mustachioed face with the big sad eyes.[94]

"When I die," he always used to tell her, "you're going to have a really interesting funeral."

It seems curious now the way he phrased it: Why you? Why not I?[95]

* * *

It was while she was with Mitch that she undertook a fast that came close to killing her.[96] Two years ago, for 48 days she subsisted on Evian water.[97] Toward the end, her blood pressure was measured at 80 over nothing. Her two children opposed what she was doing. Her son, Shamus, now 20 and a shoe salesman at Lord & Taylor,[98] asked her to please eat. Her 21-year-old daughter, Carrie Sunshine, a teacher of aerobics,[99] was puzzled because in the past all the fasts were geared toward a certain goal, like when Mitch stopped eating in order to get Reagan to hand over the old Federal City College building, which became the nation's largest shelter for the homeless ("180,000 square feet!" as Carol is fond of saying),[100] but this one seemed to be for its own consciousness-raising sake. At first their mother handled her hunger by reading cookbooks and preparing huge feasts for other people, but slowly her energy waned and by the end she did not even have the strength to stand up and weigh herself. In her room there is a photograph of her toward the end of the fast, just a head shot as she lay in her hospital bed. Her face is colorless and gaunt, all deep hollows and dulled eyes. When she is asked how she could justify a gesture of this magnitude

---

89. More physical description of Fennelly. "Trademark" suggests she smiled a lot, probably for the media.

90. A song popular in the 1970s.

91. A comedian and antiwar protestor.

92. The actor who played Snyder in the made-for-television movie.

93. The reference to a public place and lots of people implies they liked to attract attention.

94. This is the first physical description Blais has given us of Snyder, and yet through the use of scenes, quotes, and the room's furnishings we feel we have already met him.

95. Note how Blais suddenly deflates the headiness of the scene in the final sentence of this section. The questions return us to the weightier mood introduced by "absolute power." They sound like Fennelly's voice, not Blais's.

96. Fennelly's fast serves as an example of the two courting death.

97. Detail suggests a materialistic side. Why not faucet water?

98. Background on son Shamus reveals an ironic twist: the child brought up on protest lines and in homeless shelters ends up selling shoes at an upscale clothing store.

99. The daughter's name reflects the mother's flower-child days, as does her job as an aerobics teacher.

100. Quote carries connotations of thinking big, of liking to make a splash.

given the still tender years of her children,[101] her response is quick and oddly sanguine: "Oh, I always knew I would never die."[102]

He sent her a booster note:

"I still love you," he wrote, "even though you don't have potassium and electrolytes. Thanks for being you."[103]

* * *

When he died,[104] Mitch Snyder had two $2 bills tucked away in his wallet; they had become thin and melty from having been folded for so long. They sit on her desk now, next to a jar of peanut butter a stranger thrust upon her when she was out shopping recently, and she wants her children to have those bills as keepsakes and as amulets.[105] Now that he is gone they can see more clearly the role he played as their honorary stepfather.[106]

Their relationship with their father, a painting contractor who now lives in Hawaii, is spotty at best. "Let's put it this way. I call him on my birthday," says Shamus, a handsome and outgoing young man who shows his humor with a telephone tape of a flushing toilet and his recorded voice asking callers to leave a message because he is busy at the moment.

He and his sister grew up in shelters and in apartments in neighborhoods where they were often the only white people. "In one place where we lived," their mother says with a touch of something in her voice that sounds like pride,[107] "their playmates were all the children of prostitutes." Carrie Sunshine, petite and pretty with a high-pitched happy voice,[108] says they never had keys to the places where they lived because the door was always open. They do not remember much about their early years in California, where their mother says[109] she went through a super homemaker stage but that her relationship with her former husband was never great and reached its ebb at a department store when she did something that displeased him and he turned to her and said, "Why can't you just be more obedient?" Seething, she turned to him and said, "Dogs are obedient!" and promptly deposited herself on all fours and started barking and tugging on his pant cuffs with her teeth.[110] Soon after that she saw a light and heard a voice urging her to leave: "I have something special for you and your children."

Carol remembers a middle-class childhood outside Los Angeles; she has two brothers who had more trouble with her father's nasty temper than she did. In fact, she thinks her young life in a male-dominated house is curiously echoed by her life in the shelter, filled as it mostly is with men. "For a long time," she says, "my parents

---

101. The writer's voice, implying a criticism of Fennelly without directly saying it.
102. Quote carries a hint of arrogance.
103. Quote shows the quirkiness of Snyder's views toward life and love.
104. Time transition.
105. The $2 bills "show" us something about both Snyder and Fennelly. They demonstrate his lack of interest in money and materialism. The fact that Fennelly wants her children (and not his) to have them as "keepsakes and amulets" carries the religious theme, of her turning the room into a shrine to Snyder. Blais uses the bills as a transition into her children's background and their relationship with Snyder.
106. "Honorary stepfather," like "unofficial widow," conveys the closeness of their relationship.
107. "Sounds like pride" is essentially saying she was bragging.
108. "Happy voice" implies a lack of depth.
109. "Says" implies the author doubts the veracity of the statement.
110. Anecdote shows the same headstrong streak that caused Fennelly to jump into a 17-foot pie.

kept hoping I'd be normal." They blame her crusading nature on a car accident she had when she was 17; she hurt her head and has never been, in their view, the same since. Carol's children find her to be so different from her parents that they often ask her, "Are you sure you weren't adopted?"[111]

When the children get to talking about Mitch, their reminiscences trip over each other and they both try to convey at once the precise experience of hearing this musically impaired man sing. He not only had no idea how to carry a tune, but he could never remember any words anyway, so his impromptu concerts consisted mostly of crooning, loudly, with a kind of dumb happiness, *da da da da* over and over.[112] He also had a habit of making the same awful jokes again and again, and when they heard one for the millionth time, they would groan, "Oh, God," and he would take that as his golden opportunity to raise his hands in mock protest: "Please, please, that's too formal. Just call me Mitch." He also had the world's worst eating habits; when he wasn't starving himself to death he would prepare huge, utterly unappetizing basins of things like Rice-A-Roni or five pounds of steamed clams and then he would wonder why no one wanted to join him at the table. His jeans were sometimes so tight he could barely walk in them, but Carrie's warning that he was probably ruining his sperm made no difference.[113] He used to say that he wasn't really a person; he was really just a cat.[114]

* * *

The final months[115] mirrored, almost mockingly, Mitch's and Carol's lives as activists: They were filled with highs and lows, tortured partings and ecstatic reunions.

In the end his transformation was a swift downward plunge from being someone tormented beyond endurance by the cruelties of the world to someone who is in turn a cruel tormentor. In January 1990 they were going to get married, then they weren't. In April Carol went to the Soviet Union to look at alcohol treatment centers and while traveling had an epiphany not unlike the one that sent her to Washington in the first place:[116] They were meant to be together as inevitably as stars and sky, dust and desert. She had a vision of them as a couple on a grand, almost historic mission: They must marry, they should even have a baby. She bought the icon of the birthing scene. And she went wild buying Russian linens, beautiful fabric that she brought back as a kind of dowry, cloth that was fresh and unsullied for both of them to admire. Samples are now draped around her room.[117]

They even set a date: September 9. He would wear his army jacket, naturally, but

---

111. Background summary used to show that she has always been headstrong and different.

112. Singing anecdote shows us a humorous, offbeat side to Snyder. The *da da da da* lets us vicariously hear him.

113. The "God" scene both shows his corny humor and the warm rapport between him and Fennelly's children. The latter is reinforced by the ease with which Carrie could tease him about ruining his sperm.

114. The cat reference recalls his suicide, committed in the presence of his cat. The statement gains more attention at the end of the paragraph.

115. Transition. The story is moving toward an ending.

116. "Sent" is the writer's voice. It seems to question the real source of both "epiphanies."

117. Sentence captures Fennelly once more getting caught up in a grand, romantic vision of her and Snyder. "They were meant" implies that she views their union as God's plan. The paired alliterations ("stars and sky, dust and desert") reinforce this romantic vision. "Almost historic mission" is again Fennelly's voice, not Blais's. The linens are another example of her love for "pretty" things.

she would go for broke and dress in white. The ceremony would be held outdoors, in public, and they would invite thousands of witnesses.[118]

But by late spring his agony made him impossible to be around. For a while Carol moved down to the first floor near the infirmary, ostensibly to keep a closer watch on that part of the shelter's operation. She started spending more time with friends outside the shelter, including a jazz musician she remains close to today. She started to fear Mitch, and at night the worst sound she could imagine was his distinctive, heavy, heel-first footstep in the hall, coming closer and closer.[119]

By June she was staying with friends away from the shelter on a routine basis. She would not tell him where she was going and she always took care to park her car, an easy-to-recognize, well-traveled silver Honda, blocks and blocks away from wherever she was.[120] She won't talk about whether he hit her,[121] but she will say that she was terrified of sudden rages, the way his face would twist itself and become unrecognizable with anger. Their last exchange was an ugly fight in which she came back to the shelter to pick up a few of her things and he stalked her down the hall, accusing her of being with someone else,[122] showering her with epithets of which she can remember one in particular: "Trash, trash, trash," over and over.[123]

That was Monday, July 2. At that moment she had no thoughts of saving him: "All I could think about was my survival."

After that he went to his room and apparently sat by the phone, waiting for her to call. The next evening, most likely, was when he killed himself by hanging. He looped an electrical cord over a pipe along the ceiling.[124]

"He had this incredible power over me," she says. "The ability to turn my head around. You see, the same rage he directed at injustice he directed at me. His incredible manipulation of public officials was the same as his incredible manipulation of me."

When she speaks about this, her voice tends to lower and she bows her head slightly: What was once thrilling seems now almost shameful.[125]

Her eyes have a sudden shine.

"He needed to own me. I had allowed him to own me. In the end, there wasn't

---

118. Further conveys the couple's love of the spotlight. The white dress provides still more evidence of a more traditional side to Fennelly.

119. The detailed description of Snyder's footsteps lets us hear him coming closer. The repetition of "closer and closer" sounds like Fennelly speaking. It lets us vicariously share her fear. It puts us in that moment.

120. The concrete description ("easy-to-recognize, well-traveled silver Honda") re-creates the scene for us. "Blocks and blocks away" sounds like Fennelly speaking. The latter repetition underscores her fear.

121. Fennelly's lack of a denial implies, without the author saying so, that he hit her.

122. Even without giving a detailed account of the final fight, Blais draws a vivid picture of Snyder and the moment. We see his expression ("twisted," "unrecognizable with anger"). We see him "stalking her down the hall" like a wild animal going after its prey.

123. While he "showered" her with epithets, it is "trash, trash, trash" that stands out for both Fennelly and the reader. The latter is achieved through repetition both of the word and of "over and over," and its placement at the end of the paragraph.

124. Note the signals ("apparently," "most likely") that the re-creation of Snyder's final moments are speculation; no one saw him. The actual suicide is detailed and visual, placing readers in the scene. The reconstruction of the latter is possible because of the physical evidence found when his body was discovered.

125. Fennelly does not mention herself in her observation that he manipulated public officials. Nevertheless, by the author's description of her lowered voice and bowed head, she implies that Fennelly recognizes their shared guilt.

anybody else. It was that I no longer wanted to be owned. I wanted to love him and be with him.

"That wasn't enough."[126]

* * *

Now,[127] if she has her way, she will soon own him. The lawyers have said there is a good chance she can become his legal widow.[128] He had a girlfriend named Mary Ellen Hombs before he met Carol, and for years and years, even though they both worked at the shelter, Carol refused to speak to her. Why not? "She was rotten to me. She wouldn't leave me alone. She harassed me. I'm sure she'd say I harassed her. That's all I have to say on the subject. Right now, we speak through our attorneys."[129]

Mitch's 1984 will made Carol and Mary Ellen joint legal representatives of his estate. The reason she wants to become his legal spouse is a point of personal pride: "I will never love any man as much as I loved Mitch, but I don't want to be known as his longtime companion when I would have been his wife if his mental illness had not intervened. I want not just the legal but also the social standing."[130] One of her consolations on sleepless nights is to summon those times of closeness in both public and private, to close her eyes against the shifting shadows and to recall the ways in which they were spouses, the exchange of rings, the actual references to being husband and wife,[131] most frequently at hospitals when in fear and panic one of them was rushing toward the other for what might be the final time.

Mitch's ashes now occupy a small table with a candle next to her bed; soot and bone, hard and soft, like silk and pearl.[132]

But that's not really him.[133] He is elsewhere, maybe everywhere.[134] The horror of the last year has shown up in her dreams. One time she had a vision of something oozing through the vents in the ceiling, something ugly and molten and throbbing, that seemed to be evil itself, evil vents, evil events. Another time she saw while she slept a mansion next to a sunlit meadow filled with happy people. Inside she saw Mitch laid out on what looked like an operating table and a medical team working on him, but what was so odd was that they seemed to be doing some kind of heart surgery, so Carol spoke to the people in the dream: "You don't understand—he hung himself, he did not have a heart attack." And the voices in the dream answered back: "We're not healing him from what others did to him but from what he did to oth-

---

126. The background loop ends, returning readers to the earlier reference to his need for power and control, to own her.

127. Time transition returns us to the present time line.

128. Blais underscores the irony of Fennelly's efforts to be declared Snyder's "legal widow," and thus "own him," by juxtaposing this with the quote about his need to own her.

129. Quote gives us a glimpse at the in-fighting within the community of activists.

130. Quote shows an obsession with appearances.

131. "Summons" and "recall" bring us back to the opening scene, of Fennelly's attempts to conjure up Snyder. The references to an exchange of rings and the references to being husband and wife reinforce Fennelly's view of herself as Snyder's real wife, his bride.

132. Snyder's ashes and the candle re-create the image of an altar and the theme of the room as shrine. With the verb "occupy," the ashes become somewhat of a personification of Snyder.

133. Fennelly's insistence that the ashes aren't Snyder implies that he and his work live on. Note the use of the present tense, which further conveys this notion.

134. A return to her romantic viewpoint: Like the stars, he is everywhere.

ers."[135] It was a relief to dream that, to be able to wake up the next day and look at his rugged image on her walls and say, "Damn you, Mitch, for dumping all this on me!"

He was cremated with a copy of his favorite movie, "It's a Wonderful Life."[136] She thought he might want the medal left on his coffin by the nameless vet to join his ashes, but she was told that the medal would outlast the flame, and so she kept it out, and when she wants to think of all the good he did for so many, she reads the note that came with it:

"You gave shelter to those who fought when the country turned its back."[137]

No, those ashes are not him.[138] Mitch to her is enthusiasm and action and one less hungry person, one more person on a clean cot for the night. Mitch is all the money that he brought in personally to the shelter and that she must find a way to bring in now. He is the reminder that there's always more work to be done: You can never do it right, never do enough. She will carry on. The last thing she wants is for anyone to think of her as weak. Here she is, health itself, filled with potassium and electrolytes,[139] and her blood pressure is perfectly respectable. His goals are hers. She is his true bride.[140]

MADELEINE BLAIS ON READING

"I never underline or highlight anything I read because I am incapable of writing in a book. Instead I go to great lengths to use those Post-its and to make notes on them and insert them next to the passages I want to return to and remember. It doesn't matter if I have multiple copies of a text or if the book I am reading has been marked by someone else. To me it is a form of defacement.

"As for influences, there are so so many that I can't begin to do your question justice without taking up more than my share of your space. I do believe that at one point in my career I had memorized Strunk and White's *Elements of Style.*"

---

135. Dreams serve as a way of "showing" that Fennelly is still haunted by the power Snyder held over her.

136. A movie about a man who is at wit's end and almost commits suicide until an angel shows him what the world would have been like without him. It starred Jimmy Stewart.

137. Note how skillfully Blais held back the contents of the note that accompanied the Bronze Medal mentioned earlier, using it at a moment of greater impact. Had she revealed the contents earlier, they would have become lost in the body of facts and details. Coming at the end of the story, they stand out and linger in the reader's mind.

138. The repetition that the ashes are not Snyder reinforces Fennelly's view that Snyder lives on. (Note the use of the present tense.) The statement also serves as a transition into a more positive litany of who and what he was. The latter serves both to sum up his work with the homeless and her commitment to carry on in his place.

139. Echoes Snyder's own words at the time of her near-fatal fast.

140. The final statement brings the story full circle, echoing the opening scene of Fennelly in her dead lover's nightgown, the one she probably would have worn on their wedding night. With this statement you sense that she "owns" him, that she *is* his bride. The statement also carries religious overtones. The Catholic Church is often referred to as "the bride of Christ."

Tim Cahill

The role of the travel writer is to transport readers to places they have never visited. To do so, the writer must show us what is interesting and unique about the place; he must take a fresh approach and avoid what other travel writers have already said; he must draw us into the story in the way that any good nonfiction writer does. In "Taquile's True Colors," Tim Cahill succeeds at doing all this.

A New York Times *book reviewer once described Cahill as "a good companion to quip with while you explore most of the continents, taking time out, as few of us rarely do, to get good and properly lost." In this story, we meet that same good travel companion who, though he doesn't get lost, does take time to dance the cowboy lambada and seek out the island's more isolated, nontouristy reaches.*

"I went to Taquile not really knowing anything about the island, except what was in a couple of guidebooks," Cahill says. "The guidebooks mentioned two cafes in town, and that is generally where you could find conversation in English, even if the speaker was German or Japanese. I avoided these places, preferring to get a feeling for the people who lived on the island, to discover what moved them."

Cahill found a sandy beach that was a two-hour walk from the more accessible parts of the island and thus seldom frequented, except on weekends and holidays. He spent most of his ten days in Taquile walking to and from the beach and chatting with people he met along the way. Three-quarters of the reporting was done in Spanish, since that is a second language for most Taquile residents. His own Spanish was fairly good when he arrived; by the time he left, he says, it was very, very good.

Although he swears he's not very good with languages, he has picked up a smattering of French, Swahili, Bhasa Indonesian, Mandarin Chinese, and Mongolian in the course of writing six books and more than 300 articles that have appeared in such publications as National Geographic, Rolling Stone, Esquire, GEO, Travel and Leisure, *and the* New York Times Book Review. *His books are* Pass the Butterwords, Jaguars Ripped My Flesh, A Wolverine Is Eating My Leg, Pecked to Death by Ducks, Road Fever, *and the best-selling* Buried Dreams.

"Dreams of far-ranging travel and adventure are fairly universal, though most of us let them die under the dark weight of responsibility," says Cahill. "This generally happens around the time of the first job. In my own case, over the past 20 years, it has been my work to explore these subterranean dreams. Because competency and courage consistently elude me in the field, others have been inspired to realize their own fantasies, reasoning, quite cogently I think, that they could hardly do worse than I have done. I like that: I like to think that I am in the business of giving people back their dreams."

A founding editor and former columnist for Outside *magazine, Cahill began his career as associate editor of* Rolling Stone. *He co-authored the Academy Award-nominated documentaries* The Living Sea *and* Dolphins, *and the Imax film* Everest *and is currently on the staff of* Men's Journal. *He is working on a book about a trek through a new National Park in Africa.*

Taquile's True Colors

THERE WAS A FREIGHT TRAIN HIGHBALLING down a track just above my roof.[1] I had been asleep and wasn't entirely sure where I was. The room I found myself in was brown adobe, very small, with one window high on the opposite wall.[2]

It was cold, near freezing, and I was lying just off the floor on a mattress of reeds covered over in thick, woolen blankets aged to the softness of cashmere. My dull headache and queasy lethargy[3] felt like altitude sickness.[4]

Some place high,[5] then. And it came back, slowly, that I was on the altiplano—the high plain that stretches from Peru to Bolivia: a harsh, windswept land set between two snowy ridges of the Andes.[6] The jewel of the altiplano is Lake Titicaca—12,507 feet above sea level—and the jewel of Lake Titicaca is the Peruvian island of Taquile, a tiny hummock of land three miles long and less than one mile wide.[7] Which, I recalled, is where I was.[8] There was no plumbing on the island, no electricity, not a single car. And no trains to rattle overhead.[9]

I glanced up at the corrugated tin roof.[10] An arc of light flickered outside the window, switched off, then flashed again, full power this time. The room went blue white, the

---

"Taquile's True Colors" first appeared in the Discovery Channel's *TDC* magazine in 1991. Reprinted by permission of the author.

1. The lead is what Cahill calls a "reverse parallelogram lead." "Unlike the lead for a daily journalism story in which all major questions—who, what, when, where—are answered, this lead is designed to raise more questions than it answers," he says. "The idea is that if the questions are compelling enough, the readers will keep reading." And read they do. Cahill hooks us with the very first sentence. Who can possibly read about a freight train highballing down a track above somebody's room and not keep going? The image is made all the more vivid by the word "highballing," which quickly establishes the voice of a writer who would be fun to travel with.

2. Cahill doesn't let up. He continues reeling us in. Like him, we wonder where we are. To find out, we must continue reading. Next, he draws a vivid picture of the room, which further serves to put us in the scene, but we still don't know where that room is.

3. The adjectives "dull" and "queasy" convey the feeling of his headache and lethargy and move us "inside" his experience.

4. The simile gives us a clue: We are somewhere high up.

5. Cahill reaches that conclusion.

6. The explanation of where we are is delivered in a sentence that unfolds slowly, in the way the realization came to Cahill. It begins with an introductory clause, followed by an adverb, which serve as a delay; then, finally, comes the answer. Since "the altiplano" won't mean anything to many of us, Cahill offers a brief explanation followed by a more detailed description that conveys a sense of the place: the land is "harsh" and "windswept."

7. Up to now, the view has been panoramic; we have not focused on a precise spot. Now Cahill begins moving in for a closer look. Think here of a camera's view from an airplane. First we get a sweeping view of the plains, then the airplane and the camera move closer and we see a lake, then we zoom in on a tiny island. At this point, we still see no details, only an outline: It is long and narrow. At the same time, Cahill begins giving us information: the names of the lake and the island and the fact they are 12,507 feet above sea level. Hence, the altitude sickness. The repetition of "jewel" conveys a sense of the beauty and uniqueness of the place: It is special.

8. Transition returns us to the opening scene and the matter of the freight train.

9. Cahill uses the expletive "there" and a careful ordering of information to create delay and suspense: There is no plumbing or electricity; there are no cars. He leaves the fact that there are no trains to the end and lets that fact stand alone in its own sentence fragment for emphasis. In doing so, he demonstrates the effectiveness of sentence fragments in the hands of a skilled writer. The question remains: What is the noise overhead? We are compelled to continue reading to find out.

10. More details place readers in the room, in the scene.

22

way things look under a stroboscope,[11] then a bomb exploded outside.[12] The freight train kept running over the roof, and I divined I was sleeping through a hail storm.[13] Some time ago, perhaps yesterday,[14] I had left the town of Puno on the shore of the lake. The boat to Taquile was a forty-foot gasoline engine affair that coughed and sputtered through a channel cut out of a sea of golden reeds. Ducks called back and forth between the sky and the reeds: *Are you feeding? We're feeding, are you feeding? We're feeding.*

As the boat cleared the reeds, the water glittered cobalt blue under cloudless skies.[15] Fifteen miles away, I could see Taquile. It seemed to sit in the middle of the lake, and the sun shone upon it like a benediction.[16] The island was little more than a spine of mountain sloping down a vertebra of rounded peaks to the shore. The land was terraced from top to bottom, and each terrace was walled waist-high with stones. Snaking through the terraces were paths lined by more stone walls. In some terraces, crops shone bright green in the sun, while in others sheep grazed on dark green grass, so that the land seemed composed of bands of alternating color.[17] The whole island looked as if it had been sculpted for aesthetic effect.[18]

Most of the passengers were Indians of the altiplano. About 1400 A.D., their ancestors were conquered by the Incas and absorbed into the empire. A century-and-a-half later, they were conquered again, this time by the Spanish. Their ancient language, Aymara, is still spoken on the altiplano, but on Taquile the people speak Quecha, the language of the Incas. Islanders consider themselves descendants of that great empire, and dress to set themselves apart. The women wear dark shawls and red skirts, several at once, so the uppermost skirt bells out in an exuberant manner. All the men wear a red or white wool cap, wool shirts and vests, dark, woolen pants, and wide, woven belts.[19]

The boat docked at a stone pier, where a flagstone path with long steps led to the village, eight hundred feet above.[20] I began trudging up the hill, gasping in the thin air. The

---

11. Cahill renders a visual re-creation of lightning viewed within a darkened room. Note how the sentence structure again imitates the quick off-and-on flashes. Though we don't yet know what it is, the description serves as a clue.

12. The explosion confirms our suspicions that we are in the midst of a thunderstorm, though we still don't know precisely what the noise on the roof is. In this description, note Cahill's vivid word choices: "corrugated" (he could have simply said "tin"), "flickered," "switched," "flashed," "full power," "exploded." The exploding bomb further establishes the writer's playful voice.

13. The freight train circles back to the opening sentence, and now Cahill answers the question: We are in the midst of a hail storm. By this time, we are captivated by the author's voice and thus willing to follow him through his stay on the island.

14. Time transition into a background loop of how he got to where he is. Notice how the uncertainty of the transition replicates his queasiness.

15. Cahill's account of his trip to the island is vivid and detailed, bringing readers with him. We hear the engine and the ducks; we feel closed in by the reeds; we see the cloudless sky and the glittering water, which calls to mind the opening jewel image. The effect is again cinematic, and we feel a sense of building anticipation.

16. The moment comes. We finally glimpse Taquile. The simile implies that the place is special, that God Himself looks out for it. "Shone" continues its jewel-like image. It also carries echoes of Psalm 67:1: "God be merciful unto us and bless us and cause His face to shine upon us."

17. The boat and the camera—and the readers—move closer. Now the island comes into focus, and we see more detail.

18. The comparison to a piece of sculpture conveys the sense that the island is perfect, a jewel.

19. The camera now turns back to the boat's passengers, and Cahill uses them to begin telling us about the people of Taquile, and their history, customs, and manner of dress. The "exuberant" skirts give us a sense of the people themselves. Note how Cahill here begins using the scenes as a frame for weaving in background information.

20. The boat lands, and we disembark for a closer look at the island and the residents.

men carried fresh fruit, bottles of water, cases of beer, cans of beans, automobile batteries, and great slabs of lumber, all wrapped in heavy wool blankets tied over their shoulders and across their chests, like a backpack. They were slender, and few were over five-and-a-half feet tall. They laughed and shouted to one another as they trotted up the slope. Barefoot women carrying gooseneck pots full of water walked by me effortlessly. All wished me a good morning, but when I tried to reply, I had nothing in my lungs to expel the words.[21]

At the summit, several men asked if I wanted to spend the night. Yes? Then I could stay with Sebastian. The price was seventy-five cents a night. One of the men led me down a sloping cobblestone walk bordered by stone fences.[22] My room was on the second story of a stone building covered in brown adobe. I climbed a small, rickety ladder, ducked through a door about two feet high, and collapsed onto the reeds,[23] feeling very sick indeed.[24]

* * *

In Taquile, families live in several small houses set around a courtyard. The walls are covered in adobe and sometimes smeared with sheep dung against the wind and cold. Each house is a single room; one is used for cooking, one for working, one for sleeping. Sebastian Yurca's compound included a larger room that he used as a restaurant to serve his guests.[25]

Sebastian's daughters seemed shy.[26] When I asked them their names, they blushed and stared at the floor and felt obliged to cover their faces with their shawls.[27] *Oh, that a man could ask such a question!*[28] They answered in whispers: Rebecca was 4; Angelica, 12; Lina, 16; Juana, 19.[29] All spoke fluent Spanish, a second language for them.[30] They pumped more light out of the kerosene lamp for me and told me I could have pancakes, potato soup, potatoes, eggs, or trout.[31] Then Juana, the eldest, noticed my condition.

---

21. As Cahill begins the 800-foot climb, he again lets us vicariously share the moment. We feel him gasping for air, we experience the effort it takes to make it to the top of the hill—an effort that is accentuated by the ease of the men and women who pass with their heavy wares. Even with their burdens, they "trot" while Cahill "trudges." Cahill begins giving us a general description of the people (they are short, slender, good-humored, physically fit, barefoot). The items they carry also provide insight into them and their culture (they may not have cars or electricity, but they do drink beer). Note that there are no individuals in this scene. Like Cahill, we are still strangers.

22. Cahill's introduction to the people of Taquile begins. No longer are we in a crowd. We are speaking now to "several" men. For the first time, we hear their voices. Note how Cahill captures the essence of the voices and the exchange without using direct quotes, perhaps because he was not taking notes. This technique is useful for times when you are not completely sure your quotes are verbatim. Here, this technique also gives us the sense that he and the men never exchanged names or got to know one another.

23. The description of the room is rendered in concrete details that enable us to see the room (second story, adobe) and his ascent on the rickety ladder. The "two foot high" doorway is obviously an exaggeration, which again establishes his voice; it also suggests he is tall.

24. "Feeling very sick indeed" ends the background loop and brings us back to the main time line.

25. Description of houses provides information about the living arrangements of the residents of Taquile and sets the stage for Cahill's visit.

26. Transition into scene.

27. The camera is now close up. Cahill offers no physical details, yet we get a real sense of the girls through their movements, which support his initial impression that they are shy: They blush, they will not look directly at him, they cover their faces. Note how he sets up their gestures for use later to show their embarrassment.

28. From their actions, Cahill imagines what they are thinking.

29. We learn their names and ages. Cahill uses no direct quotes, yet re-creates a sense of their voices.

30. The fact that they speak a "second language" indicates their education. It also suggests that Cahill conducted his interviews in Spanish, a fact that could further explain the absence of direct quotes.

31. Insight into diet.

She'd seen it often enough: a gringo[32] with a bad headache and no appetite. Altitude sickness: the *sorache*.[33] She brought a cup of hot water and set a few sprigs of mint in it to steep. *Mate de muña*, she said, was good for pain. Women drank strong *mate de muña* when they gave birth.[34] I sipped the tea, had a bowl of bland but filling potato soup, and watched the girls go about their work in the warm light of the lantern.

Lina was weaving one of the men's red belts on a wooden loom using a lamb's bone polished sharp and smooth. The designs were intricate: a bird, a diamond radiating rays, a circle divided into six parts. The belt, she explained, was a kind of agricultural calendar: When the scissor-billed bird laid its eggs, it was time to plant. The diamond was Inti, the sun, the god of the Incas. The circle represented Taquile, which was divided into six regions. In certain years, terraces in some regions were to remain fallow—Lina was weaving dots in those—while others could be planted. A woman would make such a belt for her husband, Lina said. It would represent a man's past, present, and future. *How long did it take to make?* Lina paused. She had never thought about it. She guessed that if she worked five or six hours a day, it would take her less than two months.[35]

The other girls had plugged a small tape player into an auto battery. They played the music of the altiplano, the high, mournful sound of flutes and drums and guitar: El Condor Pasa, a kind of national lament of the altiplano. Paul Simon's words had nothing to do with the Peruvian version, but they caught the mood: *I'd rather be a hammer than a nail.* It was the music of a conquered people, plaintive and melodic and somehow triumphant.[36]

The two oldest girls wore colorful tassels at the corners of their shawls. Juana said the tassels meant they could date boys. Single men, she said, wore hats that were white at the tip. The clothes one wears indicate not only marital status, but age group, social position, and relative wealth. Girls who wear the tassels, Juana told me, are said to be in flower. A married woman cannot wear tassels.[37]

"You mean," I asked, feeling much better after my mint tea, "that when you get married, all the color goes out of your life?"[38]

This comment was treated as the height of flirtation. Juana dissolved into giggles and felt forced to again hide her face behind her shawl. My headache was now only a minor annoyance, and I sought to make the girls giggle and hide their faces. *Did Juana have a boyfriend?* Oh, blush, giggle-giggle, hide behind the shawl, whisper to Lina. *And Lina?* The girl went through an agony of exquisite embarrassment. *Such a question!* It was only possible to look at the floor. *A boyfriend! The very thought.*[39]

There was a new tape on, a Peruvian version of the lambada, and Juana asked if I could dance. It occurred to me that in South America, the lambada, as they say in the

---

32. Spanish for white man.

33. He offers translation for *sorache* and the diagnosis for his headache and queasiness.

34. Provides cultural insights.

35. Belt serves as a vehicle for explaining agricultural and domestic practices.

36. Cahill uses music to characterize the people of Taquile. The description gives us a sense of what it sounded like. The contrast of the tape player and the somewhat primitive music and makeshift battery become symbolic of the island's extremes.

37. Uses tassels to insert information on island culture.

38. Note that Cahill uses direct quotes for his own dialogue, since he can be certain of those quotes. It shows his mischievous nature. He is having fun with this encounter.

39. Cahill makes use of his earlier setup to convey the girls' embarrassment. The scene shows as much about his personality as it does theirs. He is a likable narrator, a good travel companion.

movies, was "forbeedin."[40] Somehow I couldn't imagine these shy young women performing a dance that looks like something a dog does to your leg.

"Can't dance," I explained.

A chorus of disbelief. If I was going to tease, said Juana, with her hands on her hips, falsely stern, then I had to dance. I stood, took her right hand in my left, and put my other hand on her back. She brushed it away. *No, sir, please don't—not like that.* This was, apparently, a lambada in which you touched your partner's hands and nothing else.

I had no idea how to proceed, and spun Juana away from me in a kind of cowboy two-step. This was received with much laughter and applause. Soon Juana was whirling this way and that, and would have looked right at home cutting the rug in any Montana saloon. *What kind of dance did I call that?*[41] A cowboy dance, I said. And so, at least once every night for the next week, Juana and I danced to the music of a tape deck connected to a car battery in a brown adobe room with the high country wind whistling outside. We danced the cowboy lambada.[42]

* * *

I had pancakes and coffee the next morning and began a walking tour of the island. In contrast to the freezing hail of the night before, the sun was hot and harsh at thirteen thousand feet.[43] About an hour from the village,[44] I heard a rhythmic tap-tap, and stumbled upon three men dressed in the basic men's costume. Alejandro and his brothers were cutting stone for the new school-house.[45] Everyone on the island donated a few hours of work to the community each week, Alejandro said. Tomorrow, other men would cut stone.[46]

There were two thousand people on the island, 318 families.[47] Because the island is small and the weather harsh, agriculture has to be strictly controlled so everyone can eat. Each Sunday, after Mass, the people meet in the central courtyard, where the events of the past week are discussed and plans are made.[48] Sometimes, men from the outside come to Taquile to "organize" the people. These men talk about inflation, insurgency, and police corruption. What do these things have to do with Taquile? There are no police on the island. The people do not want police. Where there are police, there are thieves. Everyone knows that.[49]

Alejandro had been tapping on a rock the size of a hassock. He used a simple hammer and chisel, gently rapping along the grain. Suddenly the rock fell apart into two pieces, each almost perfectly square. He began trimming one of them, and I recalled that the Incas were perhaps the finest stone workers in pre-Columbian America.

---

40. The writer's voice, echoing the phony Spanish accents in old south-of-the-border movies.

41. We can both see and hear this delightful scene, and this serves to draw us further into the story. While there is no conflict or drama here, we are compelled to keep reading for the sheer enjoyment of it.

42. Cahill offers a compressed—yet vivid—repetition of the scene to duplicate the way it is repeated night after night throughout his week-long stay. The picture of this lumbering man and this young girl dancing the cowboy lambada lingers in our minds as the scene and his first night ends.

43. Transition into day two. Cahill describes weather both to provide information about the island and to set up the scene.

44. Time and place transition.

45. The scene unfolds for us in the way it did for Cahill. We first hear the sounds of the chiseling, then we see the three men, then we learn their names and what they are doing. Again note the absence of direct quotes.

46. Information on island practices.

47. Statistics.

48. Explanation of island government.

49. Alejandro's indirect quote seems to be the combined voices of Taquile's people.

The sun disappeared behind a cloud and the temperature dropped fifteen degrees. I dug around in my pack for a jacket, but Alejandro and his brothers continued working. Whether it's seventy-five degrees during the day or thirty degrees at night, men never wear jackets, nor do they strip off a shirt or vest. Layers of heavy wool, finely made, seem to create a kind of microclimate around the body.[50]

Why was it, I asked Alejandro, that the people of Taquile were so honest they didn't need police? Alejandro said that if a man steals a sheep, he is taken before the community at the Sunday meeting and forced to carry the sheep on his back six times around the square, while the twelve authorities—the men who govern the six parts of the island—whip him with heavy woven ropes as he passes. If a man kills another man's sheep, he makes the same humiliating walk with the intestines of the sheep wrapped around his head. Then he is taken to the mainland. That man can never return. "So you see," Alejandro said, "we have no need for police."[51]

Alejandro himself was running for the position of first lieutenant governor, the highest authority on the island.[52] *What were the issues?* "Natural fibers," he replied without hesitation. "Natural colors." Some islanders, it seemed, were knitting hats or scarves with synthetics. They might even use artificial dyes to color the fabrics, then sell them to tourists like myself. Alejandro thinks tourists can buy such things anywhere. When the political men came to organize the island, Alejandro asked them, *And where do you stand on natural color?* The men had no answer. They knew nothing of Taquile. The people asked them to go away.[53]

People are so short-sighted, said Alejandro. There was television everywhere in the world; why would we need it here? Or loud music? It was a quiet island, very traditional, and it should be kept that way.[54] Yet all the young men of his island want to visit Lima, if only for a few days. For them, Lima is a kind of Disneyland of danger and violence, of strange, gratuitous wonders.[55] So when Alejandro decided it was time for him to see the great city, he approached the local shaman, or paq'o,[56] and asked his advice.[57]

The paq'o sat at a table and spread out three leaves of the sacred coca plant.[58] He placed a coin on the middle leaf; this represented the all-seeing eye of God. A crucifix was placed below the coin: this indicated Alejandro was Catholic. The leaf to the left was turned over so the dull side was up; it represented bad luck and trouble. The leaf on the right lay shiny side up. If God and the spirits willed it, the right leaf would triumph, and Alejandro could go to Lima without worry.

The paq'o placed five leaves in Alejandro's right palm. He closed his eyes and emptied his hand in a sweeping gesture, so that the leaves fell across the coin and the crucifix. The paq'o examined how they had fallen: all shiny side up—a very good sign. The

---

50. Scene used to work in background information.
51. Quote provides information on island practices and conveys, with some humor, the residents' way of thinking, their logic. By being a direct quote, the last sentence gains added emphasis.
52. Information.
53. Alejandro's explanation again "shows" us the people's way of thinking. While it is mostly indirect quote, the use of quotation marks for "natural fibers" indicates the fervor of their conviction. The concern over the natural fibers and colors also conveys the tranquil, unspoiled nature of the island. Here is a place where the most pressing issues are over synthetics and artificial dyes.
54. More information and insight.
55. The island may be traditional, but its youth—like young people everywhere—yearn to go where the excitement is.
56. Translates "paq'o" for future reference.
57. Transition into background loop that will explain Alejandro's convictions.
58. "Sacred" explains the status of the coca plant.

leaves traced a line below the crucifix, pointing to the shiny leaf at the right. Alejandro Flores would have good luck in Lima.[59]

Lima.[60] The air in that great city was thick and dirty. Still, the bright, colored lights glittered at night because there was electricity everywhere. On Taquile, there is no electricity, and a man can see the stars.[61]

One day during the visit to Lima,[62] a tall, thin, foreign man stopped Alejandro on the street. He was excited about something, and Alejandro thought perhaps he was crazy or drunk. No, the man said, please don't go. Please—where had Alejandro gotten the wool to weave his belt?

From sheep, of course.

His sheep?

Yes, everyone on Taquile raised sheep.

And how did they spin the wool? By machine?

No, by hand—mostly clockwise.

Mostly?

Sometimes, Alejandro explained, the wool is spun in the opposite direction when it is to be used to finish the edge of a garment. The backward spin creates good luck and wards off evil spirits.[63]

The man stared at Alejandro as if he'd just said something amazing like, "I can fly like a bird when I please."[64]

The man wondered if Alejandro's clothes had been woven on a wooden loom, whose four posts were pounded into the ground.

That was true.

And the colors—this golden yellow came from the leaf of a tree, boiled for several hours?

Yes.

And the red came from the beetle of the cactus plant? Cochineal?

Yes. Alejandro allowed the beetles to infest his cactus. Sometimes his wife took one or two of the insects and squeezed them to extract a bright red juice for painting her lips and nails. To color wool with cochineal, Alejandro dried the beetles in the sun, then boiled them for several hours until he had a pot of the most beautiful red dye on earth.

The foreign man knew about the process, which surprised Alejandro. He knew the color was fixed with salt, fermented potato water, and fermented human urine. He knew that, with few exceptions, Alejandro made textiles exactly as they had been made in the altiplano several thousand years ago. Those ancient textiles, the man said, were among the finest ever produced anywhere.[65] Perhaps Alejandro could come to his country. There were many scholars who would want to speak with him, and many people who would come to see him create his art.

Which is how Alejandro Flores of Taquile Island[66] traveled to England for three

---

59. Anecdote reveals Alejandro's belief system and that of the island. Even though he is Catholic, he is superstitious and believes in shamans.

60. Place transition.

61. Alejandro's point of view. The bright lights can limit what you see.

62. Transition into scene.

63. Reiterates his superstitious nature.

64. The author's voice.

65. Scene between Alejandro and the man in Lima provides information on Taquile and its heritage.

66. The use of Alejandro's full name and Taquile Island, rather than simply "Taquile," reflect the respect he was shown in England.

months to demonstrate pre Columbian techniques of weaving. There were articles in newspapers and magazines about him, with pictures of Alejandro dressed the way he had always dressed. People recognized him on the street, and some could speak Spanish: they called him a great artist and shook his hand.[67]

It had been an interesting trip. There were huge buildings, and things called escalators, and strange food, and beer to drink. Alejandro was glad he went, but he was happy to come back to his quiet island where there were no police and no one lied, where potatoes tasted the way potatoes should and a man could see the stars every night.[68]

The paq'o had been right: Alejandro hadn't had any trouble in Lima. What he had learned there, and in England, was that life on Taquile was good. It was worth preserving the traditions that set the island apart from the rest of the world. The difference was encompassed in Alejandro's single issue in his campaign for first lieutenant governor: natural color.[69]

* * *

On my walks around the island,[70] I often met women in their seventies tending sheep. It was a matter of some comedy on Taquile: Quecha grandmothers, people said, complain all day long. The old women seem to be in on the joke and conspire to amuse everyone. Speaking Spanish with a guttural Quecha accent, they protest the hardships of life in a merry sing-song manner.[71] *The village is so far away. My son has gone to Puno to work and I have no one. The sheep know I can't see very well anymore and hide from me.* When walking with a man from the village, we laughed together about the grandmothers' complaints. That was expected of me. Privately, I thought about these old women walking barefoot over rocky hillsides at thirteen thousand feet with the wind driving a cold rain before it. What's so funny about that?[72]

For the most part, however, I met young girls like Alejandra, a ten-year-old who was tending a small flock. She was both curious and shy, so she hid behind a stone arch while she spoke to me, peeking out every once in a while in an unconsciously flirtatious manner.

The sheep belonged to her father's brother. She was watching them while her uncle helped her father. Today, the men were on the other side of the island, turning over the soil in four big terraces, planting maize and potatoes with foot plows as people had since the time of the Incas. It would be easier, Alejandra said, to prepare the land if her father owned a cow that he could yoke to a plow. They were saving for one even now. Alejandra wore a woven bag on her hip from which she pulled newly washed black wool. Stretching it out in a long cord, she wrapped it around a top-like bobbin in a quick, complicated maneuver, and set the top spinning on a flat rock. Her young fingers were nimble and she

---

67. Handshake reaffirms respect and supports Alejandro's claims that he was referred to as "a great artist."

68. Paragraph offers Alejandro's view of England. "Huge buildings," "things called escalators," "strange food" suddenly make what is normal for the reader seem foreign and strange in the way they were for Alejandro. By contrast, Taquile comes across as the norm so that we too feel relieved to return home, to Taquile. It also captures the essence of the island. The reference to the stars echoes the earlier comment about Lima, implying that you can't see them in England either.

69. The background loop ends. The placement of "natural color" at the end of the sentence and the section give it added emphasis, conveying the theme of Taquile's colors being the true colors.

70. Transition compresses time and experiences.

71. "Merry sing-song manner" lets us hear the grandmothers' voices.

72. The author's question becomes our question.

did the work unconsciously as she spoke. The wool would be knitted into hats, and woven into belts and blankets. Perhaps tourists would buy her work.[73]

Occasionally, a sheep tried to wander past her, and she hissed at it loudly. The animal fell all over itself getting back to its fellows. The worst thing the sheep did, Alejandra said, they did on hot days like this (it was about 70 degrees). Wandering down to the lake to drink, the brainless beasts would hurl themselves into the cool water. Then you'd have to stand on a rock and stare into twenty feet of clear water to see the sheep on the bottom, white or black against green, mossy rocks, held down by all that water-logged wool.[74]

Alejandra was only ten and yet doing work for her family. I thought she must be proud of herself. This, Alejandra said from behind the arch,[75] was not so. There were eight children in her family. It was hard to keep everyone fed. Last year, Alejandra had been allowed to go to school; now, because the family needed money for a cow, she had to work. Her older brothers got to go to school, but she had to spend her days with these sheep: *los stupidos*. Her old teachers, she said, had come every week from Puno. They spoke such beautiful Spanish. She wanted to go to school and become a teacher who spoke beautiful Spanish.[76]

More likely, Alejandra would grow up frustrated in her ambitions. Taquile is the very definition of insularity. People do not marry off the island; foreigners (that is, people not born on Taquile) are not allowed to buy land. Sometimes a man will come back from Lima with strange ideas. He will wear the clothes of Lima—stone-washed jeans, cotton shirts, shoes instead of leather sandals—but soon enough, withering under constant disapproval, he finds himself falling back into the island's familiar rhythms. And a little girl who wanted to be a teacher: she would be thought of as egotistical and silly.[77]

I didn't want to think about that, because I found the people in general so happy, so handsome. I wanted to believe that there were no problems at all on Taquile.[78]

* * *

Don Pedro, a talkative man of 75 in vibrant good health, told me that people almost never die on Taquile. The last time a person died was two years ago, and the woman had been 105. In point of fact, I had talked to a man who had recently lost his 73-year-old grandmother, but I had no wish to dispute the matter with Don Pedro. It seemed a pleasant fiction, and one likely to prolong his life.[79]

Agriculture, said Don Pedro, was very important. Every February, the people went to the highest flat spot on the island, the Mulasina Pata, and made a sacrifice to Pachamama—Mother Earth.[80] They killed a baby llama, lamb, and alpaca, wrapped

---

73. The scene is vividly drawn. We see Alejandra hiding behind the arch and recall the earlier scene with Sebastian's daughters. We see her nimble fingers working the yarn. In the course of this, we learn more about Taquile's agriculture.

74. The details of the "green, mossy rocks" and the white or black sheep enable us to see the animals at the bottom of the lake. "Water-logged" echoes the girl's view of them as "brainless beasts."

75. The reminder that Alejandra says this from behind the arch again places us in the scene with Cahill.

76. Alejandra's voice. The repetition of "beautiful Spanish" conveys a longing on her part to return to school.

77. Provides information on island traditions and views.

78. Author directly addresses us and in saying this implies that as idyllic as it seems, Taquile is not without its problems.

79. Author inserts information gleaned from an earlier encounter to "show" the preposterousness of Don Pedro's statement. It is information that will serve the author later in the story.

80. Provides translation of "Pachamama."

them in serpentine paper, and buried them in three small graves, along with some coca leaves and corn beer. The last time a tourist came to Don Pedro's remote farm—he thought that might have been fourteen years ago—there had been bad crops for a year. I said I would go, but Don Pedro was already on another subject.

Hail storms, like the one the other day, could kill crops very easily. Happily, this storm had hit during planting season, not when the crops were high in the fields. What caused the worst hail storms, said Don Pedro, was when a young, unmarried girl got pregnant and aborted herself. These irresponsible girls buried the babies without a proper Catholic baptism. Then the hail would come for days, until the girl confessed and showed the authorities where the baby was buried. It was then baptized, and the hail would stop.[81]

I had a vision of the men of the village digging in the wet ground, with lightning striking all about . . . holy water sprinkled on rotting flesh . . . but Don Pedro was talking about lightning now. Once, many years ago, a woman had been struck by lightning at her wedding. "On May third," I said. Everyone on Taquile, I had just learned, gets married on May third.[82] Don Pedro, who didn't like to be interrupted, stared at me as if I had just informed him that water is wet.[83]

"Yes," he said, "May third." After that, there were three years of good crops. Then lightning had killed a cow, and there were three years of bad crops. Now, when a person is struck by lightning, a family will grieve, but the island is reassured. If a cow is killed by a bolt from the sky, however, there are many rituals to perform: taking a cake to the spot, building a small altar, and obtaining the blessing of a priest's representative.[84]

There was no priest on the island, and no doctor—only a public health nurse—but the paq'o was very good. Even when a man had been to the doctor in Puno and was still sick, the paq'o could help. The sick man might be given a white guinea pig to put in a small bag and hold to his heart for twelve hours; all the man's sickness would infect the guinea pig, and the paq'o could then dissect the animal and find what was wrong with the man. The paq'o could prescribe certain herbs.[85] No one died on Taquile.[86]

I asked Don Pedro if he could introduce me to the paq'o.

"You have seen him," Don Pedro said. "You have seen his face."

* * *

I danced one last cowboy lambada[87] with Juana and wandered back toward my room. A vicious storm had passed over the island earlier, and now it had moved far to the south. Lightning was striking behind the snowcapped mountains of Bolivia. The storm was so far away that I couldn't hear the thunder, but every five seconds or so the sky exploded, and a mountain—blue white—shivered on the horizon.

---

81. Word choices ("happily," "these irresponsible girls") carry Don Pedro's voice.

82. Explanation.

83. Author's voice.

84. Cahill avoids the temptation to insert commentary here and let's the absurdity, and humor, come across in the facts.

85. Again, he lets the people's beliefs speak for themselves.

86. Because Cahill has already set up the death of the 73-year-old woman, we realize the preposterousness of this statement. By letting it stand alone without comment, the humor hits even harder.

87. Transition into final scene echoes back to the beginning. There is no need to play it out in detail because we still carry the vivid images in our mind. Also, he is preparing us for the ending, and to have elaborated here would have distracted from the sense of the story drawing to a close. The repetitions in these final paragraphs give the story a circular feeling of completion (the lambada, the thunder, the blue-white of the mountain, the stone fences, and the circular relationship between the sheep and the fields).

The island, it seemed to me then, was a living, breathing thing. The stone fences were pleasant to look at, but they also kept the sheep out of the crops. When the fields lay fallow, they would feed the sheep; in turn, the sheep would fertilize them with their droppings. And the wool of the sheep was woven into textiles that received a man at birth, clothed him through life, and protected him on his journey to the next world.[88]

At dinner, I had asked Sebastian Yurca what the island needed more than anything else. "Natural color," he had replied. Above, the sky was clear and black, full of luminous and unfamiliar stars. At this altitude, they did not twinkle. They were great globules of light, and their colors were brilliant: white, blue white, red, green, gold. Natural colors.[89]

A man, I thought, could see the lights of Lima. Or he could see the stars.[90]

TIM CAHILL ON READING

"In college, I wanted to write the (ahem) great American novel. I came across a book by Tom Wolfe called *The Kandy-Kolored Tangerine-Flake Streamline Baby*. It was his first collection of magazine stories, and I was amazed that 'you could do that,' by which I mean, write journalism in a stylish and insightful manner. About the same time, I came on a book called *Desert Solitaire* by Ed Abbey. There is a story in there called 'The Dead Man at Grandview Point.' It is staggeringly good, and it was stylish journalism—a story about life and death, really—and I saw that you could write about the outdoors in a literate manner.

"As for old favorites that might help me: I think writing is writing, whatever the subject matter, and have many favorites, all of different styles. *Huck Finn* remains the pivotal American novel (though the ending sucks). *Heart of Darkness* is one of the greatest stories ever written, Hemingway's 'A Clean, Well-Lighted Place' is right up there, *Anna Karenina* is a model of intricate structure, and for pure guilty pleasure, I like Elmore Leonard.

"I don't underline, though I find myself memorizing great lines and analyzing techniques. (Incidentally, I find it difficult to read an author I admire, then write the next morning without, inadvertently, sounding like that writer.)"

---

88. Neatly, beautifully, Cahill summarizes the life cycle of the wool and clothing.

89. Sebastian's answer—again in quotation marks for emphasis—brings us back to the unspoiled nature of Taquile. The brilliance of the stars brings to mind Cahill's initial description of the island as a jewel.

90. Final line echoes the earlier references to the stars and the serenity of Taquile. It comes to us somewhat unexpectedly and lingers pleasantly in our minds.

James Conaway

In writing memoir, the challenge is to make your experience as interesting to readers as it is to you. James Conaway achieves this in "Absences" through vividly drawn scenes that allow readers to witness vicariously the gradual loss of his father to Alzheimer's disease, and thus come to care about him. The writerliness of Conaway's prose—the word choices, the imagery, the syntax, the rhythm—also compels us to read for the sheer pleasure of the language.

Conaway himself believes that good memoir should capture both a person and a time vital to the author. "The best approach to autobiography is, paradoxically, a story about someone else to whom the writer is attached emotionally, as I was to my father," he says. "Writing about his illness and death was less of an idea than a necessity that arose out of the confusion it entailed. I wrote this piece almost reflexively, trying to match the feeling of that time with an appropriate voice but unsure that it would work for anyone else until the piece was accepted and then published."

Response to the article, which appeared in Harper's, came from men and women of all ages and geographical locations, prompting Conaway to write Memphis Afternoons, a book-length memoir, using his father and family as a kind of organizing principle, with revelations about himself emerging as counterpoints to time and place.

"Remembering the way it was seemed impossible at first," he says, "but dealing with the past every day in the writing gradually pulled memories from obscurity, many of them revealed in dreams that, by day, took on the characteristics of reality."

To write the book, Conaway also interviewed relatives and friends to flesh out the details. He dipped into a collection of family memorabilia and letters, including those exchanged by his parents during World War II, and newspaper clippings, not for quotes but for familiarity with the past.

"In the end," he says, "a memoir is a conglomeration of yearning, pleasure, and pain reconstructed from the emotional absence of the past."

In addition to Memphis Afternoons, Conaway is the author of two novels and seven nonfiction books, including The Kingdom in the Country and the best-selling Napa: The Story of an American Eden. His articles have appeared in many publications, including the New York Times Magazine, Atlantic, the New Republic, National Geographic Traveler, Smithsonian, Civilization, and Outside. He has served as Washington editor for Harper's and as a columnist and staff writer for the Washington Post. He is currently a contributing editor for Preservation. He was a Wallace Stegner Writing Fellow at Stanford University and a recipient of a Felicia Patterson Fellowship. He spends most of his time in rural Virginia and is currently completing a sequel to Napa.

Absences

On Losing, by Degrees, One's Father

I HAD BEEN GOING HOME to Memphis for twenty-five years when I first noticed that my father was losing his mind.[1] I say first noticed, but the signs had for a long time stretched across the sheets of graph paper on which he occasionally wrote letters—he was an engineer but would not have used formal stationery in any case—in a hand so crabbed that the letters grew increasingly brief and finally ceased.[2] I should have asked why; I should have put aside the concerns of my own life and formally recognized the little routine absences that were leading, inexorably, to an absence of life.[3]

In truth, I knew little about my father's ailment, not enough to admit that "it"[4] even existed beyond the natural mental perambulations[5] of an independent[6] old man who had lived within the bounds of propriety, disappointment, and some hardship.[7] There were other signs: a hesitancy on the telephone, an awkwardness with numbers[8]—for years it had been his business to calculate how much refrigerated air a Memphis skyscraper needed to remain habitable[9]— and a slight stammer.[10] I attributed that to bourbon and learned too late it had little to do with that recreational beverage.[11] What it had to do with has a name but the name is irrelevant, even harmful, since the naming

---

"Absences" first appeared in *Harper's* in 1991. Reprinted by permission of the author.

1. The first sentence hooks readers both by its straightforward statement of fact and its choice of words. Describing someone as "losing his mind" is more dramatic, and intriguing, than to say he is suffering from Alzheimer's disease. The decision not to use the word "Alzheimer's" reflects the way we avoid talking openly about mental illnesses; it also replicates how little we know about the disease.

2. Conaway draws us into his experience—and thus the essay—by letting us vicariously share the first outward signs of his father failing. His description of the letters is so detailed and visual that, as readers, we feel we actually see them: the graph paper, the crabbed handwriting, the way they taper off. They become a metaphor for his father: like them, he is gradually drifting away. Note how with the one word "crabbed" Conaway captures the penmanship of an elderly man. He also uses the letters to begin laying out his father's background: he was an engineer.

3. Note how the rhythm of this sentence echoes the thought patterns of someone agonizing over something. The first clause is short, abrupt, in the way we often castigate ourselves on first coming to a realization; the second clause moves at a more thoughtful pace as we ponder the course we should or should not have taken. The cascading nature of this second clause also propels readers to the unavoidable ending: the absence of life. Placed at the end of the sentence, and the paragraph, this realization gains added force. It both stuns the reader and lingers in his mind. There is a writerliness to Conaway's turning of phrases ("the concerns of my own life," "the little routine absences"), which make them as pleasant to read aloud as good poetry.

4. Conaway again avoids the word "Alzheimer's," echoing how little he—and most of us—know about it. It also reflects our reluctance to say the word aloud.

5. "Perambulations" fits both the subject matter and the tone of the essay. It carries connotations both of a mind wandering and an elderly person.

6. Tells us something about his father's nature.

7. List succinctly sums up his father's life. Conaway holds back the details of those proprietary boundaries and the disappointments and hardships, thus compelling us to continue reading. Note how the insertion of "some" slightly breaks the rhythm and causes the hardships to linger in the reader's mind.

8. We learn more of his father's symptoms and thus more about Alzheimer's.

9. More of his father's background.

10. Still another symptom.

11. "Recreational beverage" is a somewhat playful, tongue-in-cheek word choice; it also hints at a southern attitude toward alcohol that Conaway will explore later in the essay.

doesn't alleviate the pain and relegates the victim, as it relegated my father, to the role of an incurable[12] in an age of medical self-congratulation.[13]

It was late autumn—monsoon season—and the ragged skies rolling out of Arkansas would have dropped tornadoes on a city less blessed than Memphis.[14] I had flown in from Knoxville in a polished steel tube,[15] owned by a bank in east Tennessee, that was filled to capacity with successful dealers in estates, real and imagined.[16] One of them would soon be indicted and sent to prison, but for the moment they were happily chasing deals around the South,[17] and I was to write about them for the *Washington Post*, my employer at the time.[18] Dad met me on the street where the bankers' limousine left me, at the wheel of his small car.[19] I knew immediately something was wrong. The face beneath the snap-brim hat seemed diminished, the eyes full of misgiving.[20] The neighborhood should have been familiar territory, but he regarded it as alien. "Hello, sonny boy,"[21] he said when I got in; I kissed him[22] and felt the stubble and smelled the remnants of my own childhood, not tobacco now, not whiskey, but the enfeebled suggestions of black coffee, Noxzema, and the dead leaves he moved ceaselessly from lawn to street.[23]

He drove without talking, concentrating on the task at hand, running a stop sign, turning a corner without regard for the oblique stream of oncoming traffic or horn blasts, passing a pedestrian who wisely decided not to challenge our passage because otherwise he would have been killed, probably not by the violence of the initial blow but by the car's dogged persistence in running him over.[24] Dad did not intend to stop until he

---

12. Conaway now tells us directly what he has implied by refraining from using the word "Alzheimer's": the consequences, and not the name, are what is important.

13. With a turn of phrase, Conaway adroitly deflates the medical world's boasts of scientific gains.

14. The first two paragraphs have acted as a summary introduction to his father's story. Now Conaway sets out to re-create the actual moment he discovered his father's ailment. He begins with a tight description of the weather to bring readers with him into the moment. Note the word choices ("monsoon," "ragged," "rolling," "dropped"), which bring the scene vividly before our eyes. We are now with him; the experience is becoming ours. Note also that the word choices have a playful edge that both reflects his attitude toward his hometown and keeps the story from becoming too depressing.

15. Poetic way of saying "an airplane." Also implies it was sleek and expensive.

16. Implies they are dreamers and, more than that, schemers. Note the pleasant sound created by the syntax: "estates, real and imagined." The placement of "imagined" at the end of the sentence gives the word added weight.

17. He confirms what was implied in the previous sentence: not all the deals were aboveboard. "Happily chasing deals" repeats the dreamer notion.

18. Background information on Conaway himself.

19. The fact that the car was small further establishes his father's situation. It also serves as a contrast to the powerful bankers and their limousine.

20. In setting the scene, Conaway has used leisurely sentences that carry us through his homecoming. He now uses an abrupt sentence to grab our attention, so that we don't miss the fact that something is wrong. The misgiving eyes, the diminished expression cause us to look Alzheimer's in the face. The concrete detail of the hat being "snap-brim" vividly conjures up a picture of his father: It is the style men of his generation wore.

21. "Sonny boy" hints of a man of a certain generation. It is a tender salutation and "shows" us something of the father-son relationship and the way even a grown son is never quite grown in a parent's eyes.

22. Reinforces an affection between the two men, that a man in his 40s would kiss his father.

23. Conaway is drawing on all the senses to place readers in the scene. We have seen and heard the old man; now the author uses touch and smell. In doing this, we too realize the father is no longer the man who favored whiskey and tobacco. The smells now are those of old age: black coffee, Noxema, and dead leaves, the latter somewhat symbolic of what the father has become.

24. A list succinctly captures the ride home in a manner that is both pathetic and humorous in the way that tragedy often borders on comedy. Conaway's exaggeration of the pedestrian's reaction and the personification of the car add to that element of humor. Conaway continues to use our senses to draw us into the scene: we see the oncoming cars out of the corner of our eyes; we hear the horns, we see the pedestrian jumping back to avoid the car.

had returned to the shelter of the carport, attached to a house that had been sleek and modern in the Sixties, set back among the trees and shrubs[25] that render east Memphis botanical anarchy in the spring and that now, in November, enfolded the low eaves in near-tropical profusion.[26]

My mother met us at the door in bathrobe and slippers—the uniform.[27] Looking after my father had become a full-time endeavor.[28] Together we got him out of his hat and raincoat and seated on the low couch, where he watched the evening news without interest. When Mom and I were alone, I said savagely,[29] "He shouldn't be driving," and she said, "It's all he's got left."[30]

* * *

He was known as Connie, and he decided to go fight the Japanese when I was a baby. I shouldn't be able to remember that day but I do:[31] hot metal stairs leading up to a railway platform in midtown, my father's smooth cheeks and shining summer dress uniform, the hat emblazoned with a gold eagle as he leans out the door of the departing train, an immaculate white wedge, smiling unhappily, one hand raised as if testing the wind.[32] Connie didn't have to enlist in the Navy, being too old for the draft and not skilled enough to be crucial;[33] my mother never forgave him.[34] As a Seabee he fought alongside the Marines on Guam and Peleliu[35] and came back to Memphis full of stories of air raids and a sun hotter than the one at home, of tropical birds that flew backward, of an enemy that holed up in caves or floated facedown, dead, in mountain pools, or appeared at dawn, naked, uniforms neatly bundled and placed on rocks, to surrender.[36] At least some of the stories were buttressed by hardware:[37] a knife made from the wreckage of a Japanese aircraft, glass balls that had held afloat the fishing nets of other yellow peo-

---

25. "Shelter" implies that home is the father's safe haven, the only place he now feels safe. The house itself provides more of his background.

26. Description of setting places readers at the scene.

27. "Bathrobe and slippers" implies the mother has lost interest in life. It is a detail that readers with elderly parents can identify with. "The uniform" carries a critical tone on the part of the author and hints at a less loving relationship than that of the father and son.

28. "Endeavor" evokes the complicated nature of caring for an Alzheimer's patient. It also carries a sense that for his mother it has become a mission.

29. "Savagely" hints at Conaway's regret for lashing out at his mother.

30. Placed at the end of the paragraph and the section, the quote gains added poignancy, greater impact. There is a haunting quality, and it lingers in our minds as the scene ends.

31. Conaway here begins a long loop, or digression, in which he will relate his father's life. He begins at a moment that contrasts with the father's present state: "Connie" as a soldier going off to war. The details of the departure have the hazy blur of a small child's memories (the shiny dress uniform, the gold eagle, the white wedge of a man, the raised hand), yet they are no less vivid, so that as readers we vicariously share the experience. In drawing the scene, Conaway continues to appeal to the readers' senses: we feel the heat of the metal steps, the smoothness of his father's shaved cheeks, we focus on the eagle's gleam.

32. The simile of Connie's wave as he and the train depart provides a memorable visual image. It causes us to draw a parallel with the current situation and how Connie is again disappearing.

33. Connie's background.

34. Statement provides insight on his mother's personality.

35. Connie's military career.

36. Conaway uses a list to relate his father's wartime experiences. Note the voice here. While there is mention of air raids and enemy soldiers floating facedown, dead, the stories do not convey a sense of the real horrors of war but instead focus on a strange, foreign world. It is the way a father would talk about his war experiences with a young child; they are the stories a child would remember. The stories carry a sense of wonder for the father as well as the child. They imply that Connie saw no real wartime action.

37. This implies some of the stories may have been exaggerated. "Buttressed" and "hardware" are vivid word choices. They reflect a certain playfulness in the writer's voice, and tell us as much about him as they do the hardware.

ple on that far ocean. Nothing reinforced the exotic quality of Connie's war more than those smooth, green globes, the smoky glass full of bubbles and strange imperfections.[38]

My mother's resentment was poured out in letters. She kept his replies wrapped in ribbon in a box on the closet floor.[39] He joined us in the house of his mother-in-law and her new husband, a house where, for him, work became the closest thing to having fun, a bulwark against a future that stretched before him, unavoidably.[40] He built and painted fences, and installed a huge attic fan that sucked moths flat against the screens,[41] and put in a bathroom upstairs. I was pressed[42] into helping whenever my older brother managed to escape. "Jimbo, would you like to bring me that hammer?" Dad would say. "Jimbo, would you like to run over there and get me that board?" "Jimbo, would you like to crawl up under there and see if you can find that goddamn roll of electrical tape."[43] In the process I learned journeyman carpentry and glimpsed in the intentness of Dad's gaze and the alacrity of his muscular hands,[44] heard in his murmured, monumental impatience, the unease that lay behind his domestic complicity.[45] I didn't know then that other men were out playing golf, shooting ducks, trolling for smallmouth bass, drinking in comfortable chairs, doing the things men did on weekends.[46]

Dad spent those years moving his file cabinets and battered desk from one building to another, taking advantage of developers' offers as Memphis shifted ever eastward. He made a modest living selling cooling devices to building contractors.[47] Even I was aware of some irony in that: His family predated my mother's in Memphis. His mother's forebear, a fierce, one-legged Confederate veteran, had once owned a sizable piece of what became Overton Park; his descendants qualified as burghers.[48]

---

38. Connie may well have brought home many more wartime mementos, but these are the ones that would have captivated a child: a knife made from an actual enemy airplane, baubles that had floated in a distant sea. The balls become real to the reader through Conaway's sensual, detailed description: we can feel the smoothness of the glass and see the imperfections. The word "strange" adds to their exotic nature. "Yellow people" echoes the attitude of Americans toward the Japanese during World War II.

39. Conaway's use of concrete detail continues to draw readers into his story. He could have simply said his mother kept his father's letters; to say that she kept them on the closet floor wrapped in ribbon creates a visual image that draws us into the scene and the essay.

40. In this paragraph, Conaway elaborates on his father's domestic life and the disappointment and hardships mentioned earlier in the essay. "Bulwark" underscores the embattled nature of his life, yet we do not see him as a fighter.

41. Conaway again pulls us into the scene with a very visual image of moths sucked against the screens of open windows.

42. "Pressed" implies Connie didn't force him to work.

43. The exchange reinforces the image of Connie as a controlled, easygoing man whose outbursts were probably limited to an occasional mild expletive. Note how skillfully Conaway "shows" this, with some humor, through dialogue. He builds toward the moment by using a series of quotes, placing the one with the expletive at the end, where it catches us off guard and thus gets more attention. The exchange also has a familiar ring: many of us have heard similar "outbursts" from our own parents. Thus, it becomes a universal experience, something we readers can identify with.

44. A glimpse at a younger, more physically fit Connie.

45. Implies that his impatience manifested itself only in mild remarks uttered under his breath. "Domestic complicity" establishes his acquiescence in an unhappy marriage. Note the pleasing use of alliteration: "muscular," "murmured," "monumental."

46. Conaway uses concrete examples of how other men pass their weekends in contrast to his father.

47. "Battered" is a vivid word choice; it also continues the image of a quietly embattled Connie. "Cooling devices" harks back to an earlier era and was probably the vocabulary of his father's generation.

48. The constantly moving file cabinets and desk and the taking advantage of developers' offers portray a man who, unlike his feistier ancestors, was always at the whim of others. Note how details make this rendering of Connie's background more vivid: the Confederate veteran is one-legged, the real estate holdings included a sizable piece of what is now Overton Park, an upscale Memphis neighborhood. We wonder what went wrong, why Connie's life took the direction it did. Conaway is gradually gaining empathy for Connie so that by the time we return to him as an older man battling Alzheimer's we care about what happens.

As the younger brother of the bluff, funny Edwin, my father grew up believing in the successful enterprise. I remember a certain windiness when Uncle Edwin entered a room.[49] He had introduced ice to the mid-South, and that had made him rich. Edwin Conaway's ice houses—barns with sweaty oak doors opening into the murk, hung with sides of beef and ham haunches and stacked blue-green slabs of ice giving off fog in layers that crept along floors and spilled over thresholds[50]—were money machines. He used them to build a fortune in stocks.[51]

My father, sixteen years younger than Edwin, had seemed destined to get rich through ice, too. First he went off to Washington and Lee; Edwin had offered to pay his way. But while in Lexington he received word that Edwin and his ice houses were in trouble—the '29 crash had caught him—and his life now took another turn. Dad left W & L to take up something more practical; he enrolled in engineering school at a state university.[52] Years later, Edwin, driving at night along a two-lane highway, far from Memphis, met on the downward slope of a hill the opposite and equal force of his own headlight-flashing sedan (the other car was driven by a drunk on the wrong side of the road) and died of it.[53]

* * *

The process of recognizing my father's predicament, if that is the right word, must be common to other families: discomfort, denial, acquiescence, grief, anger.[54] The doctors were particularly inept, ranging from the affable family physician, who assured us that all old people lose their memories and functions, to a tactless psychiatrist whose specialty was assisting the aged; he wore a heavy gold ID bracelet and demanded that my father count backward from 100 and, in the midst of Dad's struggling to do so, proudly proclaimed dementia.[55]

Money was a problem.[56] Though the disease had a name it had no cure, and so my

---

49. Even though the character of Edwin is "on stage" only briefly we get a vivid sense of what he was like, beyond what he did. Conaway accomplishes this with three words: "bluff," "funny," "windiness." "Bluff" conjures up images of a man who is overweight, outgoing, and a little loud.

50. Conaway's description is both visual and sensual so that even readers who have never been inside an ice house know what it was like. We can both see and feel the "sweaty oak doors"; the word "murk" conveys the cold, dark, and dampness. The sides of beef, the ham haunches, the fog rising from the "blue-green slabs of ice," creeping along the floors and over the threshold put us there. We continue to be with the writer in his journey back to the past. The experience is ours.

51. Edwin's background.

52. We now learn how Connie's life took the turn it did. He was a victim of the Depression. The promise of a more prosperous and perhaps easier life was dashed.

53. Conaway could have written that Edwin died when his car was hit head-on by a drunk driver. Instead, through sentence structure, he re-creates the sequence of the event, skillfully holding the collision and death for the end, where it gains more impact. The sentence begins with Edwin driving along a two-lane highway in the dark. Conaway then inserts "far from Memphis," more as a delay than to situate us geographically, since we never learn where the road was. He picks up with the verb "met," but again holds back about what Edwin met by describing the downward slope of the hill, thus forcing us to read to the end. The moment of impact is rendered poetic with a turn of phrase that hints of Edwin's windiness. The description ends abruptly, as did Edwin, with "and died of it." His death ends the background loop.

54. The essay and the narrative return to the main story line: Connie's battle with Alzheimer's. Here, Conaway universalizes the story, both by recognizing it as a common predicament and by listing emotions all of us can identify with, whether or not we have lost a loved one to this disease.

55. Conaway deftly supports his statement of the doctors' ineptness by offering proof: The first physician insists that all old people lose their memories; the second one bases his diagnosis of dementia on his father's inability to count backwards from 100. The description of the first doctor as "affable" carries a ring of insincerity. Both the word "specialty" and the gold bracelet imply the doctor is in it for the money.

56. The juxtaposition of the bracelet and the family's financial hardships create an even stronger indictment of the doctors.

father could not be committed to the hospital [57] For this reason the government could not be induced[58] to help pay. It fell to my mother, also in her seventies,[59] to care for an invalid who increasingly failed to remember names, hid the mail, shuffled and sometimes stumbled, defied the most potent pharmacopoeia to keep her awake, dribbled his food, railed at her for the loss of his right to drive and other frustrations, and eventually threatened violence if the increasingly phantasmagoric landscape would not hold still.[60] Yet she refused to entomb him in a nursing home.[61] They owned the house but could not afford both it and a nurse, and buying a smaller place was a subject that could not be discussed calmly. Mom talked instead of nonexistent equity, including stock in a moviemaking company that supposedly had Goldie Hawn in tow, sold to my mother by another specialist in assisting the aged.[62] Those lucre-driven arguments released a rancor in me that I will always regret.[63]

During visits to Memphis my brothers and I shot pool with Dad, always the best. We watched him clean the table with displays of his beautiful follow-through as he disregarded color and numbers on the balls, sinking the cue ball off the eight and the eight off the eleven and so on until he lost interest and we started the game all over again.[64]

Once, when I announced I was going to take a shower, Dad said, "Don't forget a spoon."[65]

He fell in love with women on sight and offered, in a friendly way, to knock me down if I didn't stop talking to the female director of the Alzheimer's clinic to whom he was suddenly attracted. He never lost his appetite while still at home, demolishing roast beef, sweet potatoes, tacos, grits, biscuits, and lemon meringue pie without discrimination or regard for the manners that had once been important, but somehow he kept growing smaller.[66]

As it happened, my mother succumbed first, to an aneurysm—a ballooning of a blood vessel[67]—in the right side of the brain. Fortunately, by then they had hired a man to work around the house, since Dad was no longer able to rake leaves;[68] it was he who found my mother in time. From the hospital, Dad somehow managed to telephone me in Washington; like a child, he asked, "Where is everybody?"[69]

---

57. Conaway repeats his earlier theme of how little weight the name carries. It reinforces the feeling of futility.

58. The use of "induce" implies an unreasonableness on the part of the government.

59. Background on his mother.

60. A recitation of symptoms gives us a tight, vivid picture of the ravages of the disease. By listing them rather than talking separately about each instance we get a greater sense of the cumulative effects and the horror of the disease.

61. The word "entomb" lends an image of nursing homes as places where the elderly are forgotten. They might as well be dead and in actual tombs.

62. A reference to the many get-rich schemes aimed at vulnerable senior citizens. "With Goldie Hawn in tow" implies she was paid to lend her name and legitimacy to the venture. "Another specialist in assisting the aged" puts the gold-braceleted doctor in the same category.

63. In baring his anger, Conaway puts us in his shoes, enabling us to empathize.

64. The pool scene "shows" that Connie can no longer do even the things he once excelled at.

65. Again, we "see" the effects of Alzheimer's.

66. This paragraph continues to show the effects of Alzheimer's and his father's wasting away. Even if we have never personally known anyone with the disease, through these vivid pictures we are seeing what it does. "Demolished" captures both the volume of food and the manner with which he ate it.

67. Defines "aneurysm" in lay terms.

68. "Shows" father's decline from what we readers first knew of him. In the beginning of the essay, driving and raking leaves was all he had left. Now he has nothing.

69. Quote shows Connie's isolation and his return to being a child. "Managed" conveys his difficulty in performing such seemingly easy tasks as making a phone call.

Mom survived the surgery but not as the person we knew, and so she was the first to be institutionalized.[70] My brothers and I found another nursing home for Dad just blocks from the corner where he met me that wet November.[71] The night before we moved him we all got a little drunk—I, my brothers, Frank and Dan, my nephew, Danny, and of course Dad.[72]

Too much has been written about whiskey in the South. It was often talked about when I was growing up and utilized at odd moments. Frank once heard our uncle, in the alcoholic blush of Christmas Eve, cradling fifths of his two favorite bourbons, proclaim to all present, "These are the standards!" The idea was that good things followed if you knew what and how to drink, and kept in practice. Dad would travel with a quart of sour mash, and he kept one in the desk drawer at his office and another in the cabinet above the refrigerator. I often saw him extract and uncork it on a tedious afternoon, an act that required neither apology nor explanation. Boys going off for the first time to Ole Miss or U.T. or Chapel Hill took with them an intimate knowledge of the mysteries of drink and were known for it.[73]

This time[74] alcohol undeniably served a purpose beyond the reach of sentiment or drugs. Dad's drinking had been severely curtailed, and now, as we sat around the kitchen table and he sipped some wine, an amazing thing happened: He shed, however briefly, the lost look of the terminally deranged and put on the old, sweet insouciance of the perennial party boy. He no longer knew our names but he did know that he belonged to us, and he teased, and cussed a bit, and even threw—gingerly—a piece of cutlery. Boys, even three generations of them together, were supposed to be cutups, a bit dangerous but adorable.[75] He had been viewed that way as a child, and by my mother too, despite their differences; and in this brief, boozy epiphany I glimpsed all that had been bundled down to me and my brothers and our children, and wondered what place on the planet could possibly replicate such a curious blend of love and delusion.

We hung my mother's oils on the wall of his room at Bright Glade.[76] One painting was of the house outside Tucson where my parents had spent a glorious year in the Thirties,[77] but Dad was not happy with his new digs. The day after we left him we received a call from the director, saying that Dad had attempted to walk out and, when detained, threatened to strike the attendant. I inferred that he had also used the racial epithet once so common in Memphis, and I went out and lectured Dad, who listened in perplexity, sitting in the stuffed chair we had hauled over from the house. I feared the staff would

---

70. With the single word "institutionalized," Conaway again levels criticism at nursing homes. It conveys a sense of warehousing the elderly.

71. By locating the home, Conaway brings us back to the story's beginning, where it all started.

72. The reference to the five of them getting "a little drunk" echoes back to Conaway's earlier reference to "that recreational beverage" and acts as a transition into an exploration of his family's attitude, and that of the South, toward alcohol.

73. We get the sense that the quart of sour mash in the drawer of Connie's battered, moving desk may have helped him through his tedium. The explanation helps us understand the scene that follows. Note the writerliness of this paragraph and its word choices: the use of "alcoholic blush" rather than drunk reflects the very attitude Conaway is describing. "Sour mash," "extract," and "uncork" are vivid, colorful words.

74. Transition out of digression back to main story line.

75. In this poignantly written scene, we see his father's last, brief respite from the grips of Alzheimer's. It provides us a glimpse of what the young Connie was like before he became encumbered with work, marriage, and a family: a party boy who could have a good time. "Cutlery" sounds less dangerous than "a knife" and thus does not detract from father and sons acting as cutups.

76. The use of the home's name, Bright Glade, provides a certain irony. What Conaway shows us is anything but bright and uplifting.

77. Conaway uses paintings to tell us more about his parents and their past.

lose patience and neglect him, but I was wrong. In my fumbling attempt to apologize for my father I must have lost my composure, and I remember a large black woman taking my hand sympathetically, as if I were the patient, and all this discord was transitory and ultimately insignificant.[78]

I saw him only a few times after that,[79] sitting in the foyer of the nursing home, where America's actuarial bias lay starkly exposed.[80] Except for Dad and one other man, the many patients were women, in wheelchairs, facing the door like a school of steelhead watching for the river to rise.[81] Dad almost always slept. First they fed him with a spoon and then with a big plastic syringe. He continued to shrink. When awake, his eyes danced desperately.[82] Pushing him along the outdoor walkway, I saw him attempt to follow the flight of a jay and imagined him living with a relentless mental strobe, each flickering image bearing no relation to what preceded or followed it.[83] He died a year after he went in, Dan holding a hand grown thin and dry as cardboard.[84]

* * *

His will was an old one, scribbled on graph paper.[85] Dad had requested cremation and the spreading of his ashes on the surface of the Mississippi River, at a point of our choosing.[86] We were told by the Coast Guard that this was not permissible but decided to do it anyway; one bleak spring day the three of us boarded a houseboat piloted by my brother's neighbor and set out from the marina on Mud Island, at the foot of the city,[87] with a small metal can that had a snap-on plastic lid. Dad's name was typed on a piece of paper taped to the lid.[88] What he'd hoped for, I think, was accord among the three of us, and maybe even some festivity. I had bought a half-pint of Jim Beam[89] but left it under the car seat.

We headed upstream. In another month the river would rise above the levee on the Arkansas bank and spread away like an inland, caramel-colored sea. A strong current rode up the stone buttresses beneath new, arching spans; we felt the tug of that dark water.[90]

---

78. Scene shows us as much about Conaway and the anguish of relatives as it does about Connie's unhappiness with the nursing home. Again, by revealing his own reaction, Conaway causes us to empathize with him. This moment lets us share the discomfort and ordeal of family members. The plight of the family is summed up by Conaway's observation that the attendant took his hand "as if I were the patient." He and his family are also victims of the disease.

79. Transition, a signal that both Connie and the essay are coming to an end.

80. A writerly way of saying that at nursing homes you can see the pitiful side of living a long life.

81. Simile evokes visual image of the residents passing their days lined up watching the door.

82. Signs of Connie's physical deterioration.

83. Drawing on his observations of his father's dancing eye movements and his own imagination, Conaway attempts to describe what his father must have been experiencing.

84. Simile of his brother Dan holding Connie's frail hand causes us to remember Conaway's image of his father waving from the departing train as he headed to war.

85. The detail of the graph paper echoes the beginning of the essay. It is in keeping with Connie.

86. In a single sentence, Conaway tells us what we need to know of the will, that Connie wanted to be cremated and his ashes scattered on the Mississippi River.

87. Conaway brings us with him on this final journey by setting the scene: it is spring, the day bleak. The three brothers and a neighbor are on a houseboat with Memphis as the backdrop.

88. Note the visual concrete detail and description of the can bearing Connie's ashes. It is small, metal, with a snap-on plastic lid. The piece of paper with his name is typed and taped on the lid, almost like the inscription on a tombstone.

89. Jim Beam is sour mash. It brings to mind the quart Connie always kept at hand and the last gathering of the father and three sons.

90. This paragraph serves both to set the scene and to delay the final scattering of ashes. The "tug of that dark water" creates images of death.

Our pilot said, "Be sure the wind's behind you."[91]

We removed the lid and sprinkled ashes in turn, starting with my older brother. Dan sank the tin; I tossed the lid, which floated my father's name briefly beneath the eye of the world before slipping under.[92]

A month later I dreamed of a man walking with assurance along an empty airport corridor carrying a hanging bag. It was Dad, thirty years younger, his hair thick on the sides, deep chestnut in color; his lean, muscular arms protruded from the rolled sleeves of his shirt with the old-fashioned wing-tip collars.[93] I was surprised to see him there because he did not like to fly—flying is expensive and tends to take you to places where you would just as soon not be[94]—and yet he was off, waving, through a dim, untended portal.[95]

A year later I dreamed of a distant city I wanted to leave, to get to a place where I had left something of significance.[96] My inquiries, made to a faceless person behind a cash register, elicited no response. Across the street sat a station wagon, red in the streaking rain; a clipboard on the seat suggested scheduling, imminent departure. A man sat in the passenger seat. "Dad," I said, and he turned and smiled, the polished rims of his spectacles gathering the light. His gray beard was trimmed to fit the squarish contours of his jaw, and he wore the tan raincoat I knew so well. He said, "Get in, son," with the friendly authority of a man who knows where he, where *we*, are going and is happy to provide deliverance and good company.[97]

JAMES CONAWAY ON READING

"The nonfiction writers who have influenced me include Thoreau, Hemingway, Mailer, and McPhee, but my nonfiction was also influenced by the fiction of Tolstoy, Faulkner, Graham Greene, and other traditional novelists."

---

91. Pilot's quote carries echoes of the familiar Irish blessing:

May the road rise to meet you
May the wind be always to your back
May the sun shine warm upon your face
The rains fall soft upon your fields
And until we meet again,
May God hold you in the palm of His Hand.

92. Connie's name floats briefly before the world, like an epitaph, before the lid slips under completely.

93. Conaway uses a dream to show us a younger, confident Connie. In spite of being a dream it becomes real because of the concrete detail: the chestnut hair, the rolled-up sleeves, the wing-tip collar.

94. Reveals Connie's attitude toward flying.

95. Again recalls the younger Connie heading off to war.

96. Symbolic of his lost father.

97. Final dream provides a circular ending. It essentially repeats the opening scene, but this time Connie is a man who is in control. We see this in the clipboard, the squarish (determined) contours of his jaw, the way he addresses Conaway as "son" rather than the less formal "sonny boy." And this time the car is not small; it's a station wagon and it's red, the symbol of power.

Joan Didion

Joan Didion is widely regarded as an astute observer of modern culture, especially that of her native state, California, the setting for "Some Dreamers of the Golden Dream." The article is about a tabloid-style murder in the San Bernardino Valley, and from the beginning it is as though we are sitting beside Didion, first driving to the scene of the crime, later in the courtroom watching the prosecutor, the defense attorney, and the parade of witnesses. We witness Sandy Slagle collapsing in her seat when the jury hands down its verdict; we hear the defendant Lucille Miller say in a voice that carried across the courtroom, "Sandy, for God's sake please don't."

Didion has long been admired for her careful attention to detail, but what makes her accomplishment here particularly remarkable is that she didn't arrive on the scene until after the trial was over. The description of the college girls camped out at the courthouse all night with their graham crackers and No-Cal hoping for a seat at the trial, the rendering of the attorneys' arguments, even the detail of the deputies' "1965 SHERIFF'S RODEO" string ties, came not from firsthand observation, but from meticulous research. Only her descriptions of the San Bernardino Valley and the murder setting came from direct observation.

"I read about the trial in the Los Angeles papers, kept thinking about it, and finally asked the Saturday Evening Post if they would be interested in a piece," she recalls. "By the time I got to San Bernardino, the trial was long over. I read the transcript in Edward Foley's (Mrs. Miller's defense lawyer) office, and the quotes pertaining to the murder or the affair with Arthwell Hayton came from the transcript. The descriptions of the scene at the courthouse during the trial came from news reports. I interviewed Edward Foley. I spoke to Don Turner, the prosecutor. I went to see Sandy Slagle. I had lunch with Howard Hertel, who covered the trial. . . . [Hertel was a reporter for the Los Angeles Times.]

"Mainly, I drove around to look at all the locations, and picked up what else I could about the place from the Chamber of Commerce. The week I spent in San Bernardino was probably in September or October 1965; I just remember it was the same time of year, the same weather, as it had been when the death occurred the year before. At some point later that fall, when I was already writing the piece, I read in the paper about Arthwell Hayton's remarriage, and made that the ending."

Thus we see Didion, the reporter, exploring every possible avenue—trial transcripts, news reports, even Chamber of Commerce handouts—to re-create a story that was far too good to pass up. That same diligence also marks her firsthand gathering of details and descriptions. She says she has been drawn to the concrete rather than the abstract as far back as her college days at Berkeley.

"My attention veered inexorably back to the specific, to the tangible, to what was generally considered by everyone I knew then and for that matter have known since, the peripheral," she once wrote. "I would try to contemplate the Hegelian dialectic and

would find myself concentrating instead on a flowering pear tree outside my window and the particular way the petals fell on my floor. I would try to read linguistic theory and would find myself wondering instead if the lights were on in the bevatron up the hill."

In spite of the reportorial skills demonstrated in her books Miami *and* Salvador *and the scores of articles she has written over the years, Didion insists she is a bad interviewer and particularly dislikes situations in which she has to talk to someone's press agent.*

"I do not like to make telephone calls, and would not like to count the mornings I have sat on some Best Western motel bed somewhere and tried to force myself to put through the call to the assistant district attorney," she wrote in the preface to Slouching Towards Bethlehem, *a collection of her articles and essays from the 1960s and 1970s. "My only advantage as a reporter is that I am so physically small, so temperamentally unobtrusive, and so neurotically inarticulate that people tend to forget that my presence runs counter to their best interests. And it always does. That is one last thing to remember:* writers are always selling someone out."

Didion has published two additional nonfiction collections and five novels, and collaborated on seven screenplays with writer-husband John Gregory Dunne. She is a frequent contributor to various periodicals, most frequently the New Yorker *and the* New York Review of Books. *She has received National Book Awards in both fiction and nonfiction and was the recipient of the 1996 Edward MacDowell Medal and the 1999 Columbia Journalism Award. She is a member of the American Academy of Arts & Letters and the American Academy of Arts and Sciences.*

Some Dreamers of the Golden Dream

THIS IS A STORY ABOUT LOVE and death in the golden land, and begins with the country. The San Bernardino Valley lies only an hour east of Los Angeles by the San Bernardino Freeway but is in certain ways an alien place: not the coastal California of the subtropical twilights and the soft westerlies off the Pacific but a harsher California, haunted by the Mojave just beyond the mountains, devastated by the hot dry Santa Ana wind that comes down through the passes at 100 miles an hour and whines through the eucalyptus windbreaks and works on the nerves. October is the bad month for the wind, the month when breathing is difficult and the hills blaze up spontaneously. There has been no rain since April. Every voice seems a scream. It is the season of suicide and divorce and prickly dread, wherever the wind blows.[1]

The Mormons settled this ominous country, and then they abandoned it, but by the time they left the first orange tree had been planted and for the next hundred years the San Bernardino Valley would draw a kind of people who imagined they might live among the talismanic fruit and prosper in the dry air, people who brought with them Midwestern ways of building and cooking and praying and who tried to graft those ways upon the land.[2] The graft took in curious ways.[3] This is the California where it is possible to live and die without ever eating an artichoke, without ever meeting a Catholic or a Jew. This is the California where it is easy to Dial-A-Devotion, but hard to buy a book. This is the country in which a belief in the literal interpretation of Genesis has slipped imperceptibly into a belief in the literal interpretation of *Double Indemnity*,[4] the country

1. Didion begins by setting the stage for the murder. There were no doubt many things she could have told us about the setting, but she has been selective (which is as important as the actual collecting of details), using those that best convey a sense of the landscape. In other words, she doesn't use details merely for the sake of using details; they do real work. She first compares the valley to the more familiar, and appealing, coastal California. In doing so, notice her word choices. For coastal California, it's "subtropical twilights" and "soft westerlies" (soft, pleasant, appealing words); the San Fernando Valley is "alien," "harsh," "haunted," "devastated" (hard, harsh, ominous words). The wind "whines" and "works on the nerves," and even if Didion hadn't told us this is a story about love and death, we would know from the tone that something bad is about to happen. Her repeated references to the wind and her use of "and" rather than commas to link "suicide" and "divorce" and "prickly dread" capture the essence of the wind working on the nerves, driving people to do rash things. Throughout the story, the wind is a constant presence, not the kind that brings relief but rather an ominous, ill wind. In creating this mood of foreboding, she is also developing tension, and we are compelled to keep reading. "The season for suicide and divorce and prickly dread" foreshadows what is to come. The phrase itself will be echoed later in the essay.

2. Now that we have the physical landscape, Didion gives us a brief history of the people who settled the valley. In doing so, she tells us what we have already gathered: This is ominous country. Note the interesting word choice of "graft" to describe the influence of the original inhabitants.

3. "The graft" acts as a bridge, or transition, between the original settlers and the current residents. "Curious" carries Didion's voice, and feelings, as do many of the word choices throughout the essays.

4. Through her selective, cumulative use of detail, Didion again captures the residents' narrow lives (they have never eaten an artichoke, they know no Catholics or Jews, they never read books). Her repetition of words, sentence structure, and ideas, and her use of "and" and "or" rather than commas pull the details together into a whole. The repetition also creates a rhythm that propels us, and the story, forward. But note how Didion avoids becoming monotonous. The third repetition becomes "this is the country"; the fourth is merely "the country." Eventually the fifth, sixth, and seventh will become "here." The insertion of a quote provides a breather before the paragraph again gathers momentum. "Double Indemnity" foreshadows what is to come.

of the teased hair and the Capris and the girls for whom all life's promise comes down to a waltz-length white wedding dress and the birth of a Kimberly or a Sherry or a Debbi and a Tijuana divorce and a return to hairdressers' school. "We were just crazy kids," they say without regret, and look to the future. The future always looks good in the golden land,[5] because no one remembers the past. Here is where the hot wind blows and the old ways do not seem relevant, where the divorce rate is double the national average and where one person in every thirty-eight lives in a trailer. Here is the last stop for all those who come from somewhere else, for all those who drifted away from the cold and the past and the old ways. Here is where they are trying to find a new life style, trying to find it in the only places they know to look:[6] the movies and the newspapers.[7] The case of Lucille Marie Maxwell Miller is a tabloid monument to that new life style.[8]

Imagine Banyan Street first, because Banyan is where it happened.[9] The way to Banyan is to drive west from San Bernardino out Foothill Boulevard, Route 66: past the Santa Fe switching yards, the Forty Winks Motel. Past the motel that is nineteen stucco tepees: "SLEEP IN A WIGWAM—GET MORE FOR YOUR WAMPUM." Past Fontana Drag City and the Fontana Church of the Nazarene and the Pit Stop A Go-Go; past Kaiser Steel, through Cucamonga, out to the Kapu Kai Restaurant-Bar and Coffee Shop, at the corner of Route 66 and Carnelian Avenue. Up Carnelian Avenue from the Kapu Kai, which means "Forbidden Seas," the subdivision flags whip in the harsh wind. "HALF-ACRE RANCHES! SNACK BARS! TRAVERTINE ENTRIES! $95 DOWN." It is the trail of an intention gone haywire, the flotsam of the New California. But after a while the signs thin out on Carnelian Avenue, and the houses are no longer the bright pastels of the Springtime Home owners but the faded bungalows of the people who grow a few grapes and keep a few chickens out here, and then the hill gets steeper and the road climbs and even the bungalows are few, and here—desolate, roughly surfaced, lined with eucalyptus and lemon groves—is Banyan Street.[10]

---

5. Note how "the golden land" is becoming an ironic thread that will echo throughout the essay.

6. The repetition of "trying" echoes the dreamers' struggle to climb the social ladder and the sense that they are, in the end, stuck in a rut. Their impermanence again comes through the details (Tijuana divorce, one in thirty-eight lives in a trailer, a divorce rate double the national average, everyone comes from somewhere else). As we continue, note the repeated references to this impermanence (the word "divorce" has appeared three times already) and the wind. It is never a breeze, never pleasant, always hot and unbearable.

7. Because of its placement at the end of the sentence and the use of the colon, the point about the movies and newspapers gains added emphasis.

8. The position of greatest emphasis in both a sentence and a paragraph comes at the end. Thus, Didion waits until the end of this long, involved paragraph to introduce the case of Lucille Miller. By this time, the tension has reached a crescendo. The statement has a way of making readers stop for a breather, but that pause is only momentary.

9. We move on from the previous sentence, expecting now to learn about the Miller case, but Didion instead holds back and starts over, again accumulating details and building tension. The delay compels us to continue reading. The use of direct address, coupled with Didion's use of present tense, creates both immediacy and intimacy with her readers. If we weren't already drawn into the story, we are now.

10. Much of Didion's writing is cinematic, perhaps an influence from her screenwriting. In the opening paragraph, she gave us a panoramic view of the landscape. Now she puts on the zoom lens and takes us closer. As we start up the hill, it is as though we are in the car and she is giving us directions. The latter helps bring order to the details she provides. (The lesson here is to use logic in weaving in your details, to give them order. For example, if you are trying to emphasize the height of a building, you would begin at the bottom with your details and work your way up.) Note the concreteness of the details (nineteen stucco tepees, the Kapu Kai Restaurant-Bar is located at the corner of Route 66 and Carnelian Avenue) and how Didion looks everywhere to gather those details: signs, subdivision flags. Again the details are doing work, giving us a feel for the tackiness (the tepees, a drag strip, a restaurant named Kapu Kai) and impermanence (the new subdivisions) of this "golden" land, which is anything but golden. Didion achieves a sense of completeness by beginning and ending the paragraph with Banyan Street. The repetition of the name (four times in a single paragraph) both emphasizes the street's role in the story and helps readers remember its name.

Like so much of this country, Banyan suggests something curious and unnatural. The lemon groves are sunken, down a three- or four-foot retaining wall, so that one looks directly into their dense foliage, too lush, unsettlingly glossy, the greenery of nightmare; the fallen eucalyptus bark is too dusty, a place for snakes to breed. The stones look not like natural stones but like the rubble of some unmentioned upheaval. There are smudge pots, and a closed cistern. To one side of Banyan there is the flat valley, and to the other the San Bernardino Mountains, a dark mass looming too high, too fast, nine, ten, eleven thousand feet, right there above the lemon groves.[11] At midnight on Banyan Street there is no light at all, and no sound except the wind in the eucalyptus and a muffled barking of dogs. There may be a kennel somewhere, or the dogs may be coyotes.[12]

Banyan Street[13] was the route Lucille Miller took home from the twenty-four-hour Mayfair Market on the night of October 7, 1964, a night when the moon was dark and the wind was blowing and she was out of milk, and Banyan Street was where, at about 12:30 a.m., her 1964 Volkswagen came to a sudden stop, caught fire, and began to burn.[14] For an hour and fifteen minutes Lucille Miller ran up and down Banyan calling for help, but no cars passed and no help came.[15] At three o'clock that morning, when the fire had been put out and the California Highway Patrol officers were completing their report, Lucille Miller was still sobbing and incoherent, for her husband had been asleep in the Volkswagen.[16] "What will I tell the children, when there's nothing left, nothing left in the casket," she cried to the friend called to comfort her. "How can I tell them there's nothing left?"

In fact there was something left,[17] and a week later it lay in the Draper Mortuary Chapel in a closed bronze coffin blanketed with pink carnations.[18] Some 200 mourners heard Elder Robert E. Denton[19] of the Seventh-Day Adventist Church of Ontario speak of "the temper of fury that has broken out among us." For Gordon Miller, he said, there would be "no more death, no more heartaches, no more misunderstandings." Elder Ansel Bristol mentioned the "peculiar" grief of the hour. Elder Fred Jensen asked "what shall it

---

11. Unlike the hard-news reporter, literary journalists—like feature writers in general—are under no obligation to be objective and hide their feelings. As Didion herself has written: "Writing is the act of saying I—of imposing oneself upon other people, of saying listen to me, see it my way, change your mind." Here we see just that. Sometimes those feelings are stated directly ("an intention gone haywire," "the flotsam of the New California"), but most often they are expressed subtly through word choice and description. The lemon trees are "unsettling," "too lush," their foliage nightmarish; the eucalyptus bark is a place for snakes to breed; the stones look "like the rubble of some unmentioned upheaval." Even the mountains loom too high, too fast, too dark. Her repetition of "too" reinforces the gloomy mood.

12. If we weren't already convinced that the place is unsettling, Didion clinches it with a suggestion that the barking dogs may actually be coyotes. Note that she does not say they *are* coyotes, she merely suggests it, but the seed has been planted in the reader's mind.

13. The scene now has been set, the tension built. Now Didion can proceed with Lucille Miller's story. Banyan Street serves as the transition from the scene-setting into the actual incident.

14. Didion again sets the scene so we can picture what happened—or what may have happened. The Mayfair Market is a twenty-four-hour market; there was no moon and that same foreboding wind was blowing. The use of "and" here propels the action and mimics the way Lucille Miller may have related it—all in one breath. In the second clause, Didion uses commas, to echo the action.

15. This sentence again sounds like Lucille Miller's version of the story: her emphasis on how long she ran up and down Banyan, the repetition of "no" conveying her insistence that help never came.

16. Didion saves the fact that Miller's husband was in the burning car for the end of the sentence, where it gains added impact and drama.

17. The repetition of "left" acts as a transition, linking this paragraph to the one above.

18. The concrete details of the "closed" and "bronze" coffin and the pink carnations draw readers into the scene, providing both image and smell.

19. While the actual names of the church elders are not entirely necessary, they put a face on the service. In keeping with her typical use of concrete detail, Didion even provides the middle initial.

profit a man, if he shall gain the whole world, and lose his own soul?"[20] A light rain fell, a blessing in a dry season,[21] and a female vocalist sang "Safe in the Arms of Jesus." A tape recording of the service was made for the widow, who was being held without bail in the San Bernardino County Jail on a charge of first-degree murder.[22]

* * *

Of course she came from somewhere else, came off the prairie in search of something she had seen in a movie or heard on the radio, for this is a Southern California story.[23] She was born on January 17, 1930, in Winnipeg, Manitoba, the only child of Gordon and Lily Maxwell, both schoolteachers and both dedicated to the Seventh-Day Adventist Church, whose members observe the Sabbath on Saturday, believe in an apocalyptic Second Coming, have a strong missionary tendency, and, if they are strict, do not smoke, drink, eat meat, use makeup, or wear jewelry, including wedding rings. By the time Lucille Maxwell enrolled at Walla Walla College in College Place, Washington, the Adventist school where her parents then taught, she was an eighteen-year-old possessed of unremarkable good looks and remarkable high spirits.[24] "Lucille wanted to see the world," her father would say in retrospect, "and I guess she found out."

The high spirits[25] did not seem to lend themselves to an extended course of study at Walla Walla College, and in the spring of 1949 Lucille Maxwell met and married Gordon ("Cork")[26] Miller, a twenty-four-old graduate of Walla Walla and of the University of Oregon dental school, then stationed at Fort Lewis as a medical officer. "Maybe you could say it was love at first sight," Mr. Maxwell recalls. "Before they were ever formally introduced, he sent Lucille a dozen and a half roses with a card that said even if she didn't come out on a date with him, he hoped she'd find the roses pretty anyway." The Maxwells remember their daughter as a "radiant" bride.[27]

Unhappy marriages so resemble one another that we do not need to know too much about the course of this one. There may or may not have been trouble on Guam, where Cork and Lucille Miller lived while he finished his Army duty. There may or may not have been problems in the small Oregon town where he first set up private practice. There appears to have been some disappointment about their move to California:[28] Cork Miller

---

20. The direct quotes do more than let us hear what was said, they serve as clues that the death was not accidental.

21. Rain during a funeral is usually viewed as unfortunate; here, it provides relief from the unrelenting wind and heat.

22. Didion uses the recording as a means of telling us the widow has been charged with murder. Note her careful placement of this revelation at the end of the sentence, the end of the paragraph, the end of the opening section, where it attains added impact, heightened drama.

23. Instead of continuing with what happened, Didion doubles back to give us Lucille Miller's background, and in the process creates a delay, forcing us to continue reading. In providing the background, Didion uses repetition to neatly tie her to the other inhabitants (Miller too came from "somewhere else," she too finds her answers in the movies).

24. The play on words creates a pleasing cadence and stresses the point that she was both high-spirited and good looking, which in the "golden land" is what counted.

25. Repetition both emphasizes her high spirits and links the two paragraphs.

26. The nickname implies that Gordon Miller was a lightweight, without the writer having to say so directly.

27. Gordon Maxwell's recollections of his daughter paint a picture of her; they also imply that he too is shallow. The word "radiant" is reminiscent of a society page wedding write-up.

28. While Didion doesn't say there was trouble in Guam, problems in Oregon, the seed is planted, causing readers to think there was. The repetition of "there may or may not have been . . ." conveys a feeling that there were indeed a lot of problems. Even "there appears to have been some disappointment," while not the same, carries a ring of repetition. Note how Didion uses these three statements about their marital problems also to provide background information.

had told friends that he wanted to become a doctor, that he was unhappy as a dentist and planned to enter the Seventh-Day Adventist College of Medical Evangelists at Loma Linda, a few miles south of San Bernardino. Instead he bought a dental practice in the west end of San Bernardino County, and the family settled there, in a modest house on the kind of street where there are always tricycles and revolving credit and dreams about bigger houses, better streets.[29] That was 1957. By the summer of 1964[30] they had achieved the bigger house on the better street and the familiar accoutrements of a family on its way up: the $30,000 a year, the three children for the Christmas card, the picture window, the family room, the newspaper photographs that showed "Mrs. Gordon Miller, Ontario Heart Fund Chairman. . . ."[31] They were paying the familiar price for it. And they had reached the familiar season of divorce.[32]

It might have been anyone's bad summer, anyone's siege of heat and nerves and migraine and money worries, but this one began particularly early and particularly badly.[33] On April 24 an old friend, Elaine Hayton, died suddenly; Lucille Miller had seen her only the night before.[34] During the month of May, Cork Miller was hospitalized briefly with a bleeding ulcer, and his usual reserve deepened into depression. He told his accountant that he was "sick of looking at open mouths," and threatened suicide.[35] By July 8, the conventional tensions of love and money had reached the conventional impasse[36] in the new house on the acre lot at 8488 Bella Vista,[37] and Lucille Miller filed for divorce. Within a month, however, the Millers seemed reconciled. They saw a marriage counselor. They talked about a fourth child. It seemed that the marriage had reached the traditional truce, the point at which so many resign themselves to cutting both their losses and their hopes.[38]

But the Millers' season of trouble[39] was not to end that easily. October 7 began as a commonplace enough day, one of those days that sets the teeth on edge with its tedium, its small frustrations. The temperature reached 102[40] in San Bernardino that afternoon,

---

29. Rather than giving us a blow-by-blow account of the Millers' marriage, Didion focuses on the points that capture its essence. Her selection of details and cultural symbols (tricycles, revolving credit, dreams about bigger houses and better streets) gives us a tight, vivid picture of the people and the neighborhood. You won't find artichokes and books here. The use of "and" rather than commas creates a wistful, romantic air. The repetition of the *b* sound and the comma stress the residents' yearning to move up the social ladder.

30. She uses a transition to indicate passage of seven years.

31. The repetition of "bigger" and "better" and the use of "the" in the list of accoutrements emphasize the Millers' obsession—and that of the other strivers in the "golden land"—with appearances and keeping up. The reference to her being Heart Fund chairman is also a setup for further use.

32. "Familiar season of divorce" echoes Didion's earlier reference. The repetition conveys both the prevalence of divorce in the "golden land" and the nonchalance toward it. When the Santa Anas blow, it's expected.

33. The repetition of "anyone" again suggests that the Miller case was simply life in the valley taken to the extreme. The reference to the heat, nerves, and migraines echoes Didion's opening description of how the wind works on people's nerves.

34. This statement of fact raises more questions than it answers. Readers wonder why this is important to Lucille Miller's story. We are forced to continue reading. As we will see, the reference is actually a setup.

35. Because of the earlier references, we are not surprised when Cork Miller's "bad summer" leads to a suicide attempt. From the beginning, Didion has lumped "suicide and divorce and prickly dread" together.

36. The repetition and play on the word "conventional" convey a sense that, in the "golden land," the Millers' troubles were not out of the ordinary. The repetition is also pleasing to the ear.

37. The full address suits the tone of the essay. After all, this is not just *any* house; it is "the bigger house on the better street" that all the seekers in the "golden land" want.

38. The references to "the traditional truce" and to "cutting their losses and their hopes" suggests that the reconciliation was a matter of convenience.

39. "Season of trouble" echoes the earlier references. The phrase is an obvious euphemism and thus comes across as Didion making fun of the Millers.

40. In setting the stage for the murder, Didion stresses the heat, which we already know drives people in the valley to do rash things.

and the Miller children were home from school because of Teachers' Institute. There was ironing to be dropped off. There was a trip to pick up a prescription for Nembutal, a trip to a self-service dry cleaner.[41] In the early evening, an unpleasant accident with the Volkswagen: Cork Miller hit and killed a German shepherd, and afterward said that his head felt "like it had a Mack truck on it." It was something he often said. As of that evening Cork Miller was $63,479 in debt, including the $29,637[42] mortgage on the new house, a debt load which seemed oppressive to him. He was a man who wore his responsibilities uneasily,[43] and complained of migraine headaches almost constantly.

He ate alone that night, from a TV tray in the living room. Later the Millers watched John Forsythe and Senta Berger in *See How They Run*,[44] and when the movie ended, about eleven, Cork Miller suggested that they go out for milk. He wanted some hot chocolate. He took a blanket and pillow from the couch and climbed into the passenger seat of the Volkswagen. Lucille Miller remembers reaching over to lock his door as she backed down the driveway. By the time she left the Mayfair Market, and long before they reached Banyan Street, Cork Miller appeared to be asleep.[45]

There is some confusion in Lucille Miller's mind about what happened between 12:30 a.m., when the fire broke out, and 1:50 a.m., when it was reported. She says[46] that she was driving east on Banyan Street at about 35 m.p.h. when she felt the Volkswagen pull sharply to the right. The next thing she knew the car was on the embankment, quite near the edge of the retaining wall, and flames were shooting up behind her. She does not remember jumping out. She does remember[47] prying up a stone with which she broke the window next to her husband, and then scrambling down the retaining wall to try to find a stick. "I don't know how I was going to push him out," she says. "I just thought if I had a stick, I'd push him out." She could not, and after a while she ran to the intersection of Banyan and Carnelian Avenue. There are no houses at that corner, and almost no traffic. After one car had passed without stopping, Lucille Miller ran back down Banyan toward the burning Volkswagen. She did not stop, but she slowed down, and in the flames she could see her husband. He was, she said, "just black."[48]

At the first house up Sapphire Avenue, half a mile[49] from the Volkswagen, Lucille Miller finally found help. There Mrs. Robert Swenson called the sheriff, and then, at Lucille Miller's request, she called Harold Lance, the Millers' lawyer and their close friend.[50] When Harold Lance arrived he took Lucille Miller home to his wife, Joan. Twice Harold

---

41. The repetition of "there was" and the recitation of chores replicate the day's tedium. The Nembutal is also a setup for later developments. Note that Didion does not say *who* picked up the Nembutal.

42. Note Didion's continued use of concrete details: Cork Miller killed a German shepherd, not simply a dog; the debts and mortgage are not rounded off, but rather given in exact dollars. The result is a more vivid scene.

43. The writer's voice. Without saying so, she is making fun of the Millers' melodrama. Cork Miller wears his problems and his headaches like the proverbial heart on the sleeve.

44. The movie title would be a good detail no matter what the film was; this particular movie was about a murder, which makes it particularly noteworthy, given the turn of events.

45. This is drawn from the trial transcript of Lucille Miller's testimony.

46. "Some confusion" and "she says" imply that Didion doesn't believe Lucille Miller's version, without the writer saying so directly.

47. While this is not a quote, it sounds like Lucille Miller's rendering of the accident. The "does not remember," "does remember" mimics her so-called "confusion."

48. The placement of "just black" at the end of the paragraph achieves heightened drama and impact.

49. The distance is important. Without saying so, Didion raises the question of why it took Lucille Miller more than an hour to find help.

50. The juxtaposition of the calls to the sheriff and the lawyer tells us, without Didion having to say so directly, that Lucille Miller is in trouble and she knows it.

Lance and Lucille Miller returned to Banyan Street and talked to the Highway Patrol officers. A third time Harold Lance returned alone,[51] and when he came back he said to Lucille Miller, "O.K. . . . you don't talk any more."[52]

When Lucille Miller was arrested the next afternoon, Sandy Slagle was with her.[53] Sandy Slagle was the intense, relentlessly loyal medical student who used to baby-sit for the Millers, and had been living as a member of the family since she graduated from high school in 1959. The Millers took her away from a difficult home situation, and she thinks of Lucille Miller not only as "more or less a mother or a sister" but as "the most wonderful character"[54] she has ever known. On the night of the accident,[55] Sandy Slagle was in her dormitory at Loma Linda University, but Lucille Miller called her early in the morning and asked her to come home. The doctor was there when Sandy Slagle arrived, giving Lucille Miller an injection of Nembutal. "She was crying as she was going under," Sandy Slagle recalls. "Over and over she'd say, 'Sandy, all the hours I spent trying to save him and now what are they trying to *do* to me?'"

At 1:30 that afternoon,[56] Sergeant William Paterson and Detectives Charles Callahan and Joseph Karr of the Central Homicide Division arrived at 8488 Bella Vista.[57] "One of them appeared at the bedroom door," Sandy Slagle remembers, "and said to Lucille, 'You've got ten minutes to get dressed or we'll take you as you are.' She was in her nightgown, you know, so I tried to get her dressed."

Sandy Slagle tells the story now as if by rote, and her eyes do not waver. "So I had her panties and bra on her and they opened the door again, so I got some Capris on her, you know, and a scarf." Her voice drops.[58] "And then they just took her."

The arrest took place just twelve hours after the first report that there had been an accident on Banyan Street, a rapidity which would later prompt Lucille Miller's attorney to say that the entire case was an instance of trying to justify a reckless arrest. Actually what first caused the detectives who arrived on Banyan Street toward dawn that morning to give the accident more than routine attention were certain apparent physical inconsistencies.[59] While Lucille Miller had said that she was driving about 35 m.p.h. when the car swerved to a stop, an examination of the cooling Volkswagen showed that it was in low gear, and that the parking rather than the driving lights were on.[60] The front wheels, moreover, did not seem to be in exactly the position that Lucille Miller's description of the accident would suggest,[61] and the right rear wheel was dug in deep, as if it had been spun in place. It seemed curious to the detectives, too, that a sudden stop

---

51. The placement of "twice" and "a third time" at the beginning of the sentences places emphasis on the two adverbs and the case's unfolding. They also set us up for the final quote.

52. The quote becomes even more dramatic with its placement at the end of the sentence, the end of the paragraph.

53. By inverting the sentence, Didion creates a transition from the "accident" to Sandy Slagle.

54. Note how "relentlessly loyal" is Didion's only description of Sandy Slagle, yet because of the quotes she comes across as a gushy young woman. The material relating to Slagle came from the trial transcripts, news reports, and Didion's own interview with the young woman.

55. Time transition.

56. Time transition.

57. Again, note the use of the exact address. This is the house where the Millers were supposed to live happily ever after.

58. The fact that Sandy Slagle tells the story "by rote" in a voice that does not waver, then drops, conjures up an image of a somewhat theatrical young woman who is enjoying her "performance," without Didion having to say so.

59. The construction of the sentence places the emphasis on the inconsistencies.

60. Didion again inverts the sentence to emphasize the actual inconsistencies in Lucille Miller's story.

61. "Did not seem" and "would suggest" are subtle ways of saying Lucille Miller is lying.

from 35 m.p.h.—the same jolt which was presumed to have knocked over a gasoline can in the back seat and somehow started the fire—should have left two milk cartons upright on the back floorboard, and the remains of a Polaroid camera box lying apparently undisturbed on the back seat.[62]

No one, however, could be expected to give a precise account of what did and did not happen in a moment of terror, and none of these inconsistencies seemed in themselves incontrovertible evidence of criminal intent.[63] But they did interest the Sheriff's Office, as did Gordon Miller's apparent unconsciousness at the time of the accident, and the length of time it had taken Lucille Miller to get help. Something, moreover, struck the investigators as wrong about Harold Lance's attitude when he came back to Banyan Street the third time[64] and found the investigation by no means over. "The way Lance was acting," the prosecuting attorney said later, "they thought maybe they'd hit a nerve."

And so it was that on the morning of October 8,[65] even before the doctor had come to give Lucille Miller an injection to calm her, the San Bernardino County Sheriff's Office was trying to construct another version of what might have happened between 12:30 and 1:50 a.m. The hypothesis they would eventually present was based on the somewhat tortuous premise that Lucille Miller had undertaken a plan which failed: a plan to stop the car on the lonely road, spread gasoline over her presumably drugged husband, and, with a stick on the accelerator, gently "walk" the Volkswagen over the embankment, where it would tumble four feet down the retaining wall into the lemon grove and almost certainly explode. If this happened, Lucille Miller might then have somehow negotiated the two miles up Carnelian to Bella Vista in time to be home when the accident was discovered. This plan went awry, according to the Sheriff's Office hypothesis, when the car would not go over the rise of the embankment. Lucille Miller might have panicked then—after she had killed the engine the third or fourth time, say,[66] out there on the dark road with the gasoline already spread and the dogs baying and the wind blowing and the unspeakable apprehension that a pair of headlights would suddenly light up Banyan Street and expose her there—and set the fire herself.[67]

Although this version[68] accounted for some of the physical evidence—the car in low because it had been started from a dead stop, the parking lights on because she could not do what needed doing without some light, a rear wheel spun in repeated attempts to get the car over the embankment, the milk cartons upright because there had been no sud-

---

62. Again the sentence ends with the most damaging evidence, where it gains heightened drama and lingers in our mind.

63. Didion's heightened formality ("what did and did not happen," "incontrovertible evidence," "criminal intent") tells us she doesn't believe Lucille Miller, even if she doesn't say so directly.

64. Because of Didion's earlier emphasis on the third return, there is no need to elaborate.

65. Transition.

66. Didion uses words of speculation ("might," "would," "somehow," "the third or fourth time, say") to indicate that the sheriff's office version is not based on hard evidence.

67. Note how the pacing of this "other" version seems to mimic the action. It begins slowly, replicating Lucille Miller plotting the murder: In the planning stages, each step of the scheme is separated by a comma ("a plan to stop the car on the lonely road, spread gasoline over her presumably drugged husband, and, with a stick on the accelerator, gently 'walk' the Volkswagen over the embankment, where it would tumble four feet down the retaining wall into the lemon grove and almost certainly explode"). The next two sentences continue at an equally tenuous pace, with commas and "would's" and "might's." Then when everything goes awry, Didion uses "and" instead of commas to accelerate the pace and the tension. The dash interrupts the momentum, just as a pair of headlights would have caused Lucille Miller to stop briefly before setting the fire. Thus, the most important and dramatic point comes at the end of the sheriff's hypothetical version, and the paragraph where it lingers in our mind and gains added emphasis.

68. The repetition of "version" serves as a transition, linking this paragraph to the previous one.

den stop[69]—it did not seem on its own any more or less credible than Lucille Miller's own story. Moreover, some of the physical evidence did seem to support her story: a nail in a front tire, a nine-pound rock found in the car, presumably the one with which she had broken the window in an attempt to save her husband. Within a few days an autopsy had established that Gordon Miller was alive when he burned, which did not particularly help the State's case, and that he had enough Nembutal and Sandoptal in his blood to put the average person to sleep, which did:[70] on the other hand Gordon Miller habitually took both Nembutal[71] and Fiorinal (a common headache prescription which contains Sandoptal), and had been ill besides.

It was a spotty case, and to make it work at all the State was going to have to find a motive. There was talk of unhappiness, talk of another man.[72] That kind of motive, during the next few weeks, was what they set out to establish. They set out to find it in accountants' ledgers and double-indemnity clauses and motel registers,[73] set out[74] to determine what might move a woman who believed in all the promises of the middle class—a woman who had been chairman of the Heart Fund and who always knew a reasonable little dressmaker and who had come out of the bleak wild of prairie fundamentalism to find what she imagined to be the good life—what should drive such a woman to sit on a street called Bella Vista and look out her new picture window[75] into the empty California sun and calculate how to burn her husband alive in a Volkswagen. They found the wedge they wanted closer at hand than they might have at first expected, for, as testimony would reveal later at the trial,[76] it seemed that in December of 1963 Lucille Miller had begun an affair with the husband of one of her friends, a man whose daughter called her "Auntie Lucille," a man who might have seemed to have the gift for people and money and the good life that Cork Miller so noticeably lacked.[77] The man was Arthwell Hayton,[78] a well-known San Bernardino attorney and at one time a member of the district attorney's staff.

* * *

In some ways it was the conventional[79] clandestine affair in a place like San Bernardino, a place where little is bright or graceful, where it is routine to misplace the future and easy to start looking for it in bed. Over the seven weeks that it would take to try Lucille Miller for murder, Assistant District Attorney Don A. Turner and defense attorney Edward P.

---

69. The repetition of the physical evidence keeps the State's version firmly in our minds, and while Didion says its case is no more credible than Lucille Miller's, she seems to be giving it more weight by giving it added emphasis.

70. The repetition of "which did" and "which did not" creates added emphasis and a rhythm that is pleasing to the ear.

71. We readers remember the earlier trip to pick up the Nembutal.

72. The repetition of "talk" carries the sense of gossip and rumor. It also sets up a pleasing rhythm.

73. The use of "and" rather than commas implies that all these sources indeed held damaging evidence, without the writer actually saying they did.

74. The repetition of "set out" re-creates a sense of the State piecing together its case.

75. Didion's recitation of Lucille Miller's material possessions echoes the earlier list of accoutrements of the family on its way up. The repeated reference to her being Heart Fund chairman implies this was, in Miller's eyes, her biggest accomplishment.

76. We get a clue to Didion's source for this information: trial transcripts.

77. The use of "and" rather than commas conveys a sense of this man having it all.

78. Now we understand the importance of the earlier reference to Elaine Hayton's death. It allows Didion to raise our suspicions about Lucille Miller's possible involvement in the death, without saying a word.

79. Didion again uses "conventional" to convey a sense that in the San Bernardino Valley, affairs, like divorce and "tensions of love and money," are not unusual.

Foley would between them unfold a curiously predictable story. There were the falsified motel registrations. There were the lunch dates, the afternoon drives in Arthwell Hayton's red Cadillac convertible. There were the interminable discussions of the wronged partners. There were the confidantes[80] ("I knew everything," Sandy Slagle would insist fiercely later. "I knew every time, places, everything")[81] and there were the words remembered from bad magazine stories ("Don't kiss me, it will trigger things," Lucille Miller remembered telling Arthwell Hayton in the parking lot of Harold's Club in Fontana after lunch one day) and there were the notes, the sweet exchanges: "Hi Sweetie Pie! You are my cup of tea!! Happy Birthday—you don't look a day over 29!! Your baby, Arthwell."[82]

And,[83] toward the end, there was the acrimony.[84] It was April 24, 1964, when Arthwell Hayton's wife, Elaine, died suddenly, and nothing good happened after that. Arthwell Hayton had taken his cruiser, *Captain's Lady,* over to Catalina that weekend; he called home at nine o'clock Friday night, but did not talk to his wife because Lucille Miller answered the telephone and said that Elaine was showering.[85] The next morning[86] the Haytons' daughter found her mother in bed, dead. The newspapers reported the death as accidental, perhaps the result of an allergy to hair spray.[87] When Arthwell Hayton flew home from Catalina that weekend, Lucille Miller met him at the airport, but the finish had already been written.[88]

It was in the breakup that the affair ceased to be in the conventional mode and began to resemble instead the novels of James M. Cain, the movies of the late 1930's, all the dreams in which violence and threats and blackmail are made to seem commonplaces of middle-class life.[89] What was most startling about the case that the State of California was preparing against Lucille Miller was something that had nothing to do with law at all, something[90] that never appeared in the eight-column afternoon headlines but was always there between them: the revelation that the dream was teaching the dreamers how to live. Here is Lucille Miller talking to her lover sometime in the early summer of 1964, after he had indicated that, on the advice of his minister, he did not intend to see her any more: "First, I'm going to go to that dear pastor of yours and tell him a few things. . . . When I do tell him that, you won't be in the Redlands Church any more. . . . Look, Sonny Boy, if you think your reputation is going to be ruined, your life won't be worth two cents."[91] Here is Arthwell Hayton, to Lucille Miller: "I'll go to Sheriff Frank

---

80. Didion conveys the predictable aspects of the affair through the use of parallel construction and the predictable repetition of "there were the. . . ."

81. Parentheses provide a quick way of inserting quotes (gleaned from trial transcripts) without losing the effect of the litany.

82. Trial transcripts provide an example of the lovers' notes.

83. "And" signals a shift in the tone of the affair.

84. The use of "there was" indicates that the acrimony, like the affair, was predictable.

85. Didion repeats what she has told us earlier: that Elaine Hayton died suddenly and that Lucille Miller had seen her the night before. The juxtaposition of the two facts raises our suspicions of a possible link, without the writer having to spell it out.

86. Didion again uses juxtaposition to heighten our suspicions. Placing "the next morning" at the beginning of the sentence emphasizes the time element.

87. Since the death occurred before Didion came on the scene, she turns to newspaper accounts for the details. Again, she lets the reported facts speak for themselves.

88. The term "the finish had been written" sounds like something scripted from a movie or a true-romance magazine.

89. Like the San Bernardino crowd, Didion looks to the movies for a comparison.

90. Didion repeats "something" for emphasis and rhythm.

91. Didion draws from the trial transcripts and newspaper coverage of the trial. (When writing stories involving past trials, remember to look up the newspaper coverage and/or court transcripts. The latter are public record and can yield quotes, details, and courtroom exhibits, such as photographs and taped conversations.)

Bland and tell him some things that I know about you until you'll wish you'd never heard of Arthwell Hayton." For an affair between a Seventh-Day Adventist dentist's wife and a Seventh-Day Adventist personal-injury lawyer, it seems a curious kind of dialogue.

"Boy, I could get that little boy coming and going," Lucille Miller later confided to Erwin Sprengle, a Riverside contractor who was a business partner of Arthwell Hayton's and a friend to both the lovers. (Friend or no, on this occasion he happened to have an induction coil attached to his telephone in order to tape Lucille Miller's call.)[92] "And he hasn't got one thing on me that he can prove. I mean, I've got concrete—he has nothing concrete." In the same taped conversation with Erwin Sprengle, Lucille Miller mentioned a tape that she herself had surreptitiously made, months before, in Arthwell Hayton's car.

"I said to him, I said 'Arthwell, I just feel like I'm being used.' . . . He started sucking his thumb and he said 'I love you. . . . This isn't something that happened yesterday. I'd marry you tomorrow if I could. I don't love Elaine.' He'd love to hear that played back, wouldn't he?"

"Yeah," drawled Sprengle's voice on the tape. "That would be just a little incriminating, wouldn't it?"

"Just a *little* incriminating," Lucille Miller agreed. "It really *is.*"

Later on the tape, Sprengle asked where Cork Miller was.

"He took the children down to the church."

"You didn't go?"

"No."

"You're naughty."

It was all, moreover, in the name of "love"; everyone involved placed a magical faith in the efficacy of the very word. There was the significance that Lucille Miller saw in Arthwell's saying that he "loved" her, that he did not "love" Elaine. There was Arthwell insisting, later, at the trial, that he had never said it, that he may have "whispered sweet nothings in her ear" (as her defense hinted that he had whispered in many ears), but he did not remember bestowing upon her the special seal, saying the word, declaring "love." There was the summer evening when Lucille Miller and Sandy Slagle followed Arthwell Hayton down to his new boat in its mooring at Newport Beach and untied the lines with Arthwell aboard, Arthwell and a girl with whom he later testified he was drinking hot chocolate and watching television. "I did that on purpose," Lucille Miller told Erwin Sprengle later, "to save myself from letting my heart do something crazy."[93]

* * *

January 11, 1965,[94] was a bright warm day in Southern California, the kind of day when Catalina floats on the Pacific horizon and the air smells of orange blossoms and it is a long way from the bleak and difficult East, a long way from the cold, a long way from the past. A woman in Hollywood staged an all-night sit-in on the hood of her car to prevent repossession by a finance company. A seventy-year-old pensioner drove his station wagon at five miles an hour past three Gardena poker parlors and emptied three pistols and a twelve-gauge shotgun through their windows, wounding twenty-nine people. "Many young women become prostitutes just to have enough money to play cards," he

---

92. The parenthetical aside shows us Sprengle's lack of scruples.
93. Through word choice and detail Didion "shows" us how trite and shallow Arthwell Hayton and Lucille Miller are.
94. Time transition.

explained in a note. Mrs. Nick Adams said that she was "not surprised" to hear her husband announce his divorce plans on the Les Crane Show, and, farther north, a sixteen-year-old jumped off the Golden Gate Bridge and lived.[95]

And, in the San Bernardino County Courthouse,[96] the Miller trial opened. The crowds were so bad that the glass courtroom doors were shattered in the crush, and from then on identification disks were issued to the first forty-three spectators in line. The line began forming at 6 a.m., and college girls camped at the courthouse all night, with stores of graham crackers and No-Cal.[97]

All they were doing was picking a jury, those first few days, but the sensational nature of the case had already suggested itself. Early in December there had been an abortive first trial, a trial at which no evidence was ever presented because on the day the jury was seated the San Bernardino *Sun-Telegram* ran an "inside" story quoting Assistant District Attorney Don Turner, the prosecutor, as saying, "We are looking into the circumstances of Mrs. Hayton's death. In view of the current trial concerning the death of Dr. Miller, I do not feel I should comment on Mrs. Hayton's death." It seemed that there had been barbituates in Elaine Hayton's blood, and there had seemed some irregularity about the way she was dressed on that morning when she was found under the covers, dead. Any doubts about the death at the time, however, had never gotten as far as the Sheriff's Office. "I guess somebody didn't want to rock the boat," Turner said later. "These were prominent people."

Although all of that had not been in the *Sun-Telegram's* story,[98] an immediate mistrial had been declared. Almost as immediately, there had been another development: Arthwell Hayton had asked newspapermen to an 11 a.m. Sunday morning press conference in his office. There had been television cameras, and flash bulbs popping[99] "As you gentlemen may know," Hayton had said, striking a note of stiff bonhomie,[100] "there are very often women who become amorous toward their doctor or lawyer. This does not mean on the physician's or lawyer's part that there is any romance toward the patient or client."

"Would you deny that you were having an affair with Mrs. Miller?" a reporter had asked.

"I would deny that there was any romance on my part whatsoever."

It was a distinction he would maintain through all the wearing weeks to come.

So they had come to see Arthwell, these crowds who now milled beneath the dusty palms outside the courthouse, and they had also come to see Lucille, who appeared as a slight, intermittently pretty woman, already pale from lack of sun, a woman who would turn thirty-five before the trial was over and whose tendency toward haggardness was beginning to show, a meticulous woman who insisted, against her lawyer's advice, on com-

---

95. Didion draws from the news to put Lucille Miller's case in context: It was just another California moment.

96. Place transition.

97. The concrete detail (the admittance of the first forty-three spectators on a first-come basis, the line beginning to form at 6 a.m., the college girls camping out all night, their diet of graham crackers and No-Cal) adds to Didion's portrait of a shallow Southern California culture. The description is drawn from news reports.

98. By using the adverbial clause at the beginning of the sentence, Didion creates a smooth transition between paragraphs and places the emphasis on the more important point: the declaration of a mistrial.

99. Sets stage for the press conference.

100. Didion uses attribution to insert description of Hayton's movements so that readers both "see" and hear what transpired.

ing to court with her hair piled high and lacquered.[101] "I would've been happy if she'd come in with it hanging loose, but Lucille wouldn't do that," her lawyer said. He was Edward P. Foley, a small, emotional Irish Catholic who several times wept in the courtroom. "She has a great honesty, this woman," he added, "but this honesty about her appearance always worked against her."

By the time the trial opened,[102] Lucille Miller's appearance included maternity clothes, for an official examination on December 18 had revealed that she was then three and a half months pregnant, a fact which made picking a jury even more difficult than usual, for Turner was asking the death penalty.[103] "It's unfortunate but there it is," he would say of the pregnancy to each juror in turn, and finally twelve were seated, seven of them women, the youngest forty-one, an assembly of the very peers—housewives, a machinist, a truck driver, a grocery-store manager, a filing clerk—above whom Lucille Miller had wanted so badly to rise.[104]

That[105] was the sin, more than the adultery, which tended to reinforce the one for which she was being tried. It was implicit in both the defense and the prosecution that Lucille Miller was an erring woman, a woman who perhaps wanted too much. But to the prosecution she was not merely a woman who would want a new house and want to go to parties and run up high telephone bills ($1,152 in ten months), but a woman who would go so far as to murder her husband for his $80,000 in insurance, making it appear an accident in order to collect another $40,000 in double indemnity and straight accident policies.[106] To Turner she was a woman who did not want simply her freedom and a reasonable alimony (she could have had that, the defense contended, by going through with her divorce suit), but wanted everything, a woman motivated by "love and greed." She was a "manipulator." She was a "user of people."[107]

To Edward Foley, on the other hand, she was an impulsive woman who "couldn't control her foolish little heart." Where Turner skirted the pregnancy, Foley dwelt upon it, even calling the dead man's mother down from Washington to testify that her son had told her they were going to have another baby because Lucille felt that it would "do much to weld our home again in the pleasant relations that we used to have." Where the prosecution saw a "calculator," the defense saw a "blabbermouth," and in fact Lucille Miller

---

101. While Didion doesn't directly say what she thinks about Lucille Miller, she allows her views to show through her description: "intermittently pretty," "whose tendency toward haggardness was beginning to show," "her hair piled high and lacquered." The fact she was "already pale from lack of sun" suggests Miller played in the sun a lot.

102. Time transition.

103. Note how dramatically this sentence unfolds, catching us by surprise at every turn. It's an excellent example of the writer revealing a little information at a time to keep us reading. Instead of telling us earlier that Lucille Miller was found to be pregnant during an examination in December, Didion holds back on the news until the defendant enters the courtroom in maternity clothes. While we are still reeling from this, she discloses that the State is asking for the death penalty—a fact that comes at the end of the sentence, where it gains more impact.

104. Didion again makes this point at the end of the sentence and the paragraph, where the irony gains impact and drama.

105. "That" serves as a tight transition, linking this paragraph to the previous sentence.

106. Didion neatly sums up the prosecution while still using details from trial transcripts to bring the two-month trial to life: the phone bill, the provisions of her husband's insurance. Note how Didion's earlier references to "double indemnity" have foreshadowed this moment.

107. Didion again sums up the defense in specific terms, thus continuing to capture the mood and sense of the trial. Because of her earlier emphasis on the way the word "love" was bandied about by Lucille's circle of friends, we do not take her attorney's insistence that she was motivated by "love" seriously.

did emerge as an ingenuous conversationalist. Just as, before her husband's death, she had confided in her friends about her love affair, so she chatted about it after his death, with the arresting sergeant. "Of course Cork lived with it for years, you know," her voice was heard to tell Sergeant Paterson on a tape made the morning after her arrest. "After Elaine died, he pushed the panic button one night and just asked me right out, and that, I think, was when he really—the first time he really faced it." When the sergeant asked why she had agreed to talk to him, against the specific instructions of her lawyers, Lucille Miller said airily, "Oh, I've always been basically quite an honest person. . . . I mean I can put a hat in the cupboard and say it cost ten dollars less, but basically I've always kind of just lived my life the way I wanted to, and if you don't like it you can take off."[108]

The prosecution hinted at men other than Arthwell, and even, over Foley's objections, managed to name one. The defense called Miller suicidal. The prosecution produced experts who said that the Volkswagen fire could not have been accidental. Foley produced witnesses who said that it could have been. Lucille's father, now a junior-high-school teacher in Oregon, quoted Isaiah to reporters: *"Every tongue that shall rise against thee in judgment thou shalt condemn."* "Lucille did wrong, her affair," her mother said judiciously. "With her it was love.[109] But with some I guess it's just passion." There was Debbie, the Millers' fourteen-year-old, testifying in a steady voice about how she and her mother had gone to a supermarket to buy the gasoline can the week before the accident. There was Sandy Slagle, in the courtroom every day, declaring that on at least one occasion Lucille Miller had prevented her husband not only from committing suicide but from committing suicide in such a way that it would appear an accident and ensure the double-indemnity payment. There was Wenche Berg, the pretty twenty-seven-year-old Norwegian governess to Arthwell Hayton's children, testifying that Arthwell had instructed her not to allow Lucille Miller to see or talk to the children.[110]

Two months dragged by, and the headlines never stopped.[111] Southern California's crime reporters were headquartered in San Bernardino for the duration: Howard Hertel from the *Times*, Jim Bennett and Eddy Jo Bernal from the *Herald-Examiner*. Two months in which the Miller trial was pushed off the *Examiner's* front page only by the Academy Award nominations and Stan Laurel's death.[112] And finally, on March 2, after Turner had reiterated that it was a case of "love and greed," and Foley had protested that his client was being tried for adultery, the case went to the jury.[113]

They brought in the verdict, guilty of murder in the first degree, at 4:50 p.m. on March 5.[114] "She didn't do it," Debbie Miller cried, jumping up from the spectators' section. "She didn't *do* it." Sandy Slagle collapsed in her seat and began to scream. "Sandy, for God's sake please *don't*," Lucille Miller said in a voice that carried across the court-

---

108. Didion continues summing up both the defense and the prosecution's arguments, drawing from trial transcripts and news reports to maintain the flavor of the trial. Note how she also alternates the two sides, just as they would have taken turns during the trial itself.

109. Because of the earlier setup, we don't put much stock in the word "love."

110. Didion uses parallel construction and repetition ("there was") to convey concisely some of the more interesting testimony. The repetition also serves to emphasize and set apart each item. By using the testimony of Wenche Berg, the governess, last, Didion is giving us information that will come in handy later.

111. Transition indicates passage of time.

112. The fact that the trial was pushed off the front page only by the Academy Awards and the death of one-half of the Laurel & Hardy comedy team provides commentary on the *Examiner* and, by implication, Southern California, without Didion making a direct statement.

113. By positioning this statement about the case going to the jury at the end of the sentence, it serves as a transition, or bridge, to the following paragraph.

114. Note the specific detail, which Didion drew from news reports.

room, and Sandy Slagle was momentarily subdued.[115] But as the jurors left the court-room she screamed again: "You're murderers. . . . Every last one of you is a *murderer*." Sheriff's deputies moved in then, each wearing a string tie that read "1965 SHERIFF'S RODEO,"[116] and Lucille Miller's father, that sad-faced junior-high-school teacher who believed in the word of Christ and the dangers of wanting to see the world, blew her a kiss off his fingertips.[117]

* * *

The California Institution for Women at Frontera,[118] where Lucille Miller is now, lies down where Euclid Avenue turns into country road, not too many miles from where she once lived and shopped and organized the Heart Fund Ball.[119] Cattle graze across the road, and Rainbirds sprinkle the alfalfa. Frontera has a softball field and tennis courts, and looks as if it might be a California junior college, except that the trees are not yet high enough to conceal the concertina wire around the top of the Cyclone fence. On visitors' day there are big cars in the parking area, big Buicks and Pontiacs[120] that belong to grandparents and sisters and fathers (not many of them belong to husbands),[121] and some of them have bumper stickers that say "SUPPORT YOUR LOCAL POLICE."[122]

A lot of California murderesses live here, a lot of girls who somehow misunderstood the promise.[123] Don Turner put Sandra Garner here (and her husband in the gas chamber at San Quentin) after the 1959 desert killings known to crime reporters as "the soda-pop murders." Carole Tregoff is here, and has been ever since she was convicted of conspiring to murder Dr. Finch's wife in West Covina, which is not too far from San Bernardino.[124] Carole Tregoff is in fact a nurse's aide in the prison hospital,[125] and might have attended Lucille Miller had her baby been born at Frontera; Lucille Miller chose instead to have it outside, and paid for the guard who stood outside the delivery room in St. Bernardine's Hospital. Debbie Miller came to take the baby home from the hospital, in a white dress with pink ribbons,[126] and Debbie was allowed to choose a name. She named the baby Kimi Kai.[127] The children live with Harold and Joan Lance now, because Lucille Miller will probably spend ten years at Frontera. Don Turner waived his original request for the death penalty (it was generally agreed that he had demanded it only, in Edward Foley's words, "to get anybody with the slightest trace of human kindness in their

---

115. By using the attribution to insert action, Didion brings us into the courtroom. The details again came from news reports.

116. The concrete detail again takes us into the moment.

117. Didion's voice and her feelings come through her description of the father. The fact that he blew his daughter a kiss "off his fingertips" makes him also look lightweight. Even to have written that he blew her a kiss, period, would have carried a slightly different connotation.

118. Place transition.

119. Didion uses the proximity to note again the irony of where Lucille Miller ends up. The use of "and" rather than commas pulls the three together into a whole. Note still another reference to Miller's Heart Fund activities.

120. The big cars "show" us that Lucille Miller isn't the only one whose life didn't end up exactly like she had dreamed.

121. The parenthetical aside is a tight way to tell us that most of the women are serving time for doing in their husbands.

122. The bumper sticker adds a touch of irony. It also provides insight into the people.

123. Didion elaborates on what was only implied by the big cars.

124. Two of the more highly publicized cases of that era.

125. Carole Tregoff provides a transition, or link, back to Lucille Miller and her own case.

126. Note Didion's continued use of detail, from news reports, to capture pivotal moments.

127. The name tells us something about Debbie: She is a product of her culture. The name sounds a little like the Kapu Kai Restaurant-Bar and some of the other phony names of the San Bernardino culture.

veins off the jury"), and settled for life imprisonment with the possibility of parole. Lucille Miller does not like it at Frontera, and has had trouble adjusting. "She's going to have to learn humility," Turner says. "She's going to have to use her ability to charm, to manipulate."[128]

The new house is empty now, the house on the street with the sign that says

PRIVATE ROAD

BELLA VISTA

DEAD END[129]

The Millers never did get it landscaped, and weeds grow up around the fieldstone siding. The television aerial has toppled on the roof, and a trash can is stuffed with the debris of family life: a cheap suitcase, a child's game called "Lie Detector." There is a sign on what would have been the lawn, and the sign reads "ESTATE SALE."[130] Edward Foley is trying to get Lucille Miller's case appealed, but there have been delays. "A trial always comes down to a matter of sympathy," Foley says wearily now. "I couldn't create sympathy for her." Everyone is a little weary now, weary and resigned, everyone[131] except Sandy Slagle, whose bitterness is still raw. She lives in an apartment near the medical school in Loma Linda, and studies reports of the case in *True Police Cases* and *Official Detective Stories.*[132] "I'd much rather we not talk about the Hayton business too much," she tells visitors, and she keeps a tape recorder running.[133] "I'd rather talk about Lucille and what a wonderful person she is and how her rights were violated." Harold Lance does not talk to visitors at all. "We don't want to give away what we can sell," he explains pleasantly; an attempt was made to sell Lucille Miller's personal story to *Life,* but *Life* did not want to buy it. In the district attorney's offices they are prosecuting other murders now, and do not see why the Miller trial attracted so much attention. "It wasn't a very interesting murder as murders go," Don Turner says laconically. Elaine Hayton's death is no longer under investigation. "We know everything we want to know," Turner says.[134]

Arthwell Hayton's office is directly below Edward Foley's.[135] Some people around San Bernardino say that Arthwell Hayton suffered; others say that he did not suffer at all.[136] Perhaps he did not, for time past is not believed to have any bearing upon time present or future, out in the golden land where every day the world is born anew.[137] In any case, on October 17, 1965, Arthwell Hayton married again, married his children's pretty governess, Wenche Berg,[138] at a service in the Chapel of the Roses at a retirement

---

128. The implication is that Lucille Miller has not changed. She will get by the same way she always has. The quotes come from interviews.

129. Didion no doubt observed this sign earlier in her research but waits for a more dramatic—and ironic—moment to use it.

130. Through selective use of detail Didion draws a vivid picture of a life that ended on a deadend street: the toppled antenna, the stuffed trash can, the cheap suitcase, the ironic—and unheeded—game. Didion gathered the details by driving around the area.

131. Didion uses repetition ("everyone" and "weary") for emphasis and rhythm.

132. The use of the magazine names again "shows" us Sandy Slagle's lack of depth.

133. The tape recorder provides color. It also "shows" us that Sandy Slagle is carrying on in the tradition of Lucille Miller and her circle. The "visitor" is actually Didion.

134. The quotes from Harold Lance and Don Turner are drawn from interviews.

135. Didion again uses juxtaposition to point out another irony.

136. Play on words provides a pleasing rhythm as well as tightly summing up the two sides.

137. The references to the "golden land" and the lack of stock put in the past echo the essay's opening. It also provides commentary on Arthwell Hayton's marriage.

138. Thus we see why the reference to Wenche Berg and her testimony is especially important to the essay.

village near Riverside. Later the newlyweds were feted at a reception for seventy-five in the dining room of Rose Garden Village. The bridegroom was in black tie, with a white carnation in his buttonhole. The bride wore a long white *peau de soie* dress and carried a shower bouquet of sweetheart roses with stephanotis streamers.[139] A coronet of seed pearls held her illusion veil.[140]

JOAN DIDION ON READING

When the writer Sara Davidson asked Didion what authors had influenced her, she responded:

"I don't think you're influenced by anybody you read after age 20. That all happens before you start working yourself. You would never know it from reading me, but I was very influenced by Hemingway when I was 13, 14, 15. I learned a lot about how sentences worked. How a short sentence worked in a paragraph, how a long sentence worked. Where the commas worked. How every word had to matter. It made me excited about words. Conrad, for the same reasons. The sentences sounded wonderful. I remember being so excited once, when I discovered that the key lines in *Heart of Darkness* were in parentheses. James, whom I didn't read until I was in college, was important to me in trying to come to terms with the impossibility of getting it right. James's sentences, with all those clauses, had to do with keeping the options open, letting the sentence cover as much as it could. That impressed me a great deal."

---

139. The account of Arthwell Hayton's wedding, with its trivial details, sounds like it comes straight out of an old-time society page wedding write-up, especially "the newlyweds were feted." This material came from a newspaper account.

140. The veil and its double-meaning "illusion" provide an ending that resonates and lingers with us. Life in the San Bernardino Valley goes on.

David Finkel

While thousands were affected by the Kosovo conflict, David Finkel draws readers into the experience by focusing on one family rather than the masses. "A Road That Never Ends" was the last in a series of articles he wrote for the Washington Post's *foreign section during the three months he spent overseas covering the refugees, first in the camps in Macedonia and Albania and then inside Kosovo. During his travels, he happened upon the village of Vlastica (the Serbian name; the village now goes by Llastice, the Albanian name), where he met up with a group of people just after they found the body of eleven-year-old Lulzim. He also located the boy's parents in a Macedonian refugee camp, where they were waiting to learn of their son's whereabouts.*

"They were the last of the refugees," Finkel recalls. "The exodus was over. The story was an attempt to explain everything that [the war and the exodus] did and did not mean."

The article is beautifully crafted, but Finkel's achievement becomes even more notable given the deadlines and conditions he worked under.

"One of the truths about doing such reporting is that the reporting itself was often the least of it," he says. "So much of a day was spent just getting wherever I was going, dealing with arrangements. It was difficult to find interpreters whose command of English allowed for nuance and whose political ideologies wouldn't conflict with my need for unbiased translation. It was difficult to do just about everything, and that's the other truth about such reporting: The difficulties were part of what made the experience of being a reporter in Kosovo so exhilarating. Every day, every experience, was a reminder of how devastating the war was to the people at the center of it, the refugees, and of the importance of telling their stories. It felt like a chance to do journalism that truly mattered."

He later returned to do a follow-up story for the Post's *Sunday magazine.*

Finkel received a Sigma Delta Chi award for his coverage of the conflict. Prior to joining the Post *as a staff writer in 1990, he worked on the* St. Petersburg Times *and the* Tallahassee Democrat. *He has been a recipient of a Penney-Missouri Award for feature writing and a distinguished writing award from the American Society of Newspaper Editors, an honor he had been a finalist for on three other occasions. He has been a finalist for a Pulitzer Prize twice. His work has been included in numerous journalism anthologies.*

A Road That Never Ends

These are the dreams of a refugee named Feti Musliu and his wife, Lutfie, in the last hopeful moments before their lives get even worse:[1]

We will go to the United States, Feti is saying. Any day now. Maybe to Boston, because I heard from a man in another tent that Boston is nice.[2]

And Feti will find a job, says Lutfie, speaking of a man whose only job so far has been to farm the same meager patch of Kosovo that was farmed by his father and grandfather.[3]

And Lutfie will have a house again, Feti says, speaking of a woman who for two months has been cooking over an open fire and has a bad burn on one of her arms to show for it.

And the children will go back to school, Lutfie says.

And we'll be out of this tent, Feti says of the place where he and Lutfie and three of their children have been living since April 16.

And Lulzim will be with us, Lutfie says, speaking of their oldest child, who is 11, whom they haven't seen since they were attacked by Yugoslav soldiers on April 13, who they think is somewhere in Kosovo with his grandfather.[4]

We were told a month ago we'd be going, Feti says, sitting in front of his tent.[5] So we're waiting.[6]

It's late June.[7] The war is over. The second exodus[8] is well underway. Everyone is going back to Kosovo, the place where the Muslius no longer want to be, so they watch everyone else leaving the camp and heading up the road, an entire world seeming to move in one direction, north this time, the first exodus in reverse.[9]

"A Road That Never Ends" first appeared in the *Washington Post* in 1999. Copyright © 1999 the *Washington Post*. Reprinted by permission.

1. The story is structured chronologically. It is written in the present tense to create more immediacy. The tension begins in the first sentence, which starts quietly and builds to a dramatic ending: "the last hopeful moments before their lives get even worse." We are compelled to read the story to find out both about their lives up to this moment and about what is about to happen.

2. Finkel uses the couple's dreams to provide information about them and their lives. While the quotes are paraphrased and not the exact words of Feti and Lutfie, they nevertheless sound like their voices.

3. The attribution is used as a means of inserting information. Thus, Finkel allows the action to continue to move forward rather than stopping for a long block of exposition.

4. The first crisis (the separation from their son) is introduced. We are forced to read on to learn the resolution. The exact date (April 13) serves as a reference point that will surface later in the narrative. Note the repetition of the sentence structure ("And Feti will . . . ," "And Lutfie will . . ."), which adds emphasis to each point, as well as linking them into one big dream.

5. Here, the attribution is used to insert movement and thus continue the forward momentum.

6. The last sentence of the quote introduces another crisis: How long will they have to wait? Again, we have to continue reading to find out.

7. This situates us in time and serves as a transition into a broader explanation of what is going on.

8. The word "exodus" conveys a sense of large numbers. It also carries echoes of the biblical exodus. "Second exodus" is also a setup that will be repeated throughout the story. Because Finkel has described it here, he can refer to it later without having to elaborate.

9. Note the use of short sentences and of commas in the last, longer sentence to heighten the drama. "An entire world" captures the magnitude of the migration and the sense that an entire country is on the move.

Except one day someone comes in the other direction, against the tide, into Stenkovic II and toward the entrance of the tent.[10]

It is the grandfather.

Who is alone.

And who is confused by what Lutfie is saying as she rushes toward him.[11]

"Where's Lulzim?" she is saying.

So confused he doesn't answer.

"Where's my son?" she asks again.

Now he does answer.

"I haven't seen him," he says.[12]

* * *

And just like that,[13] the truth of a war that is over, but won't be over for a long time,[14] closes in on another family.

How bad will it be in the final accounting?[15] No one can know, not yet, which is the story of Kosovo right now. The sorting. The reckoning. Already, there have been enough answers to allow the inevitable drift in attention in Washington, in the rest of Europe, in any place that isn't the Balkans. Yes, there were atrocities. Yes, there are mass graves. Yes, the stories of fires were true, and ruined villages were true, and torturings were true, and rapes were true, and murders were true; and yes, the refugees will return.[16]

The end.[17]

But meanwhile,[18] every day, come discoveries that, to outsiders, may seem numbingly repetitious—another grave site, another collapsed house, another charred land-

---

10. The preposition "except" draws attention to the lone man going against the traffic. His approach gains further impact by being isolated in a separate paragraph. Note the cinematic nature of this sentence, the way the camera follows his approach: First, we see someone in the distance, then he approaches the camp, then he enters the tent. The tension is heightened by the accumulation of prepositional phrases and the fact we cannot see who the man is. Finkel could easily have written: "Except one day Feti sees his father coming from the other direction . . . ," which would have undermined the suspense. Note how he ties the man's approach to the exodus with the repetition of "direction," drawing the contrast with the word "other."

11. The realization that it is the grandfather and that he is alone gains added impact by being divided into clauses, with each placed on a separate line. The effect is much more dramatic than combining them into one long sentence: "It is the grandfather, who is alone and who is confused by what Lutfie is saying as she rushes toward him."

12. The tension continues to build, both because of the short sentences, on separate lines, and because Finkel withholds the fact that the grandfather has not seen Lulzim until the last line, where that fact stands out starkly.

13. Transition from one family to a more general exposition about the war.

14. The repetition and play on words emphasize the fact that while the fighting may be over it will be a long time before life returns to normal.

15. Finkel could have simply made the statement that no one knows what the final assessment of the war will be. By posing the question, he seems to echo what is on the minds of both the refugees and the readers, thus drawing us further into the story.

16. As the digression continues, note the repetition of words and sentence structure to drive home points. First, there is the repetition of the prepositional phrases to emphasize the fact that everybody but the refugees has forgotten about the war. The parallel construction and repetition of "yes" and "true" drive home the reality of the atrocities reported by the news media. Note how Finkel gives added emphasis to the fact that the refugees will return by placing it at the end of the list and by breaking the expected pattern and returning to "yes."

17. After the previous paragraph with its long sentences and long litany, "the end"—isolated on its own line, in its own paragraph—gains added impact. Because of its juxtaposition with the litany of atrocities, however, we do not believe it. The horror—like the story—is not over.

18. Transition returns us to the digression. It is not the end after all.

scape—but to the families making them aren't repetitious at all.[19] Because beyond the broad outlines are details that make each family's journey home heartbreakingly fresh.[20]

In the tiny village of Vlastica,[21] where the Muslius lived until it was abandoned in early April,[22] the first people back discover that the particular grave site in their particular collapsed house contains 13 bodies, including that of a 2-year-old boy who reportedly was shot in the forehead. Twice.[23]

And how, they wonder, looking at bones in the rubble, does someone shoot a 2-year-old boy even once?[24]

And the following day, when a man named Shyqri Veseili returns to Vlastica, he discovers that Serbs not only burned his house, stole his cattle, stole his tractor, stole his refrigerator, burned his hay and burned his stockpiled corn, they also stole 19 of his 20 blankets.[25]

And why, he wonders, amid all the things to wonder about, would they leave one blanket behind?[26]

And the following day, when a man named Besim Musliu[27] returns, he discovers that in the ransacking of his family's house, the Serbs not only tipped over furniture, tossed around clothing, ripped books and smashed pictures, they fired two bullets into one end of a baby's cradle, the end with a design of hand-painted flowers.[28]

And[29] where to begin, Besim wonders—and then he does what he was sent to do, which is to begin looking for his nephew Lulzim.[30]

This was the family's decision,[31] made in the confines of a hot, dark tent as a grandfather rested from his trip. There was no way of knowing where Lulzim might be, so it was decided that Feti and Lutfie should remain in Stenkovic II in case they were listed on a flight to the United States, and that Besim, who is Feti's brother and who wanted to return to Vlastica anyway, would go back and look for a boy who might be anywhere at all.[32]

Back he went then, to a village that is a half-mile long, had a prewar population of

---

19. Repetition—even of the word "repetitious"—drives home the horror of the discoveries. It also conveys a feeling that the atrocities are unending.

20. Transition begins moving the story from the general back to the specific.

21. Place transition returns us to the Muslius' story, though not to the family itself.

22. Background information.

23. The repetition of "particular" serves to move us from a group shot to one home, then to one two-year-old boy. Note the impact of isolating "twice" at the end of the paragraph. It would have been far less effective to say "shot twice in the forehead" or even "shot in the forehead twice."

24. This is the voice of the villagers, but it is also the question on our minds. Thus, we empathize and are drawn further into the story.

25. Because it is easier for readers to empathize with an individual than with an entire village, Finkel focuses on one man's plight. Note how he uses the device of a list and repetition to drive home what happened with more force. He repeats "stole" three times, shifts to "burned" to avoid monotony, then returns to "stole" to end his account. The placement of the blankets at the end of the sentence and the slight variation in form (they also stole . . .) gives added emphasis to the puzzling nature of this theft.

26. The villagers' voice, and our own.

27. The use of the man's name ties him to Feti and Lutfie Musliu, though we do not yet know the relationship. By withholding this information, Finkel forces us to continue reading.

28. The specific detail of the bullet holes and the cradle's floral design reinforces the senselessness of war. Because the tie between this scene and Feti and Lutfie has still not been explained, we continue reading.

29. The conjunction "and" at the beginning of this and the four previous paragraphs links the individual experiences into a whole.

30. We learn finally that Besim is looking for Lulzim. The question of the relationship has been answered, but we still don't know what has happened to the boy. Thus, the tension continues to build.

31. Transition into explanatory digression.

32. Digression explains how Besim happened to be in Vlastica looking for Lulzim.

2,100 and dead-ends into a high hill, which is where all 2,100 people went into hiding in late March when mortar shells began descending on Vlastica from the Serbian village just up the road. Over the next few days, when it became apparent that the villagers would be living in the hills for a while, they began going back at night to get clothing, cooking supplies, sheets of plastic to fashion into shelters, even a few cows so they would have milk.[33]

Then, in early April, Yugoslav soldiers and Serbian militiamen descended on the village and set house after house ablaze.

Then,[34] on April 13 at 11 a.m.,[35] they came up into the hills, firing.[36]

Two hours earlier,[37] Lulzim had been sent down toward a stream with two cows sorely in need of water.[38]

Now it is 2 1/2 months later,[39] and Besim, not knowing where else to go, walks from his house into the village, and from the village up to the hill, and there, near the top, on the other side from where everyone was that day, is Lulzim.[40]

And it takes only a moment to realize what must have happened.[41]

That, alone when the shooting began, he must have begun running up this lonesome hill toward his family.[42]

That[43] the bullet that caught up with him must have come from somewhere below, because there is an entry hole in the left side of his head, just below the ear, and an exit hole in the right side, almost at the top.[44]

That he has been dead for a long time because his body is at the base of a thorny bush that has since sprouted blossoms and grown in around him.[45]

He is on his back, in a blue sweatshirt and rust-colored corduroy pants, one cuff of which is still tucked into a red rubber boot, the other of which came free,[46] perhaps as he ran, perhaps as he collapsed, exposing an inch of leg that is now nothing more than two clean, white bones. And his skull has become detached from his body. And his teeth have come loose and are scattered around in the dirt.[47]

And what can Besim do other than what he does?[48]

---

33. Background information on the village and the events that transpired there. Note how the hill is used as a transition to an explanation of the people leaving the village.

34. The repetition of "then" conveys a sense of events unfolding.

35. Because of the earlier setup, we know this is the day the Muslius last saw Lulzim.

36. Because of its placement at the end of the sentence, "firing" lingers in our minds.

37. Time transition.

38. Concrete detail lends drama to the last sighting of Lulzim.

39. Transition shows passage of time.

40. The cinematic quality of this sentence allows us to follow Besim's movements and thus lets the tension build. Because the discovery of Lulzim is delayed until the end of the paragraph, the moment gains added drama. Even now, however, Finkel withholds information. Rather than saying, here is Lulzim's body or his remains, he simply says there is Lulzim. We feel a momentary relief that maybe he is OK. We are compelled to continue reading.

41. The tension continues to build because the author withholds "what" has happened.

42. The action slows down as Finkel relates what happened. Note the writer's control, how he continues to give the information a little at a time to maintain the suspense. This also places us in Besim's footsteps, letting us make the grim discovery as he does.

43. The repetition of "that" creates a cumulative effect, underscoring the horror of Lulzim's last moments.

44. The precision of the details gives us a graphic picture. We see what Besim sees.

45. The description of the flowering bush is an unexpected detail. It confirms how long Lulzim has been dead. It also becomes symbolic: In the midst of death, life goes on.

46. The vivid details remind us that this body was once a boy, once flesh and blood. The red rubber boots will serve the writer later in the story.

47. Finkel uses the position of the body to speculate on what may have happened to Lulzim. The details of the clean, white bones, the detached skull, the scattered teeth convey the horror of war.

48. The rhetorical question provides momentary relief from the grimness of the scene.

He weeps for a boy whose life lasted 11 years 44 days.[49]

Besim descends the hill.[50]

He comes back with another man to help him, followed by his wife, who brings a sheet, and their 2-year-old daughter, who is holding a photograph of Lulzim, which she keeps looking at as she also looks at his bones.[51]

Down the hill again, this time with the body.

They stop at the mosque, burned and ruined like everything else, where they find an old coffin that they wipe clean with fistfuls of grass and wildflowers.[52]

They carry Lulzim into the ruined house, putting the coffin in the room with the cradle,[53] and then Besim heads back toward Stenkovic II to tell Feti and Lutfie.[54]

* * *

Who, a day after Besim left for Vlastica, see another figure coming against the tide toward their tent.[55]

Not Besim,[56] but someone who lives just south of the Stenkovic II in the Macedonian capital of Skopje.

For more than the obvious reasons,[57] it is so hard being a refugee. There is such a dearth of reliable information. Instead, there are so many rumors. There is a rumor,[58] for instance, that the only way to get on a humanitarian flight to the United States is to pay a bribe to the tall man with the blond hair who circulates through the camp wearing a doctor's jacket.[59] Three hundred Deutschmarks, or about $150,[60] is the going rate for a family, Feti was told, which he would gladly have paid except where in the world would he get 300 Deutschmarks?

There were also the rumors about Lulzim. That he was safe, according to a relative in Germany,[61] who Feti managed to call one day after waiting in line for three hours for a phone.[62] The relative said he'd heard this from someone else, who had heard it from someone else,[63] and Feti and Lutfie, unable to leave the camp, hung on to that particular rumor as tightly as they could.

And now comes a new rumor[64] to consider, delivered by the man from Skopje, whom Feti knows only slightly, that Besim is waiting for him on the other side of the bor-

---

49. The use of days emphasizes just how short Lulzim's life was.

50. Finkel again uses short sentences and short paragraphs to heighten the drama.

51. The description of the child holding Lulzim's photographs provides a poignant image of war. There is a sense that, in this war, the bones could have easily been hers.

52. The detail of the grass and the wildflowers creates a more vivid picture than simply saying they cleaned an old coffin. It places us in the scene.

53. The cradle and the coffin provide a dramatic juxtaposition. Lulzim's life ends where it began.

54. Transition moves us from the village back to the refugee camp, and to Feti and Lutfie.

55. The focus is now back on Feti and Lutfie, and their point of view. Note how this sentence echoes their earlier sighting of the grandfather. Even though we now know what has happened to Lulzim, we can sense their anticipation.

56. Because it is not Besim, we continue to feel their anticipation. We know that they still do not know the fate of their son.

57. Transition into explanatory digression.

58. The repetition of "rumor" emphasizes the fact that they are rampant.

59. Anecdote illustrates the unreliable nature of information.

60. Conversion of Deutschmarks.

61. This rumor serves as a transition from the digression back to Lulzim.

62. Provides information on conditions in Stenkovic II.

63. Demonstrates how secondhand the information is.

64. The fourth repetition of "rumor" returns us to the present time line and the scene with the man who has just returned from Skopje.

der. That the guards wouldn't let him back across. That he called with a message: Find Feti and tell him to come as fast as he can, and to look for a white car.[65]

And when Feti hesitates, wondering if this could be true, the man tells him the rest of what Besim said, and that's how Feti and Lutfie find out about Lulzim, from a man they hardly know standing awkwardly at the entrance to their tent. Who tries to comfort them and then drives them toward the border, which, in the midst of this second exodus, has degenerated into chaos.[66]

There are convoys of NATO trucks, which are trying to squeeze by convoys of relief trucks, which are trying to squeeze by convoys of gravel trucks, all of which[67] are trying to get through a border manned by overwhelmed guards who are yelling over the sounds of grinding gearboxes and honking horns.[68] In an attempt at control, a pecking order has been established that goes from NATO soldiers, to relief workers, to journalists, to, finally, at the end of the list, the refugees themselves,[69] who are jammed into too many taxis to count, and panel trucks loaded down with impossible numbers of them, all staring blankly ahead in the deepening dusk as they wait to lurch forward another measly inch. Every so often it happens, the line actually moves, meaning another car has made it past the border officials. But mostly everyone sits, just sits, for hours, for most of a day, in a line stretching more than a mile, not knowing when they will get across.[70]

And now, at the back of the line, comes the next car, this one with three children and two weeping parents.[71] One of whom gets out and explains to the people in front of him that his son is dead, that he was 11 years old, that they are going home to bury him,[72] and each person who hears this weeping man motions him ahead. Car by car, plea by plea, Feti and Lutfie make it across the border,[73] and now they find Besim, and now they are heading in the direction they hoped never to go again, toward home.[74]

Passing the first of the burned cars.

Passing the first of the minefields, and the first burned house.

Passing the first military checkpoint, and the first field that should be filled with yellowing wheat by this time of year, but contains only weeds.[75]

---

65. The repetition of "that" and the use of sentence fragments creates drama. They also carry a sense both of the man's excitement as he relates the message and of him perhaps being out of breath. Note how Finkel holds back the full message, compelling us to keep reading.

66. "Second exodus" echoes the earlier reference and shifts the scene from the specific (Feti and Lutfie) to the general (the masses of refugees).

67. The repetition of "convoys" and "which" creates a visual image of a road clogged with trucks. Note how Finkel varies the last repetition ("all of which") to end on a more emphatic note.

68. The vivid word choices and the variety of sounds allow us to experience the pandemonium.

69. Note that the description here is general, to convey the sense of masses trying to move. The references are all general ("NATO soldiers," "relief workers," "journalists," "refugees"). We see no faces, no individuals. The descending order of the list infers that the refugees are a low priority, that they are treated not unlike cattle.

70. The description vividly captures the waiting, the slow progress ("another measly inch," "meaning another car has made it past the border"). Repetition ("sits") and the use of commas (". . . sits, just sits, for hours, for most of a day . . .") help create that sense of waiting.

71. With this sentence, the focus gradually moves from the general back to the specific. First, our attention is directed to the back of the line, then we focus on a car, then on three children, then on two weeping parents. We are back with Feti and Lutfie.

72. The structural repetition of "that" replicates Feti repeating his story.

73. "Car by car, plea by plea" lets us follow Feti's progress to the front of the line, to the border.

74. At this point, we are in the car with Feti and Lutfie, we are heading to Vlastica with them. Their dread is captured by setting "toward home" apart with a comma and placing it at the end of the sentence.

75. The repetition of "passing the first . . ." and the placement of its discovery on a separate line creates a sense of the Muslius driving slowly through their ravaged homeland. We, too, discover each horror as they do.

Through all of this,[76] no one talks. They just look out the windows as the sky keeps blackening and closing in, and now they are passing through Pasjane,[77] the Serbian village closest to Vlastica, which they haven't seen since April 13 when, from up on the hill, they watched a line of cars moving their way. Followed by gunshots. Followed by panic. Followed by their screaming Lulzim's name and hearing nothing in response except more gunshots. Followed by running. Followed by Yugoslav soldiers rounding them up and herding them to the border. Followed by two months in a tent, wondering, wondering. Followed by this moment of untriumphant return as they turn down the potholed road from Pasjane to Vlastica,[78] a moment in which there are no sounds at all, other than a steady night wind and a car moving beyond a dark village of drawn curtains.

It is darker still when they get to Vlastica, where the only light comes from several cooking fires set among the ruins by the few people who have returned.

And then they get to their house, where it is darkest of all,[79] where the only light is from the small flame of a single cigarette lighter, bending from the wind coming through the broken windows, which is how they are able to look at their son.[80]

* * *

Then comes morning, and they can see everything.[81]

The two bullet holes. The two red boots. The sheet covering the coffin, which Lutfie embroidered as a gift to Feti for their wedding. The ruined cradle, which held their children. The ruined house Feti has always lived in,[82] and the ruined town, and the house up the road with the 13 bodies, and the burned mosque in the center,[83] which is where Feti is heading now to retrieve an Albanian flag that someone has put near the top of the minaret. He wants it for the coffin, to place atop the embroidered sheet, and as he walks looking shell-shocked into the mosque, another villager with his own ruins, his own miseries,[84] is kind enough to climb the charred stairway that is filled with burned birds and bring it down to him.

"I hope no one minds," Feti says, as if there were anyone around to mind that or anything at all, and from there, escorted now by several villagers, he goes to the cemetery to pick out a gravesite. It is toward the edge of town, just past the hind piece of a rotting

---

76. "Through all this" pulls all the fragments together into the whole picture.

77. Pasjane serves as a transition into the events of April 13.

78. The repetition of "followed by . . ." provides a dramatic vehicle for compressing time and returns us from April 13 to the present time line. With each repetition, the drama builds.

79. As the car nears home, the movement slows and the mood becomes increasingly dark and somber. Part of this is accomplished through adjectives: Pasjane is "a dark village"; Vlastica is even darker; their home "is darkest of all."

80. The overall effect is cinematic, with the camera slowly moving closer. We first see the dark village of drawn curtains, then we see cooking fires, then the single flame of a cigarette lighter. Even though we have been moving closer, Finkel nevertheless catches us unaware when he uses the lighter as a link to Feti and Lutfie's first glimpse of their son. This moment gains added impact from this element of surprise and its placement at the end of the sentence.

81. Time transition also ushers in a change of mood, from darkness to light. What was concealed in darkness now becomes a stark reality.

82. Because of the earlier description, there is no need for detailed rendering here. Instead, like a camera, Finkel focuses on what would first catch our eye: the bullet holes, the two red boots. Then he pulls back to show the sheet covering the coffin, the cradle, and the house itself. He uses each item to tell us something about Feti and Lutfie. The repetition of "ruined" emphasizes the magnitude of the destruction.

83. Note how Finkel uses the description as a transition back into the narrative, the action.

84. There is no need to describe fully the other villager because the focus here is on Feti. To do so would be to weaken the drama of the moment. "His own ruins, his own miseries" conveys a sense of his burden and tells us all we need to know.

horse on the side of the road and just before the village school, burned now, every window broken,[85] where Lulzim was midway through fifth grade.[86] Feti goes to the corner of the cemetery closest to the schoolyard, and that's where he and the others begin to dig.

While back at the house,[87] the women of the village are talking about Lulzim:

That he was such a good student, an aunt says, he brought his schoolbooks with him when everyone was driven up into the hills.

That he was such a fast runner, Lutfie says, "I never believed a bullet could reach him."[88]

While in the ruins of the house next door,[89] the men are gathered separately, as is the custom,[90] as if custom could bring sense to anything like this, having their own conversation:

"Do we remove the clothes?" someone asks.

No, they finally decide.

"Do we wash the body?"

"We cannot wash only bones," someone says.

"It will be easy to carry him," someone else says, "there's not much left of him,"[91] and now comes word that the grave is ready; and now the men are lifting the coffin; and now the women are gathered around Lutfie, who is crying so hard she can barely say her last words to her son, which are, "My poor boy"; and now the men hoist the coffin; and now they take turns carrying it along the road; and now an 11 year old is being placed in the ground; and now come the scrapes and thuds of dirt being shoveled and dropped; and now come the hums of mumbled prayers.[92]

"Come out, come out of the grave," one of the villagers sings, and now comes the sound of a father in tears; and now it is later, much later, after the funeral, toward sundown,[93] and Feti is by himself at the grave.

Earlier in the day, he'd said, "there's nothing here," and in the hours since the only change has been the creation of a new hill, which is where he now stands, saying goodbye.[94]

Because the next morning, he and his family leave Vlastica again.

Heading south.

Out of Kosovo.

Into Macedonia.

Back into Stenkovic II.[95]

* * *

85. The detail places us in the scene.
86. Description is used to insert background information.
87. Place transition.
88. Finkel uses the women's conversations to tell us more about Lulzim.
89. Place transition.
90. Information.
91. The dialogue is self-contained and dramatic. There is no need for the writer to elaborate. To do so would undermine the power of the moment.
92. "Now" is repeated for emphasis. The repetition heightens the drama. It also seems to echo a tolling church bell.
93. Transition compresses time and moves us from the burial to the scene of Feti at his son's grave.
94. The falling rhythm of the sentence and the placement of "saying goodbye" at its end add to the poignancy of the father's last words with his dead son.
95. Finkel again breaks the sentence into prepositional phrases placed on separate lines to create a transition that replicates the family's journey back to Stenkovic II. The impact is far more dramatic than one long sentence: "Because the next morning, he and his family leave Vlastica again, heading south out of Kosovo into Macedonia, back into Stenkovic II."

Where as June ends, and July begins,[96] they remain, waiting for their flight to the United States, to Boston, to a job, to a school that isn't burned, to a house that is neither in ruins nor a tent.[97]

Soon, perhaps in a week or so, Stenkovic II will be empty. It has been open since late March, and in that time more than 60,000 refugees have passed through. There have been 28 births. There have been four deaths. There have been 1,500 tents put up and eight tents lost to fire. There have been more than 150,000 blankets given out, and 7,000 foam mattresses, and 6,000 sleeping bags, and in one week alone, the refugees received 116,000 loaves of bread, 48,000 liters of milk, 53,000 oranges, 15,000 pounds of canned fish and 70,000 diapers.[98]

That was in late May, when the camp was nearing its highest one-day population of all, 23,200.

And now[99] there are only a few thousand people left, most of whom will be back in Kosovo in the next few days. The United States will continue evacuation flights every so often for the time being, but Kosovo is the destination now, and the camp, once so frantic, so wretched, so desperate, so hopeless,[100] is at times almost pleasant. Everywhere, people are packing. Everywhere, there are squares in the dirt marking where there are no longer tents, and piles of old blankets waiting to be disposed of, and everywhere the feel is of return, of repatriation, of resolution[101]—except in one tent, where the exodus is still underway.[102]

That's who the Muslius are, then, the last of the refugees.[103]

The ones who have come to Stenkovic II twice.

The ones with the mother who is saying, "They didn't need to kill him," and the father who is so lost at the moment he is saying nothing at all.[104]

How to describe what is inside of him now? What he feels made of?[105] That's what Feti wishes he could explain.

Is it anger?

"No," he says.

Is it hate?

"No."

Loneliness?

"I don't know," he says, closing his eyes, hoping he will see something to help him,

---

96. Transition shows passage of time.

97. List provides efficient means for conveying information.

98. List again serves as a convenient device for providing information about the camp and the refugees. Note that we have again moved from the specific (the Muslius) to the general (the refugee camp).

99. Time transition.

100. List enables the writer to describe the camp tightly. The repetition of "so" emphasizes the conditions.

101. "Everywhere" is repeated for dramatic effect. The first "everywhere" conveys a sense of widespread activity; the second, captures the feel of the abandoned grounds; the third, the feeling of relief and resolution, with the latter reinforced by the three prepositional phrases and alliteration.

102. The end of the sentence acts as a transition out of the digression, returning us to the Muslius, whose future has not been resolved.

103. This straightforward sentence provides information, that the Muslius are the only ones left in the camp, but more importantly it signals the approaching end to the story. We can feel the momentum winding down.

104. The repetition of "the ones . . ." is used for dramatic effect, to build toward the ending.

105. The questions are Finkel's, and yet they carry Feti's voice and come across as the grieving father agonizing to himself.

but even in that private darkness[106] there are no dreams to see, not at the moment, so he opens his eyes and, unable to stop himself, begins crying anew. Because he knows.

"Sadness," he says. "Nothing else."[107]

DAVID FINKEL ON READING

"My early influences were a trio of writers at the *Miami Herald:* Barry Bearak, Sara Rimer and Maddy [Madeleine] Blais. They were doing things with journalism, presenting it in a kind of literary narrative form, that I hadn't seen before. This was in the 1970s, when I was in college. Next group: magazine writers who, like me, were covering the case of serial murderer Ted Bundy but, unlike me, were writing about it in a way that gave deeper understanding to me than I was giving in my own reporting and writing. Since then, the influences are too numerous to catalog. There's stuff in the *Post* every day that inspires me. I read certain magazines cover to cover; I have a shelf of nonfiction books I refer to constantly when I'm writing; and I have similar shelves of fiction. In addition, I keep near my desk a thickening folder of pieces of journalism that I look at whenever I feel stuck in either my reporting or writing. They are pieces of varying lengths and approaches, all of which knocked me out on first read and subsequent reads, and all of which make me want to try to get it right one more time."

---

106. "Private darkness" vividly, yet concisely, captures the father's grief.

107. This simple quote captures the essence of the moment better than anything Finkel could have written. There is a stark, haunting quality to the three words, heightened by their placement on a separate line. They linger with us, as all good endings should.

Jon Franklin

In 1978, when Jon Franklin embarked on "Mrs. Kelly's Monster," he had recently become interested in applying classic Chekhovian story form to newspaper journalism and, to that end, had undertaken a series of practice pieces for Baltimore's Evening Sun. *He had written four such stories—including one about a dog catcher and another about a road crew—and was looking for a fifth project: something with a beginning, a middle, and an end, and something that was highly paced so he could introduce elements of rhythm. He was also contemplating beginning an occasional series about the brain and was eager to find something to kick it off. When a public relations person suggested he spend time with brain surgeon Thomas Ducker, he realized this could be the subject he had been looking for.*

As the paper's science writer, Franklin was already trusted by Baltimore's medical community, so that obtaining the kind of access he needed did not present the hurdle a lesser known reporter might have faced. He and Ducker agreed that Franklin would cover an operation in which the outcome was uncertain and write about it exactly as it happened, with no promise that the doctor would have final approval or even see the story before it was published.

On the day of surgery, Franklin showed up armed with a reporter's notebook, since this was before he had begun using a tape recorder. The procedure took place in a teaching operating room, so that what Dr. Ducker saw through the operating microscope was displayed on a television monitor. As the operation proceeded, Franklin wrote down everything, being careful to note exact times. He remembers writing so fast he barely had time to think.

Even though he and Dr. Ducker had gone into the operation unsure of its outcome, the turn of events nevertheless took Franklin by surprise. When he walked out of the operating room, he was still trying to accept the fact that Mrs. Kelly was dying.

"I had somehow assumed that the operation would work out okay and have a happy ending," he says. "Now I had this terrible feeling that I had lost my story. It was an awful day. Here a woman had died and I was feeling sorry for myself because I didn't have a story and, yet, that's how I felt. I went over it and over it, and it wasn't until seven or eight that evening that I realized I did have a story. It was just different than I thought. It was, in fact, a better story, one in which Dr. Ducker, not Mrs. Kelly, was the protagonist.

"Of all the lessons I learned on that story, the most powerful was that stories change . . . and a good writer lets them. In order to go into the story, I needed to have a certain hypothesis about what it would be and then, in order to grasp the better story, I had to let go of the first one. I have since learned that lesson many times. When a story changes on you, always let go of your hypotheses and follow the story. What you find will be much better than what you abandoned."

Franklin wrote the story over the next two days, and toward the end began to sense, for the first time in his life, that he was going out onto a stage. By the time he finished, his heart was racing. In need of reassurance, he printed out the story, took it home, and read it over the telephone to Ducker. When he finished, there was silence on the other end of the line, and then Ducker said, "Well, that's pretty much how it was."

The story earned Franklin a Pulitzer Prize for feature writing. Before leaving the Sun, he went on to win a second Pulitzer for explanatory journalism. He has since published five books, including Writing for Story *and* The Molecules of the Mind, *and headed the creative nonfiction writing program at the University of Oregon. He is also founder and moderator of WriterL, the Internet listserver for professional nonfiction writers, and the Philip Merrill Professor of Journalism at the University of Maryland. He has been named one of the top newspaper writers in America by the editors of* Brill's Content.

Mrs. Kelly's Monster

IN THE COLD HOURS OF A WINTER morning Dr. Thomas Barbee Ducker, chief brain surgeon at the University of Maryland Hospital, rises before dawn.[1] His wife serves him waffles but no coffee.[2] Coffee makes his hands shake.[3]

In downtown Baltimore, on the 12th floor of University Hospital,[4] Edna Kelly's husband tells her goodbye.[5] For 57 years Mrs. Kelly shared her skull with the monster:[6] No more. Today she is frightened but determined.[7]

It is 6:30 a.m.[8]

"I'm not afraid to die," she said[9] as this day approached. "I've lost part of my eyesight. I've gone through all the hemorrhages. A couple of years ago I lost my sense of smell, my taste. I started having seizures. I smell a strange odor and then I start strangling. It started affecting my legs, and I'm partially paralyzed.

"Three years ago a doctor told me all I had to look forward to was blindness, paralysis and a remote chance of death. Now I have aneurysms; this monster is causing that. I'm scared to death . . . but there isn't a day that goes by that I'm not in pain, and I'm tired of it. I can't bear the pain. I wouldn't want to live like this much longer."[10]

As Dr. Ducker leaves for work, Mrs. Ducker hands him a paper bag containing a peanut butter sandwich, a banana and two fig newtons.[11]

(Editor's Note: These annotations have been prepared with the help of Jon Franklin and his own annotations from Writing for Story, Atheneum, 1986. Adapted with permission of Scribner, a division of Simon & Schuster.)

"Mrs. Kelly's Monster" first appeared in the *Evening Sun* in 1978. It was subsequently published in *Writing for Story* (NAL-Plume). Copyright © 1978 the *Baltimore Sun.* Reprinted by permission of the *Baltimore Sun.*

1. The story is structured chronologically, covering a little more than seven hours. It is written in the present tense to create more immediacy. Franklin begins by establishing the setting—a cold, winter morning, before dawn. It is understood that we are in Ducker's home.

2. Note the concreteness of Franklin's details: his wife didn't just prepare him breakfast, she served him waffles and no coffee. Franklin uses food symbolically, as a life process. In the morning the food is warm and served lovingly. Later in the story it will be dry, cold, and packed anonymously in a paper bag.

3. The implication here is that it's important that Ducker's hands don't shake. Franklin withholds the reason why, forcing us to continue reading. Thus, the element of tension is introduced.

4. Place transition. The reference to University Hospital links Mrs. Kelly to Ducker.

5. "Goodbye" builds on the tension introduced with the shaking hands.

6. Franklin introduces the idea that Mrs. Kelly *is* her brain, a theme he will continue throughout the story. He uses her term "the monster" both to avoid the more unwieldy medical terminology ("arteriovenous malformation") and to enhance the sense of impending danger.

7. A straight news lead sets out to answer questions; this lead—like all good feature leads—raises more questions than it answers and forces us to continue reading. Why is it important that Ducker's hands not shake? How will Mrs. Kelly fare in her battle with the monster?

8. Franklin introduces the time to establish a pacing device that he will use throughout the story. "Pacing must begin before the need for it becomes apparent," says Franklin. "This story picks up a definite beat later. It begins here, with the stipulation of an exact time. To make it an odd number, such as 6:32, would have been enameling the lily, and would have lost the effect when the story shifts to specific time later, as the pace increases."

9. Background flashback drawn from earlier interview. Note that the attribution is in the past tense because the material is not part of the main time line.

10. Quote provides insight into Mrs. Kelly's mindset as she heads into surgery.

11. Transition returns us to the main time line. It also moves Ducker and the story from home to work. Again note the concreteness. The bag does not contain merely a sandwich, a piece of fruit, and two cookies. Franklin is setting this up for later use.

Downtown,[12] in Mrs. Kelly's brain, a sedative takes effect.

Mrs. Kelly was born with a tangled knot of abnormal blood vessels in the back of her brain. The malformation began small, but in time the vessels ballooned inside the confines of the skull, crowding the healthy brain tissue.[13]

Finally, in 1942, the malformation announced its presence[14] when one of the abnormal arteries, stretched beyond capacity, burst. Mrs. Kelly grabbed her head and collapsed.[15] After that the agony never stopped.

Mrs. Kelly, at the time of her first intracranial bleed, was carrying her second child. Despite the pain, she raised her children and cared for her husband. The malformation continued to grow.

She began calling it "the monster."[16]

Now, at 7:15 a.m. in operating room eleven,[17] a technician checks the brain surgery microscope and the circulating nurse lays out bandages and instruments.[18] Mrs. Kelly lies still on a stainless steel table.

A small sensor has been threaded through her veins and now hangs in the antechamber of her heart. The anesthesiologist connects the sensor to a 7-foot-high bank of electronic instruments. Oscilloscope waveforms begin to build and break. Dials swing. Lights flash. With each heartbeat a loud speaker produces an audible popping sound.[19] The steady pop, pop, popping[20] isn't loud, but it dominates the operating room.

Dr. Ducker enters the O.R. and pauses before the x-ray films that hang on a lighted panel. He carried those brain images to Europe, Canada and Florida in search of advice, and he knows them by heart. Still, he studies them again, eyes focused on the two fragile aneurysms that swell above the major arteries. Either may burst on contact.

The one directly behind Mrs. Kelly's eyes is the most likely to burst, but also the easiest to reach. That's first.[21]

The surgeon-in-training who will assist Dr. Ducker places Mrs. Kelly's head in a clamp and shaves her hair. Dr. Ducker checks to make certain the three steel pins of the vice have pierced the skin and press directly against Mrs. Kelly's skull. "We can't have a millimeter[22] slip," he says.

---

12. Place transition.

13. Background information drawn from earlier interviews.

14. Franklin personifies the malformation so that the monster becomes a living being. This will continue throughout the story.

15. Rather than telling us how Mrs. Kelly felt, Franklin "shows" us with her actions: she grabbed her head and collapsed. The effect is far more powerful and convincing.

16. Transition out of the background flashback.

17. Time and place transition. Note that the time is becoming more specific. The tempo is building.

18. Rather than simply saying the surgical team prepared the operating room, Franklin shows them in action and, by doing so, brings readers with him into the scene.

19. Franklin continues to draw the scene. Note how he works to give us a sense of the scene without burdening us with unnecessary details. We don't need to know precisely what the electronic instruments looked like—only that they loomed seven feet high. We don't need to know how many dials or lights there were—only that they were swinging and flashing. The scene is vibrant and alive. We see the swinging dials and flashing lights; we hear the popping of the heart. We are in that operating room.

20. Franklin sets up the "pop, pop, popping" of the heart, which he will use later both as a pacing device and to build tension.

21. The job of a science writer is to translate technical terms into lay language so that readers understand what is going on. Here Franklin explains what is going on in a clear, but unobtrusive way that comes across like Ducker's thoughts.

22. Here the writer intentionally introduces the somewhat unfamiliar word "millimeter" so that it will be more familiar later during more critical moments.

Mrs. Kelly, except for a six-inch crescent of scalp, is draped with green sheets. A rubber-gloved palm goes out and Doris Schwabland, the scrub nurse, lays a scalpel in it. Hemostats snap over the arteries of the scalp. Blood spatters onto Dr. Ducker's sterile paper booties.[23]

It is 8:25 a.m. The heartbeat goes pop, pop, pop, 70 beats a minute, steady.[24]

Today Dr. Ducker intends to remove the two aneurysms, which comprise the most immediate threat to Mrs. Kelly's life. Later, he will move directly on the monster.

It's a risky operation, designed to take him to the hazardous frontiers of neurosurgery. Several experts told him he shouldn't do it at all, that he should let Mrs. Kelly die. But the consensus was that he had no choice. The choice was Mrs. Kelly's.[25]

"There's one chance out of three that we'll end up with a hell of a mess or a dead patient," Dr. Ducker says. "I reviewed it in my own heart and with other people, and I thought about the patient. You weigh what happens if you do it against what happens if you don't do it. I convinced myself it should be done."[26]

Mrs. Kelly said yes. Now Dr. Ducker pulls back Mrs. Kelly's scalp to reveal the dull ivory of living bone. The chatter of the half-inch drill fills the room,[27] drowning the rhythmic pop, pop, pop[28] of the heart monitor. It is 9 o'clock when Dr. Ducker hands the two-by-four-inch triangle of skull to the scrub nurse.

The tough, rubbery covering of the brain is cut free, revealing the soft gray convolutions of the forebrain.

"There it is," says the circulating nurse in a hushed voice. "That's what keeps you working."

It is 9:20.[29]

Eventually Dr. Ducker steps back, holding his gloved hands high to avoid contamination. While others move the microscope into place over the glistening brain the neurosurgeon communes[30] once more with the x-ray films. The heart beats strong, 70 beats a minute, 70 beats a minute.[31] "We're going to have a hard time today," the surgeon says to the x-rays.

Dr. Ducker presses his face against the microscope. His hands go out for an electrified, tweezer-like instrument.[32] The assistant moves in close, taking his position above the secondary eyepieces.

Dr. Ducker's view is shared by a video camera.[33] Across the room a color television

---

23. Note both the details and the active verbs (here and throughout the story) that bring the scene to life. The sheet is green, the palm is rubber-gloved, the booties are sterile and paper.

24. Before the action picks up, Franklin repeats the time and the heartbeat to establish them more firmly as pacing devices. He also sets up the device of "pop, pop, pop" to indicate that the heart is beating 70 beats a minute, which is normal. This will serve him later when the situation becomes tense.

25. Explanatory information gleaned from interviews to orient the reader.

26. The quote was obviously addressed to Franklin, but he wisely keeps himself out of the story and lets Ducker address the reader directly. Still another way to handle this would be to paraphrase the quote so that it comes across as Ducker's thoughts.

27. The vivid description and word choices let us both see ("the dull ivory of living bone," "the two-by-four-inch triangle of skull") and hear ("the chatter") what is going on. We are firmly in the operating room.

28. Because of the earlier setup, the "pop, pop, pop" tells us all is well. The heartbeat is normal.

29. The time is getting more specific. The surgeon and the story are moving into more dangerous territory.

30. "Communes" conveys the image of Ducker quietly studying the x-ray.

31. The repetition reminds us of what is normal. It also foreshadows problems and thus builds tension.

32. A good medical writer describes the instrument in terms lay readers can visualize.

33. Because Franklin will not be able to stand next to Ducker during the surgery, he introduces the video camera, which will provide his view of the procedure and thus the reader's.

crackles,[34] displaying a highly-magnified landscape[35] of the brain. The polished tips of the tweezers move into view.

It is Dr. Ducker's intent to place tiny, spring-loaded alligator clips[36] across the base of each aneurysm. But first he must navigate a tortured path[37] from his incision, above Mrs. Kelly's right eye, to the deeply-buried Circle of Willis.[38]

The journey will be immense. Under magnification, the landscape of the mind expands to the size of a room. Dr. Ducker's tiny, blunt-tipped instrument travels in millimeter leaps.[39]

His strategy is to push between the forebrain, where conscious thought occurs, and the thumblike projection of the brain, called the temporal lobe, that extends beneath the temples.[40]

Carefully, Dr. Ducker pulls these two structures apart to form a deep channel. The journey begins at the bottom of this crevasse. The time is 9:36 a.m.[41]

The gray convolutions of the brain, wet with secretions, sparkle beneath the powerful operating theater spotlights. The microscopic landscape heaves and subsides in time to the pop, pop, pop[42] of the heart monitor.

Gently, gently, the blunt probe teases apart the minute structures of gray matter, spreading a tiny tunnel, millimeter by gentle millimeter[43] into the glistening gray.

"We're having trouble just getting in,"[44] Dr. Ducker tells the operating room team.

As the neurosurgeon works, he refers to Mrs. Kelly's monster as "the AVM," or arterio-venous malformation.[45] Normally, he says, arteries force high-pressure blood into muscle or organ tissue. After the living cells suck out the oxygen and nourishment the blood drains into low-pressure veins, which carry it back to the heart and lungs.

But in the back of Mrs. Kelly's brain one set of arteries pumps directly into veins, bypassing the tissue. The unnatural junction was not designed for such a rapid flow of blood and in 57 years is slowly swelled to the size of a fist.[46] Periodically it leaked drops of blood and torrents of agony. Now the structures of the brain are welded together by scar tissue and, to make his tunnel, Dr. Ducker must tease them apart again.[47] But the brain is delicate.

---

34. "Crackles" again lets us hear, as well as see, what is going on.

35. "Landscape" conveys a sense of the vastness of the brain as seen through the microscope and on the television screen. It is the beginning of a metaphor of the brain, or mind, as "landscape," and the procedure as an exploration or journey.

36. Surgical instrument described in terms readers can visualize.

37. The word choices "navigate" and "path" are in keeping with the landscape metaphor.

38. Note that Franklin does not attempt to explain the Circle of Willis. Instead, he will wait until the moment when he can more easily "show" us what it is.

39. The landscape-journey metaphor is more fully developed. Under the microscope, the focus shifts from Ducker to the instrument. Franklin now uses his earlier setup of "millimeter" to make the point that what looks like a leap on the screen is actually very small.

40. Explanation offered in terms readers can grasp. It is provided before the real action gets under way.

41. The time is now very specific. The exploration has begun.

42. Because of the earlier setup, "pop, pop, pop" becomes shorthand for the fact the heart is beating normally.

43. Earlier setup of "millimeter" now lets Franklin show how very small the area really is. The repetition ("gently, gently" and "millimeter by gentle millimeter") serves both to show the tediousness of the procedure and to heighten tension. The repetition of g and m sounds is pleasing to the ear and adds to the sense of drama.

44. Ducker's quote foreshadows future problems; the tension builds. Readers are hooked; they must continue reading to learn the outcome.

45. Readers now learn the scientific name for the monster. "AVM" will provide another simple way to refer to it elsewhere in the story. The explanation serves as a transition into more background.

46. Everyday comparison helps readers visualize the monster.

47. Transition back to main time line.

The screen of the television monitor fills with red.

Dr. Ducker responds quickly, snatching the broken end of the tiny artery with the tweezers. There is an electrical bzzzzzt[48] as he burns the bleeder closed. Progress stops while the blood is suctioned out.

"It's nothing to worry about," he says. "It's not much, but when you're looking at one square centimeter, two ounces is a damned lake."[49]

Carefully, gently, Dr. Ducker continues to make his way into the brain. Far down the tiny tunnel the white trunk of the optic nerve can be seen. It is 9:54.[50]

Slowly, using the optic nerve as a guidepost,[51] Dr. Ducker probes deeper and deeper into the gray. The heart monitor continues to pop, pop, pop, 70 beats a minute, 70 beats a minute.[52]

The neurosurgeon guides the tweezers directly to the pulsing carotid artery, one of the three main blood channels into the brain.[53] The carotid twists and dances[54] to the electronic pop, pop, popping. Gently, ever gently, nudging aside the scarred brain tissue, Dr. Ducker moves along the carotid toward the Circle of Willis,[55] near the floor of the skull.

This loop of vessels is the staging area from which blood is distributed throughout the brain. Three major arteries feed it from below, one in the rear and the two carotids in the front.

The first aneurysm lies ahead, still buried in gray matter, where the carotid meets the Circle. The second aneurysm is deeper yet in the brain, where the hindmost artery rises along the spine and joins the circle.

Eyes pressed against the microscope, Dr. Ducker makes his tedious way along the carotid.

"She's so scarred I can't identify anything," he complains through the mask.

It is 10:01 a.m. The heart monitor pop, pop, pops with reassuring[56] regularity.

The probing tweezers are gentle, firm, deliberate, probing, probing, probing,[57] slower than the hands of the clock.[58] Repeatedly, vessels bleed and Dr. Ducker cauterizes them. The blood loss is mounting, and now the anesthesiologist hangs a transfusion bag above Mrs. Kelly's shrouded form.[59]

Ten minutes pass. Twenty. Blood flows, the tweezers buzz, the suction hose hisses.[60] The tunnel is small, almost filled by the shank of the instrument.

---

48. The sound brings readers into the scene.

49. Quote serves as a reminder that under the microscope everything looks bigger, and the problem seems worse.

50. The time is again specific, as the action moves into more critical regions.

51. The word choices ("tunnel," "guidepost") continue to be appropriate to the landscape metaphor.

52. Franklin uses "pop, pop, pop" and the repetition of "70 beats a minute" both to show that Mrs. Kelly is still all right and to remind us of what is normal. Later, when the pace picks up, he can use the device to indicate trouble without the need for lengthy explanations.

53. Even as the action progresses, Franklin continues to provide brief explanation to orient readers.

54. Note the vivid verbs that breathe life into those arteries.

55. Franklin returns to the Circle of Willis. Now that it is in the picture he shows us what it is and where it is located—a much simpler task now that readers are somewhat oriented with the brain.

56. The reassurance serves as just the opposite. Juxtaposed with the specific time, it signals trouble ahead.

57. Repetition heightens tension.

58. Franklin uses a comparison familiar to readers to show how slowly the tweezers probe.

59. Earlier in the story, Franklin wrote of Mrs. Kelly being "draped" with a sheet; now her "form" is "shrouded." He is subtly foreshadowing.

60. Because nothing critical happened during this period, Franklin compresses time to give us a sense of what happened without rendering a blow-by-blow account. It is important to omit or to summarize events that aren't critical so that the really important moments stand out. If every scene, every moment is given equal weight, the important ones become lost or overwhelmed. Note, however, that this compressed time is no less vivid (blood flows, tweezers buzz, the hose hisses) than the fuller scenes.

The aneurysm finally appears at the end of the tunnel, throbbing, visibly thin, a lumpy, overstretched bag, the color of rich cream,[61] swelling out from the once-strong arterial wall, a tire about to blow out, a balloon ready to burst, a time-bomb the size of a pea.[62]

The aneurysm isn't the monster itself, only the work of the monster, which, growing malevolently, has disrupted the pressures and weakened arterial walls throughout the brain. But the monster itself, the x-rays say, lies far away.[63]

The probe nudges the aneurysm, hesitantly, gently.

"Sometimes you touch one," a nurse says, "and blooey, the wolf's at the door."

Patiently, Dr. Ducker separates the aneurysm from the surrounding brain tissue. The tension is electric.

No surgeon would dare go after the monster[64] itself until this swelling killer is defused.

Now.[65]

A nurse hands Dr. Ducker a long, delicate pair of pliers.[66] A little stainless steel clip, its jaws open wide, is positioned on the pliers' end. Presently the magnified clip moves into the field of view, light glinting from its polished surface.

It is 10:40.

For eleven minutes[67] Dr. Ducker repeatedly attempts to work the clip over the neck of the balloon, but the device is too small. He calls for one with longer jaws. Soon that clip moves into the microscopic tunnel. With infinite slowness, Dr. Ducker maneuvers it over the neck of the aneurysm.

Then, in an instant, the jaws close and the balloon collapses.

"That's clipped," Dr. Ducker calls out. Smile wrinkles appear above his mask.[68] The heart monitor goes pop, pop, pop, steady.[69] It is 10:58.

Dr. Ducker now begins following the Circle of Willis back into the brain, toward the second, and more difficult, aneurysm that swells at the very rear of the Circle, tight against the most sensitive and primitive structure in the head, the brainstem.[70] The brainstem controls vital processes, including breathing and heartbeat.[71]

The going becomes steadily more difficult and bloody. Millimeter, millimeter after treacherous millimeter the tweezers burrow a tunnel through Mrs. Kelly's mind. Blood flows, the tweezers buzz, the suction slurps. Push and probe. Cauterize. Suction. Push and probe. More blood.[72] Then the tweezers lie quiet.

---

61. Comparison of the unfamiliar to the familiar.

62. Writer again compares the swelling to things familiar to the reader. The repetitiveness of the comparisons drives home the point that the aneurysm is about to explode.

63. Background explanation.

64. Although "AVM" is Ducker's term, Franklin here uses "the monster" because the real struggle is between the surgeon and the malformation.

65. "Now," isolated in its own paragraph, underscores the drama of the moment and heightens the tension. The effect is almost as if the readers hold their breath, awaiting the outcome of Ducker's next move.

66. Franklin again uses a familiar item to describe the unfamiliar.

67. By meticulously keeping track of the time throughout the procedure, Franklin is here able to tell us precisely how long the maneuver took. His advice to young writers: "When you've got rapid action, keep writing down times in your notebook. Later, you can select what you need for pacing."

68. Ducker scores a momentary victory. He and the tension briefly relax.

69. Because of the setup, there is no need to tell us that the heartbeat is normal. All is well.

70. The tension again builds as Ducker confronts the second aneurysm—the most difficult and dangerous.

71. A reminder for readers of the critical nature of the brainstem.

72. Compressed time. Again, note how vividly it is rendered.

"I don't recognize anything," the surgeon says. He pushes further and quickly finds a landmark.

Then, exhausted, Dr. Ducker disengages himself, backs away, sits down on a stool and stares straight ahead for a long moment. The brainstem is close, close.[73]

"This is a frightening place to be," whispers the doctor.

In the background the heart monitor goes pop, pop, pop, 70 beats a minute, steady. The smell of ozone and burnt flesh hangs thick in the air. It is 11:05 a.m., the day of the monster.[74]

The operating room door opens and Dr. Michael Salcman, the assistant chief neurosurgeon,[75] enters. He confers with Dr. Ducker, who then returns to the microscope. Dr. Salcman moves to the front of the television monitor.

As he watches Dr. Ducker work, Dr. Salcman compares an aneurysm to a bump on a tire. The weakened wall of the artery balloons outward under the relentless pressure of the heartbeat and, eventually, it bursts. That's death.

So the fragile aneurysms must be removed before Dr. Ducker can tackle the AVM itself.[76] Dr. Salcman crosses his arms and fixes his eyes on the television screen, preparing himself to relieve Dr. Ducker if he tires. One aneurysm down, one to go.

The second, however, is the toughest. It pulses dangerously deep, hard against the bulb of nerves that sits atop the spinal cord.

"Technically, the brain stem," says Dr. Salcman. "I call it the 'pilot light.' That's because if it goes out . . . that's it."[77]

On the television screen the tweezer instrument presses on, following the artery toward the brainstem. Gently, gently, gently, gently[78] it pushes aside the gray coils. For a moment the optic nerve appears in the background, then vanishes.

The going is even slower now. Dr. Ducker is reaching all the way into the center of the brain and his instruments are the length of chopsticks.[79] The danger mounts because, here, many of the vessels feed the pilot light.[80]

The heartbeat goes pop, pop, pop, 70 beats a minute.[81]

The instrument moves across the topography of torture, scars everywhere, remnants of pain past, of agonies Mrs. Kelly would rather die than further endure. Dr. Ducker is lost again.

Dr. Salcman joins him at the microscope, peering through the assistant's eyepieces.

---

73. Repetition emphasizes the closeness and heightens the tension. How many times should a writer repeat a word? Most writers say it is something you develop an ear for, a sense that you should repeat it so many times and not one time more.

74. This and the exact time seem to foreshadow a victory for the monster.

75. Franklin introduces Dr. Michael Salcman before he becomes involved in the actual action. Note that he uses only a brief identification and no description. To describe him would interrupt the action; it is also unnecessary since everyone is in scrubs. If he had entered in a three-piece suit, then a description would have been in order.

76. Explanation.

77. Dr. Salcman's comparison of the brainstem to a pilot light provides both information and a setup for later use.

78. Repetition heightens drama, and again, just the right number of *gentlys*.

79. Comparison of an unfamiliar instrument to something familiar.

80. The setup reinforces the danger.

81. The beat remains normal, but Franklin now gives it its own paragraph, as it assumes a greater role in the story.

They debate the options in low tones and technical terms.[82] A decision is made and again the polished tweezers probe along the vessel.

Back on course, Dr. Ducker works his tunnel ever deeper, gentle, gentle, gentle as the touch of sterile cotton. Finally the gray matter parts.

The neurosurgeon freezes.[83]

Dead ahead[84] the field is crossed by many huge, distended ropelike veins.

The neurosurgeon stares intently at the veins, surprised, chagrined, betrayed by the x-rays.

The monster.[85]

The monster, by microscopic standards, lies far away, above and back, in the rear of the head. Dr. Ducker was to face the monster itself on another day, not now. Not here.

But clearly these tangled veins, absent on the x-ray films but very real in Mrs. Kelly's brain, are tentacles of the monster.[86]

Gingerly, the tweezers attempt to push around them.

Pop, pop, pop . . pop . . . pop . . . . pop . . . . pop.[87]

"It's slowing!"[88] warns the anesthesiologist, alarmed.

The tweezers pull away like fingers touching fire.

. . . . pop . . . pop . . pop . pop, pop, pop.

"It's coming back," says the anesthesiologist.

The vessels control bloodflow to the brainstem, the pilot light.[89]

Dr. Ducker tries to go around them a different way.

Pop, pop, pop . pop . . pop . . . pop . . . .

And withdraws.[90]

Dr. Salcman stands before the television monitor, arms crossed, frowning.

"She can't take much of that," the anesthesiologist says. "The heart will go into arrhythmia and that'll lead to a . . . call it a heart attack."

Dr. Ducker tries a still different route, pulling clear of the area and returning at a new angle. Eventually, at the end of a long, throbbing tunnel of brain tissue, the sought-after aneurysm appears.

Pop, pop, pop . pop . . pop . . . pop . . . .

The instruments retract.

---

82. Because what the two discussed might confuse the reader without adding anything to their understanding or to the action, Franklin omits it. On the matter of what to use in a story and what to leave out, Franklin says: "The iron rule is that if you don't need it to make the climax work, then you don't need it at all."

83. By setting this brief sentence off in its own paragraph, Franklin heightens the drama. Somewhat like the earlier "Now," it causes readers to gasp or to hold their breath. We must read on to see what Ducker has confronted.

84. "Dead ahead" is a term used for navigating topography. Here, given the subject matter, it has added meaning.

85. Note how Franklin creates tension by delaying telling us that the ropelike veins are the monster. Again, the words are set apart in their own paragraph. The effect is far more dramatic than if he had written: "Dead ahead is the monster."

86. The moment of crisis in the story has arrived.

87. Because of the earlier setup there is no need to explain that Mrs. Kelly's heartbeat slows down when Ducker's tweezers attempt to maneuver around the tentacles.

88. The quote confirms that "pop . . pop . . . pop . . . . pop . . . . pop" indeed means the heart has slowed down. As the action escalates, there will be no need to explain setup.

89. The earlier setup of the pilot light emphasizes the danger.

90. A pattern has been established. When the instrument retracts, the beat returns to "pop, pop, pop." As the story reaches its most critical moment, there is no need for explanation due to the carefully executed setups. The sentences can remain short, brisk, to heighten the tension.

"Damn," say the neurosurgeon. "I can only work here for a few minutes without the bottom falling out."

The clock says 12:29.

Already the gray tissue swells visibly from the repeated attempts to burrow past the tentacles.

Again the tweezers move forward in a different approach and the aneurysm reappears. Dr. Ducker tries to reach it by inserting the aneurysm clip through a long, narrow tunnel. But the pliers that hold the clip obscure the view.

Pop, pop . pop . . pop . . . pop . . . .

The pliers retract.

"We're on it and we know where we are," complains the neurosurgeon, frustration adding a metallic edge to his voice. "But we're going to have an awful time getting a clip in there. We're so close, but . . ."

A resident who has been assisting Dr. Ducker collapses on a stool. He stares straight ahead, eyes unfocused, glazed.

"Michael, scrub," Dr. Ducker says to Dr. Salcman. "See what you can do. I'm too cramped."

While the circulating nurse massages Dr. Ducker's shoulders, Dr. Salcman attempts to reach the aneurysm with the clip.

Pop, pop, pop . pop . . pop . . . pop . . . .

The clip withdraws.

"That should be the aneurysm right there," says Dr. Ducker, taking his place at the microscope again. "Why the hell can't we get to it? We've tried, ten times."

At 12:53, another approach.

Pop, pop, pop . pop . . pop . . . pop . . . .

Again.

It is 1:06.

And again, and again, and again.

Pop . . . pop . . . pop, pop, pop . . . pop . . . pop-pop-pop . . .[91]

The anesthesiologist's hands move rapidly across a panel of switches. A nurse catches her breath and holds it.

"Damn, damn, damn."

Dr. Ducker backs away from the microscope, his gloved hands held before him. For a full minute, he's silent.[92]

"There's an old dictum in medicine," he finally says. "If you can't help, don't do any harm. Let nature take its course. We may have already hurt her. We've slowed down her heart. Too many times." The words carry defeat, exhaustion, anger.

Dr. Ducker stands again before the x-rays. His eyes focus on the rear aneurysm, the second one, the one that thwarted him. He examines the film for signs, unseen before, of the monster's[93] descending tentacles. He finds no such indications.

Pop, pop, pop, goes the monitor, steady now, 70 beats a minute.

"Mother nature," a resident growls, "is a mother."

---

91. Rather than show us every try, Franklin compresses time, and in doing so heightens the tension. To play out every attempt would become monotonous and less effective.

92. Silence can be as dramatic as what is said, and this is such a case. Note the use of Franklin's careful cataloging of time and how it serves him here. To write that Ducker is silent for a full minute is far more powerful than to simply say he is silent.

93. Note that the monster is no longer the "AVM." It is Ducker's monster as much as it is Mrs. Kelly's.

The retreat[94] begins. Under Dr. Salcman's command, the team prepares to wire the chunk of skull back into place and close the incision.

It ends quickly, without ceremony. Dr. Ducker's gloves snap sharply as a nurse pulls them off. It is 1:30.[95]

Dr. Ducker walks, alone, down the hall, brown paper bag in his hand. In the lounge he sits down on the edge of a hard orange couch and unwraps the peanut butter sandwich. His eyes focus on the opposite wall.

Back in the operating room the anesthesiologist shines a light into each of Mrs. Kelly's eyes. The right pupil, the one under the incision, is dilated and does not respond to the probing beam. It is a grim omen.

If Mrs. Kelly recovers, says Dr. Ducker, he'll go ahead and try to deal with the monster itself, despite the remaining aneurysm. He'll try to block the arteries to it, maybe even take it out. That would be a tough operation, he says without enthusiasm.

"And it's providing that she's in good shape after this."

If she survives. If. If.

"I'm not afraid to die," Mrs. Kelly had said. "I'm scared to death . . . but . . . I can't bear the pain. I wouldn't want to live like this much longer."[96]

Her brain was too scarred. The operation, tolerable in a younger person, was too much. Already, where the monster's tentacles hang before the brainstem, the tissue swells, pinching off the source of oxygen.

Mrs. Kelly is dying.

The clock on the wall, near where Dr. Ducker sits, says 1:40.

"It's hard to tell what to do. We've been thinking about it for six weeks. But, you know, there are certain things . . . that's just as far as you can go. I just don't know . . ."

He lays the sandwich, the banana and the fig newtons[97] on the table before him, neatly, the way the scrub nurse laid out the instruments.[98]

"It was triple jeopardy," he says finally, staring at his peanut butter sandwich the same way he stared at the x-rays. "It was triple jeopardy."

It is 1:43, and it's over.

Dr. Ducker bites, grimly, into the sandwich.[99]

The monster won.

JON FRANKLIN ON READING

"I don't make notations nor, as much as I favor the habit, do I specifically steal techniques from other writers. I'm just not orderly enough to do that. Basically I absorb them and how they think about their subjects, and then, of course, their techniques appear in my

---

94. The word choice here is fitting. Ducker's confrontation with the monster has been a battle.

95. The removal of Ducker's gloves provides a dramatic and symbolic end to the action, the procedure. The story's crisis has reached a resolution. Ducker has accepted defeat. Note that the time is no longer on a separate line.

96. The quote serves as a flashback, or a reminder, that Mrs. Kelly went into the surgery fully aware of the risks. The reminder is necessary, says Franklin. "Otherwise, our hero becomes tarnished by failure. One of the points of the piece is that he is *not* tarnished, because he tried."

97. This returns us to the beginning and gives the story a circular feeling of completion.

98. The description adds drama to his actions; it also returns us to the beginning of the surgery as does the way Franklin compares Ducker's staring at the sandwich to the way he looked at the x-rays.

99. The monster has won, but Ducker will go on. The sandwich symbolizes life.

own work. I find it odd that nobody ever accused me of sounding like those people, but nobody ever has.

"The writers who were of great importance to me were the early structuralists such as Chekhov and O. Henry, a whole lot of writers who wrote short stories for the *Saturday Evening Post,* and of course Hemingway, Steinbeck, Maugham, and that bunch. Lawrence Durrell. Henry Miller. Clavell. Sherwood Anderson. The list is endless. Nonfiction writers include H. L. Mencken and, of course, Wolfe. I was also a movie projectionist in the mid- and late 1950s and was greatly influenced by the tightly plotted, meaningful movies of that day. And, of course, Mark Twain, Mark Twain and Mark Twain.

"I also stole liberally from popular poets. They include, most especially, Poe, Housner, Frost and Robert Service. In particular, I stole their rhythms and the way they connected rhythms to stories. I stole blank verse from Shakespeare. I stole something from the French playwright Moliere."

Tom Hallman, Jr.

To write "A Life Lost . . . and Found," Tom Hallman immersed himself in Gary Wall's world for eighteen months, as the former Blue Cross claims analyst struggled to build a new life. While nonfiction writers sometimes must reconstruct the past in such cases, Hallman was in the enviable position of watching almost all the events unfold. He accompanied Wall to doctors appointments and sat in on interviews with his counselors and job coaches. He was present when Wall ate breakfast and dinner and when he cleaned his apartment. He tagged along with Wall to his athletic club and even to singles events at church. In between, he interviewed friends, relatives, co-workers, and neighbors; he examined medical records, family documents, and police files related to Wall's accident. On the few occasions when Hallman was unable to be with Wall or when he felt his presence would be inappropriate or might change the outcome of the story, he reconstructed events from notes, recorded messages, diary entries, and interviews with Wall and whoever else was involved. The interviews almost always took place within forty-eight hours of the actual event.

"Many journalists who want to write these narratives fail to realize the importance of reporting," says Hallman, a senior reporter specializing in features/narratives for the Portland Oregonian. *"I was a police reporter for nearly a decade. My editor didn't care about the words as much as the facts. I came of age in this business as a reporter and it has served me well."*

With its universal theme of finding and defining a life—something we all have to do, Gary Wall's story became more than simply that of a disabled man. "The fears and challenges Gary faces are on the surface quite different than ours," Hallman says. "And yet at their most basic they are similar. That's why Gary's combination of courage and strength, which develop as the story progresses, resonates with readers." The story earned Hallman a position as a finalist for the 1998 Pulitzer Prize for feature writing, a prize he captured in 2001 for his poignant profile of a disfigured 14-year-old boy.

Before joining the Oregonian *in 1980, he was a copy editor for Hearst Magazines' Special Publications in New York and a reporter for the* Hermiston Herald *in Hermiston, Oregon, and the* Tri-City Herald *in Kennewick, Washington. He was a finalist for still another Pulitzer for beat reporting and has won feature-writing awards from the American Society of Newspaper Editors, the National Society of Professional Journalists, and the Penney-Missouri competition. He has also won the National Scripps Howard Journalism Award for Business Writing. Three of his stories have been reprinted by* Readers Digest; *one was featured on ABC's "20/20." He has been named one of the top newspaper writers in America by the editors of* Brill's Content.

A Life Lost . . . and Found

A BED, A DRESSER AND AN OVERHEAD LIGHT. The bedroom was as barren as a $30-a-night motel room.[1]

The only personal touch was a photograph taken during a rafting trip on the Clackamas River. The picture showed him grasping an oar and standing between three men and two women. He was smiling. He kept the picture because it was his last link to a lost life.[2]

Other artifacts—service papers from the Navy, pictures from around the world, yearbooks filled with the best wishes of old friends—lay buried at the bottom of a closet.[3]

The man who lived here[4] kept a small tape recorder beside his bed, and on it he recorded his thoughts and feelings. He played the tape back to himself—listening to his voice was better than silence.[5]

Gary Wall reported for work at noon, but he set his clock radio for 7 a.m. so that he could spend the morning trying to remember who he was.[6] In the morning, his mind was empty, like a computer that needed rebooting.[7]

He turned off the radio and lay quietly in bed. On his headboard shelf was a black, pocket-sized datebook.[8] He reached for it to see what he had written the night before.

The page was blank.[9]

He turned it to start a new day.

February 14, 1997.

Valentine's Day

He prayed, asking for strength and courage, then closed his eyes, trying to remem-

---

1. Hallman begins the story by setting a scene that slowly draws us into Gary Wall's world. Note how the first two sentences convey the barrenness of the bedroom through structure as much as content. They, like the room, are spare and direct. The commas and the lack of adjectives add to that effect. To use "and" in the list ("a bed and a dresser and an overhead light") would create a cumulative effect, making the three items seem like more, as would adjectives ("a double bed," "a four-drawer dresser"). The adjective "overhead" is necessary to distinguish the light from a lamp. The motel room simile is a fitting comparison and one that brings a definite image to the reader's mind. There is a haunting quality and a tension to these opening sentences, and the next two paragraphs, which draw us into the story, partly because of the spare style and partly because this opening raises more questions than it answers. Like Wall, we don't know who *he* is. We are compelled to continue reading.

2. The phrase "his last link to a lost life" heightens the tension and raises more questions: What does Hallman mean, he lost his life? How did it happen? Will he recover it?

3. Hallman uses the photograph and papers to begin telling us about "this man": We learn that he has served in the navy, he has traveled around the world, and he likes rafting.

4. The phrase "the man who lived here" carries an air of mystery, and thus forces us to read on to learn his identity. To have used Wall's name would have lessened the impact and the tension.

5. The dash sets off, and thus emphasizes, the fact that he listens to recordings of his own voice to break the silence. The fact that he does this is curious and forces us to keep reading.

6. Hallman finally reveals Gary Wall's name, but we still don't know *who* he is. We, like Wall, will learn this a little at a time.

7. The computer simile is an apt comparison; both it and Wall have memories that need rebooting. Since most of us are familiar with computers and rebooting, we can grasp just how blank Wall's mind is.

8. Hallman uses adjectives sparingly. The description of the datebook emphasizes its importance. It is Wall's lifeline and will appear throughout the story.

9. Hallman begins to move us closer into Wall's point of view so we can vicariously feel what his life is like.

ber if he'd dreamed during the night. Nothing.[10] There had been no dreams in six years, not since the day he died.[11]

* * *

From his bed,[12] Gary saw a small yellow Post-it note stuck to the inside of his paneled bedroom door. He had written to himself: "Turn off the kitchen light." He got out of bed and walked into the hallway, where he found a second note: "Turn off the coffee maker." As he made his way through his Northeast Portland apartment, he followed a trail of more than 60 such notes: "Turn on the dishwasher." "Get gas." "Clean the refrigerator."[13]

At breakfast[14] Gary swallowed a ginkgo biloba tablet—he'd been hoping the Chinese herb would help him remember. He gave it 30 minutes to enter his bloodstream, then tested its effectiveness by reading Bible passages[15] and seeing if he could repeat them out loud. Some days he saw improvement. But then he'd wonder how a 39-year-old man could forget to turn off the kitchen light.

Like all mornings,[16] this Friday passed slowly. He read his Bible and listened to a soft-rock radio station. He walked through his apartment reading notes and following instructions. He activated his answering machine out of habit. He received only one call a day. Every night at 6:35 his mother checked on him, and he was always there.

He locked his apartment and walked past his car. Although he'd learned how to drive again,[17] Gary rode the train to work. While other passengers read the newspaper or thumbed through a paperback, he studied his datebook.[18]

Gary was worried about the napkins the supplier was supposed to store in a cupboard in the Blue Cross lunchroom. They had started turning up under the sink, and he kept forgetting where they were stored. He stuck a yellow note to the sink, but the night crew kept taking it off. He complained to the supplier, who got mad and told him to just remember. But the problem had been keeping him up nights and making him doubt the effectiveness of the ginkgo. Today he wrote in his datebook: "Napkins under the sink."[19]

Gary got off the bus downtown, walked into his building and took the elevator to the seventh floor. He punched in and changed into his overalls.

After he'd been rehired, he often stopped on the floor where he had worked as a claims analyst, back when he wore a coat and tie to work.[20] He had been in rehabilitation

---

10. By setting the word "nothing" apart, Hallman emphasizes the fact that Wall had no dreams. To make that statement in a complete sentence would not carry the drama or impact of the lone, isolated word.

11. Hallman ends the section on a dramatic note that heightens tension. Wall is obviously alive. What does Hallman mean, "the day he died?" It echoes back to the lost life and lingers with us. Again, we are forced to read on.

12. Transition.

13. The Post-it notes continue creating tension. We know what they say, but why does Wall need them? They begin showing us how blank his mind is, that he needs reminders for even the most basic routines. Hallman drives home the extent of the problem with the fact there are 60 such notes. Here is a case in which being more precise (67 notes) would not carry the same weight as "more than 60 such notes." The trail of notes also takes us with Wall through his apartment.

14. Transition.

15. The use of the biblical passages also tells us Wall is religious.

16. Transition moves the story forward; it also tells us that what we are witnessing is routine.

17. Hallman continues to feed us information about Wall: Whatever happened to Wall six years earlier left him unable to drive.

18. The reference to the datebook and the fact that Wall "studied" it begins to show us the role it plays in his life. For him to have glanced at it would not carry the same message.

19. Hallman provides an example of Wall's datebook notations. With it and the Post-its, we are beginning to grasp that the problem is his memory. Still, we don't know how he lost it. We keep reading.

20. Hallman uses Wall's movements to fill in more of his past.

for nearly two years; so when he reappeared, there were handshakes and slaps on the back. Over time, though, things changed. His old colleagues transferred or moved on. New employees saw only a stranger in a janitor's suit. Gary stopped going to his old floor.

He used to say hello to employees he met on his rounds, but that ended when he heard two women talking about him. One said it looked as if Gary had a light on, but that no one was home. He'd been a friendly extrovert. But in his new life strangers made him nervous. He feared they assumed he was stupid or retarded. And so, over time, Gary Wall became a loner.

He was the quiet guy picking up cigarette butts in front of the Regence Blue Cross Blue Shield of Oregon building.[21] He stood about 5-foot-7 and had a slight build and a smile that women once had called sweet.[22] When someone stared at him, though, he averted his eyes and looked like an abused dog who cowers before a raised hand.[23] He was an invisible man, moving silently among them, listening to their conversations and their laughter as he wiped down tables and straightened chairs.

On the way home that Friday almost two years ago he wrote himself a note:[24] "I did the best job I knew. To live is good in itself."

He wanted to put the note on the inside of his bedroom door so that it would be the first thing he'd see each morning. He opened his front door and was putting away his coat when the answering machine's red light caught his eye.

He pushed the button.

"Hi, Gary. . . ."

It was a woman.

"Your assignment at Blue Cross has ended," she said. "Do not report to work on Monday."[25]

* * *

Monday drifted into Tuesday and into Wednesday. A week went by.[26] Gary ended up at his mother's house, where he sat on the sofa and ruminated like a man in the throes of a failed love affair. What had gone wrong? What could he have done differently? The napkins, he told his mother. It must have been the napkins.[27]

On a day in early March,[28] while his mother was off on an errand, he opened a scrapbook she kept. It was his story. On the first page was a press release from the Gresham Police Department.

On June 16, 1991, Gresham police officers responded to a serious motor-vehicle accident at S.E. 202nd Ave. and S.E. Stark St. at about 12:30 p.m.[29]

---

21. We finally learn what his current job is.

22. We get our first glimpse at what he looks like. Note the brevity. What he thinks and does is more important to the story than what he looks like.

23. Simile vividly conveys Wall's apprehension.

24. Transition indicates when the story's action is taking place and serves as a setup for the note.

25. Hallman again ends the section on a dramatic note, where it compels us to move on to the next section.

26. Transition shows the passage of time. By compressing time rather than giving us a detailed account of each day, Hallman causes the more interesting, important moments to stand out.

27. While this is not a direct quotation, it sounds like Wall speaking and is drawn from an interview in which he reconstructed the visit with his mother.

28. Time transition.

29. Hallman uses the clipping to tell us finally what happened. He also uses it to trigger Wall's memory and thus provide information.

He turned the pages. He thought it strange how he could forget to turn off the kitchen light and yet remember details about the day the man he was died.[30]

Sunday.

Home from church.

Mom called.

Come over for lunch. Sun roof open.

Listening to music.[31]

Mr. Wall was transported by Life Flight Air Ambulance to Oregon Health Sciences University Hospital, where he remains in critical condition.[32]

The other car crushed the left side of his car. His head slammed into the doorjamb. Rescuers had to cut him free. On the flight to the hospital his heart stopped twice. His jaw was broken. His arm was slashed. And his brain had been smashed against the inside of his skull. He lay in a coma for seven days. His eyes opened after a week, but he didn't speak for two months. His first word was "Mom."[33]

He had to remember how to swallow. How to control his bowels and bladder. For two months he wore a diaper. He fell out of chairs and had to learn to walk. A therapist set a fork, pen and scissors in front of him and asked him to pick up the fork. He had no idea what a fork looked like. Or a toothbrush. Or a shoe.[34]

Therapists taught him how to tie his shoes. They trained him to stay on the sidewalk instead of blundering into traffic. This is a quarter, they told him. This is a $1 bill. Here's how you make change.[35] Nearly two years after the wreck he was declared rehabilitated. His brother helped him invest $180,000 in settlement money in mutual funds to pay for living expenses and future medical bills. He received $700 a month in disability income from Social Security.

He didn't look different, but he was. If he was making lunch and he answered the telephone, he'd forget to finish the lunch. Doctors called it short-term memory loss.[36] He wasn't stupid—the knowledge was in his brain, but he couldn't retrieve it. He'd remember junior high school but forget if he'd paid his bills.[37] He could deal with the memory loss only by writing yellow notes and keeping detailed datebooks and a computer diary. Blue Cross rehired him and found a job he could handle—a janitor in the lunchroom where he used to eat when he was a claims analyst.

What frightened him, though, was that he had lost the essence of himself. His sense of humor was gone. Subtleties in conversation and gestures were lost on him. He realized that he was missing the things that had made him Gary Wall. One by one his friends stopped calling. The man they had known no longer existed.[38]

---

30. Hallman takes us inside Wall's thoughts. "The day the man he was died" echoes the earlier references to Wall's lost life and his "death." Hallman uses it to move us from the present time line into a background loop.

31. Note how Wall's thoughts are written as fragments to mimic the way memories come to us.

32. More of the newspaper account of his accident provides background explanation.

33. Hallman draws from medical records to piece together what transpired after the accident. The fact that Wall's first word was "Mom" comes at the end of the paragraph, where it gains impact.

34. The use of short sentences and sentence fragments again mimic Wall's thoughts. It also lends drama.

35. Note how specific Hallman is in his rendering of Wall's rehabilitation. By including this snatch of conversation, he lets us "hear" what happened, and thus we feel like part of the scene.

36. We finally get a diagnosis, in a layman's terms.

37. Hallman provides concrete examples of how the memory loss affected Wall so that we can more fully grasp the problem.

38. The background loop ends on a dramatic note, which continues to make clearer the earlier references to death and a lost life. Somewhat like a cliffhanger in a serial, it compels us to continue reading.

* * *

After he lost his Blue Cross job,[39] the life he'd so carefully reconstructed splintered. Gary felt as if he were being held inches below the surface of a river, so close to safety, but drowning still the same.[40]

As the weeks passed,[41] he could not help reflecting on where he should have been in life. After graduating from Gresham High School, he'd joined the Navy and became a hospital corpsman. He had traveled the world. When he left the service, he returned to Portland to work in a hospital, and later, in a laboratory where he was the assistant section head. He took the claims-analyst job to broaden his knowledge of medicine.[42]

With the future apparently hopeless and the past too painful to recall, Gary turned his thoughts inward in the same way a prisoner in solitary confinement keeps company with only his heartbeat.[43] He started hearing irritating noises from his neighbor's apartment. He called 9-1-1 to say the tenant was grinding glass. But police arrived and found nothing. When he heard the sound again, he called his mother, Doris Shaw. She came over, talked with the neighbor and apologized for the intrusion. Gary was convinced he was losing his mind. He called to tell her that two men on the bus had stared at him. He thought they were going to attack him. His mother asked him what they said or did. Nothing, he told her. But he knew. He knew.[44] Black was now white. Up was now down.[45]

Even the Post-it notes seemed to fail him. He'd call his brother for advice, and write down the information. But he'd have to call the next day and ask the same questions again. He called his mother as often as seven times a day. And the noises didn't stop. His brother spent the night in his apartment but heard nothing.

His family grew concerned, and in the early summer of 1997 his mother contacted Dr. Danielle L. Erb, a Portland doctor who specialized in helping brain-damaged patients rebuild their lives. She had been Gary's doctor since 1996.

Gary's file revealed that during his weeklong coma, he did not open his eyes even when doctors inflicted pain to get a response. A series of X-rays determined there was bleeding in his brain from above his eyes to behind his ears. The damage was to the frontal lobe, the last portion of the brain to develop and the part that makes adults emotionally and intellectually different from children. The lobe[46] makes it possible to remember past events and to use them for determining present and future behavior. That lobe is where adults wrestle with choices. That's where hindsight takes place. That's where human beings organize and carry out multiple tasks, an ability Erb calls "executive function." A child can handle one assignment at a time, while an adult can juggle numerous projects, shifting from one to the other with ease. Gary could not rely on his memory to put events into context. Nor could he use executive function.[47]

---

39. Transition back to the present time line.
40. The simile vividly captures how Wall felt. It is in keeping with the imagery of death Hallman has used earlier and is thus appropriate to the mood and focus of the story.
41. Passage of time.
42. Hallman uses Wall's thoughts and memories to reveal his past.
43. The prisoner image captures Wall's isolation. Its placement at the end of the sentence strengthens the impact. Consider how much less effective (and clumsy) it would have been to write: "Gary turned his thoughts inward in the same way a prisoner in solitary confinement keeps company with only his heartbeat as the future became hopeless and the past too painful to recall."
44. Sounds like Wall's voice.
45. Hallman provides a concise analysis of the situation.
46. Up to now Hallman has used Wall's memories to convey information. Now he uses his medical records.
47. Hallman explains Wall's condition and how the brain functions in simple, everyday terms.

In many ways, he was a child. A child afraid of two strangers on a bus.[48]

* * *

Gary Wall stood with his mother in the basement lobby of the Legacy Good Samaritan Hospital & Medical Center's neurological science center, waiting to see Dr. Erb. Other brain-injured patients surrounded them. The high-ceilinged room was dead quiet. A man waited with his wife and two young children. Another man sat in a wheelchair. A woman stared at the floor while her husband, seated next to her, read a magazine. None exchanged glances with any of the others. They all sat in their own worlds.[49]

Gary grew agitated. When he started rehashing his job at Blue Cross and the noises in his apartment, his mother shook her head in frustration. She was grateful when a nurse appeared. The woman led them down a long hallway and into a small room. Gary sat on a molded plastic chair and shrank into a corner, next to his mother. He fidgeted and stared at the ground, silent.[50]

They both looked up when Erb opened the door. She was 5-foot-8 and slender, with curly brunette hair that fell to her shoulders. She was in her late 30s and known in the field as talented, no-nonsense and all business. She sat down on a wheeled stool and scooted close, knee to knee with Gary, a manila folder stuffed with his medical records unopened on her lap. She brushed back her hair and smiled the kind of smile a woman saves for a friend.[51]

"Gary, how are you doing?" she asked.

Gary opened his datebook.[52] He fumbled through the pages.

"I'm doing fine," he said. "And . . ."

He fell quiet, and Erb waited for him to fill the gap.

"You know I liked my job at Blue Cross," Gary said. "I think that . . ."

Erb raised her hand.

"Gary, what are you doing these days?"

He looked at his datebook.

"I went to church."

"What else?"[53]

Gary shrugged his shoulders.

"I keep myself busy."

He looked in his datebook.

"I went to church twice last week."

"Gary, I'm concerned how you're filling your day. What are you doing?"

---

48. The comparison provides insight into Wall's problem and is another dramatic section ending.

49. Hallman uses the same spare, direct style to re-create the waiting-room scene, and yet his carefully chosen details draw us into it. The high ceiling enables us to picture the room itself; "dead" captures the silence. The description of the people is enough to let us visualize them caught in their separate worlds, but not so much that it slows down the action.

50. This again demonstrates Hallman's close observation and his ability to choose those details which will best capture the scene. We can see Wall being led down the "long" hallway, then "shrinking" into a corner of the "small" room. We sense his apprehension as he "fidgets" and "stares" at the floor—both verbs are examples of the vivid word choices used throughout the story.

51. The specific detail (the unopened folder on her lap, the gesture of brushing back her hair, the warm smile) again puts us into the scene.

52. Because of the earlier setup there is no need to explain the significance of the datebook. We know he is looking to it for answers.

53. Because there are only two speakers, it is not necessary to use attribution after each quote. The rule is to use enough attribution to keep the speakers clear, but not to do so unnecessarily.

For the next several minutes[54] Gary rambled about reading the Bible and creating computer files and writing letters he planned to send to Blue Cross administrators.[55] The words themselves made sense, but Gary jumped from subject to subject, getting lost on tangents. Erb opened his medical records and scanned them, listening to Wall but not paying attention.

"Because of your disability, you want to make sure you understand things," Erb said. "You want things logical. Gary, science is logical. People are not. What happens are variables. Every human reacts differently to the same situation. You believe something should be Z. And when it isn't, you interpret it as something wrong. And then things snowball for you."

Gary brought up the missing napkins. He told her how he tried to find them. His voice rose. He scooted the chair forward, closer to Erb. He looked up from the floor, and he waved his arms as he spoke. He told Erb that losing the napkins could have been the real reason Blue Cross let him go.

"You're talking about specific examples," she said, "and I am talking about generalities."

Gary deflated. His eyes dropped back to the floor. He slouched[56] in his chair. When he did speak, his voice was so soft that Erb had to lean in to hear.[57]

"Dr. Erb," he asked, "do I have a mental illness?"

Erb reached forward. She touched Wall's knee.[58]

"Gary, you are not mentally ill," she said. "You have a traumatic brain injury."

Gary looked up at her. He tilted his head to the side. His eyes opened wide.

"Honest?"

"Yes."

"I've always thought I was mentally ill."

"No, you're not."[59]

Erb shut Wall's folder.[60]

"Gary, look at me," she said. "This is important. You are not sick in the brain. You are not a schizophrenic or psychotic. You are not retarded. You have a brain injury. But you can have a life.[61] A different life than most of us, but still a life. It will be up to you to determine what kind of life you find."

* * *

---

54. Transition indicates passage of time.

55. Hallman uses "and" rather than commas to capture the sense of Wall rambling and jumping from subject to subject.

56. More vivid verbs ("scooted," "deflated," "slouched") bring this scene to life.

57. Note how carefully Hallman builds the setup for Wall's question, making an already powerful quote even more dramatic. He begins with a short, introductory clause that mimics Wall's hesitancy before speaking and, in doing so, heightens the drama. The inversion places the emphasis on the softness of his voice so that his tone precedes his actual words and lets us hear him speak.

58. Rather than immediately following with Erb's response, Hallman again uses the delay of her movements to let his words resonate.

59. Hallman has established the speaking pattern, so there is no need for attribution after each quote.

60. We see still another example of Hallman's close observation to movement, which allows him to re-create the scene and not simply the dialogue.

61. Notice how Hallman uses Erb's actual words to create a turning point. Up to now, the writer has depicted Wall's life as being over. While he could not make up this quote, he wisely chose to use it at the end of a section, where it gains added impact. Thus, we leave the section—and the doctor's visit—feeling that Wall's life is changing. The road won't be easy, but we know he'll make it. We don't know precisely *how* it will change and so are compelled to continue reading.

In the weeks that followed his. visit with Dr. Erb,[62] Gary Wall quit hearing noises. Strangers on a bus no longer bothered him.

Erb had given him hope.

The worried phone calls to his mother ended. Their relationship subtly shifted away from caretaker-patient and back toward mother-son.

She had him over for dinner one night, and, when the plates were cleared,[63] told him a story from her life when she was married and living in California with her first husband.

She told her son that she decided she had to divorce her husband because he was abusive. She was 29 and had four children and no way to support them. The only job she'd held was as a teen-ager working as a waitress at a drive-in. She went to a state welfare office and told a caseworker that she needed money, but she also needed to learn a skill. Teach me, she said.

The agency placed her in a program that provided welfare benefits, but also put her to work as a hospital clerk. Eventually the hospital hired her. Eleven years later she was an assistant supervisor in charge of 40 employees.[64]

"I know all about starting over," she told her son. "Don't let yourself be pushed down, Gary. Try. You will fail. But try again. You will make it. You are my son, and I believe in you."

Gary had been dry-eyed since the accident. But tears welled in his eyes. He told his mother he was proud of her, too.

"You've been a good mother," he said.

The next day[65] he sat at a desk in his apartment and wrote himself a yellow note: "Increase effectiveness by strength and realization of who I am and what I can do."[66] He stuck the note to his bedroom door so that it would be the first thing he would see each morning.

He knew he needed a plan and a structure to follow. He needed a job. Social Security limited how much he could earn, but he needed to work not only for the money, but also to find his place in the world.[67]

He contacted Ben Koerper, a counselor with Oregon's Vocational Rehabilitation Division. Wall had met Koerper after he'd finished his rehabilitation and was working in a head-injury program with Goodwill Industries. Gary had such a hard time solving even simple problems that program administrators labeled him unemployable. But then Blue Cross rehired Gary as a janitor.[68]

Koerper was unsure of exactly what Gary could do. Head injuries are difficult to evaluate because no one knows what's missing. It's as if a telephone book has pages ripped out, but no one realizes what's gone until it's time to make a call.[69]

Koerper enrolled Gary in a group of disabled job-seekers. Some had back injuries.

---

62. Passage of time.

63. While the detail of the dishes isn't crucial to the story, it nevertheless puts us inside the scene.

64. The detail of the mother's story lends a greater ring of truth. The repetition of "told" pulls it together into a cohesive whole. It reminds us that *she*—not Hallman—is telling us this story.

65. Time transition.

66. Even the Post-its have taken a positive turn, signaling change.

67. The placement of his quest at the end of the sentence and the paragraph gives it added emphasis and also creates a transition into his quest.

68. Hallman uses Koerper as a means for weaving in more of Wall's background.

69. The telephone book comparison draws on an experience we all have had to help us comprehend the problem.

Others had lost limbs. A few had debilitating diseases.[70] The group, which was led by counselors, met to find ways they could work again.

On the first day,[71] the meeting room felt like a singles bar where people feel as if everyone is checking them out when they walk into the place.[72] Gary avoided looking anyone in the eye and found a seat in the middle of a long conference table. He sat quietly as the table filled up around him. Other participants found common ground by making small talk about sports or the weather.[73] Gary wished the class would begin so that he wouldn't feel so self-conscious.[74] He opened his datebook and read two notes he had written to himself that morning.

"Change."

"Talk."[75]

He took a deep breath and turned to an older man to his left.

"Hi," he said. "I'm Gary."

They shook hands.

"So what do you think of this class?" the man said.

Gary didn't know what to say.

The man looked at him, waiting.

"Well?" he said.

Gary blushed and stared at his datebook. The man shook his head, turned to a woman on his left and started talking with her. When the man wasn't looking, Gary wrote himself a third note: "Always have something to say."

The counselors walked into the room and announced the group would meet twice a week from 8:30 to 11 a.m.

Gary raised his hand.

"Do you have any paper?"

A counselor slid four sheets[76] across the table.

"We assume that when you come here you are ready to work."

Gary raised his hand again.

"What time are we supposed to be here?"

"8:30."

He wrote it in his datebook and underlined it twice.

After talking about how to look for a job, the counselors took several students, including Wall, to an outer office.[77] They used a computer to search a database of available jobs. Gary punched in his qualifications. Three jobs popped up on the screen: Glass-former. Engine-installer. Doughnut-maker.[78]

He sat for a second, staring at the screen. Without writing anything down, he rose

---

70. The brief sentences emphasize the group's diversity. It is also a pleasing change of pace.

71. Transition moves us into the first meeting.

72. Another comparison makes the unfamiliar familiar.

73. The actual examples offer evidence that the talk was indeed mundane and thus makes even this brief scene vivid.

74. We again move inside Wall's mind and vicariously share the moment.

75. Because of the earlier setup, there is no need to elaborate on the datebook.

76. The specific detail makes this small gesture more vivid.

77. Note how the sequence of this sentence follows the actual action: the counselor talks about how to look for a job, then he gathers the students and leads them to an outer office, where the action in the next sentence takes place.

78. The fragments replicate the jobs popping up on the computer screen. Thus, we are seated before the computer with Wall; we are in this scene.

from his chair and walked back to the conference room. He stared out the window and watched the traffic along Southeast 122nd Avenue.

When the class was over, Gary walked out to his car.[79] Inside he saw a sticker in the center of the steering wheel: "Get gas." He sat in the driver's seat and watched his classmates walk to their cars. Several continued the friendly conversations they'd begun inside. He started his car and prepared to go back to his apartment. He pulled the sticker from the wheel, crumpled it in his fist and threw it out the window.[80]

* * *

For six years Gary Wall had remained hidden from the world. But his sessions at the Vocational Rehabilitation Division made him realize that he wanted a life.[81]

He pulled Post-it notes off his apartment walls to see if he could function without them. He started with little things, like turning off the kitchen light, and found he could remember. As the months passed,[82] the number of notes scattered through his apartment dropped from 60 to 40.

He pried himself out of his apartment and began three-times-a-week workouts at an athletic club.

Other clients found work and moved on. But he stayed. Koerper sent Gary to CCI Enterprises Inc., a private nonprofit agency that offers intensive help to disabled people.

Gary connected with a counselor named Lori Jean Conover. She spent several weeks getting a sense of Gary's abilities. While he prepared a resume, Conover scoured the metropolitan area for jobs.[83] She found two, and asked Gary to bring his resume and meet her at an Elmer's restaurant near his apartment.

They found a booth and sat across from each other. When the waitress left the coffee, she told Gary that she found his brown jacket attractive.[84] He looked up, stammered something and blushed.

Conover dropped a stack of papers on the table, and Gary looked like a man who had done something stupid and was going to hear about it from his wife.[85] He said nothing while Conover kept up a steady stream of conversation about jobs, interviews and what she had planned for him. She studied Gary's resume and said she'd refine it for him and return it when he came to her office for a practice interview.

"At what point in an interview do I mention my disability?" Gary asked.[86]

"If you have a disability that doesn't interfere with your ability to do the job, you don't have to tell," Conover said. "People who are disabled often appreciate a job in a way that others do not. Employers are aware of that and sometimes take being a little slow as a tradeoff."

Conover told Gary that she had two stock-clerk jobs at Safeway and Target. She had picked up an application from Safeway but wanted him to get one from Target. Gary

---

79. The inversion of the sentence again follows the action, while also creating a bridge to the car and the next sentence.

80. Hallman ends the scene, and the section, with another vivid moment. Wall will attempt to make it without the Post-its. Will he succeed? We must continue reading to find out.

81. The statement echoes the earlier references and reaffirms the change.

82. Transition indicates passage of time as well as Wall's improvement.

83. Again the inverted sentence provides a smoother transition into the one that follows.

84. This detail hints that Wall has outwardly changed.

85. The comparison vividly conveys the look on Wall's face.

86. The critical question comes at the end of the paragraph, where it gains greater impact.

started to write the information down but dropped his datebook. He ducked under the table to find it.

"What am I supposed to do?" he asked when he emerged.[87]

"Get an application from Target."

He wrote that down.

"Target would be a good place to work," he said. "I want a 401(k) plan."

"Gary, I have to be honest with you," she said. "Most part-timers don't get that kind of benefit."

"Oh," Gary said.

He slumped into the booth.

"But Gary, either one of these would be great jobs for you," Conover said. "Don't give up."

"I have to get an application where?"

"At Target."

"When?"

"Monday."

He wrote it in his datebook.

"And what time are we meeting next week?"

"At 10 in the morning."

He flipped through his pages.

"What week?"

"Next week."

"What time?"[88]

"At 10."

He closed his datebook. Their business done, they sat quietly, drinking their coffee. Gary wanted to say something to her, but the words wouldn't come.

"Well," he finally said. "I guess I better get busy." He took his bill and shook hands with Conover. After paying the cashier, he walked outside and stood on the sidewalk.

The car?

Where had he parked his car?[89]

He scanned the parking lot.

He was lost. Nothing looked familiar.

He moved away from the front door so Conover wouldn't see him. And for the next 10 minutes, Gary Wall wandered the parking lot, looking for his car.[90]

* * *

Of all the things Gary Wall had lost[91] with his old life, he missed his friends the most.[92] He told himself that he needed people in his new world. At the brain-injury support-group meetings, he forced himself to talk with his neighbors.

He was drawn to Jim Hardman, and, eventually, the two sat next to each other at

---

87. Hallman lets the attribution do double duty by using it to include Wall's movement.

88. Wall's repetition of questions "shows" us that the struggle isn't easy, and he must work at it.

89. The questions serve to take us inside Wall's head, as well as the scene.

90. The section ends with another dramatic moment. Wall is lost, but this time we know he will be OK.

91. The repetition of "lost" serves as a transition, linking the car to his other losses and moving the story forward.

92. The inverted sentence provides a smooth transition from him forcing himself to talk to neighbors to an example of him actually doing so. This kind of structural linking makes for a more cohesive story.

every meeting. Hardman was eight years older than Gary. He had injured his brain in a 1972 car accident, and his memory loss was worse than Gary's. He also suffered seizures that made it impossible for him to drive. He had two daughters and had been married at the time of the wreck. His wife later divorced him. He could not work and lived in a small house by himself.

One night Hardman told Gary that he liked him but didn't know what he could offer as a friend. His memory, he said, was so poor that he often forgot what he and Gary talked about.

Gary persisted.[93] He found things that he and Hardman could do together. They went to dinner or to Gary's apartment to watch a video. Their conversations were stilted. Sometimes it seemed as if they were amateur radio operators talking on different frequencies.[94] But Gary didn't mind. Hearing a voice other than his own made his apartment feel full of life.[95]

Gary was at his athletic club one morning when a woman walked up to him and said hello.

He was stunned.

No one ever talked to him at the club.

She introduced herself as Diane Foster and said she recognized him from church. Gary didn't know what to say. He forced himself to calm down, to pretend he was talking with Hardman.[96] He and Foster talked for about 15 minutes[97] before she left for work.

As she walked away, something stirred deep inside Gary.[98] As a young man, there had been plenty of women. Before the accident, he had broken up with a serious girlfriend. He'd heard she was now married and had a daughter.

But Gary hadn't spent any time with a woman who attracted him since his accident.

He was self-conscious, afraid women would think him odd. Even simple flirting was difficult. Unstructured social settings, with their lack of rules, confused him. He couldn't banter or understand the nuances that define a relationship between a man and a woman.

This Diane Foster awakened something in Gary Wall, something he thought was dead.[99]

He learned Foster was in a Bible-study group at church. He joined.

At his first meeting,[100] he made his way to the table where Foster sat. They said hello again. Each week a church leader would give the group an assignment to read, write about and then discuss.

Gary could never finish his work. During the meetings he had a hard time answer-

---

93. The scene "shows" us Wall's improvement—a good example of the power of "showing" instead of "telling." We can see the change for ourselves.

94. The simile aptly conveys a sense of their attempts at conversation.

95. The statement echoes earlier references and thus contributes to the story's cohesiveness.

96. The use of a comma rather than "and" gives us a sense of him forcing himself to stop and gather his thoughts.

97. The time here is important. It "shows" Wall being able to conduct what for him is a more lengthy conversation. This is progress.

98. The inverted sentence places the emphasis on the main point: Wall is attracted to Diane Foster. The inversion also creates a transition between the paragraphs and moves the story forward.

99. Again, note the placement of the most important point at the end of the sentence where it gains greater impact. The repetition of "dead" echoes the earlier references and contributes to the story's cohesiveness.

100. Place transition.

ing questions. He rarely said anything and had difficulty concentrating on the discussion as it bounced from one person to another.

One night,[101] several members turned on Gary, complaining that he was never prepared and hardly seemed interested in what they were doing.

He later remembered how ashamed he had felt. How he had considered saying nothing, just quitting the group and going home.[102]

But Foster was there. He decided she was worth the risk.

"I'm sorry," he said. "I have a brain injury."

And then they were apologizing to him.

After the meeting, Diane sought out Gary. She told him that 10 years earlier she had been in a car accident. Her brain bounced off the inside of her skull, tearing tissue. For two weeks after the wreck, she felt simple-minded. She called a brain-injury support group.

She asked Gary about his accident, his past and how he functioned. He told her, the first time he had been so open with a woman other than his mother. Diane told him he was doing fine, and to not worry about the study group.

They started talking on the telephone. Eventually, Gary gathered his courage and asked if Foster would like to meet him for lunch at a restaurant after church.[103]

She said yes.[104]

He didn't dare call it a date. The word itself scared him. He woke up early and searched his closet looking for the perfect outfit: A shirt that looked stylish, pants that made him look trim. He spent extra time in the bathroom. He ran through imaginary conversations in his mind, thinking of things he could say, telling himself to not be nervous. At lunch, Gary was cautious.

"I hope you don't mind me asking this?" he'd say before asking a question.

When lunch was over, they agreed to split the bill. Gary was flustered. Did that mean this was a date or not? Should he shake her hand or hug her? He could not read her. Nothing made sense.[105]

He shook her hand.

When he got home he stewed for an hour and then called her. If he had done, or said, anything wrong, he apologized.

"It's the brain injury," he said.

"Gary, don't worry," she said. "You were fine."[106]

* * *

Gary visited a Target and a Safeway near his apartment. Safeway looked easier. To him, stock clerks appeared to concentrate on specific aisles and spent most of their time loading shelves, as he used to do at Blue Cross. He knew he could do that job. At Target, the clerks seemed to move throughout the store and frequently had to help customers.[107]

---

101. Time transition.

102. The use of sentence fragments and the comma replicate Wall's thoughts. We feel we are inside his head.

103. Note how Hallman's spare, direct sentences continue to propel the story forward at a nice clip, carrying readers with him.

104. This marks another turning point in Wall's life. Hallman sets it off in its own paragraph to add emphasis.

105. The questions and short sentences capture the feel of Wall's thoughts and doubts.

106. The quote provides a dramatic end for the section.

107. We are again inside Wall's head, allowing us to vicariously share the moment.

He decided on Safeway. And then he reconsidered.[108] For the first time in years, he thought about his future. He wanted more out of life. He talked with Diane Foster and said he wanted to break out of his isolation. He wanted to be in the world. He called Lori Jean Conover to tell her that he was going to apply at Target.

Conover called the store manager to tell her about CCI Enterprises Inc. and Gary. The manager agreed to interview Gary but made no promises. Conover told Gary she'd happily go along.

Gary thought about it. Having Conover along would relax him. He needed her. But he knew she would not be around forever. He needed to do this by himself.[109] He called to tell Conover he would go to Target alone.

"Why?" she asked.

"Because I want to be needed."[110]

"Of course you'd be needed," Conover said.

"I don't want sympathy," Gary added. "Everyone feels sorry for someone like me. I don't want a job because they feel sorry. I want the job because they think I can help the company."

Conover asked him if he was sure of what he was doing. He would have one chance at this job.[111]

"Yes," he said. "I don't want to be a sympathy hire."

"It's your decision, Gary."

She met Gary at the CCI office, where she briefed him on Target's history and its philosophy toward customers. She worked with him on his interviewing and then set up a practice interview. Conover and Mary Oliver, another counselor, told Gary to wait in an outer office while they settled in a conference room to play the part of Target managers. They sat at a long table and called Gary into the room. He stood with his hands in his pockets.

"Hello, Gary," Conover said. "This is my associate, Mary."

They shook hands.

"Please," Conover said, "have a seat."

He pulled a chair out.

"Gary, could you tell us about your background," Conover said, "and how it relates to this position?"

"I did stock and cleaning," he said. "And . . ."

His voice trailed off. He sat silently for several seconds, lost.[112] Then he blurted out the only thing he could think of: "I wonder if you have a job description?" he asked.

"No," Oliver said.

Gary sat back. He took a deep breath.[113]

"I worked at Blue Cross for three years," he said. "And I cleaned the cafeteria and was in charge of restocking items."

Conover looked at a piece of paper in front of her.

"What is important to you in a job?" Conover asked.

---

108. The short sentence, followed by the sentence fragment, conveys a sense of Wall stopping, then reconsidering his decision.

109. The short sentences duplicate Wall's thoughts and place us inside his head.

110. There is no need for attribution here. We know there are only Conover and Wall on the telephone.

111. The indirect quote sounds like Conover's voice.

112. By setting "lost" apart with the comma, Hallman lets us share Wall's feeling of being lost.

113. The short, abrupt sentences heighten the drama and the tension. We wonder if Wall will recover.

Gary thought for a moment.

"I was way too isolated in my last job," he said. "This sounds strange, but I would like a job where I could say hi to people."

He watched Conover take notes.

"Gary," Oliver asked, "how would you deal with an unhappy customer?"

Gary didn't know what to say. The night before he had read a magazine article on the 10 most-asked interview questions. This wasn't on it. He shifted in the chair. He looked to Conover, who suddenly became interested in a paper in front of her. Random thoughts reeled in his mind.[114] "I've got to think," he said. "OK, that deals with miscommunication. I understand conflict resolution. As a matter of fact, I took a test at church. I typed it up last night. It was a full-page document on conflict resolution and . . ."

He was losing it and knew it. He slapped his hands on his legs.

"Wait, wait," he said.

He took a deep breath.[115]

"Let me start over. OK, an unhappy customer, right?"

Oliver nodded.

"I . . . I . . ."

Gary shrugged his shoulders. He didn't know what to say. He was fooling himself. He heard Conover cough and looked at her. He stared into her eyes, and it seemed as if she nodded. Then again. Two small nods.[116]

Gary turned to Oliver.

"An unhappy customer?"

"Yes," she said.

"I'd talk with them and see why they were unhappy," Gary said.

He took another deep breath.[117]

"And then, then I'd go to the managers to see if they could figure out a way to make the customer happy."

Conover broke out in a smile. She gave Gary a thumbs-up sign.

He smiled, too.[118]

* * *

In December 1997,[119] Gary Wall walked into the Target store on Northeast 122nd Avenue and Glisan Street[120] for his interview with the store manager. The night before he had prayed, asking God for one favor.[121]

He spent about an hour with the manager. Later that day, when Conover called him, he told her that he thought the interview had gone well. The questions and his answers

---

114. Hallman "shows" us Wall growing flustered: he shifts (nervously) in his chair; he looks to Conover, who does not come to his rescue. "Reel" vividly captures his inner turmoil.

115. The deep breath serves as a delay and allows the tension to build. We have to wait a moment to see what he does.

116. Wall's thoughts place us in this scene. We are vicariously living the moment with him.

117. The deep breath again allows the tension to build. Wall has begun to recover, but we must wait to see if he can complete his thought successfully.

118. The smile carries a sense of relief and accomplishment and gains added impact at the end of the section.

119. Time transition.

120. The precise location vividly brings the scene to life.

121. Hallman holds back on the outcome of the interview, forcing us to continue reading.

were a blur. He remembered only that the manager said she'd make a decision in a few days. Gary was at home when he got the call: Report to work on Monday.[122]

There were so many things to remember: Time cards, paychecks, his uniform and name tag.[123] He sat and watched a videotape that outlined the store's policies and procedures. There was a set way to do everything. His boss, John Payne, took Gary to the automotive department and showed him how to move products from the back to the front so that the shelves looked neat.

And so his new life began.[124]

He'd show up for work, and other employees would ask him how he was doing. He got to know the woman behind the desk. In the changing room he heard his co-workers talking about what they were doing with their lives. And he decided he wanted to be like them.

He called Andy Thomas, a man he had known even before the accident. Thomas had been the one friend who had maintained contact with Gary after the wreck. They went out to dinner, and soon began getting together once a week for coffee.

He talked frequently with Diane Foster, whom he considered not a girlfriend, but a friend, a woman who had shown him that he had attractive qualities. She invited him to a Fourth of July party. Thomas had him join a weekly group that played cards. When someone at work asked what he had done that weekend, Gary had something to say.

He enjoyed work. But it was hard to deal with customers. He'd be restocking motor oil when someone would walk up and ask where the sheets or televisions were. He had no idea. He used the intercom to call for customer service. He sensed his co-workers were annoyed with him, and that bothered him.[125]

He found a piece of paper and walked the entire store to make a detailed map. Each night he studied it. He would ask himself questions. Where were the cameras? Towels? Toothpaste?[126] In time he quit asking for help.

One weekend,[127] Andy Thomas told him about a Christian dance for single men and women. They went. He saw her standing across the dance floor. She was smaller than he was, about 5-foot-4, with light brown hair that touched her shoulders. He decided he had nothing to lose and walked up to her.[128]

"Would you like to dance?" he asked.

"Yes," she said.

Her name was Susan Lassman. They danced once and went their separate ways. But Gary went to more dances, and he usually ended up dancing a few times with her. During the breaks, they found a table to talk. Lassman, a divorced woman 11 years older than Gary, was taken with this man's gentleness. Others wanted to move so fast. Or they assumed Lassman wanted more than she did. Gary was content to talk and listen. He told

---

122. While this is not a direct quote, it has the ring of the manager's voice. The drama of the moment is heightened by its placement at the end of the sentence and the use of the colon.

123. List provides a convenient way to sum up the things he had to remember.

124. The moment we have been waiting for arrives. Hallman sets it off in its own paragraph to heighten the drama.

125. Hallman gives us a concise, yet no less specific, rundown of Wall's new life (a Fourth of July party, a weekly card group, locating the sheets and televisions).

126. The questions take us inside Wall's thoughts and allow us to share the experience.

127. Transition.

128. This scene has a cinematic quality. Like Wall, we first see Lassman from across the dance floor, then we get a closer look at her. We don't learn her name until Wall approaches her and asks for a dance. As they become acquainted, we too learn more about her—much the way we get to know people in real life.

her about his accident. She said she knew nothing about brain injuries. He told her about his struggles, the Blue Cross job and his new place at Target.

Lassman told Gary that he was different than any man she had known. The others, she said, all brought pasts with them: an ex-wife, a failed relationship, bad memories. Gary, she said, had no past.[129] Yes, he admitted, he was starting over.

He could tell that she liked him, liked him[130] in a way that no woman had since the wreck. When Gary was with her, he felt intelligent and well-read. He found it easier to express himself.

She called him one day to meet her at Clackamas Town Center. They window-shopped and talked. While they were walking, Gary reached out to take her hand in his. He fumbled briefly, embarrassed. How did a man hold a woman's hand?[131] He waited for her to pull away. And then he felt her slowly squeeze his fingers.

Eventually, Gary invited her to his apartment to watch videos. And at dances they no longer sat out the slow numbers. Gary didn't have to come up with words to describe his emotions.

At work, Payne gave Gary more assignments, sending him out to all areas of the store. He learned how to use a word processor and a hand-held inventory computer. He was put in charge of specific floor displays.

As the weeks passed,[132] he discovered he didn't know enough about the items Target sold. So he rummaged around the warehouse and found product information publications sent by manufacturers. During his lunch break he read them. He took them home at night. When Payne mentioned that some companies sent instructional CD-ROMs to the store, Gary asked if he could take them home to study on his home computer. Then, if someone asked about a ceiling fan, Gary would know how it worked and which fan was the better buy.[133] When customers asked him something, he stopped what he was doing and gave them his full attention. To them it seemed as if he was being extra polite. He was, but he also had to concentrate so he wouldn't get confused. Customers liked his attention and help. They wrote letters to management. He got a raise.[134]

In August 1998[135] his family threw Gary a 40th birthday party at his mother's. The most important people in his life surrounded him: His mother, friends, people from church and, of course, Susan Lassman. They barbecued steaks and played Pin-the-Tail-on-the-Donkey, which made everyone laugh.[136]

A few weeks later,[137] Gary received an evaluation from Target. He was rated as excellent and got a second raise.

That was about the time that Lassman called to tell him that she had a boyfriend. She said she wanted to remain friends. Sure, Gary said, sure.

He sat alone in his apartment and wondered what he had done wrong. If there was something he could have changed. He realized there was nothing. He had sought a life

---

129. Her statement becomes ironic. What was a liability for Wall is now an asset.
130. The repetition of "liked" suggests she liked him a lot.
131. Again, the question draws us inside Wall.
132. Passage of time.
133. The concrete examples make Wall's progress more believable and real.
134. News of the raise gains more impact set aside in its own, spare sentence at the end of the paragraph.
135. Time transition.
136. In one short sentence we get the essence of the party due to Hallman's use of concrete detail: barbecued steaks, Pin-the-Tail-on-the-Donkey.
137. Time transition.

and found one. He had rediscovered that a life is filled with hope and disappointment, of dreams and realities, of joy and pain.[138]

That was life. Now he had to go live it.[139]

Tom Hallman, Jr. on Reading

"Most of the writers who influenced me were from magazines: Tom Junod who was with GQ and is now with Esquire. Many of the narrative writers in Sports Illustrated. Jon Franklin, the writer and author who has led the way for many writers around the country. Rick Bragg and Michael Winerip at the New York Times."

---

138. Lassman's call presents a new obstacle, but Wall overcomes it, confirming that he is in control.
139. The ending brings us back to the beginning. He has found a new life and he is living it.

Walt Harrington

Walt Harrington is a masterful reporter, and nowhere is that more apparent than in "True Detective." The weekend before he embarked on the project, he read a half-dozen mystery novels in which the main character was a homicide detective, and he realized that what made the books work was the extraordinarily detailed description. As a result, he doubled his normal reporting efforts to collect that same kind of graphic detail. He conducted several in-depth interviews with V. I. Smith about his life, and then, for the next two weeks, Smith's world became his world. He showed up every day at 3 p.m. and did what the detective did. If Smith worked until 11 p.m., Harrington worked until 11. If Smith worked until 4 a.m., Harrington worked until 4 a.m., and if the detective worked all night, so did Harrington.

All the while he was asking questions nonstop and taking notes. In addition to the notes, he tape-recorded more than twenty hours of police conversations on the street, in the squad room, and in the police cruiser, as well as interrogations of suspects and chaotic raids. He also took dozens of photos at crime scenes and Homicide North, which he later studied with a magnifying glass for details.

"It's quite likely that things are going so quickly and you're taking notes, but you don't really know what you're going to use at the time," Harrington told a reporter for IRE after the story appeared. "That's why I have the tape recorder going and take pictures. I use tapes less for sit-down interviews than for being on the scene when things are happening and I know I can't get it all. I've learned over the years if you don't have the tape recorder going that reconstruction of the scene through notes is less textured."

In reporting, Harrington is especially aware of how the senses bring a scene alive for readers. "As journalists, we tend to use our eyes too much, they're our primary vehicle," he says. "But we over rely on it. We should still be visual, but every chance we get we should try to remember to throw in other senses to make the piece come alive in different ways."

Harrington spent a week transcribing tapes. Then he read through all the materials he had gathered, taking notes on the important things he needed to include and the scenes that came together well—a process he follows for all his projects. He then worked out his lead and the foreshadowing.

"Once I do that," he says of his writing process, "I get a feel for the story and it starts to come. I try to organize my material on Monday, Tuesday, and Wednesday and start writing Thursday and Friday. By the middle of the next week, I have an 8,000 word piece that I consider to be a solid draft. This is then the time when it's edited, reworked, rewritten and when I take people's suggestions."

The story first appeared in the Washington Post Magazine, *where Harrington was a staff writer for nearly fifteen years. He is the author of* Crossings: A White Man's Journey Into Black America; American Profiles: Somebodies and Nobodies Who Matter; *and* At the Heart of It: Ordinary People, Extraordinary Lives. *He also edited the anthology* Intimate Journalism: The Art and Craft of Reporting Everyday Life.

Harrington is the recipient of numerous journalism awards, including the Sigma Delta Chi Distinguished Service Award, two National Association of Black Journalists writing awards, Northwestern University's John Bartlow Martin Award for Public Interest Journalism, and three national Sunday magazine writing awards. Crossings *was awarded the Gustavus Myers Center Award for the Study of Human Rights in the United States. Harrington is a professor of journalism at the University of Illinois at Urbana-Champaign and is currently working on a book tentatively titled* Journey to the Everlasting Stream: A True Story of Rabbits, Guns, Blood & Modern Manhood.

True Detective

A MAN GOES 22 YEARS WITHOUT BEING AFRAID, without giving his own death a glance, without worrying that the map of the city's criminal ways and rhythms that he has always carried in his head might be obsolete.[1] A man goes 22 years climbing the ladder from beat cop to blue-boy elite, to homicide detective. A man goes 22 years to earn a reputation as a "90%er"—a detective who puts the souls of nearly all his victims to rest by closing the book on their murders.[2] A man goes 22 years, and then the waters he inhabits shift and roil with unpredictable currents, until murder isn't murder anymore, isn't a biblical sentence that friends and lovers and fathers and sons impose on each other in storms of rage and recrimination. A man goes 22 years and finds himself leaning casually over a corpse on Halley Terrace in Southeast Washington, D.C., about to be made aware. That man—Detective Victor "V. I." Smith—flips back the dead man's coat and sees a blue-black machine gun, an Uzi, cocked and ready to fire.[3]

Detective V. I. Smith is fearless, at least his police buddies think he's fearless. He has waltzed into Barry Farms, one of the roughest housing projects in Washington, at 4:00 in the morning, disappeared for an hour and returned with his suspect in tow. He has raided crack houses alone, lined up the drug heads and sweated them for reconnaissance on the spot. V. I.'s cop friends can't imagine him being afraid of anything.[4] But tonight, after Halley Terrace, V. I. talks and talks about his shock at seeing that Uzi. About how six of his last seven murder victims have been packing guns. He doesn't reveal it to his comrades, but V. I. realizes that for the first time in 22 years as a Washington cop, he was afraid. Oh, maybe he'd been afraid before and hadn't realized it, imagined his feeling was

---

1. The repetition of "a man goes 22 years" draws readers into the story by creating suspense: What happens to this man during that 22nd year? With each repetition of the phrase, the tension and suspense build, pulling the reader deeper into the story. The suspense is heightened by the fact that readers don't know *who* the man is. To use his name at the beginning of the paragraph would lessen the effect. The list of participial phrases also lures readers further, into the paragraph, as each item grows more ominous and longer in length. The repetition of "without" adds drama and is pleasing to the ear.

2. Police lingo ("beat cop," "blue-boy elite," "90%er," "closing the book") places readers in the detective's world and creates the tone of a mystery novel. Even the unfamiliar term "90%ers" is defined in terms appropriate for that world.

3. Strong verbs ("shift" and "roil") cause the pace to accelerate and sweep readers toward the end of the paragraph. That momentum is enhanced by the use of "and" rather than commas in the list of "friends and lovers and fathers and sons." Harrington briefly slows the pace with "finds himself leaning casually over a corpse" before readers come to the zinger ending. In getting to that ending, he uses delay to create tension. Readers have to wait as the detective flips back the dead man's coat, wait as he sees the machine gun, wait as he sees that the gun is an Uzi, and then, wham, we see the Uzi is cocked and ready to fire. The writer has carefully placed this important detail at the *end* of the paragraph, the position of greatest emphasis. We are as startled as V. I. Smith must have been. It is also a dramatic place to introduce Smith. The overall effect of this sentence is cinematic, with the sequence replicating the movement of a movie camera.

4. Word choices re-create the texture of Smith's world: "police buddies," "in tow," "sweated them," "reconnaissance." "Waltzed" reflects his fearlessness. The listing of cases also offers proof of that fearlessness.

excitement or readiness or the flow of adrenaline. But there's no mistaking or denying the emotion that surged through V. I. Smith on Halley Terrace tonight: It was fear.[5]

* * *

Two years later[6] . . . everything squeaks. The heavy doors squeak. The metal swivel chairs squeak. The drawers in the metal desks squeak. The file drawers squeak. The keys of the old manual upright squeak. The room—No. 5058, dubbed Homicide North[7] because it is isolated two floors above D.C.'s other homicide offices in the city's Municipal Center—is a concerto of squeaks. Its other noises—the hollering voices, the clamoring phones, the electric typewriters, *Gilligan's Island* laugh-tracking on the beat-up TV, the two coffeepots spitting mud, the hand-held walkie-talkies belching static—all add layer upon layer of volume, creating finally a kind of jangled symphony.[8]

What will stop this din and turn the entire room of nine men prayerfully silent are three words their ears are tuned to as if they were set on a private frequency: "stabbing" or "shooting" or "homicide." When the police radio dispatcher speaks any of these words, everything stops, hands reach for tiny volume knobs on radios and everybody waits. Usually, it's a false alarm and, just as abruptly, the noise once again envelops the momentary silence like a stadium cheer after the crack of a long ball.[9]

The men in Homicide North are tonight "on the bubble"—cop talk meaning that their squad of detectives is on call to investigate the city's next murder.[10] Detective Jeff Mayberry, a short, wiry, close-cropped, jet-propelled 34-year-old in a tight blue sports coat, is riding the top of the bubble in his rotation as lead investigator on whatever horror is next offered up from the bowels of the city. He has ridden the bubble aloft for four duty days now—and no murder. At least none on his 3-to-11 shift.

---

5. "Talks and talks" and the repetition of "about" mimics the way people behave when they have been frightened: they tend to talk nonstop. "For the first time in 22 years" echoes the opening paragraph and underscores the significance of this incident. Harrington describes V. I.'s earlier brushes with fear in a casual manner that sounds like V. I.'s voice. The effect is to downplay these incidents and thus heighten the impact of this night's realization. Again, that moment comes at the end of the paragraph, where it gains greater impact. Note how much less dramatic it would have been to write: But there's no mistaking or denying that it was fear surging through V. I. Smith on Halley Terrace tonight.

6. Time transition. In the first three paragraphs, Harrington has suspended time, using material from interviews to reconstruct an incident that occurred two years earlier. He now moves into the main time frame, or what writer-educator Mark Kramer refers to as "the moving now," and the material gathered by immersion reporting.

7. This early setup of "No. 5058" and "Homicide North" provides a device for quick, future references.

8. Detailed description and vivid word choices appeal to the readers' senses and capture the gritty texture of the detectives' world. Readers can *hear* the squeak of the heavy doors, the swivel chairs, the desk drawers, the typewriter keys; they can *hear* the coffeepots "spitting," the walkie-talkies "belching static," and thus are drawn into the scene. The repetition of "squeaks" supports the observation that "everything squeaks" and lends a sense of drama. (How do you know how many times to repeat a word? There is no formula, says Harrington; you have to develop an ear.) The mud comparison comes from one of Harrington's favorite Tom Waits lyrics "Give me a cup of mud."

9. The placement of "'stabbing' or 'shooting' or 'homicide'" at the end of the sentence causes the words to stand out the same way they rise above the belching static. The colon forces readers to stop and give the words their undivided attention. By inverting the next sentence, Harrington calls attention to the dramatic pause that accompanies such dispatches. Note how much stronger the impact is than if he had written: Everything stops, hands reach for tiny volume knobs on radios and everybody waits when the police radio dispatcher speaks any of these words. His description of what transpires reflects the writer's close observation of his subjects' mannerisms. The effect is to let readers vicariously share that moment. The stadium-cheer simile aptly captures the momentary suspension of noise.

10. "On the bubble" is defined at a quiet moment so that an explanation won't be necessary when the real action gets under way. The phrase is repeated in the next two sentences to set up a pattern of repetition and thus demonstrates how it will be used, to indicate a time of waiting.

"You believe it?" he asks in frustration. No murder in a town that sees almost four murders every three days![11]

"You're bad luck," comes the rejoinder of his partner, Joe Fox, a respected and bearded 41-year-old bear of a detective who has a compulsive squint that constantly edges his wire-rimmed glasses up the bridge of his nose.[12] He is called neither "Joe" nor "Fox." He is called "Joefox."[13]

"Screw you, Joefox," Mayberry says.

Seated at the end of a row of desks in a corner under a wash of fluorescent light in front of pale curtains that hang off their track is V. I. Smith, looking out of place in this seedy domain.[14] At age 46, he's quiet and self-contained, talking softly into the receiver of the old phone atop his desk, which isn't unkempt like most of the others. He's chatting with a woman who lives on W Street NW. She has been peeking out her window tonight to see if the drug boys V. I. wants to bust and shake down for tips about a recent murder are hanging on the street. They aren't.[15]

Leaning on his elbows at his desk, talking into the phone, V. I. looks less like a tough city cop than, say, a prosecuting attorney or an FBI agent. He's 6' 4". Naked on the scale,[16] he goes a trim and powerful 230, only 10 pounds over the weight he carried as a freshman basketball star at Howard University nearly three decades ago.

His face is wide and handsome, chiseled. It smiles rarely. In temperament, V. I. is terminally cool, never nervous or edgy. The more excited he gets, the more deliberately he speaks. And the more deliberately he speaks, the more trouble whomever he's speaking to is probably in. Even V. I.'s laugh is deliberate, with each "hah" in his slow "hah-hah-hah" being fully enunciated. In dress and style, he resembles a new-breed jazz player: His hair and mustache are short and neat, his shirt is crisp, his tie is knotted tightly and never yanked loose at his neck, and his suit, usually bought at Raleighs, is always well-tailored and never cheap. Unlike some of his detective pals, V. I. would never wear brown shoes with a blue suit.[17] He dresses to the nines because, having grown up

11. By keeping Mayberry's description tight, the writer does not interrupt the action. That description, however, is vivid and begins introducing us to one of the "supporting" characters in V. I.'s story. The details of his close-cropped hair, his tight sports coat, and the fact he is "jet propelled" all tell us something about what kind of man he is. The image is more vivid and precise than simply saying he had brown hair and wore a sports coat. Mention of him going four days without a murder sets the stage for action and creates tension. That and the brief exchange that follows also show the detectives' mindset. Crime statistics reflect the writer's background research.

12. Tight description of Joe Fox gives readers a feel for the man: he is respected and has a habit of squinting and edging his glasses up the bridge of his nose. The latter again shows the writer's attention to mannerisms that capture the characters' personalities.

13. Referring to the characters by the names they themselves use ("Joefox," "Mayberry," "V. I.") puts readers in their world.

14. Writer uses a cinematic technique to gradually move the camera in on V. I. First we see the room, then Mayberry, then Joefox, then V. I.'s corner of the room, then the focus of this profile: V. I. Smith.

15. The writer describes V. I. in action, talking on the phone, leaning on his elbow, so that the story is not interrupted. The details the writer chooses begin revealing V. I.'s personality: his neatness in the midst of the "seedy" office (note word choice), his self-confidence, the soft voice he uses to address the woman on the phone. Besides being a colorful detail, the description of the woman peeking out the window is also a setup for a future reference.

16. "Naked on the scale" sounds like V. I.'s voice.

17. Harrington uses description both to characterize V. I. and to begin introducing his background. Note the small details that set him apart from the other detectives: the way he laughs, the way he knots his tie, the quality of his clothes, the fact he would never wear brown shoes with a blue suit. Raleighs was an upscale men's clothing store in Washington, D.C. In learning what V. I. looks like, we are also discovering his personality. The replication of his laugh lets us hear him.

on the streets of black Washington, he knows that a man who dresses well is ascribed a dose of respect in that world, and every small advantage counts, especially these days.[18]

The guys in the office call V. I. "the Ghost," because they rarely know what he's doing from minute to minute. With his reputation as one of Washington's best homicide detectives, V. I. comes and goes at Room 5058 pretty much as he pleases. But if the radio calls out a murder, he's on the scene, appearing as if from nowhere, like an apparition.[19] Of Washington's 65 homicide detectives, V. I. Smith figures he's the only one without a regular partner. That's because Joefox, who came with V. I. to homicide seven years ago on the same cold Tuesday in February, used to be his partner, until the green and gung-ho Mayberry arrived from uniform four years ago and was assigned to Joefox for diapering.

Joefox and V. I. eventually took the kid aside and told him how it was going to be: The three of them would be partners, meaning that any one man's case was also the case of the other two. If Mayberry listened and studied and showed respect, he would learn the art and science of unraveling the darkest of human behaviors from two of the masters. And that's how it came down, with Mayberry now a fine detective in his own right. So when Mayberry is riding the bubble, Joefox and the Ghost are riding with him.[20]

When the bubble seems to burst tonight, it's no thriller.[21] A man named Willis Fields, who lived in a Washington boarding house, died at the Washington Hospital Center burn unit today, and the death was passed on to Detective C. J. Thomas, whose job it is to investigate and certify natural deaths.[22] But in the hospital file he discovered that the 56-year-old man had told a nurse that "they" had poured alcohol on him and set him afire. Willis Fields was in the hospital 10 days, but his story fell through the cracks. Nobody called the police about his allegation, which means the inquiry will start nearly two weeks cold, no leads, only an address.[23]

"C. J., why is it every one a these things you do, you always get us?" asks Mayberry. "Remember that guy on Suitland Parkway? Been there two years? Six shots to the head?"

"And what did you tell me?" C. J. asks.

"Man, that's a natural!"

"Well, here we go," says V. I., in his smooth, lyrical baritone as he palms a radio, unconsciously pats his right breast coat pocket for evidence of his ID wallet, pats his left breast coat pocket for evidence of his notebook and heads out the door in his athlete's saunter, a stylized and liquid stroll, a modern cakewalk.[24]

The address for Willis Fields is wrong—2119 11th St. NW is a vacant lot. "They probably got it turned around," V. I. says, as the threesome mills about the grassy lot, looking lamely around, shrugging. It's just before dusk and the hot summer day has begun to cool, but except for a man staring at them intently from the sidewalk in front

---

18. The final sentence reflects the writer's sit-down interviews with V. I.

19. Background continues to "show" readers how V. I. operates. The "Ghost" nickname provides a quick, easy way to refer to him later in the story.

20. The trio's background is rendered in a tone and vocabulary that sounds like the voices of V. I. and Joefox ribbing their junior partner. Note the word choices: "diapering," "the kid," "two of the masters."

21. "When the bubble seems to burst tonight" returns us to the main time line and acts as a transition into the case of Willis Fields.

22. Note that C. J. Thomas is identified but not described. His role in the story is so minor we don't really need to "see" him.

23. The case summary sounds like C. J. briefing the homicide detectives. "They" implies that Willis was too afraid to name names. "Two weeks cold, no leads, only an address" carries the ring of a thriller.

24. V. I. is again described in action so that the story is not interrupted. The comparison to a stylized cakewalk (a 19th century African American dance) gives us a vivid picture of how he moves.

of the Soul Saving Center Church of God across the street, the block is empty of people, quiet.[25] V. I. knows this neighborhood. He spent years living nearby as a kid, attending Garnet-Patterson Junior High over at 10th and U streets, Bell High School at Hiatt Place and Park Road and Cardozo High just up the hill at 13th and Clifton streets.[26] This block of 11th Street isn't Beverly Hills, but it's a stable block that doesn't fit V. I.'s image of the crime at hand. An old man is more likely to be set on fire on a block where guys hang out drinking liquor, where there's a lot of street action. He nods down the road. That sounds more like the block back at 11th and U, with a corner market and a liquor store nearby.[27] Sure enough, when the office checks the address the detectives were given, it's wrong. Willis Fields lived at 1929—near the corner of 11th and U.

* * *

Being in his old neighborhood makes V. I. nostalgic.[28] As a boy, he seemed to live everywhere in Washington—Southeast, Northeast, here in Northwest, as his mother and father struggled and moved up from dumpy apartment to less dumpy apartment. Sometimes, he and his brothers sacked out four to a mattress. But in the '50s, V. I.'s daddy—a laborer by day, a cabby by night—bought a big old house on Adams Street in LeDroit Park, near First and W streets Northwest, and the kids finally slept two to a room.

The man who grew up to be a cop was no choirboy. He didn't worry about his grades, he cut classes to play basketball, he learned to palm loaded dice, he hustled pool. By age 16, V. I. was frequenting the now defunct Birdland and Rio nightclubs on 14th Street with his older buddies. And it was at one such club that his friend Jimmy got killed. They were hanging with a fool of a friend, who flipped his cigarette butt toward the bar and hit a dude in the neck. When the guy flicked out the narrow blade with the pearl handle, everybody scrambled, but Jimmy didn't scramble fast enough. He took the knife deep in his back, stumbled outside and bled out his life on the sidewalk.

After that, V. I. was more judicious about the company he kept. A lot of guys he hung with eventually went bad in the ways kids went bad in those days—stealing purses, robbing people on the street. But not V. I. For some reason—maybe because his daddy was so strict—V. I. was always afraid of the police. While other guys figured the cops would never catch them, V. I. figured the cops would always catch him.

One incident had frightened him good: A woman was raped in his neighborhood, and the police rounded up anybody on the street close to the rapist's description and took them to the old 10th Precinct. V. I. sat in a holding room until 3:00 a.m., when the cops told him he could go home—they'd caught their man. That night made V. I. a believer in the "wrong place, wrong time" theory of city life. A guy had to think ahead, anticipate, cut trouble off at the pass, stay off the streets and away from guys bound for infamy. Or go down, too.[29]

After a stint in the military, after attending Howard University, after becoming a basketball celebrity on the playgrounds of Washington and before graduating from Ameri-

25. The sensory details ("just before dusk"; "the hot summer day has begun to cool"; the quiet, empty block with one man "staring . . . intently from the sidewalk in front of the Soul Saving Center Church of God") place readers in the scene.

26. V. I.'s familiarity with the neighborhood provides a transition into a background digression.

27. Harrington uses interview material to reconstruct V. I.'s thoughts.

28. Place transition.

29. V. I.'s old neighborhood provides another opportunity to weave in background on him and his family and an anecdote that sounds like his voice.

can University, V. I. was sworn in as one of the city's early black cops.[30] Only a few days later, he attended the funeral of a boyhood friend, a kid nicknamed Porgy, a kid V. I. had learned to avoid. Porgy had graduated from purses to stickups, and he was killed in a gun battle with police. Almost 25 years later, V. I. has never stopped believing that with a few unlucky breaks, a few poor choices, he, too, could have gone down the toilet like Porgy. To this day, he can arrive on a street corner and find a young man who has just bled out his life on the sidewalk, and think: *But for the grace of God . . .*[31]

* * *

At 1929 11th St., nobody answers the door.[32] So the detectives spread out and canvass the street, talking to neighbors. They have the office run the license plates of nearby parked cars, checking for the name Willis Fields. When an elderly man walks into the yard at 1929, Mayberry asks if he knows him.[33]

"Yeah, I know 'im."

"When's the last time you talked to Willie?"

"The Sunday 'fore last."

"Who's he hang with?"

"He works at Ben's Chili Bowl."

"Where you live?"

It turns out the man lives in the room next to the one once occupied by Willis Fields. He says Fields has no girlfriend and few male friends, that nobody ever visits his room and that he smokes cigars and hits the bottle hard.[34] The detectives want to get inside Fields's room to check for signs of a fire, because if he was burned in his room—fell asleep smoking and drinking liquor on the bed—it would show that he could have gotten burned on his back by accident, not malicious design.[35] But the man says Fields's room is locked and that the landlady is out.

"What happened to 'im?" the man asks.

"He didn't tell ya?" asks V. I., careful to reveal no information likely to make its way into the street gossip mill.

"Hell if I know."

At Ben's Chili Bowl a block away on U Street,[36] they ask their questions again. The whole time, V. I. is building scenarios, theories, in his mind. Say Fields had a buddy who often came to visit him at Ben's, but who hasn't stopped by in the last couple weeks. Good chance that guy knows something. Or say a woman always seemed to visit Fields on his payday. She's a good possibility. Or maybe Fields complained to a co-worker about somebody who'd been bothering him. Or mentioned somebody who owed him money. What-

---

30. The use of a list allows the writer to present tightly—yet in an interesting manner—biographical information. Note how he slightly alters the last item in the list to keep it from becoming monotonous.

31. Anecdote dramatizes the world V. I. grew up in and the path his own life could have taken. The story is related in street slang ("down the toilet," "stickups") so that we feel we are hearing V. I. tell the story.

32. Place transition. Note how Harrington uses similar transitions throughout the story to orient readers. We always know *where* we are.

33. The last sentence sets up the dialogue.

34. List is an economical way to sum up what the man told V. I. "Hits the bottle hard" echoes what must have been the man's actual words.

35. Harrington draws from his conversations with V. I. to replicate the latter's thinking and to explain his actions.

36. Place transition.

ever the story, V. I. knows from experience that men like Fields usually lead very simple lives. They go from their rooms to their jobs to the liquor store and back to their rooms.[37] So that's the bird dog's trail.[38] Unfortunately, nobody at Ben's knows much about Fields either, except that he has been missing.

"Ooohhh, booooy!" says Mayberry.

As a murder, this case has "unsolved" written all over it. And unless V. I., Mayberry and Joefox declare it a homicide, it will likely be forgotten. There's been no publicity, no relatives or political heavyweights demanding action. If Fields's death were declared a natural, his demise would slip into bureaucratic oblivion. It wouldn't take up their time or mess up their statistics with an unsolved murder. It would—poof—disappear. Except for one detail: Some dirtbag might have turned Willis Fields into a human torch, and catching the scum would bring great satisfaction. The idea is downright inspirational. Because in an era when most of the homicides V. I. gets are drug boys wasting drug boys, bandits beefing each other through the nose of a 9 mm, or hotheads retaliating after some trivial insult, this Willis Fields case is, well, intriguing, a puzzle with most of the pieces missing. The men need to hit 1929 again, talk to the landlady, get into Fields's room.[39] But in the meantime—since Willis Fields is still not an official homicide—Mayberry, Joefox and the Ghost are back on the bubble.[40]

The call comes at 9:50 p.m. . . .[41]

* * *

When the men arrive at Rhode Island Avenue and Brentwood Road NE,[42] the scene, as it always does, seems not real, somehow outside of time and place, like a page brought to life from a paperback novel:[43] The shooting ground is cordoned off in a triangle of yellow plastic tape (POLICE LINE DO NOT CROSS), and squad cars and cruisers are parked every which way, as if they'd landed as randomly as dice thrown in a tornado's game of craps.[44] The crowd of mostly women and youngsters is congregated in the vague and dreamy light of street lamps beneath huge and gnarled trees in the scrub-grass yard of the L-shaped Brookland Manor apartments. A police helicopter flutters overhead, its searchlight scorching a block nearby.[45] The cops know this stretch of Rhode Island as a

---

37. Harrington again is able to reconstruct V. I.'s thoughts from information gleaned from interviews.

38. Transition out of V. I.'s thoughts, back to the main time line, or scene.

39. "As a murder" moves readers back into V. I.'s thinking and that of his colleagues. Note how the language ("dirtbag," "drug boys," "wasting," "hotheads," "hit") echoes theirs. Also note how the list tightly compresses information: "The men need to hit 1929 again, talk to the landlady, get into Fields's room."

40. "Back on the bubble": The trio is again on call for the next murder. This serves as a transition back into the main time line.

41. The time orients readers; the use of an ellipsis echoes the "dum-de-dum-dum" of old-time radio dramas.

42. Place transition.

43. Simile is appropriate to the tone and subject matter of the story. It also plays off the readers' familiarity with mystery novels.

44. Concrete details (the triangle of yellow tape, the haphazard police cars) bring readers into the scene. The comparison to randomly thrown dice again helps us visualize the scene.

45. Harrington continues to describe the setting, providing a detailed picture of the crime scene. Note both the word choices and the specific detail: the composition of the crowd, the nature of the street light, what the trees looked like, even the fact that the apartment buildings were L-shaped. He uses the latter detail throughout the story to help readers follow the action. Much of the detail comes from photographs. The word "flutters" conjures up an image of a helicopter hovering overhead; "scorching" describes the glare of the spotlight.

drug market, and that's the first scenario V. I.'s mind starts to build. One shot, large caliber, left side of the head. That's all he knows.[46]

V. I. steps into the triangle and begins to think in the language of the scene before him. On the sidewalk begins the pool of blood, not red, but a thick, syrupy black. The blood has cascaded over the curb and run southwest with gravity for about five feet, where a pile of leaves and debris has dammed its flow. The young man who was shot was alive when the ambulance left, but this is a large pool of blood, and V. I. figures Mayberry is off the bubble. On the sidewalk is a footprint in blood. Could be that of the victim, the shooter, a witness, a passerby, an ambulance attendant. A few feet away is a lonely quarter, heads up. On a waist-high embankment, where the sidewalk meets the yard about six feet from the street, stand a Mountain Dew bottle and a can of Red Bull malt liquor.[47]

The details seem trivial, but a homicide detective's life is a sea of details, a collage of unconnected dots gathered and collated. In the end, most will turn out to be insignificant. But at the time, a detective cannot know the revelatory from the inconsequential. He must try to see them all, then hold them in his mind in abeyance until the few details that matter rise forth from the ocean to reveal themselves. V. I. begins to link the dots in the scene before him. For instance, a man who is shot at such close range was either hit by someone he trusted or by someone who sneaked up on him. Maybe the Mountain Dew and the Red Bull belonged to the victim and to one of his friends, who were sitting on the embankment looking toward the street, talking, laughing. From the darkened yard behind them the shooter moved in. The victim fell forward, his head landing at the curb and spurting blood with each heartbeat. His buddy bolted. If the dots are connected correctly, that buddy is a witness. If not, he could be the shooter.[48]

Suddenly, from the crowd in the dreamy light on the scrub-grass yard, comes a long, awful scream. In five seconds, it comes again. And then a woman runs wildly through the crowd, crashing into people as she goes. She disappears into a door at the elbow of the L-shaped Brookland Manor.[49]

On the chance that this might be a drug-boy shooting, V. I., Mayberry and Joefox will not wander through the crowd or canvass the apartments looking for witnesses tonight. Until a few years ago,[50] it was virtually unheard of for witnesses to be killed, but today they are crossed off like bad debts. Witnesses know it, cops know it, shooters know it. It's simply too dangerous for witnesses to be seen talking to the cops after a shooting,

---

46. Material from interviews is used to reconstruct V.I.'s thinking. The staccato sentence structure ("One shot, large caliber, left side of the head") mimics the way he and his fellow detectives think—they go right to the important facts; no dealing with the many unimportant or superfluous details.

47. Harrington uses the triangle to place his character. The graphic description of the crime scene is drawn from photographs taken by the writer and examined with a magnifying glass and from revisiting the scene in daylight. Note how the concrete details (the quarter laying heads up, the footprint, the Mountain Dew bottle, the can of Red Bull malt liquor, the blood's path) put readers in that scene. Harrington determined the direction of the blood flow by later looking at a map. Because of the earlier setup of "on the bubble," there is no need for explanation now that the action is under way.

48. The familiar dot metaphor provides a means of quickly describing how V. I. processes the details he collects. Harrington then offers an actual example of V. I. connecting "the dots" in this case. Thus readers are prepared for future references. The particular speculations here are those provided by V. I. and his partners in interviews. Harrington's goal here was to get at how police work is done in the context of an overarching mindset.

49. Harrington's use of a tape recorder enables him to time the woman's scream and thus draw a more vivid scene, allowing readers to share the experience vicariously. Note how the word choices also help draw the scene ("dreamy light," "a long, awful scream," "woman runs wildly . . . crashing into people") and how the writer again makes use of "the elbow of the L-shaped" project to place the action more specifically.

50. Transition from the scene into background information gleaned from interviews.

especially at night when the drug boys are out.[51] V. I. plans to return tomorrow afternoon to do his canvass. But after hearing the woman scream, he invokes another law of experience: "You get people cryin', they gonna tell ya somethin'."[52]

With this in mind,[53] V. I. saunters toward the door at the building's elbow and the crowd parts and murmurs as he passes.[54] On the darkened stairs up to the second floor, a place filled with the smells of a dozen dinners cooking,[55] he finds the woman's mother, who says her daughter knew the victim but doesn't want to talk to the police. V. I. doesn't push. He gets the daughter's name, her apartment number. One of the problems these days is that victims and suspects are usually known on the streets only by nicknames that the cops don't know. So V. I. asks if the victim had a nickname. The mother says, "KK."

* * *

The wanton killings of the last few years have changed everything. From 1964 to 1987, the number of Washington homicides fluctuated between 132 and 287, with 225 posted in 1987. In their first two years as detectives, the eager V. I. and Joefox drove around with their radio microphone in hand so they could lay claim to any murder as soon as it came down. Then, in 1988, homicides skyrocketed to 369—then 434, 474 and 483 in the following years, with the pace flagging only slightly so far this year. The police closure rate plummeted: By the end of 1991, only 65% of homicides from 1990 and 54% from 1991 had been closed by police, compared with 80% of homicides from 1986.

As homicides have gone berserk, so have the lives of V. I. and his fellow detectives. A cop used to have time to investigate his murders, interview everybody, build a case. In the old days, murder was more often a domestic affair, and a victim's killer was often found among his family. But by 1991, only 4% of Washington homicides were domestics, while more than three-quarters were attributed to drugs, robberies, burglaries, arguments or non-drug-related retaliations. All of which means that for most homicides today, detectives no longer have a neat list of identifiable suspects but a barrage of friends, enemies, business partners and competitors to investigate. Even with more detectives, the cases are constantly rolling over one another, with new murders arriving before old ones are solved. Sometimes, V. I. sits down and pores through his old files so he doesn't plain forget a case.[56]

And the drug-boy and bandit killings are so much more complicated than the old "mom-and-pop murders." V. I. has a case in far Northeast, where a bunch of guys opened fire on a crowd one evening, killing a young man and wounding three others. On its face, it looks like a drug-boy shooting. But the chain of events is also intertwined with the lives, loves, personalities and values of an array of individuals. The case began, according to the tips V. I. has collected from informants, a week before the shooting, when a woman

---

51. By using the detectives' own vocabulary ("cops" and "crossed off like bad debts"), Harrington seems to capture their thoughts.

52. V. I.'s thoughts are reconstructed from interviews.

53. Transition back to the scene.

54. The use of "the elbow" again helps readers place V. I.'s movements.

55. The writer gives us a succinct, yet vivid sensory image of the building the woman runs into: the darkened stairs, the second floor, "a place filled with the smells of a dozen dinners cooking."

56. By this point, Harrington has a firm grasp on his readers. It is now safe for him to insert background information on Washington homicides, without running the risk of losing both his audience and the personal story of V. I. in the "public policy" aspects of the murder explosion. Says Harrington: "Too often humans are used in stories as stick figures to supposedly illuminate policy issues. A writer-reporter should make a firm decision about which will come first in his story before he starts, or the deep human story will inevitably be lost."

friend of a suspected drug dealer was beaten by another woman. The suspected drug dealer went gunning for his friend's assailant, but shot the wrong woman. A male friend of the woman who was mistakenly shot then interceded in her behalf with the shooter, who apparently took this as a threat. With several buddies, he sought out and killed the male friend of the woman who had been mistakenly shot, before the guy could ice him. And that's a simple case.[57]

V. I. has had cases that intertwine with as many as a dozen other murders—shootings, retaliations, shootings, retaliations.[58] He has cases where families have been wiped out. A young man was killed, and his brother was set to testify against the shooter and then the brother was killed. Another brother was set to testify against that brother's shooter and he was killed. A sister was set to testify against that brother's shooter and she, too, was shot.[59] There's little moral outrage about many killings because of what V. I. calls "victim participation"—meaning the victims are often as sleazy as their killers.[60] Nowadays, half the battle is finding some reason to lock up a suspected killer on another charge to get him off the street so witnesses will cooperate and so they will be safe. This onslaught has erupted in only a few years.

But that's not the worst of it: Worse yet is what has happened inside V. I.'s heart and his head. He goes to the home of dead kids these days, knocks on the door and tells a mother and father that their child has been killed, and they say, "Yeah, okay." Without a hint of emotion, they close the door. The homicide detective's code of honor has always been that he identifies with the dead, swears to find the killer. These days, that's harder and harder. It's hard to get worked up over the injustice of a dead man who may have killed one or two or three people himself.

But that's not the worst of it: Worse yet is that V. I. has had witnesses he promised to protect get killed. After he promised! So, after 24 years of putting his honor and duty on the line at any time, night or day, V. I. Smith stopped promising. He began saying only that he would do what he could. He has been forced to make his own moral choices outside the expectations of the law: He has let murderers stay free rather than risk the lives of more witnesses.

But even that's not the worst of it: Worse yet[61] is that in the last few years, V. I. Smith—tough, cool, brave—has ridden home late at night and broken down in tears of private bereavement: The fabric of the city where he grew up, the city he loves, has been shredded, destroyed. People on the outside haven't grasped this yet, haven't felt the deadening weight of this sadness, this heartsickness.[62]

* * *

---

57. Harrington uses a case to illustrate the point that today's murders are more complicated. Note the continued use of police slang to maintain the tone.

58. "Shootings, retaliations, shootings, retaliation" echoes the pattern and repetition of the murders.

59. This case supports the point that families have been wiped out. This and the previous case help us understand why V. I.'s views on murder and victims have changed.

60. "Victim participation" echoes the dehumanized bureaucratic voice used to describe this horrible human tragedy.

61. Repetition serves to emphasize how all this has changed V. I.'s life. It also creates drama. Note how Harrington slightly varies the third repetition to break the rhythm and thus stress the fact that what follows is, indeed, the worst of all.

62. Harrington takes a comment made by V. I. in passing during a sit-down background interview ("I've even cried on the way home") and heightens the impact—and the drama—by using harder-hitting words ("broken down," "private bereavement") and juxtaposing the remark with V. I.'s "tough, cool, brave" persona.

From Brookland Manor,[63] V. I. takes only a nickname. He is famous for crashing cases at the scene, not waiting until tomorrow to investigate. He theorizes from the dots[64] and pushes every lead to the limit. He can't interview witnesses tonight, but maybe the detectives dispatched to the hospital have a lead he can push. Maybe a brother or the mother or father of the victim named names, know somebody who was beefing with the victim, gave the cops a line.[65] V. I. heads back out the door, through the parting crowd, to see what Mayberry and Joefox have learned.[66]

"He's gonna live," Mayberry says.

"That right?" V. I. asks without emotion. He glances at the pool of blood: KK is one lucky dude. Then he heads for his cruiser. He will not spend one more millisecond connecting the dots of this picture. It is an attempted murder now, another cop's glory, another cop's worry. They are still on the bubble. . . .[67]

* * *

At 1929 11th St.,[68] the landlady is home. She seems to stop breathing when they tell her Willis Fields is dead. With her hands covering her cheeks she leads the detectives up an oddly tinted turquoise stairway to his dowdy, sweltering room. One life, one room. A round white clock on the wall reads 10:55. On the dingy carpet lie one razor blade, a bottle cap and a few toothpicks. Half a dozen shirts hang on a rack, along with a single pair of pants, dirty. A lamp without a cover, an unmade bed, a small bottle of Listerine, nearly empty, three unopened bars of soap, a loaf of Wonder Bread. On the wall are a calendar and a newspaper photo of a woman in black hat, underwear and stockings. Atop the television are three pens, a pencil, a nail clipper, a wristwatch, six cigars and two packs of matches. On the nightstand is a red address book.[69] In it are the names of people listed as owing Fields money.

"Whatever happened didn't happen here," says V. I., which means the death of Fields is probably a murder.[70] V. I. starts theorizing, figuring maybe Fields went on a drinking binge and demanded money from one of his debtors, who went off. Lighting someone on fire isn't an efficient way to kill; it's more a murder of passion.[71] As the detectives are about to leave, call it a day's work at 11:35 p.m.,[72] the landlady's brother arrives.

On the last Saturday of Willis Fields's life, the brother says, he had come out of the apartment he shares with his sister, headed to catch a plane for vacation. He found Fields passed out drunk on the exterior steps going up to his room. He mentions two men—

---

63. Transition from the background information to the main time line.
64. Because of the earlier setup, the dots need no explanation.
65. The nickname is used to insert an explanation of how V. I. operates: in other words, how he connects the dots. "Beefing with the victim" and "gave the cops a line" are street slang.
66. Transition from digression back to scene.
67. "On the bubble" serves as shorthand: Mayberry and his partners are back on call for the next murder. This and the concise lists (see #46) show how cops only worry about what they need to worry about. It's a way of compartmentalizing information that keeps them on target, or as Harrington puts it: "a way of clear thinking and priority and not burdening themselves with extraneous concerns and worries."
68. Place transition.
69. Concrete details place readers at the scene. They also provide a neat summation of Willis Fields's life, or as Harrington writes, "One life, one room." The writer wanted, he says, for Fields's room and his life to seem "achingly sad and desperate." He was in the room for no more than five minutes; he reconstructed the setting from a half-dozen photographs that he examined under a magnifying glass. The clock also provides the time.
70. Harrington clarifies V. I.'s quote.
71. V. I.'s thoughts are reconstructed from interviews.
72. The time orients readers. The detectives have been on the scene for 40 minutes.

Robert and Theodore, whom Fields often hung out with on the street. He talks for a long time and the detectives are about to leave when the brother, in an aside,[73] says, "He was layin' right there in the doorway, and this old fag was tryin' to frisk him." Mayberry, Joefox and V. I. look at each other in wonder at what people can forget to mention.

"You know his name?" Joefox asks.

"Naw, he be down the street."

"Did Fields go in the house then?" V. I. asks.

"Stump can answer that," the brother says, explaining that he left Willis Fields in the care of one of Fields's friends, who happened along the Saturday before last, a man nicknamed Stump. V. I. knows that none of the people mentioned or interviewed so far tonight is a suspect, and he figures Stump isn't either, but a trail's a trail. He says of Stump, "That's where we gotta start."

* * *

For days more,[74] Mayberry, Joefox and the Ghost are on the bubble. *Amazing!* Still no murders on 3-to-11. Just the luck of the draw. But when a man and his squad are on the bubble, it's hard to do much police work, because when the call comes, everything else must be dropped. V. I. has nonetheless arranged for the squad to squeeze in a quick raid one night, sweep in with some uniformed cops in marked cruisers and hit the drug boys hanging on W Street, where his source is still peeking out the window and reporting back.[75] Two guys argued on that street a while back and one ended up killing the other. At least that's how V. I.'s informants have explained the murder, but he has "no eyes"— no witnesses willing to testify.[76]

His plan is to sweep in, make everybody hug the ground, scare up some guns and drugs, drag the crew downtown and start sweatin' 'em about the murder. When a guy's looking at 5-to-10[77] on a federal firearms rap, his memory can improve dramatically. Very little planning goes into such a raid. Eat some pizza, watch the Redskins, or *Top Cops*, or *Road Warrior*—then hop in the cars and do it.[78] Although V. I. figures maybe a quarter of the guys on that street will be strapped with guns or have a gun hidden nearby, no detective will wear a bulletproof vest.[79] All in a day's work. But night after night, the drug boys don't cooperate, and the street stays empty. Word comes back to V. I. through the drug boys' girlfriends that pals of the dead man are planning a retaliatory drive-by shooting and everybody is staying scarce.

While on the bubble,[80] V. I. works his case in far Northeast. He conspicuously cruises the neighborhood, which is a signal to his informants that he wants them to call. V. I. will collect reconnaissance as well as spread rumors—gossip that will get more people talk-

---

73. "In an aside" conveys the offhand manner in which the brother says this.

74. Transition shows passage of time. It leads us into a summary of what V. I. and his partners did during that time. Since their activities were mostly routine, there is no need to develop them into fuller scenes. Learning what to summarize or leave out of a story is important. If everything the writer observes is included and given equal weight, or space, the truly important moments will fail to stand out.

75. Because of the earlier setup, we do not need an explanation of the woman peeking out the window.

76. Harrington translates police slang.

77. Police lingo for a 5-to-10-year prison sentence.

78. Both the content and the structure of the list of sentence fragments capture the impromptu nature of the raid.

79. The fact the detectives don't wear bulletproof vests "shows" they are "tough, cool, brave." It also sets us up for a later, critical moment.

80. Transition again compresses time.

ing so his real informants will have cover, gossip that may make the shooter fear his own friends and allies are turning against him. Some guys will flag down V. I. In the street and talk to him. These are young men who have their own troubles with the law and who can tell their friends they were discussing their cases, asking V. I. to put in a good word with a judge or a prosecutor. V. I. often does. But the way the game is played, he wants payback—the names of potential witnesses, the name of a shooter, the details of the Byzantine events that often lead up to a killing.[81]

"You owe me big time," V. I. tells one young man.

"That last thing didn't work. They done me."

V. I. is unmoved. "I can't save you twice. But I did it the first time. So stay in touch. I can make it worth your while. I gotta get some eyes."[82]

It seems that nobody helps the cops anymore just because it's the right thing to do. "You ain't got nobody helpin' ya now," V. I. says. "Nobody gives a crap. You gotta make everybody do what you want 'em to do. And you gotta be real mean to get results." The drug-boy killings have spooked everybody. V. I. can't blame folks. But that has meant more and more of his encounters with potential witnesses are hostile. More and more, he has to threaten people to get their cooperation. He has to get them subpoenaed before the grand jury and then warn them that they can be charged with perjury if they don't tell the truth. And these are innocent people. He has even hinted that a witness's name might leak out before a suspected shooter has been jailed, unless that witness agrees to testify after the guy is locked up. He must sometimes act threatening to even the most harmless of people,[83] which is what happens on the Saturday afternoon[84] V. I. swings by the home of the last man known to have seen Willis Fields alive. Stump, a 64-year-old man whose real name is Earl Johnson, is off his porch and headed for his front door the instant V. I.'s cruiser pulls to the curb. V. I. halts the retreat.

"Need to talk to you. Detective Smith, Homicide."

"You wanta come inside?"

"No, sir, you gonna have ta come with me." V. I. opens the creaking front-yard gate and gestures toward his cruiser.

Stump is disoriented. "I gotta tell my wife."

"You can call her from downtown."

"I don't know nothin'."

"We gonna just talk about it."

"I don't know nothin'."

Stump looks up at his wife, who is peering down from a second-story window.[85] V. I. could have interviewed Stump at home, but he believes people are a lot like animals: They're more comfortable in their own territory. He wants them uncomfortable, so they drive off toward the station. Suddenly, the word "stabbing" squawks from the cruiser radio.[86]

---

81. The cruises through the neighborhood provide an opportunity to insert an explanation of how V. I. works with informants. Part of Harrington's goal in the story was to show readers how cops actually *do* their jobs and how they *think* about their work—to make the process explicit.

82. The scene provides an example of V. I. dealing with an informant.

83. The digression continues to describe how V. I.'s job and his dealings with witnesses have changed.

84. Transition out of the digression, back to the time line.

85. Note how Harrington refrains from interrupting the action with a description of Stump. We will get that later.

86. The radio transmission creates tension: the stabbing could be a murder, but there's no need to say so. Because of the setup way back at Homicide North, we already know that the mere word stops everything.

"You got a condition?"[87] V. I. asks the dispatcher.

"I didn't do nothin'," Stump says from the backseat.

"Hey, Stump, we know you all right, man." V. I. says this in a more friendly tone, trying to calm the man down. Then he heads for the scene of the stabbing, doing 85 mph on the Southwest Freeway. He arrives at M and Half streets SW. The victim is gone and only a dab of blood stains the sidewalk. He will live.[88]

Still on the bubble . . .

Seated back at Homicide North,[89] staring into the middle distance and wringing thick and worn hands, Stump is not a happy camper. He's a short man with a good belly, a mustache and short graying hair. He wears his blue-and-white cap backwards. He wears blue work pants and a white short-sleeved shirt. A ring of keys hangs off his belt.[90]

"Never did a crime in my life," Stump says to the air.[91]

"You know Fields?" V. I. asks.

"Right. But what happened to him, I don't know."

As these things often go, however, Stump knows more than he knows he knows. He says that before the detectives came around asking questions, a man nicknamed Bo had told him that Fields had been set on fire.[92] V. I. knows from the hospital report that an unidentified person drove Fields to the hospital. He figures Fields must have told that person what happened. And he figures that person might have told others.[93]

"You can't set me up for no murder," Stump says.

"I'm not tryin' ta charge you with murder," V. I. says, knowing that indeed Stump is not a suspect. "Did you ask Bo how he knew Fields got burned?"

"He said it was over on 18th Street."

"Did he tell ya who Fields was with?"

"He never did tell me that."

"How'd he know about it?"

"I don't know."

"You know who lives up on 18th?"

"I don't."

V. I. then takes Stump out cruising the neighborhood for Bo, but they don't find him. "I wanta go home," Stump says.

"That's where we're on the way to."

Says V. I., "Bo is the next guy to talk with."

* * *

Back at the office,[94] V. I. find Joefox and Mayberry yukking it up. As V. I. has been working the fringes of other cases while riding the bubble, they, too, have been working other cases. Joefox is telling about his informant who called and said his mother was sick in an-

---

87. Police slang for a case.

88. Since the stabbing victim will apparently live, there is no need to develop the case into a full scene. Also, as with the earlier shooting, it illustrates how cops only worry about what they need to worry about: this is not my case, I'll put it out of my mind.

89. Place transition.

90. Harrington now describes Stump during a lull in the action.

91. "To the air" shows Stump's nervousness. We get the sense of him needing to fill the vacuum with words.

92. To keep from overdoing the dialogue (and thus weakening the impact of more interesting exchanges), Harrington summarizes Stump's explanation.

93. V. I.'s thoughts are reconstructed from interviews.

94. Place transition.

other city and that he needed $300 for airfare to visit her. He said he hated to be a snitch, but that his mother was very sick. Then he gave Joefox the address of a shooter Joefox was after. Even before patrolmen could make the arrest, Joefox's informant walked into the office looking for his finder's fee.[95]

"They're still out tryin' ta get 'im," Joefox said.

With that, the informant picked up Joefox's phone, rang a number and asked for the shooter by name. They chatted. "See, I told ya he's still there," the man said after hanging up.

"Man, they got caller ID?" asked an incredulous Joefox.

"Ah, I don't think so."

Anyway, the cops got a shooter, the informant got his cash, and presumably, a sick mother got a visit from a devoted son.

* * *

It's unimaginable that Mayberry, Joefox and the Ghost won't draw a murder tonight, Saturday night. But in the meantime, before the intrigues of darkness set in, V. I. heads out to Northeast Washington to meet Detective J. O. Johnson.[96] They're off to look for Tony Boyce and Eldee Edwards, who are wanted for obstruction of justice for allegedly threatening a witness scheduled to testify in a grand jury investigation into a murder in which Edwards is a suspect.

The detectives cruise East Capitol near 17th Street, where Tony lives. They hope to find him on the street. It's safer to make an arrest outside.[97] Besides, if they raid the men's homes and come up empty, the men will learn the cops are on their tails and maybe take an extended vacation. V. I. interviewed Tony a couple days ago,[98] hoping to get him to give up his buddy Eldee, but Tony hung tough. He told them to bug off, that if they were gonna arrest him, then arrest him. And call his lawyer. He wasn't tellin' 'em anything.[99] V. I. let Tony go. But he doesn't like it when cops are treated rudely, and he's back today[100] with a warrant. Because it's late afternoon on Saturday, there will be no judges available to process Tony's case until Monday, which means he'll cool in jail for at least the weekend. When they finally spot Tony walking up East Capitol, V. I. pulls a U-turn and hops out.[101]

"How ya doin'?" V. I. asks in a friendly voice.

"I'm fine," says Tony, momentarily confused. He's a short, thin 31-year-old man wearing a white Champion T-shirt, blue jeans shorts and lavender Saucony running shoes. He has a dark blue wrap on his hair. His nails are long, his body lithe and taut.[102]

"I got a warrant for ya."

"For my arrest?"

---

95. The case reunites us with Joefox and Mayberry. It also allows Harrington to work in a brief, colorful scene that shows the trio has other work going on and some of the screwballs they end up dealing with.

96. Transition into a new place and a new case.

97. Harrington takes the opportunity for a brief digression into the advantages of making arrests on the street.

98. Transition into digression.

99. Rather than using dialogue, Harrington compresses what Tony said, yet by using his vocabulary it carries the ring of Tony's voice ("bug off," "he wasn't tellin' anything," "if they were gonna arrest him, then arrest him").

100. Transition back to the scene.

101. The word choices continue to carry the tone of a mystery ("pull a U-turn").

102. Harrington takes advantage of Tony's momentary confusion to describe him.

"Yep."

V. I. is downright cheerful. He gently turns Tony toward the trunk of a car, has him lay down the leather-bound Bible[103] he's carrying and clamps the cuffs on him behind his back. A man walks up and gruffly asks what's happening.

"They arrestin' me!" Tony says, emotional now, with an edge of fear in his high-pitched voice. "I don't know why."

V. I.'s entire manner changes. "Sir!" he says to the man in a deep and suddenly ominous voice, stepping toward him with the full authority of his 230 pounds.[104] "You wanta walk wherever you walkin', because you gonna be the next one that's locked up." The man opens his mouth to speak, but before the words emerge, V. I. says, "*Walk wherever you walkin'! I don't wanta hear 'bout it.*" The man does not move, and V. I. goes stone calm. "Turn and go," he says in almost a whisper. "Turn and go." And the man does.[105] Just then, a woman arrives and says she is Tony's mother. Because she is polite, because a mother has the right to worry about her son, V. I. is polite in return.

"I'll call you," he says.

After Tony is taken away in a paddy wagon, J. O. and V. I. head for the last known address for Eldee Edwards. Now that Tony has been taken, there's no hope of surprising his friend. J. O. goes to cover the back door and V. I. climbs the steep steps to the row house's front porch. To his right is a gray cat sunning itself on a stone railing. To his left, beneath a striped awning, sits an old man in a green metal chair.[106] V. I. asks if he has seen Eldee, and the old man nods.

"Where's he at? In the house?"

"No."

"When's the last time you saw 'im?"

"Two days ago, three days ago."

"Who's home now?"

"My daughter."

"How old's she?"

"Forty."

Walking into a strange house is a dangerous play, and V. I. has asked the old man these questions as reconnaissance. He believes the old man is telling the truth, although he has learned not to rely too heavily on his intuition in such matters because any cop who thinks he can't be successfully lied to is a fool. V. I. has been tricked more times than he cares to remember. "Lookin' at a jail sentence," he says, "makes people great liars." He knocks hard on the door eight times. No answer. He waits, opens the door, knocks hard nine times and hollers, "Hello!" No answer. He walks in the door. A narrow hallway leads back to a kitchen, rooms are off to the left, a stairway rises on the right. On the floor are two unopened gallons of fresh paint.[107]

---

103. The Bible and Tony's delicate physique seem out of sync with his alleged criminal behavior and his tough and foul-mouthed manner when he was pressed.

104. V. I.'s tone of voice and his movements place readers at the scene. We can see and hear him, just as we hear the fear in Tony's voice.

105. Since only V. I. is speaking here, Harrington weaves the dialogue and action together.

106. Harrington discovered the cat while examining a photograph he took at the scene. That and the description of the man in the chair place readers at the scene.

107. A tape recorder and a camera captured the details (the number and timing of the knocks, the unopened cans of paint) that enable Harrington to vividly recreate this scene. His goal here was the precise detail of a detective novel, which would not have been possible without the use of a recorder.

The place brings a flash of déjà vu,[108] because it was in just this kind of house that, as a young uniformed cop, V. I. had decided to play hero when he got a report of a burglary in progress. When nobody answered the door in the darkened house, he didn't announce that he was a policeman for fear of warning the burglar, and he walked in. When he flicked on the light, he looked up the stairway to see an old woman huddled terrified on her knees and an old man standing resolutely with a shotgun aimed down the stairwell's tunnel at the intruder—[109] Patrolman V. I. Smith.[110]

"Hello!" he hollers again, and his voice rings like a trumpet in the cavernous hallway. No answer. He waits four seconds and hollers "Hello" again. He waits six seconds and yells, "Anybody home?" He waits five more seconds and yells "Hello," louder this time. His back pressed against the wall, his gun still in the holster, he starts slowly up the stairs. As he goes, he glances calmly back and forth from the first to second floors.[111] Finally, a woman appears on the upstairs landing, and V. I. introduces himself as a policeman.

"I'm looking for Eldee."

"Eldee has not lived here in four or five years," she says, seeming miffed at the question.

"How frequently you see him?"

"Maybe three times a week."

"You got a phone number?"

"No. He lives in Southeast. That's all I can tell ya."

J. O. Johnson has joined them in the foyer now, and he isn't happy with what he's hearing. "I talked to you the other day myself, and I had a little confidence in what you was tellin' me, but now you make me think that you're not bein' truthful."

The woman starts to interrupt, "You know . . ."

J. O. cuts her off, "We're tryin' to be nice about it."

The woman snickers.

"We haven't been here at four o'clock in the mornin' and wake everybody up in the house and turn the house upside down lookin' for Eldee. I'm sure you don't want us to do that."

"I don't think that you supposed to be doin' that."

"You don't know what we *supposed* to be doin'. I'm askin' you to get in touch with him and have him call me. Tonight."

"Okay," she says, clearly angry.

In the car,[112] V. I. says, "He's probably in and outta there."

"I can tell ya one thing," J. O. says, "when I break back in here 'bout 4:00 in the morning . . ."

Says V. I., "She doesn't believe."

When Eldee doesn't call later that night,[113] J. O. will take his warrant and a crew of cops and hit the last known address of Eldee Edwards in the early morning hours. He will get everybody out of bed, secure them downstairs and search for Eldee. He will not find

---

108. Transition into a flashback.

109. The anecdote creates tension as V. I. now enters the house. Will he again run into the other end of a gun barrel?

110. The "camera" follows the shotgun's aim down the stairs to V. I. and leads us out of the digression.

111. Note how the precise detail creates tension—detail that would have been nearly impossible without the use of a tape recorder.

112. Place transition.

113. Time transition.

him. But afterward, V. I. will figure the folks in that house will be more likely to lean heavily on Eldee to turn himself in. They will have been made believers.[114]

But right now, back at Homicide North,[115] V. I. looks straight into the eyes of Tony Boyce, who is sitting with his right elbow on his knee, his chin on his fist and his left hand cuffed to his chair. V. I. says nothing. He gets a cup of coffee, checks the score of the Eagles-Jets game on the tube.[116] Then he reads Tony his rights and tells him he'll be arraigned Monday morning.

"Monday morning?" Tony asks, shocked. "Does my lawyer know?"

V. I. asks Tony if he has his lawyer's phone number.

"Not here."

V. I. shrugs.

"Why didn't you arrest me yesterday?" Tony asks, finally realizing that he'll spend at least the weekend in jail.

V. I. shrugs again.

After the paperwork is done and Mayberry takes Tony, who has abandoned his cool and loosed a blast of obscenity,[117] down to a cell, Joefox says, "He'll have a lotta company down there."

"Saturday in the big house!" says V. I. And then, out of character, he throws back his head and roars with laughter.

Incredibly, 11:00 comes and goes.[118] They are still on the bubble. . . .[119]

* * *

Over the years,[120] V. I. has had some spectacular cases. Soon after he came to Homicide in 1986, when he was barely off the natural death detail, he solved a series of killings in which a man in a dark van was abducting women and murdering them. The seven-year-old brother of one dead woman had mentioned to V. I. that his sister kept her boyfriends' phone numbers on the back of matchbooks and that they were spread all over the house. V. I. had the boy collect them in a bag, and the next day he began calling numbers, posing as a doctor tracking a case of venereal disease. After 17 calls, V. I. found a man who had seen the woman the night she died. Before the day was over, V. I. had interviewed him, discovered the name of another man the dead woman had been with that night, located his dark van and gone with his squad to arrest him.[121]

Just last winter, V. I. and Joefox were assigned by Chief Isaac Fulwood Jr. himself[122] to handle a high-publicity multiple murder on P Street NW, in which a man, woman and child were found slain in a car. They were a brother and sister and her two-year-old son.

---

114. The digression jumps ahead in time.

115. Transition back to the main time line, to a new location.

116. V. I.'s actions "show" him letting Tony stew.

117. "A blast of obscenity" captures the sense of Tony unleashing a string of obscenities more effectively than using the actual words in a series of quotes. The device also solves the problem of how to handle foul language in a family newspaper.

118. This situates us in time. V. I.'s shift is now over.

119. "Still on the bubble" sustains the suspense. When will the next murder occur?

120. Transition into a digression.

121. At this point, we are hooked, and Harrington can digress into some of V. I.'s past cases. An important part of the story is how murder has changed in recent years, how this has changed V. I. and, by extension, all of us who see it only from a distance. The background cases are necessary to establish the larger context of V. I.'s personal story through the nature of his past police experiences and the values he has held compared with what has now changed in police work and values.

122. "Himself" emphasizes the importance of this case.

When the body of the child, who had been suffocated, was taken from the backseat, it looked to V. I. as if the boy were only asleep. He felt the righteousness rise in him, felt his revulsion for the random injustice, felt as if this could happen to his own family, his own friends. There was no "victim participation." And when V. I. and Joefox went to the home of the dead to inform their parents, who were also the boy's grandparents, the family cried, sobbed as humans should, must, if they are to be human. V. I., Joefox and Mayberry, the entire squad, worked day and night for four days. As their reward, as affirmation of their own humanity, they locked up the alleged son-of-a-bitch killer, who's now awaiting trial and facing the possibility of life in prison.[123]

That's what has changed.[124] So many murders seem to count for nothing today. They don't embody the eternals of love and devotion and loss, recall the immeasurable value of one life, no matter how seemingly insignificant, announce through quick justice that living is safe and predictable and violence an aberration, thereby cauterizing the psychic wounds of the living. No, these murders trumpet the evil, insidious reverse: Life is cheap, easily forgotten, humanity is a fraud.[125] At the front lines of this diminution, V. I. Smith feels his own humanity under assault, feels the fire of indignation in his belly going cold. His deep fear is that, at the front lines, he is taking only the early hit for an entire society. Because what's happening to V. I. Smith is happening to everyone who reads the paper or watches the TV news. His numbed heart is but an early warning.[126]

"If you see the motives for why people are killing people out there now, you say to yourself, 'How can you do anything about somebody who's thinkin' like this?' It's valueless. You go into a crack house two or three months after it's got rollin' and find a family with young girls 15, 16 years old who have lost everything. They've lost their dignity. They've lost their will. They've lost themselves.

"And what have you accomplished being a policeman? You're on TV: 'We got one of the biggest cocaine raids we've had and locked up two New Yorkers.' But you've left the victimized family devastated and haven't given them any alternative. But I don't have time to worry about people anymore. And it's a goddamned shame. I've gotten to the point where I'm not really comfortable doing what I do anymore. I've gotten to the point where I sense fear. And I've never done that before. You can't predict who's out there anymore. Everything has gone to extremes."[127]

* * *

On the next 3-to-11 shift,[128] with Joefox home sick, the bubble finally bursts at 5:30 p.m.,[129] probably too early for a drug-boy killing. On the way to the scene in an apartment on 29th Street SE, just off Pennsylvania Avenue,[130] V. I. starts theorizing. *Female*

---

123. The case of the dead child provides an opportunity for further exploring the change in murder cases. Because of the nature of the crime, we can identify with V. I.'s revulsion. We share his righteousness.

124. Transition.

125. Harrington lays out a belief system most readers will identify with.

126. Harrington universalizes the story: What is happening to V. I. is happening to us all. We share his indignation.

127. Because readers are caught up in the story, Harrington can now use a disembodied quote in which V. I. is obviously addressing the narrator, and not a character in the story. Such quotes, sometimes referred to as "talking-head" quotes, can at times pull readers out of a scene. By not using attribution here, Harrington succeeds at making it come across as V. I. thinking out loud to himself. Still another way of handling this would have been to paraphrase the quotations while preserving the flavor of V. I.'s voice.

128. Transition indicates passage of time.

129. Orients us time-wise.

130. Places us geographically.

victim, inside her apartment, shot once in the head. When a person is killed inside her home, the case is usually easier, because it's a snap to discover the last person to see the victim alive. It's also daylight, which makes any investigation easier still, and most promising, this killing is in a normally quiet neighborhood, which hints at an old-fashioned, mom-and-pop murder, a murder of passion.[131] When Mayberry and V. I. walk into the door of apartment 101,[132] they find half a dozen cops, like gawkers at a car crash,[133] milling around. Mayberry orders everybody out.

The dead woman is lying in the middle of the room, halfway between the front door and the rear patio doors, one of which has been knocked off its track. It is an ugly scene, with brain and skull splattered on the wall and floor. The room is dark, but they don't touch the light switches for fear of smudging any prints. They wander the apartment with flashlights and find a framed photo of a woman. Mayberry flashes a light on the dead woman's face to be certain it is her.[134]

In a matter of minutes, the dots are made whole:[135] The woman, Crystal Johnson-Kinzer, and a male friend had walked in the door and been attacked. The male friend had escaped as shots were fired. The woman did not. Outside the patio balcony, detectives scour the yard and garbage cans for clues. They find a footprint with a distinctive circle in the tread imprinted on the hood of a gray Toyota parked beneath the balcony.[136]

When the victim's family arrives, there is—as there should be—[137] great anguish. For months, they say, Crystal had been harassed by her husband, from whom she was separated. She'd quit a job, moved across town to this apartment, gotten a court order for him to stay away. Crystal's brother is screaming at the police: "She called y'all! And now look! Y'all come when it's too late!" He is weeping and hitting his forehead with his fist. Crystal's father, wearing the gray uniform of a working man, stands perfectly still, stunned silent. Her mother, with a rose bandanna wrapped on her head, shuffles about without expression, wiping her face again and again with a tissue. The fiancée of Crystal's brother—a woman who is a look-alike for Crystal, a woman who was often mistaken for her twin—is holding a diapered baby and sobbing.[138]

---

131. V. I.'s thoughts are drawn from interviews. Here and in other places his thoughts are expropriated and given to the narrator to establish an authoritative narrative voice that the reader accepts with confidence. In a sense, the reader is tricked into forgetting that V. I. and the others are the source, thus blurring the voice of characters and narrator into one authoritative treatment.

132. Transition out of digression.

133. Simile provides a shorthand image of the officers milling about.

134. Since Harrington is not allowed to enter the crime scene, he reconstructs it from what he can observe from outside and from information (including crime lab photos) he later obtained at police headquarters. Note that it is not as detailed as the earlier scenes he observed firsthand.

135. Because of the earlier setup about connecting the dots, we know that V. I. is piecing together what happened. The "dots" are an excellent example of the use of repetition to tie together threads introduced throughout a story into an overall theme without the writer having to do so in a more obvious, direct manner.

136. The clue is detailed and specific ("a footprint with a distinctive circle," "a gray Toyota"). The detail is important; it also serves as a setup for later use in the story.

137. V. I.'s aside strikes a sympathetic chord with readers.

138. The material for this scene was gathered by Harrington as he stood outside observing the family from about 15 feet away. He vividly captures the emotion through selective use of detail: the brother screaming, weeping, hitting his fist against his forehead; the father standing stunned, still; the mother shuffling about, lost, wiping away her tears. Note how Harrington gives the description of the father an interpretive spin by saying he wore "the gray uniform of a working man" rather than simply a gray uniform. The bandanna and the tissue offer a tight, vivid picture of the mother. The description of the fiancée holding the diapered baby would itself be compelling; the fact she looked like the murder victim adds extra force. This fact was gleaned from a later conversation with the brother. Harrington's handling of this scene provides a good example of how to make the best of what you can find by changing gears when you are cut out of a situation.

Amid this horror,[139] V. I. is invigorated, renewed. *This poor woman!* She could have been *his* sister, *his* daughter! A sweet 22-year-old girl with a good job as a telephone operator. She loved smooth jazz, John Coltrane. She was studying cosmetology at night. She came from a nice, protective family. She had stopped at her apartment to change clothes and head out for a picnic at her brother's. She does not deserve this. This murder is "real"—with a good guy and a bad guy. Crystal's death must be avenged.

Says V. I., "You don't get many like this anymore."[140]

* * *

Back at Homicide North,[141] the details are gathered and collated,[142] family and friends are interviewed, the husband's undistinguished police record is pulled. At 12:17 a.m.,[143] V. I. has finished writing the arrest warrant for Kodie Cotrell Kinzer, age 21, last known address in Silver Spring.[144] It's the home of Kinzer's grandmother, and V. I. figures it's probably where he ran to, because that's just what shooters usually do.

"They wanta go home," V. I. says.

"We gotta start the hunt!" says Mayberry, excited.

When they arrive at the Georgetown home of the judge who will sign the arrest warrant, V. I. notices for the first time that it is a lovely, perfectly clear and starry night, cool, with a light breeze. The Georgetown street is quiet, except for the soothing mantra of crickets and the conversation of what look to be two drunken college boys stumbling home. As V. I. walks through the manicured garden courtyard to the judge's town house, he sees yard after yard marked with signs that read "Electronic Security by Night Owl." It's the kind of neighborhood V. I. hasn't seen much of in his job. As the judge puts down his book and reads the warrant, V. I. studies the high, elegant ceilings in the judge's home. "You wouldn't be needin' our services too often in this neighborhood," he says, and the judge laughs, although V. I. is not joking.[145]

The Montgomery County[146] police are waiting for the three-car caravan of detectives that arrives about 2:00 in the morning.[147] Taking down a suspected murderer is still an exotic event in suburban Montgomery, and the sergeant on duty is talking about whether he should call in the SWAT team and waiting for a captain to arrive to take responsibility for the decisions.

"They don't get to do this much," Mayberry whispers.

"It's comin'," V. I. answers ominously. "Believe me, it's comin'."[148]

Despite the delay, the detectives will not complain. V. I. doesn't want neighboring police telling stories about how Washington's cowboy cops came out and broke protocol

---

139. Transition into a digression.

140. V. I.'s thoughts are used to provide more information about Crystal and to bring us back to the larger story, the way murder has changed.

141. Place transition.

142. Repetition of the "dot" metaphor.

143. The time orients us. It also shows that the detectives have worked overtime. They have been working the case for 6 hours and 47 minutes.

144. "Last known address" carries the tone of a thriller. Silver Spring, Maryland, is a suburb just over the District of Columbia line.

145. The visit to the judge's Georgetown home serves as a contrast to V. I.'s world; it also shows us another step in the legal justice process. It is not critical enough to the story to warrant a full-blown scene.

146. The county where Silver Spring is located.

147. Establishes time.

148. Quote echoes Harrington's earlier point that V. I. is "taking only the early hit for an entire society."

or acted arrogant. So they wait . . . and wait . . . and wait.[149] Finally, it is decided that several more cars of Montgomery cops, all of whom don bulletproof vests,[150] will surround the apartment, and V. I. will call in on a telephone and announce the raid. This gentlemanly approach runs against every grain in Mayberry and V. I., who back home would take a couple of uniformed cops and knock on the damned door.[151] On the phone, V. I. talks to a young man who says Kodie Kinzer isn't home and that Kinzer's grandmother is too frail to be awakened with the shock of a police raid. V. I. asks the youth to come outside, which he does. He's a nice kid, clean-cut, polite.[152]

"Did you see Kodie last night?" V. I. asks gently.

"I came in like *late*, 'bout 1:00 or 2:00."

"Was he in bed?"

"Yes, sir."

"Where does he usually sleep?"

"Huh?"

"Where does he usually sleep?"

"He sleeps on the couch."

"He doesn't have a room?"

"No, he's like a pass-through."

"You know of any girlfriends he might be stayin' with?"

"I couldn't tell ya."

"How old is Kodie's grandmother?"

"She's 'bout 70."

"Is she in pretty good health?"

"Ah, not really, that's why I say I didn't wanta scare her."

"Do you expect him to come back tonight?"

"Uhm, I don't think so."

"Why not?"

"Huh?"

"Why not?"

"Ah, 'cause, ah, he was, uhm, talkin' about he was gonna go over his friend's house or somethin'."[153]

"You ever meet his wife?"

"Nah, I never met her. I heard of her name before."

V. I. looks at Mayberry. "Think we oughta wake Grandma up?" Mayberry shrugs, but he is thinking of a line from the movie *Dirty Harry:* "I gots ta know." And he knows V. I. is thinking the same thing.[154] The kid seems honest, but V. I. has learned not to always trust his intuition. They didn't come all the way out here with seven, eight police cars to be talked away at the door. V. I. is being gentle, getting the kid used to the idea.[155]

---

149. Passage of time.

150. Because of the earlier setup, we realize that V. I. and his partners *aren't* wearing bulletproof vests. Thus, the tension builds.

151. "Damned door" is the trio's voice and if not their exact words drawn from a direct quotation, their sentiments.

152. The description is kept tight so it will not slow down the action.

153. The *ahs* and *uhm* are left in the quote because they "show" us the young man is lying. Harrington would not have been able to reconstruct this without a tape recorder.

154. Mayberry's thoughts are drawn from an interview.

155. The aside explains what V. I. is up to.

"Captain, whataya think?" V. I. asks, bringing the Montgomery brass into a decision that he has already made. The captain nods, and V. I. turns back to the youth. "Think it would be a problem if we talk to Kodie's grandmother?"

The young man looks suddenly shaky. "See, all these people . . ."[156]

V. I. cuts him off. "There ain't gonna be all these people."

"I don't, I don't know . . ."

V. I. cuts him off again, this time in a voice that has once again gone stone calm: "Look, man, this is somethin' we gotta do. Prolongin' the situation isn't gonna do any good. Let's go."

Inside, buried beneath a pile of blankets, they find Kodie Kinzer. Minutes later, he's led away, his head tilted downward mournfully. He's wearing yellow shorts, a white T-shirt, white socks and no shoes. When V. I. leaves the apartment, he's carrying a pair of black Adidas with three white stripes adorning the uppers and a distinctive circle on the sole.[157] It will be up to Forensics to evaluate whether they could have left that footprint on the car beneath Crystal Johnson-Kinzer's balcony. But V. I. says, "I remember that tread."

* * *

It is nearly dawn by the time[158] V. I. and Mayberry finish interviewing Kodie Kinzer, who denies that he killed Crystal. When the detectives head back to Homicide North, leaving Kinzer in a Montgomery cell awaiting extradition to Washington, the city is just waking up. The sky is brightening in the east, and people are standing at bus stops in twos and threes. A laundry truck is picking up, a Coke truck is dropping off, and the lights of sleeping cars are awakening along the roads. Outside police headquarters, a rat scurries along the sidewalk, stops, gazes about at the emerging daylight and dives into the bushes for cover.

Life as it should be.[159]

In the next few weeks,[160] V. I. will keep tugging at threads in his murder case in far Northeast—the one that began when a suspected drug dealer shot the wrong woman. Before that chain of misery and foolishness concludes, five people will end up shot. He'll keep working the murder of Willis Fields, never finding Bo, the man who told Stump that Fields was attacked on 18th Street. But no matter. Bo was simply repeating street rumor passed on by lots of other people. V. I. will discover that somebody who lives on 18th Street owed Fields money. But it will be a long time, if ever, before that murder is avenged. In the meantime, Tony Boyce will stay in jail for weeks and be indicted for obstruction of justice. Eldee Edwards will be arrested and indicted for murder. In a few days, Kodie Kinzer will arrive at the D.C. jail, where he will await trial after his indictment

---

156. The ellipsis supports Harrington's observation that the young man is shaky.

157. The scene from within the house is summed up in one brief sentence because Harrington did not have access to the inside. Once Kinzer moves outside within Harrington's sight, the description again becomes detailed. Note how he saves the detail of the circle on the shoe sole until the end of the description—and the sentence—for greater impact. Because of the earlier clue, readers automatically make the connection.

158. Time transition.

159. The scene of a new day conjures up the notion of good triumphing over evil. V. I.'s side has won this round. Or, as Harrington writes, "Life as it should be," which is meant to take the point of the story back to the general public, the readers.

160. Time transition jumps ahead.

for murder. Soon, Mayberry, Joefox and the Ghost will collect half a dozen new homicides, all of which will look like drug-boy killings.[161]

But that's all in the future.[162] This morning, just back from the hunt, V. I. and Mayberry still have their damned paperwork to do. And in Room 5058, the coffee is cold.[163] But that's okay. It has been a good night—an old-fashioned night, a night that affirmed the world's predictability, justice and humanity, that healed the psychic wounds of the living, that again brought feeling to the numbed heart of Detective Victor "V. I." Smith. This horrific night has made him feel better. It has made him feel human again.[164]

WALT HARRINGTON ON READING

"It wasn't classic literary journalism that first got my attention in the mid-1970s but humanized public affairs books such as *The Final Days* by Woodward and Bernstein; *The Power Broker* by Robert Caro; and *The Best and the Brightest* by David Halberstam. *Let Us Now Praise Famous Men* by James Agee also got my attention early, as did the usual suspects—McPhee, Talese, Wolfe, Capote, E. B. White's essays, A. J. Liebling's *The Sweet Science*, Hersey's *Hiroshima*. Like so many other journalists of my age, I was deeply influenced by Wolfe's 1974 collection *The New Journalism*, the articles as well as the essays. I can't give you chapter and verse, but I began reading *Esquire* in the early 1970s before I had any idea I would be a journalist or what kind of journalist I would be, and I always loved the treatments, although I don't think I understood why. Later, I found travel and nature literature to be awfully helpful in learning to use detail in service to ideas—Peter Matthiessen's *The Snow Leopard;* Edward Abbey's *Desert Solitaire;* Wendell Berry's nature essays; Aldo Leopold's *A Sand County Almanac.*"

---

161. Harrington jumps ahead to tie together the story and to create a sense of resolution, not just for the Johnson-Kinzer case but for the story.

162. Transition from the flash-forward back to the present time line.

163. "5058" and the cold coffee take us back to where the story began, at Homicide North, bringing us full circle.

164. The story ends with a sense of resolution. V. I. has avenged the death of an innocent young woman. For the time being, at least, "life is as it should be."

Tracy Kidder

Choosing a point of view, says Tracy Kidder, is a matter of finding the best place to stand as the storyteller. That choice affects everything else, including voice, he says, and it should not be determined by theory, but by immersion in the material itself. In his own writing, he has made the decision sometimes by instinct, sometimes by experimenting. When he began Among Schoolchildren, *he assumed he would approach it from the viewpoints of a number of characters. But as soon as he started writing, he ran into problems.*

"Every page I wrote felt lifeless," he said in a TriQuarterly Review essay. "Finally, I hit on a restricted third-person narration. The approach seemed to work. The world of that classroom seemed to come alive when the view of it was restricted mainly to observations of the teacher and to accounts of what the teacher saw and heard and smelled and felt. This choice narrowed my options. I ended up writing something less comprehensive than I'd planned. The book became essentially an account of a year in the emotional life of a schoolteacher."

As the excerpt "September" demonstrates, the result is a book that transports readers into teacher Chris Zajac's classroom and causes us to feel like we, not Kidder, are looking over her shoulder. Indeed, there are times we feel we are viewing the students and the world through Zajac's eyes. To achieve so intimate a point of view, Kidder spent an entire school year in Zajac's fifth grade class, missing only two days—one to play hooky, the other because he was sick. He was given a desk at the front of the classroom next to the teacher, where his vantage point was fairly close to hers. The two talked constantly about what was going through her mind when a particular incident occurred. He also talked to the children, visiting some of their homes, as he did Zajac's.

Kidder felt a keen responsibility in writing about children, even more than he does for his adult subjects, and to protect them he changed all their names and left unmentioned the year in which the action took place. Even now, he is hesitant to talk about them for fear of divulging more than he should.

While the narrow point of view resulted in a book slightly less comprehensive than he had planned, he never set out to write a tract about education. With this and all his books, he has preferred to write about the particular rather than the general. As he told Publishers Weekly: *"I hoped that by looking at one class closely, I could say a lot about education generally, and that I wouldn't have to say it, it would all be there."*

According to Kidder, he tries to write the kind of books he likes to read, and what he likes is storytelling as gracefully accomplished as good fiction. Using that approach he has managed to turn the stories of building a house, designing a computer, and living in a nursing home into best-selling books. He has been rewarded with the Pulitzer Prize in general nonfiction and the National Book Award for The Soul of the Machine, *and National Book Critics Circle nominations for* House *and* Among Schoolchildren, *which also won the Robert F. Kennedy Book Award. His two most recent books are* Old Friends, *set in an old-age home, and* Home Town, *a portrait of Northampton, Massachusetts,* centered on a local police officer. He is also the author of The Road to Yuba City *about a murder case in California.*

In addition to his books, Kidder is a contributing editor for Atlantic Monthly *and has written for other periodicals, including the* New Yorker, *the* New York Times Book Review, Granta, *and* TriQuarterly Review. *His publications include three fictional short stories, which appeared in* Atlantic. *He was the 1994 editor for* The Best American Essays.

September

MRS. ZAJAC WASN'T BORN YESTERDAY. *She knows you didn't do your best work on this paper, Clarence. Don't you remember Mrs. Zajac saying that if you didn't do your best, she'd make you do it over? As for you, Claude, God forbid that you should ever need brain surgery. But Mrs. Zajac hopes that if you do, the doctor won't open up your head and walk off saying he's almost done, as you just said when Mrs. Zajac asked you for your penmanship, which, by the way, looks like who did it and ran. Felipe, the reason you have hiccups is, your mouth is always open and the wind rushes in. You're in fifth grade now. So, Felipe, put a lock on it. Zip it up. Then go get a drink of water. Mrs. Zajac means business, Robert. The sooner you realize she never said everybody in the room has to do the work except for Robert, the sooner you'll get along with her. And . . . Clarence. Mrs. Zajac knows you didn't try. You don't just hand in junk to Mrs. Zajac. She's been teaching an awful lot of years. She didn't fall off the turnip cart yesterday. She told you she was an old-lady teacher.*[1]

* * *

She was thirty-four. She wore a white skirt and yellow sweater and a thin gold necklace, which she held in her fingers, as if holding her own reins,[2] while waiting for children to answer. Her hair was black with a hint of Irish[3] red. It was cut short to the tops of her ears, and swept back like a pair of folded wings.[4] She had a delicately cleft chin, and she was short—the children's chairs would have fit her.[5] Although her voice sounded conversational, it had projection. She had never acted. She had found this voice in classrooms.

Mrs. Zajac seemed to have a frightening amount of energy. She strode across the room, her arms swinging high and her hands in small fists. Taking her stand in front of the green chalkboard,[6] discussing the rules with her new class, she repeated sentences, and her lips held the shapes of certain words, such as "homework,"[7] after she had said them. Her hands kept very busy. They sliced the air and made karate chops to mark off boundaries. They extended straight out like a traffic cop's, halting illegal maneuvers yet to be perpetrated. When they rested momentarily on her hips, her hands looked as if they

From *Among Schoolchildren* by Tracy Kidder. Copyright © 1989 by John Tracy Kidder. Reprinted by permission of Houghton Mifflin Company. All rights reserved.

1. Kidder begins, as the school year does, with a lecture by teacher Chris Zajac. The colorful first-day-of-school monologue quickly draws us into the story and gives us a feel for her personality. It also establishes the point of view: We will see the story through her eyes. The author's point of view was pretty close to hers; he sat out the year in a desk right next to the teacher's. The monologue is actually a compilation of things Zajac said during the early days of the school year.
2. The comparison helps us picture her gesture.
3. The adjective provides not just description, but information about Zajac's background.
4. The simile again lets us get a clearer picture of what Zajac looks like.
5. The use of the children's chairs is a fitting choice to give us an idea of Zajac's size.
6. Note the specific detail. It is not just a chalkboard, but a *green* chalkboard. The specificity brings us inside that particular classroom.
7. Zajac's lips obviously held the shape of other words. Kidder uses "homework" to do double duty. It both describes her manner of speaking and conveys information about her. Even before we come to the final quote in the paragraph, we know Mrs. Zajac is a firm believer in homework.

were in holsters.[8] She told the children, "One thing Mrs. Zajac expects from each of you is that you do *your* best." She said, "Mrs. Zajac gives homework. I'm sure you've all heard. The only meanie gives homework." *Mrs. Zajac.* It was in part a role.[9] She worked her way into it every September.

At home on late summer days like these,[10] Chris Zajac wore shorts or blue jeans. Although there was no dress code for teachers here at Kelly School, she always went to work in skirts or dresses. She dressed as if she were applying for a job, and hoped in the back of her mind[11] that someday, heading for job interviews, her students would remember her example. Outside school, she wept easily over small and large catastrophes and at sentimental movies, but she never cried in front of students,[12] except once a few years ago when the news came over the intercom that the Space Shuttle had exploded and Christa McAuliffe[13] had died—and then she saw in her students' faces that the sight of Mrs. Zajac crying had frightened them, and she made herself stop and then explained.

At home, Chris laughed at the antics of her infant daughter and egged the child on. She and her first-grade son would sneak up to the radio when her husband wasn't looking and change the station from classical to rock-and-roll music. "You're regressing, Chris," her husband would say.[14] But especially on the first few days of school, she didn't let her students get away with much. She was not amused when, for instance, on the first day, two of the boys started dueling with their rulers. On nights before the school year started, Chris used to have bad dreams:[15] her principal would come to observe her, and her students would choose that moment to climb up on their desks and give her the finger, or they would simply wander out the door. But a child in her classroom would never know that Mrs. Zajac had the slightest doubt that students would obey her.

The first day,[16] after going over all the school rules, Chris spoke to them about effort.[17] "If you put your name on a paper, you should be proud of it," she said. "You should

8. Kidder's description of Zajac's arms is delightful to read and further engages us in the story and the scene. It also shows us Zajac in action. The comparisons to karate chops and traffic cops and holsters help us picture precisely how she used her arms. The entire passage demonstrates Kidder's close observation of telling mannerisms.

9. Note the continued comparison to acting. She had never acted, but teaching was a role she had perfected. The classroom was her stage.

10. Transition into a brief digression on Zajac.

11. Here we see Kidder moving us even more into Zajac's point of view, giving us her thoughts—thoughts he obtained throughout the year by asking her what was going through her mind when a particular incident occurred. Sometimes he asked in the course of their many interviews before and after school; sometimes during whispered conversations in the classroom while the children were engaged in something. "You know, sort of, Do you believe what he just said?" Kidder explains. "Or she'd say, I'm trying to do such and such. That sort of thing."

12. Kidder continues to round out his characterization of Zajac. First he describes her physical appearance, then her voice and the way she moves. Now he delves into the inner Zajac: her thoughts and emotions. Some of these insights came through interviews, some from firsthand observation.

13. Christa McAuliffe was a New Hampshire high school teacher chosen to accompany the crew of astronauts on the 1986 mission of the Challenger Space Shuttle, which exploded shortly after liftoff.

14. This passage does double duty. It continues to round out Zajac's personality, and it tells us about her family.

15. Kidder continues to draw from every avenue—even Zajac's dreams—to create a three-dimensional character, but unlike the fictional character, he relies on facts and observations for his material.

16. Transition out of the digression, back to the classroom and the first day of school.

17. Before using a quote or a scene, a writer must prepare the reader by setting the stage with a paraphrase, a description, or a summation. Here Kidder does a setup for the scene that follows.

think, This is the best I can do and I'm proud of it and I want to hand this in." Then she asked, "If it isn't your best, what's Mrs. Zajac going to do!"

Many voices, most of them female, answered softly in unison, "Make us do it over."

"*Make you do it over,*" Chris repeated. It sounded like a chant.[18]

"Does anyone know anything about Lisette?" she asked when no one answered to that name.

Felipe—small, with glossy black hair—[19]threw up his hand.

"Felipe?"

"She isn't here!" said Felipe. He wasn't being fresh. On those first few days of school, whenever Mrs. Zajac put the sound of a question in her voice, and sometimes before she got the question out, Felipe's hand shot up.

In contrast, there was the very chubby girl who sat nearly motionless at her desk, covering the lower half of her face with her hands.[20] As usual, most of their voices sounded timid the first day, and came out of hiding gradually. There were twenty children. About half were Puerto Rican. Almost two-thirds of the twenty needed the forms to obtain free lunches. There was a lot of long and curly hair. Some boys wore little rattails. The eyes the children lifted up to her as she went over the rules—a few eyes were blue and many more were brown—looked so solemn and so wide that Chris felt like dropping all pretense and laughing. Their faces ranged from dark brown to gold, to pink, to pasty white, the color that Chris associated with sunless tenements and too much TV. The boys wore polo shirts and T-shirts and new white sneakers with the ends of the laces untied and tucked behind the tongues. Some girls wore lacy ribbons in their hair, and some wore pants and others skirts, a rough but not infallible indication of religion—the daughters of Jehovah's Witnesses and Pentecostals do not wear pants.[21] There was a lot of prettiness in the room, and all of the children looked cute to Chris.

So did the student teacher, Miss Hunt,[22] a very young woman in a dress with a bow at the throat who sat at a table in the back of the room. Miss Hunt had a sweet smile, which she turned on the children, hunching her shoulders when they looked at her. At times the first days, while watching Chris in action, Miss Hunt seemed to gulp. Sometimes she looked as frightened as the children. For Chris, looking at Miss Hunt was like looking at herself fourteen years ago.[23]

The smell of construction paper, slightly sweet and forest-like, mingled with the fading, acrid smell of roach and rodent spray. The squawk box on the wall above the closets, beside the clock with its jerky minute hand, erupted almost constantly, adult voices pag-

---

18. The comparison lets us hear *how* she says this.

19. Kidder uses dashes to insert a brief description, which serves to begin making Felix more than just a name. He will flesh out the children just as he has Zajac.

20. Kidder's close attention to mannerisms continues to establish Zajac's point of view. It's as if we are looking over her shoulder, out at the class. A few sentences down we will see still another example of the writer telling the story through her eyes when he writes "the eyes of the children lifted up to her. . . ."

21. Up to now, Kidder has focused on individuals. Here, he gives us an overall sense of the class and its socioeconomic makeup. In doing so, he is no less detailed. The boys wear new white sneakers with the untied laces tucked behind the tongues; the girls' ribbons are lacy; some are children of Jehovah's Witnesses and Pentecostals.

22. Transition from the students to Miss Hunt, the student teacher.

23. Kidder gives us a tight description of Miss Hunt and her mannerisms, focusing on the ones that would have stood out at first sight: the bow at the neckline of her dress, the smile, the hunched shoulders, the gulp, the frightened look. The mannerisms are ones we'll see in action throughout the excerpt. Note how he shows us these traits through Chris Zajac's eyes and point of view.

ing adults by their surnames and reminding staff of deadlines for the census forms, attendance calendars, and United Way contributions.[24] Other teachers poked their heads inside the door to say hello to Chris or to ask advice about how to fill out forms or to confer with her on schedules for math and reading. In between interruptions, amid the usual commotion of the first day, Chris taught short lessons, assigned the children seat work, and attended to paperwork at her large gray metal desk over by the window.[25]

For moments then, the room was still.[26] From the bilingual class next door to the south came the baritone of the teacher Victor Guevara, singing to his students in Spanish. Through the small casement windows behind Chris came sounds of the city—Holyoke, Massachusetts—trailer truck brakes releasing giant sighs now and then, occasional screeches of freight trains, and, always in the background, the mechanical hum of ventilators from the school and from Dinn Bros. Trophies and Autron, from Leduc Corp. Metal Fabricators and Laminated Papers. It was so quiet inside the room during those moments that little sounds were loud: the rustle of a book's pages being turned and the tiny clanks of metal-legged chairs being shifted slightly.[27] Bending over forms and the children's records, Chris watched the class from the corner of her eye.[28] The first day she kept an especially close eye on the boy called Clarence.[29]

Clarence was a small, lithe, brown-skinned boy with large eyes and deep dimples. Chris watched his journeys to the pencil sharpener. They were frequent. Clarence took the longest possible route around the room, walking heel-to-toe and brushing the back of one leg with the shin of the other at every step—a cheerful little dance across the blue carpet, around the perimeter of desks, and along the back wall, passing under the American flag, which didn't quite brush his head. Reaching the sharpener, Clarence would turn his pencil into a stunt plane, which did several loop-the-loops before plunging in the hole.[30]

The first morning,[31] Chris didn't catch one of the intercom announcements. She asked aloud if anyone had heard the message. Clarence, who seemed to stutter at the start of sentences when he was in a hurry to speak,[32] piped up right away, "He he say to put the extra desks in the hall." Clarence noticed things. He paid close attention to the inter-

---

24. Now that we have been introduced to Zajac, Hunt, and the students, Kidder stops to draw the setting into clearer focus. In describing the classroom, notice how he appeals to all our senses. We *smell* the construction paper and pesticide; we *hear* the squawk box and the disembodied announcements (and note the concreteness of these—census forms, attendance calendars, United Fund contributions); we *see* the clock's jerky minute hand. Through the use of the senses, he places us in the classroom and into the scene.

25. Now he sets the classroom in motion. Rather than giving us a detailed rendering here, he uses summary to convey the essence of how the time was spent—in other words, a general picture.

26. Transition moves us from the general back to the actual scene.

27. Kidder again uses sound to place us in the classroom, at that particular moment. In doing so, he is also providing physical description (the room has casement windows, the metal-legged chairs, the children poring over books) and information about the area (it is located in an industrial neighborhood). By using the scene to weave in this description and information, Kidder keeps the action and the story moving forward, without interruption.

28. Kidder again places us squarely in Zajac's point of view.

29. Transition to Clarence.

30. Now we get a description of Clarence, who will become one of the central figures. Again, note Kidder's close, careful observation and how he shows Clarence in action so that the story continues to move forward, carrying readers with it. The comparison of the stunt plane helps us see and identify with the moment. Which of us hasn't seen this same, little maneuver? Note how Kidder again uses Clarence's actions to continue describing the room.

31. Transition from the general to a specific moment.

32. Kidder describes how Clarence speaks to enable us to hear his voice now and throughout the story. Thus when Clarence repeats "he," there is no need to interrupt the quote with an explanation.

com. His eyes darted to the door the moment a visitor appeared.[33] But he paid almost no attention to her lessons and his work. It seemed as if every time that she glanced at Clarence he wasn't working.[34]

"Take a look at Clarence," Chris whispered to Miss Hunt. She had called Miss Hunt up to her desk for a chat. "Is he doing anything?"

The other children were working. Clarence was just then glancing over his shoulder, checking on the clock. Miss Hunt hunched her shoulders and laughed without making a sound.[35] "He has such huge eyes!" she said.

"And they're looking right through me," said Chris, who lifted her voice and called,[36] "Clarence, the pencil's moving, right?" Then Chris smiled at Miss Hunt, and said in a half whisper, "I can see that Clarence and I will have a little chat out in the hall, one of these days."

Miss Hunt smiled, gulped, and nodded, all at once.[37]

* * *

Chris had received the children's "cumulative" records,[38] which were stuffed inside salmon-colored folders known as "cumes."[39] For now she checked only addresses and phone numbers, and resisted looking into histories. It was usually better at first to let her own opinions form.[40] But she couldn't help noticing the thickness of some cumes. "The thicker the cume, the more trouble," she told Miss Hunt. "If it looks like *War and Peace* . . ." Clarence's cume was about as thick as the Boston phone book.[41] And Chris couldn't help having heard what some colleagues had insisted on telling her about Clarence. One teacher whom Chris trusted had described him as probably the most difficult child in all of last year's fourth-grade classes. Chris wished she hadn't heard that, nor the rumors about Clarence. She'd heard confident but unsubstantiated assertions that he was a beaten child. These days many people applied the word "abused" to any apparently troubled student. She had no good reason to believe the rumors, but she couldn't help thinking, "What if they're true?" She wished she hadn't heard anything about Clarence's past at this early moment. She found it hard enough after thirteen years to believe that all fifth graders' futures lay before them out of sight, and not in plain view behind.[42]

She'd try to ignore what she had heard and deal with problems as they came. Clarence's were surfacing quickly.[43] He came to school the second morning without having done his homework. He had not done any work at all so far, except for one math as-

---

33. Kidder continues to tell us about Clarence. The brevity of the sentences conveys a sense of Zajac reaching conclusions about him, and thus lets us see him through her eyes.

34. This longer, last sentence in the paragraph confirms that we have been watching Clarence through Zajac's eyes. It also moves us from the more general description of his mannerisms back to the specific scene.

35. Because of the earlier setups, we know where the clock is. We also understand why Miss Hunt hunches her shoulders.

36. Kidder uses the attribution to insert a description of Zajac's movements.

37. Because of the earlier setup of Miss Hunt's mannerisms, we know she is uneasy.

38. Transition into a digression on Clarence.

39. Again note the concrete detail (salmon-colored folders). Explaining the nickname "cumes" will allow Kidder to use the short name to refer to them later.

40. Zajac's thoughts, gleaned from interviews.

41. Even if we have never been to Boston, the comparison gives us a vivid picture of how thick Clarence's cumes are.

42. Zajac's thoughts continue to allow us to see the story from her point of view.

43. The sentence shows the passage of time and acts as a transition into the second day.

signment, and for that he'd just written down some numbers at random. She'd try to nip this in the bud.[44] "No work, no recess," she told Clarence late the second morning. He had quit even pretending to work about half an hour before.[45]

Just a little later, she saw Clarence heading for the pencil sharpener again. He paused near Felipe's desk. Clarence glanced back at her. She could see that he thought she wasn't looking.

Clarence set his jaw. He made a quick, sharp kick at Felipe's leg under the desk. Then he stalked, glancing backward at Chris, to the pencil sharpener. Felipe didn't complain.[46]

Maybe Felipe had provoked the kick. Or maybe this was Clarence's way of getting even with her for threatening to keep him in from recess. It wasn't a pleasant thought. She let the incident pass. She'd have to watch Clarence carefully, though.[47]

The afternoon of that second day of class,[48] Chris warned Clarence several times that she would keep him after school if he didn't get to work. Detention seemed like a masochistic exercise. Sometimes it worked. It was a tool she'd found most useful at the beginning of a year and after vacations. In her experience, most children responded well to clearly prescribed rules and consequences, and she really didn't have many other tangible weapons. The idea was to get most of the unpleasantness, the scoldings and detentions, out of the way early. And, of course, if she threatened to keep Clarence after school, she had to keep her word. Maybe he would do some work, and she could have a quiet talk with him. She didn't plan to keep him long.[49]

The other children went home, and so did Miss Hunt.[50] Chris sat at her desk, a warm late-summer breeze coming through the little casement window behind her. She worked on her plans for next week, and from under cover of her bowed head, she watched Clarence.[51] The children's chairs, the plastic backs and seats of which came in primary colors, like a bag full of party balloons, were placed upside down on the tops of their desks. Clarence sat alone at his desk, surrounded by upended chairs. He had his arms folded on his chest and was glaring at her.[52] The picture of defiance. He would show her. She felt like laughing for a moment. His stubbornness was impressive.[53] Nearly an hour passed, and the boy did no work at all.[54]

Chris sighed, got up, and walked over to Clarence.

He turned his face away as she approached.

Chris sat in a child's chair and, resting her chin on her hand, leaned her face close to Clarence's.

He turned his farther away.

"What's the problem?"

---

44. Sets up quote.

45. Rather than play out everything that happens in detail, Kidder focuses on the more interesting, telling moments. By doing so, these moments are given added weight and thus stand out.

46. Now Kidder slows down the time, allowing us to see this little scene unfold through Zajac's eyes.

47. More interior Zajac thoughts, gathered through interviews.

48. Time transition.

49. Rather than Kidder himself telling us how Zajac operates, he filters it through her point of view. As a result, we continue to feel as if we are in that room, looking over her shoulder.

50. Passage of time and transition into the scene.

51. We see the scene through Zajac's eyes.

52. Kidder again uses the action to include more description of the room, even the breeze coming through the window. The party balloons provide a colorful comparison; they are also appropriate to a story about elementary school children.

53. Short sentences again mimic Zajac's thought patterns.

54. Kidder compresses time.

He didn't answer. His eyelashes began to flutter.[55]

"Do you understand the work in fifth grade!"

He didn't answer.

"I hear you're a very smart boy. Don't you want to have a good year? Don't you want to take your work home and tell your mom, 'Look what I did'?"[56]

The fluorescent lights in the ceiling were pale and bright. One was flickering. Tears came rolling out of Clarence's eyes. They streaked his brown cheeks.

Chris gazed at him, and in a while said, "Okay, I'll make a deal with you. You go home and do your work, and come in tomorrow with all your work done, and I'll pretend these two days never happened. We'll have a new Clarence tomorrow. Okay?"

Clarence still had not looked at her or answered.

"A new Clarence," Chris said. "Promise?"

Clarence made the suggestion of a nod,[57] a slight concession to her, she figured, now that it was clear she would let him leave.

Her face was very close to his. Her eyes almost touched his tear-stained cheeks. She gazed. She knew she wasn't going to see a new Clarence tomorrow. It would be naive to think a boy with a cume[58] that thick was going to change overnight. But she'd heard the words in her mind anyway. She had to keep alive the little voice that says, Well, you never know. What was the alternative? To decide an eleven-year-old was going to go on failing, and there was nothing anyone could do about it, so why try? Besides, this was just the start of a campaign. She was trying to tell him, "You don't have to have another bad year. Your life in school can begin to change." If she could talk him into believing that, maybe by June there *would* be a new Clarence.[59]

"We always keep our promises?" Chris said.

He seemed to make a little nod.

"I bet everyone will be surprised. We'll have a new Clarence," Chris said, and then she let him go.[60]

2

When Chris had first walked into her room—Room 205—back in late August, it felt like an attic.[61] The chalkboards and bulletin boards were covered up with newspaper, and the bright colors of the plastic chairs seemed calculated to force cheerfulness upon her. On the side of one of the empty children's desks there was a faded sticker that read, OFFICIAL PACE CAR.[62] A child from some other year must have put it there; he'd moved on, but she'd come back to the same place. There was always something a little mournful about com-

---

55. The fluttering eyelashes bring us, like Zajac, close to Clarence.

56. Because Clarence is not answering, there is no need for attribution.

57. The specificity of it being a slight nod conveys his reluctance to concur.

58. Because of the earlier setup, there is no need to explain what "cume" means in the midst of the scene.

59. Zajac's thoughts, picked up from interviews.

60. The section ends on a poignant note that lingers with us as we move on to the next section. It also creates tension. Will we see a new Clarence tomorrow? Will his educational future change? We are compelled to keep reading.

61. Transition into a digression, or flashback, about Zajac's preparation of her classroom. The comparison of the deserted room to an attic quickly creates a picture in our minds. Note how much more effective it is for Kidder to work this information in here rather than beginning his chronology in August. By opening with the more interesting and dramatic scenes of the first and second day, he has drawn us into the story and can now weave in background such as this.

62. The detail of the old sticker reminds us of the classroom's past life.

ing back to an empty classroom at the end of summer, a childhood feeling, like being put to bed when it is light outside.[63]

She spent her summer days with children, her own and those of friends. While her daughter splashed around in the wading pool and her son and his six-year-old buddies climbed the wooden fort her husband had built in their back yard, she sat at the picnic table and there was time to read—this summer, a few popular novels and then, as August wore on, a book called *The Art of Teaching Writing*, which she read with a marking pencil in hand, underlining the tips that seemed most useful. There was time for adult conversation, around the swimming pool at her best friend's house, while their children swam. In August she left Holyoke and spent a couple of weeks near the ocean with her husband and children, on Cape Cod. She liked the pace of summer, and of all the parts of summer she liked the mornings best, the unhurried, slowly unfolding mornings, which once again this year went by much too fast.[64]

Chris looked around her empty classroom. It was fairly small as classrooms go, about twenty-five by thirty-six feet. The room repossessed her. She said to herself, "I can't believe the summer's over. I feel like I never left this place." And then she got to work.[65]

She put up her bulletin board displays, scouted up pencils and many kinds of paper—crayons hadn't yet arrived; she'd borrow some of her son's—made a red paper apple for her door, and moved the desks around into the layout she had settled on in her first years of teaching. She didn't use the truly ancient arrangement, with the teacher's desk up front and the children's in even rows before it. Her desk was already where she wanted it, in a corner by the window. She had to be on her feet and moving in order to teach. Over there in the corner, her desk wouldn't get in her way. And she could retire to it in between lessons, at a little distance from the children, and still see down the hallway between her door and the boys' room—a strategic piece of real estate—[66] and also keep an eye on all the children at their desks. She pushed most of the children's small, beige-topped desks side by side, in a continuous perimeter describing three-quarters of a square, open at the front. She put four desks in the middle of the square, so that each of those four had space between it and any other desk. These were Chris's "middle-person desks," where it was especially hard to hide, although even the back row of the perimeter was more exposed than back rows usually are.[67]

When the room was arranged to her liking, she went home to the last days of summer.

* * *

Chris let the children choose their own desks the first day.[68] On the morning of the second, she announced, "I'm going to make a few changes in seats right now. Some of you are too short for where you are. There's nothing wrong with being short. Mrs. Zajac's

---

63. We are inside Zajac's head. The simile is one we can all identify with. It helps us grasp her feelings.

64. Kidder compresses Zajac's summer to give us the essence of how she spent her time away from her students.

65. We are again looking at the classroom through Zajac. In the course of doing so, we also see what the room looks like, its size.

66. Kidder uses dashes to insert an explanation of the role of the boys' room.

67. Kidder uses Zajac's arrangement of the room to describe it. He also puts us inside her head by giving us her logic.

68. The digression, or flashback, continues with Kidder quickly taking us through the first and second days and eventually working us back to the point where the digression began, the beginning of the third day.

short." She directed traffic[69] as, without audible protests but with a lot of clanging of metal,[70] the children pushed their chairs like vendor's carts across the blue carpet. Shortness had little to do with where she placed them, but it was too soon to tell them most of the real reasons.

She knew all of their names by that second morning. She wasn't any better than most people at remembering names, but in a classroom that knack is a necessity and naturally acquired. Confronting a new class isn't like meeting strangers at a party. Inside her room, Chris didn't have to think as much about how she looked to the children as how they looked to her.[71]

Here they were, and they were, as always, compelling. Four years ago these children were still learning to dress themselves. Four years from now these cute little ten- and eleven-year-olds would be able—but not disposed, she hoped—to produce children of their own. Some of their voices hadn't changed yet, but they were only pausing here on their way to adolescence.[72]

One boy, Julio, had the beginnings of a mustache. Julio was repeating fifth grade. He wrote in one of his first essays:

Yesterday my mother and my father unchul cusint me we all went to springfield to see the brudishduldog and rode piper ricky stemdout ladey is fight for the lult

She put Julio in one of the middle-person desks.[73] ("He's sort of a special project, and I also know he's got to be pushed. He's very quiet. He doesn't bother anyone. That was the problem last year, I'm told. He didn't bother anyone. He just didn't *do* anything.")[74]

Kimberly, whom Chris had noticed squinting yesterday and who confessed she'd lost her glasses, got a seat on a wing of the perimeter, up near the board.

Chris moved Claude to the wing farthest from her desk. ("Because he seems to be the type who would be up at my desk every minute, and if he's going to drive me crazy, he's going to do it over there.") Claude was a pale boy with elfin ears. He had spent most of the first day picking at his lip and making it bleed.[75] When Chris took the globe out of her closet and carried it up to the front table, Claude piped up, "My uncle got a big globe like that. It cost about, let's see, a hundred and ninety-two dollars. It stood up this high."

"Oh, my," said Chris. She smiled.[76]

She had caught Courtney not paying attention several times yesterday. Courtney was small and doll-like, with a mobile, rubbery face—she had a way, when worried, of

---

69. Because of Kidder's earlier description of Zajac's arms, we see the traffic cop at work.
70. We again hear, as well as see, the movement in the room.
71. The comparison is one we can all identify with. We can appreciate the difference.
72. In one brief paragraph, Kidder quickly captures the essence of the children as a group. What the children were four years ago and what they will be by the end of the next four is a startling thought that had probably not crossed our minds. While Zajac hopes they won't be engaging in sex, there is a sinking realization they probably will be. Some of the girls will be mothers.
73. Now as Zajac assigns the children to their desks, Kidder gives us a description and some background on each. First comes Julio.
74. More of Zajac's logic again enables us to share this moment through her. Kidder inserts her thoughts in parentheses so as not to stop the action.
75. This detail offers more evidence of Kidder's close observation. It puts us into the scene that second day.
76. This little exchange keeps the action moving and again draws us into the scene.

making her mouth an O and moving it over to one side.[77] Courtney wore what looked like long underwear, clinging to her skinny frame. ("I look at Courtney and I think, 'I hope she stays in school.' If school doesn't become important for her, and she doesn't do better at it, she'll have a boyfriend at fourteen and a baby at sixteen. But, you never know.")[78] Courtney got a middle-person spot.

Chris put Robert in another of the hot seats. Robert was a burly child with a cume almost as thick as Clarence's.[79]

She sent handsome, enthusiastic Felipe to a spot between Margaret and Alice. Felipe seemed to be very talkative and excitable. He was probably used to being the center of attention. Chris guessed, "He's easily influenced by the people around him. If he sits between twits, he'll be a twit." Placed between two obviously well-mannered children, Felipe might be an asset. ("People think that teachers want a room full of girls with their hands folded in their laps. I don't! You like a lively room.")

Alice and Margaret, both from what was called the upper-class Highlands, were obviously friends. But to Chris, it seemed as though Margaret hovered near Alice, aware of Alice when Alice didn't seem to be aware of Margaret. Margaret would need to learn some independence. Felipe would be a buffer between the two girls. ("I want to separate Margaret from Alice, but not too far.")[80]

Several children seemed quick academically, especially Alice and Judith, a Puerto Rican girl with long, dark, curly hair and penetrating eyes. Judith was easy to spot. On the second day, Chris organized an exploratory math game called Around the World, a game like Musical Chairs, in which the players advance around the room on the strength of their right answers. In Chris's experience, one child rarely beat everyone. Yet Judith did, not once but twice. In victory, Judith walked quickly back to her desk, a little unsteadily on medium high heels, which emphasized the sway of her hips, and with her head laid against one shoulder, as if she were trying to hide her face. Every child clapped for Judith. Felipe cheered loudly. So Judith was popular, too, Chris thought. Also curiously reserved. The girl didn't even smile at the applause.

Chris moved Judith next to Alice. ("Judith's exceptional, and I want Alice to get to know an Hispanic kid who's at her level.") Maybe Judith and Alice would become friends. At any rate, they made a comely picture, the silky-haired and pink-cheeked Alice with freckles around her nose, from the Highlands by way of Ireland long ago, and the pale-skinned and dark-eyed Judith, from the Flats by way of Juncos on the island of enchantment (as Puerto Rican license plates say), sitting side by side.

Chris put Clarence in the remaining middle-person desk.[81]

* * *

---

77. This one mannerism brings Courtney to life before our very eyes. We've seen people make that O; we can picture her. It continues to add life to the scene.

78. More of Zajac's thoughts, as expressed in conversation with Kidder.

79. Because we know about Clarence's cume, we understand that Robert is also a troubled child. There is no need to elaborate.

80. Kidder continues to weave in Zajac's strategy and in doing so "shows" us she is a good teacher.

81. The digression and placement of students brings us back to Clarence, and where the action left off. We are ready—and eager—to see if the new Clarence will appear on the third day. Note how Kidder does not go into the placement of all twenty children, but rather focuses on the ones who will become key players in the story, and he provides enough to give us a feel for Zajac's thinking.

On the third day of school, a Friday, several children including Clarence came in without homework,[82] and Chris told them that they were in for recess. Holding midday detention would cost her half her lunch break, but what mattered now, it seemed to her, was that they realize that she cared whether they did their work.[83] Clarence objected to the news about being in for recess. He threw an eraser at one classmate and punched another. Chris didn't see him do that; she'd left the room for a moment. A couple of the children told on him. Chris thought, "I have to put a stop to this now."[84]

So much, she thought, for her talk yesterday about a new Clarence today. She called him to her desk. He came, but he stood sideways to her, chin lifted, face averted. She told him, in a matter-of-fact voice that wasn't very stern, that he could put someone's eye out by throwing things, and that he could not hit anyone. He didn't say a word. He just stared away, chin raised, as if to say,[85] "I'm not listening to you."

Chris had to move Felipe's desk again that day, to a spot nearer hers. Felipe was chattering too much.

"Good," hissed Clarence when Felipe pushed his desk to its new spot.

"Why is that good, Clarence?" Chris asked.

He didn't answer.

But it was obvious to her. Clarence felt wronged. He felt glad that someone else was getting punished, too.

All of the children kept in for recess worked hard, except for Clarence. She had put up lists of the work that children owed on the upper right hand corner of the board, and "Clarence" appeared on every list. He did a little work after lunch, but he came to a full stop when, late in the day,[86] she asked the class to write a paragraph and draw some pictures to describe their visions of the lives of Native Americans. She told them that later, after they'd learned all about Native Americans, they'd look back at these paragraphs and pictures and probably have a good laugh. All the other children got to work, quite happily, it seemed. Clarence said he didn't understand the assignment. She explained it again, twice. Finally, she told him that she'd have to keep him after school again today if he didn't get to work on the paragraph. She called him to her desk and said, "Clarence, you are making a choice between going home with your friends and staying here after school. You're a bright boy. Why don't you just pick up your pencil and write?" She hoped he would. She didn't want to stay after school on a Friday.[87]

She watched Clarence. He sauntered back to his desk. On the way, with an angry swipe, Clarence brushed all the books and papers off Robert's desk. Then he sat down and glared at her.[88]

Chris turned for another whispered conference with Miss Hunt, about scheduling. The other children bent their heads over their papers, working out their impressions

---

82. Transition back to the present time line. We quickly learn that there is no new Clarence. The plot thickens. We are curious to follow his development.

83. We are drawn more closely into Zajac's head.

84. Kidder is able to keep this incident (which he no doubt observed firsthand) in Zajac's point of view by telling us a couple of the other children told on Clarence.

85. The phrase "as if to say" lets us know that Kidder is only speculating from the boy's mannerisms.

86. Indicates passage of time. Kidder is skipping less interesting and important moments in the day.

87. We continue to experience the scene through Zajac.

88. As we continue, notice the vivid word choices Kidder is using to capture the students' movements. Clarence saunters, he takes a swipe at the books and papers on Robert's desk, he glares at the teacher.

about Indians. Chris saw Clarence take out his ruler and put it on top of his pencil. Grinning, he tapped the ruler with his finger. It spun like a helicopter blade.[89]

Chris watched the ruler spin. She understood this as defiance. The lines were being drawn.[90]

The intercom called the last bus. The children who lived near the school—"the walkers"[91]—lined up at the door. Clarence headed for the closet and took out his brown vinyl aviator jacket.[92] It was new and had epaulets. It was a little big for him, and made him look even younger than he was.

"Where do you think you're going, Clarence? I don't know why you think you need your coat." She never liked to hear that ironic sound in her voice, but she felt annoyed. Because this boy would not work, she had to stay after school.[93]

Clarence threw himself into his chair. He sat with his jacket in his lap and watched the other children file out the door.

It was just like yesterday.[94] Chris sat at her desk and did some paperwork while watching Clarence. Now and then she said, without looking up, "The pencil's moving. Right, Clarence?" She could see that it wasn't, but her voice was not ironic. It carried the same sort of message as yesterday's: "Let's assume that you are going to do the work."

Clarence's paper lay on his desk. He hadn't written anything on it. He didn't even look at it. He gazed, mouth slightly ajar, at nothing. Then he glared at her, then stared off. From her desk, his face appeared as if suspended in the forest of inverted chairs.

Children get dealt grossly unequal hands, but that is all the more reason to treat them equally in school, Chris thought. "I think the cruelest form of prejudice is . . . if I ever said, 'Clarence is poor, so I'll expect less of him than Alice.' Maybe he won't do what Alice does. But I want his best."[95] She knew that precept wasn't as simple as it sounded. Treating children equally often means treating them very differently. But it also means bringing the same moral force to bear on all of them, saying, in effect, to Clarence that you matter as much as Alice and won't get away with not working, and to Alice that you won't be allowed to stay where you are either. She wanted Clarence to realize that he would pay a price for not doing his best and for misbehaving. If she was consistent, Clarence might begin to reason that he could make school a lot easier by trying to do his work. If she got him to try, she could help him succeed, and maybe even help him to like school and schoolwork someday.[96]

But this was Friday.[97] Chris never stayed after school on Friday. She felt worn out. The first few days always made her yearn for a sofa and some pillows. Her feet ached. She had earned her Friday afternoon away from here and Clarence. Why had she put herself in this position? On a Friday!

---

89. Zajac saw this maneuver, and so did Kidder. The comparison to a helicopter blade is appropriate to the subject matter. It also reminds us of the stunt plane.

90. The short sentences again give us the feel of Zajac quickly assessing the situation and reaching conclusions.

91. Dashes provide a quick, simple way to insert explanation.

92. Now we know just how appropriate the stunt plane and helicopter comparisons are. This concrete detail also gives us a vivid picture of Clarence.

93. We share Zajac's irritation.

94. This reference provides a sort of shorthand referring to the fuller scene without Kidder having to elaborate.

95. Here Kidder inserts an actual quote rather than translate it into Zajac's thoughts.

96. Zajac's more idealistic thoughts.

97. While Zajac has those loftier thoughts, she is nevertheless miffed about having to remain after class on a Friday.

Clarence's teacher last year had said that Clarence cried a lot. The teacher was no fool, but Chris just bet that she, and the teachers before her, had too often relented at the sight of Clarence's tears, just as Chris had yesterday when she'd asked for a new Clarence. She would not relent again. She looked across the room at Clarence and flexed the muscles in her jaw. She felt testy. Just then, it seemed like the best way to feel: *All right, buster. What you need is what I've got.* Chris took a deep breath and let it out. Then she got up and strode across the room, her hands in fists.[98]

Clarence jerked his head away as she approached.

"Are we going to go through this every day, Clarence?"

She grabbed a chair and sat down beside him, leaning her head forward and a little to one side to get it close to his. He turned his farther away. "I can wait you out as much as you can wait me out. If this is not done Monday"—she tapped the blank paper on his desk—"plus all the other work you owe me, you won't have recess. And you'll be after school. You are *going* to do it."

Tears began to streak his cheeks again.

"Secondly," Chris began, and she let her voice rise.[99] It was all right to let it rise; this offense was more severe. "If you're mad at Mrs. Zajac, you deal with me. You don't take it out on others! You raise a hand again to anybody and you're out of here. Do you under-*stand?*"

He had turned his face all the way around, so that she was looking at the back of his head.

Chris's voice came down. "I tried yesterday to be nice to you, and said, 'Let's start over.' But you don't want that. Now, Monday, this work is going to be done. Do you understand?"

He didn't speak.

"Now, go," she said.

Clarence jumped up and ran out the door. From the hallway, echoing back up the stairs, came his voice. There were tears in it. It was a sharp little cry. "I *hate* Mrs. Zajac!"[100]

*   *   *

Chris sat for a while in the child's chair that she'd pulled up to Clarence's desk. She sat there, looking out the door, until the worst of her defeated feeling passed. It was the sort of feeling that follows domestic quarrels. You feel that you have every right to speak angrily to your child or your parents, and when you do and a wound appears, you suddenly see the situation altogether differently. She hadn't been able to sympathize fully with Clarence until now, when she had hurt him.[101]

She couldn't help getting angry sometimes, and sometimes getting angry worked. Usually, the sort of child who got her angry was the sort of child who got angry back. They could wrangle openly. Together, they could clear the air. But Clarence wasn't that

---

98. The fists "show" she feels testy.

99. Note how the verb choices "show" how Zajac's patience isn't what it was the first time Clarence was kept after school. On the first day, she sighed, walked over to Clarence, and sat in a child's chair with her face close to his. Today, she grabs a chair, taps the blank paper on his desk, her voice rises.

100. Another section—and day—comes to a dramatic end that compels us to keep reading to find out what happens next in the saga of Mrs. Zajac and Clarence.

101. This scene lets us share Zajac's moments alone, as well as her thoughts. The comparison to a domestic quarrel is one we can all identify with. Thus we know how she feels.

child, and mistaking anger for reason was always dangerous. Clarence needed firmness, but she wondered if he hadn't seen too much anger from adults already.

I hate Mrs. Zajac![102] Once she heard the cry, she could imagine any number of gentler words she could have used on him, and all of them seemed better than the ones she'd chosen. By yelling it on the stairs, he let her know she'd wounded him and didn't give her a chance to make repairs. He won that skirmish.[103]

There were a lot of stories about Clarence around. One school department psychologist remembered him as a kindergartner and remembered being struck by the eagerness with which he climbed into her lap. There seemed to be a desperate quality about Clarence's search for love. Chris would have felt better if she could have told herself that Clarence really did dislike her. But, of course, that wasn't what he meant. He *hated* her. Had he attached himself that strongly to her already? This was only the third day of school. If things went on this way with Clarence, it was going to be an exhausting year.[104]

Chris got up and walked over to her desk. She stared out the window. It was one long, rectangular sheet of smoky, slightly scratched plexiglass flanked by two small casements. The windows opened onto the playground below: a field of grass with a baseball diamond and a concrete basketball court in one corner and a few scrawny young trees on the edges along the chain link fence. The playground ended at a line of warehouses and factories. One factory building was old, of dingy brick, with its ground-floor windows covered in plywood. Another, Laminated Papers, had pale green walls the color of hospital corridors. The factory roofs hid all views of the wide, brown Connecticut River, rushing down from the huge falls, which once powered all of industrial Holyoke. Under a string of high-tension wires, a lumpy horizon of trees, the only full-grown trees in sight, rose from the Chicopee bank of the river. Chris stared out at the hospital-green walls of the Laminated Papers building.[105] Clarence is an angry child, she thought. Angry at the whole world. Worst of all was that stony, averted face he wore when she tried to talk to him. How could she ever get close enough to reason with a child who put up a barrier like that?

Anger wouldn't work, obviously, nor would endless sessions of detention—they would simply make her feel resentful, too. Maybe she should simply warn him that he was getting F's. No, that wouldn't work either. On his first report card he'd flunk everything, and that would tell him the same old news, that he didn't have to do the work because he couldn't.

3

After spending most of six hours alone with children in one room, a teacher needs to talk to another adult, if only to remind herself that she still is an adult. Chris needed to talk more than most people. She couldn't sort out her thoughts until she had turned them loose into the air. She hated, not solitude, but the silences that cover up emotions. This evening especially she would have to talk.[106]

When she got home her husband, Billy, was there already. Billy was about six feet,

---

102. The repetition of "*I hate Mrs. Zajac!*" echoes how Clarence's outburst stays with her and bothers her.
103. Earlier, after the ruler incident, Kidder wrote that the lines were being drawn. Now he—and Zajac—continue the combat metaphor.
104. Zajac's thoughts and feelings continue drawing us into the scene and the story.
105. Kidder uses Zajac's moment of reflection to weave in more description of both the classroom and the neighborhood.
106. The insight on Zajac also acts as a transition, moving her and the story from the classroom to home.

with prematurely gray hair and an open, youthful face. He was a good listener.[107] The first year or so of their marriage, she would bring home teacher stories and halfway through would pause to check. She'd say accusingly, "You weren't listening, Billy."

"Yes, I was," Billy would reply. "You were telling me that so-and-so was throwing snots around the room."

Actually, it had turned out that Billy remembered the names of her difficult pupils years after she had managed to forget them herself.

Billy understood how badly Chris needed to talk. The few times when he felt truly angry at Chris, he would break off the argument and simply walk away from her. Chris would then chase Billy around the house. She wouldn't be able to help herself. She had to keep on talking at those times. Otherwise, the argument would fester.

Chris found Billy in the kitchen and told him all about this day: Clarence's tears, Clarence's stoniness, Clarence's exit. "I don't know, Billy. Every year you get one, and every year it's the same. But it's discouraging."

She went on: "I wasn't trained for this. I was trained to teach, not to deal with kids like this. And they stick them in your room, and you're supposed to perform miracles. Plus teach all the others."[108]

Poor Billy. She talked about Clarence all weekend. "Guilt," she said. "Guilt plays a large part in my life." She might as well have brought Clarence home for those two days. She kept seeing the big eyes exuding tears, and hearing the sharp, wounded voice saying, "I *hate* Mrs. Zajac!" She was angry at herself about her timing, too. You never scold a child on Friday afternoon and give yourself two days to brood about it. She knew better than to do that.[109]

* * *

On Monday morning,[110] Chris told Pam Hunt, the student teacher, "This week I'm going to kill him with kindness. But if he lays a hand on another kid, I'm going to step on him. I'm not going to have a child afraid to come to school because Clarence is going to hit him. I'm not going to let him out of doing his work, but this week I'm just going to keep putting his name on the board and reminding him, and try that for a week."[111]

Pam pursed her lips and nodded.

When Clarence ambled in, walking heel-to-toe as if to music only he could hear,[112] Chris said, "Good morning, Clarence! How are you this morning?"

It seemed as though Friday had never happened. Clarence grinned at her. Chris smiled over her blotter at the after-image. Those dimples of his were so deep she could see them from behind.

Clarence did a 360-degree turn, a pirouette with arms outstretched, and like an airplane coming in for a landing,[113] dropped his books on his desk. Then he took his coat

---

107. Kidder takes this opportunity to tell us more about her husband, Billy.

108. This is a scene Kidder observed.

109. Kidder gives us the essence of the rest of the weekend, gleaned from talking to Zajac after the fact. Note how the third repetition of "I hate Mrs. Zajac!" causes the outburst to linger with us just as it does Chris Zajac.

110. Time transition into a new scene, a new day.

111. Kidder gives us Zajac's new strategy right up front. We are forced to continue reading to see if it works.

112. This detailed little description gives us a vivid picture of Clarence entering the classroom. The verb "amble" is right on target.

113. Kidder continues the aviation metaphor. The lesson here: Try to maintain the same metaphor to describe the same situation or character.

to the closet. Now he was gazing at the week's luncheon menus that were taped up on the closet door. He rubbed his little belly, his hand moving in a circle over it. "Mmmm! Applesauce!" he said.

He really was extraordinarily cute, Chris thought. But in a moment, she would have to ask him for the work he hadn't done last week.[114]

TRACY KIDDER ON READING

"I don't underline much or make notations—at least not in books that I think or hope have literary value. I do underline when I'm doing research, when, that is, I'm reading books and articles purely for the information in them. I don't think I've ever turned to stories or books to learn particular techniques. To me, that seems like a bad idea. I do believe that people can be helped to learn to write, but I don't believe there are universal formulas for accomplishing that and I don't believe that any very analytical approach is wise. Technique, I think, is something one absorbs from other writers, reinventing along the way. I do believe in reading for that purpose and also for inspiration. There are various authors who have made me want to try my own hand. The lists have changed over the years. Hemingway and Fitzgerald when I was in school; Conrad in my early twenties; Orwell (his nonfiction) and A. J. Liebling and Tom Wolfe (some of his nonfiction) and John McPhee and Norman Mailer when I first discovered nonfiction narrative. Right now I'm reading and re-reading Graham Greene, my current favorite writer. A few years ago it was Nabokov and the great Italian poet Eugenio Montale. . . . Reading is a part of writing and vice versa. I chose to think that there's mystery involved in both."

---

114. The section ends on a cliffhanger that leaves us wanting more. Is this a new Clarence? What will happen when she asks for his work? We are compelled to read the rest of the book.

Jane Kramer

Over the years, Jane Kramer has introduced New Yorker readers to an assortment of fascinating "characters." There have been hapless Texas cowboys, kidnapped Moroccan brides, Dadaist German spies, African rockers performing in Paris—individuals she has encountered both in this country and in Europe, where she lives half of each year. The eccentric vintner Armande Douhairet, she says, came to her as an unexpected gift during a weekend visit in Burgundy with friends in the wine trade there.

"At some point over the weekend somebody said, Let's go see Armande. So we all went," Kramer recalls. "Armande was enchanting. Her style, her conversation, her situation. And of course her wines. I made up my mind, then and there, to write about her, though it took a few trips over the course of a year, and the beginnings of a friendship between us, to persuade her."

To Kramer, Armande illuminated a world, or rather, many worlds. There was the world of La France Profonde, or "Deep France"; the world of making great Burgundy and the Enlightenment tradition as it shaped the lives and politics and perspectives of provincial families like Armande's; the world of big money and land grabs, of all the people who wanted Armande's seven hectares; the world of French women—especially old spinsters like Armande—and what the French call their formation, their education and survival, their sense of who they are; and, finally, there was, to Kramer, the world-in-the-head of one dazzling character.

Once Armande agreed to the story, Kramer returned to Burgundy for about a month, staying with the friends who had introduced them—a connection that proved invaluable in solidifying Armande's trust. Kramer conducted the interviews in French, a language she speaks fluently, visiting Armande most days, but, she stresses, not every day.

"There is a rhythm to this sort of prolonged, deeply personal (you could say, deeply intrusive) encounter," she explains. "A reporter learns very quickly to gauge the moment when a subject's psychic fatigue sets in; to leave then; to return when the subject begins to miss the interest (remember, Armande had a very lively curiosity, and, as a stranger, I was at least as exotic to her as she to me) and attention and conversation. It has to do with a sense of appropriate timing, and for the work I do, it's probably the single most important talent to have. Some subjects are marathons. You talk to the point of exhaustion. Others—Armande was one of these—are more like small daily walks around the park, and your understanding deepens gradually, and depends on the pace at which ease and familiarity grows."

Kramer spent the rest of her time getting to know Burgundy and the other vintners, from the most celebrated to the most artisanal. The whole experience was essentially an education—Kramer's favorite part of any long project. She learned how wine is made, and about soil and temperature and tasting.

When it came time to write, the hardest part was determining how to tell the story.

"French isn't a language with a rich vocabulary, like English; it's a language of so-

phisticated syntactical play," says Kramer. "The particularity of a certain voice—Armande's, in this case—doesn't always lie in the words chosen but in a particular way of phrasing, a particular syntactical strategy used to arrange a limited vocabulary into what you could call 'an attitude.' Armande was a natural ironist, but her ironies were grammatical, and sometimes there was no way to convey them—that is, to convey her particularity of voice and character—through direct literal quotation.

"I found that in many cases I could actually be more faithful to Armande by slipping her phrasing into my own paraphrase, a snippet of a quote into a paraphrase of a sentence that expressed Armande. Armande was lively. I didn't want to weigh her down, or to drown her in the imprecision of precise translation (the way I might have had to do if she were an astronomer, say, or a politician). My own choices involved when to quote and when to approximate—when to fold her voice into mine."

It was a challenge Kramer met with ease. By the time we finish the story, it's as if we too have shared a petit cocktail with Armande, a level of intimacy Kramer has been praised for in her profiles. She is particularly noted for her seamless style, which comes across as effortless, but in reality is the result of painstaking revision. She once told an interviewer, "I spend as much time editing and reworking a piece as I do writing it the first time."

A staff writer for the New Yorker since 1964, she is perhaps best known for her "Letters From Europe," which have appeared regularly since 1981. She is the author of eight books, including The Politics of Memory, Europeans, Unsettling Europe, and The Last Cowboy. Her book about a militia in the American West will be published next spring.

She has won an American Book Award, a National Magazine Award, a Front Page Award, an Overseas Press Club of America Citation for Excellence, and an Emmy for the documentary "This Is Edward Steichen," among other honors. In 1993, she became the first American, and the first woman, to win the Prix Européen de l'Essai, Europe's most prestigious award for nonfiction.

Armande

ARMANDE does not go down to her cellars much, now that she is eighty-three and has a titanium pin in her hip and needs a cane for walking. She never liked the cellars anyway.[1] There were treacherous stone steps and dangling spiderwebs and mold all over the 1906 Volnay[2] that her father reserved from the *millésime* when she was born, thinking, perhaps, to open it for Armande's wedding, or the birth day of her first child. She says that the damp, yeasty smell of the wine *caves,* ten feet underground, always made her sneeze and that tasting gave her hiccups and then, too, as far as Armande is concerned, there was something unpleasant about the rituals of tasting—the men standing in a circle in their suits and ties, shivering in the chill, rolling the tart new wine around their mouths, like mouthwash, and spitting it out between the barrels and into dark corners. She does not think that a lady should have to watch men spitting wine into corners.[3] "*Ça ne m'apporte rien,*" she says. "It does nothing for me."[4] When clients come to the village now, wanting to taste her Volnay or Pommard or her special Meursault-Santenots[5]—or just to talk to Armande, who has a reputation among wine people and is known in Burgundy simply as Mademoiselle—she will greet them in her parlor, sitting on a rubber tube, her cane at hand, and even offer them a cheese biscuit and a glass of the ratafia she produces, on the

---

"Armande" first appeared in the *New Yorker* in 1990. Reprinted by permission of the author. (Editor's note: This story has been cut because of space limitations. The cuts are indicated by ellipses.)

1. The opening sentence draws us into the story as much by what it omits as what it includes. We don't learn who Armande is (not even her last name), what kind of cellar she has, where the cellar is located, or why her going—or not going—down there is relevant. Thus, we are compelled to continue reading. Like most stories, there are any number of ways Kramer could have begun, but the wine cellar proves an excellent choice because it supports the focus and enables the author to tell us about both Armande and her vineyard: her employees, her customers, her neighbors, the people who court her for her land. The sentence starts with a simple statement, then builds, beginning an energy that drives the entire story. Here, this energy is accomplished through the use of "and" rather than commas. To use commas after each item in the list would cause readers to pause; "and" sweeps us and the story along. The detail that the pin was titanium stands out like a jewel. Kramer could have simply written that Armande had a pin in her hip. The fact that it is titanium sets Armande apart and reflects her sense of humor. We get the feeling that this is the way she herself refers to the pin. Already she is more interesting than just any old lady with a broken hip.

2. Kramer begins a pattern, albeit it a subtle one, of making a short, straightforward statement of fact, followed by longer, rolling sentences that elaborate on that statement and create an energy that propels the story—and the reader—forward.

3. The next three sentences explain why Armande doesn't like the cellar. The forward movement of the first sentence is again achieved with "and" and with the accumulation of facts. "Perhaps" is a subtle signal that the father's thoughts are speculation. The forward progression and the accumulation of facts continue in the second, longer sentence, but note here how Kramer inserts an occasional aside, set off by commas (and even a dash), for emphasis. The third sentence in the series is shorter and more straightforward, bringing us to the end of Armande's explanation of why she doesn't like the cellar. The vivid word choices ("sneeze," "hiccup," "spitting") and colorful material begin telling us about Armande in a manner that captures her irreverent nature. The choice of words and anecdotes also establishes a witty, yet sophisticated tone throughout the story.

4. Kramer uses French words and phrases for flavor throughout the story. As the story progresses, we will see that she translates only those terms non-French-speaking readers may have difficulty understanding. Even when Kramer provides a translation, she does so unobtrusively, and informally; we scarcely realize that she is doing so.

5. Like all good detail, the specific varietals are more vivid than a general "her wine." They also tell us what wines Armande produces.

side, from her marc and the must of the pressing, but unless she knows them well and likes them she does not go down to the cellars with them.[6] When it is time to taste, she calls Francis, her tractor man and new *caviste*,[7] to escort them—to rinse the glasses and siphon the wine from the casks and take the orders and sometimes, in the end, to fill a pail and splash some water onto the splattered floor near the tasting table.[8]

Armande does not walk easily at all. She has a bad left leg, and a year and a half ago she fell and broke her right hip and needed an operation—which, she says, is how she got enough titanium inside her to send her straight to Heaven.[9] She has a lot of stories about her broken hip. She likes to tell people that she broke it[10] dancing with a handsome African she met in Senegal during the *troisième âge* tour she took with the widow of a winegrower from Auxey-Duresses, off Route 973, toward La Rochepot. Or she says that she had her accident reaching to switch channels from "Les Enfants du Rock," on Antenne 2, to the pornographic movie on La Cinq.[11] Her stories make her clients uncomfortable—which may be why she tells them. She has no patience with the sort of discreet and embarrassed conversation people reserve for old women, and especially, as she puts it,[12] for plain old virgins like herself. Armande is smart. She knows that everybody[13] in the village—and, indeed, everybody in Burgundy who cares about wine and vines and vineyards—is waiting to see what Mademoiselle decides to do with her property. Armande has fifteen acres in vine here. She has fifteen acres of Volnay, Pommard, Meursault, and Monthelie, her own *appellation village*—which means that she has fifteen of the most coveted acres in the world.[14] There were never any children or grandchildren to inherit them. She has one sister, in the south, with a retarded daughter, and, in a village where there are usually ten or fifteen families bottling, as she does, under the Monthelie name, she has no cousins left—and, in fact, no relatives at all.[15] Armande was not courted as a girl, but she is courted[16] now—too much, she says, for a spinster of eighty-three who was never, as she puts it, "*gracieuse.*" She gets Christmas cards from Japanese businessmen and family news from California ranchers. German millionaires send her expensive patent-leather belts (she has a weakness for good black patent leather),[17] and Belgian

---

6. This echoes the earlier point about Armande not going to the cellar and thus contributes to the cohesiveness of the paragraph.

7. Because *caviste* is similar to "cellar," or "cave," Kramer has no need to provide a translation.

8. Kramer uses a list to describe economically the *caviste*'s duties. "Splattered" is a colorful word choice—in keeping with both the tone of the story and Armande's attitude toward the tasting ritual.

9. "Enough titanium inside her to send her straight to Heaven" sounds like Armande's voice, even though it is not a direct quote.

10. Repetition of words and phrases is a device literary journalists and other feature writers use, often instinctively, to achieve various effects. Here, the repetition of "broke" creates both cohesiveness and a pleasing rhythm.

11. Armande's stories add color to the profile. They also reflect her personality and thus tell us something about her. While most of us may not be familiar with Route 973 or Antenne 2 or La Cinq, the concrete detail makes both the profile and Armande's stories more vivid. There is no need to translate "Les Enfants du Rock." Even readers not conversant in French can figure that out.

12. Tells us in an interesting way that this is Armande's own self-description, thus indicating she is irreverent even about herself.

13. Kramer repeats "everybody" for emphasis.

14. If readers haven't figured out just why everybody is so interested in Armande, this emphasizes the point—and the focus—of the profile.

15. Kramer again uses a list connected by "and" to economically provide information about Armande's family and to maintain the story's energy and forward momentum, but note how she uses brief asides for variation and to insert information. The thing to remember here is that too much of a good thing can lose its effectiveness. You must learn to pace yourself, and this again is something a writer must develop a feel for.

16. Here, the repetition of "courted" maintains the story's impish tone.

17. The parenthetical aside is an economical way to insert information about Armande.

doctors send cases of her favorite beer, and there are Sunday afternoons when some of the most important priests in Beaune[18] drive out to Monthelie to promise her Heaven if she gives her vines in charity to the Beaune Hospices.[19] In age and indecision and discomfort, Armande has become powerful in Burgundy. People are careful around her now. They try to ingratiate themselves. They are relentlessly respectful, and have lost the wit to amuse her. Even the neighbors are careful. They have stopped swearing too much and telling the terrible jokes Armande loves and the terrible dirty stories,[20] and Armande has to amuse herself with stories of her own. Her stories give her courage. They are small acts of defiance, a whistling in the dark of her own solitude,[21] a way of saying, "Attention! Mademoiselle Douhairet is still in charge of her own life and her own cellars and her own vines."

* * *

Everybody who loves wine loves Burgundy, or claims to love Burgundy, or knows, at least, that loving Burgundy is the mark of a worldly *amateur*. The Burgundians think that Celts settled what is now Autun in order to be near the vineyards here, and that Romans stopped and built a great city for the same reason. Armande, as a schoolgirl, read all about the Romans in Burgundy. She liked the Romans much more than she liked the Merovingians and Carolingians who ruled Burgundy after them. She suspects that, Germans being Germans,[22] those Frankish clans were like the clients from Stuttgart and Cologne who arrive at all hours of the day and night and ask for tastings and then, when they have got drunk at her expense, leave without buying anything. She suspects that they were rude and proprietary and more interested in plunder than in the old Burgundian arts of viticulture and vinification.[23] People are always asking Armande how it feels to be the custodian of land like hers, land with so much history attached to it. They want to know what she thinks about Romans and Merovingians in her back yard, or about owning the kind of vines Petrarch had in mind when he was trying to talk the Avignon pope into coming home and wrote to say what a terrible thing it was—keeping the Church from Rome because of an unholy fondness for Burgundy. Petrarch did not approve of people like Urban V who couldn't live without Burgundy[24] "*qui beatam sine Beuna vitam agi posse diffidunt*"[25]—and Armande agrees with Petrarch. She likes to say[26] that she can live quite nicely with her Belgian beer, some Alsatian table wine, and an occasional Bordeaux, and, if it comes to choosing Burgundies, she prefers a good Échézeaux to her own Pommard, which most people think is wonderful but to her mind is too aggressive, something for Belgians and Germans. It may be that, having no heirs, no issue, no one to

---

18. Kramer has again woven in examples of the individuals who court Armande—in other words, she has gone from the general to the specific. The examples are concrete and colorful and thus captivate readers. Who could possibly put aside a story with this cast of characters?

19. "Promise her Heaven if she gives her vines in charity to the Beaune Hospices" probably expresses Armande's sentiments, but is Kramer's voice. This tells us as much about her sense of humor as it does Armande's.

20. Kramer's examples of the neighbors' caution tell us as much about Armande as it does them: She is a little risqué.

21. This familiar metaphor conveys Armande's unease with the people's sudden propriety.

22. A subtle way to introduce Armande's distaste for Germans.

23. The alliteration, or repetition of *v*, has a pleasing quality.

24. In this paragraph, Kramer weaves in history of the region, as filtered through the points of view of Armande and the Burgundians. She does so in a manner that maintains the story's irreverent tone or voice so that it becomes an integral part of the story, not a history lesson that is cut and pasted in.

25. Kramer varies her use of foreign phrases, providing the translation before the actual phrase.

26. "Likes to say" implies this is an opinion she often expresses.

inherit,[27] she has dismissed history, and, with it, her own failure to account for herself with another generation of winegrowers. She is fierce about her land, but the fact that it has probably been in vine for two thousand years does not intimidate her at all.[28] She is much less reverent than the wine merchants and the wine writers who gather in her *caves*, gargling and sniffing,[29] to compare her Volnay '83 and her Volnay '85 or discuss the qualities of her two new Monthelie Premiers Crus—her Monthelie-Duresses and her Monthelie-Le Meix Bataille—hoping all the while for a taste of one of the 1949s in the small *cave* where she keeps her private stock.[30]

Armande likes drinking. She drinks, by her reckoning, about a bottle of wine a day, but she does not go down to the *caves* and choose a 1959 Volnay or a 1978 Monthelie from her reserve. Toward six, she opens the window and shouts down to Francis to bring the open bottles from the day's tastings, and then she empties them into a kitchen pitcher and stirs everything around and fills her glass. She calls it her *petit cocktail.*[31]

* * *

The village of Monthelie[32] once belonged to the Benedictine abbey in Cluny. The village church, where Armande goes to Mass, was built by a Cluny abbot in the twelfth century—it has a square bell tower and a pretty, patterned, tile steeple,[33] like other churches in the style that has come to be known as Cluny Romanesque—and, as far as anyone in the village knows, the vines in what are now Armande's vineyards were cultivated for six centuries by monks and vassals of the abbot and of the local bishops and monsignors who were the *seigneurs en partie* and, like the abbot, made fortunes from the wine they sold. Armande's family—her mother's family—arrived in Monthelie in the sixteenth century. Armande does not know where they lived before, or how they made their money or got their land. She knows only that they came when Monthelie passed out of the abbot's hands, and that they took the village name (which, depending on whom you ask, is either Celtic and means "the hill by the road" or Greek and means "the mountain of the sun god"),[34] and that they built their house and bought their land and started vinifying well before the French Revolution—which is when most of the other vineyards in Burgundy were divided and sold. She is not much interested in ancestors. As far as Armande is concerned, the interesting Monthelies are the Monthelies she has known, and the interesting villagers are the villagers she knows now. Henri Meyer, who lives across the road and is sixty-nine and used to make the most beautiful wine barrels in Burgundy. Germaine de Suremain, who lives in the local château and is eighty-five and cruised the fjords with Armande on one of her best vacations. The two sisters who visit regularly in

---

27. The repetition stresses the fact she has no children. It also has a pleasing rhythm. Note how each repetition grows in length: the first mention has two syllables, the second has three, the last has six, thus giving emphasis to the last.

28. "At all" provides an informal, conversational tone. It also adds emphasis.

29. More irreverent word choices that capture Armande's voice.

30. The concrete details make the story more vivid and tell us more about Armande's winery.

31. This tight little anecdote draws a vivid picture of Armande, which we readers can visualize. Note the active verbs ("opens," "shouts," "empties," "fills") that bring the scene to life. It tells us as much about her personality as it does her routine. *Petit cocktail* is a setup for quick, future references.

32. This begins a digression into Armande's village and her family. The line-break acts as a transition.

33. List provides a means of concisely describing the church. For all its brevity, however, note how specific the details are.

34. Parenthetical insert is a convenient way of working in an interesting piece of information.

the afternoon and always sell Armande four bars of lemon soap and give the money to a charity for disabled dogs.[35]

There are two hundred people in Monthelie. At election time, anyone who wants to join the town council signs his name on a list of candidates at the *mairie*,[36] and the villagers with the most votes run Monthelie until they are tired of the meetings and can persuade their neighbors to replace them. The only politics that most people in the village care about are wine politics, although Armande herself has a weakness for Margaret Thatcher.[37] She suspects that women are better at running things than men—she is, by her own admission, very good at business, very talented and very crafty[38]—and then, too, she has heard that Mrs. Thatcher does not believe in "1992" and European unity and all the other *gigantesque* projects of the Common Market and the European Parliament. Armande says that a country where winemakers from Beaune do not talk to winemakers from Nuits-Saint-Georges is not likely to settle on a common currency with the Germans or agree to an English quarantine for its dogs or adjust its pensions to keep the Italians happy.[39] Burgundians are proprietary. Burgundians from the strip of red, gently sloping soil that runs for thirty miles from Marsannay through Santenay and is known as the Côte d'Or, and, by *appellation* and common wisdom, produces the great Burgundy wines, are particularly proprietary. The thirty-two communes of the Côte d'Or are the only communes in France that refuse to let the government's agricultural-land board (it is called SAFER, after Société d'Aménagement Foncier et d'Établissement Rural) intervene in arguments over vineyard sales and land prices, and they are always arguing. They even argue about whether the wine is more agreeable on their northern slope, which they call the Côte de Nuits, or on their southern slope, which they call the Côte de Beaune.[40] Armande's father, Louis Douhairet, married into the Monthelie vineyards and thus into the Côte de Beaune. He came from Joncy, in the Chârolais, where the arguments were about cows, but he took up the cause of the Côte de Beaune, and Armande remembers that he would not let a Côte de Nuits in the house, let alone into his cellars. He used to say that when a boy from Beaune married a girl from Nuits-Saint-Georges it was a marriage of foreigners, and there is some of that same stubborn loyalty in Armande, despite her trips to Senegal and her fondness for a good bottle of Échézeaux and her spotty[41] sense of history. Armande belongs to what people here call *la France profonde*—Deep France.[42] She has chosen her corner of the earth, and she is profoundly located in it. She

---

35. In introducing Armande's neighbors, Kramer provides a brief, yet specific description of each to set one apart from the other. In *The Art of Fiction*, John Gardner advised fiction writers to give minor, walk-on characters at least one memorable trait. The same advice is equally important for nonfiction writers. While readers often have difficulty remembering names, these identifying characteristics can help them keep track of who is who. They also add color. Note the wonderful, quirky word choice "disabled dogs." It further establishes Kramer's voice and her own sense of humor.

36. There is no need to translate here. Given the context, *mairie* is a word even readers who speak no French can make out.

37. Former British prime minister Margaret Thatcher—another strong female.

38. The repetition of "very" adds emphasis and rhythm.

39. In keeping with the tone of the story and Armande's point of view, Kramer combines the quirky (quarantining of dogs) with the serious (common currency) in describing the issues facing the Common Market.

40. Kramer uses the communes' inability to agree on anything to weave in information on the region. Côte de Beaune also serves as a transition into Armande's father.

41. "Spotty" is a colorful word that seems fitting for both a character like Armande and the tone of the story.

42. Kramer translates for non-French-speaking readers who might not readily grasp what *la France profonde* means. Note how she then has fun with a play on the word "profound."

says that once—she was eighteen or nineteen, and romantic[43]—she wanted to take orders and become a nun and put on starched medieval habits, like the *bonnes sœurs* at the Hospices, and belong to God and do gracious deeds among the poor,[44] but her father told her she was too eccentric, too particular, *trop personnelle,* for convent life, and after that, she says, the land claimed[45] her. . . .

Armande was born in the Douhairet family house in Joncy.[46] The house was only thirty-five miles from Monthelie, but it took the better part of a day to get here when you were in a wagon drawn by a couple of fat farm horses, and Armande thought of Monthelie as a kind of country place, a place to play, somewhere for weekends and summers. Joncy was different. Joncy was a serious plains town, with wide, straight streets and a *place* with chestnut trees,[47] and the Douhairet house in Joncy was a serious house. It sat in a square garden on the *place,* and it was clearly the important house in town—the house where the doctor lived, or the dentist, or the *notaire,* and kept an office with a Louis XVI desk and dark, musty velvet curtains.[48] Louis Douhairet was, in fact, a doctor. He had a big practice of his own and six hundred acres of Charolais farmland and pastures and one of the first cars in Joncy[49] *or* Charolles. Dr. Douhairet was a paterfamilias in what could be called the French-provincial style. He thrived on the ceremonies of small-town life. Whenever there was a speech to make or an official gift to give or a war memorial to dedicate or an important visitor to welcome to Joncy, it was Dr. Douhairet who presided. Being a doctor suited him, because it added so many ceremonies of its own. Births, deaths, measles, whooping cough, and the 1918 flu—he made them all small state occasions, occasions for his high hat and his black frock coat and his brocaded vest, occasions for a slick of pomade on his twirled Burgundy mustache and a trim at the barber's for the pointed Burgundy goatee he wore until his beard turned white and he let it grow and kept it forked and Biblical.[50] Armande says that her father was a *grosse bête—a personnage.* He believed in his life and his prominence. Every year, he would summon the best photographer in Beaune and call the family together for a portrait. They would gather by the car—the first was a stately, open De Dion-Bouton—and, at the count of three, point appreciatively at one of its splendid features, at the leather seats or the spoked wheels or

---

43. For variety, Kramer uses dashes, rather than parentheses, to set off inserted information. The aside carries the flavor of Armande's voice. Dashes and parentheses are useful devices that can add verve to your writing, but remember to use them sparingly. Otherwise, they can clutter and slow down your readers.

44. While Armande's ambition to become a nun was obviously fleeting, Kramer nevertheless includes it because it's such an unexpected piece of her past. It also serves as a setup for future references. The sentence construction seems to mimic the turn of events: the first portion is connected by "and," creating the feel of a young woman caught up in a romantic dream; "but" brings that dream abruptly to an end. "Too eccentric, too particular" sounds like her father's voice. Because of the context, there is no need to translate *bonnes sœurs.*

45. "Claimed" captures in a single word her tie to the land.

46. Armande's birth serves as a transition into a description of Joncy, the family house, and her parents.

47. There are many things Kramer could tell us about Joncy. She selectively chooses those elements that will give us an overall sense of the place, the most telling being its serious personality.

48. The description of the family house is equally brief, and yet we get a sense that it was big and impressive from the fact it was the most important house in town, the kind of house the local doctor or dentist would live in. The detail of Louis XVI furniture and dark, musty, velvet curtains further give us a feel for what it was like.

49. The land and the car are evidence of his success. The latter also conveys a sense that he liked attention, a trait his love of ceremony confirms.

50. Kramer's description (the high hat, frock coat, twirled mustache, and pointed goatee) gives us both a vivid picture of Dr. Douhairet and a feel for his personality. It was drawn from photographs.

the sweep of the walnut running board,[51] and the year was thus recorded, and joined the other years in the top drawer of a lemonwood Charles X secretary in Dr. Douhairet's study.

Alix Douhairet began her married life with her hair rolled into a tight brown top-knot and her waist laced into a trousseau of high-neck, leg-of-mutton-sleeve summer dresses—beautiful white lawn dresses, with lace insets and embroidery. Twenty-five years and two daughters later, she was a plump, glaring, corseted bourgeoise—a column of thick, pale crêpe and dangling bugle beads and T-strap shoes digging into swollen ankles.[52] Armande and her sister had what Armande calls the Monthelie face, which was a small, sharp, bright-eyed, Burgundy face, and the Douhairet shape, which was the squat, solid shape of Charolais plains people. They had high, broad shoulders and high, thick waists and solid calves, and they looked embarrassed in their cloche hats and their ripply flapper frocks, as if the pretty, frivolous new clothes they always wore for their photographs betrayed them, and made them awkward and mannish.[53] Armande had, to her mind, one good point. She was a *rousse*. She had beautiful red hair,[54] which would have been lost under the nun's coif of her girlhood fantasy[55] and was in fact lost to the bobs and hats of her short, mild blooming. Her mother tried to show her off. She looked for suitors. She took the girls to summer at the beach and bought them bathing suits—navy maillots with no sleeves and racy pant legs—and rented cabañas and umbrellas for them, but she was not successful. Then she tried Paris. She sent Armande, at seventeen, to spend a year with her brother, Louis Monthelie, who was an important Paris doctor and kept an apartment at 87 Rue de Passy and entertained a lot of glamorous Parisian people. Louis Monthelie's specialty was stomachs—livers and intestines,[56] Armande says—and he was known as a scientist. He spent his time at the Passy flat consulting with other scientists and peering at cells under his brass[57] microscope, and it was believed by all the Douhairets in Joncy and all the Monthelies in Monthelie that a year in his instructive, sophisticated company would give Armande an edge on the local girls in the matter of husbands.

In the end,[58] it was her sister who married. Armande came home, and thought about the *bonnes sœurs* at the Hospices,[59] and then she started thinking about Monthelie—started counting the years in *millésimes* and the seasons of the year by the winegrowers'

---

51. The picture-taking anecdote provides an opportunity to describe the De Dion-Bouton, a car that will be unfamiliar to most readers. Note how the specific details of the photograph (the family pose, the features of the car) allow us to "see" the picture for ourselves. The description is drawn from the actual photograph. The specific details of where the photographs were kept (top drawer, lemonwood Charles X secretary, in Dr. Douhairet's study) reinforce the doctor's pride in his automobiles.

52. Photographs again enable Kramer to describe Mme. Douhairet, both as she appeared at the time of her marriage and twenty-five years later.

53. We get our first physical description of Armande, and it is of her as a young woman. Nevertheless, we've already gotten a feel for what she is like because of the cane and her irreverent disposition, which in this case is more important than whether she had bifocals and long hair pulled into a bun.

54. Kramer unobtrusively translates *rousse*.

55. Because of the earlier setup, there is no need to elaborate further on the nun fantasy.

56. The word ("stomachs—livers and intestines") here is more colorful and appropriate to the story's tone than "gastroenterologist." It also sounds like what Armande might have said.

57. Note how Kramer continues to use concrete detail to make the story vivid and real to her readers.

58. Transition.

59. Because of the earlier setup, there is no need to explain or elaborate on *bonnes sœurs*.

rituals of pruning and turning and trimming and picking.[60] She never talked about her Paris year. She says now she never really liked Paris. She can tell you about the day the vines flowered in 1929, but she cannot remember what she did in Paris or whom she met or what she saw. She has shaken Paris from her memory the way you shake the dust from a dry mop—in a kind of mental tidying.[61] She is always shaking out her memory, making it neat and acceptable, something to live with. She was in love once. Some of the neighbors talk about a young man—a suitor, maybe—who called on Armande between the wars and then died in an accident, but none of them except Germaine de Suremain is old enough to remember Armande well between the wars, and Mme. de Suremain does not gossip. The neighbors do not ask Armande. Armande's lapses are unconditional. She has armored[62] herself in a kind of topsy-turvy[63] senility, and breaks the rules of her own old age by recalling the present in limpid and precise detail and forgetting almost everything about her childhood and girlhood and, indeed, her first thirty or forty years.

Armande was thirty-four when the Germans occupied[64] Monthelie. The line between Vichy France and Occupied France had cut through Burgundy at Givry, and it separated Monthelie from Joncy and the Monthelies from the Douhairets, and most of the village men were either prisoners of war or conscript labor in the wheat fields of the plains or in German factories. Every other Saturday, Armande and her mother (her father had died in 1933)[65] would travel from Joncy to Monthelie to see the man who managed the estate for the family, and, if there were no Germans in residence, spend the weekend at the Monthelie house. Usually, there were Germans. There was a cavalry company of a hundred and twenty men and fifty horses quartered in the village, and over the years of the Occupation five commandants set up housekeeping in the house and policed the neighborhood from the winemaker's office. "*Il y avait de la boue,*" Armande says. There was filth in Monthelie.[66] The Germans took everything they liked, and what they liked in Monthelie was the 1923s and the 1929s in Armande's cellars. Armande likes to describe the German officers, in their high boots, marching down the stone steps to steal her wine. They always banged their heads on the second arch[67]—the stairway has a rare double-vaulted ceiling—and Armande made up her mind, right away, not to warn them. She calls it her Resistance. When she sends a client to the *caves* to taste, she will say "*Attention la tête!*"[68] and tell him about that second arch and her Resistance, and begin to laugh, remembering all those Germans and their banged heads, seeing them, in her mind's eye, unconscious in a great heap at the bottom of the treacherous stairs.[69]

It was during the war that Armande decided to run the family vineyard. She says she

---

60. A more interesting way of saying she turned her attention to the vineyard. Again, note the use of "and" to move the sentence—and the story—along energetically.

61. The metaphor suits both Armande and the tone of the story. It is a colorful, no-nonsense way of saying that Armande doesn't dwell on things she doesn't care about.

62. "Unconditional" and "armored" convey Armande's stubbornness.

63. "Topsy-turvy" suits the playful tone of the story.

64. Here we get at the heart of why Armande despises Germans.

65. Parenthetical expression provides a way to insert information economically, without interrupting the anecdote and the energetic flow of the story.

66. Because *Il y avait de la boue* is not a phrase non-French-speaking readers are likely to understand, Kramer provides a translation.

67. The head-banging is a colorful detail. It is also a setup for a future reference.

68. There is no need to translate because Kramer has told us about the head-banging on the arch. Even readers not conversant in French will know *attention*; they can figure out that *la tête* means "head."

69. Note how, throughout the story, Kramer uses vivid anecdotes and moments both to engage us and to tell us about Armande.

was the first Monthelie in a hundred years to do it, family tradition being for the men to go to Beaune and practice law, the way her grandfather had, or to go to Paris and practice medicine, like her uncle, leaving a winemaker in charge and a *caviste* living in the courtyard—one with a wife to keep the linens changed and the kitchen stocked and the house ready for a family visit. The Monthelie men came home to harvest, and they enjoyed the vinifying, but it was a matter of pride for them to have what in Burgundy is called a double profession. In Burgundy, you had vines for your "*côté paysan*," Armande says, and a respectable profession for your "*côté gentilhomme*." No one, though, had thought of educating Armande to a profession. She was educated to wine, *faute de mieux*, by the boredom of spinsterhood, by the war, and by her Uncle Louis, who had decided one day to apply "scientific method" to the family wines, and had installed a little laboratory in his bedroom at Monthelie, with a microscope like his Paris microscope[70] and a Bunsen burner and a stack of test tubes, and started analyzing soil and studying grape sections and mixing nutrients and trying to discover the perfect temperature for fermenting Pinot Noir in order to produce a perfect bouquet and a perfect *robe*—which is to say a perfect color. Armande could play Ravel on the piano and she knew whole passages of Saint-Simon by heart, but she had no other competence, and no real experience of the world, despite her summer at the beach and her Paris year and the terrible daily strain of German soldiers falling down the cellar stairs.[71] She says now that she wanted to be like Victor Hugo. She wanted to drain the world in great, long, thirsty gulps, as if it were a glass of Échézeaux, or a Richebourg '34. . . .

She began the year the war ended—the year her uncle died and her workers came out of hiding along with the other local *résistants* who had managed to stay alive during the Occupation. Her idea was to leave the vines to her winemaker and to take over the accounts and the clients and the marketing for her mother. Being a Leo[72]—August 14th is her birthday—she never doubted she could do it. Her sister, who was a Scorpio, had no interest in the vineyard. She lived near Beaune then with her family, but she only came home to Monthelie once or twice a year, to check the books—to check on her inheritance, Armande says—and, little by little, Armande took over. When their mother died, in 1958, she put the house in Joncy on the market. She packed the family photographs and the three green Nevers tureens with angels for handles and the lace collars and fichus left over from her mother's trousseau and invited the neighbors in to say goodbye. There are still people in Joncy who reckon time according to the day Armande followed the movers to Monthelie in her car. "That was before Mademoiselle moved to Monthelie," the butcher will say when he is reminiscing. Or "That was two Easters after Mademoiselle went away."

Armande was the last Douhairet in Joncy. The first was a knight who arrived with his lord five centuries ago, and stayed to farm, and the locals say that there were always Douhairets in Joncy until Armande moved. Armande is not a sentimental person. Her regrets are practical. She regrets the five hundred bottles of 1947 Volnay-Champans that popped their corks and the two hundred bottles of 1986 Meursault-Santenots that fell and broke and the 1987 Pommards that seem to have skipped their malolactic fermentation. She regrets the land she could have bought and didn't, and the clients she chased away because they came at lunchtime and she was cooking *pommes frites* and couldn't be

---

70. Because of the earlier "brass" detail, we remember that microscope!
71. This echoes the earlier anecdote. Thus, there is no need to elaborate.
72. Implies Armande is superstitious without saying so directly.

interrupted while the oil was hot. But she does not regret the life she left when she added a hyphen to the family name and registered her vineyard as the Domaine Monthelie-Douhairet and moved her narrow lemonwood bed into the master bedroom of the Monthelie house and added a chaste canopy—like one a nun would have, only purple satin.[73]

* * *

The house is near the end of the village, at the edge of the Volnay massif, looking out over a valley known to geologists as the Auxey-Duresses fault and to wine people as a stretch of chalky soil planted mainly in Pinot Noir and producing some nice village reds—not very distinguished, Armande says, but punchy.[74] It is a pretty, postcard village, with its church and its small château and its terracing of old stone houses with fat chimneys and red tile roofs.[75] The vines start almost exactly where the houses stop. There are a couple of fruit trees, for *crème de pêche* and the other Burgundy liqueurs,[76] and then the vines, the rows of vines, slipping down onto the plains and disappearing. Wine villages are like that. Quaint, practical, and unadorned. "*Pas d'histoires*," Armande would say. No nonsense.[77] The land is too valuable for nonsense. No one in Monthelie would think of taking any of it out of vine to build a shop, say, or a new house—which may be why the village stays so picturesque and is a little strange, as if time had stopped here in some other century. It has not changed much in three hundred years. The roof of Armande's house is still covered with its first red tiles. The walls still turn, following the old Auxey road, to meet the barn and form a courtyard that you still enter through a pair of creaking wooden doors, wide enough for an ox-drawn barrel wagon. There is a pale-blue 1988 Renault sedan in the barn now—Armande likes big cars, and she especially likes buying new ones—and Francis and his girlfriend are moving into rooms next to it that must have housed a *femme de la basse-cour* back in the days when there were chickens and geese and pigs in the stalls and coops that Francis uses now for bottling and labelling and filling orders. There is a freight elevator now, too. Armande ordered it for her old *caviste* when he was nearing sixty and, to her mind, getting on. She called an outfit[78] in town that specialized in freight elevators, and a few days later some men appeared in hard hats and shook the village drilling from the labelling room past her private *cave* to the cool, deep vault where Armande keeps the barrels of her new wine.

The elevator[79] doesn't bother Armande. She keeps a kind of upstairs-downstairs relation[80] with the working winery below her in the courtyard. She communicates with the courtyard through an open window,[81] and the courtyard communicates with Armande by way of a steep outdoor stairway that runs up the wall of her house to her front door. The stairway confirms the hierarchies in a small, close world. There are

---

73. Note how Kramer has continued her pattern of making a short statement, followed by longer elaborations that are propelled forward by the use of "and" rather than commas. The final dash sets apart the point that the canopy was like a nun's, only purple satin, causing that detail to linger in our minds. Note, too, that the use of repetition has continued throughout the story. Here "regret" is repeated both for emphasis and because the repetition of words and sounds creates a pleasing quality.

74. While this is not a direct quote, it sounds like Armande's voice.

75. "Postcard" immediately creates a picture of the village in readers' minds. The details that Kramer chooses are indeed the ones that would stand out on a postcard.

76. A subtle way of translating *crème de pêche*.

77. Translation.

78. Armande's voice.

79. The repetition of "elevator" acts as a transition, linking this paragraph to the previous one.

80. A concise way to convey her relationship with the employees. It is also a setup for future references.

81. This echoes the beginning description of Armande calling down for her *petit cocktail*.

times when all the people of a vineyard meet on common ground—the harvest, say, and the harvest feast, which is traditionally a wine feast, with rich Burgundian wine dishes like *œufs en meurette* and *coq au vin* for the pickers.[82] Armande used to produce a grand feast in the days when her pickers worked for the estate, but she stopped cooking when she started using day labor. First she used Gypsies who were moving north, following the harvest. Now she calls a contractor in Dijon, and he sends her a busload of itinerant farm workers and local university students, earning extra money before the semester starts. She gives them their *grand vin ordinaire,* and she drives to Beaune twice a day and collects their meals—copious meals, which start with charcuterie and go on to stew and flageolets and then to cheeses and dessert[83] from something called a production kitchen, and after the harvest she sends them home. She does not romanticize the people who work the land for her, although she likes it when students come to harvest. A group of students picked for her this year, and brought their girlfriends, and she let them camp all over the house and, on the last day, called her butcher in Meursault and ordered them her favorite cold cuts—headcheese and rillettes and jellied ham and sausage.[84] She says that she prefers a student's sharp mind to a peasant's strong arm and is not much moved by the sight of peasants "toiling in the vines," the way the poets and novelists are.

Every year[85] at the Paulée de Meursault, which is a big winegrowers' banquet where everyone spends the afternoon eating and gossiping and singing and getting drunk on everyone else's best vintages, a visiting writer is presented with a plaque and a hundred bottles for his contribution to what could be called the French agricultural novel, and Armande buys the novels and reads them and gets her sentimental satisfactions that way. She has read Jacques Chapus and Jean Raspail and the Burgundy writer Henri Vincenot, whose peasants are pious and noble and earthy and wise and so strenuously good that they read like Tolstoy cast in argot. She has a weakness for genre—but not at home, tracking mud on the living-room rug. She prefers it in books and berets and an occasional exchange of weather forecasts at the butcher's. Like most French people, she believes, at heart, more in common etiquette than in common ground.[86] She is at home to the butcher and the barrelmaker and the old sisters selling soap, but the peasants who pick her grapes do not sit down if they have business "upstairs"[87] in Armande's house. They stand and state that business with their caps in hand,[88] and once they have stated it they go downstairs.

Armande runs the Domaine Monthelie-Douhairet from the dining-room table. It is not her favorite table—it belongs to a set of gloomy oak dining-room furniture that her grandfather bought, and no one ever bothered replacing—but when people describe her it is usually at that table, sitting straight in a tall, carved chair, with her ledger open and her papers and waybills all spread out around her and a *petit cocktail* by her right hand.[89]

---

82. The dash sets the example apart and calls attention to it.
83. The specific details of the meals make them vivid.
84. Again, note the concrete detail.
85. Transition.
86. The repetition creates a pleasing play on words.
87. The single word "upstairs" reminds us of her upstairs-downstairs relationship with her employees.
88. The detail of the workers standing with caps in hand conjures up a vivid image, allowing readers to picture the scene.
89. The specific detail of this description enables readers to see Armande at work: her erect posture; the tall, carved chair; the open ledger; the bills spread out about her; the *petit cocktail.* Note how very specific Kramer is. The cocktail is in her *right* hand. The use of dashes stresses the fact that her grandfather bought the table.

She has never used the office. She says that maybe the Germans spoiled the office for her. One of the German commandants kept his bed there, and another used it for interrogations, and after that no one in the family managed to restore it, so to speak, to the rest of the house. Armande tried once, after her mother died. She took an old picture of her father (he was dedicating a monument, and Armande thought he looked intrepid)[90] and had it enlarged and hung it up and waited for the ghosts of the five commandants to disappear, but nothing happened, and, besides, by then she was beginning to like working where she was.[91]

Armande did not bring much of her own to Monthelie—no dowry, no nursery furniture, none of the things that refresh a house and a heritage when a young woman takes it over and starts a family and dispels the tyranny of other, earlier women with new plates and new curtains and a new man and a change of wallpaper.[92] In France, in Armande's day, being a spinster meant being a kind of custodian. Armande did not decorate[93] her life. She did not really replace anything or restore anything or throw anything away or have a barn sale and start over with a lot of empty room.[94] It was considered unseemly and aggressive, and even a little suggestive, for a mademoiselle like Armande to announce herself, like a bride. The price of her plainness was to look after another woman's household until a real bride—a niece, or a nephew's wife—could claim it, and this, mainly, is what Armande did. At fifty-two, she dug herself a secret garden—fitted her bedroom out with purple satin and old lemonwood and crystal perfume bottles[95] and closed the door and put the key in her pocket, and then she turned over the rest of the house to the conventions of spinsterhood, to the mixture of bric-a-brac and decorum, of fringed velvet and chairs in circles and coy tourist souvenirs, that marks the houses of old women who live alone. The things she buys now are mostly the objects of illness and age and solitude.[96] The new, raised toilet. The color television with its remote control. The reclining orthopedic chair that covers the Chinese rug between her grandmother's statue of two children on a marble couch and the inlaid fruitwood chest with the Empire clock and candelabras. The laminated plastic-wood tea tables, easy to clean, for serving ratafia to clients.[97] The giftshop pottery—the pitchers and coliseums and minarets from her *troisiéme âge* tours which have replaced the children's drawings and the shells and stones

---

90. Not just *any* photo of her father; rather one of him doing what he loved most—dedicating a monument, a detail that echoes the earlier reference. As we proceed through the story, note how these echoes to earlier references add to the story's cohesiveness.

91. Note how Kramer uses "and" to connect the elements of this sentence, but inserts commas and asides for pacing, causing readers to linger slightly over key moments. The sentence also echoes the beginning of the paragraph, giving it a nice, circular sense of completion.

92. The repetition provides a pleasing quality to this list, but notice how Kramer varies the last—and longest—item, saying "none of" rather than "no." By doing so, she avoids monotony and stresses the final item, which becomes its own detailed list. The repetition also adds emphasis.

93. Still another vivid verb that is perfectly suited to Armande.

94. Here, Kramer uses "or," rather than commas, for an effect opposite to that achieved with "and." "Or" tends to cause us to pause a bit more dramatically, and emphatically, than a comma.

95. Details are vital to a story, and knowing *which* ones to omit is even more important. There are no doubt many things Kramer could have told us about Armande's bedroom, but the three she chooses tell us a lot about Armande: the purple satin show us a flamboyant side, the old lemonwood furniture shows us a practical side, the crystal perfume bottles show an unexpected liking for fine things.

96. This serves somewhat as a transition from her past back to the present day.

97. Note here how Kramer uses short sentences rather than a list with items joined by "and" for emphasis and to provide a picture of Armande in her old age. The description of each object is, as usual, detailed, making it vivid.

and bits of junk that families collect on vacations and that become totems, intimate and exclusive.[98]

Armande is stubborn about her pottery. She wants it to have its proper place and its own importance. She is especially fond of her ashtrays. They are covered with little risqué Burgundian epigrams and make her clients laugh. She keeps them in the library, with the family treasures[99]—the signed paisley shawl and the green silk Persian prayer rug and the lace bridal gloves from Tenerife and the Baby Jesus, under a bell jar,[100] and the Monthelie family set of the Encyclopédie. The set is priceless. It was the third set off the press—it was ordered when Diderot was selling subscriptions to finance the project, and over the years it was delivered to Monthelie, book by book, in twenty-eight volumes—and the Monthelie paterfamilias of the moment was so pleased with his purchase that he ordered a second set,[101] as a kind of backup, which Armande keeps hidden in a deep bookcase, behind the first. Armande says that the Monthelie men were Enlightenment men. They made a religion of understanding. They believed in rational man and the perfected mind, and in their own ability to think their way to truth, to *maîtriser*[102] their ignorance, the way the Monthelie women believed in miracles and the power of a wax Jesus strewn with seed pearls and silk flowers under a bell jar,[103] and they put together a library to cover every human "science" from Philosophy to Trigonometry to Justice. The Germans who passed the library every day for four years on their way to the office were too busy looking for secret cellars and hidden wine to pay much attention to Diderot,[104] or to the history of salt, or to the entire chronology of the universe in one volume.[105] As far as Armande can remember, the only book they took was a book of La Fontaine's fables, and, even so, they missed the important La Fontaine, the one with the forty etchings. She says that aside from the La Fontaine the collection has not been altered or expanded in two hundred years, and she is right, from the looks of it. She herself would never think of adding to it. She may keep her ashtrays in the library, and she stores her hip X-rays in a manila envelope on a shelf next to the Encyclopédie, but the books she reads now—the *romans policiers* and the Prix de la Paulée novels and the book about Louis XIV being a Mormon with seventy-two children—are piled on the sideboard in the parlor, where, to her mind, it is "*plus amical.*"[106]

In a way, the library is too much of a family shrine for Armande. She visits it with friends, and she likes to show it off to clients, but she is not at home there. She says that it has nothing to do with the rest of the house. It is too perfect. It is a calm, small, beautifully proportioned room, with a parquet floor and pale cherry panelling—a room for the eighteenth century and for browsing through Diderot with a glass of the same Volnay that Thomas Jefferson liked to drink.[107] Armande's great-great-uncle Charles Clé-

---

98. The repeated references to Armande's *troisième âge* tours and the comparison of the knickknacks to the children's drawings and keepsakes of other families tell us that those trips were the highlight of her life.

99. The fact that she keeps these risqué ashtrays with the family treasures underscores just how much she enjoys being a little bawdy, a little shocking.

100. The Baby Jesus is a setup for future references.

101. A colorful, telling detail: Armande comes from a long line of eccentrics.

102. *Maîtriser* is close enough to "master" to need no translation.

103. Now we understand the significance of the Baby Jesus under the bell jar.

104. The frequent references to Germans reinforce her distaste for them.

105. This detail comes from Kramer actually flipping through the volumes.

106. This sentence is both humorous and revealing: Armande is no intellectual. She prefers detective novels and scandal. There is no need to translate either *romans policiers* or *plus amical.* Even readers who don't understand French will know what they mean.

107. The fact that Thomas Jefferson drank Volnay is unexpected information. While not critical to the story, it is nevertheless interesting and indicates the wine's longstanding esteem.

ment restored it. He was a bibliophile, and a scholar, and a scientist, and he worked in a famous chemistry laboratory in Autun. Armande says that for a while he had the library with him in Autun but that in the end he brought it "home," and the Monthelie women "let in the Jesuits."[108] Letting in the Jesuits meant letting in the Church. The men in Armande's family used to say that if you slammed the door on the Jesuits the women opened the window and they came in anyway. Armande likes to repeat that. It pleases her to think of the Monthelie men now, looking down from their Seat of Reason (which is where she assumes they are) when the priests arrive in Monthelie on a Sunday afternoon for a glass of ratafia and a game of cards and a little cautious conversation about the final disposition of the Monthelie vines. . . .[109]

Hervé Gaboreau, who runs the Crédit Agricole in Nuits-Saint-Georges, says that the Côte d'Or is the only place he knows where no one—absolutely no one[110]—wants to leave the land. In Poitou, where he was born, there is a kind of attrition, but in Burgundy every generation of winegrowers settles down on top of the generation before it, and Gaboreau says it reminds him of a court society that hasn't prepared its succession. He figures that ninety-five per cent of the young winegrowers on the Côte d'Or are living on their parents' land or their wives' parents' land, or have income from a second profession, and that the rest are marginal, with nothing to guarantee their future. Death taxes are progressive in France. They go up quickly, and it is unlikely that a young man, having paid them, will have money left for buying land from the rest of his family. It is more likely that he will have sold his own land, or part of his land, to pay those taxes in the first place. The young don't buy in Burgundy anymore—banks, even agricultural banks like Crédit Agricole, do not lend money to young people any more willingly than they lend money to poor people—and this is one reason everybody is interested in the disposition of the Domaine Monthelie-Douhairet. In the past, good vineyards were often contested, but they rarely left a family entirely. Great vineyards were almost never sold. Three years ago, a tiny parcel of Richebourg and Échézeaux went on the market, and a vintner named Jean Grivot, from Vosne-Romanée, bought it, and the newspapers said it was the first sale of a piece of Richebourg in fifty-three years.[111]

Today, the Burgundians are buying out of Burgundy—into Oregon and Australia. They say that they support their Burgundy "habit" with their vineyards abroad. They love the kangaroos in Australia, and they love le dynamisme américain, but the truth is they do not expect to find anything so particular and so satisfying as their life at home. They want to share their villages with a dozen other winegrowers whose vines have a different age from theirs, and whose caves have a different yeast, and whose barrels have a different flavor, and whose winemaking books have a different family secret. The formulas that interest them lately have less to do with enzymes and malolactic fermentation than with payment schedules and credit sources and investment capital that will somehow make their thirty miles of limestone and marlstone extend forever. They can put out a nice Grand Cru for thirty francs a bottle and sell it at once for a hundred and fifty (and their bankers say that most of them do, and that the ones with no entailments on their land

---

108. The time to use a direct quote is when your subject expresses something in a way that you, the writer, can't improve on, and that's the case here. Kramer then clarifies (in a manner suitable to the story's tone) and uses it to tell us about the Monthelie women's religious bent.

109. The reference to the Sunday afternoon visits echoes the earlier reference to the priests' visits.

110. Dashes are used to emphasize the point.

111. This digression explains why Armande's land is so much in demand, why she is courted. It also provides information on the French wine industry.

are making fortunes).[112] But if that wine has what is called a "difficult adolescence"—if it sits, pallid, for its first six or seven months in bottle[113]—and buyers and writers taste it during those months and word gets around, its price can drop, just like that, and Burgundy suffers.

Armande says that the trouble with Burgundy, and the beauty of Burgundy, is that everything depends on what happens to a few grapes on their way down a very small slope that is exposed and barren on the top and sodden on the bottom. Some people would dispute that Burgundy. There are people who still like to think of Burgundy as circling France—stretching all the way east to Switzerland and north to Belgium and Holland, the way it did in the days of the dukes and Chancellor Rolin. There are people who say that you have to start in Chablis and go south to Beaujolais, and that everything in between is Burgundy—which, from the point of view of the wine, is true. But the heart of Burgundy is really that small slope called the Côte d'Or. Everyone in the wine business wants a piece of it, and there isn't enough of it for the families that are already there.

* * *

Armande and her sister stopped talking once. It was in 1980. Armande was running the land she had inherited and the land her sister had inherited as one estate, and giving her sister half the profits, and the two of them had just agreed to save taxes by turning the estate into what the French call a *société d'exploitation,* with Armande renting the vineyard, in effect, from their company. She was ready to sign the papers—she was in fact on her way to Beaune to sign them—when her sister changed her mind. She offered her land to Armande for ten million francs, which at the time was two million dollars, and gave Armande twenty-four hours to reply. Armande says that she took a piece of paper and did some calculating and decided that, with loans at the bank costing about eight per cent, and the income from two million dollars' worth of the Côte d'Or running, at best, four per cent, it would take her twenty years even to be able to meet her interest payments—and she said no. Her sister sold most of the land to a speculator from Meursault (who turned it around a few months later for a big profit), and for a while Armande and her sister stopped talking.[114] It was the first argument over land in the family, but, then, as Armande says, the family was lucky. No one before had had to make a living from it. It was only Armande who lived, as the French say, *de ses vignes.*

Today,[115] Armande is land rich. Her parcels of Pommard alone are worth about eighty-five thousand francs an *ouvrée*—an *ouvrée* is the yield in wine from one day's work by one man, and Burgundians use it when they talk land prices, despite the fact that the yield on any estate varies with the year and the age of the vines and the technology[116]—and that means that if she were buying right now they would cost her more than a hundred and thirty thousand dollars an acre. Armande makes a lot of money. It is the local habit to deny it, but most people in Burgundy with family land make a lot of money.[117] They do not make nearly enough, though, to buy more land at today's prices.

---

112. Kramer uses parentheses to insert a brief aside from another interview, without interrupting the flow of the story.

113. The wine term "difficult adolescence" adds flavor to the story, but needs to be translated into everyday language for lay readers.

114. Kramer ends the anecdote at the point where it began, giving it a sense of wholeness and cohesiveness.

115. Time transition.

116. Because the explanation of *ouvrée* is a little lengthy, Kramer sets it off with dashes.

117. The repetition of "makes a lot of money" emphasizes the point.

(An *ouvrée* of Grand Cru on the Côte de Nuits costs sixty-five thousand dollars, which makes the land worth more than half a million dollars an acre, and wine-growers say that the only way to break even buying land like that is to find customers stupid[118] enough to pay you five or six times what your neighbor charges for the same wine.) When Armande talks about her sister now, she shrugs and says, "My sister doesn't love the land." Her sister was a disappointment, like any other disappointment. It was the surprise that hurt her. Once the surprise was gone, she got over it. She regrets, sometimes, that she didn't try to buy her sister's parcel of Volnay-Frémiets, because she likes Volnay, but she is not bitter. She knows that Burgundians are venal, and in a way she approves, and, then, too, she is proud of having been decisive, of having settled the question of two million dollars' worth of land in—by her own reckoning—six or seven minutes.[119]

Living so long alone, Armande is used to making difficult decisions by herself.[120] She was the first person to produce a Monthelie white. None of the neighbors tried before her. The neighbors thought that she was being foolish. But she had read in *Le Bien Public*, the Dijon paper,[121] that white wines were getting fashionable, and she noticed that her best clients—the ones she always invited to sit down in the parlor for a glass of ratafia[122]—were beginning to ask if perhaps she had some white open, so she thought she would do well with a Monthelie white, and she was right. Every year now, she goes to the *mairie* in Monthelie and declares thirty-five barrels of white and eighty-five barrels of red, which is what the *appellation* board allows her to produce, and stashes a few more barrels for "personal emergencies,"[123] and she says that the Monthelie white starts selling right away. She counts her new white wine among the important decisions she has taken, on a level with her latest Renault and her freight elevator[124] and the air-conditioner she installed in her *caves* four years ago and the pale-gray blouse, with dark-gray insets in the sleeves, that she bought for too much money at the Louis Féraud boutique in Beaune and wore to the 1988 Paulée. She has never had trouble making decisions before, but she is having trouble now.[125] She thinks about her sister's land, chopped up and in the hands of strangers, and it makes her uneasy. She does not much mind what happens to the Monthelie house. The library is already willed, and she has presented her wooden press—it is a huge old squirrel-wheel press—to the Hospices. But she minds what happens to the Domaine Monthelie-Douhairet. She does not want her vineyard to die when she does.[126]

* * *

The people who work for Armande are known in the neighborhood as "Mademoiselle's team," and they are an odd lot, assembled over time and bound mainly by their affection

---

118. The word "stupid" suits the story's irreverent tone.

119. Armande's pride in making what turned out to be a faulty decision in six or seven minutes shows us something about her personality. It is also humorous.

120. The repetition of making difficult decisions serves as a transition.

121. It is more vivid to include the actual name of the newspaper rather than simply saying "the Dijon paper."

122. "The ones she always invited to sit down in the parlor for a glass of ratafia" is a colorful—and very Armande—way of identifying her best customers.

123. Armande's voice.

124. These echo earlier references. The overall list reveals a lot about her values.

125. Decision-making again serves as a transition into her current predicament. The repetition also adds to the cohesiveness.

126. This brings us back to the crux of the story and the real tension that drives it forward: What will happen to Armande's land?

for her and a determination to protect her from each other. She has special arrangements with them all. She says it is a matter of old ties and responsibilities, and of keeping the state out of her affairs, but it is clear that she is jealous of her arrangements. She likes the complicity. Everyone connected to the vineyard has a secret, or thinks he has a secret, and everyone enjoys, or thinks he enjoys, her confidence. Armande believes that it gives her staff a lively interest in the business.[127]

Her old *caviste* was called Fernand.[128] He lived in the courtyard from 1956 until he moved to Bresse, a month after the vinification this year, and he and his wife, Denise, raised six children and several litters of Brittany spaniels in the rooms next to the garage,[129] but twenty-two years ago Fernand had a heart attack and officially retired, and for twenty-two years everyone in Monthelie pretended that Fernand and Denise were simply camped in the courtyard, waiting for their house in Bresse to be painted. Fernand came from Bresse. He used to be a chicken farmer, raising *poulets de Bresse*, on a diet of milk and corn. It broke his heart when people in Paris and Lyons started buying cheap, feed-yard chickens instead of fine, fat, farm chickens like his, and he sold his coops and moved to Burgundy, with a letter from his parish priest to a priest in Volnay who knew that Armande was looking for somebody to run her cellars. Armande says that Fernand was a very handsome young man. He pressed the grapes himself. He would take off his clothes and lower himself into a smelly vat and jump for hours on a crust of crushed, fermenting grapes, until he was exhausted and the crust broken and the grapes pressed back into their juices, and Armande would always come down to the barn to watch him, because she liked the sight of such a fine, *interesting* male body at work. He gave up pressing five years ago—ordered a fancy vat for the *pigeage* and an automatic *pigeur* to crush the pips and electric pumps to bring the juices to the surface. He says he had to stop, because of his bad heart, but Armande likes to say she made him stop because he was getting old and a little flabby and not so handsome naked. She lost interest, and replaced him with a machine.[130]

Fernand preferred the old ways of making wine. He said that a pair of feet were better than any pump—that feet pressed better and mixed better and added a tang that no oenologist could reproduce—and that a pair of hands were better than any machine for sorting labels and pasting them on bottles. He was always wandering around in the winery, in his slippers and his blue overalls and a floppy poplin hat that he had bought for shooting, looking for something his hands could do. Up to the end, he would still "fine" wine by beating four egg whites and putting them in the wine barrel and letting the impurities adhere,[131] and he would still clean barrels with an old iron tool that looked like

---

127. The trick to writing good humor is to lay out the facts and let them speak for themselves. If they are indeed funny, the reader will come to that conclusion without the writer having to be obvious. Here Kramer enhances that humor with the inclusion of contradictory asides: "Everyone connected to the vineyard has a secret, or thinks he has a secret, and everyone enjoys, or thinks he enjoys, her confidence."

128. After an introductory paragraph, Kramer sets out to elaborate on the employees, introducing them one by one. First comes Fernand.

129. The juxtaposition of the children and Brittany spaniels implies that Armande places children and dogs on the same level.

130. Another example of Kramer's humor coming through in the material. The art of this comes from the selection of material: the image of a nude young man crushing grapes, Armande coming to the barn to watch him, her joke about replacing him with a machine.

131. Kramer unobtrusively explains what "fine" means. In doing so, she is specific: *four* egg whites, not just egg whites.

a pitted scythe,[132] and he would still mend a forty-year-old wooden vat rather than ferment his wine in an expensive new steel one.

Armande has eight fermenting vats, and by now two of them are steel—lined with enamel and warmed and cooled by circulating water.[133] There is a new Swiss Grand Cru press, which works by air pressure (next to the old press, which worked on oil pressure, like a furnace),[134] and there is a new bottling machine, and, of course, the air-conditioner.[135] Fernand didn't like them much, but Francis likes them. Francis is twenty-two and holds practical views—which are that steel vats are easier to maintain than wooden vats, and that air-conditioners are useful in the heat and the cold, and that the only thing to be said for jumping up and down in a vat of fermenting grapes is that it keeps you in shape for rugby.[136] . . .

Armande likes Francis's good nature and his red cheeks and his eager face.[137] She likes the fact that he works in the *caves* on Saturdays, receiving clients, because Fernand would never work Saturdays after he retired. And she especially likes it that Francis is moving to Monthelie with his girlfriend, because to Armande's mind a *"union libre"* will add some spice to village life.

Francis says he never expected anyone as old as Armande. He worried that Armande, being old and Catholic, would disapprove of a *caviste* with a girlfriend, but Armande said right away that given what she had seen of marriage she was "for free love,"[138] and that was when Francis knew that *"le courant passait entre nous"*—which is a way of saying there were good vibrations[139]—and he took the job. He loves the vineyard. There is no land in his family—his father was a car mechanic, and his mother works as a secretary at the Beaune Ponts et Chaussées[140]—but there was no business in the family, either. He enrolled at the Lycée Viticole in Beaune, and stayed for three years, and then he worked in a vineyard and winery in Saint-Romain. Working like that—working a little on the land, then a little in the *caves*[141]—he started to distinguish between the people who liked growing grapes and the people who liked making wine. He started to distinguish, he says, between the cultivators and the cooks. Right now, the job of cultivating vines absorbs him. He says if your graft is weak, or your subsoil, or if you cheat on the trimming to get a bigger harvest, there is not much you can do in a winery—even a winery full of fancy machines and fancy wine scientists—to produce a decent bottle.

Francis's mentor[142] in wine is Armande's friend André Porcheret. Porcheret worked for ten years as *maître des vignes* and chief winemaker for the Hospices, which have a hundred and twenty-five acres in vine on the Côte de Beaune, and now he works for

---

132. The simile compares the tool to something familiar to most readers. The choice of a scythe is fitting since it, too, is an agricultural tool.

133. The aside describes the steel vats and what they do, thus educating lay readers.

134. Again, a comparison of the unfamiliar with the familiar.

135. Air-conditioner serves as a transition into Francis, the present *caviste*.

136. Kramer uses a list to tightly summarize the differences between Fernand and Francis. Here she again precedes each "and" with a comma, which causes us to linger on each difference.

137. The momentum picks up again with "and" and the omission of the commas.

138. While *union libre* should be clear to readers who don't understand French, Kramer nevertheless provides a delayed translation.

139. Kramer again translates an expression that would probably not be clear to the non-French-speaking reader.

140. Dashes provide an economical way to insert background information here.

141. Kramer creates a pleasing sort of progressive repetition: She first repeats "working" and then from the second phrase, picks up "little" for the second repetition.

142. Francis serves as a transition into André Porcheret.

Lalou Bize-Leroy, of the Domaine de La Romanée Conti, who bought a neglected estate on the Côte de Nuits last year and turned it over to Porcheret to nurture. Porcheret comes from a village near Saint-Romain. His parents were sharecroppers. They rented vines *en métayage*,[143] and never made any money, and every one of their seven children left the land except him. He says that for a while he thought he would rather see the world than stay in Burgundy. He was twenty-four and working for a wine company called Clerget, and when a chance came to drive the company truck to Paris he took off with a consignment of wine and stopped at a *routier* bar and started drinking and playing pinball and looking at the Paris girls, and the next thing he knew it was eight days later and the truck was lost and the wine with it, and he thought that the Champs-Elysées was the Avenue de la République in Beaune.[144] He is fifty-two now, a big, impatient, opinionated, exuberant man who speaks his mind with a roaring Burgundy accent and has a lot of local authority and is devoted to Armande. He has been working with Armande in his free time for over ten years. They met one day to settle some boundary markers between Armande's Volnay-Champans and a parcel of Volnay that belonged to the Hospices, and after that he started stopping by, after work on Thursdays, to advise her. Once you talk to her, you want to help her, is the way he explains it.[145] Soon he was looking after Armande's vines. . . .

Armande worried that maybe Mme. Bize-Leroy would be jealous of the time her *vigneron* spent on the vines of an old mademoiselle with a strong character of her own. Porcheret never worried. His interest in Monthelie-Douhairet gives him something of his own, and he is passionate about it. He says that when a busload of pieceworkers arrives at Noëllat to harvest grapes or work the bottling line, he thinks about the harvest at Armande's—about how everybody, even the pieceworkers, makes a family for Mademoiselle. The harvest this year was early and dry, and the grapes were heavy and sweet, and Porcheret brought in a fortune in grapes and sent them through his new steel chute onto his new sorting table and pressed them with his new automatic press[146]—the one with "three-dimensional drainage"—and part of him wished he were at Monthelie, bossing everyone around, while Fernand beat the egg whites and Francis raced all over the place on his tractor and Mademoiselle sat upstairs, with a *petit cocktail*, entering each truckload of grapes in the 1989 ledger.[147]

The man who supervises the harvest at Armande's is an old friend of hers, whom I will call Claude.[148] Claude has been vinifying for Armande for nearly twenty years, and Porcheret is equivocal about him, because Claude has a degree, and Porcheret does not think much of people who learn their wine-making from textbooks. Porcheret says that the "experts" produced by wine schools like the Lycée Viticole in Beaune and wine-science departments like the one at the University of Dijon or Montpellier are "like the doctors who give you twelve shots in the ass after you've got better"—by which he means that when your soil is good and your summer has been hot and it has not rained at the harvest there is not much for an oenologist to do except to say that the wine needs

143. Here the translation precedes the French: They worked the vineyard as sharecroppers.
144. Kramer uses "and" to move this colorful anecdote forward energetically.
145. Rather than use a direct quote, Kramer paraphrases in such a way that she maintains his voice.
146. The repetition of "new" emphasizes the point that Noëllat is a more state-of-the-art winery.
147. This concise description of Armande's operation echoes earlier references, tying the pieces of the story together and thus creating cohesiveness.
148. "Whom I will call Claude" is a skillful way of saying Kramer changed his name.

work,[149] and hope that his clients believe him. Claude once worked for a big shipper on the Côte d'Or. He was *maître des chais*—a kind of warehouse production manager.[150] He had hundreds of thousands of bottles of stock to account for, and two hours of tasting every day, and an assembly line that could turn out eight or ten thousand bottles an hour during the bottling season, and he started coming to Armande's "for the human scale." It was good for his nerves, he says, and good for his morale, to work in a *cuverie* where you didn't have to rush the wine—where you could say that the wine was too *mou*, that it had to wait for another few months in barrel.[151]

Claude was always having to rush the wine at his shipper's. It frustrated what he calls his oenological interest in the things you can do for a wine when it is in a vat or a barrel, or even in a bottle. He likes to think of himself, making wine, as a father watching over a sleeping child, or a child who has just left home for a pitiless world. "The wine is out in the world, all alone," he says whenever he has an audience. "We are not there to defend it, but we are *morally* responsible."[152] Claude is a smooth man and a smooth talker, and, like Mme. Bize-Leroy and a lot of wine people, he has invented a vocabulary for his self-interest. He loves to talk what Burgundians call serious wine talk when he visits Armande, with his white hair groomed and his corduroys pressed and a V-neck pullover that makes him look like an aging blind date—and Armande loves to torment him.[153] When Claude sighs and tells her that her village wine is "artisanal and true," she says that her wine was meant to be "drunk and pissed in a single day." When he talks about "*l'élevage du vin*," she says that the word "*élevage*" reminds her of a cow.[154] But she depends on him. She says he is fussy about corks—Armande still frets about the Volnay-Champans that popped its corks[155]—and fussy about grafting. Burgundians have been grafting since phylloxera arrived on the Côte d'Or, in 1878. They use American rootstock and graft it with Burgundy clones, and then they plant the graft in soil that has been "disinfected" and analyzed to a depth of two or three feet.[156] Claude is fond of the process. He likes running into the laboratory in Beaune to choose the clones and discuss the magnesium reports. He says it keeps him in the avant-garde.

Claude used to visit Armande on Friday, after work, and come back for the day on Saturday, but he is restless, now that he has retired from the wine shipper and has no warehouse to inspect, and he tends to drop in on odd days and at odd hours. It distresses[157] Armande, who likes to stagger the visits of her admirers. Armande preferred it when she could count on a visit from Porcheret on Thursday night and a visit from Claude on Friday and a visit from one of the Beaune priests on Sunday, and knew that

---

149. Kramer's clarification of what Porcheret means also provides information on winemaking. In using Porcheret's views on experts, he serves as a transition into Claude.

150. The aside translates *maître des chais* in an informal manner in keeping with the tone of the story.

151. A loose translation of *mou*.

152. Here Kramer uses a direct quote because, beyond what he is actually saying, it conveys a lot about Claude. As she then tells us directly: "he is a smooth man and a smooth talker." It also demonstrates his "invented" vocabulary.

153. This tight little passage gives us a delightful picture of his visits and implies a flirtation between him and Armande.

154. This exchange says as much about Armande as it does Claude. Besides providing an example of her teasing, it shows that she is down-to-earth and prefers a more no-nonsense way of talking about wine. As we have already seen, she does not put on airs.

155. This repetition implies that this is an episode she dwells on.

156. Informs readers about winemaking.

157. "Distresses" is the perfect word choice for an elderly French lady—more fitting or on-target than, say, "upsets" or "bothers."

nobody would overlap. She worries that Claude will find out about Porcheret's interest in the estate (which, of course, he has), or that Porcheret will tell people that Claude is working for her (which, of course, they know already),[158] and that somehow she will lose control. People in the wine trade used to tell Armande that with Claude doing the wine-making and Fernand looking after the wine in barrel it was safe to say that her wines "made themselves," from vintage to vintage. But Armande is fond of Claude, and she understands his disappointments. He had wanted to be a winegrower himself. His parents were winegrowers. They were brave people—*résistants*. There were always three or four *résistants* hiding in their house during the Occupation, and Claude, who was a boy when the Germans came, carried messages for the *résistants* and brought them food. The Germans put him to work as a field hand, and then they sent him as a laborer to Germany. He says that all he thought about during those years was coming home to his parents' vineyard. They had twenty acres in vine—twenty acres and four children—and by the time Claude had finished the *lycée*[159] and apprenticed in town, washing bottles and cleaning barrels, it was clear that four children couldn't live off twenty acres, not if they wanted families of their own. He ceded his part to his oldest brother, and went to college to earn a diploma that would let him work for someone else. . . .

* * *

Armande's uncle was one of the first growers on the Côte de Beaune to commercialize his wines. He started bottling to sell in 1934. He had mainly French clients, and never a big production. He kept his red wines for three years—two in barrel and one in bottle—before he sold them, and he put a lot away for himself, but he had a following, and it included a New York wine importer who started buying the family's wine. Armande inherited a couple of private Swiss and Belgian clients but no important foreign connection to replace what she called "my uncle's American," and she liked most foreigners, because foreigners liked buying. She especially liked Americans. She liked the way they did business. (Claude had told her that if you went bankrupt in America all you had to do was change your company name and you could start over.)[160] Americans took getting used to, she said, but over the long term they were amusing.

The fact that Armande was alone and available gave her what the French would call a *fidèle clientèle*.[161] Most winegrowers didn't open their doors from Saturday noon to Monday morning—weekends in the French provinces are private, family times, and not for business—but Armande had no family to fill her weekends, and she would open *her* doors at any hour of the day or night, and word got around. She says that once she bought her elevator her weekends were "bathroom to cellar." She was always shouting into the courtyard[162] at eleven on a Saturday night to tell some German stockbroker or honeymooning American couple to wait a minute, she would be right down, and then rushing into the bathroom to change from her nightgown into a skirt and sweater. She says that she had no choice, that whenever she turned anyone away he would simply appear again, at six in the morning, ready to taste. Her favorite American was a Mormon

---

158. The asides add information and humor and are much more interesting and in keeping with the tone than longer explanations.

159. We all know what *lycée* means. No need to translate here.

160. This aside again tells us something about Claude and how he views the world.

161. Most of us can make out *fidèle clientèle*. No need to translate.

162. Because of the earlier setup, we can visualize Armande opening the window and shouting down to the courtyard.

plastic surgeon who specialized in grafting big toes onto fingers that had lost a joint.[163] She met him through one of his French colleagues—an old Monthelie client who brought him to her—and he started coming every year, and Armande says that every year he came with a different wife. He told Armande that he liked to find a wife and keep her for a few years and a few children and then "retire" her and take a new one—someone younger and fertile. Armande claims that by the time he met her he had seven wives at home and seventeen children and a proscribed fondness for good Burgundy.[164] He got her interested in Mormons. "*Ce n'est pas une mauvaise idée, sept femmes,*" she says. "*C'est pour leur race.*" Whenever he appears now, with a new wife, she takes him aside and tells him to come alone next time. She says if he comes alone he can find a French wife—and that way he will have saved on airfare.

* * *

Five years ago,[165] Armande met Russell Hone and started exporting seriously. Russell is a forty-five-year-old Scot in the wine trade. He made his reputation in Burgundy in the seventies—he was working for a Bordeaux wine broker who wanted to expand into Burgundy—when he discovered a cellar of rare wines in the town of Gueugnon, bought them up at a couple of dollars a bottle, and sold them at Christie's for his firm at roughly fifty times the price. By the time Armande got to know him, he had settled in Burgundy. He was divorced and living in Bouilland, a half hour from Monthelie, with an American woman named Rebecca Wasserman, who had a wine-brokerage business and bought from growers like Armande on behalf of stores and clients and importers abroad. Becky Wasserman ran her business out of an old stone farmhouse, and she was someone unique to the Burgundy wine trade, someone "in the American style," people said. She was a small, pretty woman with a soft voice and a mop[166] of curly hair and a kind of assurance about wine that nobody expected in a foreigner. She had an enormous influence in Burgundy, despite the fact that she was not only American and a woman but a divorced American woman, raising two boys on her own. She was known for her "nose." She sought out the good, small, independent Burgundy *vignerons* who had been selling mainly to old family clients, and introduced them abroad to people who would never have tasted their wines without her, people whose Burgundy had been the famous vintages and the famous names. Russell had heard about Armande from a friend in Becky's office—had heard that a Mlle. Douhairet had some very nice 1982s and that he ought to try them.[167] When he finally met her—"met this very old lady with a lot of humor," Russell says—he remembered the name and the year and asked to visit her in Monthelie. Armande was delighted with Russell. He was a dry, shy, courteous, compassionate man—and he took to her.[168] He liked her company. She was unpretentious and direct, like the people in Scotland. He wished her well, and he worried about her wine and her future, and so he began stopping by, trying not to interfere, trading wine gossip and advice and listening while she sorted out whatever problems were on her mind and needed solving.

---

163. Can't you hear Armande reveling in this! No wonder she likes this man.
164. By combining these three items in the same list, Kramer shows us how Armande puts his love of Burgundy on the same level with his wives and children.
165. Transition.
166. This word fits the story's tone and implies that Becky Wasserman is, like Armande, a down-to-earth, no-nonsense woman.
167. While this is not a direct quote, it carries the flavor of Russell Hone repeating it.
168. The dash separates the fact that he liked her and thus emphasizes it.

At first, whenever he came to see her Armande would call the neighbors and show him off. "Come see my tall Scotsman," she would say, and the neighbors would come, because there was no one in Monthelie nearly as tall as Russell Hone, and never had been, and the neighbors were hoping he would roar or howl or do something ferocious, like the warriors in "Macbeth." . . .

By now,[169] there is a great bond between Russell and Armande. Armande stood up for him last spring when he and Becky Wasserman got married—she bought two new dresses, one for the *mairie* and one for the wedding lunch[170]—and in a way it made them family. Russell and Becky keep an eye on her. They take her to the Burgundy parties, and see to it that she is in the foreign wine catalogues and that the foreign buyers taste her wines—and if the buyers have no time for Monthelie they arrange tasting at their own house.[171] They like her wines. Becky says that years of making tough, radical decisions are in those wines. People are buying them now in Washington and San Francisco and London and Tokyo,[172] and Armande wonders if they are satisfied, if they wouldn't be just as happy with some good Belgian beer and an occasional white from Alsace—like her. She worries about her Japanese clients, because she knows there is not much room in Japan, and she has no idea where they are going to store their bottles. She worries about all her clients. She says it is part of the service. She knows that there are days when a wine tastes good and days when the same wine tastes awful. You can never predict them.[173] So she worries about her clients, and she worries[174] about the critics who have been coming around, now that she is—as she likes to tell Porcheret—"international." The wine critics make her nervous. They can easily hit the bad day, and, as far as Armande is concerned, they never say the really interesting things anyway. They never sniff the air in her cellar, the way Becky did last spring, and say that the yeast there is like a wonderful interpretation of a Mozart sonata.[175] A wine critic is more apt to say that her cellar is "rustic." Robert Parker, the American wine critic, called it rustic. He came to Burgundy last year and tasted Armande's 1986 reds and gave them a middling score, and then he called her Monthelie "cheesy and musty" and said that her Monthelie Premier Cru smelled like damp chestnuts and her Volnay-Champans like feces—that they were worth trying if you wanted to know how red Burgundies must have tasted eighty years ago. Armande went to the tasting with Porcheret and Claude, and sat through it with her hand on her cane, looking stoic.[176] She says now it was a wonder everything didn't taste like feces, because by the time Mr. Parker got to her wines he must have tasted thirty or forty others. . . .

* * *

169. Transition.

170. While this aside is not critical to the story, it shows us that this was an important occasion for Armande and thus how she feels about Russell Hone and Becky Wasserman.

171. Following her pattern, Kramer follows up on the statement that they keep an eye on Armande with a sentence listing examples of precisely how they look out for her.

172. The use of "and" rather than commas gives the feeling of people all over the world buying Armande's wine.

173. This brief passages adds to our understanding of wine.

174. The repetition of "worries" emphasizes just how much Armande worries about her customers.

175. Becky's comparison of the yeasty smell of a wine cellar to a Mozart sonata is a delightful addition to the story and gives us a glimpse into her personality. The fact that Armande repeats this conveys her fondness for Becky.

176. The detail of her hand on the cane and the stoic look conjures up an image of the moment for readers.

Armande has a lot more stories to tell,[177] now that she is international. She has stories about Belgians who will only buy deep-red wine that looks like blood, and stories about Germans who get sick from her Meursault-Santenots, and stories about Englishmen who serve it as an aphrodisiac. She has stories about Japanese businessmen sending Burgundy to their friends so that their friends can calculate, in yen, exactly how much (or how little) the businessmen regard them. She has stories about Americans who shop with a scorecard culled from Robert Parker in their pocket—they want to get the most points, on a scale from fifty to a hundred, for the least money—and stories[178] about Englishmen who don't like to pay their bills. She says you have to watch the English when they start to pretend that paying bills, or even talking about paying bills, is bad manners, something gentlemen don't do. Once, an English importer bought a hundred cases of her Monthelie '85—it was selling for thirty-five francs a bottle then, and everyone wanted it—and liked it so much he ordered more. He came back with a truck, and wanted to drive right off with her last seventy cases, and avoid the broker's fee.[179] Armande said no. She said no that week to the Englishman, and no to the American Embassy, which had ordered fifty cases and wanted Armande to file tax-free forms because the Embassy, on the Avenue Gabriel in Paris, was really the United States, and no[180] to a winegrower from Mercurey who wanted to "let Mademoiselle retire," and to rent her land for one of his children. She was exhausted and cross. She missed the biweekly Saturday-night Mass at the Monthelie church, and had to make do with a television Mass at eleven on Sunday morning, on Antenne 2. She has an invalid's dispensation to worship, as it were, on television. She takes it when she has to, but she doesn't feel right, and she certainly doesn't feel rewarded—only that another duty has been performed. Armande believes that church is for Masses and television is for dirty movies, like the movie that made her trip, changing channels, and caused the problem to begin with. . . .[181]

The grower from Mercurey never got very far with Armande. He was what the French call a *gros paysan*—a rich peasant.[182] He had a big family, with a lot of cousins and a lot of vines, and he was very commercial. Armande had heard that he liked to hand out fancy promotion flyers, in four languages, about all the three-star Michelin restaurants that served his wine. His interest in Armande's vines was practical. His son was already working on the family land, and he wanted to settle vineyards on his three daughters, like dowries. He worked it out according to their charm and their prospects, and approached Armande. It wasn't easy to see Armande. No one he asked would introduce him, and when he finally called her it did not go well, because Mlle. Douhairet[183] told him she was going to live forever, and he told her, straight out, "*Ce n'est pas évident.*" Armande repeated the story to her neighbors, who thought that if she was ever going to rent or sell her land she should think of someone close to home, someone like Michel Lafarge, in Volnay, where there were forty winegrowers and all the land was taken. Lafarge had four

---

177. The stories echo back to the profile's beginning, contributing to cohesiveness.

178. The *repetition* of "stories" and the recitation of examples demonstrate that she does indeed have "a lot more stories."

179. Kramer entertains us with an anecdote to illustrate Armande's point about Englishmen. Note how the specific detail ("a hundred cases," "Monthelie '85," "thirty-five francs," "her last seventy cases") makes the story even more vivid.

180. The repetition of "no" adds emphasis.

181. This echoes the story's beginning and how she came to break her hip.

182. Translation.

183. The use of "Mlle. Douhairet," rather than "Armande," conveys a sense of the haughty tone she must have used with the Mercurey grower.

children, too, and twenty-five acres—some of them touching Armande's parcels of Volnay. Lafarge was a neighbor. He was someone to count on. You could taste the "style" in his wines, and he was sure to understand Armande's style, and the special robes that distinguished the wines of Monthelie-Douhairet, and try to preserve them. He would agree with Armande that a real oenologist is someone formed by his own *caves* and his own land and his own family.[184]

Armande added the name to a mental list of people she calls "interested parties," along with the Beaune priests, and the man from Tokyo with the unpronounceable name[185] who had a business importing wine and surfboards, and the Belgian doctors with an investment club, and the Germans who were longing to tell their friends in Stuttgart that they were Burgundy winegrowers, and the three large young men from California who arrived at her house one day—one of them in a ponytail and jeans and earrings—and showed her pictures of their own vineyard, which turned out to be the size of Burgundy.[186]

* * *

All the attention was invigorating for Armande. It revived her at a time when her hip hurt and her leg was giving her a lot of trouble, and she was having a hard job getting used to the idea that after twenty-two years Fernand's house in Bresse was finally painted—that Fernand was packing up and leaving Monthelie and going home.[187] She went to the hairdresser in Meursault and had a permanent and a henna rinse,[188] and then she started driving the blue Renault for the first time since her operation—and brought in her share of the best harvest on the Côte d'Or in thirty years. Armande's is not a great vineyard— *pás superstar,* they say in Pickwicks—but there are wine people who think that arguing about "great" and "good" on the Côte d'Or in a year like 1989 is splitting hairs, and even Armande had to admit that her 1989 Volnay and her 1989 Pommard, and even her 1989[189] Monthelie, were going to be fine. "Nice and scruffy," she called the Monthelie, quoting the one wine writer she approves of, for his manners—an Englishman named Clive Coates, who comes visiting every year and takes notes in her *caves* in such a neat, tiny hand that he reminds Armande of Maître Prélot, the Beaune *notaire.* But once the vinification was over Armande was alone a lot, waiting for winter, waiting for Fernand to go, waiting for Francis to "redecorate" the rooms next to the garage with what she imagined would be rugby posters and the various accessories of a *union libre,* waiting[190] for the doctors to decide if it was worth opening the veins in her bad leg—her eighty-three-

---

184. This passage about Lafarge sounds like the neighbors saying this to Armande. This sense is conveyed through "He was someone to count on," "you," and "sure." The repetition of "his own" sounds like the neighbors trying to convince Armande.

185. "Unpronounceable name" lets us hear Armande's voice.

186. Note how specific Kramer is in her listing of "interested parties."

187. Fernand's move and the echoes of earlier references give us a sense that the story is winding down. Kramer is preparing us for an end.

188. At eighty-three, Armande still colors her hair, she is still a *rousse.* The story is almost over, and this and the cane and the description of her as a young woman are the only physical details Kramer has given, yet they are enough. With them and with her superbly conveyed personality, we are satisfied. The goal of every good profile should be to let readers vicariously come to know the subject, and this one has succeeded marvelously at doing that.

189. The repetition of "1989" emphasizes the fact that it has been a very good year for wine.

190. The repetition of "waiting" conveys the feeling of time weighing heavily on Armande.

year-old[191] bad leg, she said—to ease the pressure. She was looking forward to the Paulée, which is always held in November, the Monday after the Hospices auction. She had reserved places for herself and Porcheret, and for the doctor who fixed her hip in Dracy—and one more place that Russell was going to use for Rusty Staub, the American baseball player, who was coming to Burgundy to be inducted into the Confrérie des Chevaliers du Tastevin, and wanted to join them—but she never received her tickets, and when she called Meursault a woman at the Paulée office told her that they were cancelling twenty local seats to make room for "important foreigners," and that four of those local seats were hers. The woman said that Armande could always come "next year," and Armande replied that she might be dead next year, and the woman said, well, in that case, she could come the year after.[192] Armande got all her seats, in the end, and Becky and Russell shared her table, and everyone drank a nice 1923 Volnay from her private *cave*,[193] but Armande was dispirited. A few weeks later,[194] Henri Meyer, across the road, noticed that her shutters were closed. It was nine-thirty on a Saturday morning, and Armande always opened her shutters at eight-thirty, even on weekends, and Henri and his wife got worried and broke into the house and found the television on and Armande lying on her orthopedic chair, with a cerebral hemorrhage.

Armande is in the hospital now[195]—a big new hospital on the edge of town which was built by the Hospices de Beaune with money from the wine auctions. It is a practical place. There are no glazed tiles dancing across the roof, the way there are at the Hôtel-Dieu that Chancellor Rolin built inside the Beaune walls. There are no Rogier van der Weyden altarpieces, like the one the Chancellor commissioned to help the Hospices patients "bear their sufferings," and no *bonnes sœurs* gliding through the wards in starched medieval habits. There is a television in Armande's room, and an old woman in the next bed, and there are always a lot of neighbors waiting in the hall to see Armande and bring her the local gossip[196]—and wonder whether a few weeks of Hospices care is going to "let in the Jesuits" in the matter of the disposition of the Domaine Monthelie-Douhairet.[197] In the old days, people who gave their vines to the Hospices got back beds and nursing in their own name. They got the right to assign those beds. It was a kind of trade—wine for care. Armande gets her care through health insurance and social security. Her interest in the Hospices, she always liked to say, was spiritual, and had to do with her "*côté chrétien.*" Maybe it was a way of making her peace with the Baby Jesus under the bell jar, who has never received her wedding token—never received a string of seed pearls or a scrap of lace for luck and babies[198]—and maybe a way of saying "*Je m'en fous*" to the Enlightenment gentlemen who made her library so boring, and maybe a way of confounding all the people who are courting her so strenuously now. Armande is getting better, but she has trouble speaking—so no one really knows.[199]

---

191. Ordinarily, once is enough to tell readers how old your subject is, but in this story the repetition indicates that Armande's age is always in the forefront of her mind and conversation.

192. An excellent example of letting humor speak for itself.

193. The detail of the 1923 Volnay conveys the specialness of the event for Armande.

194. Time transition.

195. Time transition.

196. "No *bonnes sœurs*" echoes the earlier setup. The repetition of "there are no . . ." has the ring of these being Armande's complaints. Note the interesting twist of ending with positive repetitions.

197. Again, an echo back to an earlier reference: Is Armande, like the other Douhairet women, going to give in to the Beaune priests? Will her vineyards go to them?

198. This echoes the earlier reference. Now we understand the significance of the strings of seed pearls.

199. The question—and tension—of whether or not Armande's land will go to the priests remains unanswered.

* * *

Just before the harvest,[200] Armande asked Becky to drive to Joncy with her. She wanted to show her the cemetery where she is going to be buried—the cemetery where her parents are buried, under a big white marble cross.[201] She didn't talk about it. The two of them made the trip a kind of outing, and talked mainly about the harvest, about whether the good weather was going to hold and the grapes would be sugary and fat. When they got to the cemetery, they stopped for a few minutes and looked at the cross, and then they turned the car around and drove home. At the cemetery, Armande repeated something her father had said, not long before he died: "Won't it be nice to spend eternity right here, in Burgundy, with flowers on your belly?"[202]

JANE KRAMER ON READING

In a 1980's interview with the *Contemporary Authors* series, Jane Kramer spoke of a great love for poetry and said she reads W. B. Yeats, John Donne, Gerard Manley Hopkins, Seamus Heaney, and Ted Hughes. Her favorite writer, she said, was the novelist George Eliot because she "writes about personal life in a moral universe. I like the moral rigor of Eliot's world. She is concerned with the ethical dimensions of personal and social behavior." She said she loves Proust, but can't stand Hemingway or Fitzgerald.

Today, Kramer says she still reads Donne and Yeats, along with contemporary poets W. S. Merwin and John Ashbery.

---

200. Time transition.

201. Just as the description of Armande's decreasing trips to the cellar was an appropriate way to begin the story, the cemetery visit supports the profile's focus (what will happen to Mlle. Douhairet's vineyard when she dies?) and thus provides closure.

202. The quote is colorful and an unexpected, but satisfying, tweak. While her father actually said it, it sounds totally like Armande. As readers, we leave the story with her words lingering in our minds.

John McPhee

When John McPhee returned from traveling 1,100 miles through the back roads of rural Georgia, he knew he had a problem: How do you write about a biologist who collects and eats road kill without offending your editor and your readers?

"If William Shawn wasn't a vegetarian, he was the next thing to it," he says of the late New Yorker editor. "I had him in mind, as well as the reader, as I was trying to find a way to make the subject of eating road kill more palatable."

The solution McPhee found was in the structure. He and his two travel companions had first eaten weasel and muskrat and assorted other critters, with a snapping turtle literally coming quite a way down the road. But since people eat turtle soup he decided to start there, both because turtle was not so off-putting as some of the other road kill they collected and ate, and because the scene itself was funny. From that point, he and the story moved on to a stream channelization project, followed by a long digression on the biologist, Carol Ruckdeschel, and her menagerie of wounded animals. By that time, he figured, enough interest had been developed in Ruckdeschel and the story to risk returning in a flashback to the weasel and the trip's actual beginning.

Before McPhee began writing "Travels in Georgia," he drew a diagram of the story's structure, as he does for all his articles. In this case, the diagram resembled a lowercase "e." Such attention to structure is a cornerstone of McPhee's work. When he returns from conducting field research, he types up his notes and then begins determining the story's structure and where all the parts will go.

Every piece of writing begins, goes along somewhere, and ends in a manner that is thought out beforehand, McPhee once told Norman Sims. "I always know the last line of a story before I've written the first one. Going through all that creates the form and the shape of the thing. It also relieves the writer, once you know the structure, to concentrate each day on one thing. You know right where it fits."

Over the years, the structures of McPhee's stories have taken many forms, including the back and forth of a tennis match, which he used to profile Arthur Ashe and Clark Graebner. In his introduction to The John McPhee Reader, William L. Howarth describes structural order as the main ingredient that attracts readers to McPhee's work. It is also one of the things that has earned him the admiration of other writers. He is considered a writer's writer by many because of his masterful craftsmanship—his seamless transitions, his apt analogies, his close attention to the smallest detail as well as the overall structure. While working on "A Sense of Where You Are," his profile of then Princeton basketball player Bill Bradley, McPhee returned to a school gym with a steel tape, borrowed a stepladder, and measured the height of the basket after Bradley insisted he had missed a series of practice shots because the hoop was an inch and a half low.

Over the years, McPhee has written about a wide range of topics, from oranges to eccentric art collectors to bizarre aeronautical experiments, but he is perhaps best known for his two decades of geological writings, which resulted in four books that were ultimately combined and extended as Annals of the Former World. The latter earned him the 1999 Pulitzer Prize for general nonfiction, which many admirers felt was long overdue.

McPhee has been a staff writer for the New Yorker since 1965 and is the author of twenty-eight books, including A Sense of Where You Are, The Pine Barrens, Oranges, The Deltoid Pumpkin Seed, Coming into the Country, and Looking for a Ship. His pieces have been collected in The John McPhee Reader, Pieces of the Frame, Table of Contents, Giving Good Weight, and most recently, The Second John McPhee Reader. His most recent book is Irons in the Fire.

He received the Award in Literature from the American Academy of Arts and Letters in 1977 and was nominated for National Book Awards in 1972 and 1974 for Encounters with the Archdruid and The Curve of Binding Energy. He teaches nonfiction writing at Princeton University.

Travels in Georgia

I ASKED FOR THE GORP.[1] Carol passed it to me. Breakfast had been heavy with cathead biscuits, sausage, boiled eggs, Familia, and chicory coffee,[2] but that was an hour ago and I was again hungry. Sam said, "The little Yankee bastard[3] wants the gorp, Carol. Shall we give him some?" Sam's voice was as soft as sphagnum,[4] with inflections of piedmont Georgia.[5]

"The little Yankee bastard can have all he wants this morning," Carol said. "It's such a beautiful day."

Although Sam was working for the state, he was driving his own Chevrolet. He was doing seventy.[6] In a reverberation of rubber,[7] he crossed Hunger and Hardship Creek and headed into the sun[8] on the Swainsboro Road. I took a ration of gorp—soybeans, sunflower seeds, oats, pretzels, Wheat Chex, raisins, and kelp[9]—and poured another ration into Carol's hand. At just about that moment, a snapping turtle was hit[10] on the road a couple of miles ahead of us, who knows by what sort of vehicle, a car, a pickup; run over like a manhole cover, probably with much the same sound,[11] and not crushed, but gravely wounded. It remained still.[12] It appeared to be dead on the road.

Sam, as we approached, was the first to see it. "D.O.R.,"[13] he said. "Man, that is a big snapper." Carol and I both sat forward. Sam pressed hard on the brakes. Even so, he was going fifty when he passed the turtle.

"Travels in Georgia" is reprinted from *Pieces of the Frame.* Copyright © 1973, 1975 by John McPhee. The piece first appeared in the *New Yorker.* Reprinted by permission of Farrar, Straus and Giroux, LLC.

1. The opening "I" places us in the car, with McPhee, so that we can vicariously share his experience. While the story is written chronologically, it is a rearranged chronology. When we begin, the trip has been under way for several days.

2. The specific details of the breakfast ("cathead," "boiled," "chicory," "Familia") make the lead more vivid and enable us to share McPhee's trip.

3. The "Yankee bastard" establishes, with humor, that McPhee is an outsider. The use of only Carol and Sam's first names establishes a comfortable, informal tone.

4. The simile fits both the subject matter and the setting. It also carries the softness of Sam's voice.

5. The description of Sam's accent conveys information about him: He is from Georgia. As the story proceeds, note how we gradually become acquainted with him and Carol. Rather than bombarding us all at once with their backgrounds and what they look like, McPhee lets us get to know them a little at a time. By holding back on precisely who they are and why they are making this trip, he compels us to keep reading. It is also the way we get to know people in real life: gradually.

6. "Doing seventy" maintains the story's informal tone and is far less stilted than saying "he was driving seventy miles an hour." It sounds like what someone would say in conversation.

7. The repetition of R creates a pleasing effect. "Reverberates" also reproduces the actual sound of the tires. Appealing to the senses is an important part of drawing your readers into a scene. While you are reporting, it is important to note not just what you see, but also what you hear, feel, and smell.

8. The detail of the sun places us in the car, in the scene.

9. Dashes are a convenient means of inserting a brief explanation of gorp.

10. McPhee uses the passive voice because the turtle was the *target* of the action, not the perpetrator, and also because we don't know who or what actually hit it.

11. Metaphors must be fresh. They also should fit your subject matter and tone, and McPhee is a master of this. Here the manhole image is appropriate for a story about a road trip; it also helps us visualize the turtle flipping through the air. The word "probably" signals that he is speculating on the turn of events.

12. Note the switch to an active verb. Now the turtle is actually the *actor.*

13. Because of its proximity to the actual phrase "dead on the road," we understand what the initials mean. There is no need to explain. Here the initials act as a setup for McPhee's use of the term throughout the story as a sort of shorthand and as a connecting theme.

Carol said, "He's not dead. He didn't look dead."

Sam reversed. He drove backward rapidly, fast as the car would go. He stopped on the shoulder, and we all got out. There was a pond beyond the turtle. The big, broad head was shining with blood, but there was, as yet, very little blood on the road. The big[14] jaws struck as we came near, opened and closed bloodily—not the kind of strike that, minutes ago, could have cut off a finger, but still a strike with power. The turtle was about fourteen inches long and a shining hornbrown. The bright spots on its marginal scutes were like light bulbs around a mirror.[15] The neck lunged out. Carol urged the turtle, with her foot, toward the side of the road. "I know, big man," she said to it. "I know it's bad. We're not tormenting you. Honest we're not."[16] Sam asked her if she thought it had a chance to live and she said she was sure it had no chance at all. A car, coming west, braked down and stopped. The driver got out, with some effort and a big paunch.[17] He looked at the turtle and said, "Fifty years old if he's a day." That was the whole of what the man had to say. He got into his car and drove on. Carol nudged the snapper, but it was too hurt to move. It could only strike the air. Now, in a screech of brakes, another car came onto the scene. It went by us, then spun around with squealing tires and pulled up on the far shoulder. It was a two-tone, high-speed, dome-lighted Ford, and in it was the sheriff of Laurens County. He got out and walked toward us, all Technicolor in his uniform, legs striped like a pine-barrens tree frog's, plastic plate on his chest, name of Wade.[18]

"Good morning," Sam said to him.

"How y'all?" said Sheriff Wade.

Carol said, "Would you mind shooting this turtle for us, please?"

"Surely, Ma'am," said the sheriff, and he drew his .38.[19] He extended his arm and took aim.

"Uh, Sheriff," I said. "If you don't mind . . ." And I asked him if he would kindly shoot the turtle over soil and not over concrete. The sheriff paused and looked slowly, with new interest, from one of us to another: a woman in her twenties, good-looking, with long tawny hair, no accent (that he could hear), barefoot, and wearing a gray sweatshirt and brown dungarees with a hunting knife in the belt; a man (Sam) around forty, in weathered khaki, also without an accent, and with a full black beard divided by a short white patch at the chin—an authentic, natural split beard; and then this incongruous little Yankee bastard telling him not to shoot the road.[20] Carol picked up the turtle by its long, serrated tail and carried it, underside toward her leg, beyond the shoulder of the

---

14. The repetition of "big" emphasizes the turtle's size.

15. The simile enables us to picture the turtle's scutes and essentially provides a definition for readers who may not know what they are. Note how McPhee's metaphors are fresh, but don't call so much attention to themselves that they interrupt the story.

16. It is important to choose quotes that convey something about the speaker beyond the words themselves. This one shows us Carol's affection for animals.

17. McPhee makes this minor character memorable with a brief description that gives us a sense of the man. Note that the description becomes part of the action: the man has trouble getting out of the car because of his weight.

18. The sentences in this little scene seem to mimic the action. The car sails past, spins about in a squeal of rubber and brakes, then pulls to a stop. Then following the action almost like a camera, we first see the car's two tones, next its dome light, then the sheriff himself. As the man moves toward us we size him up: his colorful uniform, the stripe on his pants' leg, the nameplate, then finally his name.

19. Note the concreteness of the detail. The man aimed not just a pistol or a gun, but a .38.

20. We get our first physical description of the trio in the car, as McPhee imagines how the sheriff sees them. He focuses on their most distinguishable features.

highway, where she set it down on a patch of grass. The sheriff followed with his .38. He again took aim. He steadied the muzzle of the pistol twelve inches from the turtle.[21] He fired, and missed. The gun made an absurdly light sound, like a screen door shutting. He fired again. He missed. He fired again. The third shot killed the turtle. The pistol smoked.[22] The sheriff blew the smoke away, and smiled, apparently at himself. He shook his head a little. "He should be good," he said, with a nod at the turtle.[23] The sheriff crossed the road and got into his car. "Y'all be careful," he said. With a great screech of tires, he wheeled around and headed on west.[24]

Carol guessed that the turtle was about ten years old. By the tail, she carried it down to the edge of the pond, like a heavy suitcase with a broken strap.[25] Sam fetched plastic bags from the car. I found a long two-by-ten plank and carried it to the edge of the water. Carol placed the snapper upside down on the plank. Kneeling, she unsheathed her hunting knife and began, in a practiced and professional way, to slice around the crescents in the plastron, until the flesh of the legs—in thick steaks of red meat—came free. Her knife was very sharp. She put the steaks[26] into a plastic bag. All the while, she talked to the dead turtle, soothingly, reassuringly, nurse to patient, doctor to child, and when she reached in under the plastron and found an ovary, she shifted genders with a grunt of surprise. She pulled out some globate yellow fat and tossed it into the pond. Hundreds of mosquito fish came darting through the water, sank their teeth, shook their heads, worried[27] the fat. Carol began to remove eggs from the turtle's body. The eggs were like ping-pong balls in size, shape, and color,[28] and how they all fitted into the turtle was more than I could comprehend, for there were fifty-six[29] of them in there, fully finished, and a number that had not quite taken their ultimate form. "Look at those eggs. Aren't they beautiful?" Carol said. "Oh, that's sad. You were just about to do your thing, weren't you, girl?" That was why the snapper had gone out of the pond and up onto the road. She was going to bury her eggs in some place she knew, perhaps drawn by an atavistic attachment to the place where she herself had hatched out and where many generations of her forebears had been born when there was no road at all.[30] The turtle twitched. Its neck moved. Its nerves were still working, though its life was gone. The nails on the ends of the claws were each an inch long. The turtle draped one of these talons over one of Carol's fingers. Carol withdrew more fat and threw a huge hunk into the pond. "Wouldn't it be fun to analyze *that* for pesticides?" she said. "You're fat as a pig, Mama. You sure lived high off the hog." Finishing the job—it took forty minutes—Carol found frog bones in the turtle. She put more red meat into plastic sacks and divided the eggs. She kept half for us to eat.[31] With

---

21. Including the gun's distance from the turtle makes the shooting scene that follows even more humorous.

22. The very short sentences further add to that humor.

23. The sheriff's quote provides our first clue to what the story is about. Note how McPhee uses the attribution to insert a description of the sheriff's movements and thus keeps the action going.

24. The structure of the sentence replicates the car's movements.

25. The simile is again right on target. It enables us to see Carol carrying the turtle.

26. McPhee's use of "steaks" and "red meat" to refer to the turtle is appropriate for the subject matter. It also provides another clue that the story is about eating road kill.

27. The sequence of the scene lets us follow the fish's movements. "Worried" is the perfect verb for capturing how they nibble at the fat.

28. The comparison helps us visualize the eggs.

29. The precise "fifty-six" emphasizes just how many eggs are crammed into the turtle.

30. McPhee is a master at educating readers without them being aware of what he is doing. Here he weaves in a brief explanation of the turtle's reproductive practices so smoothly, we don't realize we have left the main time line.

31. The eggs provide an even stronger clue to what the story is largely about.

her knife she carefully buried the remaining eggs, twenty-eight or so, in a sandbank, much as the mother turtle might have been doing at just that time. Carol picked away some leeches from between her fingers. The leeches had come off the turtle's shell. She tied the sacks and said, "All right. That's all we can say grace over. Let's send her back whence she came." Picking up the inedible parts—plastron, carapace, neck, claws—she heaved them into the pond. They hit with a slap and sank without bubbles.[32]

* * *

As we moved east,[33] pine trees kept giving us messages—small, hand-painted signs nailed into the loblollies. "HAVE YOU WHAT IT TAKES TO MEET JESUS WHEN HE RETURNS?" Sam said he was certain he did not. "JESUS WILL NEVER FAIL YOU." City limits, Adrian, Georgia. Swainsboro, Georgia. Portal, Georgia. Towns on the long, straight roads of the coastal plain. White-painted, tin-roofed bungalows. Awnings shading the fronts of stores—prepared for heat and glare. Red earth. Sand roads. Houses on short stilts. Sloping verandas. Unpainted boards.[34]

"D.O.R.," said Carol.[35]

"What do you suppose that was?"

"I don't know. I didn't see. It could have been a squirrel."

Sam backed up to the D.O.R. It was a brown thrasher. Carol looked it over, and felt it. Sam picked it up. "Throw him far off the road," Carol said. "So a possum won't get killed while eating him." Sam threw the bird far off the road. A stop for a D.O.R. always brought the landscape into detailed focus. Pitch coming out of a pine. Clustered sows behind a fence. An automobile wrapped in vines. A mailbox. "Donald Foskey." His home. Beyond the mailbox, a set of cinder blocks and on the cinder blocks a mobile home.[36] As Sam regathered speed, Carol turned on the radio and moved the dial. If she could find some Johnny Cash, it would elevate her day.[37] Some Johnny Cash was not hard to find in the airwaves of Georgia. There he was now, resonantly singing about his Mississippi Delta land, where, on a sharecropping farm, he grew up. Carol smiled and closed her eyes. In her ears—pierced ears—were gold maple leaves that seemed to move under the influence of the music.

"D.O.R. possum,"[38] Sam said, stopping again. "Two! A grown one and a baby." They had been killed probably ten minutes before. Carol carried the adult to the side of the road and left it there. She kept the baby. He was seven inches long. He was half tail.[39] Although dead, he seemed virtually undamaged. We moved on. Carol had a clipboard she used for making occasional notes and sketches. She put the little possum on the clipboard and rested the clipboard on her knees. "Oh, you sweet little angel. How could any-

---

32. The image of the remains sinking without bubbles bears testimony to McPhee's close observation.

33. Place transition.

34. Rather than playing out the entire trip in detail, McPhee compresses time and miles. To do so, he uses road signs, town names, and details that capture the essence of the Georgia countryside. The sentence fragments create a sense of the various sights popping in and out of view as we whiz by.

35. Because of the earlier setup, there is no need to explain that they've come upon another road kill.

36. McPhee uses the stop to weave in more description of the landscape.

37. This detail gives us further insight into Carol's personality. Note that we still don't know her—or Sam's—last name or their occupations or why we are in this car.

38. Another D.O.R. The obsession of the car's occupants with road kill is beginning to set off bells. Still, we don't know precisely why they are interested in dead animals. McPhee again uses the attribution to insert action.

39. McPhee's description is brief yet gives us a clear picture of the baby possum and its long tail. He could have simply said she kept the baby; by describing it he draws us into the scene.

body run over *you?*" she said. "Oh, I just love possums. I've raised so many of them. This is a great age. They are the neatest little animals. They love you so much. They crawl on your shoulder and hang in your hair. How people can dislike them I don't understand." Carol reached into the back seat and put the little opossum into a container of formaldehyde. After a while, she said, "What mystifies me is: that big possum back there was a male."[40]

Bethel Primitive Baptist Church. Old Canoochee Primitive Baptist Church. "THE CHURCH HAS NO INDULGENCES." A town every ten miles, a church—so it seemed—every two. Carol said she frequently slept in church graveyards. They were, for one thing, quiet, and, for another, private. Graham Memorial Church of the Nazarene.[41]

Sam and Carol both sat forward at the same moment, alert, excited. "D.O.R. Wow! That was something special. It had a long yellow belly and brown fur or feathers! Hurry, Sam. It's a good one." Sam backed up at forty miles an hour and strained the Chevrolet.

"What is it? What is it?"

"It's a piece of bark. Fell off a pulpwood truck."[42]

The approach to Pembroke[43] was made with a sense of infiltration[44]—Pembroke, seat of Bryan County. "Remember, now, we're interested in frogs," Sam said, and we went up the steps of Bryan County Courthouse. "We understand there is a stream-channelization project going on near here. Could you tell us where? We're collecting frogs." It is hard to say what the clerks in the courthouse thought of this group—the spokesman with the black-and-white beard, the shoeless young woman, and their silent companion. They looked at us—they in their pumps and print dresses—from the other side of a distance.[45] The last thing they might have imagined was that two of the three of us were representing the state government in Atlanta.[46] The clerks did not know where the channelization was going on but they knew who might—a woman in town who knew everything. We went to see her. A chicken ran out of her house when she opened the screen door.[47] No, she was not sure just where we should go, but try a man named Miller in Lanier. He'd know.[48] He knew everything.[49] Lanier was five miles down the track—literally so. The Seaboard Coast Line ran beside the road. Miller was a thickset man with unbelievably long, sharp fingernails, a driver of oil trucks. It seemed wonderful that he could get his hands around the wheel without cutting himself, that he could

---

40. The clipboard and formaldehyde tell us Carol's interest is more than a hobby. The fact she knew the adult possum was a male indicates she knows quite a bit about wildlife. We are learning more about her.

41. This time McPhee uses churches to compress time and miles. He also takes the opportunity to work in another piece of information about Carol.

42. The false alarm adds a touch of humor and shows the pair's eagerness.

43. Place transition.

44. "Sense of infiltration" creates an air of intrigue and compels us to keep reading. We still don't know what they are up to.

45. Somewhat the way a caricature artist highlights the features that distinguish one individual from another, McPhee uses the details that best capture the scene in the courthouse: the bearded man, the barefoot woman, the silent McPhee, the courthouse employees in their print dresses (more vivid than mere dresses), their chilly reception.

46. McPhee gives a little more information: Carol and Sam are somehow connected to the state of Georgia and are collecting frogs.

47. The chicken makes another walk-on character memorable.

48. The quote is paraphrased, but it nevertheless carries the sound of the woman's voice and thus places us in the scene. We can see her standing with the screened door partially open, conversing with the trio.

49. Rather than giving us a blow-by-blow account of the exchange, McPhee reduces it to its essence: Miller knew everything they wanted to know.

deliver oil without cutting the hose.[50] He said, "Do you mind my asking why you're interested in stream channelization?"

"We're interested in frogs," Sam said. "Snakes and frogs. We thought the project might be stirring some up."

Miller said, "I don't mind the frog, but I want no part of the snake."

His directions were perfect—through pine forests, a right, two lefts, to where a dirt road crossed a tributary of the Ogeechee.[51] A wooden bridge there had been replaced by a culvert. The stream now flowed through big pipes in the culvert. Upriver, far as the eye could see, a riparian swath had been cut by chain saws. Back from the banks, about fifty feet on each side, the overstory and the understory—every tree, bush, and sapling—had been cut down. The river was under revision. It had been freed of meanders. It was now two yards wide between vertical six-foot banks; and it was now as straight as a ditch. It had, in fact, become a ditch—in it a stream of thin mud, flowing.[52] An immense yellow machine, slowly backing upstream, had in effect eaten this river. It was at work now, grunting and belching, two hundred yards from the culvert. We tried to walk toward it along the bank but sank to our shins in black ooze.[53] The stumps of the cut trees were all but covered with mud from the bottom of the river. We crossed the ditch. The dredged mud was somewhat firmer on the other side. Sam and I walked there. Carol waded up-current in the stream. The machine was an American dragline crane. The word "American" stood out on its cab in letters more than a foot high. Its boom reached up a hundred feet. Its bucket took six-foot bites.[54] As we approached, the bucket kept eating the riverbed, then swinging up and out of the channel and disgorging tons of mud to either side.[55] Carol began to take pictures. She took more and more pictures as she waded on upstream. When she was fifty feet away from the dragline, its engine coughed down and stopped. The sudden serenity was oddly disturbing. The operator stepped out of the cab and onto the catwalk. One hand on the flank of his crane, he inclined his head somewhat forward and stared down at Carol. He was a stocky man with an open shirt and an open face, deeply tanned.[56] He said, "Howdy."

"Howdy," said Carol.

"You're taking some pictures," he said.

"I sure am. I'm taking some pictures. I'm interested in the range extension of river frogs, and the places they live. I bet you turn up some interesting things."

"I see some frogs," the man said. "I see lots of frogs."

---

50. McPhee takes Miller's most striking feature—those long fingernails—and makes another minor character memorable. He then has fun with the nails, wondering the kind of things that might go through our head.

51. Miller's directions provide a place transition. Note how McPhee uses detail to move us from one place to the next, continuing to give us a feeling for the terrain.

52. In describing the changes the river has undergone, McPhee is essentially "showing" us what channelization is.

53. Note how "black ooze" conveys a sense of gunk you could sink shin-deep in better than the word "mud."

54. McPhee's specificity (the height of the letters, the reach of the boom, the size of the bites) captures just how big the crane is.

55. McPhee uses personification to bring the crane to life: it takes bites, it grunts, it belches, it disgorges—all eating terms that fit the overall subject matter. They are also colorful verbs that vividly bring the scene to life.

56. The description here is tight, yet specific (Carol's position in the river, the placement of the operator's hand, the inclination of his head, the fact he has to look down to speak to Carol), allowing us to witness the exchange. The man's physical description is brief, yet through McPhee's careful selection of detail gives us a clear feeling both for his manner and appearance. The repetition of "open" adds a pleasing rhythm to the description.

"You sure know what you're doing with that machine," Carol said. The man shifted his weight.[57] "That's a *big* thing," she went on. "How much does it weigh?"

"Eighty-two tons."

"Eighty-two *tons?*"

"Eighty-two tons."

"Wow! How far can you dig in one day?"

"Five hundred feet."

"A mile every ten days," Sam said, shaking his head with awe.[58]

"Sometimes I do better than that."

"You live around here?"

"No. My home's near Baxley. I go where I'm sent. All over the state."

"Well, sorry. Didn't mean to interrupt you."

"Not 't all. Take all the pictures you want."

"Thanks. What did you say your name was?"

"Chap," he said. "Chap Causey."[59]

We walked around the dragline, went upstream a short way, and sat down on the trunk of a large oak, felled by the chain saws, to eat our lunch—sardines, chocolate, crackers, and wine.[60] Causey at work was the entertainment, pulling his levers, swinging his bucket, having at the stream.[61]

If he had been at first wary,[62] he no doubt had had experience that made him so. All over the United States, but particularly in the Southeast, his occupation had become a raw issue. He was working for the Soil Conservation Service, a subdivision of the United States Department of Agriculture, making a "water-resource channel improvement"—generally known as stream channelization, or reaming a river. Behind his dragline, despite the clear-cutting of the riverine trees, was a free-flowing natural stream, descending toward the Ogeechee in bends and eddies, riffles and deeps[63]—in appearance somewhere between a trout stream and a bass river,[64] and still handsomely so, even though it was shaved and ready for its operation.[65] At the dragline, the recognizable river disappeared, and below the big machine was a kind of reverse irrigation ditch, engi-

---

57. McPhee includes not only what was said, but the speakers' movements, allowing us to witness the scene. The lesson here is to remember in observing a scene to record your subjects' actions (their movements, their facial expressions, their tones of voice) as well as their words.

58. Because the conversation has only been between Carol and the operator, there has been no need for attribution. When Sam enters the exchange, it becomes necessary. Note how McPhee again uses the attribution to show us Sam's reaction and thus continues to put us in the scene.

59. Up to now, the operator has been referred to only as "the man" and "he" because we, like the trio, don't know his name. We now get an introduction; from now on in the story, he will become "Chap Causey." The lesson here: When an unfamiliar character enters your story, don't use his or her name until you and your subject know it. Just think about how we meet people in actual life. When we see a stranger at a cocktail party, we know only what he or she looks like. If we stand close enough, we may even overhear what he or she is saying, but unless someone at the party identifies the person, we learn his or her name only after we introduce ourselves.

60. Specific details bring this brief scene to life: the oak tree trunk, what they ate for lunch.

61. This informal expression not only suits the story, it tells us something about McPhee. He's a casual, comfortable man.

62. McPhee uses Causey as a transition into a digression on channelization and this particular project, all the while maintaining the same tone and mood of the story. We scarcely know we've taken a brief detour from the main time line, or what writer-educator Mark Kramer refers to as the "moving now."

63. The paired couplings—and the choice of details—give us a picture of the stream. They also create a poetic rhythm, which is pleasing to the ear—as fine writing should be.

64. The comparison with the trout stream and the bass river further enable us to envision the stream.

65. The surgery metaphor vividly conveys what the stream is in store for and carries negative connotations.

neered to remove water rapidly from the immediate watershed. "How could anyone even conceive of this idea?" Sam said. "Not just to do it, but even to *conceive* of it?"

The purpose of such projects was to anticipate and eliminate floods, to drain swamps, to increase cropland, to channel water toward freshly created reservoirs serving and attracting new industries and new housing developments. Water sports would flourish on the new reservoirs, hatchery fish would proliferate below the surface: new pulsations in the life of the rural South. The Soil Conservation Service was annually spending about fifteen million dollars on stream-channelization projects, providing, among other things, newly arable land to farmers who already had land in the Soil Bank. The Department of Agriculture could not do enough for the Southern farmer, whose only problem was bookkeeping. He got money for keeping his front forty idle. His bottomland went up in value when the swamps were drained, and then more money came for not farming the drained land. Years earlier, when a conservationist had been someone who plowed land along natural contours, the Soil Conservation Service had been the epicenter of the conservation movement, decorated for its victories over erosion of the land. Now, to a new generation that had discovered ecology, the S.C.S. was the enemy. Its drainage programs tampered with river mechanics, upsetting the relationships between bass and otter, frog and owl. The Soil Conservation Service had grown over the years into a bureau of fifteen thousand people, and all the way down at the working point, the cutting edge of things, was Chap Causey,[66] in the cab of his American dragline, hearing nothing but the pounding of his big Jimmy diesel while he eliminated a river, eradicated a swamp.

After heaving up a half-dozen buckets of mud, Causey moved backward several feet. The broad steel shoes of the crane were resting on oak beams that were bound together in pairs with cables. There were twelve beams in all. Collectively, they were called "mats."[67] Under the crane, they made a temporary bridge over the river. As Causey moved backward and off the front pair of beams, he would reach down out of the sky with a hook from his boom and snare a loop of the cable that held the beams. He snatched them up—they weighed at least half a ton—and whipped them around to the back. The beams dropped perfectly into place, adding a yard to Causey's platform on the upstream side. Near the tree line beyond one bank, he had a fuel tank large enough to bury under a gas station,[68] and every so often he would reach out with his hook and his hundred-foot arm and, without groping, lift the tank and move it on in the direction he was going. With his levers, his cables, his bucket, and hook, he handled his mats and his tank and his hunks of the riverbed[69] as if he were dribbling a basketball through his legs and behind his back. He was deft. He was world class.[70] "I bet he could put on a baby's diapers with that thing," Sam said.

Carol said, "See that three-foot stump? I sure would like to see him pull *that* out." She gestured toward the rooted remains of a tree that must have stood, a week earlier, a hundred and fifty feet high. Causey, out of the corner of his eye, must have seen the ges-

---

66. McPhee again uses Chap Causey as his transition out of the background explanation. The transition is so skillful we are hardly conscious that we ever left the main time line. In telling us about S.C.S., he leaves until last the fact that the agency has fifteen thousand employees, then moves us to the one currently in the picture—Chap Causey—and the story is back to the "moving now."

67. This description of the crane is vivid and alive—and interesting to read.

68. The comparison to the gas-station tank helps us visualize just how big the tank is.

69. The accumulation of detail here, coupled with the use of "and" rather than commas, conveys a sense of him skillfully handling a lot of tasks at once.

70. The basketball simile shows us just how adept Causey is. It also captures his ability to juggle things all around him.

ture. Perhaps he just read her mind.[71] He was much aware that he was being watched, and now he reached around behind him, grabbed the stump in his bucket, and ripped it out of the earth like a molar.[72] He set it at Carol's feet. It towered over her.[73]

After a modest interval, a few more buckets of streambed, Causey shut off the dragline and stopped for an adulation break. Carol told him he was fabulous. And she meant it. He was. She asked him what the name of the stream was. He said, "To tell you the truth, Ma'am, I don't rightly know."[74]

* * *

Carol said, "Do you see many snakes?"

"Oh, yes, I see lots of snakes," Causey said, and he looked at her carefully.

"What kinds of snakes?"

"Moccasins, mainly. They climb up here on the mats. They don't run. They never run. They're not afraid. I got a canoe paddle in the cab there. I kill them with the paddle. One day, I killed thirty-five moccasins. People come along sometimes, like you, visitors, come up here curious to see the digging, and they see the dead snakes lying on the mats, and they freeze. They refuse to move. They refuse to walk back where they came from."

If Causey was trying to frighten Carol, to impress her by frightening her, he had picked the wrong person.[75] He might have sent a shot or two of adrenalin through me, but not through Carol. I once saw her reach into a semi-submerged hollow stump in a manmade lake where she knew a water snake lived,[76] and she had felt around in there, underwater, with her hands on the coils of the snake, trying to figure out which end was front. Standing thigh-deep in the water, she was wearing a two-piece bathing suit. Her appearance did not suggest old Roger Conant on a field trip. She was trim and supple and tan from a life in the open. Her hair, in a ponytail, had fallen across one shoulder,[77] while her hands, down inside the stump, kept moving slowly, gently along the body of the snake. This snake was her friend, she said, and she wanted Sam and me to see him. "Easy there, fellow, it's only Carol. I sure wish I could find your head. Here we go. We're coming to the end. Oh, damn. I've got his tail." There was nothing to do but turn around. She felt her way all four feet[78] to the other end. "At last," she said. "How are you, old fellow?" And she lifted her arms up out of the water. In them was something like a piece of television cable moving with great vigor. She held on tight and carried her friend out of the lake and onto the shore.

---

71. Since we nonfiction writers can't ethically make things up, this is an excellent way to get around the problem of what your subject might be thinking when you really don't know. The "must" and "perhaps" clearly let readers know McPhee is merely speculating.

72. Another one of McPhee's fresh, on-target similes. Pulled up roots and all, the stump surely must have resembled an extracted molar.

73. The comparison conveys the size of the stump.

74. Here, McPhee compresses the dialogue so that the most important—and telling—quote stands out. Its placement at the end of the section also adds emphasis.

75. McPhee uses the exchange about snakes as a transition into a lengthy digression about Carol and the story's origins. McPhee's reaction echoes what our own reaction would probably have been. As the digression proceeds, we begin to see that the story is more about Carol than Sam.

76. The snake anecdote provides colorful support for McPhee's statement that Carol is not afraid of snakes.

77. The scene becomes an opportunity to give us a fuller physical description of Carol.

78. The specific detail makes the scene more vivid. A four-foot snake is more intimidating than one that is one or two feet long and thus makes McPhee's point about Carol.

At Carol's house,[79] Sam and I one night slept in sleeping bags on the floor of her study beside Zebra, her rattlesnake. He was an eastern diamondback, and he had light lines, parallel, on his dark face. He was young and less than three feet long. He lived among rocks and leaves in a big glass jar. "As a pet, he's ideal," Carol told us. "I've never had a diamondback like him before. Anytime you get uptight about anything, just look at him. He just sits there. He's so great. He doesn't complain. He just waits. It's as if he's saying, 'I've got all the time in the world. I'll outwait you, you son of a bitch.'"

"He shows you what patience is," Sam said. "He's like a deer. Deer will wait two hours before they move into a field to eat."

In Carol's kitchen was the skin of a mature diamondback, about six feet long, that Sam and Carol had eaten in southwest Georgia, roasting him on a stick like a big hot dog, beside the Muckalee Creek.[80] The snake, when they came upon him, had just been hit and was still alive. The men who had mortally wounded the snake were standing over it, watching it die. A dump truck full of gravel was coming toward the scene, and Carol, imagining the truck running over and crushing the diamondback, ran up to the men standing over it and said, "Do you want it?" Surprised, they said no. "No, *Ma'am!*" So she picked up the stricken snake, carried it off the road and back to the car, where she coiled it on the floor between her feet. "Later, in a gas station, we didn't worry about leaving the car unlocked. Oh, that was funny. We do have some fun. We ate him that night."

"What did he taste like?" I asked her.[81]

"Taste like? You know, like rattlesnake. Maybe a cross between a chicken and a squirrel."

Carol's house, in Atlanta, consisted of four small rooms, each about ten feet square—kitchen, study, storage room, bedroom. They were divided by walls of tongue-and-groove boards, nailed horizontally onto the studs. A bathroom and vestibule were more or less stuck onto one side of the building. She lived alone there. An oak with a three-foot bole stood over the house like an umbrella and was so close to it that it virtually blocked the front door. An old refrigerator sat on the stoop. Around it were the skulls of a porpoise, a horse, a cow, and a pig. White columns adorned the façade. They were made of two-inch iron pipe. Paint peeled from the clapboard. The front yard was hard red clay, and it had some vestigial grasses in it (someone having once tried a lawn) that had not been mowed for possibly a decade. Carol had set out some tomatoes among the weeds. The house stood on fairly steep ground that sloped through woods to a creek. The basement was completely above grade at the rear, and a door there led into a dim room[82]

---

79. Transition into a visit to Carol's house and another anecdote. The fact that the snake has a name and McPhee refers to it as "her rattlesnake" tells us about Carol's attachment to animals. The detailed description of the snake sets the scene more vividly than simply referring to the reptile as a rattlesnake, which many writers would have been content to do.

80. McPhee is easing us into the eating of road kill. Because he waits until we are engaged in the story and because he makes the incident seem so casual (we think of the hot dog, we see the peaceful creek setting), we accept it as almost routine. Presented earlier in the story, the same incident would probably cause most us to flinch.

81. We identify with the question. It is probably what we too would ask.

82. McPhee includes the details that best convey a sense of the house: the tongue-and-groove walls, the refrigerator on the stoop (note how the word fits this particular house and story—this is no veranda), the sprawling oak, the iron-pipe columns, the overgrown yard, the skulls of the various animals. The whole scene points to Carol's very basic, close-to-the-earth lifestyle.

where Carol's red-tailed hawk lived.[83] He was high in one corner, standing on a pipe. I had never been in the immediate presence[84] of a red-tailed hawk, and at sight of him I was not sure whether to run or to kneel. At any rate, I could not have taken one step nearer. He was two feet tall. His look was incendiary. Slowly, angrily, he lifted and spread his wings, reached out a yard and a half. His talons could have hooked tuna. His name was Big Man. His spread-winged posture revealed all there was to know about him: his beauty—the snowy chest, the rufous tail; his power; his affliction. One of his wings was broken.[85] Carol had brought him back from near death. Now she walked over to him and stood by him and stroked his chest. "Come on, Big Man," she said. "It's not so bad. Come on, Big Man." Slowly, ever so slowly—over a period of a minute or two—the wide wings came down, folded together, while Carol stroked his chest. Fear departed, but nothing much changed in his eyes.

"What will he ever do?" I asked her.

She said, "Nothing, I guess. Just be someone's friend."

Outside the basement door[86] was a covered pen that housed a rooster and a seagull. The rooster had been on his way to Colonel Sanders' when he fell off a truck and broke a drumstick. Someone called Carol, as people often do, and she took the rooster into her care. He was hard of moving, but she had hopes for him. He was so new there he did not even have a name. The seagull, on the other hand, had been with her for years. He had one wing. She had picked him up on a beach three hundred miles away. His name was Garbage Belly.

Carol had about fifteen ecosystems going on at once in her twenty-by-twenty house. In the study, a colony of dermestid beetles was eating flesh off the pelvis of an alligator. The beetles lived in a big can that had once held forty pounds of mincemeat. Dermestids clean bones. They do thorough work. They all but simonize the bones. Carol had obtained her original colony from the Smithsonian Institution. One of her vaulting ambitions was to be able to identify on sight any bone that she happened to pick up. Also in the can were the skulls of a water turkey, a possum, and a coon.[87]

The beetles ate and were eaten. Carol reached into the colony, pulled out a beetle, and gave it to her black-widow spider.[88] The black widow lived in a commercial mayonnaise jar. Carol had found her in the basement while cleaning it up for Big Man. The spider's egg was getting ready to hatch, and when it did thousands like her would emerge into the jar. Efficiently, the black widow encased the beetle in filament gauze that flowed from her spinnerets.

Carol then fed dermestids to her turtles. She had three galvanized tubs full of cooters and sliders, under a sunlamp. "They need sun, you know. Vitamin D." She fed der-

---

83. Note how matter-of-factly McPhee introduces Carol's menagerie, as if it were the most natural thing in the world to have a hawk and a rattlesnake as pets. He lets the fact that she has them speak for itself.

84. The word "immediate presence" captures both McPhee's awe and the magnificence of the hawk. To say he had never seen a red-tailed hawk would have set an entirely different mood and scene.

85. Note both the vividness of McPhee's description and the ordering of it. By saving Big Man's spread-winged posture until last, it and his broken wing also serve as a smooth, natural transition back to Carol and the visit to her house.

86. Place transition, into more of Carol's menagerie.

87. McPhee maintains his same informal tone to explain how Carol's ecosystems work. Note how he brings each creature to life: we learn their origins, their function in the system, even where they reside. Details like the forty-pound mincemeat can and, later, the mayonnaise jar add color. "Simonize" is the perfect verb choice, and a fresh one. We automatically think of polishing a car and realize that's what the beetles do to the bones.

88. He offers an example of the ecosystem at work.

mesilds to her spotted salamander, and to her gray tree frog. Yellow spots, polka dots, on black, the salamander's coloring was so simple and contrasting that he appeared to be a knickknack from a gift shop, a salamander made in Japan.[89] The tree frog lived in a giant brandy snifter, furnished with rocks and dry leaves. With his latex body and his webbed and gummy oversized hands, he could walk right up the inside of his brandy snifter, even after its shape began to tilt him backward, then lay a mitt over the rim and haul himself after and walk down the outside.[90] He could walk straight up a wall; and he did that, while digesting his beetle. He had been with Carol three years. He was a star there in her house. No mayonnaise jar for him.[91] He had the brandy snifter. It was all his and would be as long as he lived.

Notebooks were open on Carol's desk, a heavy, kneehole desk, covered with pens, Magic Markers, brushes, pencils, drawing materials. The notebooks had spiral bindings and were, in part, diaries.[92]

17 April. Okefenokee. Caught two banded water snakes, one skink. . . .

18 April. To King's Landing. Set three line traps baited with peanut butter, caught a rather small moccasin AGKISTRODON coming from under shed. Put out ninety-five set hooks baited with pork liner. To gator hole. Tried to use shocker, after putting up seines across exit. No luck!

19 April. D.O.R. *Natrix rigida,* glossy water snake; *Farancia abacura,* mud snake; *Elaphe guttata guttata,* corn snake. . . .

21 April. S. W. Georgia. D.O.R. vulture, ½ mi. E. Leary, Hwy 62, Calhoun County. Fresh. Possum D.O.R. nearby. . . .

The notebooks were also, in part, ledgers of her general interests.

Dissolve mouse in nitric acid and put him through spectrophotometer—can tell every element.

A starving snake can gain weight on water.

Gray whales are born with their bellies up and weigh a ton, and when they are grown they swim five thousand miles to breed in shallow lagoons and eat sand and stand on their tails and gravity-feed on pelagic crabs.

And the notebooks were, in part, filled with maps and sketches. Making a drawing of something—a mermaid weed, the hind foot of an opossum, the egg case of a spotted salamander, a cutaway of a deer's heart—was her way of printing it into her memory. The maps implied stories. They were of places too specific—too eccentric, wild, and

---

89. McPhee provides a whimsical description of the salamander that is both delightful to read and helpful in allowing us to picture it.

90. Note the word choices ("furnished," "over-sized hands," "mitts") McPhee uses to bring the tree frog to life and to convey how, in Carol's eyes, he's far more than a frog: he's almost human. The description of the little guy making his way up and out of the brandy snifter is a delight to read and demonstrates McPhee's close, patient observation. This close observation to detail and movement is one of the things that makes this story such a jewel and an excellent learning tool for aspiring nonfiction writers.

91. The use of sentence fragments is usually a no-no, but in the hands of a seasoned writer they can be effective, as McPhee demonstrates here. The mayonnaise jar comment is funnier and more emphatic when set aside in this way. The lesson here: When using sentence fragments, be sure they really work.

92. A good nonfiction writer looks to any and every source for information. Here, McPhee uses Carol's notebooks to tell us about her life, her interests, her personality. They also reveal her deep interest in wildlife and her work in biology.

minute—to show up as much of anything on other maps, including a topographical quadrangle. They were of places that Carol wanted to remember and, frequently enough, to find again.[93]

12 May. Caught *Natrix erythrogaster flavigaster,* red-bellied water snake 9:30 A.M. Saw quite a large gator at 9:35. Ten feet. Swarm of honeybees 25 feet up cypress at edge of creek. Large—six-foot—gray rat snake in oak tree over water. *Elaphe obsoleta spiloides.* Tried unsuccessfully to knock it into canoe. Finally climbed tree but snake had gone into hole in limb. . . .

26 June. Sleep on nest where loggerhead laid eggs Cumberland Island, to protect eggs from feral hogs. Return later find that hog has eaten eggs. Shoot hog. . . .

27 August. Oconee River. Saw *Natrix* wrestling with a catfish in water. *Natrix* was trying to pull fish out on bank. Snake about 2½ feet. Fish 8 inches. Snake finally won. Didn't have heart to collect snake as he was so proud of fish and wouldn't let go even when touched. Camped by railroad bridge. Many trains. Found catfish on set hook, smoked him for supper. . . .

The rods of the vertebrate eye provide scotopic vision—sight in dim light. Nocturnal animals that also go out in daylight need slit eyes to protect the rods. Crocodiles. Seals. Rattlesnakes. Cottonmouths.

13 June. North Georgia. Oh, most glorious night. The fireflies are truly in competition with the stars At the tops of the ridges it is impossible to tell them apart. As of old, I wished for a human companion. On the banks of a road, a round worm was glowing, giving off light. What a wonderful thing it is. It allows us to see in the darkness.

Above the desk, tacked to a wall,[94] was the skin of a bobcat—D.O.R. two miles west of Baxley, Highway 341. "I was excited out of my mind when we found him," Carol said. "He was the best D.O.R. ever. It was late afternoon. January. He was stiff, but less than a day old. Bobcats move mostly at night. He was unbloody, three feet long, and weighed twenty-one pounds. I was amazed how small his testicles were. I skinned him here at home. I tanned his hide—salt, alum, then neat's-foot oil. He had a thigh like a goat's— so big, so much beautiful meat. I boiled him. He tasted good—you know, the wild taste. Strong. But not as strong as a strong coon."

Zebra lifted his head, flashed his fangs, and yawned[95] a pink yawn. This was the first time in at least a day that Zebra had moved. Carol said the yawn meant he was hungry. Zebra had had his most recent meal seven weeks before. Carol went over to the gerbil bin to select a meal for Zebra. "Snakes just don't eat that much," she said, shaking her head in dismay over the exploding population of gerbils. She tossed one to a cat. She picked up another one, a small one, for Zebra.[96] "Zebra eats every month or two," she went on. "That's all he needs. He doesn't do anything. He just sits there." She lifted the lid of Zebra's jar and dropped the gerbil inside. The gerbil stood still, among the dry leaves, looking. Zebra did not move. "I'm going to let him go soon. He's been a good friend. He really has. You sometimes forget they're deadly, you know. I've had my hand down inside

---

93. McPhee inserts some explanation into the role of the maps and sketches.
94. Transition from the notebooks, back to the actual flashback scene at Carol's house.
95. Because McPhee has already introduced Zebra by name, there is no need to remind us he's the rattlesnake. Note how he uses the verb "yawn" to make the snake seem more human and likeable.
96. Again, we see an example of how the ecosystems work.

the jar, cleaning it out, and suddenly realized, with cold sweat, that he's poisonous. Ordinarily, when you see a rattlesnake you are on guard immediately. But with him in the house all the time I tend to forget how deadly he is. The younger the snake, the more concentrated the venom."[97]

The gerbil began to walk around the bottom of the big glass jar. Zebra, whose body was arranged in a loose coil, gave no sign that he was aware of the gerbil's presence. Under a leaf, over a rock, sniffing, the gerbil explored the periphery of Zebra's domain. Eventually, the gerbil stepped up onto Zebra's back. Still Zebra did not move. Zebra had been known to refuse a meal, and perhaps that would happen now. The gerbil walked along the snake's back, stepped down, and continued along the boundary of the base of the jar, still exploring. Another leaf, another stone, the strike came when the gerbil was perhaps eight inches from Zebra's head. The strike was so fast, the strike and the recovery, that it could not really be followed by the eye. Zebra lanced across the distance, hit the gerbil in the heart, and, all in the same instant, was back where he had started, same loose coil, head resting just where it had been resting before. The gerbil took three steps forward and fell dead, so dead it did not even quiver, tail out straight behind.[98]

Sam had once told me how clumsy he thought rattlesnakes were, advising me never to walk through a palmetto stand third in a line, because a rattlesnake, said Sam, takes aim at the first person, strikes at the second, and hits the third.[99] After watching Zebra, though, I decided to go tenth in line, if at all. Carol seemed thoughtful. "I've had copperheads," she said. "But I'm not really that much on snakes. I'm always worrying that someday I'll come home and find the jar turned over and several cats lying on the floor." That night, on the floor in my sleeping bag, I began to doze off and then imagined rolling over and knocking Zebra out of his jar. I spent most of the night with my chin in my hands, watching him through the glass.

There was a baby hawk in a box in the kitchen, and early in the morning he began to scream. Nothing was going to quiet him except food. Carol got up, took a rabbit out of the refrigerator, and cut it up with a pair of scissors. It had been a rabbit D.O.R.[100] The rabbit was twice the size of the hawk, but the hawk ate most of the rabbit. There followed silence, bought and paid for. In the freezer, Carol had frogs' legs, trout, bream, nighthawk, possum, squirrel, quail, turtle, and what she called trash fish. The trash fish were for Garbage Belly. The destiny of the other items was indistinct. They were for the consumption of the various occupants of the house,[101] the whole food chain—bird, am-

97. Note how McPhee uses the quote both to convey information and as a delay. By postponing telling, or showing, us what happens to the gerbil, he compels us to continue reading.

98. McPhee continues to build tension in this wonderful scene, which again demonstrates his close attention to detail and movement. Like the gerbil, McPhee moves slowly and gingerly, all the while building the tension, drawing us into the scene and causing us to hold our breaths, to wait for the strike. He follows the gerbil's move over every leaf, every rock, every inch of the snake's back. He describes Zebra's loose coils. He even suggests that this might be one of those times Zebra refuses a meal. He sets us up with "another leaf, another stone" so that the actual strike comes as unexpectedly for us as it did for McPhee. He then quickly recapitulates the strike and finishes off the scene, with Zebra back in repose and the gerbil flat out, dead. Note how McPhee has kept the scene light, almost humorous, with the final touch being the detail of the gerbil's tail.

99. McPhee uses Sam's anecdote as explanatory information, but, as we will see, it is also a setup for further use later in the story.

100. Note how the use of "D.O.R." acts as a continuing link, tying this to the earlier part of the story and the actual road trip.

101. Again, note how the phrase "occupants of the house" humanizes Carol's menagerie and contributes to the story's informal tone.

phibian, beast and beetle, reptile, arachnid, man.[102] A sign over the kitchen sink said "EAT MORE POSSUM," black on Chinese red.[103]

In the bedroom[104] was a deerskin. "I saw blood on the trail," Carol said. "I knew a deer wouldn't go uphill shot, so I went down. I found it. It wasn't a spike buck, it was a slickhead. It had been poached. I poached it from the poacher." On the walls were watercolors and oils she had done of natural scenes, and three blown-up photographs of Johnny Cash. A half-finished papier-mâché head of Johnny Cash was in her bedroom as well, and other pieces of her sculpture, including "Earth Stars," a relief of mushrooms. Carol looked reverently at the photographs and said that whenever she had had depressing and difficult times she had turned to Johnny Cash, to the reassurances in the timbre of his voice, to the philosophy in his lyrics, to his approach to life. She said he had more than once pulled her through.

Carol grew up in Rochester, New York, until she was twelve, after that in Atlanta. Her father, Earl Ruckdeschel, worked for Eastman Kodak and managed the Atlanta processing plant.[105] She was an only child. Animals were *non grata* at home, so she went to them. "You have to turn to something. There was a lot of comfort out there in those woods. Wild creatures were my brothers and sisters. That is why I'm more interested in mammals than anything else. They're warm-blooded. Fish are cold-blooded. You can't snuggle up with a fish." Her parents mortally feared snakes, but she never did. Her father once made her a snake stick. Her mother told her, many times a month and year, that it was not ladylike to be interested in snakes and toads. Carol went to Northside High in Atlanta. After high school, for five years, she worked at odd jobs—she fixed car radios, she wandered. Then she went to Georgia State University, studied biology, and married a biologist there. He was an authority on river swamps, an ecologist—a tall, prognathous, slow-speaking scientific man. His subspeciality was cottonmouths. He had found an island in the Gulf that had a cottonmouth under every palmetto, and he lived for a time among them. He weighed and measured them one by one. He was a lot older than Carol. She had taken his course in vertebrate zoology. The marriage did not really come apart. It evaporated. Carol kept going on field trips with him, and she stayed on at Georgia State as a biological researcher.[106] The little house she moved into could not have been better: low rent, no class, high privacy, woods, a creek. And it was all her own. A cemetery was across the street. She could sleep there if she wanted to get out of the house. On Mother's Day, or whenever else she needed flowers, she collected bouquets from among the graves. From time to time, she wandered away. She had a white pickup truck and a German shepherd. His name was Catfish, and he was "all mouth and no brains." Carol and Catfish slept on a bale of hay in the back of the truck, and they went all over, from the mountains to the sea. They fished in the mountains, hunted in the sand hills, set traps in the Okefenokee Swamp.[107] She began collecting specimens for the Georgia State University

---

102. Humor is best understated. Here, McPhee simply tags "man" onto the end of the food chain and lets it speak for itself.

103. Another example of the varied sources McPhee has drawn upon to paint a portrait of Carol. While the sign itself could be sufficient, the fact it is black on Chinese red lets us see it.

104. Transition.

105. Twenty pages into the story, after we're thoroughly caught up in it, McPhee takes time to begin giving us Carol's background and, for the first time, her last name.

106. In providing Carol's background, note how selectively McPhee uses those details and facts that explain her interest in wildlife, especially snakes. We now also learn what she does for a living.

107. List provides means to sum up the adventures of Carol and Catfish.

research collection Most she found dead on the road.[108] Occasionally, she brought new specimens into the collection, filling in gaps, but mainly she replenished exhausted supplies—worn-out pelts and skulls. There was always a need. An animal's skin has a better chance against a Goodyear tire than it does against the paws of a college student. She had no exclusive specialty. She wanted to do everything. Any plant or creature, dead or alive, attracted her eye.

She volunteered, as well, for service with the Georgia Natural Areas Council, a small office of the state government that had been established to take an inventory of wild places in Georgia worth preserving, proclaiming, and defending. While she travelled around Georgia picking up usable D.O.R.s for the university, she appraised the landscape for the state, detouring now and again into river swamps to check the range of frogs.[109] Sam Candler, who also worked for the Natural Areas Council,[110] generally went with her. Rarely, they flew in his plane. For the most part, they were on the road. Sam had a farm in Coweta County. He had also spent much of his life in the seclusion of Cumberland Island, off the Georgia coast. He was a great-grandson of the pharmacist who developed and at one time wholly owned the Coca-Cola Company, so he could have been a rampant lion in social Atlanta, but he would have preferred to wade blindfolded through an alligator swamp with chunks of horsemeat trussed to his legs. He wanted to live, as he put it, "close to the earth." He knew wilderness, he had been in it so much, and his own outlook on the world seemed to have been formed and directed by his observations of the creatures that ranged in wild places, some human, some not. Sam had no formal zoological or ecological training. What he brought to his work was mainly a sense of what he wanted for the region where he had lived his life. He had grown up around Atlanta, had gone to Druid Hills Grammar School and to Emory University and on into the Air Force. He had lived ever since on the island and the farm. His wife and their four children seemed to share with him a lack of interest in urban events. The Natural Areas Council had been effective. It had the weight of the government behind it. Georgia was as advanced in this respect as say, Indiana, Illinois, Iowa, and New Jersey, where important conservancy work was also being accomplished on the state-government level, and far more advanced than most other states. There was much to evaluate. Georgia was, after all, the largest state east of the Mississippi River, and a great deal of it was still wild. Georgia forests, mountains, swamps, islands, and rivers—a long list of sites of special interest or value—had become Registered Natural Areas. Sam and Carol had done the basic work—exploring the state, following leads, assessing terrain, considering vegetation and wildlife, choosing sites, and persuading owners to register lands for preservation.[111]

Sam had been a friend of mine for some years, and when he wrote to say that he was now travelling around the state collecting skulls and pelts, eating rattlesnakes, preserving natural areas, and charting the ranges of river frogs, I could not wait until I could go down there and see.[112] I had to wait more than a year, though, while finishing up some work. I live in Princeton, New Jersey, so I flew from Newark when the day came, and I nearly missed the plane. Automobiles that morning were backed up at least a mile from the Newark Airport tollbooths (fourteen tollbooths, fourteen lanes), and the jam was just as thick on the paid side as it was on the unpaid side—thousands and thousands of

---

108. The phrase "dead on the road" echoes the earlier references and neatly ties the story together.
109. Now we more fully understand the reason for the road trip.
110. We move onto Sam and his background and last name.
111. McPhee uses a list to tightly summarize Carol and Sam's work in preserving natural habitats.
112. McPhee explains this particular trip's origins.

murmuring cars, moving nowhere, nowhere to move, shaking, vibrating, stinking, rattling.[113] *Homo sapiens* D.O.R.[114] I got out of my car and left it there, left it, shamefully, with a high-school student who was accepting money to drive it home, and began to make my way overland to the terminal. I climbed up on bumpers and over corrugated fences and ducked under huge green signs. I went around tractor trailers and in front of buses.[115] Fortunately, Sam had told me to bring a backpack. Carrying a suitcase through that milieu would have been like carrying a suitcase up the Matterhorn.[116] Occasionally, I lost direction, and once I had to crawl under a mastodonic truck, but I did get through, and I ran down the cattle-pen corridors of the airport and, with a minute to go, up the steps and into the plane—relieved beyond measure to be out of that ruck and off to high ground and sweet air,[117] taking my chances on the food.[118] Sam and Carol met me, and we went straight to the mountains, stopping all the way for D.O.R.s.[119] That night, we ate a weasel.[120]

In a valley in north Georgia,[121] Carol had a cabin that was made of peeled logs, had a stone fireplace, and stood beside a cold stream. We stayed there on the first night of a journey that eventually meandered through eleven hundred miles of the state—a great loop, down out of the river gorges and ravine forests of the mountains, across the granitic piedmont and over the sand hills and the red hills to the river swamps and pine flatwoods of the coastal plain. Sam had a canoe on the top of the car. We slept in swamps and beside a lake and streams. Made, in part, in the name of the government, it was a journey that tended to mock the idea of a state—as an unnatural subdivision of the globe, as a metaphor of the human ego sketched on paper and framed in straight lines and in riparian boundaries behind an unalterable coast. Georgia. A state? Really a core sample of a continent, a plug in the melon, a piece of North America. Pull it out and wildcats would spill off the high edges. Alligators off the low ones. The terrain was crisscrossed with geological boundaries, mammalian boundaries, amphibian boundaries—the range of the river frogs. The range of the wildcat was the wildcat's natural state, overlaying segments

---

113. The chronology actually begins here, with the Newark traffic jam and McPhee's flight to Georgia. Note how this scene is as concrete and vivid as those on the actual road trip: the number of tollbooths, the extent of the traffic jam. He captures the scene, even the sounds ("murmuring," "rattling"), smell ("stinking"), and movement ("shaking," "vibrating") of the cars in a list of participles. The repetition "moving nowhere, nowhere to move" captures the complete standstill.

114. "D.O.R." acts as a connecting thread, linking the airport fiasco to the road trip and the rest of the story, this time with added humor: "*Homo sapiens* D.O.R."

115. McPhee's rendering of his ordeal to get to the airport is both vivid and delightful and, through his careful selection of detail, allows us to follow the whole experience. As he makes his way up and over and through the obstacle course, we are somewhat reminded of the gerbil making its way over the leaves and rocks and Zebra's back. Will he make it? The use of "and" rather than commas makes the course seem all the more insurmountable.

116. The Matterhorn simile fits the subject matter and drives home his point.

117. Note how this long sentence replicates his actions. It rushes headlong and breathlessly ahead as he dashes for the plane and then pauses momentarily at the prepositional phrase ("with a minute to go") set off by commas, before proceeding at a more leisurely pace as he makes his way to higher ground.

118. The comment becomes especially humorous and ironic, given the food he'll be eating as the trip progresses.

119. Rather than give us a detailed account of the trip's first day, McPhee compresses the time, focusing on the most important point: They picked up a lot of road kill.

120. By this time, we—and his vegetarian editor—are thoroughly hooked, and McPhee can now safely introduce the weasel. What some readers might have found offensive earlier is now more apt to be acceptable. Nevertheless, note how casually he drops in the fact they ate weasel. Because of his own nonchalance, we too accept it as almost routine.

121. Place transition.

of tens of thousands of other states, one of which was Georgia. The State of Georgia. Governor Jimmy Carter in the mansion in Atlanta.[122]

The first thing Sam and Carol wanted to assess on this trip was a sphagnum bog in Rabun County, off the north side of the Rabun Bald (4,696 feet).[123] The place seemed marginal to me, full of muck and trout lilies, with swamp pinks in blossom under fringe trees and smooth alders, but Sam and Carol thought it ought to be registered, and they sought out the owner, a heavy woman, greatly slow of speech, with a Sears, Roebuck tape measure around her neck.[124] She stood under a big white pine by the concrete front porch of her shingled house on a flinty mountain farm. Sam outlined the value of registering a natural area for preservation beyond one's years. She looked at him with no expression and said, "We treasure the bog." He gave her an application. ("Being aware of the high responsibility to the state that goes with the ownership and use of a property which has outstanding value in illustrating the natural history of Georgia, we morally agree to continue to protect and use this site for purposes consistent with the preservation of its natural integrity.")[125] Perhaps she could consider it with her husband and his brothers and nephews when they came home. One day soon, he would stop back to talk again.[126] She said, "We likes to hunt arrowheads. We treasure the bog."

The D.O.R.s that first day included a fan belt Sam took for a blacksnake—jammed on his brakes, backed up to see—and a banana peel that Carol identified, at first glimpse, as a jumping mouse.[127] Eager was the word for them. They were so much on the hunt. "It is rare for specimens to be collected this way," Carol said. "Most people are too lazy. Or they're hung up on just frogs or just salamanders, or whatever, and they don't care about other things. Watching for D.O.R.s makes travelling a lot more interesting. I mean, can you imagine just *going* down the road?"

We went around a bend in a mountain highway and the road presented Carol with the find of the day. "D.O.R." she said. "That was a good one. That was a *good* one Sam, hurry back. That was a weasel."[128]

Sam hurried back. It was no banana peel. It was exactly what Carol said it was: *Mustela frenata*, the long-tailed weasel, dead on the road.[129] It was fresh-killed, and—from the point of view of Georgia State University—in fine condition. Carol was so excited she jumped. The weasel was a handsome thing, minklike, his long body a tube roughly ten by two, his neck long and slender. His fur was white and yellow on the underside and dark brown on his back. "What a magnificent animal!" Carol said. "And hard as hell to trap.

---

122. Instead of immediately going into the actual finding and eating of the weasel, McPhee gives us a tight, yet vivid overview of the road trip and the state of Georgia. He uses the metaphor of the plug of watermelon to make his point that Georgia could tell us about the North American continent itself.

123. The story resumes its account of the road trip. Even though we are now at the beginning of the actual trip, we are still in the midst of the loop that began with the snapping turtle, Chap Causey, and snakes.

124. Another minor character becomes memorable, thanks to the Sears, Roebuck tape measure and her drawl.

125. The application's actual wording provides information and adds flavor. By enclosing it in parentheses, it does not interfere with the forward movement of the story.

126. Rather than include the exchange, McPhee paraphrases what Sam said, phrasing it in a way that it sounds like him speaking.

127. McPhee again compresses the D.O.R.s, both to stress the pair's eagerness and to make the more memorable finds—like the weasel—stand out.

128. McPhee catches us off guard. Because of his well-placed delay (the overview of the trip, the description of Georgia, the fan belt), we do not expect to come upon it so soon. Now we share the experience in detail.

129. Again, the unifying refrain. This time McPhee spells it out rather than using the initials, and in doing so, avoids the smell and mangled connotations usually associated with road kill.

Smell his musk. The scent glands are back here by the tail." While backing up after seeing him, she had hoped against hope that he would be a least weasel—smallest of all carnivores. She had never seen one. The least weasel diets almost exclusively on tiny, selected mice. This one would have eaten almost anything warm, up to and including a rabbit twice his size. Carol put him in an iced cooler that was on the back seat. The cooler was not airtight. Musk permeated the interior of the car. It was not disturbing. It was merely powerful.[130] Carol said they had once collected a skunk D.O.R. They had put it in a plastic bag within a plastic bag within four additional plastic bags. The perfume still came through.[131]

Carol's valley[132] resisted visitors. It was seven miles from a paved road. It was rimmed with mountains. It was the coldest valley in Georgia. A trout stream cascaded out of the south end. Ridges pressed in from east and west. The north was interrupted by a fifty-five-hundred-foot mountain called Standing Indian. Standing Indian stood in North Carolina, showing Georgia where to stop. The valley was prize enough. Its floor was flat and green with pastureland and shoots of new corn. Its brooks were clear. Now, in May, there would be frost across the fields in the morning, heavy and bright, but blossoms were appearing on the dogwoods and leaves on the big hardwoods—only so far up the mountains, though; it was still winter on Standing Indian, stick-figure forests to the top. Sam had flown over this whole area, minutely, in his Cessna—Mt. Oglethorpe to the Chattooga River, Black Rock Mountain to the Brasstown Bald. He said there was no valley in Georgia like this one in beauty or remoteness. It was about two miles long and a half mile wide. Its year-round population was twelve. Someone else, somewhere else, would have called it by another name, but not here. Lyrical in its effrontery to fact, the name of the valley was Tate City.[133] On our way in, we stopped to see Arthur and Mammy Young, its senior residents. Their house, until recently, had had so many preserves stacked on boards among the rafters that the roof sagged. Their outhouse straddled a stream. Their house, made of logs, burned to the ground one day when they were in town, eighteen miles away. Now they lived in a cinderblock hut with a pickup truck outside, fragments of machinery lying on the ground, hound dogs barking. The Youngs were approaching old age, apparently with opposite metabolisms, he sinewy, she more than ample, after sixty years of cathead biscuits.[134] Inside, Arthur rolled himself a cigarette and sat down to smoke it beside his wood-burning stove. Near him was a fiddle. Sam said that Arthur was a champion fiddler. Arthur went on smoking and did not reach for the fiddle. He exchanged news with Carol. Christ looked down on us from pictures on each wall. The room had two kerosene lanterns, and its windows were patched with tape. "I always wished I had power, so I could iron," Mammy said. "When I had kids. Now I don't care."[135] Dusk was near and Carol wanted time in the light, so we left soon and went on up the valley, a mile or so, to her log cabin.[136]

---

130. McPhee continues to work at making the weasel acceptable fare: it is "fresh-killed," "in fine condition," "handsome." He also uses the occasion to educate us, telling us about the animal's size, coloring, odor, and eating habits.

131. The musk provides a place to work in another anecdote.

132. The reference reminds us that we are still in the valley in north Georgia, where Carol has a cabin.

133. Earlier McPhee wrote that stops always brought the landscape into focus, and so it is here as he captures the essence of Carol's valley: the rim of mountains, the cascading stream, Standing Indian, the dogwood blooming only so far up the mountain, the stick-figure timber, the morning frost, the one dozen inhabitants.

134. Arthur and Mammy Young stand out because of their hovel in the midst of this natural beauty, though the extremes of their sizes is memorable.

135. Instead of fully playing out the scene, McPhee gives us the more interesting details: the fiddle and the fact Arthur never plays it, the pictures of Christ, and the lack of electricity.

136. Place transition.

A wooden deck reached out from the cabin on stilts toward the stream. The place had been cut out of woods—hemlock, ironwood, oak, alder, dogwood, rhododendron. A golden birch was standing in a hole in the center of the deck. Carol got out the weasel and set him, paws up, on the deck. Sam unpacked his things and set a bottle of The Glenlivet near the weasel, with three silver cups. I added a bottle of Talisker. Sam was no bourbon colonel. He liked pure Highland malt Scotch whisky. Carol measured the weasel. She traced him on paper and fondled his ears.[137] His skull and his skin would go into the university's research collection. She broke a double-edged Gillette blade in half the long way. "Weasels are hard to come by, hard to scent, hard to bait," she said. "We've tried to trap a least weasel. We don't even have one. I hate to catch animals, though. With D.O.R.s, I feel great. We've got the specimen and we're making use of it. The skull is the most important thing. The study skin shows the color pattern."[138]

With a simple slice, she brought out a testicle; she placed it on a sheet of paper and measured it. Three-quarters of an inch. Slicing smoothly through the weasel's fur, she began to remove the pelt. Surely, she worked the skin away from the long neck. The flesh inside the pelt looked like a segment of veal tenderloin.[139] "I lived on squirrel last winter," she said. "Every time you'd come to a turn in the road, there was another squirrel. I stopped buying meat. I haven't bought any meat in a year, except for some tongue. I do love tongue." While she talked, the blade moved in light, definite touches. "Isn't he in perfect shape?" she said. "He was hardly touched. You really lose your orientation when you start skinning an animal that's been run over by a Mack truck." From time to time, she stopped for a taste of The Glenlivet, her hand, brown from sun and flecked with patches of the weasel's blood, reaching for the silver cup. "You've got to be careful where you buy meat anyway. They inject some animals with an enzyme, a meat tenderizer, before they kill them. *That* isn't any good for you."[140] Where the going was difficult, she moistened the skin with water. At last it came away entire, like a rubber glove.[141] She now had the weasel disassembled, laid out on the deck in cleanly dissected parts. "I used to love to take clocks apart," she said. "To see how they were built. This is the same thing. I like plants and animals and their relationship to the land and us. I like the vertebrates especially." The weasel's tailbone was still in the skin. She tugged at it with her teeth. Pausing for a sip, she said that sometimes you just had to use your mouth in her line of work, as once when she was catching cricket frogs. She had a frog in each hand and saw another frog, so she put one frog into her mouth while she caught the third. Gradually, the weasel's tailbone came free. She held it in her hand and admired it. "Some bones are real neat," she said.[142] "In the heart of a deer, there's a bone. And not between the ventricles, where you'd expect it. Some animals have bones in their penises—raccoons, for example, and weasels." She removed the bone from the weasel's penis. It was long, proportionately speaking, with a hook at the penetrating end. It was called a baculum, she said, which meant "rod" in Latin. She would save it. Its dimensions were one way to tell the weasel's

137. The detail of the weasel lying paws up, the Gillette razor blade, and Carol measuring, tracing, and fondling its ears place us in the scene. The expensive Scotch and silver cups provide an interesting, and thus memorable, contrast.
138. The research center's use of D.O.R. skeletons and pelts provides justification and explanation.
139. The veal simile fits the subject matter.
140. Another attempt to make their eating of the weasel acceptable.
141. The comparison helps us envision how the skin came away from the body.
142. Carol's awe and admiration help put readers at ease.

age. Baculums are also involved in keying differences in species.[143] Sam said he kept a raccoon's baculum in his wallet because it made a great toothpick. Carol turned the pelt inside out and folded the forepaws in an X, standard procedure with a study skin. She covered it with a deep layer of salt and packed it away.

The dusk was deep then. Carol had finished working almost in the dark. The air was cold. It was on its way to thirty. Sam had a fire going, inside, already disintegrating into coals. The smell of burning oak was sweet. We went into the cabin. Carol put the weasel on the tines of a long fork and roasted it over the coals.

"How do you like your weasel?" Sam asked me.

"Extremely well done," I said.

Carol sniffed the aroma of the roast.[144] "It has a wild odor," she said. "You *know* it's not cow. The first time I had bear, people said, 'Cut the fat off. That's where the bad taste is.' I did, and the bear tasted just like cow. The next bear, I left the fat on."

The taste of the weasel was strong and not unpleasant. It lingered in the mouth after dinner. The meat was fibrous and dark.[145] "It just goes to show you how good everything is," said Carol. "People who only eat cows, pigs, sheep, chickens—boy, have those people got blinders on! Is that tunnelization! There's one poisonous mammal in the United States: the short-tailed shrew. And you can even eat that."

Sam built up the fire.

"How can you be sure that something is not too old?" I asked.

"My God, if you can't tell if it's bad, what's the difference?" said Carol.

Sam said, "If it tastes good, don't knock it."

"People don't make sense," Carol said. "They hunt squirrels, but they wouldn't consider eating a squirrel killed on the road. Only once have I ever had competition for a D.O.R. A man wanted a squirrel for his black servant, and we had a set-to in the road."

There were double-deck bunks in the corners of the room. The corners were cold. We pulled three mattresses off the bunks and put them down side by side before the fire. We unrolled our three sleeping bags. It had been a big day; we were tired, and slept without stirring. Sam dreamed in the night that he was eating his own beard.[146]

With a load of honey and cathead biscuits,[147] gifts of Mammy Young,[148] we went down out of the valley in the morning, mile after mile on a dirt road that ran beside and frequently crossed the outlet stream, which was the beginnings of the Tallulah River. Some twenty miles on down, the river had cut a gorge, in hard quartzite, six hundred feet deep. Warner Brothers had chosen the gorge as the site for the filming of a scene from James Dickey's novel, *Deliverance*. This mountain land in general was referred to around the state as "*Deliverance* country." The novel seemed to have been the most elaborate literary event in Georgia since *Gone with the Wind*. *Deliverance* was so talked about that people had, for conversational convenience, labelled its every part ("the owl scene," "the banjo scene"). It was a gothic novel, a metaphysical terror novel, the structural center of which involved four men going through the rapids of a mountain river in canoes. They

---

143. Still another example of McPhee educating while entertaining his readers. We are learning, though we are scarcely aware of it.

144. McPhee continues to use food terms to make eating the weasel more palatable for readers.

145. McPhee delicately skips the actual eating of the weasel and only describes the taste and texture.

146. The section, and the first day, ends on a humorous note that demonstrates McPhee's resourcefulness in using material. Here he makes good use of a dream.

147. Transition into day two.

148. The name "Mammy" is unusual, so we know without explanation whom he is talking about.

were attacked. The action climax occurred when one of the canoemen scaled the wall of a fantastically sheer gorge to establish an ambush and kill a mountain man. He killed him with a bow and arrow. Carol and Sam, like half the people in Atlanta and a couple of dozen in Hollywood, called this "the climb-out scene," and they took me to see where Warners would shoot. The six-hundred-foot gorge was a wonder indeed, clefting narrowly and giddily down through the quartzite to the bed of the river that had done the cutting. Remarkably, though, no river was there. A few still pools. A trickle of water. Graffiti adorned the rock walls beside the pools. There was a dam nearby, and, in 1913, the river had been detoured through a hydropower tunnel. Steel towers stood on opposite lips of the chasm, supported by guy wires. A cable connected the towers. They had been built for performances of wire walkers, the Flying Wallendas.[149] Nearby was the Cliffhanger Café. A sign said, "Enjoy Coca-Cola. See it here, free. Tallulah Gorge. 1200 feet deep." The Georgia Natural Areas Council looked on. Too late to register that one. The eye of the Warner Brothers camera would, however, register just what it wanted to select and see, and it would move up that wall in an unfailing evocation of wilderness. I was awed by the power of Dickey. In writing his novel, he had assembled "*Deliverance* country" from such fragments, restored and heightened in the chambers of his imagination. The canoes in his novel dived at steep angles down breathtaking cataracts and shot like javelins through white torrents among blockading monoliths. If a canoe were ten inches long and had men in it three inches high, they might find such conditions in a trout stream, steeply inclined, with cataracts and plunge pools and rushing bright water falling over ledges and splaying through gardens of rock.[150] Dickey must have imagined something like that and then enlarged the picture until the trout stream became a gothic nightmare for men in full-size canoes. A geologically maturer, less V-shaped stream would not have served. No actual river anywhere could have served his artistic purpose— not the Snake, not the Upper Hudson, not even the Colorado—and least of all a river in Georgia, whose wild Chattooga, best of the state's white-water rivers, has comparatively modest rapids. The people of the *Deliverance* mountains were malevolent, opaque, and sinister. Arthur and Mammy Young.[151]

There were records of the presence of isolated cottonmouths on Dry Fork Creek, in wild, forested piedmont country east of Athens. Dry Fork Creek, a tributary of a tributary of the Savannah River, was about halfway between Vesta and Rayle, the beginning and the end of nowhere.[152] We searched the woods along the creek. It would not have been at all unusual had we found the highland moccasin (the copperhead) there, for this was his terrain—*Agkistrodon contortrix contortrix*. What we were looking for, though, was the water mocassin (the cottonmouth), inexplicably out of his range. Cottonmouths belong in the coastal plain, in the rice fields, in the slow-moving rivers—*Agkistrodon piscivorus pis-*

---

149. McPhee, the good guide, takes us with them out of the valley, describing the terrain and its history and the most interesting moments as he goes. Within this long digression, note how many mini-digressions he makes, weaving in background, explanation, anecdotes, interesting tidbits, wherever the opportunity presents itself. Because he does this so smoothly and with care to maintain the tone and vivid writing, we seldom realize we've left the main time line. Here he uses the 600-foot depth of the gorge as a transition into and out of a digression into the movie *Deliverance*. The pools and trickle of water provide an opportunity to tell about the damming of the river, the towers and the guy wires to talk about the Flying Wallendas. The detours are themselves interesting, but they also show us the spoiling of this natural setting and the need for Carol and Sam's efforts.

150. McPhee replicates the sense of white water with a list of participial phrases connected by "and."

151. McPhee uses *Deliverance* to return us to Arthur and Mammy Young and the valley.

152. McPhee's playful voice comes through "a tributary of a tributary" and "the beginning and the end of nowhere."

civorus. Seeing a cottonmouth in a place like this would be a rare experience, and Carol fairly leaped into the woods. For my part, I regretted that I lacked aluminum boots. Carol was wearing green tennis shoes. Sam's feet were covered with moccasins.[153] Carol rolled every log. She lifted anything that could have sheltered a newt, let alone a snake. By the stream, she ran her eye over every flat rock and projecting branch. Always disappointed, she quickly moved on. Sam sauntered beside her. The flood plain was beautiful under big sycamores, water oaks, maples: light filtering down in motes, wet leaves on the ground, cold water moving quietly in the stream.[154] But the variety of tracks she found was disturbingly incomplete. "There, on that sandbar—those are possum tracks. Possums and coons go together, but that's just possum right there, no way about it. And that is not right. There shouldn't be a bar like that with no coon tracks on it, even if the water goes up and down every night. Possums can live anywhere. Coons can't. Coon tracks signify a healthy place. I don't much like this place. It's been cut over. There are no big dead trees."[155] One big dead tree with a cottonmouth under it would have changed that, would have glorified Dry Fork Creek for Carol, coons or no coons—*piscivorus piscivorus* caught poaching, out of his territory, off the edge of his map, beyond his range. I felt her disappointment and was sorry the snakes were not there. "Don't be disappointed," she said. "When we go down the Cemocheckobee, cottonmouths will show us the way."[156]

Buffalo disappeared from Georgia in early Colonial time. William Bartram noted this when he visited the colony and wrote *Travels in Georgia and Florida, 1773–74*. Bartram, from Philadelphia, was the first naturalist to describe in detail the American subtropics. After his book reached London, sedentary English poets cribbed from his descriptions (Wordsworth, for example, and Coleridge). Ten miles south of Dry Fork Creek, Sam, Carol, and I crossed Bartram's path. In Bartram's words, "We came into an open Forest of Pines, Scrub white Oaks, Black Jacks, Plumb, Hicory, Grapes Vines, Rising a sort of Ridge, come to a flat levill Plain, and at the upper side of this, levell at the foot of the hills of the great Ridge, is the great Buffiloe Lick, which are vast Pits, licked in the Clay, formerly by the Buffiloes, and now kept smoothe and open by Cattle, deer, and horses, that resort here constantly to lick the clay, which is a greesey Marle of various colours, Red, Yellow & white, & has a sweetish taste, but nothing saltish that I could perceive." Bartram was describing what is now Philomath, Georgia 30659—a one-street town consisting of thirty houses and a buffalo lick.[157] Philomath was established, early in the nineteenth century, as a seat of learning—hence the name. The town was the address of an academy whose students, in time, vanished like the buffalo. Now it was a place of preeminent silence under big oaks, and as we glided into town we were the only thing that moved. Ninety blacks, fifty whites lived there, but no one was out in the midday shade. The almost idling engine was the only sound. In an L-shaped elegant clapboard house, built in 1795, lived Dorothy Daniel Wright.[158] Sam and Carol, having read Bar-

---

153. The detail of the trio's shoes tells us, without need for explanation, how each one feels about the prospect of encountering cottonmouths.

154. In the midst of looking for snakes, McPhee again stops to bring his surroundings into focus in a sentence that captures the beauty: the light filtering through the trees, the wet leaves on the ground, the quietly moving stream.

155. With Carol's quote, we get another brief wildlife lesson.

156. The quote foreshadows and sets up expectations.

157. McPhee draws from an eighteenth-century naturalist to give us a detailed description of what the area once looked like. The ZIP code creates an interesting transition from what was to what is.

158. McPhee inverts the sentence to move us gracefully from a wide shot of the town to Dorothy Daniel Wright.

tram's description and having determined that the buffalo lick was still intact, wanted to see it and, they hoped, to register it as a Georgia Natural Area. Miss Wright was the person to see. It was her lick. She was in her upper sixties. Her hair was white and swept upward, and crowned with a braided gold bun. Her welcome was warm. She showed us the lick.[159] Cattle and deer had licked it slick all through her girlhood, she said. Now it was covered with grass, some hawthorn and sumac, and dominated by an immense, outreaching laurel oak. Carol squatted flat-footed, knees high, and dug with her hands for various colors of clay. She ate some blue clay, and handed pieces to me and Sam. It was sweet, bland, alkaline, slightly chewy. "My first thought was 'soapy,'" she said. "I expected it to get stronger, but it didn't. The final thought was 'sweetness.'" She put a bit more in her mouth and ate it contemplatively. There was, apparently, no sodium chloride in this ground. Phosphate, sodium, and calcium are what the buffalo licked. Where did they get their salt? "Twelve miles away there was salt," Miss Wright said. "Twelve miles is nothin' to a buffalo roamin' around. Between the two licks, they got all the minerals they needed for their bovine metabolism." Miss Wright had taught biology and chemistry in various high schools for forty-three years. She was eager to register the Great Buffalo Lick Natural Area, which had once been a boundary-line landmark separating the Georgia colony from the territory of the Creeks and Cherokees. She took us home to a lunch of salad and saltines. Into the salad went mushrooms, violets, and trout lilies that Carol had gathered in the mountains the day before.[160]

Leaving Philomath, heading south,[161] Sam commented how easy and pleasant that experience had been and how tense such encounters could sometimes be. He talked about a redneck peanut farmer in south Georgia, owner of a potential Natural Area. This redneck had taken one look at Sam's beard and had seemed ready to kill him then and there.

"What is a redneck, Sam?"

"You know what a redneck is, you little Yankee bastard."

"I want to hear your definition."

"A redneck is a fat slob in a pickup truck with a rifle across the back. He hates 'niggers.' He would rather have his kids ignorant than go to school with colored. I guess I don't like rednecks. I guess I've known some."

"Some of my best friends are rednecks," Carol said.[162]

D.O.R. blacksnake,[163] five miles south of Irwinton—old and bloated. "I'll just get it off the road, so its body won't be further humiliated," Carol said. Across a fence, a big sow was grunting. Carol carried the snake to the fence. She said, "Here, piggy-poo, look what I've got for you." She tossed the snake across the fence. The sow bit off the snake's head and ate it like an apple.[164]

"Interesting," Carol said, "that we can feed a rotten snake to something we in turn will eat."

---

159. Note how McPhee shifts to short sentences as Carol and Sam get down to business: *Miss Wright was the person to see. It was her lick. She showed them the lick.* Once they see the lick, the sentences again grow longer.

160. You won't find violets and trout lilies in many salads. They are vivid details to include, and they again show us just how close to nature Carol lives.

161. Transition out of the scene and back to the road.

162. Beyond the words themselves, this exchange provides insight into both characters.

163. The focus returns to road kill.

164. Simile provides a clear image of the pig biting into the snake and is appropriate to the tone and subject matter.

I said I would rather eat the buffalo lick.

Carol said, "I'll tell you the truth, I've had better clay."

We were out of the piedmont and down on the coastal plain, into the north of south Georgia. The roadside ads were riddled with bullet holes. "PREPARE TO MEET JESUS CHRIST THE LORD." "WE WANT TO WIPE OUT CANCER IN YOUR LIFETIME." "WE CANNOT ACCEPT TIRES THAT HAVE BEEN CAPPED AS TRADE-INS."[165]

Johnny Cash was back. Indians were now his theme. He was singing about a dam that was going to flood Seneca land, although the Senecas had been promised title to their land "as long as the moon shall rise." Cash's voice was deeper than ever. He sounded as if he were smoking a peace pipe through an oboe. Carol hugged herself. "As long . . . as the moon . . . shall rise . . . As long . . . as the rivers . . . flow."

"DON'T LOSE YOUR SOUL BY THE MARK OF THE BEAST."

We ate muskrat that night in a campsite on flat ground beside Big Sandy Creek, in Wilkinson County, innermost Georgia—muskrat with beans, chili powder, onions, tomatoes, and kelp. "I have one terrible handicap," Carol said. "I cannot follow a recipe." The muskrat, though, was very good. Carol had parboiled it for twenty minutes and then put it through a meat grinder, medium grind.[166] Firewood was scarce, because the area was much used by fishermen who were prone to build fires and fish all night. Carol went up a tall spruce pine, and when she was forty feet or so above the ground she began to break off dead limbs and throw them down. She had to throw them like spears to clear the living branches of the tree. Pine burns oily, but that would not matter tonight. The muskrat was in a pot. Sam and I built up the fire. He pitched a tent.

To pass time before dinner, I put the canoe into the river and paddled slowly downstream.[167] Carol called to me from the tree, "Watch for snakes. They'll be overhead, in the limbs of trees." She was not warning me; she was trying to raise the pleasure of the ride. "If you don't see the snake, you can tell by the splash," she went on. "A frog splash is a concentrated splash. A snake splash is a long splat." Gliding, watching, I went a quarter of a mile without a splash or a splat. It was dusk. The water was growing dark. I heard the hoot of a barred owl. Going back against the current, I worked up an appetite for muskrat.[168]

After dinner,[169] in moonlight, Sam and Carol and I got into the canoe and went up the river. A bend to the left, a bend to the right, and we penetrated the intense darkness of a river swamp that seemed to reach out unendingly. We could only guess at its dimensions. Upland swamps occur in areas between streams. River swamps are in the flood plains of rivers, and nearly all the streams in the Georgia coastal plain have them. They can be as much as six miles wide, and when the swamps of two or more big rivers connect, the result can be a vast and separate world. The darkness in there was so rich it felt warm. It was not total, for bars and slats of moonlight occasionally came through, touched a root or a patch of water.[170] Essentially, however, everything was black: black water, black vegetation—water-standing maples, cypress—black on black.[171] Columnar trunks were all around us, and we knew the channel only by the feel of the current, which

---

165. McPhee again uses religious road signs to compress time and miles.
166. More precise detail.
167. McPhee inverts the sentence both to create a smoother transition and to position him and the canoe next to Carol's warning.
168. Transition back to the muskrat.
169. Time transition.
170. The use of the second comma and the "or" give us the sense of those occasional patches of moonlight.
171. Repetition of the word "black" conveys just how dark it was.

sometimes seemed to be coming through from more than one direction. Here the black water sucked and bubbled, roiled by, splashed[172] through the roots of the trees. Farther on, it was silent again. Silent ourselves, we pushed on into the black. Carol moved a flashlight beam among the roots of trees. She held the flashlight to her nose, because the eye can see much more if the line of sight is closely parallel to the beam. She inspected minutely the knobby waterlines of the trees. Something like a sonic boom cracked in our ears. "Jesus, what was that?"

"Beaver."

The next two slaps were even louder than the first. Carol ignored the beaver, and continued to move the light. It stopped. Out there in the obsidian was a single blue eye.

"A blue single eye is a spider," she said. "Two eyes is a frog. Two eyes almost touching is a snake. An alligator's eyes are blood red."[173]

Two tiny coins now came up in her light. "Move in there," she said. "I want that one."

With a throw of her hand, she snatched up a frog. It was a leopard frog, and she let him go. He was much within his range. Carol was looking for river frogs, pig frogs, carpenter frogs, whose range peripheries we were stalking. She saw another pair of eyes. The canoe moved in. Her hand swept out unseen and made a perfect tackle, thighs to knees. This was a bronze frog, home on the range. Another pair of eyes, another catch, another disappointment—a bullfrog. Now another shattering slap on the water. Another. The beaver slapped only when the canoe was moving upstream. The frog chorus, filling the background, varied in pitch and intensity, rose and fell. Repeatedly came the hoot of the barred owl.

Sam dipped a cup and had a drink. "I feel better about drinking water out of swamps than out of most rivers," he said. "It's filtered. No one ever says a good word for a swamp. The whole feeling up to now has been 'Fill it in—it's too wet to plow, too dry to fish.' Most people stay out of swamps. I love them. I like the water, the reptiles, the amphibians. There is so much life in a swamp. The sounds are so different. Frogs, owls, birds, beavers. Birds sound different in swamps."

"You see a coon in here and you realize it's his whole world," Carol said.

"It's a beautiful home with thousands of creatures," Sam said.

With all this ecological intoxication, I thought they were going to fall out of the canoe.

"Life came out of the swamps," Sam said. "And now swamps are among the last truly wild places left."

We went back downstream. Tobacco smoke was in the air over the river. Occasionally, on the bank, we saw an orange-red glow, momentarily illuminating a black face. Fishing lines, slanting into the stream, were visible against the light of small fires. The canoe moved soundlessly by, and on into the darkness. "The groids sure love to fish," Sam murmured. The moon was low. It was midnight.[174]

* * *

Now, at noon, a hundred miles or so to the southeast and by another stream, we were sitting on the big felled oak, pouring out the last of the wine, with Chap Causey moving to-

---

172. That water comes to life through the use of vivid verbs: "sucked," "bubbled," "roiled," "splashed."
173. The quote is interesting for the information it conveys. It also serves as a setup for the frogs.
174. The long digression ends and we are ready to pick up where we left off.

ward us a foot at a time in his American dragline crane.[175] He swung a pair of mats around behind him and backed up a bit more, and as he went on gutting the streambed the oak began to tremble. It must have weighed two or three tons, but it was trembling and felt like an earthquake—time to move. Carol picked up a piece of dry otter scat. She bounced it in the palm of her hand and looked upcurrent at the unaltered stream and downcurrent into the new ditch. She said, "You can talk about coons' being able to go off into the woods and eat nuts and berries, because they're omnivores. But not this otter. He's finished." She broke open the scat. Inside it were fishbones and hair—hair of a mouse or hair of a young rabbit. There were fish otoliths as well, two of them, like small stones.[176] She flung it all into the stream. "He's done for," she said, and waved goodbye to Chap Causey.

On down the dirt road[177] from the stream-channelization project, we saw ahead a D.O.R.

"Looks like a bad one," Carol said.

Sam stopped. "Yes, it's a bad one," he said. "Canebrake. Do you want to eat him?"

Carol leaned over and looked. "He's too old. Throw him out of the road, the poor darlin'. What gets me is that some bastard is proud of having run over him. When I die, I don't want to be humiliated like that."

Sam threw the rattlesnake out of the road. Then we headed southwest through underdeveloped country, almost innocent of towns—Alma, Douglas, Adel, Moultrie, a hundred miles from Alma to Moultrie.

D.O.R. king snake, blue jay, sparrow hawk, wood thrush, raccoon, catbird, cotton rat. The poor darlin's. Threw them out of the road.[178]

A.O.R. hobo—man with a dog. "Oh, there's a good guy," Carol said as we passed him. "He has a dog and a bedroll. What else do you need?"

D.O.R. opossum. Cook County. Three miles east of Adel. Carol spoke admiringly of the creature flexibility of the opossum. Among the oldest of mammals, the possum goes all the way back to Cretaceous time, she said, and, like people, it has never specialized, in a biological sense. "You can specialize yourself out of existence. Drain the home of the otter. The otter dies. The opossum, though, can walk away from an ecological disaster. So much for that. Try something else. He eats anything. He lives almost anywhere. That's why the possum is not extinct. That's why the possum has been so successful." One place this particular possum was never going to walk away from was Georgia Highway 76. Technology, for him the ultimate ecological disaster, had clouted him at seventy miles an hour.[179]

Between Moultrie and Doerun, in the watershed of the Ochlockonee,[180] was a lake in a pine grove surrounded by fifty acres of pitcher plants. They belonged to a couple named Barber, from Moultrie, who had read about the Natural Areas Council and had offered their pitcher plants to posterity. Sam and Carol, posterity, would accept. This was

---

175. McPhee again uses Chap Causey to return us to the main time line.
176. For those of us who don't know what "otoliths" are McPhee uses a simile to show us what they look like.
177. Place transition.
178. McPhee uses towns and road kill to compress time, all the while maintaining the story's flavor. Here he repeats Carol's expression "the poor darlin's" and the fact they threw the critters off the road.
179. The D.O.R. opossum serves as a transition into and out of a brief digression on possums. In taking us out of the digression, note how McPhee structures the sentence so that we gracefully move from the possum back onto the highway, and the action, going seventy miles an hour.
180. Place transition into a scene and a digression on pitcher plants.

the largest colony of pitcher plants any of us was ever likely to see. Bright-green leaves, ruddy blooms, they glistened in the sun and nodded in the breeze and reached out from the lakeshore like tulips from a Dutch canal. Barber cut one off at the base and held up a leaf—folded upon itself like a narrow goblet, half full of water. The interior was lined with bristles, pointing downward. In the water were dozens of winged creatures, some still moving, most not. Barber had interrupted a handsome meal. His pitcher plants, in aggregate, could probably eat a ton of bugs a day. Sam said he sure was pleased to be able to make the pitcher plants a Georgia Natural Area. Carol saw a tiny water snake. She picked it up. It coiled in her hand and snapped at her. She talked gently to it until it settled down. "Are you going to be good now?" she said. She opened her hand, and the snake sat there, placidly, on her palm. The Barbers did not seem charmed. They said nothing and did not move. Carol set down the snake. It departed, and so did the Barbers. They went back to Moultrie in their air-conditioned car, leaving us their lake, their pines, their pitcher plants.[181]

We jumped into the lake with a bar of soap and scrubbed ourselves up for dinner. In places, the lake was warm from the sun and in places cold from springs. We set up the tent and built a fire. The breeze was cool in the evening in the pines. Carol's stomach growled like a mastiff. She said that when she was hungry she could make her stomach growl on cue. It growled again. She had a tape recorder in the car. Sam got it and recorded the growls, which seemed marketable. He said they could scare away burglars. We fried beefsteaks and turtle steaks[182] under a gibbous moon. We buried the fossils of pleasure: three cow bones and a bottle that had held The Glenlivet. Frogs were hooting. There were no owls. We slept like bears.[183]

At six in the morning,[184] we got into the canoe and moved slowly around the lake. Sam cast for bass. He could flick his lure seventy feet and drop it on a pine needle. He could lay it under stumps with the delicacy of an eyedropper, or drive it, if he wanted to, halfway down the lake. He caught two bass. One wrapped itself hopelessly into a big waterlogged multiple branch. We pulled the branch up out of the water. The bass had himself woven into it like a bird in a cage. Under the blue sky and star-burst clusters of longleaf pine—pitcher plants far as you could see, the lake blue and cool—we cooked the bass in butter and ate it with fried turtle eggs. Then we fried salt-risen bread in the bass butter with more turtle eggs and poured Tate City honey over the bread. Chicory coffee with milk and honey. Fish-crackling off the bottom of the pan.[185]

The yolk of a turtle egg cooks readily to a soft, mushy yellow. The albumen, though, pops and bubbles and jumps around the pan, and will not congeal. No matter how blazing the heat beneath it may be, the white of the egg of the snapping turtle will not turn milky and set. It will jump like a frog and bounce and dance and skitter all over the pan until your patience snaps or the fire dies.[186] So you give up trying to cook it. You swallow it hot and raw.

* * *

---

181. Like the snake and the Barbers, we back out of the pitcher scene.
182. We return to the turtle steaks we left at the story's beginning and round out that day.
183. The voice of our congenial tour guide.
184. Time transition into day four.
185. Knowing when sentence fragments will work and when they won't is something you have to develop an ear for. Make sure you have that ear before you risk it.
186. Like those obstinate egg whites, this sentence skitters and dances because of its animated verbs and connecting "and"s; then, like the fire, it comes to an end.

D.O.R. cat, D.O.R. dog.[187] Near the Mitchell County line. Carol sighed, but no move was made to stop. We were heading west on 37 to check out a river that the Natural Areas Council had been told was like no other in Georgia. Florida was only forty miles away. The terrain was flat and serene between the quiet towns—Camilla, Newton, Elmodel. Cattle stood on light-green grassland under groves of dark pecans. Sometimes the road was a corridor walled with pines. Sometimes the margins opened out into farms, then closed down toward small cabins, more palisades of pine.

D.O.R. gray squirrel. "We could eat him," Carol said.

"We've got enough food," said Sam.

More pines, more pecans, more farms, a mild morning under a blue-and-white sky. Out of the sky came country music—the Carter Sisters, Johnny Cash, philosophy falling like hail: "It's not easy to be all alone, but time goes by and life goes on . . . for after night there comes a dawn. Yes, time goes by and life goes on."[188]

D.O.R. fox squirrel. Baker County. He was as warm as in life, and he was in perfect shape. Kneeling in the road, Carol held out his long, feathery silver-gray tail so that it caught the sunlight. "There aren't many things prettier than that," she said. "Makes a human being sort of jealous not to have a pretty tail like that." Gently, she brushed the squirrel and daubed blood from his head. He looked alive in her hands. She put him in a plastic bag. The ice was low. We stopped at the next icehouse and bought twenty-five pounds.

D.O.R. nighthawk, fresh as the squirrel. Carol kept the hawk for a while in her lap, just to look at him. He could have been an Aztec emblem—wings half spread, head in profile, feathers patterned in blacks and browns and patches of white. Around the mouth were stiff bristles, fanned out like a radar screen, adapted for catching insects.[189]

D.O.R. box turtle.

D.O.R. loggerhead shrike.

D.O.R. gas station. It was abandoned, its old pumps rusting; beside the pumps, a twenty-year-old Dodge with four flat tires.

D.O.R. cottonmouth. Three miles east of Bluffton. Clay County. Finding him there was exciting to Carol. We were nearing the Cemocheckobee, the river we had come to see, and the presence of one cottonmouth here on the road implied crowded colonies along the river. There was no traffic, no point in moving him immediately off the road. Carol knelt beside him. "He was getting ready to shed. He would have been a lot prettier when he had," she said. The skin was dull olive. Carol felt along the spine to a point about three-quarters of the way back and squeezed. The dead snake coiled. "That is what really frightens people," she said. She lifted the head and turned it so that we could see, between the mouth and the nostrils, the deep pits, sensory organs, through which the striking snake had homed on his targets. Slowly, Carol opened the creature's mouth. The manuals of herpetology tell you not to do that, tell you, in fact, not to touch a dead cottonmouth, because through reflex action a dead one can strike and kill a human being. Now a fang was visible—a short brown needle projecting down from the upper jaw. "You have to be very careful not to scratch your finger on one of those," Carol said. She pressed with her fingertips behind the eyes, directly on the poison sacs, and a drop of milky fluid fell onto a stick she held in her other hand. Four more drops followed, forming a dome of venom.

187. Transition back to the road, but like the car, the story won't stop to examine these D.O.R.s.
188. McPhee continues compressing time and miles, using music on the radio and the terrain to do so.
189. McPhee takes time to describe those road kills the car's passengers stop for.

"That amount could kill you," she said, and she pressed out another drop. "Did you know that this is where they got the idea for the hypodermic syringe?" Another drop. "It has to get into the bloodstream. You could drink all you want and it wouldn't hurt you." She placed the cottonmouth off the road. Carol once milked honeysuckle until she had about two ounces, which she then drank. The fluid was so concentratedly sweet it almost made her sick.[190]

Carol's purse fell open as we got back into the car, and out of it spilled a. 22-calibre revolver in a case that looked much like a compact. Also in the purse was a Big Brother tear-gas gun, flashlight bulbs, chapstick, shampoo, suntan lotion, and several headbands. Once, when she was off in a swamp frogging and salamandering, a state trooper came upon the car and—thinking it might be an abandoned vehicle—rummaged through it. He found the purse and opened it. He discovered the pistol, the chapstick, the shampoo, et cetera, and a pink garter belt and black net stockings. He might have sent out a five-state alert, but Carol just then emerged from the swamp. She was on her way, she told him, to make a call on Kimberly-Clark executives in an attempt to get them to register some forest and riverbank land with the Natural Areas Council, and for that mission the black net stockings would be as useful as the pistol might be in a swamp or the chapstick in a blistering sun. "Yes, Ma'am." The visit to the Kleenex people was successful, as it happened, and the result was the Griffin's Landing Registered Natural Area, fifty acres—a series of fossil beds on the Savannah River containing by the many thousands *Crassostrea gigantissima*, forty-million-year-old oysters, the largest that ever lived.[191]

Down a dirt road, across a railroad track, and on through woods that scraped the car on both sides, Sam worked his way as far as he could toward the river's edge.[192] We took down the canoe, and carried it to the water. The Cemocheckobee was a rejuvenated stream. Widening its valley, long ago, it had formed relaxed meanders, and now, apparently, the land was rising beneath it, and the river had speeded up and was cutting deeply into the meanders. The current was strong—nothing spectacular, nothing white, but forceful and swift. It ran beneath a jungle of overhanging trees. The river was compact and intimate. The distance from bank to bank was only about thirty feet, so there could be no getting away from the trees. "I'd venture to say we'll see our share of snakes today," Carol exulted. "Let's go! This is cottonmouth country!" Carol shoved up the sleeves of her sweatshirt over her elbows. Sam went to the car and got a snakebite kit.[193]

I had thought I might be apprehensive about this part of the journey. I didn't see how I could help but be. Now I realized that I was having difficulty walking toward the river. "Sam," I said, "wouldn't you prefer that I paddle in the stern?"[194] I had put in many more hours than he had in canoes on rivers, so it seemed only correct to me that Sam should sit up in the bow and fend off branches and cottonmouths while I guided the canoe from the commanding position in the rear.

---

190. The cottonmouth provides an opportunity to weave in more information, including the honeysuckle anecdote.

191. McPhee uses the pistol incident to weave in the contents of Carol's purse, a colorful anecdote, and information on the Griffin's Landing Registered Natural Area.

192. McPhee again inverts the sentence to provide a transition into the next paragraph and scene and to place the river's edge at the end, and thus create another natural transition into the canoe and the next sentence.

193. Carol's quote and the snakebite kit create tension. We are compelled to read on to see if they encounter snakes.

194. We continue to experience the story through McPhee. His reactions become ours. Because of Sam's earlier comments about the clumsiness of the rattlesnake, we understand why McPhee wants to paddle. There is no need to explain, and an explanation would undercut the humor.

"I'll go in the stern," said Sam. "Carol will go in the middle to collect snakes. You go in the bow." So much for that. It was his canoe. I got in and moved to the bow. They got in, and we shoved off.

The canoe found the current, accelerated, went downstream fifty feet, and smashed into a magnolia branch. I expected cottonmouths to strike me in both shoulders and the groin. But the magnolia proved to be snakeless. We shot on through and downriver. We could not avoid the overhanging branches. The current was too fast and there were too many of them. Once or twice a minute, we punched through the leafy twigs reaching down from a horizontal limb. But I began to settle down. There weren't any snakes, after all—not in the first mile, anyway. And things Carol was saying made a difference. She said, for example, that snakes plop off branches long before the canoe gets to them. She also said that cottonmouths rarely go out onto branches. They stay back at the river's edge and in the swamps. Snakes on branches are, in the main, as harmless as licorice. Bands of tension loosened and began to drop away. I looked ahead. At the next bend, the river was veiled in a curtain of water oak. I was actually hoping to see a snake hit the surface, but none did.[195] We slipped through and into the clear.

This was heavy current for a river with no white water, and when we rested the river gave us a fast drift. Scenes quickly changed, within the steep banks, the incised meanders, against backgrounds of beech and laurel, white oak, spruce pine, Venus maidenhair, and resurrection fern. We came upon a young coon at the foot of a tree. He looked at us with no apparent fear. We pulled in to the bank. "Hey, there, you high-stepper, you," Carol said. "Get up that tree!" The coon put a paw on the tree and went up a foot or two and looked around. "Why aren't you afraid?" Carol went on. "Are you O.K., cooner?" The raccoon's trouble—probably[196]—was that he had never seen a human. He was insufficiently afraid, and Carol began to worry about him. So she got out of the canoe and went after him. The coon moved up the tree fifteen feet. The tree was a slender maple. Carol started up it like a rope climber. The coon stayed where he was. Carol said, "I'm not climbing the tree to make him jump out. I'll just go high enough to let him know he ought to be afraid of people." When she got near him, the coon scrambled to the high branches, where he hung on to one and swayed. Carol stopped about twenty-five feet up. "Hey, coon! We're no good. Don't you know that?" she called to him. Then she slid on down. "Let that be a lesson to you!" she called from the bottom.[197]

We moved on downstream, passing blue-tailed skinks and salamanders, animal tracks on every flat. A pair of beavers dived into the water and went around slapping the surface, firing blanks.[198] Carol saw the mouth of their den, and she got out of the canoe, climbed the bank, and stuck her head inside. She regretted that she had not brought a flashlight with her. We moved on. We passed a banded snake sitting on a limb. He produced mild interest. Fear was gone from me. It had gone off with the flow of the river. There was a light splash to the right—as if from a slide, not a dive. No one saw what made it. "Otter," Carol said. "Pull in to the opposite bank—over there. Quickly!" We stopped the canoe, and held on to bush stems of the riverbank and waited. Nothing happened. The quiet grew. "The otter will come up and look at us," Carol said. We waited. Smooth,

---

195. Carol's explanations provide information. They also serve as a vehicle for change in McPhee's reactions—and ours, though I'm still not so sure I would have been hoping to see a snake hit the water.

196. "Probably" indicates McPhee is speculating. He obviously can't know this for sure.

197. This scene is almost cinematic, with McPhee following in detail every move by Carol and the raccoon. He even describes the tree. Thus we follow the action as though we too were on the ground watching.

198. The metaphor lets us hear the slapping.

the river moved—never the same, always the same.[199] No otter. "He is an extraordinarily intelligent and curious animal," Carol said. "He could go off somewhere, if he wanted to, just to breathe. But he wants to see us. He will not be able to stand it much longer. He will have to come up." Up came a face, chin on the water—dark bright eyes in a dark-brown head, small ears, wide snout: otter.[200] His gaze was direct and unflinching. He looked at us until he had seen his fill; then he went back under. "Wouldn't you like to live in this creek?" Carol said. "You'd never get lonely. Wouldn't you like to play with the otter?"

A waterfall, about twelve feet high, poured into the river from the left. Two hundred yards downstream, another fall dropped into the river from the right. The feeder streams of the Cemocheckobee were not cutting down as fast as the river itself, and these hanging tributaries poured in from above, all the way down. We now moved through stands of royal fern under big sycamores and big beeches, and past another waterfall. "This is otter, beaver, coon heaven," Carol said. Her only disappointment was the unexpected scarcity of snakes. She said she had seen more than her share of "magnolia-leaf snakes" that day. Her imagination, charged with hope and anticipation, could, and frequently did, turn magnolia leaves into snakes, green upon the branches. I found myself feeling disappointed, too. Only one lousy banded snake. The day was incomplete.

Sam said the threat to this river was the lumber industry. Logging was going on in the forests on both sides, and he would try to persuade the lumbermen to register the river—and its marginal lands—before the day came when it would be too late. While he was speaking, I saw a snake on a log at the water's edge, and pointed to it, interrupting him.

"Is that a banded snake?"

"That is not a banded snake," Carol said.

"Is it a bad one?"

"It's a bad one, friend."

"Well, at last. Where have you been all day?"[201]

He had been right there, of course, in his own shaft of sun, and the sight of a shining aluminum canoe with three figures in it was not going to cause him to move. Moving back was not in his character. He would stay where he was or go toward something that seemed to threaten him. Whatever else he might be, he was not afraid. He was a cottonmouth, a water moccasin. Carol was closer to him than I was, and I felt no fear at all. Sam, in the stern, was closest of all, because we were backing up toward the snake. I remember thinking, as we moved closer, that I preferred that they not bring the thing into the canoe, but that was the sum of my concern; we were ten miles downstream from where we had begun. The moccasin did not move.[202] We were now right next to it. Sam reached toward it with his paddle.

"Rough him up a little to teach him to beware of humans," Carol said. "But don't hurt him."

Under the snake Sam slipped the paddle, and worked it a bit, like a spatula, so that

---

199. The short sentences and sentence fragments carry a feel of anticipation, of waiting. The one-word variation in the phrase, "never the same, always the same" reflect the subtle changes in the river. It also has a pleasing ring.

200. Note how gently the description unfolds: First we see the face surface, chin on the water; then we gradually take in his features until we have the otter. Note, too, McPhee's use of the word "chin," humanizing the intelligent critter.

201. McPhee's transformation is complete. He's no longer an outsider.

202. Through observation, McPhee gives us the snake's reaction as well as his own.

e came up onto the blade. Sam lifted the cottonmouth into the air. Sam rocked
lle. "Come on," he said. "Come on, there. Open your mouth so John can see the
cotton."

"Isn't he magnificent?" Carol said. "Set him down, Sam. He isn't going to open his
mouth."

Sam returned the moccasin to the log. The canoe moved on into a gorge. The walls
of the gorge were a hundred feet high.

* * *

The Cemocheckobee was itself a feeder stream, ending in the Chattahoochee,[203] there in
southwestern Georgia, at the Alabama line. An appointment elsewhere with the Chattahoochee—a red-letter one for Sam and Carol—drew us back north. The Chattahoochee
is Georgia's most prodigious river. Atlanta developed where railheads met the river. The
Chattahoochee rises off the slopes of the Brass-town Bald, Georgia's highest mountain,
seven miles from North Carolina, and flows to Florida, where its name changes at the
frontier. It is thereafter called the Appalachicola. In all its four hundred Georgia miles,
what seems most remarkable about this river is that it flows into Atlanta nearly wild.
Through a series of rapids between high forested bluffs, it enters the city clear and clean.
From parts of the Chattahoochee within the city of Atlanta, no structures are visible—
just water, sky, and woodland. The circumstance is nostalgic, archaic, and unimaginable.
It is as if an unbefouled Willamette were to flow wild into Portland—Charles into
Boston, Missouri into Omaha, Hudson into New York, Delaware into Philadelphia,
James into Richmond, Cuyahoga into Cleveland[204] (the Cuyahoga caught fire one day,
and fire engines had to come put out the blazing river). Atlanta deserves little credit for
the clear Chattahoochee, though, because the Chattahoochee is killed before it leaves the
city. It dies between Marietta Boulevard and South Cobb Drive, just below the Atlanta
Water Intake, at the point where thirty-five million gallons of partially treated sewage
and forty million gallons of raw sewage are poured into the river every day. A short distance below that stand two enormous power plants, whose effluent pipes raise the temperature of the river. A seven-pound brown trout was caught recently not far above the
Water Intake. It is difficult to imagine what sort of fin-rotted, five-legged, uranium-
gilled, web-mouthed monster could live in the river by Georgia Power. Seen from the air
(Sam showed it to me once in his plane), the spoiling of the Chattahoochee is instant,
from river-water blue to sewer ochre-brown, as if a pair of colored ribbons had been
sewn together there by the city.[205]

Now a sewer line was projected to run upstream beside the river to fresh subdivisions that would bloom beyond the city's perimeter highway. The sewer would not actually be in the water, but, unless it could be tunnelled or not built at all, it would cause the
clear-cutting of every tree in a sixty-foot swath many miles long. A segment of the sewer
was already under construction. The Georgia Natural Areas Council was among the lead-
ership in an effort to put down this specific project and at the same time to urge a bill

---

203. McPhee uses the Cemocheckobee to build a bridge to the outing with then-Governor Jimmy Carter.
The Cemocheckobee feeds into the Chattahoochee, which leads into McPhee's description of the spoiling of
the river in Atlanta, which in turn leads to the proposed sewer line and the Georgia Natural Areas Council's op-
position. This then leads to the canoe trip with Carter and an unexpected ending to the road kill story.

204. The list of cities and their rivers makes clear the Chattahoochee's tie in Atlanta.

205. McPhee delays the description of the point of pollution until the end of the paragraph where it has
more impact.

through the legislature that would protect permanently the river and its overview. Sam had asked Jimmy Carter to come get into a canoe and shoot the metropolitan rapids and see for himself the value and the vulnerability of the river. Carter was willing. So, in three canoes, six of us put in under the perimeter highway, I-285, and paddled into Atlanta.

Sam had Carter in his bow. Carter might be governor of Georgia but not of Sam's canoe. Carol and I had the second canoe. In the third was a state trooper, who had a pistol on his hip that could have sunk a frigate. In the stern was James Morrison, of the federal government, the Bureau of Outdoor Recreation's man in Atlanta. He wore wet-suit bootees and rubber kneepads and seemed to be ready to go down the Colorado in an acorn.

The current was strong. The canoes moved smartly downstream. Carter was a lithe man, an athletic man in his forties—at home, obviously enough, in boats. He was wearing a tan wind-breaker, khaki trousers, and white basketball shoes. He had a shock of wind-tossed sandy hair. In the course of the day, he mentioned that he had grown up in Archery, Georgia, by a swamp of the Kinchafoonee and the Choctawhatchee. He and his friend A. D. Davis, who was black, had built a twelve-foot bateau. "When it rained and we couldn't work in the fields, we went down to the creek and set out set hooks for catfish and eels, and we drifted downstream in the bateau hunting ducks with a shotgun. We fished for bass and redbellies, and we waded for jack. The bateau weighed eighty pounds. I could pick it up." Archery was three miles west of Plains, a cross-roads with a short row of stores and less than a thousand people. Sam, Carol, and I had passed through Plains— in fifteen seconds[206]—on our way north. An enormous red-lettered sign over the stores said, "PLAINS, GEORGIA, HOME OF JIMMY CARTER." Carter had played basketball at Plains High School, had gone on to Annapolis and into nuclear submarines, and had come back to Plains in 1953 to farm peanuts and to market them for himself and others, businesses he continued as he went on into the legislature and upward to become governor. The career of his boyhood friend had been quite different.[207] The last Carter had heard of A. D. Davis, Davis was in jail for manslaughter.

Now, on the Chattahoochee, the Governor said,[208] "We're lucky here in Georgia that the environment thing has risen nationally, because Georgia is less developed than some states and still has much to save." With that, he and Sam went into the largest set of rapids in the city of Atlanta. The rip was about a hundred yards long, full of Vs confusing to the choice, broad ledges, haystacks, eddies, and tumbling water. They were good rapids, noisy and alive, and strong enough to flip a canoe that might hit a rock and swing broadside.

In the shadow of a two-hundred-foot bluff,[209] we pulled out on a small island to survey the scene. Carol said the bluff was a gneiss and was full of garnets. The Governor had binoculars. With them, he discovered a muskrat far out in the river. The muskrat was gnawing on a branch that had been stopped by a boulder. "He's sniffin' around that little old limb on top of that rock," Carter said. "Maybe he's eating the lichens off it. Look, there's another. Who owns the land here?"

---

206. McPhee's precision captures just how small Plains is.

207. In 1973 when the story first appeared in the *New Yorker*, Carter was virtually unknown outside of Georgia. Thus, McPhee provides a quick synopsis of his background.

208. McPhee uses the attribution before the quote to create a transition out of Carter's description and background back to the canoe trip.

209. Place transition.

"Various people," Morrison said. "Some are speculators. A lot of it is owned by Alfred Kennedy."

"Kennedy?"

"A director of the First National Bank," Carol said.

"Is he a good guy, so far as conservancy goes?"

"From what I hear, he's too busy making money."

"Sometimes it's better to slip up on people like that," Carter told her. "Rather than make an issue of it right away." He spoke in a low voice, almost shyly. There was a touch of melancholy in his face that disappeared, as it did frequently, when he grinned. A trillium caught his eye. He asked her what it was, and she told him. "And what's that?" he said.

"Dog hobble," Carol said. "*Leucothoë.* Look here." She pointed at the ground. "A coon track."[210]

The canoes moved on, and the next stop was a visit with a fisherman who was casting from the bank. He was middle-aged and weathered, a classical, prototype fisherman, many years on the river. He was wreathed in smiles at sight of the Governor. I looked hard at Sam, but nothing in his face indicated that he had planted the man there. The fisherman, Ron Sturdevant, showed the Governor a Kodacolor print of a twenty-three-inch rainbow he had recently caught right here under this bluff. "I guess I'm glad I met you," Sturdevant said. "I'm glad you're taking this trip. I'm worried about the river."

"I hope we can keep it this way," Carter said.

We climbed from the river through a deep wood of oaks and big pines to a cave in which families of Cherokees had once lived. It was about a hundred feet up. The view swept the river, no structures visible. "Who owns this place?"

Sam said, "Alfred Kennedy."

"And he hasn't even slept here," said Carol.

"Have you slept here, Carol?" the Governor asked her.

"Many times," she told him. "With a dog named Catfish."

Morrison said, "There's gold here, around the Indian cave. It's never been mined."

"That would be a good way to keep this place undisturbed," Carter said. "To announce that there was gold up here."

Back on the river,[211] he used his binoculars while Sam paddled. He saw four more muskrats and an automobile, upside down in the water, near the far bank. He also saw a turtle.[212]

"What kind is it?" Carol asked him.

"If I knew what kind it was, I could tell you." He handed the binoculars across to her, too late.

"I've been down through here and seen fifteen turtles with bullet holes in their shells," Carol told him.

"What kind?" Carter said.

"Cooters and sliders."

There was a racket of engines. Out of nowhere came two motorcyclists riding *in* the river. A mile or so later, we took out, beside an iron bridge. Carol said she had washed her hair any number of times under that bridge.

---

210. Because of the earlier scene and setup, we understand, without need for explanation, the significance of the coon tracks.

211. Transition to resume the canoe trip.

212. The juxtaposition of detail "shows" the spoiling of the river without need for explanation.

The Governor invited us home for lunch. The mansion was new—a million-dollar neo-Palladian Xanadu, formal as a wedding cake,[213] and exquisitely landscaped. Carol and Sam and I were ropy from a thousand miles of mountains, rivers, and swamps. None of us had changed clothes in nearly a week, but we would soon be eating grilled cheese sandwiches at a twenty-foot table under a crystal chandelier.[214] The Governor, for that matter, did not look laundered anymore—mud on his trousers, mud on his basketball shoes.[215] We parked in back of the mansion. A backboard, hoop, and net were mounted there. A ball sat on the pavement. Before going in, we shot baskets for a while.

"The river is just great," the Governor said, laying one in.[216] "And it ought to be kept the way it is. It's almost heartbreaking to feel that the river is in danger of destruction. I guess I'll write a letter to all the landowners and say, 'If you'll use some self-restraint, it'll decrease the amount of legal restraint put on you in the future.' I don't think people want to incur the permanent wrath of the governor or the legislature."

"I've tried to talk to property owners," Carol said. "To get them to register their land with the Natural Areas Council. But they wouldn't even talk to me."

The Governor said, "To be blunt about it, Carol, why would they?"

The Governor had the ball and was dribbling in place, as if contemplating a property owner in front of him, one-on-one. He went to the basket, shot, and missed. Carol got the rebound and fed the ball to Sam. He shot. He missed, too.[217]

JOHN MCPHEE ON READING

John McPhee was not influenced by any one writer. "I think as a would-be writer, you react to what you like and that influences you," he says. "You also react to what you don't like and that too influences you. You react both positively and negatively to what you read, and it all shapes you as a writer."

McPhee was, however, particularly drawn to the *New Yorker* and its long factual pieces and knew in college that was what he eventually wanted to write.

---

213. Without ever seeing a picture of the governor's mansion, we nevertheless get an impression of it from the Palladian-Xanadu and wedding-cake comparisons.

214. McPhee's choice of details (the unbathed trio, the twenty-foot table, and the crystal chandelier) provide a memorable shot of the luncheon.

215. The repetition of "mud" is pleasing to the ear; it also "shows" us that Carter didn't mind getting dirty.

216. Attribution keeps the action moving.

217. Just as Carol and Sam and others in the conservation movement win some and lose some in their efforts to register land for preservation, so Carter misses a shot. Thus, what at first might seem like an unexpected ending becomes subtly symbolic and satisfying.

Michael Paterniti

The seed for "Driving Mr. Albert" was planted almost ten years ago when Michael Paterniti first heard a rumor that the pathologist who performed the autopsy on Albert Einstein had absconded with the brain and subsequently cut it into pieces that were then scattered hither and yon. The greater part of the brain, rumor had it, belonged to the pathologist, who had since disappeared, along with the brain. For Paterniti, tracking down the pathologist—and the brain—became an obsession. Eventually he came into possession of a telephone number, which he proceeded to call with regularity—never getting an answer or an answering machine. Every time he passed the phone, he would dial the number. Finally, he scored. The trip cross-country with the pathologist and the brain was an unexpected bonus, proving once more just how a writer's persistence can pay off.

Says Paterniti: "I was thirty-two and at a crossroads in my life, and along came Dr. Thomas Harvey, all of eighty-four, who leapt into a rental car with a virtual stranger, plunked Einstein's brain in the trunk, and was raring and ready for an eleven-day, cross-country safari to see Einstein's granddaughter in Berkeley, California. That trip became a kind of pilgrimage, and Dr. Harvey became a man of ultimate faith, as he'd believed in his holy relic, the brain, and safeguarded it for nearly five decades."

The trip itself provided more than enough material for a good magazine article, but Paterniti didn't stop there. Once home, he read books and articles about Einstein, talked to people who had known him, and studied up on the late scientist's theories. He tracked down individuals who had known Dr. Harvey as a young man and ones who knew him now. He even asked Dr. Harvey to describe the autopsy in detail and then observed one himself to make sure he had the details right.

"When I sat to write, I did so with little design or intention," he says. "What eventually emerged, after much puzzling, was this article. Because Einstein ghosted every line, and because Harvey was such an enigma, I felt this incredible freedom to experiment with the form, to try to make something that felt both literary and journalistic, but that also added up to a soulful tale. In the end, too, I most simply hoped it was a good read."

Using the trip as a frame, Paterniti deftly weaves in all this, so by story's end we learn about Thomas Harvey, Albert Einstein, his theory of relativity, the atomic bomb, and much, much more.

The resulting article, which appeared in Harper's, *won a National Magazine Award and has since been expanded it into a best-selling book by the same title. Paterniti is a former executive editor of* Outside *magazine. His work has appeared in the* New York Times Magazine, Rolling Stone, Details, *and* Esquire, *where he is a Writer at Large.*

Driving Mr. Albert

A Trip Across America With Einstein's Brain

PRINCETON, NEW JERSEY. FEBRUARY 17, 1997.

In the beginning, there was a brain. All of the universe was the size of this brain, floating in space. Until one day it simply exploded. Out poured photons and quarks and leptons. Out flew dust particles like millions of fast-moving birds into the expanding aviary of the cosmos. Cooked heavy elements—silicon, magnesium, and nickel—were sucked into a small pocket and balled together under great pressure and morphed with the organic matter of our solar system. Lo, the planets!

Our world—Earth—was covered with lava, then granite mountains. Oceans formed, a wormy thing crawled from the sea. There were pea-brained brontosauri and fiery meteor showers and gnawing, hairy-backed monsters that kept coming and coming—these furious little stumps, human beings, us. Under the hot sun, we roasted different colors, fornicated, and fought. Full of wonder, we attached words to the sky and the mountains and the water, and claimed them as our own. We named ourselves Homer, Sappho, Humperdinck, and Nixon. We made bewitching sonatas and novels and paintings. Stargazed and built great cities. Exterminated some people. Settled the West. Cooked meat and slathered it with special sauce. Did the hustle. Built the strip mall.[1]

And in the end, after billions of years of evolution, a pink two-story motel rose up on a drag of asphalt in Berkeley, California. The Flamingo Motel. There, a man stepped out onto the balcony in a bright beam of millennial sunlight, holding the original universe in his hands, in a Tupperware container, and for one flickering moment he saw into the future. I can picture this man now: he needs a haircut, he needs some coffee.[2]

But not yet, not before we rewind and start again.[3] Not long ago. In Maine on a bus.

"Driving Mr. Albert: A Trip Across America With Einstein's Brain" first appeared in *Harper's* in 1997. Copyright © 2000 Michael Paterniti. Used by permission of Dial Press/Dell Publishing, a division of Random House, Inc. (Editor's note: This story has been cut because of space. The cuts are indicated by ellipses.)

1. Paterniti sets out to encapsulate the history of the universe in a few paragraphs, "to accelerate time, to connect the primal explosion of our cosmos to Albert's brain, which itself was full of brilliance and wit." He says: "I was hoping for energy, absurdity, and feeling, all at once, by warping time in a way that set this brain as the ur-vessel of the universe." He does this brilliantly, displaying his own wit and imagination and, in the process, thoroughly engaging his readers. Who can resist a metaphor that likens dust particles to fast-moving birds and the cosmos to an aviary? Note how his use of short sentences and sentence fragments conveys a sense both of awe and of the universe exploding and all manner of wonders pouring forth. In the second paragraph, the tacking on of words and phrases mimics the unfolding of evolution: "Our world—Earth—was covered with lava, then granite mountains"; "hairy-backed monsters that kept coming and coming—these furious little stumps, human beings, us." Then with a very few, carefully chosen words ("fornicated," "fought," for example), he captures the history and development of man. In doing so, note how Paterniti is both concrete and quirky. We named ourselves not only Homer and Sappho but Humperdinck and Nixon. We barbecued, we did the hustle, we built the all-American strip mall. Paterniti is having fun, and so are the readers. We are hooked and ready to accompany him through the story.

2. Paterniti brings his history and the story back to the present, and the brain: the Flamingo Motel in Berkeley. Again, note the concrete—and wacky—details: the motel is pink and named "Flamingo" (no bland Holiday Inns for this story), the "original universe" is in a Tupperware container (not merely a refrigerator container), the man needs a haircut and a cup of coffee.

3. Paterniti begins a long flashback, or loop. Later we will return to the moment on the balcony, which will serve as a sort of bookend. The body of the story is written in present tense, creating immediacy.

In Massachusetts on a train. In Connecticut behind the wheel of a shiny, teal-colored rental car. The engine purrs. I should know, I'm the driver. I'm on my way to pick up an eighty-four-year-old man named Thomas Harvey, who lives in a modest, low-slung 1950s ranch that belongs to his sixty-seven-year-old girlfriend, Cleora.[4] To get there you caroom through New Jersey's exurbia, through swirls of dead leaves and unruly thickets of oak and pine that give way to well-ordered fields of roan, buttermilk, and black snorting atoms—horses.[5] Harvey greets me at the door, stooped and chuckling nervously, wearing a red-and-white plaid shirt and a solid-blue Pendleton tie that still bears a waterlogged $10 price tag from some earlier decade. He has peckled, blowsy skin runneled with lines, an eagle nose, stubbed yellow teeth, bitten nails, and a spray of white hair as fine as corn silk that shifts with the wind over the bald patches on his head.[6] He could be one of a million beach-bound, black-socked Florida retirees, not the man who, by some odd happenstance of life, possesses the brain of Albert Einstein—literally cut it out of the dead scientist's head.[7]

Harvey has stoked a fire in the basement, which is dank and dark, and I sit among crocheted rugs and genie bottles of blown glass, Ethiopian cookbooks, and macramé.[8] It has taken me more than a year to find Harvey, and during that time I've had a dim, inchoate feeling—one that has increased in luminosity—that if I could somehow reach him and Einstein's brain, I might unravel their strange relationship, one that arcs across this century and America itself.[9] And now, before the future arrives and the supercomputers of the world fritz out and we move to lunar colonies—before all that hullabaloo[10]—Harvey and I are finally sitting here together.

---

4. The loop and the trip begin. Paterniti continues to use short sentences and elliptical fragments to move the story along at a fast clip. With three prepositional phrases, he compresses time and miles ("In Maine . . . ," "In Massachusetts . . . ," "In Connecticut . . .") while maintaining the flavor of the trip: he traveled by bus, by train, and finally by "teal-colored rental car." Note how the phrases grow in length as he moves forward to the present, until he is writing in complete sentences. The effect is somewhat cinematic, with the camera moving quickly over the shots of Paterniti making his way toward Dr. Harvey and slowing as he reaches the Princeton suburbs. Again, note his use of details, the description of the house and the ages, which will play a role throughout the story.

5. Throughout the story, Paterniti will give us vivid descriptions of the landscapes he drives through, making us feel like we are in the car with him. He no doubt passed many things on his way to the girlfriend's house, but it is the swirling leaves, the thickets of oaks and pines, and the snorting horses that capture the flavor of the countryside. Note his use of "atoms" to describe those horses, a word choice that fits the story's subject.

6. Just as Paterniti allowed his description of the developing universe to unfold, so he does with that of Dr. Harvey in two long sentences that capture both the details that liken him to the "million beach-bound, black-socked Florida retirees" (the silky white hair, the "peckled, blowsy skin runneled with lines," the stooped posture) and the one that sets him apart as an eccentric (the plaid shirt and tie with its waterlogged price tag). The description allows us both to see and hear Harvey and his nervous chuckle. By the end of the story Paterniti will have presented a fascinating, three-dimensional "character." Note the vivid word choices throughout: "purr," "caroom," "peckled," "blowsy," "runneled," some of them of Paterniti's own making.

7. This paragraph builds to a crescendo, ending on the point Paterniti wants to stress: This man is the owner of Einstein's brain. Then, while we are reeling from that, he hits us with the fact that this man not only possesses the brain, he cut it out of Einstein's head. Both points gain emphasis and drama by coming at the end of this long, building paragraph.

8. Just as Paterniti brought us along with him through the New Jersey countryside, so he takes us into the 1950s ranch-style house with his description of the fire, the dank darkness, and the details that "show" Harvey as a throwback: the crocheted rugs, the blown-glass bottles, the macramé.

9. We get a concise summary of the story's origins and its goals: to explore Harvey's relationship with Einstein.

10. Note how Paterniti continues to bring lofty ideas back to the ordinary with words like "fritz" and "hullabaloo." Even the reader with no deep interest in Einstein and the theory of relativity will be engaged by this story.

That day Harvey tells me the story he's told before[11]—to friends and family and pilgrims[12]—one that has made him an odd celebrity even in this age of odd celebrity.[13] He tells it deliberately, assuming that I will be impressed by it as a testament to the rightness of his actions rather than as a cogent defense of them. "You see," he says, "I was just so fortunate to have been there. Just so lucky."

"Fortunate" is one word, "improbable" is another.[14] Albert Einstein was born in 1879 with a head shaped like a lopsided medicine ball. Seeing it for the first time, his grandmother fell into shock. "Much too fat!" she exclaimed. "Much too fat!" He didn't speak until he was three, and it was generally assumed that he was brain-damaged. Even as a child, he lived mostly in his mind, building intricate card houses, marveling at a compass his father showed him. His faith was less in people than in the things of the world. When his sister Maja was born, young Albert, crestfallen, said, "Yes, but where are its wheels?"[15]

As a man, he grew into a powerful body with thick arms and legs. He liked to hike and sail but spent most of his life sitting still, dreaming of the universe. In 1905, as a twenty-six-year-old patent clerk in Bern, Switzerland, he conceived of the special theory of relativity and the equation $E = mc^2$, a supposition that all matter, from a feather to a rock, contains energy. And with his theories that predicted the origin, nature, and destiny of the universe,[16] he toppled Newton and nearly three hundred years of science. When the first glimmer of relativity occurred to him, he casually told a friend, "Thank you. I've completely solved the problem."

So complex were his findings that they could only be partially understood and verified fourteen years later. Then, of course, Albert Einstein instantly became famous. His mischievous smile beamed from newspapers around the world. A genius! A Nobel Prize! A gurumystic who had unlocked the secrets of God's own mind.[17] There were suddenly hundreds of books on relativity. Einstein embarked on a frenzied world tour, was feted by kings and emperors and presidents,[18] gamboling into the world's most sacred halls in a sockless state of bemused dishevelment. He claimed he got his hairstyle—eventually a wild, electric-white nimbus—"through negligence" and, explaining his overall sloppiness, said, "It would be a sad situation if the wrapper were better than the meat wrapped

---

11. Paterniti begins one of a series of short loops that make up the story. Structurally, the story is arranged chronologically, following his journey with Harvey and Einstein's brain. Into this, he weaves information (gleaned from research and interviews) about the scientist and the pathologist so that by the end of the story we have gotten to know about both men and even about the theory of relativity.

12. The use of "and" rather than commas conveys just how many times Harvey has told this story.

13. The repetition of "odd celebrity" emphasizes the oddity of his fame. It also creates an interesting rhythm.

14. The repetition of "fortunate" creates a transition, or bridge, to move us from Harvey to Albert Einstein and a digression that takes us from his birth through his death and the removal by Harvey of his brain.

15. In giving us a biography of the famous scientist, Paterniti selectively chooses those details that will provide a down-to-earth picture of this eccentric man. Thus, in the course of learning about Einstein's life, we also come to know him as a human being. Those details are also the ones that are most apt to engage us in the story: the fact that he didn't speak until age three and was considered brain-damaged, the fact that he was captivated by a compass, the quotes by him and his grandmother. While you might be inclined to think those quotes are too colorful and off-the-wall to be true, not so. Paterniti read "tons of bios" and interviewed people who once knew Einstein. The young Albert indeed said of his sister: "Yes, but where are its wheels?"—proof again that fact can be more colorful than fiction. The lesson here: Leave no stone unturned in your research; you never know what you might turn up.

16. Since this is a story for a lay audience, Paterniti provides a simple, straightforward explanation of the theory of relativity.

17. Paterniti captures the flavor of the headlines and captions from around the world.

18. The use of "and" rather than commas conveys a sense of just how widely Einstein was feted.

inside it." He laughed like a barking seal, snored like a foghorn, sunbathed in the nude. And then took tea with the queen.[19]

Everywhere, it was Einstein mania. People named their children after him, fawned and fainted upon seeing him, wrote letters inquiring if he really existed. He was asked to "perform" at London's Palladium for three weeks on the same bill as fire-eaters and tightrope walkers, explaining his theory, at the price of his asking. "At the Chrysanthemum Festival," wrote one German diplomat stationed in Japan, "it was neither the empress nor the prince regent nor the imperial princes who held reception; everything turned around Einstein." A copy of the special theory of relativity in Einstein's scrawl was auctioned off for $6 million. And the New York Times urged its readers not to be offended by the fact that only twelve people in the world truly understood the theory of "the suddenly famous Dr. Einstein."[20]

In the years to follow,[21] Einstein's fame would only grow. He would vehemently criticize the Nazis and become a target for German ultra-nationalists, who waited outside his home and office, hurling anti-Semitic obscenities at him. When they made him a target for assassination, he fled to the United States—to Princeton, New Jersey[22]—and became an American citizen. He was called "the new Columbus of science." David Ben-Gurion offered him the presidency of Israel (to everyone's relief, he declined).[23] His political utterances were as good as Gandhi's. Before Michael Jordan was beamed by satellite to China, before Marilyn Monroe and the Beatles and Arnold Schwarzenegger, Albert Einstein was the first transglobal supercelebrity.[24]

In the last years of his life, he was struck with frequent attacks of nausea, the pain flowering between his shoulder blades, culminating in diarrhea or vomiting. An exam revealed an aneurysm in his abdominal aorta, but Einstein refused an operation and anticipated his own demise. "I want to be cremated so people won't come to worship at my bones," he said. On the night before he died, April 17, 1955, lying in bed in Princeton Hospital, Einstein asked to see his most recent pages of calculations, typically working until the end. His last words were spoken in German to a nurse who didn't know the language, though sometime earlier he had told a friend, "I have finished my task here."

The next morning, April 18[25] when the chief pathologist of the hospital—our Harvey, then a strapping forty-two-year-old with Montgomery Clift good looks[26]—arrived for work, Einstein's body was laid out, naked and mottle-skinned, on a gurney. "Imagine my surprise," Harvey says to me now. "A fellow up in New York, my former teacher Dr.

---

19. Somewhat like a caricaturist, Paterniti focuses on Einstein's most recognizable—and human—features: the hair and his sloppiness. The quotes reveal both his eccentricity and his sense of humor. Note how Paterniti's exaggerated similes make Einstein's laugh and his snoring more humorous. Note also how the juxtaposition of Einstein's sunbathing in the nude and his taking tea with the queen adds to the humor.

20. In this paragraph, Paterniti goes from the general to the specific, using concrete examples (gleaned from biographies and newspaper clippings) of the Einstein mania.

21. The transition compresses time. In this paragraph Paterniti again goes from the general to the specific, offering examples that show Einstein's growing fame.

22. Paterniti uses dashes to insert information.

23. This time Paterniti uses parentheses to work in an aside.

24. The comparison to Michael Jordan, Marilyn Monroe, et al., conveys a sense of the movie-star kind of supercelebrity bestowed on Einstein.

25. Note how specific Paterniti is with the dates. This is when the two men's paths will cross, the crucial moment in terms of the brain.

26. The description allows us to see what Harvey looked like at the time of this critical moment and serves as a contrast with the man we see today. The comparison is again to a movie star—fitting for a man destined to do the autopsy on someone who had become a supercelebrity.

Zimmerman"—and an acquaintance of Einstein's[27]—"was going to do the autopsy. But then he couldn't get away. He rang me up, and we agreed that I'd do it." Harvey says that he felt awe when he came face-to-face with the world-famous physicist, the voice of conscience in a century of madness, who had bewildered the world by suggesting that time should be understood as the fourth, and inseparable, dimension. Now he lay alone in the pale light, 180 pounds of mere matter.[28]

Harvey took a scalpel in his hand and sliced Einstein open with a Y incision, scoring the belly, the skin giving like cellophane,[29] then cut the rib cartilage and lifted the sternum. He found nearly three quarts of blood in Einstein's peritoneal cavity, a result of the burst aneurysm, and after investigating his heart and veins concluded that, with an operation, the physicist might have lived for several more years, though how long was hard to tell "because Einstein liked his fatty foods," in particular goose scratchings.[30]

Working under the humming lights, his fingers inside Einstein's opened body, juggling the liver, palpating the heart,[31] Harvey made a decision. Who's to say whether it was inspired by awe or by greed, beneficence or mere pettiness? Who's to say what comes over a mortal, what chemical reaction takes place deep in the thalamus, when faced with the blinding brightness of another's greatness and, with it, a knowledge that I/you/we shall never possess even a cheeseparing of that greatness?[32]

Working quickly with a knife, Harvey tonsured the scalp, peeled the skin back, and, bearing down on a saw, cut through Einstein's head with a quick, hacking motion. He removed a cap of bone, peeled back the meninges, then clipped blood vessels and bundles of nerve and the spinal cord. He reached with his fingers deeper into the chalice of the man's cranium and simply removed the glistening brain. *To keep for himself.* Forever. In perpetuity. Amen.[33]

What he didn't count on, however, was that with this one act his whole world would go haywire. Apparently, word got out through Zimmerman that Harvey had the brain, and when it was reported in the *New York Times* a day later, some people were aghast. Einstein's son, Hans Albert, reportedly felt betrayed. Harvey claimed that he was planning to conduct medical research on the brain, and, in an agreement eventually struck with Hans Albert over the phone, he assured that the brain would only be the subject of medical journals and not become a popcultural gewgaw, as the Einsteins most feared. Sometime after the autopsy, Harvey was fired from his job for refusing to give up the brain.

Years passed, and there were no papers, no findings. And then Harvey fell off the

---

27. Paterniti uses dashes to insert explanation into a direct quote.

28. Paterniti places this description at the end of the paragraph where it becomes more dramatic.

29. The simile brings us into the scene, drawing on something familiar to show us how easily the skin gave. To write more realistically, Paterniti had Harvey describe the autopsy. He himself also attended one to make sure he got the details right—something all writers might want to consider before reconstructing such a procedure.

30. If we've thought about Einstein only as a scientist and a genius, this detail makes him more human.

31. Paterniti brings us into scene, allowing us to *hear* the humming lights and feel Harvey palpating the heart.

32. The "I/you/we" puts us in Harvey's place and causes us perhaps to empathize with whatever drove him to remove the brain. Note both how Paterniti uses a change in Harvey's own brain as a possible explanation for what he does.

33. Paterniti dramatically builds to the moment of the taking, providing a detailed description of Harvey opening first the scalp, then the skull, then removing the famous brain—and keeping it for himself. The act takes on religious overtones with the comparison of the skull to a chalice and the prayer-like quality of the ending: "Forever. In perpetuity. Amen."

radar screen. When he gave an occasional interview—in articles from 1956 and 1979 and 1988—he always repeated that he was about "a year away from finishing study on the specimen."*

Forty years later—after Harvey has gone through three wives, after he has sunk to lesser circumstances, after he has outlived most of his critics and accusers, including Hans Albert—we are sitting together before a hot fire on a cold winter day.[34] And because I like him so much, because somewhere in his watery blue eyes, his genial stumble-footing, and that ineffable cloak of hunched integrity that falls over the old, I find myself feeling for him and cannot bring myself to ask the essential questions:

Is Harvey a grave-robbing thief or a hero? A sham artist or a high priest? Why not heist a finger or a toe? Or a simple earlobe? What about rumors that he plans to sell Einstein's brain to Michael Jackson for $2 million? Does he feel ashamed? Or justified? If the brain is the ultimate Fabergé egg, the Hope diamond, the Cantino map, the One-Penny Magenta stamp, "Guernica," what does it look like? Feel like? Smell like? Does he talk to it as one talks to one's poodle or ferns?[35]

We conclude the visit by going out for sushi, and over the course of our conversation he mentions a handful of people he hopes to see out in America before he dies. "Yessir, I'd really like to visit some folks," he says. They include a few neuroanatomists with whom he has brain business,[36] some friends, and, in Berkeley, Evelyn Einstein, Hans Albert's daughter and the granddaughter of Albert. Harvey has wanted to meet her for many years. Although he doesn't say why, I think he might be trying to face down some lingering guilt, some late-in-life desire to resolve the past before his age grounds him permanently and, with his death, the brain falls into someone else's hands. Perhaps, too, he wants to make arrangements for someone to take over the brain, and Evelyn is going to be interviewed for the job.[37] Whatever the reason, by the meal's end, doped on the incessant tinkling of piped-in harps and a heady shot of tekka maki, Harvey and I have somehow agreed to take a road trip: I will drive him to California.[38]

And then, one afternoon soon before our departure, Harvey takes me to a secret location—one he asks me not to reveal for fear of thieves and rambunctious pilgrims—where he now keeps the brain.[39] From a dark room he retrieves a box that contains two glass jars full of Einstein's brain.[40] After the autopsy, he had it chopped into nearly two hundred pieces—from the size of a dime to that of a thick turkey neck—and since then

---

*According to newspaper accounts following Einstein's death, mystery immediately shrouded the brain. Dr. Zimmerman, on staff at New York City's Montefiore Medical Center, expected to receive Einstein's brain from Harvey, but never, in fact, did: Princeton Hospital decided not to relinquish the brain. Harvey, however, also decided not to relinquish the brain and at some point removed it from the hospital. (Author's note.)

34. Transition shows passage of time, capturing the essence of what transpired: Harvey's marriages, his diminished lifestyle, and the passing of his critics. Thus, the mini-loop ends, bringing us back to the current time line.

35. Throughout much of the story, we vicariously share Paterniti's experiences. Here, he asks the questions we are asking, the ones we want answered: Why did Harvey do it? What does it look, smell, and feel like? In doing so, Paterniti has fun. Does Harvey talk to it like one talks to a poodle or a pet fern? By comparing the brain to the ultimate Fabergé egg, the Hope diamond, etc., we grasp its value—if you can really place a price tag on it.

36. "Brain business" fits the story's informal, nonscientific tone.

37. "I think" and "perhaps" let us know that Paterniti is merely speculating about Harvey's thoughts—one way of handling your subject's thoughts when you can't get inside his head.

38. Paterniti uses a colon to give this development added drama.

39. Harvey's reasons for the secrecy gain added emphasis and intrigue by being set off by dashes.

40. By beginning this sentence with a prepositional phrase, Paterniti adds to the feeling of stealth. It also places the two jars of brain at the end of the sentence, where they gain added emphasis.

he has given nearly a third of it away to various people. He flashes the jars before me but only for a second, then retreats quickly with them. The brain pieces float in murky formaldehyde, leaving an impression of very chunky chicken soup.[41] But it happens so quickly, Harvey so suddenly absconds with the brain, that I have no real idea what I've seen.

When I show up at his house a few weeks later in a rented Buick Skylark, Harvey has apparently fished several fistfuls' worth of brain matter from the jars, put them in Tupperware filled with formaldehyde, and zipped it all inside a gray duffel bag.[42] He meets me in his driveway with a plaid suitcase rimmed with fake leather and the gray duffel sagging heavily in his right hand. He pecks Cleora good-bye. "He's a fine Quaker gentleman," she tells me, watching Harvey's curled-over self shuffle across the pavement. He rubs a smudge of dirt off my side mirror, then toodles around the front of the car.[43] When he's fallen into the passenger seat, he chuckles nervously, scratchily clears his throat, and utters what will become his mantra, "Yessir . . . real good."[44] And then we just start driving. For four thousand miles. Me, Harvey, and, in the trunk, Einstein's brain.[45]

Toward Columbus, Ohio. February 18, 1997.

We morph as one. Even if we are more than a half century apart in age, he born under the star of William Howard Taft and I under the napalm bomb of Lyndon Baines Johnson, if he wears black Wallabees and I sport Oakley sunglasses, if he has three ex-wives, ten children, and twelve grandchildren and I have yet to procreate, we begin to think together, to make unconscious team decisions.[46] It seems the entire backseat area will serve as a kind of trash can. By the time we make Wheeling, West Virginia, it's already strewn with books and tissuey green papers from the rental-car agreement, snack wrappers, and empty bottles of seltzer,[47] a hedge against "G.I. upset," as Harvey puts it.[48] An old rambler at heart, he takes to the road like it's a river of fine brandy,[49] seems to grow stronger on its oily fumes and oily-rainbow mirages, its oily fast food and the oily-tarmacked gas plazas[50] that we skate across for candy bars and Coca-Colas while the Skylark feeds at the pump. By default, I take charge of the radio—working the dial in a schizophrenic riffle from NPR to Dr. Laura and, in between, all kinds of high school basketball, gardening shows, local on-air auctions, blathering DJs, farm reports, and Christian call-in shows.[51]

---

41. The comparison of the floating brain pieces to chunky chicken soup helps us visualize what Paterniti sees in his fleeting glance. We get a sense of the brain, but we don't get a good look at it.

42. Specific details bring us to the scene: Paterniti arrives not in just a rented car, but a rented Buick Skylark, and the now familiar Tupperware is zipped inside a gray duffel bag.

43. Fresh, vivid verbs give us a real sense of Harvey and his movements and mannerisms: "pecks," "shuffle," "toodles."

44. Paterniti introduces one of Harvey's favorite phrases, setting it up for future use.

45. The trip begins with the three characters in place: Harvey, Einstein's brain, and Paterniti, who will enable us to share his experiences vicariously.

46. Paterniti helps us imagine this odd couple on the road by pointing up their differences in age, style, and marital experience, thus adding to the humor.

47. Since the Buick will be a principal setting for the trip, Paterniti gives us a detailed description of its back seat to bring us into the scene.

48. The quote adds color; it also gives us a feel for Harvey.

49. The comparison to a river of fine brandy aptly conveys Harvey's enjoyment.

50. The repetition of "oily" to describe the fumes, mirages, fast food, and gas plazas brings home the reality of the road: that it's really far from a river of fine brandy.

51. The radio gives us both the flavor of the trip and the countryside.

Harvey is hard-of-hearing in his right ear and, perhaps out of pride or vanity, refuses to wear a hearing aid, so I've brought tapes too, figuring he might do a fair amount of sleeping while, as designated driver, I might do more staying awake. I've got bands with names like Dinosaur Jr., Soul Coughing, and Pavement, and a book-on-tape, *Neuromancer*, by William Gibson. Harvey himself is partial to classical music and reads mostly scientific journals and novels by Kay Boyle.[52]

And although we are now bound by the road—Einstein's brain, Harvey, and me— he studiously avoids all discussion of the brain.[53] Earlier, however, he ticked off twelve different researchers to whom he had given slices of the brain. According to Harvey, one of them, Sandra Witelson from McMaster University in Hamilton, Ontario, organized his ephemera and articles on the brain into a scrapbook, and he turned over nearly a fifth of the brain to her. "She has one of the biggest collections of brains around," he says, proudly. "She gets them from a local undertaker."[54] (Later, when contacted, Witelson said that Harvey's assertions about her were "incorrect.")[55]

In most cases, Harvey has made it sound as if he himself handpicked these people after reading their work, though by some of their own admissions, a number of them had contacted him first. One neuroanatomist, a Berkeley professor named Marian Diamond, had written a paper claiming that she had counted in Einstein's brain a higher than normal number of glial cells, which nourish the organ.[56] The only other paper written to date, by a researcher at the University of Alabama named Britt Anderson, stated that Einstein had a thinner cortex than normal. "You see," says Harvey enthusiastically, "we're finding out that Einstein's brain is more unusual than many people first thought." But a professor of neurobiology at UCLA, Larry Kruger, calls the "meagre findings" on the brain "laughable" and says that when Diamond herself delivered her paper, the audience found it "comical," because "it means absolutely nothing." (When I asked Diamond, a woman with impeccable credentials, about this, she claimed that Kruger had "a lack of inhibitor cells" and said, "Well, we have to start somewhere, don't we?")[57]

Despite my expectations that Harvey will sleep a good deal, what I soon realize is that he's damn perky for eighty-four and never sleeps at all.[58] Nor talks much. In this age of self-revelation, he eschews the orotundity of a confessor. He speaks in a clipped, spare, almost penurious way—with a barely perceptible drawl from his midwestern childhood—letting huge blocks of time fall in between the subject and the verb, and then between the verb and the modifier of a sentence. He pronounces "pleasure" *play-sure*, and "measurements" *may-sure-mints*. When my line of questioning makes him uncomfortable, he chuckles flatly like two chops of wood, "Heh-heh," raspily clears his throat, then says, "Way-ell . . ."[59] And just steps aside to let some more time pass, returning to his map, which he studies like it's a rune. Through the window he watches Pennsylvania pass by: its barns and elaborate hexes, signs for Amish goods, the Allegheny Mountains rising

52. Paterniti again shows us the contrast in their tastes.
53. Paterniti uses Harvey's reluctance to talk about the brain to weave in a brief digression on the various people he has given slices to.
54. While the quote isn't directly related to Harvey and Einstein's brain, it is about brains, and it's far too colorful to leave out.
55. Paterniti uses parentheses to insert Witelson's denial, without interrupting the story's flow.
56. Paterniti supplies a brief, simple explanation of glial cells.
57. Parentheses are used to insert a quote from another interview.
58. The mini-loop ends, and the story returns to the main time line.
59. This description of the way Harvey talks gives us a feel for the man and also serves as a setup, enabling us to "hear" him as the story progresses.

like dark whales out of the earth, lost behind the mist of some unseen blowhole. He watches Ohio all pan-flattened and thrown back down on itself.[60] And he blinks languidly at it. But never sleeps.

I admit: this disappoints me.[61] Something in me wants Harvey to sleep. I want Harvey to fall into a deep, blurry, Rip Van Winkle daze, and I want to park the Skylark mothership on top of a mountain and walk around to the trunk and open it. I want Harvey snoring loudly as I unzip the duffel bag and reach my hands inside, and I want to—what?—touch Einstein's brain. I want to touch the brain. Yes, I've said it. I want to hold it, coddle it, measure its weight in my palm, handle some of its 15 billion now-dormant neurons.[62] Does it feel like tofu, sea urchin, baloney? What, exactly?[63] And what does such a desire make me? One of the legion of relic freaks who send Harvey letters asking, sometimes begging, for pieces of the brain? One of the pilgrims who come from as far away as Japan or England or Australia to glimpse it?

For Harvey's sake, I act like I haven't given the brain a second thought, while he encourages stultifying state-long silences[64] and offers the occasional historical anecdote. "Eisenhower's farm was in these parts, I believe." Or, "In the days of the canal . . ." The more the idea persists in my head, the more towns slip past outside the window, the more I wonder what, in fact, I'd really be holding if I held the brain.[65] I mean, it's not really Einstein and it's not really a brain but disconnected pieces of a brain, just as the passing farms are not *really* America but parts of a whole, symbols of the thing itself, which is everything and nothing at once.[66]

In part, I would be touching Einstein the Superstar, immediately recognizable by his Krameresque hair and the both-at-once mournful and mirthful eyes.[67] The man whose apotheosis is so complete that he's now a coffee mug, a postcard, a T-shirt. The face zooming out of a pop rock video on MTV's Buzz Clip for a song called "MMMBop." A figure of speech, an ad pitchman. The voice of reason on posters festooning undergrad dorm rooms. Despite the fact that he was a sixty-one-year-old man when he was naturalized as an American citizen, Einstein has been fully appropriated by this country, by our writers and moralists, politicians and scientists, cult leaders and clergy. In the *fin-de-siècle* shadows of America, in our antsy, searching times, Einstein comes back to us both as Lear's fool and Tiresias, comically offering his uncanny vision of the future while cautioning us against the violence that lurks in the heart of man. "I do not know how the

---

60. Paterniti uses Harvey to work in a description of the passing countryside, and thus compress time.

61. The colon helps emphasize Paterniti's disappointment.

62. Look how Paterniti builds to this wonderful moment of confession. He begins with a short, straightforward sentence, stating he wants Harvey to sleep. Then he repeats himself, this time piling on the details and using "and" rather than commas to build the momentum, as though he is hurtling madly toward something and can't stop until he opens the trunk. Then he begins again, piling on still more details. When he comes to the critical moment, he uses dashes to slow us down for the confession—that he wants to touch Einstein's brain. Then he repeats the confession in a short, concise sentence for emphasis. Once the confession is out in the open, he continues to build on it, this time using a list to pile on the things he wants to do to the brain. The repetition and exaggeration add to the humor. The tension of whether or not Paterniti will ever get to see-touch-feel-coddle the brain will help propel the story, and the readers, forward.

63. The questions draw us inside Paterniti and his experience. They are ones we might also ask.

64. "State-long" is an exaggerated and humorous way to convey Harvey's periods of silence.

65. The tension continues to build, forcing us to continue reading to find out if Paterniti ever gets to touch the brain.

66. The farm comparison is a poetic and fitting way of explaining the current state of Einstein's brain.

67. Paterniti uses his hypothetical touching of the brain to work in a digression on the commercialization of Einstein.

Third World War will be fought," he warned, "but I do know how the Fourth will: with sticks and stones."

To complete his American deification, Einstein has been fully commodified and marketed, earning millions of dollars for his estate. Bought and sold back to us by the foot soldiers of high capitalism, Einstein's name and image are conjured to sell computers and CD-ROMs, Nikon cameras and myriad baubles. In fact, a Los Angeles celebrity-licensing agency handles his account.

But why so much commotion over a guy with sweaty feet and rumpled clothes? The answer is perhaps found in a feeling that Einstein was not one of us. It seems we regard him as being supernatural. Because he glimpsed into the very workings of the universe and returned with God on his tongue, because he greeted this era by rocketing into the next with his break-through theories, he assumed a mien of supernaturalism. And because his tatterdemalion, at times dotty, demeanor stood in such stark contrast to his supernaturalism, he seemed both innocent and trustworthy and thus that much more supernatural. He, alone, held the seashell of the century to his ear.[68]

Einstein is also one of the few figures born in the last century whose ideas are equally relevant to us today. If we've incorporated the theory of relativity into our scientific view of the universe, it's Einstein's attempt to devise a kind of personal religion—an intimate spiritual and political manifesto—that still stands in stark, almost sacred contrast to the Pecksniffian systems of salvation offered by the modern world. Depending on the day's sex crimes and senseless murders, or the intensity of our millennial migraine, we run the real risk of feeling straitjacketed and sacrificed to everything from organized religion to the nuclear blood lust of nations to the cult visionaries of our world and their various vodka-and-cuckoo schemes, their Hale-Bopp fantasies.

Thus Einstein's blending of twentieth-century skepticism with nineteenth-century romanticism offers a kind of modern hope. "I am a deeply religious nonbeliever," he said. "This is a somewhat new kind of religion." Pushing further, he sought to marry science and religion by redefining their terms. "I am of the opinion that all the finer speculations in the realm of science spring from a deep religious feeling," he said. "I also believe that this kind of religiousness . . . is the only creative religious activity of our time."

To touch Einstein's brain would also be to touch the white dwarf and the black hole, the Big Bang and ghost waves.[69] To ride a ray of light, as Einstein once dreamed it as a child, into utter oblivion. He imagined that a clock placed on the equator would run more slowly than a clock placed at one of the poles under identical conditions. Einstein claimed that the happiest thought of his life came to him in 1907, at the Patent Office in Bern, when he was twenty-eight and couldn't find a teaching job. Up to his ears in a worsted wool suit and patent applications, a voice in his mind whispered, "If a person falls freely, he won't feel his own weight." That became the general theory of relativity. His life and ideas continue to fill thousands of books; even today, scientists are still verifying his work. Recently, a NASA satellite took millions of measurements in space that proved a uniform distribution of primordial temperatures just above absolute zero; that is, the

68. Paterniti, the writer, tries to make sense of why someone like Einstein would become a superstar. Notice his use of "perhaps" and "seems" to signal that he is speculating. In doing so, note the elevated diction (he glimpsed into the workings of the universe and returned "with God on his tongue") that persuades us to come to Paterniti's conclusion: that Einstein held "the seashell of the century to his ear." While the writer may begin the paragraph with a touch of humor (the sweaty feet and rumpled clothes), the rest of it, and the two that follow, take a serious turn.

69. The comparisons act as a bridge to an exploration of some of Einstein's thoughts and ideas, expressed in down-to-earth terms that the nonscientific among us can understand.

data proved that the universe was in a kind of postcoital afterglow from the Big Bang, further confirming Einstein's explanation for how the universe began

It would be good to touch that.[70]

We disembark that first night at a Best Western in Columbus, Ohio. As we open the trunk to gather our bags, I watch Harvey take what he needs, then leave the gray duffel there, the zipper shining like silver teeth in the streetlight.[71]

"Is it safe?" I ask, nodding my head toward the duffel.[72]

"Is what safe?" Harvey asks back, gelid eyes sparking once in the dark. He doesn't seem to know or remember. He's carried the contraband for so long he has come to consider himself something of a celebrity. No longer defined by the specimen, *he* has become the real specimen. A piece of living history. On tour. In his glen-plaid suitcase, he carries postcards of himself.

Inside his motel room with the brain,[73] Harvey gathers the sleep of the old. Next door I am exhausted yet wide awake. I am thinking of the brain, remembering that after more than 8 million people had marched to their deaths in the fields of Europe during World War I, Einstein's theory of relativity allowed humanity, in the words of a colleague, to look up from an "earth covered with graves and blood to the heavens covered with the stars." He suddenly appeared on the world's doorstep, inspiring pan-national awe and offering with it pan-national reconciliation—a liberal German Jew who clung to his Swiss citizenship and renounced violence.[74] What better way to absolve oneself of all sins than to follow a blameless scientist up into the glimmering waters of time and space?[75]

Another contemporary of Einstein's, Erwin Schrödinger, claimed that Einstein's theory of relativity quite simply meant "the dethronement of time as a rigid tyrant," opening up the possibility that there might be an alternative Master Plan. "And this thought," he wrote, "is a religious thought, nay I should call it *the* religious thought." With relativity, Einstein, the original cosmic slacker, was himself touching the mind of a new god, forming a conga line to immortality through some wrinkle in time. "It is quite possible that we can do greater things than Jesus," he said.[76]

That, finally, was Einstein's ultimate power and hold on our imagination. Eternity— it would be good to touch *that* too.[77]

Kansas City, Missouri. February 19, 1997.

Across Indiana, Illinois, and Missouri, beneath scudding clouds and clear shots of sunlight, the chill air fragrant with manure and feed. We pass over the chocolate, moiling Mississippi, drive near the towns of Emma, Bellflower, Peruque, and Auxvasse. . . . On the radio, we get the farm reports: lean hog futures down five-eighths; feeder cattle futures up a half. Corn futures and soybean and cocoa, up two-eighths, down a third, even.

---

70. Transition out of the digression back to the main time line. The repetition adds to the cohesiveness.

71. The simile is both fresh and fun. It's as though the zipper is smirking at Paterniti.

72. Paterniti uses the attribution to insert a description of Harvey's movement. The use of the dialogue and the scene draws us further into the story.

73. Place transition. Note the inclusion of the brain. It too is a character in this story.

74. Paterniti uses his own musings to weave in more insight on Einstein, drawn from his research.

75. The question carries the sense of being Harvey's thoughts without saying it is.

76. Paterniti again draws from his research to weave in more analysis of Einstein's theory of relativity. Note, however, how he throws in quirky words and phrases here and there ("conga line," "some wrinkle in time") to maintain the story's down-to-earth tone.

77. The placement of this thought at the end of the paragraph, the end of Paterniti's pondering, gives it added emphasis and drama. It lingers in our mind, as it must on Paterniti's, as he drifts off to sleep.

January sugar and March corn; September rice and December cotton[78]—all of them attached to a momentary price that may right now be making someone rich as it bankrupts someone else.

"Look at that cow!" exclaims Harvey.[79]

And it is quite a cow! On this, our third day together, something is beginning to happen out here between us, the three of us. Time is slowing, it seems, or expanding to fill a bigger sky, a more open landscape. The got-to-be-there self-importance of the East, its frantic floodlight charge, has given way to a single lit parlor lamp. And under it, a cow or one silver tree in the wind or the rusted remains of an old tiller seems more holy, even mythic. It's not that the Midwest lacks bustle; it's just that away from the cities, the deadlines are imposed by the earth and its seasons. I slip off my watch and feel myself beginning to slow into Harvey time.

We are, in fact, retracing Harvey's route when he came west from New Jersey in the 1960s, after eluding those who themselves desired the brain.[80] Within weeks of Einstein's death, after it was reported that the brain had been taken from the body, a group of leading brain researchers met in Washington, D.C. It was an august, winning collection of men: Doctors Webb Haymaker and Hartwig Kuhlenbeck, Clem Fox and Gerhardt von Bonin, Jerzy E. Rose and Walle Nauta.[81] And necessarily among them, but perhaps regarded with a tinge of condescension, this slightly awkward, nervously chuckling half-doctor, this Irregular Sock, this pathologist from a small-town hospital connected only by the same name to the hallowed halls and elite eating clubs of Princeton University. When Webb Haymaker, who represented the U.S. Army, demanded the brain, Harvey simply refused to hand it over. Heh-heh.[82] When Haymaker got angry, Harvey didn't budge. And now who laughs last? Who's dead, each last one of them, and who's out here busting for California with the brain, inhaling Frostees and baked potatoes, hoovering Denny's pancakes and green salads and chicken noodle soup?[83]

"Harvey didn't know his ass from his elbow from the brain," says Larry Kruger, who at the time was a postdoctoral fellow with Jerzy Rose at Johns Hopkins. "Harvey refused to give up the brain even though he wasn't a neuropathologist, and then all bets were off. I mean, what were you going to do with it anyway? I heard he kept it in his basement and would show it to visitors. I guess some people show off a rare edition of Shakespeare. He would say, 'Hey, wanna see Einstein's brain?' The guy's a jerk. . . . He wanted fame and nothing came of it."*[84]

---

*Later, when I visit Kruger in Los Angeles, among the clutter of his office, which includes an oversize book entitled *A Dendro-cyto-myeloarchitectonic Atlas of the Cat's Brain*, he's a bit more judicious. "What [Harvey] did is probably illegal," he tells me. "I guess he must be a slightly strange guy. . . . Had he been smart, he would have given it up and moved away from it, but he was grandstanding, and I presume he paid a price for it." (Author's note.)

78. Paterniti uses the names of states and towns to compress time and miles, while still maintaining the flavor of the trip. The radio farm reports place us in the Buick Skylark.

79. The quote shows Harvey's almost childlike fascination with seemingly everyday things and thus continues fleshing out his personality.

80. The drive through the Midwest provides a vehicle for working in what happened to Harvey after he took the brain, information gleaned from the pathologist and from reading books on Einstein.

81. While the names flesh out the meeting, the bigger reason for using them is as a setup for future references throughout the story.

82. The tight description gives us a vivid picture of the awkward young doctor. The term "Irregular Sock" is a colorful way of conveying his awkwardness in this celebrated group of scientists. Because of the earlier setup, we can hear his nervous "heh-heh" without Paterniti having to elaborate.

83. These questions sound like the morphed voice of Harvey and Paterniti.

84. We get an outsider's view of Harvey.

Meanwhile, Harvey bristles at such suggestions, regards himself as destiny's chosen one, the man who forever belongs with Einstein's brain, for better or for worse.[85] In a way, it is a tale of obsessive love: Humbert Humbert and his Lolita.[86] But Harvey sees it more prosaically: "Yup, I was just so fortunate to be the one to walk in the room that morning," he repeats again and again. Prior to that April morning in 1955,[87] Harvey's life hardly augured greatness as much as stolid servitude and an abiding curiosity in science. He had met Einstein only once, to take blood from him, and, expecting his usual nurse for such a menial chore, the ever-lustful scientist saw Harvey and blurted, "You've changed your sex!" Summing up his years as a pathologist, Harvey says, "It was great to try to figure out what killed someone."

Sawed-off statements like these initially make it easy to, well, feel underwhelmed by Harvey. In part, it is simply Quaker modesty, a respectful reticence, beneath which glimmers a diamond-sharp, at times even cunning man who has survived over four decades with the brain. Harvey grew up in a Kentucky line of dyed-in-the-wool Quakers, then moved to Hartford, Connecticut, when his father got a good job with an insurance firm. Later, he attended Yale, where he contracted tuberculosis, spent over a year in a sanatorium, and when he returned, gave up his dreams of doctoring and turned to pathology because "the hours were less demanding." He lists that year of sickness and the later revocation of his medical license as among the greatest disappointments of his life. Did he pay a price for the brain? Perhaps. He was soon fired from his job at the hospital and divorced from his first wife. In the next years he drifted through jobs at state psychiatric hospitals and medical labs, another wife, and then picked up and moved west to start a general practice in Weston, Missouri, which eventually folded. Later, he lost his medical license after failing a three-day test and was forced to work the late shift as an extruder at a plastics factory in Lawrence, Kansas. All of it after the brain, perhaps because of the brain.[88]

Nonetheless, a life isn't one paragraph long, and we might also consider Harvey a happy man, with each move maybe feeling himself to be on to the next adventure, with each wife and child perhaps feeling himself loved. Still, I try to picture him standing before Einstein's body—in that one naked moment.[89]

Only occasionally can you glimpse through the embrasures of an otherwise perfectly polite person to see the cannons aimed out, only in a certain glint of light do the eyeteeth become fangs. We are driven by desire and fear. Only in our solitary hungers do we find ourselves capable of the most magnificently unexpected sins. . . .

TOWARD DODGE CITY, KANSAS. FEBRUARY 21, 1997.

We wake in Lawrence to a nuclear-powered snow, driving horizontally, starring the windows with ice, piling up until the Skylark looks like a soap-flake duck float in a Memorial Day parade gone terribly wrong. Everything is suddenly heaped in the frigid no-smell

---

85. Paterniti lets Harvey answer his critics.

86. The comparison to the Nabokov characters adds understanding and humor.

87. Transition into digression on Harvey and his background.

88. Note how selective Paterniti is in giving us Harvey's background, using only those details that relate to his disposition (the Quaker upbringing), his medical training, and the brain.

89. That one naked moment becomes even more dramatic and memorable because of its placement at the end of the paragraph. Set off by the dash, it lingers in our minds and becomes both awkward and humorous—the adjective "naked" causes us to picture Harvey standing there literally naked.

of winter, cars skidding, then running off roadsides into gulleys. The snow falls in thick sheaves, icicles jag the gutters. It feels like Lawrence is going back to a day, 500,000 years ago, when it was buried under hundreds of feet of ice.[90]

We take shelter in our adjoining rooms at the Westminster Inn, are slow to rise. When we do, Harvey is bright-eyed and spunky as we find the good people of Kansas doing what they do in a blizzard: eating pancakes. The Village Inn Pancake House Restaurant is packed: college students and retirees, all flannel-shirted, how-are-ya's ricocheting everywhere; steak-and-egg specials zooming by on super-white plates. Some of the old men wear Dickies workpants and baseball caps with automotive labels; the undergrads sport caps emblazoned with team names or slogans like WHATEVER or RAGE or GOOD TO GO. Even in the no-smoking section everyone smokes[91]—one of Harvey's pet peeves.

Our routine in restaurants follows a familiar pattern: Harvey meditates over the menu, examining it, dissecting, vectoring, and equating what his stomach really wants. I get a newspaper and usually skim through the first section before he's ready. Even as James Earl Ray is planning to go on *The Montel Williams Show* to plead for a new liver and two teenagers are indicted for the murder and dismemberment of a man in Central Park, there's an ongoing existential debate raging in Harvey's head: salty or sweet, eggs or waffles with maple syrup.[92]

Occasionally, after a particularly deliberate order, he'll deliberately change it.[93] Our waitress is a pathologically smiley K.U. student, well-versed in the dynamics of a breakfast rush, the coffee-craving, caffeine-induced chaos of it all. She waits as Harvey takes a second look at the menu. It could be that an actual week passes as he clears his throat a couple of times, then ponders some more, but she smiles patiently and then chirps back, "Eggs over easy, bacon, wheat toast, home fries. More coffee?"

This town was once the setting for a Jason Robards made-for-television movie called *The Day After*. In it, the sturdy people of America's Hometown were blown to smithereens in a nuclear attack, and the few who survived wandered in a postapocalyptic stupor, in rags, bodies flowered with keloid scars. That Lawrence would become connected in the nation's psyche with nuclear devastation and that Einstein's brain, the power that unknowingly wrought the bomb, rested here for six or seven years is a small pixel of irony that seems to escape Harvey.[94] When I ask him about it, he says, "Way-ell, I guess that's true." And starts laughing.

The truth is that Einstein himself was confounded by the idea that his theory of relativity had opened up a Pandora's box of mutually assured annihilation. In a 1935 press conference, in which he was asked about the possibility of an atomic bomb, the physicist said that the likelihood of transforming matter into energy was "something akin to

---

90. Note the fresh description: "nuclear-powered snow" (a fitting adjective for this story), "the frigid no-smell of winter," "icicles jag the gutters." It puts us in the scene.

91. Paterniti's selective use of concrete details again puts us into that Lawrence, Kansas, restaurant: we see the flannel-shirted retirees, the steak-and-egg specials, the super-white plates, the undergrads in sloganed billed caps, the smoke. He uses the latter to tell us something about Harvey.

92. Rather than simply describing the scene, Paterniti lets us know this is a pattern, and in doing so lets us see more of Harvey's personality. "Dissecting, vectoring" come from Harvey's world and add to the scene's humor, as does the "existential debate" over salty or sweet. The tidbits from the news further help to put us in this scene.

93. Paterniti continues to have fun with Harvey, with a play on the word "deliberate."

94. The movie and the fact that Harvey and the brain once resided in Lawrence provide an opportunity for a digression on Einstein's relationship, or lack thereof, to the atomic bomb.

shooting birds in the dark in a country where there are only a few birds." Four years later, however, the Nazis had invaded Poland, and Einstein, the celebrated pacifist, signed a letter to President Roosevelt advocating the building of an atomic weapon. When the letter was personally delivered to Roosevelt, the President immediately saw the gravity of the situation—that if the Americans had just thought to build a bomb, perhaps the Nazis, with great scientists such as Heisenberg, were well on their way to completing one—and ordered his chief of staff to begin immediate top-secret plans that led to the building of an atomic weapon. Sometime later, on a mesa in New Mexico, rose the Town That Never Was, Los Alamos, and, under the guidance of Robert Oppenheimer, came Little Boy and Fat Man, the bombs that would eventually decimate Hiroshima and Nagasaki, respectively.

Einstein, who was thought to be a Communist sympathizer by the FBI and an untrustworthy, outspoken pacifist by the Roosevelt Administration, was not part of Oppenheimer's team. In fact, he had nothing to do with the bomb whatsoever, though even today his name is connected to it. The letter to Roosevelt haunted him and his family and, in one case, incited a physical attack against Einstein's son, Hans Albert. Writing to Linus Pauling, Einstein called the letter the "one mistake" of his life. When the bomb was dropped on Hiroshima—on August 6, 1945—Einstein heard the news after waking from a nap at Saranac Lake. "Oy vay," he said wearily. "Alas." . . .[95]

We drive south to Dodge City,[96] the Oglala aquifer under our wheels, huge cow-uddered[97] clouds overhead. On the radio: steer calves and heifers for sale, Red Angus bulls, yearlings with good genetics and quality carcass.[98] Later, Bobby Darin singing "Beyond the Sea," Harvey tapping a finger on his knee, the brain sloshing in its Tupperware.[99] In this happy moment, we could probably drive forever.

By twilight,[100] a nocturne of autumn rain on the roof of the Skylark. We pass a pungent nitrogen plant, itself like a twisted metallic brain. Water towers gleam in the silver light like spaceships, telephone poles pass like crucifixes, and grain elevators rise like organ pipes from the plains.[101]

Out here, too, just before Dodge City and a most delicious slab of Angus fillet, before a night at the Astro Motel and a dawn that brings a herd of 18-wheelers hurtling for Abilene, we see a rainbow and come face-to-face with Harvey's blighted ambition. "I remember more rainbows in Kansas than any other state," he says, blinking his moist eyes at the brilliant beams of blue and green, orange and yellow. "I used to try to photograph rainbows, but they never turned out."[102]

SOMEWHERE EAST OF LOS ALAMOS, NEW MEXICO. FEBRUARY 22, 1997.

A confession: over the last days, at truck stops and drive-thrus, at restaurants and random road meetings, I've kept our little secret—that we've got Einstein's brain stashed in the trunk—and it's taken its psychic toll. There have been moments when I've been alone

---

95. Note the very specific detail of where Einstein was and what he was doing when he learned of the Hiroshima bomb. The quote adds a human touch to the moment.
96. Place transition.
97. Another fresh, quirky adjective.
98. The radio is again used to compress time.
99. We never forget the third party in this threesome.
100. Time transition.
101. A series of fresh similes captures the passing landscape.
102. The day ends with a memorable rainbow, a memorable quote. We again glimpse Harvey's simple awe.

with the brain—Harvey in a rest room or visiting a friend—when I've opened up the car trunk and looked in, pinched the cold zipper between my thumb and forefinger, but then couldn't bring myself to unzip the duffel and unsheath[103] the brain. Too much of a violation, an untenable breach in our manly society, even as Harvey covets for himself the gray matter upon which our private Skylarkian democracy is founded. In fact, we've been together now for nearly five full days, and he won't show me the brain. When I bring it up in conversation, he doesn't want to talk about it. When I ask him what parts of the brain we're traveling with exactly, he says he doesn't know and changes the subject. It is as if I am trying to find the secret center of his power. Which I am.[104]

Leaving the Astro Motel the next morning, I unexpectedly spill my guts at the front desk, as I return our room keys to the manager. I tell him we've got the brain in the trunk, adding that we're headed to California to show it to Einstein's granddaughter. The manager, an affable, middle-age man, stops for a moment and looks at me sideways, realizes I'm serious, and tries to be hospitable. "Einstein, huh? That guy knew something," he says, folding his arms, shifting his weight. "That guy really did have a brain. But I wouldn't have wanted to live with him. You know . . . a little weirdy." He spins his finger in a cuckoo circle around his ear. "I have a nephew who is kind of a genius, but he hasn't flaked off yet. I met a guy in California who was so smart he couldn't talk. He sure could tell you how to look at the moon, but he couldn't tell you how to tie your shoes."[105]

I'm not sure that I feel better, though I know that, in his way, he has tried to help. But does he scribble down our license-plate number as we leave? . . .

We gas down into Oklahoma (through Tyrone, Hooker, Guymon, and Texhoma) and then the Texas Panhandle (edging the Rita Blanca National Grasslands, through Stratford, Dalhart, and Nara Visa)—all of it flat, with oil rigs like metronomes. I've taken to photographing Harvey by various signs and monuments along the road, and when we drift by a huge wooden cowboy with two guns blazing out across the empty plains, Harvey poses between his legs. By the New Mexico border, the wood-frame farmhouses have transmogrified into adobe. In Tucumcari, almost on cue, there is red dirt and tumbleweed. We drive through ruts and washes, over tableland and mesa. Here the hills are testicular, the ancient mounds mons-like, but all of it has a dead, washed-out sexuality, decayed from a time when this place was overrun by dinosaurs.[106] We climb the crags that rim Pajarito Plateau to Los Alamos—the gridded, repressed hothouse that wrought Little Boy and Fat Man.[107] In the rush of cacti, my frustration with Harvey's Humbertness,[108] with his protective zeal when it comes to the brain, has bled into a kind of benev-

---

103. Paterniti continues his fresh, vivid verbs: "stashed," "pinched," "unsheath."

104. Paterniti returns to his curiosity about the brain, and the tension resumes: Will he get to see and touch the brain? Will he eventually violate that "manly society" and take a peek? We must read on to find out.

105. Paterniti works in another scene. In doing so, note how he draws us into the moment by setting the scene (at the front desk, with the author returning the key) and by letting us see what the characters look like ("an affable, middle-age man"—not simply "the manager") and do ("spins his fingers in a cuckoo circle"), as well as what they say (the dialogue). The final quote is a gem.

106. Rather than giving us a blow-by-blow account of the trip, Paterniti compresses time and miles by using the names of towns and providing a sweeping description: "all of it flat, with oil rigs like metronomes." As we near their destination, Los Alamos, he slows down and brings the landscape into focus, selectively choosing the details that will give us a sense of what it is like: adobe houses, red dirt, tumbleweed, the tableland and mesa. While Paterniti took many pictures of Harvey by various roadside signs and monuments, he chooses the one of Harvey between the legs of the giant cowboy to show the offbeat pathologist's unsophisticated nature.

107. Because of the earlier setup, there is no need to explain Little Boy and Fat Man. We know they are the bombs dropped on Hiroshima and Nagasaki.

108. Again, because of the earlier reference, we understand what the writer means by Harvey's "Humbertness."

olent respect, an idea that Harvey actually may be a revolutionary hero. For wasn't he the one who thumbed his nose at the great U.C. Army doctor, Webb Haymaker,[109] upped the establishment, and legged it out West on an end around with the brain? Maybe he thought he was protecting the brain from the so-called experts, or saving the brain of one of the world's greatest pacifists from the clutches of the U.S. military. Wouldn't that make him the perfect Einsteinian hero?[110] . . .

Perhaps this is why Harvey felt that Einstein's brain, one of the most powerful engines of thought ever on earth, deserved a committed curator, an unpartisan keeper, an eccentric brother whose sole purpose would be to unlock the biological secrets of Einstein's brain by placing it in the hands of a chosen few. Einstein himself had called his brain his laboratory, and with it had pondered the blueness of sky, the bending of starlight, the orbit of Mercury. And maybe, if Harvey knew nothing else, he knew enough to make sure that Einstein's brain didn't get sucked into the maw of the System.[111]

This is my line of thought as we zag through saguaro and scrub brush, in the shadow of the Jemez Mountains. When I look over at Harvey, he has momentarily nodded off for the first time all trip. I've sort of nodded off, too. On a straightaway, I look at the speedometer: we're going 115 miles an hour.[112]

LOS ALAMOS, NEW MEXICO. FEBRUARY 22, 1997.

At Los Alamos, we visit the Bradbury Science Museum. Not unexpectedly, the first exhibit is Einstein's letter to President Roosevelt.[113] Harvey stands before it, nodding seriously, then moves on. The museum is a three-room pavilion walled with text and grainy black-and-white photographs that detail the scientific, as well as human, challenges of building the bomb, while lionizing the patriotic men and women who contributed to the Manhattan Project. But the museum—and the culture of Los Alamos as a whole—is most glaringly defined by what its curators seem to have selectively forgotten about the bomb.[114]

For what the Bradbury Science Museum doesn't show is an August 1945 morning in central Hiroshima, trolleys packed with people, thousands of schoolgirls doing community service in the streets. It doesn't show the B-29, the *Enola Gay*, floating above at 31,000 feet, then releasing four tons of metal through the air, Little Boy. It doesn't show the side of the bomb with its autographs and obscene messages (one starts, "Greetings to the Emperor . . .") and emblazoned with the crude naked likeness of Rita Hayworth.[115]

What the museum forgets to show is the forty-three seconds of utter silence, the time it takes Little Boy to drop on the city, and then perhaps the loudest second of the

---

109. There is no need to explain Webb Haymaker because of the earlier reference.

110. The questions are the writer's voice, his thoughts.

111. More of Paterniti's thoughts. Note how they are at once lofty ("with it had pondered the blueness of the sky, the bending of starlight") and down-to-earth ("an eccentric brother," "to make sure Einstein's brain didn't get sucked into the maw of the System"), and how they also draw on Einstein's own words ("had called his brain his laboratory").

112. The speed brings another section to a memorable ending. After his lofty thoughts we aren't surprised that his mind really wasn't on driving.

113. Because of the earlier reference, there is no need to explain Einstein's letter to Roosevelt.

114. Paterniti uses the museum and the letter to work in a graphic description of the bombing of Hiroshima. He draws from his reading to reconstruct the scene, choosing those details that will draw us into the experience just as we've been drawn into the road trip.

115. The autographs, obscene messages, and naked Rita Hayworths on the side of Little Boy show us the bravado and callousness of the men flying the mission.

twentieth century, a blast that equals 12,500 tons of TNT. It doesn't show ground zero, at Aioi Bridge, the birds incinerating in the air, people flaming like candles, others swelling like bronze Buddhas. And this is just the beginning.

It doesn't show the firestorm that soon pulverizes the city, the atomic winds that turn into a tornado in the north part of town. The nine of ten bodies dead within a mile of the blast, the 200,000 people who will finally be counted dead, and the black, sticky rain, carrying radioactive fallout, that beats relentlessly down on the survivors. It doesn't show the naked man, skin hanging from his body like a kimono, with his eyeball in his hand. It doesn't show the 70,000 rubbled buildings and the people trapped beneath them. Afterward, it doesn't show Nagasaki and the 140,000 more Japanese who will die in like fashion.[116] One can spend hours in the museum—as Harvey does, finally exiting, exhilarated, buzzed about the wonders of technology[117]—but this devastation remains invisible.

We spend the night at the ranch of some friends of mine near Cerrillos[118]—a thirtyish couple, Scott and Clare. We share a terrific meal, and Harvey is particularly animated, fired on red wine,[119] talking at length about the brain, about how he came by it and how, after fixing it with formaldehyde (his one mistake was injecting the brain with warm formaldehyde instead of cold formaldehyde, thus hastening its denaturation),[120] he photographed the brain. "It's a real traysure,"[121] he says. "I've gotten to meet many famous people, many who knew Einstein."

Later,[122] I leave the room to make a phone call, and when I return Harvey and Clare are alone at the table, flushed with excitement, absolutely twittering about the brain. They lower their voices when I come in, raise them when I leave again. Later, I feel compelled to ask Clare some questions: What is Harvey's magic? Does the brain turn her on? Does she feel hypnotized? "He's a very, very interesting man," she says. "And for some men chivalry is not dead. Did you see him pull out my chair for me before dinner?"

Before bed, we take a hot tub. I'm confident that Harvey will sit this one out, but, no sir, he doesn't. Shambles out in a borrowed bathrobe and swim trunks, dips a toe in the boiling water. It's a pretty chilly night, stars glazed in the sky like cold coins on black ice, and it's hard not to worry about the physiological ramifications of dropping an eighty-four-year-old body into 104-degree water. But Harvey just throws himself in like a heavy stone.[123] "OH, OH, HEH-HEH. WOW, THAT'S HOT. WOW, WOW, WOW!!!" We simmer for a while, and, chitchatting over the bubbler, it slips out that, in my earlier absence, Harvey opened the duffel for my friends, unpeeled the Tupperware top, fingered chunks of the brain, expansively answered questions. This hits me hard. In fact, I take it as a personal injury. I want to say something about how unfair it is that I would have driven 2,000 miles so far and not been allowed to examine the brain, while my friends, doing nothing

---

116. The repetition of "it doesn't show" emphasizes the horrors and serves as a constant reminder that they have been ignored by the museum, which has attempted to put a good face on the bomb. "Afterward" varies the repetition and conveys a sense of going through the litany all over again. Paterniti draws from photographs and written accounts for his vivid descriptions.

117. The dashes serve to emphasize Harvey's reaction.

118. Place transition.

119. "Fired on red wine" conveys a sense of the wine loosening Harvey's tongue.

120. Parentheses provide a way of working in this aside without interrupting the scene.

121. Because of the earlier setup, we can hear Harvey's voice.

122. Time transition.

123. This funny scene is made funnier by Paterniti's exaggerated martyr tone: "They lower their voices when I come in, raise them when I leave"; "This hits me hard. In fact I take it as a personal injury." Note, however, that he doesn't overdo it. Writing humor takes a careful, easy hand.

but being their friendly selves, got to see the brain instantly. But when I look over at Harvey, he has his eyes closed, in a wonderful trance, his pale body streaming out from him underwater. I wait for as long as I can take it really, expecting to outlast him, as a kind of revenge. But damn if he doesn't seem to gain strength. Finally, grudgingly, I lift myself from the tub, from its magic eternal spring, and splosh inside, leaving him in the dark waters, keening softly with pleasure—ahhh, play-sure[124]—alone beneath the comos. . . .[125]

LAS VEGAS, NEVADA. FEBRUARY 23, 1997.

The city is a coronation of shimmering brightnesses, like so much shattered glass thrown by the fistful over a sandy floor, a high-desert Hong Kong of possibility. "Sunday midnight is our busiest time of the week," says the woman who checks us in to the Excalibur Hotel/Casino. "There's no freaking explaining it."[126] We've driven to Las Vegas in a dopamine infusion of orange light, nerved on Coca-Cola, gorged on pizza, the Skylark smelling vaguely stale. The brain sloshing in the padded cranium of the trunk.[127] . . .

And now, in the casino at midnight:[128] we stand amid ballyhooing hordes of pale-skinned Easterners and leather-skinned Westerners, bikers and accountants, cowboy-hatted and big-haired and bald as cue balls,[129] imperial on free drinks,[130] soaring on the oxygen-enriched air pumping into the casino to keep people awake, everyone taking a stab at Instamatic riches.[131] Harvey seems overwhelmed, his sensibilities so jangled that he schlepps[132] straight up to one of our cheesy eighteenth-floor rooms—rooms that are tricked out like a cardboard-castle set for a high school production of *Camelot*. He refuses help with his luggage, has the brain slung over his shoulder in the duffel, tosses it in the closet.[133]

Wide awake, I go back downstairs and roam all night, remembering that Einstein put little faith in games of chance. About quantum mechanics, a theory that allowed for unpredictable outcomes, he once said that God does not play dice with the universe.[134] Yet Las Vegas is all about dice. And all about a perverse kind of hope too. One man at a five-dollar blackjack table, a short, tightly bundled guy who smells of lime aftershave, is abstractly addressing the male dealer in gambler clichés and porn-movie dialogue. "Oh yeah, baby! . . . Yeah, baby! . . . Give it to me! . . . Hit me! . . . Oh yeah! . . . Hold right there! . . . Feels good!"[135]

Soon, he is sitting alone. As are others like him. These are men so sunk down inside themselves that they don't give a prostitute working the place a second look when she cozies up to them. Personally, I'm feeling pretty good, lose some quick money at the roulette table, and then, feeling a little less good, regroup in the Minstrel's Lounge. Maybe

---

124. Because of the earlier setup, we hear Harvey's voice.
125. The reference to the cosmos brings us back to Einstein.
126. The description is concise yet captures the essence of Las Vegas. The clerk's quote puts us there.
127. The brain continues to be a present third passenger. Note the comparison of the trunk to a skull.
128. Time and place transition.
129. The use of "and" rather than commas conveys a sense of the assorted types in the crowd. Of course you'd expect a sea of cowboy hats and teased hair.
130. "Imperial on free drinks" aptly conveys the air of superiority that often comes with alcohol.
131. A fresh way of describing hitting the jackpot.
132. The verb gives us a vivid picture of Harvey's walk.
133. The "camera" keeps the brain in sight.
134. Paterniti uses the visit to the casino to weave in a bit of Einstein material from his research and thus bring the Las Vegas visit back to the story's focus.
135. Paterniti has given us an overview of the crowd; now he uses the zoom lens to re-create a scene.

I've been alone with Harvey too long, probably I need friends, but I find myself asking an older couple about Einstein.[136] The man looks at me suspiciously. "I don't know anything about him really, and I don't care one way or the other. I'm just trying to have fun," he says in a Yankee accent.

"I don't know anything either," chimes his wife cheerfully. "Just that he was a genius or something."

After the hot-tub revelation, I no longer feel compelled to keep our secret. I am traveling with the man who owns Einstein's brain, I say, and we are going to California to show it to Einstein's granddaughter. The man folds his arms and looks at me straight on. "Whatever makes you happy," he says.

At an empty blackjack table, I ask a dealer, a Korean guy with a mustache, about Einstein. "I don't know anything about him," he says, "but that man over there should be able to help you." He points to his manager, a white guy with a mustache. He barely lets me finish before responding. "Haven't seen him in here tonight. Sorry, pal."

I try again, with the friendliest-looking man I can find. He's middle-age and round-bellied, like his group of friends, all wearing Bucky Badger sweatshirts. I smile at them, ask their pardon, phrase my question more carefully this time.

Mr. Badger furrows his brow. "Why do you want to know?" he demands. "Has anyone ever told you about $E = mc^2$? Has anyone in this casino bothered to tell you that?"

I explain that in fact no one has, that I myself am traveling with Einstein's brain. At the mention of the brain, he doesn't miss a beat, becomes impatient. "Let's bury the damn brain and be done with it," he says, as if he's been in on the debate since day one.

I try one last time, a cocktail waitress with a tornado of blond hair. She stands in a short black-and-gold dress, looking like someone's risqué aunt in age denial at a wedding. When I ask her if she happens to know what Albert Einstein is famous for, her jaw drops. "You're kidding?" she asks. "You must be kidding me. Is there a hidden camera around here? You're the fifth guy to ask me that tonight, and frankly I'm offended." Her voice is pinched with anger. "You know what? I do know who he is . . ." She and I have known each other less than twenty seconds, and yet it feels as if we've lived a life-time of emotions. "He invented the atom bomb, and I happen to think he's terrible."[137]

In the morning,[138] Harvey and I go for breakfast. There are huge lines trailing out of the Roundtable Buffet and Sherwood Forest Café, and so we watch a juggler dressed in green tights work the crowd—"Oh boy, whatta juggler!" says Harvey. Later, we gather our bags and head through the casino for the castle door. As usual, Harvey refuses help with his luggage, has the brain slung over his shoulder. We pause at a bank of slot machines. A group of grandmothers from Iowa give Harvey a quick once-over, then go back to their spinning lemons and limes and sevens. I pull a couple of coins from my pocket. "For good luck," I tell him. Until now, Harvey hasn't been keen on gambling, but for my sake he slides a quarter in the slot machine and reluctantly pulls the lever. In a way, however, Harvey has been a high-stakes gambler all along, having risked everything on one bet many, many years ago. And even though his slot windows display only unmatched fruit, he leaves the casino with his own jackpot safely stashed in the gray duffel, his step oddly

---

136. Since Las Vegas has no real tie to Einstein, Paterniti creates his own by asking the gamblers about the famous scientist.

137. Note how Paterniti gives the gamblers a face. He speaks to an older couple with a Yankee accent, a Korean guy with a mustache, a middle-age and round-bellied guy, a cocktail waitress with blond hair and a short black-and-gold dress. He uses the round-bellied guy's T-shirt as another quick means of identification.

138. Time transition.

light as he slips over the Excalibur's rich purple carpet and out into the blinding sunlight and sandpapery air.[139]

LOS ANGELES, CALIFORNIA. FEBRUARY 24, 1997.

Down through the brown, low-slung, burned-out flats of the Mojave, passing the Soda and Cady Mountains, along Ivanpah and Silver Lakes, powdered white and dinosaur-bone dry, through the broken-winged, blue-shadowed towns of Baker and Yermo and Barstow, by the world's largest thermometer (electronically measuring temperatures to 140 degrees),[140] then up over Cajon Summit—all of it like a grim, parched-mouth, sun-bleached day-after-Las-Vegas hangover until suddenly Los Angeles explodes in a flash of lush green palm trees and red taillights at rush hour, the California sky tilting ultraviolet over the Pacific.[141] Harvey reads from the map the whole way, literally reads to me like it's the story of Job. . . .

When we finally escape the highway, we're somewhere in West Hollywood,[142] though we are looking for Santa Monica and the ocean. At a gas station, I approach a stocky, balding guy in short sleeves and a tie. He works for Kodak as a field engineer. He gives me directions and then asks where I'm from. Once he's registered our vitals, the expression on his face looks like a billboard for the country of the dumbfounded. "No fuck, you got Einstein's brain right over there?" he says. "No fucking way. Right in that trunk? The car with the little old man? Are you making a fucking movie of this? Holy fuck." He pulls out a business card with a picture of himself on it, sporting a full head of half-synthetic hair. "That was in my Hair Club days," he says, without hesitation. "You gotta put me in this fucking article. I'm the guy who gave you directions to the ocean. Einstein's fucking brain! What the fuck next? Aliens, right?"[143]

About five blocks down, we realize that Hair Club[144] has given us bum directions. We drift to the curb and ask help from the first person who appears on the other side of our rolled-down window: a cross-dresser in body-hugging, black leather with thin, shaven legs that seem six feet high and a tiara of some sort in his hair. He's an attractive woman and knows it and acts like he's been expecting us, bends into the window seductively, and gives precise directions, then says, "Hurry now, y'all don't want to miss that romantic sunset over the Pacific." After a half block, Harvey glances once over his shoulder. "Well, we sure asked the right person," he says, with no irony intended. We drive the brain[145] down Sunset and Wilshire, Rodeo and Hollywood, and finally hole up in Santa Monica.

We've come to L.A. so that Harvey can meet one of the doctors to whom he once sent slices of Einstein's brain for research. Yet Harvey can't seem to reach him—can't recall his name when I ask. Meanwhile, I've made plans to meet Roger Richman, the president of his own celebrity-licensing agency and the man who represents the beneficiaries of the estate of Albert Einstein, which itself is presided over by Hebrew University in

---

139. Paterniti again brings this stopover back to Harvey and the brain.
140. The thermometer adds the flavor of roadside attractions to the drive into Los Angeles.
141. Paterniti chooses three things to give us a first glimpse of Los Angeles: the palm trees, rush-hour traffic, and a Pacific sunset.
142. Place transition.
143. Paterniti again manufactures a way to tie the scene to his focus.
144. Since we don't know the guy's name, Hair Club is a recognizable description.
145. The brain remains a presence.

Jerusalem. Richman polices trademark infringements, hawks[146] trade shows for Einstein contraband, and decides just how the image of the physicist will be used in advertisements and on merchandise around the world. When I first called Richman from Kansas and told him that I was heading his way with Harvey and the brain, he was curt. "The brain is at the Smithsonian," he said. "And I'd rather not have you bring that man along."

And although the brain has never been near the Smithsonian, actually,[147] and is authentically still in our trunk, I'm forced to make up some polite excuse when I leave Harvey—something about seeing a friend.[148] I drop him at the beach, where he finds a senior center and spends the day writing postcards, making pals, playing cards.[149] Then I guiltily head over to Richman's Beverly Hills office.[150]

Richman, fifty-three, is a big, powerful man with big, powerful[151] ideas and a full head of thickly parted, natural hair. He wears an Izod-type green short-sleeve shirt. He greets me by saying, "You got the brain with you?" And then he starts laughing.

He ushers me into his office, a spacious, cluttered room strewn with unlicensed celebrity products, and before we begin our interview he puts a tape recorder next to mine, turns it on, and, in this most self-referential of cities, announces that he is taping for the autobiography he intends to write someday. "I would like to say that I'm a marketing genius," he announces. . . .

Of all his clients, Einstein is the biggest. Richman employs five law firms domestically and as many abroad to police him, paying up to $40,000 a month for their services. He shows me a stack of papers, dictionary thick.[152] "All of these are Albert Einstein infringements," he declares proudly. He shows me a famous photograph of Einstein sticking his tongue out. "We never allow this picture to be used," he says fussily. "You know people come back to me and say, 'Who are you to say that we can't use this when he stuck his tongue out and he knew photographers were there?' and I say, 'Hey, I'm running a public trust; it's incumbent upon me to protect these people.' "

Richman won't reveal how much money he and Hebrew University make from Einstein, but he admits it's more than from any other client. When I ask if the figure is in the millions, he simply says, "I wouldn't say *millions*." I remind him that Einstein never allowed his name or image to serve as a product endorsement during his life. "Money only appeals to selfishness and irresistibly invites abuse," the physicist said. "Can anyone imagine Moses, Jesus, or Gandhi with the moneybags of Carnegie?"[153] So wouldn't he object to himself selling Nikon cameras now? Richman dismisses this idea out of hand and assures me that all the profits go to scholarships at Hebrew University.

Then, to show me just how bleak a world without Roger Richman can be, he leads me to a large cardboard box across the room. It's full of black-market desecrations—"horrible, horrible stuff," Richman says. A greeting card with Mae West urinating through an hourglass, one of Marilyn Monroe snorting cocaine. There's John Wayne toilet paper ("It's rough!—It's tough! And it doesn't take crap off anyone!") and a vial of Elvis's sweat ("Now you can let his perspiration be an inspiration") and a box of cotton

---

146. More fresh, vivid verbs: "polices," "hawks."
147. Paterniti deftly corrects Richman and again reminds us the brain is still in the trunk.
148. This tacked-on phrase carries the flavor of Paterniti making an excuse.
149. The lack of the final "and" in this list implies that these are only some of the things Harvey does while Paterniti is out.
150. Place transition.
151. The repetition carries the sense that this guy is a little windy.
152. The description helps us visualize just how thick the stack of papers is.
153. Evidence of Paterniti's research.

balls emblazoned with the words BRANDO'S BALLS. But the *pièce de résistance,* the *succès de scandale,* is wrapped in paper with rubber bands around it. "I always keep him in his house," says Richman. "I never take him out."

Richman places it in my hands, and I unwrap it slowly to find eight inches of hard rubber topped by the smiley-faced head of President Ronald Reagan. It was this very dildo that Richman waved on the floor of the California statehouse to make his point[154]—"I HAVE HERE IN MY HANDS A SEXUAL DEVICE," he bellowed to the shocked assemblage—and that pleases him.

Once the Gipper has been wrapped and replaced in the box, we tour the rest of the office. And Richman gallops on: "We're planning a major celebration of the millennium. We're doing mailings to advertising agencies reminding them that it's coming, that we represent all these people, that they should be celebrating this past century." . . .

Finally I ask Richman why our country is overly obsessed with celebrity today, why celebrity, as much as a Vegas jackpot, has become the Jell-O mold of the American dream. He begins by quoting Thoreau: "The mass of men lead lives of quiet desperation."

"They'll never be an Elizabeth Taylor," he says. "Their hopes are their dreams and their dreams are on TV and their dreams are watching these beautiful chests walking into the Academy Awards in gorgeous gowns and they live for that. That's why Communism failed. [It] never gave people any hope. That's why democracy has been so successful. The American dream, it's based on hope . . . as long as you have money, you go right to the top."

He continues. "When I travel into the heartland of America—I go backpacking a lot—and talk about what I'm doing, oh, these people, they won't let me shut up. They just ask question after question after question. I'm like a hero to them. Around here, no one cares. Dead stars, oh, forget it. You're an agent for the dead, you're a joke, c'mon."

But Richman is convinced that he's having the last laugh, in no small part thanks to Einstein, who's gone global.[155] In Japan, Einstein's image is used in a commercial for a video game called 3DO; in Hungary, his mug is plastered on billboards for a local telephone company; in South Africa, he advertises insurance. "He's the most widely recognized human being that ever lived," declares Richman. "In China"—where Richman has recently brokered a deal for Einstein T-shirts—"they're limited to one child per family, and every single parent calls their one child 'my little Einstein.'" He smiles at the thought.

"China is a cultural wasteland," he says emphatically. "They've never heard of John Wayne. They've never heard of Steve McQueen. They've never seen any of their movies. But Einstein, they know."[156]

SAN JOSE, CALIFORNIA. FEBRUARY 26, 1997.

Harvey is to give a talk on Einstein's brain in San Jose. Before we left Princeton, he rooted through the letters he keeps in a shoe box—letters from an oddball collection of fans and groupies, critics and psychos, everywhere from Denmark to New Zealand, everyone from angry rabbis demanding the brain for burial to elegiacal schoolkids cutely waxing juvenile about trying to figure out relativity[157]—and called a woman named Sarah Gonzalez,

---

154. The concrete details both add color to the story and show us the tackiness in celebrity merchandise.
155. The story returns to Einstein.
156. Paterniti wisely allows the irony of this quote to speak for itself.
157. The aside gives us a picture of the colorful mix of people who've written Harvey over the years by showing us the extremes. We know by implication there has been everything in between.

someone he doesn't know but who had written to him a few years ago randomly asking for a piece of the brain. When she heard from Harvey, she felt that the Lord God had intervened on her behalf. Ever since his call, she has been busy informing San Jose of our arrival, contacting the mayor and the local media, trying to set up a dinner party for leading lights in the community, and arranging for Harvey and Einstein's brain to visit with students at Independence High School, one of the biggest in the country.

Gonzalez has reserved us rooms at the Biltmore Hotel, but when we arrive around 2:00 A.M., out on some industrial edge of San Jose, there is only one available room left, with a single bed. "Why, I'm sure it's a big one," says Harvey with a nervous chuckle.

I ask for a cot. And by the time I roll it into the room, the gray duffel[158] is up on the television with the weather on and Harvey is snorkeling[159] through his suitcase, each item of his clothing—his silk pajamas, a 49ers sweatshirt, his slippers, and a dress shirt—wrapped in cellophane. He has brought two suits for tomorrow, neatly folded like big bat wings in his case, a black winter worsted wool and a baby-blue leisure-type suit that puts me in mind of a carnival barker or a midwestern aluminum-siding salesman.[160]

I collapse on the cot, and no sooner do I hit the pillow than I'm wide awake. But I keep my head buried as Harvey putters about the room. I can hear him running water in the sink, clearing his throat, ironing. I can hear him rustling through his cellophane-wrapped clothes, then perusing his various articles on Einstein, preparing for his lecture. I can hear something that sounds like an electric toothbrush. Before the sun rises, he finally beds down, and his breathing slows and then grows deeper like a river running into pools. Instead of snoring, there's a sweet lowing in his theta-gasps for air, and finally it puts me to sleep too. When I wake to the crunching of Harvey eating caramel corn,[161] it's 8:00 A.M., and he's half-dressed, having opted for the black suit with black suspenders and a gray turtleneck, though the weather is verging on summer. Sarah Gonzalez calls and announces that she's in the lobby, nearly an hour early. While Harvey primps,[162] I go to meet her. She's the only person at the bar, busily doing something with her hands. When I come closer, I realize that she is pressing on a set of acrylic fingernails. For a moment, she doesn't notice that I'm standing there, and we both admire her handiwork. When she looks up, she seems surprised. "Oh," she says, extends an automatic hand with half new nails and half bitten ones, and peeks around me for Harvey and the brain.[163]

Sarah Gonzalez is a short, pretty, quick-moving Filipino woman with black-and-gold sunglasses and an ostentatious emerald car.[164] In her mood and mannerisms she reminds me of a brushfire in a high wind.[165] She personifies the immigrant's dream. A former executive secretary, she is now the president of her own company, Pacific Connections, which markets biomass energy conversion—or, as she puts it, "turning cornstalks to megawatts." Next week, she tells me, she will be in Manila meeting with the Fil-

---

158. The duffel bag has been so tied to the brain that a reference to it immediately conjures up the brain itself.

159. Another fresh, vivid verb.

160. The clothes and the cellophane give us a sense of Harvey's personality. The bat-wing image helps us picture the folded suits.

161. The caramel corn is still more evidence of Harvey's eccentricity.

162. The verb "primps" implies a certain prissy, prima-donna side.

163. The fingernail scene is another of Paterniti's unexpected bonuses, the kind a writer can never plan for.

164. In describing Sarah Gonzalez, Paterniti chooses the features that will best give us a sense of what she is like: the fact she is Filipino, the sunglasses, the ostentatious car.

165. The metaphor is fresh and fitting. It seems to capture her personality perfectly.

ipino president, Fidel V. Ramos, in hopes of bringing the gift of energy—more lights and televisions—to her country of birth

When Harvey comes chugging out, she blanches, then starts forward. "Dr. Harvey, I presume," says Gonzalez, clucking and bowing her head, "I can't believe there is someone living and breathing who was so close to Einstein." Harvey has removed the brain from the gray duffel and now holds the Tupperware container in his hand, though the plastic is clouded enough that you can really only see urine-colored liquid inside.[166] Suddenly, it feels as if we're not fully clothed. Even as Harvey palms the brain in the lobby, I feel a need to hide it. Gonzalez herself doesn't notice and rushes us into her Mercury Grand Marquis. She's a woman who enjoys the liberal use of first names. "Mike, what do you think of this scandal, Mike?" she asks. "This—how do you say?—campaign-contribution scandal, Mike?" She is perhaps the most persistently friendly person I've ever met.

Harvey sits in the front bucket seat, sunk down in the fine Italian leather, the fabric of his own suit, by comparison, dull and aged; there's a tiny hole in one knee of his heavy suit pants.[167] He clears his throat repeatedly and starts to chuckle. "Do you know a fella named Burroughs, William Burroughs?" She's never heard of him. Harvey tries again.

"Where does Gates live?"

"Bill Gates, Dr. Harvey? That would be Seattle, I think. Isn't that right, Mike? Seattle, Mike?"

"I thought that fella lived right here in Silicon Valley," says Harvey, hawkeyeing the streets suspiciously. A little later on, Harvey's more at ease, sets himself chuckling again. "Those are the funniest looking trees," he says.

"They are palm trees, Dr. Harvey," says Gonzalez.[168]

We are given a brief tour of "old San Jose"—a collection of Day-Glo houses that look brand new—then stop at Gonzalez's house, a comfortable though tightly packed bungalow on a cul-de-sac where she lives with her husband and five children, two of them teenagers. A full drum kit is set up in the living room. One gets the impression that when this house is full there's probably nothing here but love and a hell of a racket. Meeting her husband, I retract her title and claim him as the friendliest person I've ever met. "Oh, Dr. Harvey, what does it feel like to be you?" he asks. He serves us cookies and milk. Finally, after photographs have been taken on the front lawn, we start to leave. Harvey reaches down and lifts a pinecone from the perfect, chemical-fed turf. He holds it up, admiring its symmetry, and for reasons of his own pockets it.

Then we drive to Independence High, where we are picked up by a golf cart at the front entrance and whisked a half mile through campus. Harvey delivers his lecture in a dim, egg-cavern room flooded with students and the smell of bubble gum. Some wear baggy Starter sweats or jeans pulled low off their hips or unlaced high-tops; some have pierced noses or tongues or eyebrows. Some are white or Asian or Latino or African American. A number of boys have shaved the sides of their head and wear moptops or Egyptian pharaoh dos; a number of the girls have dyed hair, all colors of the rainbow.[169]

---

166. The moment we have been waiting for arrives, but instead of the brain, all we really see is what Paterniti sees: cloudy, urine-colored liquid. Thus the quest to really see the brain continues, and along with it, the tension. We must keep reading to see if he gets a closer look.

167. Note the "telling" detail.

168. The fact that Harvey doesn't know a palm tree again shows us the narrowness of his world.

169. Note Paterniti's careful observation. The smell of bubble gum places us inside that auditorium. He then chooses those details—the dress, the nationalities, the hairstyles, the body piercings—that capture the crowd.

The teachers shush everyone, but the hormonal thrum here defies complete silence, and there's a low-level sputter of laughter like a car chuffing even after the ignition's been turned off. And then suddenly Sarah Gonzalez is introducing Harvey, the gold of her glasses flashing success, and Harvey, shaped like a black candy cane, is stumping to the podium, looking every bit the retired undertaker.[170] He clears his throat and chuckles and then clears his throat again. He runs his hands up and down the side of the podium and focuses on a spot at the back of the room, rheumy-eyed, squinting.[171] These are the thirteen-, fourteen-, and fifteen-year-olds of America—hundreds of clear eyes reflecting back at him, brains obsessed with Silverchair, Tupac, Blossom, and Brandy[172]—and Harvey seems at a loss, begins a droning, discombobulated, start-and-stop remembrance[173] of Albert Einstein almost as if he's talking to himself.

"The Great Scientist would eventually come up with the equation $E = mc^2$, and how he did that I'll never know, heh-heh . . .

"He was a friendly person. Real easy to talk to, you know. Wore flannels and tennis shoes a lot . . .

"I was just real lucky to be at the right place at the right time . . ."[174]

Einstein's animated face is flashed on a screen, Harvey's impassive one beneath it. When Harvey senses he's losing his audience, he tells them about the autopsy, about the Great Scientist lying on the table and how his brain was removed. "He liked the fatty foods, you know," says Harvey. "That's what he died of." He starts slowly for the Tupperware and the entire audience lean forward in their seats, crane their necks, hold their collective breath. For the first time, there is complete silence.

He pops the lid and unabashedly fishes around for some of the brain, then holds up a chunk of it. It's almost like a dream—illogically logical, shockingly normal. My first real glimpse of the Tupperwared brain and it is with three hundred other strangers.[175] One girl squeals, and general chaotic murmurings fill the room. Kids come to their feet in waves of "ohhhhs" and "ahhhs." The smell of formaldehyde wafts thickly over them, a scent of the ages, and drives them back on their heels.[176]

Harvey natters on, but no one is really listening now, just gasping at these blobs of brain. "I took the meninges off. . . . This is a little bit of the cortex. . . . He had more glial cells than the rest of us—those are the cells that nourish the neurons . . ."

They are transfixed by the liver-colored slices[177] as if it were all a macabre Halloween joke. They are repulsed and captivated by the man whose fingers are wet with brain. Sarah Gonzalez stands up, slightly disheveled, flushed in the face. "Children, questions! Ask Dr Harvey your questions!"

One swaggering boy in the back of the room raises his hand, seemingly offended: "Yeah, but like, WHAT'S THE POINT?"

---

170. The comparisons to a black candy cane and retired undertaker help us visualize Harvey making his way to the podium.

171. The word choices ("shush," "thrum," "sputter," "chuffing," "rheumy-eyed") bring this scene to life.

172. Paterniti hints that what's on these students' minds is a far cry from the theory of relativity.

173. Before he gives us Harvey's actual words, Paterniti describes his delivery so that when he actually speaks we can hear what he sounds like.

174. Because of the setup, we can hear Harvey's nervous laugh. The ellipses capture his start-and-stop delivery.

175. The moment finally comes: Paterniti gets to see the brain. He uses the fact that his first real glimpse comes in the midst of 300 strangers to down-play it and then keep us reading in hopes of a closer look.

176. The sounds and smell bring us into the scene.

177. "Liver-colored" helps us imagine what the slices of brain look like.

Harvey doesn't hear, puts his hand behind his ear to signal that he doesn't hear, and a teacher sitting nearby translates. "He wants to know what the point is," says the teacher politely.

Harvey hesitates for a second, then almost seems angry. "To see the difference between your brain and a genius's," he shoots back.

The crowd titters. A girl throws a high five at her best friend. "Dang, girl."

The old man is cool!

Another boy in the back stands. "I was told, like, Einstein didn't want people to *take* his brain."

Again the teacher translates, and as soon as Harvey processes the question he bristles. "Where are you getting your information?" he says.

"My world-government teacher," the boy says.

Harvey ponders this, then responds, as if it's answer enough, "In Germany, it's very common to do an autopsy and take the brain out."

When the period ends, the students storm Harvey and the brain. They want to know how long he's had it (forty-two years). If he plans to clone it ("Way-ell, under the right conditions someday, I suppose it might be done"). Whether an evil dictator such as Qaddafi might try to get his hands on it ("Heh-heh-heh").[178] I try to get close, but the crowd is too thick, the crush to see the brain too great, and so I stand on the edges with Gonzalez. Even as Harvey gambols outside later, a few students come up and a boy says, "Yo, man, where you going next? Can we follow?" Harvey flushes with triumph, stammers that he doesn't really know where he's going now, as Sarah Gonzalez leads him to a seat in a waiting golf cart.

When we pull away, I wonder what we must look like to the students waving goodbye. Harvey rides shotgun as always, with the Tupperwared brain on his lap—a man beyond their own grandfathers, someone from a different dimension in space and time really, lit down here for a weird moment at Independence High, then away again, vanishing on a golf cart down the cement superstring sidewalks of their world.[179]

BERKELEY, CALIFORNIA. FEBRUARY 27, 1997.

We've reached the end of the road. Evelyn Einstein greets us at the door to her bayside apartment complex in a black jumper, wearing two Star Trek pins and globe earrings.[180] Nearly a head taller than Harvey, she is a big-boned fifty-six-year-old, though looks younger, with a short bob of brown hair. Due to a series of illnesses over the last few years, she walks in small steps and breathes heavily after the slightest exertion. She gives off an aura of enormous sadness, though her powers of humor and forgiveness seem to run equally as deep. Despite the distress that Harvey's removal of the brain caused her father—Hans Albert—and the rest of the family, she has invited him to her house.

Evelyn is known to be the adopted daughter of Hans Albert, though the circumstance of her lineage is a bit clouded. At least one doctor, Charles Boyd, tried but failed to match the DNA of Albert's brain matter and Evelyn's skin because of suggestions that

---

178. Paterniti compresses the scene by inserting the answers and Harvey's laugh in parentheses. He maintains the flavor by phonetically spelling out "way-ell" and "heh-heh-heh."

179. Paterniti again waxes philosophical as he brings the scene to an end, just where it began, in the golf cart.

180. The detail of the pins and earrings fits the subject matter and reflects Einstein's influence on his granddaughter.

Evelyn might actually be Albert's daughter. And although Albert's DNA was too dena-
tured to decipher, the attempt led to something of a row.[181] Even as Evelyn characterizes
Boyd's theory as "unfortunate and unfounded," however, her resemblance to Einstein,
the mirthful play of light in her heavy-lidded eyes and the Picasso shape of her face, is
uncanny. Evelyn herself ruefully says, "If you believe in what Albert said about time, then
I'm really his grandmother anyway."

From her light-filled living room, you can see the skyline of San Francisco, Angel Island rising from the sun-flecked blue bay; Mt. Tamalpais lurking in the distance. Among
artifacts and antique clocks, Evelyn offers us seats. We have come a long way and yet it
feels like Harvey would like to be anywhere else but here. Evelyn sits down. I fall onto the
plush couch. Harvey remains standing.

Evelyn tells us about what it was like to grow up as an Einstein, how her life became
an exercise in navigating the jagged shoals of her family. Her father had inherited a degree
of his own father's cold distance—she refers to her grandfather only as Albert or Albie—
and Evelyn found herself shipped off to school in Switzerland. She came back to Berkeley
for college, had a bad marriage, lived for a year on the streets, then later worked as a cop
in Berkeley and afterward with cult members and their families. She has very few re-
membrances of her grandfather. Most of the letters he'd once sent her were stolen.

As she says this, Harvey still stands frozen in the middle of the room, speechless. Evelyn does what she can to politely ignore him, asks me innocuous questions about the trip,
waiting for him to sit, too. But he doesn't. He just stands there, his arms limply at his side.
He breathes more quickly. Somewhere in his head, virulent, radioactive cells of what?
guilt? proliferate and mushroom. He stands awkwardly in the middle of the room and
just won't sit, can't sit, holds the brain in its Tupperware, trembling in his left hand. Having arrived here, does he now have second thoughts? Could he ever have imagined, those
forty-two years ago, when he cut the brain from Einstein's head, that he would now be
standing here before Evelyn Einstein with it in his hands?[182]

The fourth time that Evelyn offers him a seat he takes it. He laughs nervously, then
clears his throat. "Real good," he says.[183] Evelyn is talking about cults, how frightening
they are and how what's most frightening about cults is that it's you and I who end up
getting sucked in, how easy mind control really is. "All my friends say I should start one,"
she says, joking. "I could channel Albert. I mean, when Linda Evans channels Ramtha she
talks like Yul Brynner. It's just hysterical. If this broad can channel a 30,000-year-old guy,
I can channel Albert."

Having summoned his courage, Harvey abruptly pulls out a sheaf of photographs
and slides with cresyl violet stains of axons and glial cells, then plunks the Tupperware
on the table. "Ah, brain time," says Evelyn, and Harvey just begins talking as if he's talking to the youngsters at Independence High School again. "This is a picture of the brain
from different aspects, olfactory nerve, and so forth." He pulls out a photo of Einstein. "I
like to show this picture because it shows him as a younger man, you know, when he first
came over to be an American. So many of the photos you see of him are when he was an
older man."

"I have a lot when he was young," says Evelyn.

---

181. The meeting with Evelyn Einstein provides an opportunity to fit in more about the famous scientist
and his family.
182. The questions take us inside Paterniti's head and thoughts.
183. Because of the earlier setup, we recognize his mantra.

"You do? I'll trade you some," says Harvey.

"Did you autopsy the whole body?"

"The whole body."

"What was that like?"

Harvey pauses a moment, clears his throat. "Why, it made me feel humble and insignificant."

"Did he have a gall bladder? Or had they taken it out?"

"I think he still had a gall bladder. Heh-heh. Yeah, his diet was his nemesis, you know, because he lived before we knew what cholesterol did to the blood, so he probably walked around with high blood cholesterol, much of it being deposited in his blood vessels. That aorta, that was just full of cholesterol plaque."[184]

Evelyn nods. "Yeah . . . well, of course, the European diet . . . my father and I would fight over fat. When we got a ham, we would cut off the fat and fry it, then fight over it. Bitterly." Evelyn smiles.

"And all that good goose grease," chimes in Harvey.

"Oh yeah. Well, in those days goose . . . well, goose is actually a lot safer than beef, a lot less cholesterol."

"Oh yeah? I didn't know that."

"It's a family that just adored fat," she says.

"I used to eat in a little inn up in Metuchen, New Jersey, where your grandfather would spend weekends, and they had these cheeses, you know, full-fat cheeses and nice wines."

"I don't know if he was into wines," says Evelyn.

"I never saw him drink it myself," says Harvey, forgetting, then perhaps remembering, that he met Einstein only once.[185] "Well, the innkeeper had a good supply of wine, and I thought it was for your grandfather. Maybe it wasn't."

There is some talk about the size of the brain. Evelyn contends that at 1,230 grams it qualifies as microcephalic according to the 1923 edition of *Gray's Anatomy*—that is, smaller than normal[186]—but Harvey insists that the brain was normal size for a man Einstein's age, given the fact that brains shrink over time. He lets her see some slides but seems unwilling to open the Tupperware. When I ask him if he'd show us pieces of the brain, he seems a bit put out, uncaps the lid for a moment, then almost immediately lids it. He offers Evelyn a piece—to which she says, "That would be wonderful"—then, curiously, never gives it to her. Evelyn seems perplexed, as am I. After all of this, it seems, Harvey has decided that there will be no show-and-tell with the actual gray matter.

"I'm amazed they didn't work with the brain earlier, right away when he died, actually," Evelyn says. Harvey gets uncomfortable again, stiffening into his pillar of salt. The words slow as they come from his mouth: something about the fissure of Sylvius, occipital lobe, cingulate gyrus.[187] All of it a part of some abstract painting, some hocus-pocus act. "It took us a while," he says finally.

And then, as we make plans to leave soon for dinner, Harvey abruptly ends the meeting. "Well, it's been a real play-sure,"[188] he says, taking us by surprise. And then he ex-

---

184. Since there are only two speakers, it is not necessary to use attribution for each quote.

185. Paterniti uses the attribution to insert a reminder that Harvey met Einstein only once.

186. Paterniti gives us the meaning of "microcephalic" in lay terms.

187. This time, Paterniti intentionally leaves the medical terms untranslated to mimic Harvey's "hocus-pocus."

188. The spelling again lets us hear how Harvey speaks.

plains: earlier, in San Jose, unbeknownst to me, he made a call to his eighty-five-year-old cousin in San Mateo and now insists that he must go spend the night there, assuming that I will take him more than halfway back to San Jose in rush-hour traffic.[189] But to come this far for only half an hour? And besides, Evelyn has made reservations for us all to have dinner. But nothing sways Harvey. I suggest that his cousin join us or that we visit his cousin in the morning after rush hour. Harvey stands firm; then I stand firm. After 4,000 miles of driving, I, for one, am eating with the granddaughter of Albert Einstein. Harvey gets on the phone with his cousin and says loudly enough so that I can hear, "The chauffeur won't give me a ride."

Ever the rambler, Harvey decides to take public transportation—BART—and then have his cousin pick him up at the station. And so he does. We pile into the Skylark and drive to a nearby station, Harvey in the back seat with the brain.[190] Although Harvey and I will meet again tomorrow for a visit with Marian Diamond, and although we will share a heartfelt good-bye as I drop him off at the train station again (he on his way to the airport to fly back home, me off to visit friends),[191] this parting feels like the real end of our trip. At the station, Harvey opens his case and presents Evelyn with a postcard: a black-and-white photo of himself looking pensive in a striped turtleneck, his ear the size of a small slipper, gazing sleepy-eyed at some form in the distance, some ghostly presence. "That's a very nice one," she says politely.

"Yessir," says Harvey. "Couldn't have been happier to meet . . ."

It all seems so anticlimactic, but so appropriate. So like Harvey. And then he's off with his suitcase full of cellophane-wrapped clothes, caught in a river of people drifting toward the escalators, spilling underground, the silver tassel of his hair flashing once, then his body going down and down into the catacomb's shadow.[192]

It's not until after Evelyn and I have had dinner that we realize the brain is still with us. In fact, it's still sitting on the car's back seat in its bubble of Tupperware, lit by a streetlight, slopping in formaldehyde. It has been there for three hours, as Evelyn told me over dessert about the ugly schisms and legal battles inside her family for letters left behind by "Albie."[193] Given Harvey's well-documented guardianship of the brain, given the fact that Einstein seems to be Harvey's invisible friend, it seems impossible that he's just forgotten it, but then maybe not. Maybe, through some unconscious lapse or some odd, oblique act of intention, he has left it for us. A passing of the brain to the next generation.[194] My giddiness is now rivaled only by my sudden paranoia. What if it gets ripped off?[195]

"He left the brain?" says Evelyn. "Does he do this often?"

"Nope," I say, and suddenly we are smiling at each other.

We don't look at it right away—right there in full view of the strolling sidewalk

---

189. Rather than spelling out Harvey's explanation, he compresses it, using the more important points.

190. The third passenger is still with us.

191. Paterniti is essentially jumping ahead to tell us how the trip ultimately ends. It's a planned strategy that will enable him to end the story at a more interesting moment.

192. We get our final glimpse of Harvey, disappearing into the subway. Paterniti reminds us again of the cellophane-wrapped clothes and Harvey's eccentricity. For a brief moment, we lose sight of the third passenger: the brain. Thus, its discovery on the back seat comes as much as a surprise for us as it does for Paterniti and Evelyn Einstein.

193. Even in the midst of this important scene, Paterniti manages to weave in more about the Einstein family.

194. Paterniti makes the moment symbolic.

195. Paterniti again uses a question to work in his own thoughts.

masses—but drive back to Evelyn's apartment by the bay. I stop in front of the building with the Skylark idling. I reach back and take the Tupperware in my hands, then unseal the lid, and, in the domelight of the car, open the container.

After all these miles, all these days on the road during which the vengeful gray duf fel taunted me, I am finally afforded the inspection I was denied back in New Mexico. The bits of Einstein's brain are pouched in a white cloth, floating in formaldehyde. When I unravel the cloth,[196] maybe a dozen golf-ball-size chunks of the brain spill out—parts from the cerebral cortex and the frontal lobe. The smell of formaldehyde smacks us like a backhand, and for a moment I actually feel as if I might puke. The pieces are sealed in celloidin—the liver-colored blobs of brain rimmed by gold wax. I pick some out of the plastic container and hand a few to Evelyn. They feel squishy, weigh about the same as very light beach stones. We hold them up like jewelers, marveling at how they seem less like a brain than—what?—some kind of snack food, some kind of energy chunk for genius triathletes.[197] Or an edible product that offers the consumer world peace, space travel, eternity. Even today, the Asmat of Irian Jaya believe that to consume a brain is to gain the mystical essence of another person. But to be absolutely honest, I never thought that, holding Einstein's brain, I'd somehow imagine eating it.[198]

"So this is what all the fuss is about," says Evelyn. She pokes at the brain-nuggets still in the Tupperware, laps formaldehyde on them. A security guard walks by and glances at us, then keeps walking. There is, I must admit, something entirely bizarre about Evelyn messing around with her grandfather's brain, checking his soggy neurons.[199] But she seems more intrigued than grossed out. "You could make a nice necklace of this one," she says, holding up a circular piece of brain. "This is pretty weird, huh?"

Watching her in the cast of domelight—an impression of her sadness returning to me, the thrill of adrenaline confusing everything—I'm overcome with a desire to make her happy for a moment. Without thinking, I say, "You should take it." Then I remind her that Harvey had offered her a piece earlier but had never given it to her. "It belongs to you anyway," I say. Weeks later, on the phone, she'll tell me, "I wish I'd taken it." But now, sitting back in the teal velour of the Skylark, she says, "I couldn't."

Instead, she puts the pieces back in the Tupperware, closes it, and hands it to me. She gets out of the car and heavily walks herself inside.

Which leaves just me and the brain.[200]

THE FLAMINGO MOTEL. FEBRUARY 28, 1997.

We[201] drive the East Shore Freeway to University Avenue—skirting the bay, all black and glassed-over, San Francisco on the other side like so many lit-up missile silos—and then

---

196. Note the delay and buildup in getting to the brain. Paterniti takes his time to build drama and thus compel us to keep reading. (Note also the adjective "vengeful." Remember the earlier description of the bag's somewhat smirking zipper?) The moment of revelation is delayed even more by the unwrapping of the cloth.

197. At last, the moment we've been waiting for: We get to see, feel, and smell the dissected brain. Now Paterniti slows down and lets us carefully "examine" it, using familiar everyday terms that enable us see what it looks like: golf balls, liver, wax, beach stones, snack food. Note how he appeals to all our senses, describing what it looks, feels, and smells like.

198. Paterniti then works in some of his loftier thoughts and a bit of trivia from his research before returning to his more down-to-earth tone.

199. If this hasn't already occurred to us, Paterniti points out the irony, so it doesn't escape us.

200. The brevity of the statement and its placement at the end of the section and the scene add to the drama, and the humor.

201. Note the plural pronoun. Harvey is not around, but the brain is.

head toward Shattuck Avenue. Although I'm exhausted, I suddenly feel very free, have this desire to start driving back across America, sans Harvey. On the radio, there's a local talk show about UFOs, an expert insisting that in February 1954, Eisenhower disappeared for three days, allegedly making contact with aliens.

Although there is no convention that we know of in Berkeley, we soon find that all the inns are full. All the inns but the Flamingo Motel[202]—a pink, cement, L-shaped, Forties-style two-story with a mod neon rendering of a flamingo. A fleabag. But it's enough. A double bed, a bathroom, a rotary phone. Some brother partyers have an upstairs room at the far end of the motel and are drinking cases of Pabst Blue Ribbon. As I carry the brain up to my room, they eye me, then hoot and toss their crushed cans over the banister into the parking lot.

Inside our room,[203] we are hit with an industrial-size wallop of disinfectant. The room is the size of a couple of horse stalls with a rust-colored unvacuumed shag rug scorched with cigarette burns. A few stations come in on the television, which is bolted high on the wall. *Nightline* is getting to the bottom of the sheep-cloning business. It's been a long day, and yet the brain has got me pumped up. I try to make a phone call, but the phone is broken.[204] I try to write some postcards, but my pen explodes. By some trick of the room's mirror, it seems that there are lights levitating everywhere. Finally, not quite knowing what to do, I go to bed. I put Einstein's brain on one pillow and rest my own head on the other one next to it, fewer than four inches away. Just to see. I've come 4,000 miles for this moment, and now all I do is fall asleep.[205] Light from the road slips over the room—a greenish, underwater glow—and the traffic noise dims. I can hear beer cans softly pattering down on the pavement, then nothing.

It's possible that in our dreams we enter a different dimension of the universe. On this night, it's possible that I suddenly have three wives and ten kids and twelve grandchildren, that I've become Harvey himself, that I open up bodies to find more bodies and open those bodies to find that I'm falling through space and time. It's possible that, in some fifth dimension, I am Robert Oppenheimer and Mahatma Gandhi, Billie Holiday and Adolf Hitler, Honus Wagner and Olga Korbut. I am Navajo and Cambodian and Tutsi. I am Tupac Amaru and NASA astronaut. I am a scatterling, I am a billionaire, I am a person in a field in North Dakota about to be abducted by a UFO.[206] It's possible, too, that I am nobody, or rather only myself, slightly dazed and confused, curled in a question mark in a pink motel with Einstein's brain on the pillow by my head.

When I wake the next morning, craving coffee, there is only the world as I know it again— the desk chair in its place, the wrappered soap in the shower, the brain sitting demurely on its pillow, the Flamingo still the Flamingo, with cigarette burns in the rusty rug. There's a sudden grand beauty to its shoddiness.

When I step outside into the bright early-morning sun of California, I have the top

---

202. We return to the Flamingo Motel. Paterniti is preparing to end the story.

203. Transition.

204. Through careful selection of detail, Paterniti puts us in that room with him: the smell of disinfectant, the grungy shag rug, the rotary telephone (not simply a telephone), the television bolted high on the wall, Ted Koppel carrying on about sheep (a stroke of luck for Paterniti, since we often associate counting sheep with falling asleep).

205. The moment Paterniti has been waiting for arrives. He is alone with the brain.

206. Though nothing really happens, Paterniti makes the most of the moment by letting his own imagination and his dreams run wild, and in so doing, turns it into a funny scene. He is Harvey, he is Robert Oppenheimer and Mahatma Gandhi—even a NASA astronaut.

off the Tupperware. And although later I will return the brain to Harvey, I am for a brief moment the man with the plan, the keeper of the cosmos. Do I feel the thing that all totems and fetishes make people feel? Something that I can believe in? A power larger than myself that I can submit to? Salvation? Have I touched eternity?[207]

I'm not sure. The beer cans strewn in the parking lot make out the rough shape of America, surrounded by pools of sudsy, gold liquid. And the birds have come down out of the sky and they're drinking from it. Even now, the universe is filling with dark matter. We are slowing down. Snowballs the size of jumbo trucks are pelting our atmosphere. Perhaps a meteor has just been bumped into a new flight pattern, straight toward Earth, and we won't know anything about it until it explodes us all, as meteors once exploded the dinosaurs.[208]

But I am here now.[209] In the now now. Day has come back up from the other side of the earth, the birds have come down from the sky. There are flashes of orange light, the air is flooded with honeysuckle. I feel something I can't quite put my finger on, something euphoric but deeply unsayable. Is it love or just not hate? Is it joy or just not sadness? For a moment, all of time seems to flow through the Flamingo, its bright edges reflecting the past and the present, travelers packing their bags and rivering into some farther future. We are always driving with our secrets in the trunk, amazed by the cows and rainbows and palm trees.[210] And do I dare to think that there will be no ending of the world, of America, of ourselves? I do. I really do. For in some recurrence, in some light wave, in some shimmer of time, we are out there now, and forever, existing, even as surely as Einstein himself continues to exist, here in my hands.[211]

MICHAEL PATERNITI ON READING

"The writers who I've read diligently include, for fiction Virginia Woolf, F. Scott Fitzgerald, Nabokov, Salinger, John Hawkes, and a score of others, each offering specific insights into plotting, atmosphere, characterization that are the basis for good storytelling. I also tend to read a lot of poetry when I'm writing. For my recent profile of President Clinton, I read Yeats, but I also constantly thumb my collections of Wallace Stevens, [Paul] Celan, Jorie Graham, and more narrative poets like Philip Levine and C. K. Williams to remind myself of the power that image and metaphor can carry in a story."

---

207. The balcony scene echoes the earlier one. The story has come full circle, but this time we understand what he means by "holding the original universe in his hand." His thoughts are at once lofty and funny.

208. He again ponders the end of the world, echoing the story's opening.

209. We return to reality.

210. This sentence reaffirms our faith—and Paterniti's—in the future and echoes back not just to the brain, but to Harvey's earlier childlike amazement.

211. Paterniti ends with Einstein's brain—and eternity—in his hands, a far stronger ending than the trip's actual ending of him putting Harvey on an airplane for his return home. The lesson here: When writing a story chronologically, a writer should be on the lookout for the best place to end it, which may not always be the same as where his or her research stopped.

Mike Sager

How do you find something interesting in the everyday life of a 92-year-old man? More than that, how do you turn it into a story other people want to read? Engaging readers in subjects they think they aren't interested in is one of the challenges (and great possibilities) of literary nonfiction, and it is precisely the one Mike Sager faced when he set out to profile Glenn Sanberg.

To write the story, Sager spent two full weeks, six to ten hours a day, with Sanberg, later returning for another thirty-six hours to gather what he calls "the sleep stuff." He admits he carried into his research a life-long aversion to old people and nursing homes.

"Spending all that time with Glenn was a lot like visiting a relative in a nursing home," he says. "Long hours, few happenings. Sickening sights and smells. The clock ticked. Fingernails drummed on the arm of the chair. Sometimes I was bored nearly to sleep. The whole time, quite frankly, I felt a little queasy, as if I was staring at my own mortality.

"But I maintained, I stuck it out. I hung around and asked questions. And more importantly, I kept my eyes and ears open and my mouth shut and I let the knowledge come to me. When I got home, I transcribed my tapes and assembled my notes. And then, I practiced something I have come to call the 'trash compactor theory of journalism.' Taken all together, compressed a bit, put in perspective, regarded from different angles, I began to be able to see the true sense of drama in Glenn's life. Sure, when I was there, it felt at times like mind-numbing dullness. But I had to get beyond that. I had to see things through Glenn's eyes instead of my own. Compressed and regarded, I found the drama in Glenn's life. The truth is, when you are 92, just waking up is a miracle. If that's not drama, what is?"

On the last day Sager spent with Sanberg, he bent over to put a plate in the dishwasher and felt something in his back pop. By the next morning he was in so much pain he had to be pushed through the airport in a wheelchair. That experience, he says, informed the whole piece. Now he knew firsthand some of how it felt to be old.

Part of what makes the story work so well is the third-person subjective that lets us vicariously share Sanberg's thoughts, dreams, and discomforts as intimately as if they were our own; part is Sager's use of concrete details to draw us into the scenes; part is the way he creates tension by feeding us a little information at a time so that we are forced to read all the way to the end.

"When I begin a story, I write for my reader," says Sager. "I want him like a hungry fisherman wants a fish. My lead is my lure. It draws the bite, sets the hook. From that moment on, word by word, sentence by sentence, I am reeling you in. At the end, if I have managed to hold on, I have you just where I want you—in the boat that I have created, thinking the thoughts that I have wrought. It is manipulation of the highest order, albeit benign. It is the ultimate power of words."

"Old" was named a finalist for a 1999 National Magazine Award, one of many honors that have come Sager's way. He has had two articles named "Notable Essays" in

Best American Essays. *Two of his stories are being developed into feature films. "Re-quiem for a Gangsta" received ASCAP's 1996 Deems Taylor Award for Distinguished Music Writing.*

Sager began his career as a copy boy for the Washington Post *after dropping out of Georgetown law school at the end of his first three weeks. Eleven months later he was promoted to staff writer, a position he held for six years. He is currently a Writer at Large for* Esquire. *A former Writer at Large for* GQ *and Contributing Editor for* Rolling Stone, *Sager has also written for* Vibe, Spy, Interview, Playboy, Regardies, Manhattan Inc., Washingtonian, *and other publications.*

Old

MORNING FILTERS THROUGH THE BEDROOM WINDOW in delicate, slanted rays, dust motes and sounds and memories drifting in the air. Doves coo, a horseshoe clangs, quails skitter across the rain gutter. The clock radio on the night table whirs and vibrates; the number card flops: 6:33.

The old man sleeps on his left shoulder on the right side of the bed. His name is Glenn Brown Sanberg. He is ninety-two. He is peaceful in repose in plaid pajamas, a colorful floral spread pulled snugly to his neck. He has white, flyaway hair and bushy eyebrows, a flaky irritation at the point on his forehead from which his pompadour once issued. His cheeks are soft and deeply furrowed, speckled here and there with brown spots. His mouth is open, top lip buckled a bit over the gum line, chin stubbled with fine white whiskers. His left hand rests upon the pillow on the unmussed side of the bed, a queen.[1]

Starlings chatter. Water gurgles in an ornamental pond. A draft horse pulls a wagon full of housewares down a cobblestone street. Glenn stirs, sighs, floats toward wakefulness.[2] He thinks of the lake cabin he once built.[3] Laying the foundation, he used a pancake turner for a trowel. He thinks of woodpeckers, of ducks, of fresh blueberries. A Studebaker with a rumble seat. A player piano in a speakeasy. Stealing apples from an orchard, buckshot whistling overhead, the double row of brass buttons on the blue serge uniform of the town constable. Smoking corn silk under the porch.[4] Joan leaning against the radiator in his office in the collection department at the Mayo Clinic, drying her stockings on a cold, rainy day.[5]

The paper thuds against the front door. Glenn's eyelids flutter. An electric golf cart

---

"Old" first appeared in *Esquire* in 1998. Reprinted by permission of the author.

1. The story is structured chronologically, following a day in the life of a 92-year-old retiree. It begins with an almost cinematic description of the room and of Sanberg. It is a tranquil picture that captures the twilight state between sleep and wakefulness. We see the delicate rays of the sun that perhaps first rouse him, then come the sounds that drift in and out of his consciousness. We then observe Sanberg before he stirs. The description is so detailed that it is as though we have tiptoed into the room and are standing over him. Sager tells us Sanberg is "old," but he could have easily omitted that adjective because the details he chooses are those of old age: the flyaway white hair and eyebrows, the flaky irritation, the receding hairline, the brown spots, the white stubble. Note that the sentences here are longer to re-create the scene's tranquility. The word choices seem to come from an earlier, more poetic era: "repose," "issued," "unmussed." It is smoother to say "the unmussed side of the bed, a queen" than to have written "the unmussed side of the queen-sized bed." Only the description of the clock radio is abrupt to mimic its movements and sounds: it "whirs and vibrates; the number card flops: 6:33." This sentence also firmly places us in a bedroom, next to someone who is about to awaken. Note, too, that the point of view here is third-person objective. We are not yet inside Sanberg, but rather we are observing him. The use of the present tense makes the experience immediate.

2. In the third paragraph, the point of view shifts to third-person subjective as the story moves inside Sanberg and we begin sharing the dreams and memories that come to him as he "floats toward wakefulness."

3. Brief reference to a cabin that will be expanded, and further explained, in later memories. Here, and throughout the story, note how Sager creates drama or suspense by carefully holding back information. Rather than telling us everything he knows in one sudden burst, he skillfully gives it to us a little at a time, forcing us to read the entire story.

4. For the most part, the paragraph is made up of fragments to mimic the way memories come to us. They are, however, no less concrete and detailed. It is not just a car with a rumble seat, but rather a Studebaker; the constable's uniform is blue serge with a double row of brass buttons.

5. The memory of Joan drying her stockings is uncharacteristically long to capture Sanberg fondly dwelling on what has become his favorite recollection: the first time he saw Joan.

hums past, tires swishing through sprinkler runoff. He thinks of an address book left behind at a riverside telephone booth, a thermos left behind at a seaside hotel. Mount Rushmore. Old Faithful. Shaking hands with Lawrence Welk. Napping on his favorite divan. The odd, modest undershirt and boxers worn by his Mormon son-in-law.[6]

He opens his eyes, blinking against the light. Through the cracks in the partially opened vertical blinds, he can see the sky, a wan blue, vectored with contrails, overhung with wispy clouds. He thinks of the cold, clear sky of a northern Minnesota winter. He thinks of Joan digging in the garden, a smudge of mud on her nose. Dad sitting in President Eisenhower's chair in the White House, a proud and grave expression on his face. Tom bagging his first buck with the Savage .303. Mickey reeling in a fat pike on a sparkling mountain lake. Little Eleanor, limp in her bed, scarlet fever. Joan falling against a door. Lucy falling against the curb. Ann Black, front row center at the Greek Week songfest, legs crossed, dark eyes beaming. Jeffy's warm, tiny hand inside of his.[7]

A lawn mower sputters and coughs, catches, begins to drone.[8] Glenn slides his left hand beneath the covers, places it palm down beside his hip. He reaches behind himself with his right arm, grabs a handful of bedspread. Pushing with one hand, pulling with the other, he rolls himself over onto his back with a grunt. There is little pain to speak of—a twinge of nagging soreness, perhaps, in the knuckles, the left shoulder, the right hip, the neck—but there is a certain acute stiffness in his muscles and ligaments and joints that enfeebles his every action, renders his every movement a task.[9] Think of the first few turns on a rusty lug after it has finally come unstuck—such is the effort.[10] Winded, Glenn lets his head settle into the pillow. He thinks of hoeing weeds in a five-acre bean patch on a hot summer day. Walking across a golf course in the early morning,[11] meeting Lucy at the fountain for a sip of water and a little hug.[12] Martin Luther King Jr. at the Lincoln Memorial. Eleanor in the car on the way to her freshman year of college: "Don't drive so fast, Daddy."[13]

---

6. The "thud" of the newspaper against the door brings Sanberg and the story more fully into the present, and the outside world and today begin mingling with his memories of the past: he hears a golf cart outside, he thinks of a lost address book. The latter triggers a recollection of an earlier loss of a thermos, which somehow triggers a fleeting memory of Mount Rushmore, then Old Faithful, then shaking hands with Lawrence Welk, then napping on his favorite divan, then a more immediate thought of his son-in-law's underwear, as he grows more fully awake. The sequence very much follows the kind of association our recollections take. Note the use of "divan," probably the word choice of Sanberg's generation.

7. Up to now, the story has focused on what Sanberg has heard and thought. Now, as he opens his eyes, Sager introduces us to what he sees, and what he sees triggers memories of other times. Sager uses these memories to begin telling us about Sanberg's past: We learn that he lived in Minnesota, that his father had ties to the White House, that Joan was probably his wife and that Tom, Mickey, Jeffy, and Eleanor were probably his children. We assume, because of the Greek Week reference, that Ann Black was a college girlfriend, but we are not sure who Lucy is. Sager holds back telling us about the fall, thus creating suspense and forcing us to keep reading.

8. Note the vivid, active word choices here and throughout the article: "sputters," "coughs," "catches," "slides." No overuse of "to be" here!

9. Sager's detailed description of Sanberg's movements lets us begin to feel what it's like to be old. We experience the effort it takes to get out of bed: the way Sanberg has to push with one hand and pull with the other just to roll over. We feel the stiffness and the "nagging soreness." The listing of body parts lets us know this stiffness and soreness is not confined to one area, so we understand why his every movement becomes a task.

10. Sager drives home his point with a metaphor that readers of all ages can grasp: the undoing of a rusty lug.

11. As Sanberg rests from the effort, he thinks of the more strenuous activities he was capable of in the past. These trigger more memories, which continue filling in his past.

12. We learn a little more about Lucy, that she and Sanberg were close. Sager continues holding back the full nature of that relationship, causing us to read on.

13. Eleanor's quote confirms that she was indeed his daughter.

Stretching both arms above his head, he yawns deeply, luxuriantly, then brings his right hand forward, uses his thumb and forefinger to wipe away the cakey dryness that has accumulated at the corners of his mouth. His hand trembles.[14] He's not sure when it began, this shaking. His son pointed it out not long ago when he came to visit. Glenn was taken aback by the revelation; he simply hadn't noticed.[15] You live in your body every day of your life.[16] Things change slowly, inexorably, in increments too small to measure. You gain weight, you lose weight, your hair falls out. Your skin slackens, your voice thins, your bones become brittle, your ankles swell. Your prostate and a piece of your colon are removed. Your back bends with the weight of gravity and passing time. You wake up twice during the night to pee; once in a while, you wet your pants. Crossing your legs has become a project that requires your hands; getting out of a chair has become a gymnastic routine; eating a bowl of soup has become a logistical feat. Whenever you go to the store, you can't remember if you have coffee at home. There are two blue cans of Maxwell House in your refrigerator, six more in your cupboard. You buy another can just to be sure. There is a tiny droplet of moisture suspended from the bottom of your nose. There is food crusted on the front of your shirt, the crotch of your pants, the tips of your shoes. You ask people questions several times over. Sometimes, just as you're asking, you realize that you've already asked this same question, that you've already heard the answer. You go ahead and ask again anyway. It's too embarrassing to do anything else.[17] Your parents and your five siblings and your spouse have all died. Your late-life companion has moved on to constant care. You visit her three times a day. She lights up when you're around. Your children have entered their own retirement years in distant states.[18] People talk to you as if you were a four-year-old; they are always trying to give you hard candies. You are old, diminished, alone. You can't even cut your own toenails. The podiatrist does it for fifty-five dollars. His nurse calls to remind you about your appointment.[19] It was thirty minutes ago.[20]

All of this happens; everything changes. But the odd part is, you don't really notice. You're aware of it, sure, but somehow it doesn't integrate. Deep down, to yourself, you are always just you, the same pair of eyes in the mirror, the same familiar voice inside your head still wondering, "When will I feel grown up?"[21]

Glenn runs his pink tongue around the inside of his mouth, tries to swallow. He is

---

14. Sager again focuses on the outward signs of old age—the cakey dryness at the corners of Sanberg's mouth, his trembling hand.

15. We then move inward, into Sanberg's consciousness, his thoughts, his bewilderment.

16. By shifting to second person, Sager makes readers experience what it is like to be 92 years old.

17. The experiences become real because they are concrete: not being able to remember if you have coffee when you already have six cans of Maxwell House at home; asking a question and then realizing too late that you already know the answer. The list is rendered in a manner that sounds like Sanberg himself rattling off a litany of old age. In it, we see glimpses of a man with a sense of humor, a man who is old but not letting it get him down ("Crossing your legs has become a project that requires your hands; getting out of a chair has become a gymnastic routine; eating a bowl of soup has become a logistical feat").

18. Sager also uses the litany to fill in more of Sanberg's background: his parents, five siblings, and wife are dead; his children are retired. We learn that his late-life companion is in constant care. We wonder if that could be Lucy. Again we must keep reading to find out.

19. The litany moves to those aspects of old age that seem to most irritate and embarrass Sanberg. Because the end of a paragraph is the position of greatest impact, these things receive added emphasis here.

20. A clue that Sanberg's memory is slipping.

21. "All of this happens" is an abrupt change of pace that snaps us to attention so that we don't miss the underlying truth: The old really don't think of themselves as old. The next sentence attempts to say this in a way that even the young can understand: You see the same eyes in the mirror, hear the same voice, still wonder, "When will I grow up?"

thirsty, but he can wait, the thought of the effort needed to get himself a glass of water[22] displaced for the moment by the pure, sensual pleasure of lingering beneath the covers with no place special to go.[23] It isn't all bad, this diminishment, this narrowing of the circle of friends and activity and influence and competence. You can see it as a long, slow march toward death. Or you can see it as a distillation, a paring down—as the last leg of a journey, the jump-off point, perhaps, for a great new adventure in the next world, a chance to reunite with your loved ones. It is truly a second childhood, only this time you're the one in charge, as long as you still live on your own, as long as you can still dress yourself and feed yourself and get to the store. As long as you still have your driver's license. You can wear the same clothes two days in a row. You can stay up half the night watching *National Geographic* videos. You can nap. You can eat dessert for dinner, pour mocha crème on your cornflakes, stay in bed until you feel like getting up.[24]

At the moment,[25] Glenn feels like staying in bed. He places his hands behind his head, interlaces his fingers. He pans the room, eyes blue and elfin, the eyes of his grandfather, a blacksmith from Sweden, and of his father, a school superintendent from Minnesota. There is Lucy's wig hanging from a hook on the towel rack in the bathroom. Joan's desk, Mother's lamp. A copy of the *Physicians' Desk Reference*. A Snoopy doll holding a tiny box of Whitman's chocolates. Portraits of Lucy's kids and grandkids and greatgrandkids. A small, silver frame on a dresser with a picture of Joan on their wedding day. Joan: She was quite a gal. She wasn't a super woman, but he never knew anybody who was more honest.[26] The first time he saw her, she was leaning against the radiator in his office in the collection department at the Mayo Clinic, drying her stockings on a cold, rainy day.[27] She could read him like a book. One night in bed, in the dark, she slapped him. He doesn't remember what the argument was about. Boy oh boy oh boy. Right on the cheek: *Slap!* That was a wake-up call. Yes sirree.[28] A female voice, digitized, robotic, calls out from the living room: "6:30 A.M."[29]

---

22. The story returns briefly to the narrative line, or as writer-educator Mark Kramer calls it, "the moving now." While the story is structured around one day, note how very little space the actual "moving now," or present action, takes up. Usually there is no more than a sentence or two before the story moves into a digression of memories, flashbacks, background. Here we have two sentences of narrative, the description of a very intimate mannerism (running the tongue around the inside of his mouth, realizing he is thirsty) that serves to move us back inside the main character.

23. We know the reluctance to leave a warm comfortable bed. We are with Sanberg. The latter serves as a transition into more of Sanberg's thoughts on the negative and positive aspects of growing old.

24. Again, Sager uses second person to bring readers into the experience. He also includes thoughts we ourselves may have had (like eating dessert for dinner and wearing the same clothes for two days). This more positive litany shows that Sanberg is playful and an optimist—a child at heart. Note the writerliness of Sager's prose: the use of repetition, the rhythm of the sentences. The repetition causes us to linger over his points; it is also pleasant to the ear due to the pacing of the sentences, as each item in the list of negatives and positives grows in length: "It isn't all bad, this diminishing, this narrowing of the circle of friends and activity and influence and competence."

25. Transition back to present-day time line.

26. Sager uses Sanberg's thoughts to describe him ("eyes blue and elfin"), to show us the furnishings of his room (the copy of *Physicians' Desk Reference*, the Snoopy doll), and to fill in his background. In doing so, we learn about both Joan and Lucy in greater detail and while we still aren't sure of his relationship to the latter, we begin to realize the intimacy of it when Sanberg focuses on her wig hanging in the bathroom. Sager again withholds an explanation of the wig, forcing us to read to the end of the story.

27. Return to Sanberg's favorite memory, of the first time he saw Joan.

28. While the anecdote about Joan slapping Sanberg is not a direct quote, it is written in what sounds like his voice: "She could read him like a book"; "Boy oh boy oh boy"; "That was a wake-up call. Yes sirree."

29. We move from the anecdotal "wake-up call" to the digitized one in the living room," which brings us back to the present time frame.

Glenn's brow furrows. He sighs. *Where am I?* he wonders.[30]

He closes his eyes. The lids tremble with concentration. You can be ninety-two years old and have your eyesight, as Glenn does, need glasses only for reading. You can have hearing good enough to pick out whispers in a crowded room, reflexes good enough to drive on busy streets. You can have a medicine chest with nary a prescription pill or bottle of ibuprofen in evidence. But when you get to be Glenn's age, things are different; things like this happen all the time: A situation comes up and suddenly you are stymied, baffled, lost, confused; the information needed proves elusive. *Why did I come into this room? When did they board up this bank? What's Tom's daughter's name? Wasn't the meeting supposed to be here? When did I order these pictures of myself from Olan Mills? Where am I?*[31]

Glenn knows that he knows the answer.[32] He knows that he knows where he lives. He just can't put his finger on it right now—this little scrap of knowledge[33] stored, along with so many other disparate pieces of information gathered over a lifetime, somewhere in the crammed and dusty attic of random rooms that is his memory, an archive[34] chockablock with electrobiochemical renderings of pictures and dates and facts and ideas, words of wisdom, personal milestones, nouns and verbs and adjectives particular to his life.[35] Like the facts that he was born in Bird Island, Minnesota, in 1905, graduated from the University of North Dakota in 1927, married Joan in 1929, just before the Depression. He was an air-raid warden in Minneapolis during World War II, stepped down as executive vice-president of the American Society of Association Executives in 1964, lost Joan in 1987. Twenty-nine years he's been retired. He knows that fact, too, can do the math in his head right now if he chooses. He knows that Tom lives in Chicago, that Jeffy lives in Oregon and deals in lumber, that Saturday is the most dangerous day of the week to drive your car. That in order to live happily in retirement, you must find something to be important to. That the best excuse is the one you never make. That you should back up your files on a floppy disk. That the knocking noise in the hot-water heater is probably due to sediment buildup. That you need to separate the laundry before you wash. That it is best to eat the biggest strawberry last. That the first income-tax law was enacted

---

30. We move back into Sanberg's thoughts and are confronted with a dilemma, or complication: "Where am I?"

31. Sager uses the question to create tension, to compel us to keep reading, and to continue telling us about Sanberg's physical and mental state. Sager again uses second person to allow us to experience the confusion that comes with not being able to remember everyday things. Note the concreteness of the situations enumerated in the list of questions (the boarded-up bank, Tom's daughter's name, the pictures from Olan Mills) and how it makes the situations more believable. The repetition of "Where am I?" gives the paragraph a circular feel and underscores the ongoing nature of the dilemma.

32. Succinctly describes the dilemma.

33. Metaphor of "this little scrap of knowledge" conjures up a lost scrap of paper and an experience that readers of all ages can have.

34. Sager uses metaphors of an archive and a crammed, dusty attic to help explain what it's like to try to find a piece of information in a mind crowded with 92 years of information. Both metaphors fit both the subject matter and the tone.

35. His description of Sanberg's memory captures the conglomeration of bits and pieces of stored knowledge both with its word choices ("chockablock") and the list of disparate kinds of information. "Electrobiochemical renderings" carries the sense of a brain working. The structure of the list seems to echo the chockablock nature of the information: the items linked by "and" give us a sense of the unending kinds of information; the use of a comma gives a sense of the mind finally succeeding in retrieving another bit of information.

by the U.S. Congress in 1862. That if you are big enough, your troubles will always be smaller than you.[36]

Lying there with his fingers interlaced behind his head, his lids trembling with concentration, Glenn searches the borders of his awareness for the information he seeks. *Come on, Sanberg, you old coot. Boy oh boy oh boy. You're in a fine state, Sanberg. You don't even know where you are!*[37]

The voice that is speaking, the old familiar one inside his head, the one he grew up with, seems oddly amused at the turn of events. A little embarrassed, a bit nonplussed, just the slightest bit self-pitying, the words punctuated with a phlegmy, nervous laugh, *Ah ha ha!*[38] You learn to go with the flow in these matters, to let nature take its course. Patience.[39] That is what you learn with age. You can rage against the dying of the light, or you can feel fortunate that it's not yet totally dark, that there's still time left and things to see, things to remember, even things to forget. Glenn thinks of the other places where he has woken up, the other places he has called home.[40] The cabin they named Spike-horn[41]—the best idea he ever had, enlisting the whole family to build from scratch a one-room cabin in the woods. The three-bedroom house in Minneapolis—he hated to leave the place, but the nation's capital was calling, and he was a man of some ambition. The trailer in McAllen, Texas, their third abortive attempt at finding a place of retirement—too many old farmers with creased necks, nothing to do, too much bingo, and too much square dancing, no way to spend the rest of your life. You don't think about it when you're young, even when you're middle-aged, even when you first retire, but if you're lucky, if you're blessed with hardy genes, as Glenn has been—and that is the only reason he can give for his longevity and good health, the fact that his father died at eighty-nine of the colon cancer they caught in Glenn a few years back, and that his mother died at ninety-three of natural causes—then your retirement years can last for a period of time that is longer than your youth, almost as long as your working adulthood. It's been almost thirty years since Glenn had to set an alarm clock.[42]

Now, as he lies in bed with his eyes closed, it comes to him at last: the answer he's been seeking, materializing out of the shadows, floating toward him like an autumn

---

36. Sager now uses Sanberg's "chockablock" archive to tell us about his life. To capture the chockablock flavor of what is stored in Sanberg's mind, Sager combines personal milestones with random facts and words of wisdom ("Saturday is the most dangerous day of the week to drive your car," "the best excuse is the one you never make"). Some of the axioms come from a series of newspaper columns Sanberg has written for various newspapers over the years.

37. This paragraph and the beginning of the next use third-person subjective to take us into Sanberg's thoughts and then switch to second person to let us share his embarrassment, irritation, and self-pity at not being able to think as fast as he once could. The voice is very much Sanberg's, talking and laughing to himself ("Come on, Sanberg, you old coot. Boy oh boy oh boy. You're in a fine state, Sanberg. You don't even know where you are!")

38. Nervous "*Ah ha ha!*" sets us up for later scenes.

39. We see that Sanberg is patient.

40. Through Sanberg's thoughts we learn some of the places where he has lived.

41. We learn more details about the cabin mentioned earlier.

42. We learn more background about him and his family, including the fact he has survived colon cancer. The last sentence is an interesting way to tell us Sanberg has been retired for thirty years. Note how often Sager ends his paragraphs with an observation, an insight, a statement, a memory that lingers in the reader's mind because of its placement.

leaf.[43] Of course, of course. Of course! *Ah ha ha!*[44] He is in Sun City, Arizona, fifteen miles northwest of downtown Phoenix. Nine thousand acres, forty thousand residents, almost all of them over fifty-five. City of Volunteers, home of the Active Retirement Lifestyle, the nation's first large-scale experiment in retirement living. Glenn's home since 1972.[45]

He studies the sky through the cracks in the blinds, a bit amused, a bit relieved. *Sanberg, you old coot! You ain't dead yet!* Doves coo, a lawn mower drones, quails skitter across the rain gutter. Another fine day in Sun City. Another fine day of retirement.[46] Another fine day to—

His brow furrows. He sighs. *What day is this?* he wonders.[47]

* * *

The waitress unlocks the door,[48] and Glenn steps lightly across the threshold. He is a handsome man, five feet ten, 190 pounds, with a prominent nose and a broad, friendly chin, another trait passed down from his father. He is wearing a crisp, pale-blue guayabera shirt that he washed and ironed himself and navy-blue flared trousers, polyester, with western stitching. He tips two fingers to his forehead in a modified salute.[49] His eyes twinkle. "Thank ya kindly, ma'am."[50]

"No problem, dear," says the woman, thin and sixtyish, with a cigarette rasp. "How you doin' this morning?"

"Pretty good for an old coot," he says cheerfully.[51]

She smiles wide, lays a hand on his shoulder. "You're just the cutest thing!"[52]

Glenn arches his bushy white eyebrows, makes his mouth an O of surprise. He attempts a step or two of soft shoe, then takes his leave, stage left, heading at his usual good clip toward the banquet room at the rear of Nancy's Country Cupboard. He has an odd, stiff, jaunty gait, torso rigid and bent slightly forward, arms pumping from the elbows, feet working from the knees, weight shifting quickly from side to side, the sole of his left shoe scuffing the floor.[53] Seeing him walk, you detect pride and good nature in the face of adversity; you sense that here is a man who understands the value of progress made one step at a time. A man undeterred by what he cannot do, focused instead on what he can, determined to do it well.[54] He holds his head high.[55]

---

43. Shadow image conveys the way the answer gradually takes shape in Sanberg's mind, the leaf simile conjures up the way it slowly floats into his consciousness.

44. Because of the early setup of "*Ah ha ha!*" we don't need to be told of Sanberg's embarrassment and unease.

45. Sager uses Sanberg's realization of where he is to provide us with information about Sun City.

46. Now that Sanberg has figured out where he is, he can again relax. Tranquility is restored. This paragraph echoes the story's opening and brings us back to the beginning of Sanberg's day.

47. Sager presents us with a new dilemma to compel us to continue reading: What day is it?

48. Place transition.

49. New scene serves to further the physical description of Sanberg. The voice here is objective, we are observing him as outsiders.

50. His mannerisms and quote imply a courtliness.

51. Quote shows both his preoccupation with age and his somewhat self-deprecating attitude toward himself.

52. The waitress's remark supports the earlier observation that outsiders treat the elderly like children.

53. The point of view remains exterior, with us as outsiders "seeing" Sanberg. The entire paragraph gives us a sense of the way he carries himself; it also shows how closely Sager has observed his subject.

54. At the end of this paragraph we see Sager making assumptions based on his observations of Sanberg. We believe him because those assumptions seem in line with views Sanberg has already expressed or "thought."

55. The concrete detail of Sanberg holding his head high reinforces the accuracy of Sager's assumptions.

Had this been a Monday morning,[56] Glenn would have driven his '91 Buick Park Avenue the three hundred yards from his garage to what he likes to call the Chamber of Commerce, the snack bar in the main building of Royal Oaks, his fifth residence since retirement. Had this been a Wednesday,[57] he would have tidied up a bit in anticipation of a visit from Maria the cleaning lady, a pretty young Mexican woman who tells him stories about her little boy. On other days, he might have had a meeting of the Lakes Club board of directors, or the Sun City Community Fund grants committee, or the New Horizons club, wherein outsiders are invited to dinner to discuss topics of general interest, from health care to the state of today's teens.

Thursdays are his busiest, with a Lions Club meeting at noon and his weekly column due at four o'clock. For almost thirty years, in various venues, Glenn has been writing a newspaper column called "Retired in Style." It began in 1952, long before he retired, as an extracurricular attempt to satisfy his lifelong desire to be a writer. A self-published weekly broadsheet containing words of wisdom, encouragement, and solidarity for busy executives like himself, it was called LIFT, as in, "Have you given someone a lift today?" A sort of support group in the form of a newsletter, with subscribers all over the country, LIFT was a bit ahead of its time in sentiment and sensibility, rather touchy-feely in an era of Sputnik and Joe McCarthy. Later, when he retired, Glenn remembered how lost his father had been without something important to do in his golden years. Never much for hobbies, he decided to make the column a late-life career. For five years, "Retired in Style" was carried by *The Arizona Republic,* the major daily in Phoenix. When the long drive downtown to drop off his offerings became problematic, he switched to the *Daily News-Sun,* the chronicle of Sun City and environs, a snappy little afternoon paper conveniently located two blocks from his house. True to his late-found profession, he waits until the last possible moment to flip on his Gateway computer, which features Windows 95, WordPerfect, and America Online. He writes about what he knows, what he thinks, what he sees, what he remembers, what he reads. Increasingly, he writes about what he's already written, borrowing material from the reams of old clippings he keeps filed in the den he uses for an office. He usually finishes thirty minutes before deadline, then drives it over. The column runs Saturdays on the front page of the second section, along with his picture.[58]

Had this been a Sunday, Glenn would have driven a hundred yards to the constant-care center and picked up Lucy for church. Though he spent most of his life with the Methodists, he now attends Faith Presbyterian, Lucy's church. He sometimes finds comfort in prayer, in the calm, meditative state it brings, in the fellowship of worship with others. He doesn't subscribe to the whole hellfire-and-brimstone story. His beliefs are centered more on the kind of living you do than on what happens when you die. He's not hung up on denomination, either. The way he figures it, God is God is God no matter what house you're in, and Lucy cared more than he did about which church they attended. Faith Presbyterian was also the sponsor of the Royal Oaks Life Care Community, where Glenn and Lucy moved three years ago when they decided to set up house to-

---

56. Sager uses Sanberg's efforts to determine what day it is to give us an account of how and where he spends his time. Thus begins a loop, or digression, that provides us with information about Sanberg's life.

57. Sager skillfully skips Tuesday.

58. In learning about his various activities, we also learn about his approach to life (he waits until the last minute to begin his column), his beliefs (he's not concerned about the hereafter), and the people in his life.

gether.[59] A sort of retirement development within a retirement community, Royal Oaks offers laundry, housecleaning, repair services, a cafeteria, social workers, and shuttle vans to shopping and doctors. Within Royal Oaks are three grades of living arrangements—ranch-style duplex garden homes, assisted-living apartments, and full-care nursing facilities. For $40,000 down, $800 a month. Glenn will have food, housing, and care for the rest of his life.[60]

As it is, today turns out to be Tuesday[61]—a fact he finally confirmed by consulting the newspaper tossed every morning from his driveway to his front door by a friendly neighbor on his daily walk—and Glenn has come to Nancy's. For twenty years, Tuesday mornings have been reserved for the Walk-Jog Club. Once upon a time, all the members would jog or walk for an hour and then convene in Nancy's banquet room for the $1.99 breakfast special. Nobody jogs anymore. The big joke these days is how they lose a half pound walking, then gain a pound and a half at breakfast. Glenn contents himself with driving the mile or so to the restaurant and walking one circuit around the parking lot. At his age, you need to get your circulation going, relieve some of the stiffness, but there's no sense getting all worked up.[62] Actuarial tables say that Glenn will likely be dead in 3.4 years.[63] He knows this. He's all right with it. As he often says: "It's been a good life."

Glenn enters the banquet room, the first to arrive. He takes a seat at one of the two large, round tables that have been set up to accommodate the group. He looks around. He sighs. He pats the tabletop like a set of bongos, pat-a-pat-pat.[64]

A man enters, takes a seat across from Glenn. He is in his early eighties. Glenn can't remember his name.[65] "Good to see you," says Glenn.

"How do?" says the man.

"Pretty good for an old coot."

"I'll say," says the man.[66] It occurs to Glenn that he was once a banker. Possibly from Chicago.[67] He is wearing his official Walk-Jog Club T-shirt.[68]

Glenn points to his own chest with a crooked finger. "Looks like I forgot to wear my T-shirt."

"Yeah, well," says the banker, pinching his T-shirt between a crooked thumb and forefinger. "I came to find out if there's anybody still alive down here."

"Alive and kickin'!" says Glenn. He pushes a fist into the air before him, rah-rah.

Soon the others begin to arrive.[69] The younger crowd, sixties and seventies, goes to

---

59. Here again, Sager is controlled in the facts he gives us about Sanberg and Lucy, continuing to hold back on telling us the complete story, and thus forcing us to keep reading.

60. He takes this opportunity to give us information about Royal Oaks Life Care Community.

61. The loop, or digression, ends with the resolution: It's Tuesday.

62. With that question answered, we return to the present-day scene at Nancy's Country Cupboard with the Walk-Jog Club. The latter serves as a means for Sager to weave in Sanberg's attitude toward fitness and mortality.

63. Here we see evidence of Sager's research.

64. "Shows" Sanberg's boredom.

65. Sanberg's inability to recall the man's name shows both his failing memory and the lack of any real connection among the residents of the retirement community. They are acquaintances and not friends, Sanberg will later acknowledge.

66. Their conversations are those of people attempting to kill time, rarely going beyond "Good to see you," "How do?" and always coming around to the topic of age and aging ("Pretty good for an old coot," "I came to find out if there's anybody still alive and kickin'").

67. "The scrap of information" that the man was a banker from Chicago gradually comes to Sanberg like something "materializing out of the shadows."

68. We see the evidence of the second childhood in the matching T-shirts they all wear.

69. Transition indicates passage of time.

one table; the others go to Glenn's. Big John is a retired attorney. Edith, in a wide-brimmed straw hat, was one of the founding members of the club. Harold is a retired Westclox executive from somewhere back east; Pearl is his wife. The banker, it turns out, is named Frank. The only other person at the table in his nineties is Reggie. He carries a wireless contraption that he places on the table; it helps him hear. His speech is nearly unintelligible, his glasses are thick, and he walks with a slow shuffle.[70] Though the median age in Sun City is about seventy-four and 25 percent of the residents are over eighty, ninety-two-year-old men who are up and around and healthy like Glenn are a rare commodity. The life expectancy of an American male today is seventy-three years. According to the Census Bureau, there are about fifty-three thousand ninety-two-year-old men in the country, but that number is increasing. All told, people over ninety are the fastest-growing demographic group in America.[71] Edith pours him a cup of decaf coffee from the carafe on the table. They wait to order. No one needs a menu.[72]

"It was a nice breezy walk, wasn't it?" says Frank. "We were bucking the breeze going, but we got a nice rear-end push on the way back."

"Is that what it was?" asks Edith, raising her eyebrows.

"Oh!" exclaims Frank. "You mean you thought that rear-end push was me?"[73]

Edith swats the air in his direction. Everyone laughs. Glenn is sitting with his arms crossed casually, like an executive at a meeting.[74] "You can't beat a little good, clean fun, now can you?" says Glenn.

"No sirree, you can't," says John.

"Nope," says Edith.

"Did I tell you about my Northern Tissue stock?"[75] asks Frank.

"Go ahead if you must," says John, rolling his eyes.

"I guess you're going to anyway," says Edith.

"I bought a hundred shares, but I got wiped out on it," says Frank. He crosses his arms, proud of himself.

"Groan!" says Glenn.

And so it goes.[76] The food comes: oatmeal and eggs and French toast, lots of warm syrup. They chat about summering in Utah, motor homes, cruises up the Colorado, bus trips to Laughlin, Nevada, to play the one-armed bandits. About the traffic on Bell Road, the exploits of sons and daughters, the times they played golf in the 115 degree heat.[77] They swap stories about the legendary Del Webb, the six-foot-four-inch former minor-league pitcher who built Bugsy Siegel's casino, who once owned the Yankees, who, almost forty years ago now, saw acres and acres of sun-bleached cotton fields in the Arizona desert and envisioned a new kind of lifestyle for people in the winter of their lives, the next logical post-Levittown step for the citizens who peopled the American century.[78]

---

70. While the characters in this scene are minor, through detail we nevertheless see them as individuals: Edith and her wide-brimmed hat; Harold, the retired Westclox executive; Frank, the banker; and Reggie, with his portable hearing aid, unintelligible speech, thick glasses, and slow shuffle.

71. Evidence of Sager's background research.

72. The detail of not needing a menu underscores the monotony and limited nature of their world.

73. Quote shows an unexpected flirtatious side to the elderly.

74. Simile conjures up a shared image among readers.

75. Another example of shallow conversation.

76. Transition.

77. Sager compresses time and dialogue to give us the essence and the tone of their conversation, without the details. By compressing the lesser moments, the more interesting exchanges that are played out in detail carry more impact.

78. Conversation is used to give us the origins of Sun City.

Sitting back with his arms crossed, tossing out a reminiscence here, a comment or a bon mot there asking a question when the conversation hits a lull, Glenn[79] has the relaxed air of a man at a cocktail party in the 1950s. You can imagine him in a dark suit and skinny tie, puffing on a pipe, passing pleasant time with pleasant associates over a manhattan, two cherries. Since he came here, in fact, Sun City has impressed Glenn as being just like that, like one big floating cocktail party without the booze, a gathering of familiar, friendly acquaintances, all of them of similar type and class and background, with shared values and customs. People from a genteel era, a time when men wore sport coats to baseball games, held doors open for ladies, paid their bills on time, gave backyard cookouts for neighbors, had a friendly word for all, whether they meant it or not.[80]

Glenn pats the tabletop like a set of bongos, pat-a-pat-pat.[81] It is a pleasant feeling, this comradeship, this diversion, this activity that takes him outside his ranch-style duplex garden home,[82] outside his own head. But it is also somewhat hollow and boring. Glenn may be old, but he still knows the difference between acquaintances and true friends, between quality time and killing time. Though he's been living among these same people for many years, he doesn't really know them, and they don't know him, his little offerings in the newspaper every week notwithstanding. They have no idea that he married into the Mayo family, helped set up the world-famous clinic's first collection department. That he started his own successful business, went on to be executive secretary of the American Collectors Association. That by the time his career was at its peak, he could claim good friends among top people in the White House.[83] Like the trophies and plaques and framed citations stored in dusty boxes in his garage, none of that matters much anymore,[84] it happened so long ago now, he can hardly remember the details. You spend thirty or forty or fifty years bulking up your résumé, throwing your weight around, polishing your reputation, playing the game, planting your legacy. It matters what you do in life, it really does—the impressions you leave, the contributions you make, the money you earn, the people you touch, the children you send off into the world. But as the end draws near, as the scope of your life narrows, none of that seems very important anymore, none of that is very important anymore. What becomes important are things like your health and the state of the weather, things like putting one foot in front of the other, making sure the chair doesn't roll out from under you when you go to stand, getting a phone call now and then from your sons or daughter, tasting a warm, sweet Entenmann's bear claw.[85] Being able to sit with yourself at the end of another day and feel that you have no regrets about the time you've spent on earth, that you've done your best to live a good life, to give others a lift.

79. In the preceding scenes, the focus has been on the group. Now Sager zooms in on Sanberg.

80. Sager uses Sanberg's demeanor ("the relaxed air of a man at a cocktail party in the 1950s") both to describe him and as a transition into a comparison of the group to "one big floating cocktail party without the booze," an image that immediately calls to mind boring, meaningless cocktail chatter. By lumping everyone together, the members of the group lose their identities as individuals, underscoring the impersonal nature of retirement community living.

81. Shows Sanberg's boredom.

82. Sanberg's current home.

83. Sanberg's musings about what his associates do and do not know about him provide a vehicle for details about his past.

84. The use of "and" rather than commas in this series creates a greater sense of Sanberg's accumulated success. That success is deflated by the abrupt statement "none of that matters anymore."

85. Shift to second person makes readers empathize. The litany of what an individual does to get ahead sounds like Sanberg's, but it is one that most readers can identify with. Note how lofty and general ("he can hardly remember the details") these things are compared to what becomes important when you get old. Here the list becomes detailed to illustrate how the little things become important to the elderly.

A woman named Barbara comes over from the younger table. She is carrying a newspaper clipping, two inches square, an obituary.[86] She is in her early sixties, the only one in the room wearing shorts.[87]

"There she is, Miss America," sings Frank.[88]

Barbara throws him a dismissive look, walks over to John, shows him the clipping. "Is this the Bob Thompson from Sun City West that used to walk with us?"

John tilts his head up, reads down through the bottom of his trifocals. "Sure," he says, "that was him."

"How old was he?" asks Edith.

"Says here he was eighty-four," says John.

"Bob Thompson?" asks Harold. "Which one was he?"

"Remember?" reminds Pearl, his wife. "Little Bob Thompson. He used to . . . what do you call that? Race walk."

"He used to jog with the boys, then his legs gave out and he got to walkin'," John confirms.

"So that was Bob Thompson," says Harold.

"Guess so," says Frank.

"Yep," says John.

"Hmmm," says Edith.

"Hey, Miss America," says Frank. "Did I tell you the one about my Northern Tissue stock?"

"Say yes!" exclaims Edith.

"Say yes!" exclaims John.

"No matter what, say yes!" exclaims Glenn.

Everybody laughs.[89]

* * *

Glenn struts into Lucy's place,[90] full of vigor and good cheer, a fresh pink rose in his hand. The room is a standard nursing-home double painted in pastels.[91] "How you doing, old gal?"

"I never know," says Lucy.[92] She is a small woman with large, brown glasses and short, gray hair, sitting on the edge of the narrow bed. She giggles a nervous laugh, *Ha ha ha.*[93]

"I like that black-and-white outfit."[94]

"Do you?" She looks down to see what she's wearing, adjusts the drape of her blouse. "I have to stop and think. Where am I? Who am I?"[95] She giggles again, *Ha ha ha.*[96]

---

86. Underscores the elderly's preoccupation with death.

87. Detail cancels our stereotype about older people. It also sets us up for the scene that follows.

88. Comment again breaks a stereotype: You are never too old to flirt. The scene carries the implication that the flirtation, however, will not be acted upon.

89. Scene focuses on preoccupation with aging and death. It is also an example of the "hollow" conversations alluded to earlier.

90. Place transition.

91. Select details tell us where we are and quickly convey what the room looks like.

92. We finally meet Lucy. Quote hints at Alzheimer's disease.

93. Sager sets up nervous laugh for later reference.

94. Quote serves both as a scene and a way to describe Lucy.

95. Quotes "show" that her memory is failing and offer a strong hint that she is suffering from Alzheimer's.

96. Because of the earlier setup of the laugh, we know she is embarrassed.

"That's all right, dear," says Glenn. "I have to do that, too." He reaches out with a trembling hand and cups her cheek.[97]

Lucy sighs, leans her face into his palm. "Oh, well," she says. She has been in the constant-care center for almost two years. Her Alzheimer's is still at an early enough stage that in her good moments, she seems to be aware of what is happening to her, this process that is slowly taking her away from the world. It seems to embarrass and frustrate her, yet at the same time she seems resigned and good-humored, willing to accept what comes. She no longer complains about the food, no longer asks about going home. Rarely is she sad or angry anymore. During her active lifetime, she was smart, pleasant, witty, a little feisty, willing to see the silver lining.[98] Now it is as if the disease is slowly distilling her to her essence, rendering her a fond memory of herself.[99] "It's really a very nice day," she says. She is a bit difficult to understand without her dentures.[100]

"A little breezy out there right now."

"It's a little tricky."

"It's always a little tricky," says Glenn. He laughs nervously, *Ah ha ha!*[101] He is embarrassed and frustrated, too. He visits three times a day. He makes it a policy to stay upbeat, though he secretly wonders sometimes why he bothers to come at all. He always hopes, whenever he walks through the door to her room, that this time things will be different, that this time Lucy will show signs of getting well. He knows she won't get well. More often than not, a few moments after he arrives, he feels ready to leave. He sticks it out anyway. It's a rough deal, this thing. Having her here is very tough. A real push/pull, if you know what he means. If he didn't show up, she probably wouldn't know. Yet something deep compels him to return time after time, day after day, with a cheery expression on his face: a deep gratitude for the years they spent together, for what they meant to each other. A deep solace in knowing that he is not alone here in Sun City.[102] He steps to the bed, turns, slowly lowers himself down next to her.

Glenn and Lucy met many years ago in Minneapolis.[103] She and her husband, they called him Bake, lived near the Sanbergs. He was an accountant for the railroad. The two couples were quite friendly, members of the same social club. Glenn and Bake hunted together. Lucy worked for a time as Glenn's secretary. Years later, her daughter had a summer job with him. When Glenn and Joan came to Sun City for the first time to check it out, the Bakers and another couple were their hosts.

When Joan died in 1987, just before Thanksgiving, Glenn got a call late at night from the hospital, saying she was gone. It all happened so fast. That summer, vacationing in Logan, Utah, she had fallen and hit her head. Four months later, she was dead. Fifty-eight years of married life were over.[104] He never thought he'd be the one who was left behind. He listened to the words, delivered by a stranger, a nurse, over the telephone. Then he re-

---

97. Gesture "shows" both the nature of their relationship and Sanberg's own frailty.

98. Up to now, most of what we learn about Sanberg comes to us through scenes and his thoughts. Sager now tells us about Lucy's ailment and her past. Because he is unable to interview her and get inside her mind in the way he has with Sanberg, he does so indirectly using information gleaned from Sanberg and her family.

99. Poetic rendering of Alzheimer's disease's toll on Lucy.

100. Detail enables us to "hear" how she speaks.

101. Again we get Sanberg's unease.

102. Point of view again becomes third-person subjective, with Sager using information from interviews to reconstruct Sanberg's thoughts and inner turmoil.

103. Sager sums up the background of Sanberg's relationship with Lucy in the next few paragraphs, so that we finally learn just who she is.

104. Return to third-person subjective to draw readers into how it felt to find himself alone.

placed the receiver on its cradle. "I'm all alone," he said, speaking out loud into the darkness. He will forget a lot of things before his time is up, but he will never forget that.[105]

It was rough for a while, real rough, boy oh boy oh boy,[106] though he came to enjoy the parade of widows with their casseroles who started showing up at his door. He learned how to sort the laundry and make coffee, how to fend for himself after so many years as a husband.[107] He was doing okay; it wasn't great, but he was getting along. Then one day he ran into Lucy. Bake had died a few years before; Joan and Glenn had helped her through her grief. Now, coincidentally, both Glenn and Lucy were on a walking kick. He began phoning her in the mornings to say he was leaving for his walk, and she'd leave, too, and they'd meet at the water fountain on the golf course, a point equidistant from their houses. At first, they'd just hang around and talk. Soon, they were giving each other a little hug. That's the thing you come to miss the most: a little hug, the warmth of someone next to you, her body against yours, her breath on your neck.[108] They began eating meals together, some days at his place, some at hers. Lucy took Joan's place in a way that was very positive, Glenn believes, and he thinks he took Bake's place in the same way. After a few years, they decided to cut out the foolishness[109] and move in together.

Before they finalized their plans, however, they went to see the pastor of Lucy's church. They told him their intention, to live together in the open, out of wedlock. He regarded them gravely. Then he cracked a smile. "Go for it!" he said. Three other words that Glenn will never forget.[110]

Glenn and Lucy had similar likes and dislikes. They both played golf and bridge, enjoyed dancing. They both cared about who was president, who was senator, what was going on in the world. She was easy to be with, very accessible, had a sense of humor, was a very sharp gal, a college graduate, very involved throughout her life with the American Field Service. You couldn't put anything over on her. She was that kind, like Joan in many respects. They went on trips to see each other's children, drove all the way to Florida, took a cruise once through the Panama Canal.[111] In the years they lived and traveled together, they slept in the same bed—he on the right, she on the left—but never had sexual intercourse. Thinking about it, Glenn wonders if it was kind of unusual to be so close and yet never be intimate in that way. Their spouses had been their lifelong lovers, their only lovers. And so it remained, though it wasn't like he couldn't have, physically—he still feels the call now and then. No matter. They were at an age in life[112] when that wasn't very important anymore.[113]

Then one day Lucy fell against the curb in the parking lot.[114] It didn't seem like that

---

105. Because of its placement at the end of the paragraph, Sanberg's quote and his realization that he is alone stand out for the reader. The fact that he will never forget that moment adds to the impact.

106. Sanberg's voice.

107. Details (sorting laundry, making coffee, widows bearing casseroles) capture the essence of what it was like to be a widower.

108. The reference to the hugs echoes references early in the story. The point of view is third-person subjective, so that we feel his need for this simple affection.

109. Sanberg's voice and word choice.

110. Repetition of "will never forget" emphasizes the importance of this moment to Sanberg.

111. Use of concise lists enable Sager to give us a tight, yet vivid rendering of their relationship and life. Each item in the lists is concrete (drove to Florida, cruise through the Panama Canal). The description of Lucy tells us as much about Sanberg as it does her.

112. Up to now, their lives have been described in compact lists. The more intimate side of their relationship is treated in more detail and through Sanberg's point of view.

113. Last two sentences are in contrast to the endings of the earlier paragraphs about the things Sanberg won't forget and thus puts the role of sex into perspective. It also carries a hint of longing on Sanberg's part.

114. We finally get the answer to the earlier reference to Lucy's fall.

big of a deal[115]—a few cuts and scratches, a badly bruised hip. But tests at the hospital revealed Alzheimer's. She never returned home. He still keeps her things in their proper places in the house, the way they were the day she left with him to go out for a simple lunch at the Lakes Club—the wig hanging from a hook on the towel rack,[116] the pictures of her family on the walls. To do otherwise would be unthinkable.

Lucy leans her head against Glenn's shoulder.[117] Glenn looks distractedly around the room. Through the doorway, he can see the slow procession of Royal Oaks residents up and down the central corridor, aged figures caterpillar-walking in their wheelchairs, pushing with their hands and padding with their feet, eyes fixed on the distance.[118] A woman is slumped in her wheelchair just outside Lucy's door.[119] She is holding a teddy bear.[120] "Help me," she calls again and again. "I have to make a BM."[121]

Glenn notices the rose in his hand, holds it out in front of Lucy. "I brought you this rose. It's from our yard."

"No kidding?"

"Yeah, right from our yard."

"Our yard?"

"The one at the house."

"It's lovely this time of year."

"Yes it is, dear, yes it is." He puts the rose on the dresser. "I had breakfast this morning with Harold and Pearl. Frank was there, too."[122]

"How are their families doing? Or are you only interested in whether or not the little boy can jump the fence?"[123]

"I guess so," says Glenn. He laughs, *Ah ha ha!*[124] Lucy looks at him questioningly. She seems to realize that she is not making sense. She laughs. *Ha ha ha.*[125]

"My whole back is bad," says Lucy.

"Itchy?"

"It's just wonderful when they come by and scratch."

"Here, allow me, madam," Glenn says with mock formality. He shifts his weight, moves his arm slowly behind her back, begins to scratch.

A look of pure bliss crosses Lucy's face. "*Ooooooooh, ahhhhhhh, ooooooo,*" she purrs. She closes her eyes, shrugs her shoulders, wriggles her back. "It's almost worth paying extra," she says. "*Ahhhhhh.*"[126]

"You can leave me a tip."

---

115. Sanberg's voice.

116. Explains the earlier reference to the wig in the bathroom and thus completes the question of who Lucy is.

117. Return to present-day scene.

118. Caterpillar metaphor captures the slow, cautious movement. Attention to detail draws vivid picture of the elderly in wheelchairs making their way down the hall.

119. At first we see the people in the hall as a group, then the camera zooms in on one memorable woman.

120. Detail enforces the return to childhood.

121. The quote "shows" helplessness and the ultimate return to childhood: infancy. At the end of the paragraph, it gains even more impact.

122. Quote hints at Sanberg's pride at being able to remember Frank's name.

123. Scene begins with normal, routine exchange. Lucy's question about the little boy catches us off guard and captures the unpredictable nature of Alzheimer's.

124. Sanberg's unease.

125. The uneasy "ha ha ha" seems to support Sager's conclusion that Lucy realizes she is not making sense.

126. Scene shows the warm, loving nature of their relationship.

"Absolutely!"

"Boy oh boy oh boy," says Glenn. He laughs, *Ah ha ho!*[127] He continues scratching.

* * *

Glenn slips beneath the floral spread,[128] rolls effortlessly onto his left side, one hand resting beneath his cheek. Street light filters through the bedroom window; a night bird sings, a single voice.[129]

Glenn breathes deeply. He thinks of the beautiful birch tree that guarded the breezeway at Spikehorn. The carpenter from across the lake thought he was crazy, but he couldn't bring himself to cut it down. He ended up building the roof with a big zigzag in it, leaving plenty of room for the stately old tree to grow.[130] He thinks of playing run-sheep-run and kick-the-can and gyp, playing trombone in the high school band, shaking hands with John Philip Sousa, listening to Stan Kenton on a superheterodyne radio. A Model T milk truck. A flapper in a beaver coat, dancing the Charleston. A thank-you note from Wendell Willkie. A letter from Bennett Cerf. Pounding nails into a scrap of two-by-four on the back porch while his mother snaps beans. Lucy in her square-dance outfit. Joan leaning against the radiator in his office in the collection department at the Mayo Clinic, drying her stockings on a cold, rainy day.[131]

Water gurgles in an ornamental pond.[132] The air conditioner kicks over, cycles up, begins to blow. Glenn sighs. He pushes his head deep into the feather pillow. It feels soft and cool. The clock radio on the night table whirs and vibrates; the number card flops: 10:35.[133]

MIKE SAGER ON READING

"Reading Tom Wolfe's *The New Journalism* literally changed my life. I had a literal epiphany, the only true one of my life. The people contained therein, and all the stuff that they wrote—they are our forefathers: Tom Wolfe, Gay Talese, Harry Crews, Joan Didion, John McPhee, Robert Caro. Get a hold of Wolfe's book, and then get a hold of all their books and read it all. More modern is Paul Theroux, one of my favorites.

"Then, after reading that, my suggestion is not to read nonfiction at all, to start reading all the fiction you can read. Old stuff. New stuff. Classic stuff. Weird stuff. Learn about drama and detail from the greats. Like Wolfe said, you take your reporting skills to gather, and then you employ the elements of a novel to render your piece.

---

127. Sanberg's unease.
128. Place transition.
129. Scene signals an approaching end to the story and echoes the beginning, giving a circular feel to the story. Now the light filtering through the window is street light, indicating it is bedtime, the end of Sanberg's day. The point of view is third-person subjective as he prepares to fall asleep: first there are the final sights and sounds of the outside world, then we move into his thoughts, which also echo earlier moments in the story and continue to tell us of Sanberg's past.
130. Tree becomes symbolic of Sanberg.
131. Sanberg's final thoughts before dozing off serve to continue filling in moments from his past. They all come back to the scene of Joan drying her stockings, so that we end the story with his fondest memory. The fact that he thinks of Lucy in her retirement years and Joan as an attractive young woman shows the difference in his feelings for the two women.
132. Repetition, from the story's beginning. Life goes on.
133. The story comes full circle as the clock on the radio flips to "10:35."

"The aim, I think, is to try and be a journalist who thinks like a novelist, an artist comfortable in the trenches. Maybe the aim is to meld the skills and techniques of a journalist with the craftsmanship and soul of a novelist.

"Along the same lines, I don't underline or read with a pen. It is overly cerebral. Anything worth remembering gets remembered without taking notes. That's the problem with journalists. They think too much with their minds and neglect their hearts. Read for pleasure, open your soul. You can teach gathering details, but you can't teach depth. Go for human over professorial. Allow your heart to be pulled along into the depths of feelings and you will see more and you will begin to understand. In other words, a literary journalist is a novelist with a tape recorder . . . a poet's heart, a reporter's worn-out shoes."

Susan Sheehan

Susan Sheehan has earned a reputation for reporting on people of the underclass. Over the years, she has written about a welfare mother, a schizophrenic woman, a daughter caring for an elderly mother, an inmate in a New York penitentiary, and Vietnamese dealing with a revolutionary war and American soldiers. In both her articles and her books, Sheehan has preferred to focus on a single individual or, in the case of "Ain't No Middle Class," a family. With multiple subjects, she says, "I have more facts but not more truth, and I would lose the vividness, the felt truth one gets only when writing about a single person."

Finding the right subject is itself an art. Intuition plays a significant role in this sort of decision, says Sheehan. To locate a family living close to the median income level, she began by figuring out the proper geography. "I felt it wasn't a big-city story," she says, "not D.C., New York, not even East Coast or West Coast, possibly Midwest or not-too-deep South. I thought of Omaha, Nashville, Des Moines, where I'd been to research a lot of my book A Missing Plane."

In the end, she settled on Des Moines and, with the help of contacts at a local housing agency, located two prospects. The first couple had only one child, the wife didn't work, and the husband's income was too high; the second—the Mertens—fit Sheehan's expectations and were willing to cooperate. After a visit to their home, she decided they were right for the story.

Sheehan then set out to capture what life was like for the working poor by reconstructing the Mertens' daily routine and their budget. To do this, she stayed in Des Moines almost a week, spending mornings with Bonita Merten, before she reported to the evening shift at Luther Park Health Center, and evenings with Kenny, after he returned home from his job setting up roadblocks. On the weekend, she accompanied the family on outings, most notably a trip to the supermarket. Later she returned for a long weekend. In between, she gathered material (including the potato scene) via long-distance telephone conversations. Her account of every dollar—and virtually every cent—the Mertens spent came from income-tax returns, paycheck stubs, receipts, and interviews.

Sheehan has been praised for her simple, matter-of-fact style and her detachment. Penn State professor R. Thomas Berner has described her as coming as close to objective writing as a human being can. Sheehan herself says she doesn't see heroes and villains, or black and white—"I see gray." Thus, instead of commenting on the Mertens' spending habits, she turned to a consumer counselor, whom she interviewed after returning home.

Although Sheehan ultimately became friends with the Mertens (as she does with most of her subjects), she refused to offer advice during the course of her reporting, adhering to the principle that a writer's presence should not affect the outcome of a story. "You have to tell the story, not change it," she once told the Washington Post's Megan Rosenfeld. "Psychiatrists can play God. Writers can't."

This kind of meticulous reporting has earned Sheehan many honors, including a Pulitzer Prize for Is There No Place on Earth for Me?, *her book about schizophrenic Sylvia Frumkin. She is the author of six other books, including* A Welfare Mother, Life for Me Ain't Been No Crystal Stair, A Prison and a Prisoner, *and* Kate Quinton's Days. *She has been a staff writer for the* New Yorker *since 1961 and a contributing writer for* Architectural Digest *since 1997. Her articles have also appeared in the* New York Times, *the* Washington Post, Atlantic, Harper's, *the* New Republic, *the* Boston Globe, *and* Washingtonian *magazine.*

She was named a Literary Lion by the New York Public Library in 1995. She has also been a Guggenheim Fellow, a Woodrow Wilson Scholar, and the recipient of the American Bar Association's Silver Gavel Award, a Sidney Hillman Foundation Award, and a National Mental Health Association Award for individual reporting. She has served as both chair and a member of the Pulitzer Prize nominating jury and as a judge for the Robert F. Kennedy journalism award.

Ain't No Middle Class

AT TEN O'CLOCK ON A TUESDAY NIGHT in September, Bonita Merten gets home from her job as a nursing-home aide on the evening shift at the Luther Park Health Center, in Des Moines, Iowa. Home is a two-story, three-bedroom house in the predominantly working-class East Side section of the city. The house, drab on the outside, was built in 1905 for factory and railroad workers. It has aluminum siding painted an off-shade of green, with white and dark-brown trim.[1] Usually, Bonita's sons—Christopher, who is sixteen, and David, who is twenty and still in high school (a slow learner, he was found to be suffering from autism when he was eight)[2]—are awake when she comes home, but tonight they are asleep. Bonita's husband, Kenny, who has picked her up at the nursing home—"Driving makes Mama nervous,"[3] Kenny often says—loses no time in going to bed himself. Bonita is wearing her nursing-home uniform, which consists of a short-sleeved navy blue polyester top with "Luther Park" inscribed in white, matching navy slacks and white shoes. She takes off her work shoes, which she describes as "any kind I can pick up for ten or twelve dollars,"[4] puts on a pair of black boots and a pair of gloves, and goes out to the garage to get a pitchfork.

In the spring,[5] Bonita planted a garden. She and David, who loves plants and flowers, have been picking strawberries, raspberries, tomatoes, and zucchini since June. Bonita's mother, who lives in Washington, Iowa, a small town about a hundred miles from Des Moines, has always had a large garden—this summer, she gave the Mertens dozens of tomatoes from her thirty-two tomato plants[6]—but her row of potato plants, which had been bountiful in the past, didn't yield a single potato. This is the first year that Bonita has put potato plants in her own garden. A frost has been predicted, and she is afraid her potatoes (*if there are any*)[7] will die, so instead of plunking herself down in front

---

"Ain't No Middle Class" first appeared in the *New Yorker* in 1995. Reprinted by permission of the author.

1. Sheehan begins with a simple, straightforward statement of fact that introduces us to both the Mertens' routine and their house. By opening the story with a description of the house, Sheehan quickly draws us into their working-class world. Her careful selection of detail (working-class side of town; the drab, off-shade of green) creates a definite image of the house, as does the fact that it was once a house for factory and railroad workers. Note Sheehan's use of repetition for cohesiveness. The second sentence repeats the word "home" from the first; the third repeats "house" from the second; the fourth uses the pronoun "it" to refer to the house.

2. Sheehan will use dashes and parentheses efficiently to work in information (even quotes) throughout the story without interrupting the main narrative. Here she uses both—parentheses within dashes.

3. Besides revealing Bonita's dislike for driving, this quote conveys the closeness between her and Kenny.

4. Throughout the story, Sheehan will reconstruct the Mertens' budget and their daily routine to show us what the lives of the working poor are like. She uses Bonita's shoes to begin disclosing the family's spending habits.

5. Transition into explanatory digression about the garden.

6. Sheehan's careful cataloging of the garden harvest provides insight into the family's lifestyle. Note the specificity of her detail. We learn not only where Bonita's mother lives, but that the town is small and a hundred miles from the Mertens. The fact that she has thirty-two tomato plants shows us just how large her garden is.

7. While the parenthetical insert is not a direct quote, it sounds like Bonita's voice, as she heads out to dig for potatoes. Although most of the scenes are drawn from the time Sheehan spent with the Mertens, she reconstructs this one from several long-distance telephone conversations, in which she prompted Bonita to recall the incident in painstaking detail. In doing such reconstruction, writers must remember that complete scenes and anecdotes are seldom revealed with a single question. Like Sheehan, you must prod for details: What was the temperature? Was there a moon? What were you wearing? What were your thoughts?

of the television set, as she customarily does after work, she goes out to tend her small potato strip alongside the house.[8]

The night is cool and moonless. The only light in the back yard, which is a block from the round-the-clock thrum of Interstate 235, is provided by a tall mercury-arc lamp next to the garage. Traffic is steady on the freeway, but Bonita is used to the noise of the cars and trucks and doesn't hear a thing as she digs contentedly in the yellow darkness.[9] Bonita takes pleasure in the little things in life, and she excavates for potatoes with cheerful curiosity—"like I was digging for gold."[10] Her pitchfork stabs and dents a large potato. Then, as she turns over the loosened dirt, she finds a second baking-size potato, says "Uh-huh!" to herself,[11] and comes up with three smaller ones before calling it quits[12] for the night.

"Twenty-two years ago, when Kenny and me got married, I agreed to marry him for richer or poorer," Bonita, who is forty-nine,[13] says. "I don't have no regrets, but I didn't have no idea for how much poorer. Nineteen-ninety-five has been a hard year in a pretty hard life. We had our water shut off in July *and* in August, and we ain't never had it turned off even once before, so I look on those five potatoes as a sign of hope. Maybe our luck will change."[14]

When Bonita told Kenny she was going out to dig up her potatoes, he remembers thinking, Let her have fun. If she got the ambition, great. I'm kinda out of hope and I'm tired.[15]

* * *

Kenny Merten is almost always tired[16] when he gets home, after 5 P.M., from his job at Bonnie's Barricades—a small company, started ten years ago by a woman named Bonnie Ruggless, that puts up barriers, sandbags, and signs to protect construction crews at road sites. Some days, he drives a truck a hundred and fifty miles to rural counties across the state to set up roadblocks. Other days, he does a lot of heavy lifting. "The heaviest sandbags weigh between thirty-five and forty pounds dry," he says. "Wet, they weigh fifty or sixty pounds, depending on how soaked they are. Sand holds a lot of water."[17] Hauling

---

8. The predicted frost provides a transition out of the garden background back to the main time line. Note the vivid use of "plunking" and its appropriateness to the subject matter. It's a working-class sort of word.

9. The vivid description draws us into the scene. We feel the evening chill; we see the dark, moonless sky, the light from the mercury lamp, the "yellowy darkness"; we hear the thrum of interstate traffic. Again, note Sheehan's word choices: "thrum" replicates the sound of the freeway traffic; "yellowy (Sheehan's word) darkness" is fresh and conveys the light cast by mercury lamps. While most of the detail was drawn from her phone interviews, Sheehan was able to describe the light and the sound of traffic from spending time in that yard.

10. Sheehan uses Bonita's own metaphor to capture her enthusiasm for digging for potatoes.

11. So how does Sheehan know Bonita said "Uh-huh" to herself if she wasn't present that evening? The answer: She *asked* Bonita for her reaction to finding the potato.

12. "Quits" again sounds like Bonita's words and fits the tone of the story.

13. Sheehan uses the attribution to weave in information.

14. A good quote should convey something about your subject beyond the information it contains. Here, by not cleaning up the grammar, Sheehan *shows* that Bonita's education is limited, without the writer having to actually say so. Note the use of words rather than numbers for the year. While newspapers usually use numerals in quotes, words are preferable in dialogue in magazines and books because people don't speak in numerals.

15. Kenny's thoughts are reconstructed from a telephone interview.

16. The word "tired" serves as a transition, linking his comments to a digression into his background. The digression, or loop, will ultimately take us into Bonita's background and earlier scenes, with the ones in September serving as bookends to open and close the story.

17. Again, note how specific Sheehan is in describing Kenny's work. The heavy sandbags and hundred-and-fifty-mile drive help us understand why he arrives home tired.

the sandbags is not easy for Kenny, who contracted polio when he was eighteen months old and wore a brace on his left leg until he was almost twenty. He is now fifty-one, walks with a pronounced limp, and twists his left ankle easily.[18] "Bonnie's got a big heart and hires people who are down on their luck," he says.

Kenny went to work at Bonnie's Barricades two years ago, and after two raises he earns seven dollars and thirty cents an hour.[19] "It's a small living—too small for me, on account of all the debts I got," he says. "I'd like to quit working when I'm sixty-five, but Bonnie doesn't offer a retirement plan, so there's no way I can quit then, with twenty-eight years left to pay on the house mortgage, plus a car loan and etceteras. So I'm look-ing around for something easier—maybe driving a forklift in a warehouse. Something with better raises and fringe benefits."

On a summer afternoon after work,[20] Kenny sits down in a rose-colored La-Z-Boy recliner in the Mertens' living room/dining room, turns on the TV—a nineteen-inch Syl-vania color set he bought secondhand nine years ago for a hundred dollars[21]—and watches local and national news until six-thirty, occasionally dozing off. After the news-casts, he gets out of his work uniform—navy-blue pants and a short-sleeved orange shirt with the word "Ken" over one shirt pocket and "Bonnie's Barricades" over the other[22]—and takes a bath. The house has one bathroom,[23] with a tub but no shower. Last Christ-mas, Bonita's mother and her three younger brothers gave the Mertens a shower for their basement, but it has yet to be hooked up—by Kenny, who, with the help of a friend, can do the work for much less than a licensed plumber.

Kenny's philosophy is: Never do today what can be put off until tomorrow—unless he really wants to do it. Not that he is physically lazy. If the Mertens' lawn needs mowing, he'll mow it, and the lawn of their elderly next-door neighbor, Eunice, as well. Sometimes he gets up at 4:30 A.M.—an hour earlier than necessary—if Larry, his half uncle, needs a ride to work. Larry, who lives in a rented apartment two miles from the Mertens and drives an old clunker[24] that breaks down regularly, has been married and divorced sev-eral times and has paid a lot of money for child support over the years. He is a security guard at a tire company and makes five dollars an hour. "If he doesn't get to work, he'll lose his job," Kenny says. In addition, Kenny helps his half brother Bob, who is also di-vorced and paying child support, with lifts to work and with loans.[25]

Around 7:30 P.M.,[26] Kenny, who has changed into a clean T-shirt and a pair of old jeans, fixes dinner for himself and his two sons. Dinner is often macaroni and cheese, or

---

18. Sheehan uses the sandbags to weave in the fact that Kenny had polio and now walks with a limp. As the story progresses, note how Sheehan's description is not the bland blue eyes and brown hair so many writers fall back on, but rather the details (Kenny's work uniform, his limp, for example) that give us a vivid picture of this working-class man.

19. Sheehan continues to provide information on the Mertens' finances. Again, note how specific she is, telling us his income down to the penny.

20. Time transition into an earlier scene.

21. The fact that the recliner is a La-Z-Boy and the TV a nineteen-inch Sylvania is more vivid than merely writing that he sits down in a recliner and turns on the television. Again, Sheehan uses dashes to insert this in-formation.

22. The details help further to put us into the scene.

23. Sheehan uses Kenny's after-work bath to work in more about the house.

24. The word "clunker" suits the story's tone and subject matter.

25. Sheehan backs up her statement with examples to show that Kenny is not lazy. This is important. When you make a judgment, be sure to back it up with the "evidence" that led you to that conclusion. The examples also "show" us that Kenny is kindhearted, almost to a fault. Again Sheehan does this by "showing" rather than telling. We already know he can ill afford to make loans to anybody.

26. Time transition.

spaghetti with store-bought sauce or stewed tomatoes from Bonita's mother's garden. He doesn't prepare salad or a separate vegetable ("Sauce or stewed tomatoes *is* the vegetable," he says); dessert, which tends to be an Iowa brand of ice cream, Anderson Erickson, is a rare luxury. Kenny takes the boys out for Subway sandwiches whenever he gets "a hankering" for one. Once a week—most likely on Friday, when he gets paid—he takes them out for dinner, usually to McDonald's. "It's easier than cooking," Kenny says.[27]

Because Bonita works the evening shift, Kenny spends more time with his sons than most fathers do; because she doesn't drive, he spends more time behind the wheel.[28] Christopher, a short, trim, cute boy with hazel eyes and brown hair, is one badge away from becoming an Eagle Scout, and Kenny drives him to many Scouting activities. This summer, Kenny drove Eunice, who is eighty-five, to the hospital to visit her ninety-year-old husband, Tony, who had become seriously ill in August.[29] After Tony's death, on September 12th, Kenny arranged for the funeral—choosing the casket and the flowers, buying a new shirt for Tony, and chauffeuring the boys to the private viewing at the funeral home. "Everyone was real appreciative," he says.

At around eight-thirty on evenings free from special transportation duties, Kenny unwinds by watching more television, playing solitaire, dozing again, and drinking his third Pepsi of the day. (He is a self-described "Pepsiholic.") Around nine-fifty, he drives two miles to the Luther Park nursing home for Bonita.[30]

* * *

Bonita Merten leaves the house before 1 P.M., carrying a sixteen-ounce bottle of Pepsi[31] (she, too, is a Pepsiholic), and catches the bus to work. She is dressed in her navy-blue uniform and white shoes. Since the uniforms cost thirty-three dollars, Bonita considers herself lucky to have been given a used one by a nurse's aide who quit, and she bought another, secondhand, for ten dollars.[32] Luther Park recently announced a mandatory change to forest-green uniforms, and Bonita does not look forward to having to shell out for new attire.

Bonita clocks in before one-forty-five, puts her Pepsi in the break-room refrigerator, and, with the other evening aides, makes rounds with the day aides. She and another aide are assigned to a wing with twenty long-term residents.[33] "The residents have just been laid down on top of their beds before we get there," Bonita says. "First, I change water pitchers and give the residents ice—got to remember which ones don't want ice, just want plain water. We pass out snacks—shakes fortified with proteins and vitamins, in

---

27. The details literally give us a taste for this working man's eating patterns. They also tell us something about his spending habits.

28. By inverting the clauses in this sentence, Sheehan emphasizes the more important point, that Kenny spends more time driving and with his sons than Bonita does. The structural repetition creates a pleasing rhythm; it also further emphasizes the two points.

29. Throughout the story we learn about not only the Mertens but their circle of friends and family.

30. A list allows Sheehan to sum up Kenny's routine quickly. She ends his day with his nightly trip to pick up Bonita, which shifts the focus from him to his wife and serves as a transition into her routine.

31. The sixteen-ounce Pepsi and the fact that both Mertens are Pepsiholics tells us something about their eating habits, as do the trips to Subway and McDonald's.

32. Sheehan uses the uniforms to continue laying out the Mertens' budget. By the time the story is finished, she will account for every penny the family spends—information she obtained from income-tax returns, paycheck stubs, and interviews.

33. Just as she did with Kenny, Sheehan takes us through Bonita's work routine to give us a feel for her job at Luther Park. Both descriptions are given chronologically, using the time to keep track of their movements.

strawberry, vanilla, or chocolate. They need the shakes, because they ordinarily don't want to eat their meals. While I'm doing that, the other aide has to pass out the gowns, washrags, and towels, and the Chux—great big absorbent pads—and Dri-Prides. They're adult snap pants with liners that fit inside them. We don't call them diapers, because they're not actually diapers, and because residents got their pride to be considered."[34]

At three-thirty,[35] Bonita takes a ten-minute break and drinks some Pepsi. "We start getting the residents up and giving showers before our break and continue after," Bonita says. "Each resident gets two showers a week, and it works out so's I have to shower three patients a day."

One aide eats from four-thirty to five, the other from five to five-thirty. Until August 1st, Bonita bought a two-dollar meal ticket if she liked what was being offered in the employees' dining room. When the meal didn't appeal to her—she wouldn't spend the two dollars for, say, a turkey sandwich and a bowl of cream-of-mushroom soup ("I don't like it at all")—she either bought a bag of Chee-tos from a vending machine or skipped eating altogether. On August 1st, the nursing home reduced meal tickets to a dollar.[36] "Even a turkey sandwich is worth that much," she says.

The residents eat at five-thirty, in their dining room. "We pass trays and help feed people who can't feed themselves," Bonita says. "Sometimes we feed them like a baby or encourage them to do as much as they can." At six-thirty, Bonita charts their meals—"what per cent they ate, how much they drank. They don't eat a whole lot, because they don't get a lot of exercise, either. We clear out the dining room and walk them or wheel them to their rooms. We lay them down, and we've got to wash them and position them. I always lay them on their side, because I like lying on my side. I put a pillow behind their back and a blanket between their legs. We take the false teeth out of those with false teeth, and put the dentures into a denture cup for those that will let us. A lot of them have mouthwash, and we're supposed to rinse their mouth. We're supposed to brush their teeth if they have them. After everyone is down, we chart. We check off that we positioned them and if we changed their liners. I'm supposed to get a ten-minute evening break, but I hardly ever take it. Charting, I'm off my feet, and there's just too much to do. Often we're short—I'll be alone on a hall for a few hours. The last thing we do is make rounds with the shift coming in. I clock out by nine-forty-five. Ninety-nine per cent of the time, Kenny picks me up. When I had different hours and he'd be bowling, his half brother Bob picked me up, or I took a cab for five dollars. The bus is one dollar, but it stops running by seven o'clock."[37]

Bonita has worked all three shifts at Luther Park. The evening shift currently pays fifty cents an hour more than the day shift and fifty cents less than the night shift, but days and nights involve more lifting. (In moving her patients, Bonita has injured her back more times than she can remember, and she now wears a wide black belt with straps which goes around her sacroiliac; she also uses a mechanical device to help carry heavy

---

34. Besides providing information about her job, the quote shows sensitivity toward her patients' feelings.

35. Time transition.

36. In her discussion of Bonita's work schedule, Sheehan works in how much she spends for meals and what she eats.

37. The time to use a direct quote rather than a paraphrase is when your subject expresses herself so well that you, the writer, can't improve on it. Bonita's quote is an excellent example. The detail with which she lays out her various chores comes as no accident. Sheehan, the interviewer, was there prompting her for that detail.

residents between their wheelchairs and their beds.)[38] Bonita's 1994 earnings from Luther Park were only eight hundred and sixty-nine dollars higher than her 1993 earnings, reflecting an hourly increase in wages from six dollars and fifty cents to six-sixty-five and some overtime hours and holidays, for which she is paid time and a half. This July 1st, she received the grandest raise that she has ever had in her life—seventy-five cents an hour—but she believes there is a hold-down on overtime, so she doesn't expect to earn substantially more in 1995. Luther Park gives her a ham for Easter, a turkey for Thanksgiving, ten dollars for her birthday, and twenty dollars for Christmas.[39]

Bonita rarely complains about working at the nursing home. "I don't mind emptying bedpans or cleaning up the residents' messes," she says. She regards her job, with its time clocks, uniforms, tedious chores, low wages, penny-ante raises, and Dickensian holiday rewards, as "a means to a life."

* * *

Bonita and Kenny Merten and their two sons live in a statistical land above the lowly welfare poor but far beneath the exalted rich.[40] In 1994, they earned $31,216 between them. Kenny made $17,239 working for Bonnie's Barricades; Bonita made $13,977 at Luther Park. With an additional $1,212 income from other sources, including some money that Kenny withdrew from the retirement plan of a previous employer, the Mertens' gross income was $32,428.[41] Last year, as in most other years of their marriage, the Mertens spent more than they earned.

The Mertens' story is distinctive, but it is also representative of what has happened to the working poor of their generation. In 1974, Kenny Merten was making roughly the same hourly wage that he is today, and was able to buy a new Chevrolet Nova for less than four thousand dollars; a similar vehicle today would cost fifteen thousand dollars[42]—a sum that even Kenny, who is far more prone than Bonita to take on debt, might hesitate to finance. And though Kenny has brought on some of his own troubles by not always practicing thrift and by not always following principles of sound money management, his situation also reflects changing times.

In the nineteen-sixties, jobs for high-school graduates were plentiful. Young men could easily get work from one day to the next which paid a living wage, and that's what Kenny did at the time.[43] By the mid-eighties, many of these jobs were gone. In Des Moines, the Rock Island Motor Transit Company (part of the Chicago, Rock Island & Pa-

---

38. Sheehan continues to accumulate the details of the Mertens' finances and their jobs to pull us into their lives. Here, she use parentheses to insert Bonita's on-the-job injuries into a rundown of salaries at Luther Park. By juxtaposing the two pieces of information, Sheehan "shows" us the physical price Bonita pays for very little financial reward.

39. Sheehan lists Bonita's bonuses at the end of the paragraph, where they gain added emphasis. She lets us grasp just how puny they are before adding her own spin on them in the next paragraph.

40. Here, Sheehan uses a digression similar to that which newspaper reporters refer to as a nut graph (in this case, graphs) in which she universalizes the Mertens' situation and explains what the story is about.

41. In laying out the couple's income, note how specific Sheehan is, using the exact dollars rather than rounding them off as writers normally do with figures. By doing this, she demonstrates how, with the working poor, every dollar counts.

42. By comparing car prices and Kenny's wages to those twenty years ago, Sheehan dramatically supports her point that the working poor are how worse off than ever.

43. Up to now, Sheehan has drawn on her interviews and observations of the Mertens; now she brings in research from other sources to explain why individuals like Kenny are facing harder times. Note how in talking about the working poor Sheehan always brings her point back to Kenny and Des Moines. The lesson here is that readers can identify much more with one individual than with a group of people.

cific Railroad) went belly up. Borden moved out of the city, and so did a division of the Ford Motor Company. Utility companies also began downsizing, and many factory jobs were replaced by service-industry jobs, which paid less. Although there is a chronic shortage of nurse's aides at Luther Park, those who stay are not rewarded. After fifteen years of almost continuous employment, Bonita is paid seven dollars and forty cents an hour—fifty-five cents an hour more than new aides coming onto the job.

Working for one employer, as men like Kenny's father-in-law used to do, is a novelty now. Des Moines has become one of the largest insurance cities in the United States, but the Mertens don't qualify for white-collar positions. Civil-service jobs, formerly held by high-school graduates, have become harder to obtain because of competition from college graduates, who face diminishing job opportunities themselves. Bonita's thirty-seven-year-old brother, Eugene, studied mechanical engineering at the University of Iowa, but after graduation he wasn't offered a position in his field. He went to work for a box company and later took the United States Postal Service exam. He passed. When Bonita and Kenny took the exam, they scored too low to be hired by the Post Office.

Although thirty-one per cent of America's four-person families earned less in 1994 than the Mertens did,[44] Kenny and Bonita do not feel like members of the middle class, as they did years ago. "There ain't no middle class no more," Kenny says. "There's only rich and poor."

* * *

This is where the $32,428 that the Mertens grossed last year went.[45] They paid $2,481 in federal income taxes. Their Iowa income-tax bill was $1,142, and $2,388 was withheld from their paychecks for Social Security and Medicare. These items reduced their disposable income to $26,417. In 1994, Bonita had $9.64 withheld from her biweekly paycheck for medical insurance, and $14.21 for dental insurance—a $620.10 annual cost. The insurance brought their disposable income down to $25,797.

The highest expenditures in the Mertens' budget were for food and household supplies, for which they spent approximately $110 a week at various stores and farmers' markets, for a yearly total of $5,720. They tried to economize by buying hamburger and chicken and by limiting their treats. (All four Mertens like potato chips.) Kenny spent about eight dollars per working day on breakfast (two doughnuts and a Pepsi), lunch (a double cheeseburger or a chicken sandwich),[46] and sodas on the road—an additional two thousand dollars annually. His weekly dinner out at McDonald's with his sons cost between eleven and twelve dollars—six hundred dollars a year more. Bonita's meals or snacks at work added up to about three hundred dollars. Kenny sometimes went out to breakfast on Saturday—alone or with the boys—and the meals he and his sons ate at McDonald's or Subway and the dinners that all four Mertens ate at restaurants like Bo-

---

44. More evidence of Sheehan's broader research.

45. Throughout the story, Sheehan works in data about the Mertens' income and how they spend it. Here she goes into a straightforward account of how every dollar they earned in 1994 was spent. Again, note how all the figures are exact (even down to pennies), both to give us a vivid picture of what it's like to live off $32,428 and to demonstrate how, at this level, every cent counts. Sheehan has always been known for her simple, unadorned style; here she is even more to the point, causing the facts and figures to hit harder.

46. Sheehan continues to use parentheses and dashes to insert information that provides insights into the Mertens and their lifestyle. Again, note how specific she is: It's not simply a cheeseburger, but rather a double cheeseburger.

nanza and Denny's[47] probably came to another six hundred dollars annually. David and Christopher's school lunches cost a dollar-fifty a day; they received allowances of ten dollars a week each, and that provided them with an extra two dollars and fifty cents to spend. The money the boys paid for food outside the house came to five hundred dollars a year. The family spent a total of about $9,720 last year on dining in and out; on paper products and cleaning supplies; and on caring for their cats (they have two). This left them with $16,077.

The Mertens' next-highest expenditure in 1994 was $3,980 in property taxes and payments they made on a fixed-rate, thirty-year, thirty-two-thousand-dollar mortgage, on which they paid an interest rate of 8.75 per cent. This left them with $12,097.

In April of 1994, Kenny's 1979 Oldsmobile, with two hundred and seventy-nine thousand miles on it,[48] was no longer worth repairing, so he bought a 1988 Grand Am from Bonita's brother Eugene for three thousand dollars, on which he made four payments of two hundred dollars a month. The Grand Am was damaged in an accident in September, whereupon he traded up to an eleven-thousand-dollar 1991 Chevy Blazer, and his car-loan payments increased to $285 a month.[49] Bonita has reproached Kenny for what she regards as a nonessential purchase. "A man's got his ego," he replies. "The Blazer is also safer—it has four-wheel drive."[50] The insurance on Kenny's cars cost a total of $798, and he spent five hundred dollars on replacement parts. Kenny figures that he spends about twenty dollars a week on gas, or about $1,040 for the year. After car expenses of $2,338 and after payments on the car loans of $1,655, the Mertens had $8,104 left to spend. A ten-day driving vacation in August of last year, highlighted by stops at the Indianapolis Motor Speedway, Mammoth Cave, in Kentucky, and the Hard Rock Cafe in Nashville, cost fifteen hundred dollars[51] and left them with $6,604.

The Mertens' phone bill was approximately twenty-five dollars a month: the only long-distance calls Bonita made were to her mother and to her youngest brother, Todd, a thirty-three-year-old aerospace engineer living in Seattle. She kept the calls short. "Most of our calls are incoming, and most of them are for Christopher," Bonita says. The Mertens' water-and-sewage bill was about fifty dollars a month; their gas-and-electric bill was about a hundred and fifty dollars a month. "I have a hard time paying them bills now that the gas and electric companies have consolidated," Kenny says. "Before, if the gas was seventy-five dollars and the electric was seventy-five dollars, I could afford to pay one when I got paid. My take-home pay is too low to pay the two together."[52] After paying approximately twenty-seven hundred dollars for utilities, including late charges, the Mertens had a disposable income of $3,904.

Much of that[53] went toward making payments to a finance company on two of Kenny's loans. To help pay for the family's 1994 vacation, Kenny borrowed eleven hundred dollars, incurring payments of about seventy-five dollars a month for two years and

---

47. The names of the restaurants and fast-food outlets give us a better sense of the Mertens' lives than more general terms like "fast-food outlet" or "chain restaurant."

48. The mileage "shows" us just how worn out the car was.

49. By laying out the Mertens' income and bills, Sheehan "shows" us the family can ill afford the Blazer.

50. Through Kenny's spending and his own quotes, Sheehan "shows" us that he does not always use good judgment, without the writer having to say so directly. Bonita's quote does the same for her.

51. Again, the facts speak for themselves. The family's judgment is not always good.

52. Kenny's uncorrected grammar adds texture to the story and "shows" us his limited education. The whole quote is a very telling one, vividly conveying the family's difficulty in stretching their income to meet their expenses.

53. "That" acts as a transition, linking this paragraph to the previous one.

three months, at an interest rate of roughly twenty-five per cent.[54] Kenny was more re-luctant to discuss the second loan, saying only that it consisted of previous loans he'd "consolidated" at a rate of about twenty-five per cent, and that it cost him a hundred and seventy-five dollars a month in payments. Also in 1994 he borrowed "a small sum" for "Christmas and odds and ends" from the credit union at Bonnie's Barricades; twenty-five dollars a week was deducted from his paycheck for that loan. Payments on the three loans—about forty-three hundred dollars last year[55]—left the Merten family with a budget deficit even before their numerous other expenses were taken into account.

Except in a few small instances (according to their 1994 Iowa income-tax return, Bonita and Kenny paid H & R Block a hundred and two dollars to prepare their 1993 re-turn, and they gave a hundred and twenty-five dollars to charity), it isn't possible to de-termine precisely what the rest of the Mertens' expenditures were in 1994. Several years ago, Kenny bounced a lot of checks, and he has not had a checking account since. Kenny exceeded the limits on both of their MasterCards a few years ago, and the cards were can-celled. Bonita has a J.C. Penney charge card but says, "I seldom dust it off." Now and then, Bonita went to a downtown outlet store, and if a dress caught her fancy she might put it on layaway.[56] On special occasions, she bought inexpensive outfits for herself and for Kenny. Before last year's summer holiday, she spent seven dollars on a top and a pair of shorts, and during the trip Kenny bought a seventy-five dollar denim jacket for himself and about fifty dollars' worth of T-shirts for the whole family at the Hard Rock Cafe. One consequence of Kenny's having had polio as a child is that his left foot is a size 5 ½ and his right foot a size 7. If he wants a comfortable pair of shoes, he has to buy two pairs or order a pair consisting of a 5 ½ and a 7. Often he compromises, buying sneakers in size 6 ½. David wears T-shirts and jeans as long as they are black, the color worn by Garth Brooks, his favorite country singer. Christopher is partial to name brands, and Bonita couldn't say no to a pair of eighty-nine-dollar Nikes he coveted last year. The Mertens spent about seven hundred dollars last year on clothing, and tried to economize on dry cleaning. "I dry-clean our winter coats and one or two dresses, but I avoid buying anything with a 'Dry-clean only' label," Bonita says.[57]

The Mertens' entertainment expenses usually come to a thousand dollars a year, but that amount was exceeded in 1994 when Kenny bought a mountain bike for every mem-ber of the family. The bikes (Bonita has yet to ride hers out of the driveway) cost two hundred and fifty-nine dollars apiece, and Kenny made the final payments on them ear-lier this year. This July, David rode Kenny's bike to a hardware store, and it was stolen while he was inside. Kenny yelled at David; Bonita told Kenny he was being too hard on him, and Kenny calmed down.

Bonita and Kenny don't buy books or magazines, and they don't subscribe to news-papers. (They routinely borrowed Eunice and Tony's Des Moines *Register* until Tony's death, when Eunice cancelled it.) They rarely go to the movies—"Too expensive," Kenny says—but regularly rent movies and video games, usually at Blockbuster. For amuse-ment, they often go to malls, just to browse, but when they get a serious urge to buy they

---

54. By inverting the sentence and beginning with the infinitive phrase, Sheehan places the emphasis on the most important point: that Kenny paid an exorbitant amount of interest on the loan.

55. Dashes allow Sheehan to quickly insert the amount of the loan payments.

56. The fact she put clothing on layaway is a telling detail, giving us a feel for the Mertens' lifestyle.

57. Sheehan continues to let the facts speak for themselves, allowing readers to draw their own conclusions about the Mertens' spending practices. The accumulation of facts in this paragraph alone gives us a vivid pic-ture of both their excesses and their hardships.

go to antique stores. Kenny believes in "collectibles." His most treasured possession is an assortment of Currier & Ives dishes and glasses.[58]

The Mertens have never paid to send a fax, or to send a package via Federal Express, and they aren't on-line: they have no computer. They even avoid spending money on postage: Kenny pays his bills in person. Bonita used to send out a lot of Christmas cards, but, she says, "I didn't get a whole lot back, so I quit that, too."[59] They spend little on gifts, except to members of Bonita's family.

Kenny knows how much Bonita loves red roses. Twenty-two years ago, he gave her one red rose after they had been married one month, two after they had been married two months, and continued until he reached twelve red roses on their first anniversary. He also gave her a dozen red roses when she had a miscarriage, in 1973, "to make her feel better." To celebrate the birth of David and of Christopher, he gave her a dozen red roses and one yellow one for each boy. And Kenny gives Bonita a glass rose every Christmas.

* * *

On a Sunday evening this summer,[60] the four Mertens went to Dahl's, their supermarket of choice in Des Moines. They bought four rolls of toilet paper (69 cents); a toothbrush (99 cents); a box of Rice Krispies (on sale for $1.99); eight sixteen-ounce bottles of Pepsi ($1.67); a gallon of two-per-cent milk ($2.07); a large package of the least expensive dishwasher detergent ($2.19), the Mertens having acquired their first dishwasher in 1993, for a hundred and twenty-five dollars; two jars of Prego spaghetti sauce ($3); a box of Shake 'n Bake ($1.99); two rolls of film ($10.38), one for Kenny, who owns a Canon T50 he bought for a hundred and twenty-five dollars at a pawnshop, and one for Christopher to take to Boy Scout camp in Colorado; a battery ($2.99) for Christopher's flashlight, also for camp; a pound of carrots (65 cents); a green pepper (79 cents); some Ziploc bags ($1.89); a Stain Stick ($1.89); a box of 2000 Flushes ($2.89); a package of shredded mozzarella ($1.39) to add to some pizza the Mertens already had in the freezer; and twelve cans of cat food ($3). Bonita bought one treat for herself—a box of toaster pastries with raspberry filling ($2.05). Christopher asked for a Reese's peanut-butter cup (25 cents), a bottle of Crystal Light (75 cents), and a package of Pounce cat treats ($1.05).[61] All three purchases were O.K.'d.

David, who is enchanted by electrical fixtures, was content to spend his time in the store browsing in the light-bulb section.[62] He was born with a cataract in his left eye, and the Mertens were instructed to put drops in that eye and a patch over his "good" right eye for a few years, so that the left eye wouldn't become lazy. Sometimes when they put the drops in, they told David to look up at a light. Today, David's main obsession, which apparently dates back to the eyedrops, is light. "We'd go someplace with David, and if there

---

58. Here we see still another example of the facts providing insight into the Mertens beyond their spending.

59. Throughout the story Sheehan uses few quotes, but the ones she does use say more about the family than the actual words, and so it is with this one.

60. Transition.

61. Earlier Sheehan told us the Mertens spend approximately $110 a week on food and household supplies. Here, she draws from a trip to the supermarket to show us precisely how that money is spent—even including brand names. While much of the Mertens' budget information is drawn from receipts, Sheehan wrote this account from her own observations. Again, note how she lets the facts speak for themselves.

62. Sheehan uses the shopping trip to weave in this poignant (and revealing) scene of David's fascination with lights. She in turn uses the scene to work in more information about David.

was a light with a bulb out he'd say, 'Light out,'" Bonita recalls. "We'd tell him, 'Don't worry about that,' and pretty soon he was saying, 'Light out, don't worry about that.'"

At twenty,[63] David looks fifteen. A lanky young man with copper-colored hair, hearing aids in both ears, and eye-glasses with thick lenses, he attends Ruby Van Meter, a special public high school for the city's mentally challenged. He reads at a fifth-grade level, and he doesn't read much. For years, the Mertens have been applying—without success—for Supplemental Security Income for David. In June of this year, when his application for S.S.I. was once again turned down, the Mertens hired a lawyer to appeal the decision. David has held a series of jobs set aside for slow learners (working, for instance, as a busboy in the Iowa state-house cafeteria and in the laundry room of the local Marriott hotel), but he says that his "mood was off" when he was interviewed for several possible jobs this summer, and he drifted quietly through his school vacation. He will not be permitted to remain in school past the age of twenty-one. If David could receive monthly S.S.I. checks and Medicaid, the Mertens would worry less about what will happen to him after they are gone. They have never regarded David as a burden, and although he has always been in special-education classes, they have treated him as much as possible the way they treat Christopher. Say "special ed" to Bonita, and she will say, "Both my boys are very special."

The Dahl's bill came to $44.75.[64] When Kenny failed to take money out of his pocket at the cash register, Bonita, looking upset, pulled out her checkbook. She had expected Kenny to pay for the groceries, and she had hoped that the bill would be forty dollars or less. But Kenny was short of money. "Aargh," Bonita said, softly.[65]

Bonita didn't want to write checks for groceries, because she has other ideas about where her biweekly paychecks—about four hundred dollars take-home—[66] should go. Most of her first check of the month goes toward the mortgage—$331.68 when she pays it before the seventeenth of the month, $344.26 when she doesn't. Bonita likes to put aside the second check for the two most important events in her year—the family's summer vacation and Christmas. In theory, Kenny is supposed to pay most of the other family expenses and to stick to a budget—a theory to which he sometimes has difficulty subscribing. "I don't like to work off a budget," he says. "I think it restricts you. My way is to see who we have to pay this week and go from there. I rob Peter to pay Paul and try to pay Peter back."[67] In practice, Kenny rarely pays Peter back. With his take-home pay averaging about two hundred and thirty-five dollars a week, he can't.[68]

* * *

When a consumer counsellor, who does not know the Mertens, was questioned about the family's current financial predicament—specifically, their 1994 income and expenditures—she made numerous recommendations.[69] Among her suggestions for major sav-

---

63. David's age serves as a transition into a description of him and his disability.

64. The total supermarket bill provides a transition out of the background digression on David and back to the scene at the grocery.

65. While Sheehan was present to observe Bonita's expression and hear her "Aargh," the writer learned what she was thinking by asking questions.

66. Sheehan uses the scene to weave in information, like the fact that Bonita is paid every other week and takes home roughly $400.

67. Sheehan backs up her observation that Kenny has trouble sticking to a budget with his own words.

68. The fact that Kenny is rarely able to "pay Peter back" gains added impact and lingers in our minds as we move on because of its placement at the end of the paragraph and section.

69. Sheehan now turns to an expert (a consumer counselor) to make sense of the family's financial situation and, by doing so, avoids making judgments of her own. Note how the inverted sentence serves as a transition from the narrative, or time line, into a lengthy explanatory digression.

ings was that the Mertens cut their food bills dramatically, to fifty-four hundred dollars a year. She proposed stretching the Mertens' food dollars by drastically curtailing their eating out and by buying in bulk from the supermarket. She said that Kenny should get rid of his high-interest loans, and use the money he was spending on usurious interest to convert his mortgage from thirty years to fifteen. The way Kenny and Bonita were going, the counsellor pointed out, they would not finish paying off their current mortgage until they were seventy-nine and seventy-seven years old, respectively. The Mertens' principal asset is eight thousand dollars in equity they have in their house. If the Mertens wanted to retire at sixty-five, they would need more than what they could expect to receive from Social Security.

The counsellor had many minor suggestions for economizing at the grocery store. The Mertens should buy powdered milk and mix it with one-per-cent milk instead of buying two-per-cent milk. They should cut down even further on buying meat; beans and lentils, the counsellor observed, are a nutritious and less costly form of protein. She recommended buying raisins rather than potato chips, which she characterized as "high-caloric, high-fat, and high-cost."

The counsellor had one word for the amount—between fifteen hundred and twenty-five hundred dollars—that the Mertens spent on vacations: "outlandish." Their vacations, she said, should cost a maximum of five hundred dollars a year. She recommended renting a cabin with another family at a nearby state park or a lake. She urged the Mertens to visit local museums and free festivals, and go on picnics, including "no-ant picnics"—on a blanket in their living room.

Kenny and Bonita were resistant to most of the suggestions that were passed on to them from the counsellor, who is funded mainly by creditors to dispense advice to those with bill-paying problems. According to Kenny, buying a dozen doughnuts at the supermarket and then taking breakfast to work would be "boring." Bonita says she tried powdered milk in the mid-eighties, when Kenny was unemployed, and the kids wouldn't drink it. She does buy raisins, but the boys don't really like them. Bonita and Kenny both laugh at the prospect of a no-ant picnic. "Sitting on the living-room carpet don't seem like a picnic to me," Bonita says.

Bonita surmises that the counsellor hasn't experienced much of blue-collar life and therefore underestimates the necessity for vacations and other forms of having fun. "We couldn't afford vacations in the eighties, and if we don't take them now the kids will be grown," she says. Kenny reacted angrily to the idea of the boys' eating dried beans and other processed foods. "I lived on powdered milk, dried beans, surplus yellow cheese, and that kind of stuff for two years when I was a kid," he says. "I want better for my boys."

Kenny acknowledges that he tried to confine his responses to the consumer counsellor's minor suggestions, because he realizes that her major recommendations are sound. He also realizes that he isn't in a position to act on them. He dreams of being free of debt. He has tried a number of times to get a fifteen-year mortgage, and has been turned down each time. "We both work hard, we're not on welfare, and we just can't seem to do anything that will make a real difference in our lives," he says. "So I save ten dollars a bowling season by not getting a locker at the alley to store my ball and shoes, and have to carry them back and forth. So I save twenty-five dollars by changing my own oil instead of going to Jiffy Lube. So what? Going out to dinner is as necessary to me as paying water bills."[70]

---

70. The Mertens' reaction to the counselor's advice "shows" us a great deal about the family's logic, without Sheehan having to pass judgment. In doing this, she is careful to show us also why they feel the way they do.

* * *

Kenneth Deane Merten was born poor and illegitimate to Ruby Merten in her mother's home, outside Des Moines, on October 5, 1944; his maternal relatives declined to reveal his father's name, and he never met his father.[71] Ruby Merten went on to marry a soldier and had another son, Robert. She divorced Bob's father, and later married Don Summers, a frequently unemployed laborer, with whom she had three more children. "Mr. Summers was so mean he made me stand up all night in the bed when I was eight years old," Kenny recalls. He has never hit his own sons, because "I know what it done to my life and I don't want it to get passed down." The family often moved in haste when the rent was due. Kenny attended eight or ten schools, some of them twice, before he completed sixth grade.

Kenny's mother died of cancer at twenty-seven, when he was fourteen. The three younger children stayed with Don Summers and a woman he married a month later. Kenny and Bob went to live with their maternal grandparents, and their lives became more stable. Even so, Kenny's school grades were low. "I had a hard time with math and science," he says. "Coulda been because of all the early moving around. I ain't stupid." He spent his high-school years at Des Moines Technical High School and graduated in 1964, when he was almost twenty.

Two days later, he found a job as a shipping clerk for *Look* magazine. He kept the job until 1969, and left only when it became apparent that the magazine was cutting back its operations. He drove a cab from 1969 to 1972, drank too much, and did what he calls "some rowdy rambling." He had put much of that behind him when he got a job as a factory worker at EMCO Industries, a manufacturer of muffler parts and machinery bolts, in the fall of 1972, shortly before he met Bonita.[72]

Bonita Anne Crooks was born on October 7, 1946, in Harper, Iowa. Her father, Cloyce Crooks, was employed all his working life by the Natural Gas Pipeline Company; his wife, Pauline, stayed home to take care of Bonita and her three younger brothers. Bonita was required to do chores, for which she was paid, and to deposit those earnings in a bank. She took tap-dancing lessons, wore braces on her teeth, and often went with her family on vacation to places like California and Texas. "Kenny's growing up was a lot worse than mine," she says. In 1965, Bonita graduated from a Catholic high school and became a nurse's aide, while living at home and continuing to bank her money. In 1971, she moved to Des Moines, and the following year she got a job as a keypunch operator for a large insurance company. Keypunching, however, proved too difficult for her (she couldn't combine accuracy with high speed), and she soon transferred within the company to a lower-paying position—that of a file clerk.

Bonita met Kenny in October, 1972, on a blind date that had been arranged by a friend of hers.[73] "I had been jilted by a younger man, and I knew Kenny was meant for me on our first date, when he told me he was born on October 5, 1944—exactly two years

---

71. In the earlier digression on Kenny, Sheehan focused on his employment and his daily routine. Here she sets out to piece together his early life so that we can understand how he came to this place in life. In so doing, she helps us better understand some of the choices and decisions he makes. Getting at motivation and what makes people tick is important to many of the stories we write. To do so requires careful—and sometimes sensitive—questions into an individual's early life: How far did you go in school? What kind of grades did you make? What did your father and/or mother do for a living? How many siblings did you have? What was your first job?

72. Sheehan uses his job at EMCO Industries as a transition from Kenny's background to Bonita's.

73. The couple's blind date again serves as a transition out of Bonita's background into the couple's courtship and early married life, as Sheehan continues this long digression in which she ultimately reconstructs their lives up to the present time.

and two days earlier than me," Bonita says. She and Kenny fell in love quickly and were married in a traditional ceremony at a Catholic church in Harper on June 30, 1973. The newlyweds set off for Colorado on their honeymoon, but Kenny's car, a secondhand 1966 Pontiac Bonneville convertible, broke down, and the couple ended up in the Black Hills of South Dakota. When they were courting, Kenny had asked Bonita what sort of engagement ring she wanted. She had declined a "chunky" diamond, and said that matching wedding bands would suffice. "I suspected Kenny had debts," Bonita says. "I just didn't know how many he had until we got home."

The couple moved into a modest two-bedroom house. Bonita kept her file-clerk job after David's birth, in April, 1975, but when she became pregnant with Christopher, who was born in November, 1979, her doctor ordered her to bed. From the window of her bedroom, Bonita could see the Luther Park nursing home being built "kinda like next to my back yard." She didn't return to the insurance company, because her pay couldn't cover the cost of daytime care for two children. Kenny was working days at EMCO, so in June, 1980, Bonita took a job on the 3-to-11 P.M. shift at Luther Park. She earned more there than she had as a file clerk. On some nights, Kenny drove a cab. He needed two jobs, because he regularly spent more than he and Bonita earned, just as he had overspent his own pay when he was single. Every year or two, he bought a new car. "I shouldn't have bought those new cars, but life with Don Summers made me feel completely insecure," he says. "Driving new cars gave me a sense of self-worth."[74]

Kenny lost his job at EMCO at the end of 1983. He says[75] that he had asked his supervisor for permission to take some discarded aluminum parts, and that permission was granted. But as he was driving off EMCO's premises with the parts in the bed of his pickup he was accused of stealing them. His supervisor then denied having given Kenny permission to take the parts. A demoralized Kenny didn't seek a new job for a year. He had already stopped driving the cab—after being robbed twice—and had started mowing lawns part time in the spring and summer, and doing cleanup work and shovelling snow in the fall and winter. Kenny's business failed—"There were too many unemployed guys like me out there." Many of his prized belongings were repossessed, among them a Curtis-Mathes stereo console. For two weeks in the summer of 1984, the Mertens were without gas or electricity or telephone service. They went on food stamps. Bonita felt guilty about going to work in air-conditioned surroundings while her husband and children were at home in the heat. Kenny felt humiliated when Bonita's parents visited their dark, sweltering house over the Fourth of July weekend. While Kenny has done better financially than most of his side of the family, it pains him that he hasn't done as well as Bonita's brothers, and that they regard him as a spendthrift and an inadequate provider.[76] "When they get down on Kenny, I feel like I'm caught between a rock and a crevice," Bonita says.

Kenny's starting salary at EMCO had been seven dollars an hour. By the time he was terminated, it was eight-ninety-five an hour. In 1985, he found several jobs he liked, but

---

74. Kenny's quote is insightful. He comes to the same conclusion we have: that much of his spending is to make up for his low self-esteem.

75. By attributing this account to Kenny, Sheehan indicates, without saying so, that this is his version and that she has no way of knowing whether or not the facts are accurate. Had she omitted the attribution and merely written that he asked his supervisor's permission, we would have concluded with more certainty that this is definitely what happened. Had she said he "claimed" he asked the supervisor's permission, the implication would have been that she didn't believe him. Thus, the word choice for such attribution is important.

76. In reconstructing events from your subjects' past, remember to ask about their thoughts and how they felt during pivotal experiences.

none paid more than seven dollars an hour.[77] One such job was with Bob Allen Sportswear, and he kept it until 1987, when he was let go during the off-season. He occasionally filed unemployment claims, and the family qualified for food stamps and received some groceries from food banks. During the rocky period between 1984 and 1988, Kenny tried to continue making payments on bills that he owed, in order to avoid having to declare bankruptcy, but his debts grew to the point where they exceeded his assets by "I think twelve or thirteen thousand dollars"; his creditors—mostly finance companies— got fed up with him, and then he had no choice. The Mertens were able to keep their house and their '79 Olds. Going on food stamps didn't embarrass them—the boys had to eat, and they went off food stamps whenever Kenny had a new job—but the bankruptcy filing was published in the newspaper and made Bonita feel ashamed.

In 1989, after seeing an ad on television, Kenny enrolled in electronics courses at a local vocational school and borrowed seventy-two hundred dollars to pay for his studies. His deficiency in math came back to haunt him, and he eventually dropped out. While at school, he had heard of an opening as a janitor at Ryko Manufacturing, an Iowa manufacturer of car washes. He eventually moved up to a factory job, working full time at Ryko in the early nineties for three years. Those years were happy ones. He got regular raises, and during the April-to-December busy season he earned a lot of overtime. In the summer of 1991, the Mertens flew to Seattle to visit Bonita's brother Todd. They had just enough money to cover one plane fare, and asked Bonita's brother Eugene to lend them the money for the three other tickets. Bonita took three months off that year; by then, she had worked full time at Luther Park for eleven straight years and needed a break. Kenny was proud to be the family's main provider, and wanted Bonita to stay home and take it easy.

In February, 1993, Ryko fired Kenny Merten. His supervisors said that the work he did on the assembly line was neither fast enough nor of a sufficiently high quality. He was earning eleven dollars and eighty cents an hour—almost thirty thousand dollars a year including overtime—when he was terminated. "In today's job market, first-rate companies like Ryko can afford to be selective," he says. "They want to hire young men."

Around the same time,[78] Luther Park announced that it intended to expand. The nursing home offered the Mertens thirty-nine thousand dollars for the house they had lived in for eighteen years. Kenny and Bonita accepted the offer, and were allowed to stay on, free of charge, for six months while they went house hunting. After they sold their house, it became apparent that they had been using it to supplement their income. The house they had bought for fourteen thousand eight hundred dollars had appreciated handsomely in value, but they had kept remortgaging, and now they owed twenty-nine thousand dollars on it. As a result, they netted only ten thousand dollars from the sale. The purchase price of the Mertens' new home was forty thousand dollars. They spent two thousand dollars from the sale of the old house on improvements to their new home, and this reduced the amount of the down payment they were able to afford to eight thousand dollars.

Kenny attempted to return to work at several of the companies where he had previously been employed, but they weren't hiring. It took him five months to find his current job with Bonnie's Barricades—far more arduous work, at lower wages than he had been

---

77. Sheehan continues to reconstruct the Mertens' past, focusing on their employment and their finances to piece together what it has been like to be among the working poor.

78. Transition.

paid at EMCO more than twenty years earlier. "I know I'll never be able to earn eleven-eighty an hour again," he says. "The most I can hope for is a seven-dollar-an-hour job that doesn't involve swinging sandbags. Maybe if I come home less tired at the end of the day, I can handle an evening job."[79]

* * *

This year did not get off to a good start for Kenny.[80] In January, he hocked two rings that Bonita had given him for a hundred dollars, in order to pay a utility bill. Then, three months later, true to form,[81] Kenny spotted two rings at a local pawnshop that he wanted Bonita to have—a hundred-and-ninety-nine-dollar opal ring and a three-hundred-and-ninety-nine-dollar diamond-cluster ring. He asked the pawnshop owner to take the two rings out of the showcase and agreed to make periodic twenty-dollar payments[82] on them until they were paid off.

Kenny was not worried about how he would pay for the rings, or how he would pay for the family's annual summer vacation. In September of last year, a few days after the Mertens returned from that summer's driving trip, his Grand Am was rear-ended. After the collision, in which Kenny hurt his back, he hired a lawyer on a contingency basis. The young man who had caused the accident had adequate insurance, and Kenny expected to be reimbursed for medical bills and lost wages. (He hadn't been permitted to lift heavy objects for several weeks.)[83] He also expected the insurance company to pay a sizable sum—ten or fifteen thousand dollars—for pain and suffering. Kenny's lawyer told him that he could expect the insurance company to settle with him by March. When the in-surance money failed to arrive that month, Kenny's lawyer told him to expect an offer in April, then in May, and then in June. In early July, the lawyer said that he could get Kenny sixty-five hundred dollars by the end of the month—just in time to save the Mertens' summer vacation. The insurance payment and the annual vacation had been the focus of Bonita's attention for seven months. "If you don't go on vacation, a year has gone by with nothing to show for it," she says.[84]

Bonita wanted the family to travel to Seattle to visit Todd because he had a new home and she was eager to see it. The Mertens made meticulous plans for a driving trip to the state of Washington. They decided they would get up at 4 A.M. on Saturday, August 5th, and drive to Rapid City, South Dakota. They would visit Mt. Rushmore, and Kenny, who has an eye for landscapes, would take photographs of the Devils Tower, in Wyoming, at sunrise and sunset. They would arrive at Todd's home on Wednesday, August 9th, spend a few days there, and return to Des Moines, by way of the Mall of America, in Bloomington, Minnesota, on August 19th.[85] Both Bonita and Kenny had arranged with their employers to take one week off with pay and one without.

---

79. Sheehan uses Kenny's observation as a transition out of the lengthy background digression.

80. Transition into more contemporary events that will ultimately move us back into the present time line. The account of Kenny buying the rings both fills us in on the Mertens' year to date and sets up the final scene of the story.

81. Sheehan's voice, revealing her own view.

82. Note the continued specific details: the price and kinds of rings, the amount of his payments.

83. Parenthetical expression explains why he lost earnings.

84. Quote speaks volumes about the couple's priorities.

85. The detailed description of Kenny and Bonita's vacation plans conveys the couple's excitement as the vacation nears and sets us up for their later disappointment.

Six days before their departure,[86] however, their lawyer called with crushing news: the insurance payment would not be arriving until September. The following evening, Bonita injured her shoulder lifting a patient at the nursing home, but she was still determined to have her vacation. Although Kenny was behind on almost all his bills—he had just borrowed seventy-five dollars from David to pay a water bill—he went to a bank and to his credit union on August 2nd to borrow twenty-five hundred dollars to cover the cost of the vacation, figuring he would pay off this newest loan from the insurance money in September. On the evening of August 2nd, Bonita reinjured her shoulder while helping another aide transfer a resident from her wheelchair to her bed.

Both the bank and the credit union turned Kenny down. Not only did he have too much outstanding debt of his own but he had also co-signed a loan on his half brother Bob's car. Without being able to borrow, the Mertens could not go on vacation. To make matters worse, Luther Park had sent Bonita to a doctor, and he informed her that she would require physical therapy three times a week for the next two weeks. The vacation would have to be cancelled. "When Kenny told me he'd been turned down for the loan, his jaw dropped about two inches," Bonita recalls. "Kenny was so shocked and disappointed for me that I couldn't be disappointed for myself."

The Mertens have had their share of disappointments, but they don't stay down long.[87] On the morning they had set aside to pack for their trip, Bonita baked banana bread. That evening, after she finished work, Kenny took the whole family out to dinner. From there they drove to Blockbuster and bought two videos—"Sister Act 2" (David had loved the original) and a Beatles movie. They also rented two movies, and a video game that Christopher wanted. The boys spent the following week at their grandmother's. During the second vacation week, Bonita took David to the Iowa State Fair, in town.[88] "Me and David really had fun together," she says.

Both Mertens spent a little money during the two weeks that they didn't go out West. Bonita made a payment to Fingerhut on a shelf that she had bought for David's room and on a game that she had bought him, and she finished paying Home Interiors for some mirrors, sconces, and a gold shelf that she had bought for her bedroom. "When I buy this stuff, I can see Kenny getting a little perturbed, but he doesn't say anything," she says. Later in August, the front brakes on Kenny's Blazer failed, and replacement parts cost about a hundred dollars. The labor would have cost him twice that much, but Eunice, the next-door neighbor, gave him some furniture that she no longer needed, and he bartered the furniture with a friend who is an auto mechanic. Kenny and Bonita agreed that driving with faulty brakes through the mountains on their way West would have been dangerous, so it was a blessing in disguise that they had been forced to remain at home.[89]

On Friday, September 22nd, Kenny, feeling unusually fatigued, decided to take the day off from work. After lunch, he drove Bonita to their lawyer's office. The insurance company had agreed to pay Kenny seventy-two hundred dollars. The lawyer would get a

---

86. Sheehan begins with the last-minute nature of the news, saving the news for the end of the sentence, where it gains added impact.

87. Transition.

88. While Sheehan doesn't provide the figures here, she is specific about what the Mertens did to make up for their lost vacation, telling us what videos the family bought and where they purchased them.

89. The fact that the couple came to view the lost vacation as a blessing bears out Sheehan's statement that they don't stay down long.

third—twenty-four hundred dollars—and Kenny owed twelve hundred dollars in medical bills, so he would net thirty-six hundred dollars. He had wanted more—to pay off more of his debts and bills—but this was three days after Bonita's lucky potato strike, and she was feeling optimistic.[90] She persuaded Kenny to put the agony of waiting behind them and to accept the offer.

The next day,[91] Kenny drove Bonita, David, and Christopher to the pawnshop.[92] The proprietor, Doug Schlegel, was expecting them. At the cash register, Doug handed Kenny a small manila envelope with the opal ring inside. "Hey, kiddo!" Kenny called out to Bonita as he removed the ring from the envelope. "Come here!"

Bonita tried to kiss Kenny, but he quickly moved away. "I love you," she said. After Bonita finished working the opal ring down the third finger of her left hand, checking to see whether it fitted properly, Doug told her, "You don't want to let it sit in the sun or put it in hot water."

"I know," Bonita said. "Opals are soft and touchy. They're my birthstone. I have one I bought for myself, but this is lots prettier."

Once the Mertens were back in the Blazer, Bonita asked Kenny, "Is the opal my birthday present?" Her forty-ninth birthday was coming up in two weeks.

"It's a pre-birthday present," Kenny replied. He didn't mention his plan to give her the more expensive ring—the one with the diamond cluster—[93] for Christmas, provided he could make the payments in time.

"Thank you, Kenny. I love you," Bonita said.

"Sure," Kenny said. "You love to pick on me and drive me crazy."

Bonita touched Kenny's hand. "Leave me alone, I'm driving," he told her.

When Kenny stopped at a red light, Bonita said, "You're not driving now." But the light suddenly turned green.

* * *

Throughout the fall,[94] Kenny Merten refused to fret over the very real possibility that he would have to file for bankruptcy again if he didn't get his financial house in order. He was thinking only as far ahead as Christmas—imagining himself putting the box that held the diamond-cluster ring for Bonita under the tree in their living room and marking it "Open this one last." Kenny predicts that when his brothers-in-law see the ring they will surely disapprove, but he doesn't care. "The rings shouldn't be in the budget, but they are," he says.

Kenny's mother's short life left him with a determination to marry once and to make that marriage succeed[95]—something that few of his relatives have done. Bonita has often said that one reason she loves Kenny is that he surprises her every once in a while.

---

90. The time line has now come full circle. We are back to where the story began and the present, September and the lucky potatoes. The story is winding down.

91. Time transition.

92. Sheehan has carefully cataloged the Mertens' histories and their finances. Now she moves into a scene to draw us back into their world. It is drawn from the writer's follow-up visit with the family, before completing the story. Because Sheehan has already told us about Kenny putting the rings on layaway, she does not need to interrupt the scene with an explanation.

93. Sheehan inserts this brief description to remind us of the even grander ring that is in store for Bonita.

94. Transition.

95. Because of the earlier background digression there is no need to elaborate on the mother's life and thus weaken the impact of the ending. Sheehan has carefully given us what we need to know during a quieter moment in the story.

"Diamonds are a girl's best friend, next to her husband," Kenny says. "And Bonita's worth that ring, every bit of it. After all, she puts up with me."[96]

Susan Sheehan on Reading

"Perhaps because I started writing for publication a year after graduating from college, and was fortunate enough to be published by the *New Yorker* two years after graduation, two of its finest writers inspired me. One is E. B. White. His prose is elegant. White's *Here Is New York* is still, to me, the best book ever written about the city. It's hard to forget lines like 'I heard the Queen Mary blow one midnight . . . and the sound carried the whole history of departure and longing and loss.' The Queen Mary is no longer (well, maybe it's parked in the waters off Long Beach, California), but the prose endures. Probably because I'm a writer my favorite lines by E. B. White are the closing lines of *Charlotte's Web*. 'It is not often that someone comes along who is a true friend and a good writer. Charlotte was both.' I try to be a true friend and a good writer."

Even now, before writing a long article or beginning a book, Sheehan takes down her paperback copy of Joseph Mitchell's *McSorley's Wonderful Saloon*. "Mitchell made so many of us realize that simplicity was a virtue, not a crime. I turn to 'Mazie' and re-read the opening sentence: 'A bossy, yellow-haired blonde named Mazie P. Gordon is a celebrity on the Bowery.' That and other opening lines of Joe's made it possible for me to begin *A Welfare Mother* with the simple line 'Carmen Santana is a welfare mother.'"

---

96. The quote provides a fresh, unexpected ending, vividly—and delightfully—capturing Kenny Merten.

Tom Wolfe

One of the problems with conventional nonfiction writing in the 1960s, Tom Wolfe wrote in The New Journalism, *was the "pale beige voice" of the narrator. It was like the standard announcer's droning voice, he said, signaling to readers "that a well-known bore was here again, 'the journalist,' a pedestrian mind, a phlegmatic spirit, a faded personality. . . ." To avoid this, he began experimenting with outlandish voices and shifting points of view. In "Yeager," we see him in top form, using the familiar, unflappable voice of an airline pilot to draw us into the story of one equally unflappable test pilot, Chuck Yeager.*

Wolfe has been called "the chief architect and advocate" of the New Journalism of the 1960s and 1970s. As such, he championed the use by journalists of fictional techniques, most notably scenes, dialogue, status details, characterization, including the characters' innermost thoughts and emotions. His own foray into what at the time was considered a fairly revolutionary form of journalism came in 1963 with an Esquire *article about custom car mania titled "The Kandy-Kolored Tangerine-Flake Streamline Baby."*

Wolfe himself has trouble describing the piece. "It was a garage sale, that piece," he wrote in The New Journalism, *"vignettes, odds and ends of scholarship, bits of memoir, short bursts of sociology, apostrophes, epithets, moans, cackles, anything that came into my head, much of it thrown together in a rough and awkward way. That was its virtue. It showed me the possibility of there being something 'new' in journalism."*

While the article did not take the form of a short story, it showed him the range of possibilities available to nonfiction writers. "What interested me was not simply the discovery that it was possible to write accurate nonfiction with techniques usually associated with novels and short stories," he wrote in The New Journalism. *"It was that— plus. It was the discovery that it was possible in nonfiction, in journalism, to use any literary device, from the traditional dialogisms of the essay to stream-of-consciousness, and to use many different kinds simultaneously, or within a relatively short space . . . to excite the reader both intellectually and emotionally."*

And use them he did. Both as a staff reporter at the New York Herald-Tribune *and in his freelance articles for* Esquire, *his writing during this period became highly experimental and distinctive, with the point of view shifting as many as three times within a short passage and punctuation sometimes running amok.*

His first book, The Kandy-Kolored Tangerine-Flake Streamline Baby, *was published in 1965, followed three years later by* The Pump House Gang *and* The Electric Kool-Aid Acid Test. *He has since published two novels,* Bonfire of the Vanities *and* A Man in Full, *and seven additional books of nonfiction, the most notable being the anthology* The New Journalism *and* The Right Stuff, *about the seven original United States astronauts.*

The latter, from which "Yeager" is excerpted, won the American Book Award for general nonfiction in 1979. It was included, along with two of his earlier books, on New

York University's Top 100 Works of Journalism in the United States in the twentieth century. Wolfe is also a recipient of the American Academy and Institute of Arts and Letters' Harold D. Vursell Memorial Award for distinguished service in the field of journalism.

While "Yeager" and the book demonstrate Wolfe's departure from the wild experimentation and punctuation that marked his earlier work, the Wolfe trademarks are nevertheless present: the meticulous reporting, the vivid and realistic dialogue, the reconstruction of scenes, the anything-but-beige voice. The excerpt, and indeed the entire book, is a testament to the potential for a writer to re-create scenes long after they occurred as vividly as if he'd witnessed them firsthand. When the book was published, Wolfe told the New York Time's Janet Maslin that reconstructing what happened fifteen years after the fact was actually easier than it would have been to write about it at the time. "A lot of the people involved could look back analytically," he said. "They were no longer caught up in the passion of the original moment, in which patriotism really overrode everything else, and a lot of things were thrown down the memory hole." Nevertheless, it was a painstaking process that involved interviewing the astronauts and their families and the many individuals intimately involved in the early era of manned rocket flight, as well as poring over transcripts of the post-flight debriefings of the astronauts.

Contrary to what we've typically been taught about approaching our subjects in appropriate attire, Wolfe presented himself to the NASA crew in his trademark three-piece suit. "It was useless for me to try to fit into the world of pilots, because I didn't know anything about flying," he told Maslin. "I also sensed that pilots, like people in the psychedelic life, really dislike people who presume a familiarity with the Lodge."

Yeager

ANYONE WHO TRAVELS VERY MUCH ON AIRLINES in the United States soon gets to know the voice of *the airline pilot* . . . coming over the intercom . . . with a particular drawl, a particular folksiness, a particular down-home calmness that is so exaggerated it begins to parody itself (nevertheless!—it's reassuring) . . . the voice that tells you, as the airliner is caught in thunderheads and goes bolting up and down a thousand feet at a single gulp, to check your seat belts because "it might get a little choppy" . . . the voice that tells you (on a flight from Phoenix preparing for its final approach into Kennedy Airport, New York, just after dawn):[1] "Now, folks, uh . . . this is the captain . . . ummmm . . . We've got a little ol' red light up here on the control panel that's tryin' to tell us that the *landin'* gears're not . . . uh . . . *lockin'* into position when we lower 'em . . . Now *I* don't believe that little ol' red light knows what it's *talkin'* about—I believe it's that little ol' red *light* that iddn' workin' right" . . . faint chuckle, long pause, as if to say, *I'm not even sure all this is really worth going into—still, it may amuse you* . . . "But . . . I guess to play it by the rules, we oughta *humor* that little ol' light . . . so we're gonna take her down to about, oh, two or three hundred feet over the runway at Kennedy, and the folks down there on the ground are gonna see if they caint give us a visual inspection of those ol' landin' gears"—with which he is obviously on intimate ol'-buddy terms, as with every other working part of this mighty ship—"and if I'm right . . . they're gonna tell us everything is copa*cetic* all the way aroun' an' we'll jes take her on in" . . . and, after a couple of low passes over the field, the voice returns: "Well, folks, those folks down there on the ground—it must be too early for 'em or somethin'—I 'spect they still got the *sleepers* in their eyes . . . 'cause they say they caint tell if those ol' landin' gears are all the way down or not . . . But, you know, up here in the cockpit we're convinced they're all the way down, so we're jes gonna take her on in . . . And oh" . . . (*I almost forgot*) . . . "while we take a little swing out over the ocean an' empty some of that surplus fuel we're not gonna be needin' anymore—that's what you might be seein' comin' out of the wings—our lovely little ladies . . . if they'll be so kind . . . they're gonna go up and down the aisles and show you how we do what we call 'assumin' the position'" . . . another faint chuckle (*We do this so often, and it's so much fun, we even have a funny little name for it*) . . . and the stewardesses, a bit grimmer, by the looks of them, than *that voice,* start telling the passengers to take their glasses off and take the ballpoint pens and other sharp objects out of their pockets and they show them *the position,* with head lowered . . . while down on the field at Kennedy the little yellow emergency trucks start roaring across the field—and even though

"Yeager" is reprinted from *The Right Stuff,* which was published in 1979 by Farrar, Straus and Giroux. Copyright © 1979 by Tom Wolfe. Reprinted by permission of Farrar, Straus and Giroux, LLC.

1. In this opening paragraph, Wolfe uses four voices and points of view: the airline pilot (in quotation marks, with his thoughts in parenthetical, italicized asides); his own, as narrator; what he refers to as the "downstage voice," which seems to be that of an on-the-scene commentator (in parentheses); and the reader, whom he denotes by second person. All four are anything but beige. Also known for his unorthodox use of punctuation, Wolfe throws in liberal doses of ellipses, not to indicate an omission but rather a pause or, as Wolfe has said, to create the effect of a skipped beat. The first voice is that of the narrator.

in your pounding heart and your sweating palms and your broiling brainpan you *know* this is a critical moment in your life, you still can't quite bring yourself to *believe* it because if it were . . . how could *the captain,* the man who knows the actual situation most intimately . . . how could he keep on drawlin' and chucklin' and driftin' and lollygaggin' in that particular voice of his—

Well!—who doesn't know that voice! And who can forget it!—even after he is proved right and the emergency is over.

That particular voice[2] may sound vaguely Southern or Southwestern, but it is specifically Appalachian in origin. It originated in the mountains of West Virginia, in the coal country in Lincoln County, so far up in the hollows that, as the saying went "they had to pipe in daylight."[3] In the late 1940's and early 1950's this up-hollow voice drifted down from on high, from over the high desert of California, down, down, down, from the upper reaches of the Brotherhood into all phases of American aviation.[4] It was amazing.[5] It was *Pygmalion* in reverse. Military pilots and then, soon airline pilots, pilots from Maine and Massachusetts and the Dakotas and Oregon and everywhere else,[6] began to talk in that poker-hollow West Virginia drawl, or as close to it as they could bend their native accents. It was the drawl of the most righteous of all the possessors of the right stuff: Chuck Yeager.[7]

Yeager[8] had started out as the equivalent in the Second World War, of the legendary Frank Luke of the 27th Aero Squadron in the First. Which is to say, he was the boondocker, the boy from the back country, with only a high-school education, no credentials, no cachet or polish of any sort, who took off the feed-store overalls and put on a uniform and climbed into an airplane and lit up the skies over Europe.[9]

Yeager grew up in Hamlin, West Virginia, a town on the Mud River not far from Nitro, Hurricane, Whirlwind, Salt Rock, Mud, Sod, Crum, Leet, Dollie, Ruth, and Alum Creek.[10] His father was a gas driller (drilling for natural gas in the coalfields),[11] his older brother was a gas driller, and he would have been a gas driller had he not enlisted in the Army Air Force in 1941 at the age of eighteen. In 1943, at twenty, he became a flight officer, i.e., a non-com[12] who was allowed to fly, and went to England to fly fighter planes over France and Germany. Even in the tumult of the war Yeager was somewhat puzzling to a lot of other pilots. He was a short, wiry, but muscular little guy with dark curly hair

---

2. "That particular voice" picks up on Wolfe's repetition of "particular" and "voice" and serves as a transition. We are back in the narrator's voice.

3. The saying echoes the particular voice we have been hearing and thus adds color to the narrator's.

4. Wolfe has fun playing around with the repetition of "up" and "down" to describe the voice's spread.

5. This is Wolfe, the narrator, but he has assumed the same exaggerated diction of "the voice."

6. The use of "and" rather than commas and the tacking on of "everywhere else" conveys just how far this West Virginia drawl spread.

7. These first three paragraphs have had a rolling momentum. Suddenly Wolfe puts on the brakes with the colon, causing us to pause and pay attention. When we come to "Chuck Yeager," the name receives added emphasis.

8. The repetition of the name serves as a transition.

9. Since most of us will not be familiar with Frank Luke, Wolfe follows up with a description that could fit both men. In doing so, note his fresh, colorful words: "boondocker," "feed-store."

10. This list of towns we've never heard of indicates just how far back in the hollows Yeager lived.

11. The first two repetitions of "gas driller" set up the expectation that Yeager too will become a gas driller, but then Wolfe catches us by surprise, using the third repetition to say he enlisted in the army air force instead. The whole play on words is fun to read and engages the reader.

12. The air force lingo adds flavor.

and a tough-looking face that seemed (to strangers) to be saying: "You best not be lookin' me in the eye, you peckerwood, or I'll put four more holes in your nose."[13] But that wasn't what was puzzling. What was puzzling[14] was the way Yeager talked. He seemed to talk with some older forms of English elocution, syntax, and conjugation that had been preserved up-hollow[15] in the Appalachians. There were people up there who never said they disapproved of anything, they said: "I don't hold with it." In the present tense they were willing to *help* out, like anyone else; but in the past tense they only *holped*. "H'it weren't nothin' I hold with, but I holped him out with it, anyways."[16]

In his first eight missions, at the age of twenty, Yeager shot down two German fighters. On his ninth he was shot down over German-occupied French territory, suffering flak wounds; he bailed out, was picked up by the French underground, which smuggled him across the Pyrenees into Spain disguised as a peasant. In Spain he was jailed briefly, then released, whereupon he made it back to England and returned to combat during the Allied invasion of France. On October 12, 1944, Yeager took on and shot down five German fighter planes in succession. On November 6, flying a propeller-driven P–51 Mustang, he shot down one of the new jet fighters the Germans had developed, the Messerschmitt-262, and damaged two more, and on November 20 he shot down four FW-190s. It was a true Frank Luke-style display of warrior fury and personal prowess. By the end of the war he had thirteen and a half kills. He was twenty-two years old.[17]

In 1946 and 1947 Yeager was trained as a test pilot at Wright Field in Dayton. He amazed his instructors with his ability at stunt-team flying, not to mention the unofficial business of hassling. That plus his up-hollow drawl had everybody saying, "He's a natural-born stick 'n' rudder man."[18] Nevertheless, there was something extraordinary about it when a man so young, with so little experience in flight test, was selected to go to Muroc Field in California for the X–1 project.

Muroc[19] was up in the high elevations of the Mojave Desert. It looked like some fossil landscape[20] that had long since been left behind by the rest of terrestrial evolution. It was full of huge dry lake beds, the biggest being Rogers Lake. Other than sagebrush the only vegetation was Joshua trees, twisted freaks of the plant world that looked like a cross between cactus and Japanese bonsai.[21] They had a dark petrified green color and horribly crippled branches. At dusk the Joshua trees stood out in silhouette on the fossil wasteland like some arthritic nightmare.[22] In the summer the temperature went up to 110 degrees as a matter of course, and the dry lake beds were covered in sand, and there would be windstorms and sandstorms right out of a Foreign Legion movie.[23] At night it would

---

13. Wolfe lets us know he's shifted point of view, but even the stranger assumes the Chuck Yeager voice.

14. The repetition of "what was puzzling" creates both a pleasing rhythm and a transition.

15. Note Wolfe's frequent repetition to "up-hollow" to remind us where Yeager comes from.

16. After describing the characteristics of up-hollow talk, Wolfe offers some examples.

17. Note how Wolfe begins and ends this paragraph with Yeager's age to stress how young he was when he made thirteen and a half kills. The use of exact dates emphasizes the short period of time. Note also how he uses commas rather than "and" to indicate the speed of the chain of events.

18. Wolfe again borrows from the up-hollow drawl for flavor.

19. The repetition of the name acts as a transition, or bridge.

20. "Fossil landscape" captures the essence of the desert.

21. The comparison to the more familiar cactus and Japanese bonsai helps unfamiliar readers picture the Joshua tree.

22. Just as Wolfe repeated "up-hollow," so he does "fossil" to keep the image in our minds. Sometimes writers can stretch too far for synonyms; a confident one is not afraid to repeat the right word when he finds it. Note also how Wolfe sustains the "crippled" metaphor.

23. While most of us have never been through a desert sandstorm, we are familiar with the ones in the Foreign Legion movies.

drop to near freezing, and in December it would start raining, and the dry lakes would fill up with a few inches of water, and some sort of putrid prehistoric shrimps would work their way up from out of the ooze, and sea gulls would come flying in a hundred miles or more from the ocean, over the mountains, to gobble up these squirming little throwbacks. A person had to see it to believe it: flocks of sea gulls wheeling around in the air out in the middle of the high desert in the dead of winter and grazing on antediluvian crustaceans in the primordial ooze.[24]

When the wind blew the few inches of water back and forth across the lake beds, they became absolutely smooth and level. And when the water evaporated in the spring, and the sun baked the ground hard, the lake beds became the greatest natural landing fields ever discovered, and also the biggest, with miles of room for error. That was highly desirable, given the nature of the enterprise at Muroc.

Besides the wind, sand, tumbleweed, and Joshua trees, there was nothing at Muroc except for two quonset-style hangars, side by side, a couple of gasoline pumps, a single concrete runway, a few tarpaper shacks, and some tents.[25] The officers stayed in the shacks marked "barracks," and lesser souls stayed in the tents and froze all night and fried all day. Every road into the property had a guardhouse on it manned by soldiers. The enterprise the Army had undertaken in this godforsaken place was the development of supersonic jet and rocket planes.[26]

At the end of the war the Army had discovered that the Germans not only had the world's first jet fighter but also a rocket plane that had gone 596 miles an hour in tests. Just after the war a British jet, the Gloster Meteor, jumped the official world speed record from 469 to 606 in a single day. The next great plateau would be Mach 1, the speed of sound,[27] and the Army Air Force considered it crucial to achieve it first.

The speed of sound, Mach 1,[28] was known (thanks to the work of the physicist Ernst Mach)[29] to vary at different altitudes, temperatures, and wind speeds. On a calm 60-degree day at sea level it was about 760 miles an hour, while at 40,000 feet, where the temperature would be at least 60 below, it was about 660 miles an hour. Evil and baffling things happened in the transonic zone, which began at about .7 Mach. Wind tunnels choked out at such velocities. Pilots who approached the speed of sound in dives reported that the controls would lock or "freeze" or even alter their normal functions. Pilots had crashed and died because they couldn't budge the stick.[30] Just last year Geoffrey de Havilland, son of the famous British aircraft designer and builder, had tried to take one of his father's DH 108s to Mach 1. The ship started buffeting and then disintegrated, and he was killed.[31] This led engineers to speculate that the g-forces became infinite at Mach 1, causing the aircraft to implode. They started talking about "the sonic wall" and "the sound barrier."[32]

---

24. Wolfe continues the fossil metaphor through his word choices: "prehistoric," "antediluvian," "primordial," "throwbacks."

25. Lists provide an economical means of describing Muroc Field.

26. Now that the "stage" is set, Wolfe moves on to the subject at hand, placing it at the end of the sentence and the paragraph for emphasis.

27. A quick definition of "Mach 1."

28. Since Mach 1 will become central to the story, Wolfe repeats the term and the definition both as a transition and to help us remember what it means.

29. Parentheses provide a means of inserting a quick explanation.

30. Wolfe provides a description of Mach 1 and its variations, which will become crucial to our understanding as the story unfolds.

31. The account of the de Havilland crash also serves as a setup for later developments.

32. Further explanation of Mach 1.

So this was the task that a handful of pilots, engineers, and mechanics had at Muroc. The place was utterly primitive,[33] nothing but bare bones, bleached tarpaulins, and corrugated tin rippling in the heat with caloric waves; and for an ambitious young pilot it was perfect. Muroc seemed like an outpost on the dome of the world, open only to a righteous few, closed off to the rest of humanity, including even the Army Air Force brass of command control, which was at Wright Field. The commanding officer at Muroc was only a colonel, and his superiors at Wright did not relish junkets to the Muroc rat shacks in the first place. But to pilots this prehistoric throwback of an airfield[34] became . . . shrimp heaven! the rat-shack plains of Olympus![35]

Low Rent Septic Tank Perfection . . . yes; and not excluding those traditional essentials for the blissful hot young pilot: Flying & Drinking and Drinking & Driving.[36]

Just beyond the base, to the southwest, there was a rickety windblown 1930's-style establishment called Pancho's Fly Inn, owned, run, and bartended by a woman named Pancho Barnes. Pancho Barnes wore tight white sweaters and tight pants,[37] after the mode of Barbara Stanwyck in *Double Indemnity*.[38] She was only forty-one when Yeager arrived at Muroc, but her face was so weatherbeaten, had so many hard miles on it, that she looked older, especially to the young pilots at the base. She also shocked the pants off them with her vulcanized tongue. Everybody she didn't like was an old bastard or a sonofabitch. People she liked were old bastards and sonofabitches, too. "I tol' 'at ol' bastard to get 'is ass on over here and I'd g'im a drink."[39] But Pancho Barnes was anything but Low Rent. She was the granddaughter of the man who designed the old Mount Lowe cable-car system, Thaddeus S. C. Lowe. Her maiden name was Florence Leontine Lowe. She was brought up in San Marino, which adjoined Pasadena and was one of Los Angeles' wealthiest suburbs, and her first husband—she was married four times[40]—was the pastor of the Pasadena Episcopal Church, the Rev. C. Rankin Barnes.[41] Mrs. Barnes seemed to have few of the conventional community interests of a Pasadena matron. In the late 1920's, by boat and plane, she ran guns for Mexican revolutionaries and picked up the nickname Pancho. In 1930 she broke Amelia Earhart's air-speed record for women. Then she barnstormed around the country as the featured performer of "Pancho Barnes's Mystery Circus of the Air."[42] She always greeted her public in jodhpurs and riding boots, a flight packet, a white scarf, and a white sweater that showed off her terrific Barbara Stanwyck chest.[43] Pancho's desert Fly Inn had an airstrip, a swimming pool,

---

33. The word "primitive" jogs our memory of the fossil wasteland, with its arthritic Joshua trees and windswept sand.

34. The repetition of "prehistoric throwback" again triggers our memory of the quonset-hut hangars and tarpaper-shack barracks.

35. Linking the rat-shack plains to Mount Olympus shows us its exalted status among the hot young test pilots.

36. The phrase becomes an ongoing motif.

37. The repetition of "tight" conveys just how snug those sweaters and pants were.

38. Tight sweaters and pants were synonymous with movie star Barbara Stanwyck. A reference to her enables readers to picture Pancho Barnes.

39. The quote illustrates Pancho Barnes's use of "old bastard" and "sonofabitch" and lets us hear her voice.

40. Dashes provide a quick way to insert a bit of information.

41. Wolfe supports his observation that Pancho Barnes was not Low Rent by including select pieces of her background.

42. Pancho Barnes no doubt had many other experiences during her forty-one years, but Wolfe chooses those that show her as a colorful adventurer.

43. Note that Wolfe does not use the adjective "tight" here. Instead he lets the Barbara Stanwyck reference jog the reader's memory.

a dude ranch corral, plenty of acreage for horseback riding, a big old[44] guest house for the lodgers, and a connecting building that was the bar and restaurant. In the barroom the floors, the tables, the chairs, the walls, the beams, the bar were of the sort known as extremely weatherbeaten,[45] and the screen doors kept banging.[46] Nobody putting together such a place for a movie about flying in the old days would ever dare make it as dilapidated and generally go-to-hell[47] as it actually was. Behind the bar were many pictures of airplanes and pilots, lavishly autographed and inscribed, badly framed and crookedly hung. There was an old piano that had been dried out and cracked to the point of hopeless desiccation. On a good night a huddle of drunken aviators could be heard trying to bang, slosh, and navigate their way through old Cole Porter tunes.[48] On average nights the tunes were not that good to start with. When the screen door banged[49] and a man walked through the door into the saloon, every eye in the place checked him out. If he wasn't known as somebody who had something to do with flying at Muroc, he would be eyed like some lame goddamned mouseshit sheepherder[50] from *Shane*.

The plane the Air Force wanted to break the sound barrier with was called the X–1. The Bell Aircraft Corporation had built it under an Army contract. The core of the ship was a rocket of the type first developed by a young Navy inventor, Robert Truax, during the war. The fuselage was shaped like a 50-caliber bullet—an object that was known to go supersonic smoothly. Military pilots seldom drew major test assignments; they went to highly paid civilians working for the aircraft corporations. The prime pilot for the X–1 was a man whom Bell regarded as the best of the breed. This man looked like a movie star. He looked like a pilot from out of *Hell's Angels*.[51] And on top of everything else there was his name: Slick Goodlin.

The idea in testing the X–1 was to nurse it carefully into the transonic zone, up to seven-tenths, eight-tenths, nine-tenths the speed of sound (.7 Mach, .8 Mach, .9 Mach) before attempting the speed of sound itself, Mach 1,[52] even though Bell and the Army already knew the X–1 had the rocket power to go to Mach 1 and beyond, if there *was* any *beyond*.[53] The consensus of aviators and engineers, after Geoffrey de Havilland's death, was that the speed of sound was an absolute, like the firmness of the earth.[54] The sound barrier was a farm you could buy in the sky. So Slick Goodlin began to probe the transonic zone in the X–1, going up to .8 Mach. Every time he came down he'd have a riveting tale to tell. The buffeting, it was so fierce—and the listeners, their imaginations aflame, could practically see poor[55] Geoffrey de Havilland disintegrating in midair. And the goddamned aerodynamics—and the listeners got a picture of a man in ballroom pumps skidding

44. Wolfe, the narrator, borrows from "the voice" and the "up-hollow" idiom.
45. The long list conveys just how weatherbeaten everything was.
46. Wolfe appeals to our ears as well as our eyes. We will hear this banging door again.
47. Another fresh Tom Wolfe concoction.
48. Note how Wolfe's fresh, vivid word choices capture the scene. "Huddle" aptly describes the drunken pilots semi-circled around the piano with arms on one another's shoulders. "Bang, slosh, and navigate" is far more on the mark than the verb "play." Cole Porter tunes are particularly reminiscent of the era and the setting.
49. There's that door.
50. Wolfe, the narrator, again appropriates "the voice."
51. The repetition of "looked like" is pleasing and playful to read. It also emphasizes Goodlin's movie-star good looks.
52. This explanation is a setup for further developments.
53. The italics are for emphasis.
54. The comparison helps us grasp the absoluteness of the sound barrier.
55. The narrator is again borrowing "the voice."

across a sheet of ice, pursued by bears. A controversy arose over just how much bonus Slick Goodlin should receive for assaulting the dread Mach 1 itself. Bonuses for contract test pilots were not unusual; but the figure of $150,000 was now bruited about. The Army balked, and Yeager got the job. He took it for $283 a month, or $3,396 a year; which is to say, his regular Army captain's pay.[56]

The only trouble they had with Yeager was in holding him back. On his first powered flight in the X–1 he immediately executed an unauthorized zero-g roll with a full load of rocket fuel, then stood the ship on its tail and went up to .85 Mach in a vertical climb, also unauthorized.[57] On subsequent flights, at speeds between .85 Mach and .9 Mach, Yeager ran into most known airfoil problems—loss of elevator, aileron, and rudder control, heavy trim pressures, Dutch rolls, pitching and buffeting, the lot[58]—yet was convinced, after edging over .9 Mach, that this would all get better, not worse, as you reached Mach 1. The attempt to push beyond Mach 1—"breaking the sound barrier"— was set for October 14, 1947. Not being an engineer, Yeager didn't believe the "barrier" existed.

* * *

October 14[59] was a Tuesday. On Sunday evening, October 12, Chuck Yeager dropped in at Pancho's,[60] along with his wife. She was a brunette named Glennis, whom he had met in California while he was in training, and she was such a number, so striking,[61] he had the inscription "Glamorous Glennis" written on the nose of his P–51 in Europe and, just a few weeks back, on the X–1 itself. Yeager didn't go to Pancho's and knock back a few because two days later the big test was coming up. Nor did he knock back a few because it was the weekend. No, he knocked back a few because night had come and he was a pilot at Muroc.[62] In keeping with the military tradition of Flying & Drinking,[63] that was what you did, for no other reason than that the sun had gone down. You went to Pancho's and knocked back a few and listened to the screen doors banging and to other aviators torturing the piano and the nation's repertoire of Familiar Favorites and to lonesome mouse-turd strangers wandering in through the banging doors and to Pancho classifying the whole bunch of them as old bastards and miserable peckerwoods.[64] That was what you did if you were a pilot at Muroc and the sun went down.

---

56. The explanation makes it clear that Yeager got nothing extra for risking his life to go beyond Mach 1.

57. Wolfe makes a statement about the army not being able to hold back Chuck Yeager, then offers anecdotes that show his penchant for pushing the envelope and ignoring orders. Such anecdotes are useful for adding color and for moving a story forward.

58. The long list, capped off by "the lot," backs up the statement that he encountered most known airfoil problems.

59. The repetition of "October 14" serves as a transition.

60. Because of the earlier setup we know what Pancho's is so that Wolfe doesn't have to interrupt the action to explain.

61. Instead of giving us a detailed description of Glennis, Wolfe tells us that she was "such a number, so striking" and lets our own minds fill in the picture.

62. The repetition of "knock back" adds to the humor.

63. This ongoing motif echoes the earlier reference to this tradition among the hot young pilots, and we fill in the rest: of course he did, everyone knocks back a few.

64. Wolfe is able to quickly capture the essence of an evening at Pancho's by repeating its identifying features. The use of "and" rather than commas pulls them all together in a unified package. We hear the banging screen door and Pancho calling everyone "old bastard and sonofabitch" and the huddle of drunken pilots torturing Cole Porter songs; we see the glares at the uncomfortable, unwelcome outsider.

So about eleven Yeager got the idea that it would be a hell of a kick if he and Glennis saddled up a couple of Pancho's dude-ranch horses and went for a romp, a little rat race, in the moonlight. This was in keeping with the military tradition of Flying & Drinking and Drinking & Driving,[65] except that this was prehistoric[66] Muroc and you rode horses. So Yeager and his wife set off on a little proficiency run at full gallop through the desert in the moonlight amid the arthritic silhouettes of the Joshua trees.[67] Then they start racing back[68] to the corral, with Yeager in the lead and heading for the gateway. Given the prevailing conditions, it being nighttime, at Pancho's, and his head being filled with a black sandstorm of many badly bawled songs and vulcanized oaths, he sees too late that the gate has been closed.[69] Like many a hard-driving midnight pilot before him, he does not realize that he is not equally gifted in the control of all forms of locomotion. He and the horse hit the gate, and he goes flying off and lands on his right side.[70] His side hurts like hell.[71]

The next day, Monday, his side still hurts like hell. It hurts every time he moves. It hurts every time he breathes deep. It hurts every time he moves his right arm.[72] He knows that if he goes to a doctor at Muroc or says anything to anybody even remotely connected with his superiors, he will be scrubbed from the flight on Tuesday. They might even go so far as to put some other miserable peckerwood in his place. So he gets on his motorcycle, an old junker that Pancho had given him, and rides over to see a doctor in the town of Rosamond, near where he lives. Every time the goddamned motorcycle hits a pebble in the road, his side hurts like a sonofabitch.[73] The doctor in Rosamond informs him he has two broken ribs and he tapes them up and tells him that if he'll just keep his right arm immobilized for a couple of weeks and avoid any physical exertion or sudden movements,[74] he should be all right.

Yeager gets up before daybreak on Tuesday morning—which is supposed to be the day he tries to break the sound barrier[75]—and his ribs still hurt like a sonofabitch.[76] He gets his wife to drive him over to the field, and he has to keep his right arm pinned down to his side to keep his ribs from hurting so much. At dawn, on the day of a flight, you could hear the X–1 screaming long before you got there. The fuel for the X–1 was alcohol and liquid oxygen, oxygen converted from a gas to a liquid by lowering its temperature to 297 degrees below zero. And when the lox, as it was called,[77] rolled out of the hoses and into the belly of the X–1, it started boiling off and the X–1 started steaming and screaming like a teakettle.[78] There's quite a crowd on hand, by Muroc standards . . .

---

65. The now familiar motif provides cohesiveness.

66. The adjective jogs our memory, and we fill in with Wolfe's earlier description of the fossil wasteland.

67. Still more reminders of his earlier description to help us visualize the scene.

68. Wolfe shifts to present tense to make this scene more immediate.

69. Note how Wolfe creates added drama by backing into this sentence. He begins by reminding us of the circumstances—Yeager has been at Pancho's all evening, singing, cussing, knocking back a few too many. At the end of this recitation, he catches us off guard: we too see the closed gate too late. Thus, by placing this at the end of the sentence, it gains added emphasis and drama.

70. The use of "and" rather than commas mimics Yeager catapulting through the air.

71. Again the narrator and "the voice," or Yeager, are one.

72. The repetition of "hurts" conveys just how bad his side hurts.

73. Wolfe continues to borrow "the voice": "miserable peckerwood," "old junker," "sonofabitch."

74. Note the use of "and" rather than commas to link the doctor's actions and words.

75. In case we've lost track, Wolfe reminds us that this is the day of the big flight.

76. Yeager's voice and point of view.

77. Wolfe explains in layman's terms what liquid oxygen is.

78. The teakettle simile lets us hear what the X–1 sounds like.

perhaps nine or ten souls. They're still fueling the X–1 with the lox, and the beast is wailing.[79]

The X–1 looked like a fat orange swallow with white markings.[80] But it was really just a length of pipe with four rocket chambers in it. It had a tiny cockpit and a needle nose, two little straight blades (only three and a half inches thick at the thickest part) for wings, and a tail assembly set up high to avoid the "sonic wash" from the wings. Even though his side was throbbing and his right arm felt practically useless, Yeager figured he could grit his teeth and get through the flight—except for one specific move he had to make.[81] In the rocket launches, the X–1, which held only two and a half minutes' worth of fuel, was carried up to twenty-six thousand feet underneath the wings of a B–29. At seven thousand feet, Yeager was to climb down a ladder from the bomb bay of the B–29 to the open doorway of the X–1, hook up to the oxygen system and the radio microphone and earphones, and put his crash helmet on and prepare for the launch, which would come at twenty-five thousand feet. This helmet was a homemade number.[82] There had never been any such thing as a crash helmet before. Throughout the war pilots had used the old skin-tight leather helmet-and-goggles. But the X–1 had a way of throwing the pilot around so violently that there was danger of getting knocked out against the walls of the cockpit. So Yeager had bought a big leather football helmet—there were no plastic ones at the time[83]—and he butchered it with a hunting knife until he carved the right kind of holes in it, so that it would fit down over his regular flying helmet and the earphones and the oxygen rig. Anyway, then his flight engineer, Jack Ridley, would climb down the ladder, out in the breeze, and shove into place the cockpit door, which had to be lowered out of the belly of the B–29 on a chain. Then Yeager had to push a handle to lock the door airtight. Since the X–1's cockpit was minute, you had to push the handle with your right hand. It took quite a shove.[84] There was no way you could move into position to get enough leverage with your left hand.

Out in the hangar[85] Yeager makes a few test shoves on the sly, and the pain is so incredible he realizes that there is no way a man with two broken ribs is going to get the door closed. It is time to confide in somebody, and the logical man is Jack Ridley.[86] Ridley is not only the flight engineer but a pilot himself and a good old boy from Oklahoma to boot. He will understand about Flying & Drinking and Drinking & Driving through the goddamned Joshua trees.[87] So Yeager takes Ridley off to the side in the tin hangar and says: Jack, I got me a little ol' problem here. Over at Pancho's the other night I sorta . . . dinged my goddamned ribs. Ridley says, Whattya mean . . . *dinged?* Yeager says, Well, I guess you might say I damned near like to . . . *broke* a coupla the sonsabitches.[88] Whereupon Yeager sketches out the problem he foresees.

---

79. Note how Wolfe has used personification to bring the X–1 to life: It looks like a fat orange swallow and screams and wails.

80. Wolfe uses the X–1's most distinctive features to give us a tight, yet vivid picture of the plane.

81. Wolfe uses a dash to set off the one critical move Yeager will have trouble executing, giving it added emphasis.

82. The narrator again uses "the voice."

83. Dashes are used to insert information.

84. The brevity of the sentence emphasizes the point.

85. Place transition moves out of the explanation and back to the scene. It resumes in present tense, for immediacy.

86. Yeager's point of view.

87. Yeager's voice and point of view.

88. Since Wolfe is reconstructing the scene and dialogue, he uses no quotation marks, but nevertheless captures Yeager's voice.

Not for nothing[89] is Ridley the engineer on this project. He has an inspiration. He tells a janitor named Sam to cut him about nine inches off a broom handle. When nobody's looking, he slips the broomstick into the cockpit of the X–1 and gives Yeager a little advice and counsel.

So with that added bit of supersonic flight gear Yeager went aloft.[90]

At seven thousand feet he climbed down the ladder into the X–1's cockpit, clipped on his hoses and lines, and managed to pull the pumpkin[91] football helmet over his head. Then Ridley came down the ladder and lowered the door into place. As Ridley had instructed, Yeager now took the nine inches of broomstick and slipped it between the handle and the door. This gave him just enough mechanical advantage to reach over with his left hand and whang the thing shut. So he whanged[92] the door shut with Ridley's broomstick and was ready to fly.

At 26,000 feet the B–29 went into a shallow dive, then pulled up and released Yeager and the X–1 as if it were a bomb. Like a bomb it dropped and shot forward (at the speed of the mother ship) at the same time. Yeager had been launched straight into the sun. It seemed to be no more than six feet in front of him, filling up the sky and blinding him. But he managed to get his bearings and set off the four rocket chambers one after the other. He then experienced something that became known as the ultimate sensation in flying: "booming and zooming." The surge of the rockets was so tremendous, forced him back into his seat so violently, he could hardly move his hands forward the few inches necessary to reach the controls. The X–1 seemed to shoot straight up in an absolutely perpendicular trajectory, as if determined to snap the hold of gravity via the most direct route possible.[93] In fact, he was only climbing at the 45-degree angle called for in the flight plan. At about .87 Mach the buffeting started.[94]

On the ground the engineers could no longer see Yeager. They could only hear . . . that poker-hollow West Virginia drawl.[95]

"Had a mild buffet there . . . jes the usual instability . . ."

Jes the usual instability?

Then the X–1 reached the speed of .96 Mach, and that incredible caint-hardlyin' aw-shuckin' drawl said:

"Say, Ridley . . . make a note here, will ya?" (*if you ain't got nothin' better to do*) ". . . elevator effectiveness *regained*."

Just as Yeager had predicted, as the X–1 approached Mach 1, the stability improved. Yeager had his eyes pinned on the machometer. The needle reached .96, fluctuated, and went off the scale.

And on the ground they heard . . . that voice:

"Say, Ridley . . . make another note, will ya?" (*if you ain't too bored yet*) ". . . there's somethin' wrong with this ol' machometer . . ." (faint chuckle) ". . . it's gone kinda screwy on me . . ."

---

89. The narrator again appropriates "the voice's" idiom.
90. Wolfe returns to past tense.
91. "Pumpkin" captures both the shape and size of the helmet.
92. Yeager's voice.
93. Wolfe put us in the cockpit and allows us to share Yeager's ride.
94. Because of the earlier account of Geoffrey de Havilland's ill-fated flight, we know that this is where the real danger begins. Thus, Wolfe stops summing up the action and plays out the scene and the dialogue to build the drama and tension.
95. The point of view shifts back and forth between Yeager and the ground engineers. Since they can no longer see Yeager, Wolfe gives us their exchange. He begins with Yeager's voice.

And in that moment, on the ground, they heard a boom rock over the desert floor—just as the physicist Theodore von Kármán had predicted many years before.

Then they heard Ridley back in the B–29: "If it is, Chuck, we'll fix it. Personally I think you're seeing things."

Then they heard Yeager's poker-hollow drawl again:

"Well, I guess I am, Jack . . . And I'm still goin' upstairs like a bat."

The X–1 had gone through "the sonic wall" without so much as a bump. As the speed topped out at Mach 1.05, Yeager had the sensation of shooting straight through the top of the sky. The sky turned a deep purple and all at once the stars and the moon came out—and the sun shone at the same time. He had reached a layer of the upper atmosphere where the air was too thin to contain reflecting dust particles. He was simply looking out into space. As the X–1 nosed over at the top of the climb, Yeager now had seven minutes of . . . Pilot Heaven . . . ahead of him. He was going faster than any man in history, and it was almost silent up here, since he had exhausted his rocket fuel, and he was so high in such a vast space that there was no sensation of motion. He was master of the sky. His was a king's solitude, unique and inviolate, above the dome of the world. It would take him seven minutes to glide back down and land at Muroc. He spent the time doing victory rolls and wing-over-wing aerobatics while Rogers Lake and the High Sierras spun around below.

* * *

On the ground[96] they had understood the code as soon as they heard Yeager's little exchange[97] with Ridley. The project was secret, but the radio exchanges could be picked up by anyone within range. The business of the "screwy machometer" was Yeager's deadpan way of announcing that the X–1's instruments indicated Mach 1.[98] As soon as he landed, they checked out the X–1's automatic recording instruments. Without any doubt the ship had gone supersonic. They immediately called the brass at Wright Field to break the tremendous news. Within two hours Wright Field called back and gave some firm orders. A top security lid was being put on the morning's events. That the press was not to be informed went without saying. But neither was anyone else, anyone at all,[99] to be told. Word of the flight was not to go beyond the flight line. And even among the people directly involved—who were there and knew about it, anyway—there was to be no celebrating. Just what was on the minds of the brass at Wright is hard to say. Much of it, no doubt, was a simple holdover from wartime, when every breakthrough of possible strategic importance was kept under wraps. That was what you did—you shut up about them. Another possibility was that the chiefs at Wright had never quite known what to make of Muroc.[100] There was some sort of weird ribald aerial tarpaper mad-monk squadron up on the roof of the desert out there . . .[101]

In any case, by mid-afternoon Yeager's tremendous feat had become a piece of thunder with no reverberation. A strange and implausible stillness settled over the event.[102]

---

96. Transition takes us out of the sky and back to earth.

97. Echoes Yeager's voice.

98. Yeager explains the real meaning of the exchange.

99. The repetition conveys the extent of the secrecy.

100. Wolfe's point of view. He indicates he is speculating with the phrases "no doubt" and "another possibility."

101. Point of view of the Wright chiefs.

102. Wolfe uses sound metaphors to describe the secrecy that surrounded Yeager's historic breaking of the sound barrier.

Well . . . there was not supposed to be any celebration, but come nightfall . . .[103] Yeager and Ridley and some of the others ambled over to Pancho's. After all, it was the end of the day, and they were pilots.[104] So they knocked back a few. And they had to let Pancho in on the secret, because Pancho had said she'd serve a free steak dinner to any pilot who could fly supersonic and walk in here to tell about it, and they had to see the look on *her* face. So Pancho served Yeager a big steak dinner and said they were a buncha miserable peckerwoods all the same, and the desert cooled off and the wind came up and the screen doors banged and they drank some more and bawled some songs over the cackling dry piano and the stars and the moon came out and Pancho screamed oaths no one had ever heard before and Yeager and Ridley roared and the old weatherbeaten bar boomed and the autographed pictures of a hundred dead pilots shook and clattered on the frame wires and the faces of the living fell apart in the reflections, and by and by they all left and stumbled and staggered and yelped and bayed for glory before the arthritic silhouettes of the Joshua trees.[105] Shit!—there was no one to tell except Pancho and the goddamned Joshua trees![106]

* * *

Over the next five months Yeager flew supersonic in the X–1 more than a dozen times, but still the Air Force insisted on keeping the story secret.[107] *Aviation Week* published a report of the flights late in December (without mentioning Yeager's name)[108] provoking a minor debate in the press over whether or not *Aviation Week* had violated national security—and *still* the Air Force refused to publicize the achievement until June of 1948. Only then was Yeager's name released. He received only a fraction of the publicity that would have been his had he been presented to the world immediately, on October 14, 1947, as the man who "broke the sound barrier."[109] This dragged-out process had curious effects.[110]

In 1952 a British movie called *Breaking the Sound Barrier,* starring Ralph Richardson, was released in the United States, and its promoters got the bright idea of inviting the man who had actually done it, Major Charles E. Yeager of the U.S. Air Force, to the American premiere. So the Air Force goes along with it and Yeager turns up for the festivities.[111] When he watches the movie, he's stunned. He can't believe what he's seeing. Far from being based on the exploits of Charles E. Yeager, *Breaking the Sound Barrier* was inspired by the death of Geoffrey de Havilland in his father's DH 108. At the end of the movie a British pilot solves the mystery of "the barrier" by *reversing the controls* at the critical moment during a power dive. The buffeting is tearing his ship to pieces, and every rational process in his head is telling him to *pull back* on the stick to keep from crash-

---

103. The ellipses are again used not to indicate an omission, but rather to replicate a dramatic pause.

104. The fact that they are pilots and it is the end of the day jogs our memory: We know it's time for Flying & Drinking and Drinking & Driving.

105. This long recitation repeating the earlier description of Pancho's Fly Inn and a night of Flying & Drinking and Drinking & Driving—all connected by "and" rather than commas—gives us the sense of it being one hell of a celebration.

106. Yeager's point of view.

107. Transition compresses time.

108. The parentheses emphasize the omission of Yeager's name.

109. The paragraph relates the aftermath of Yeager's feat.

110. Sentence serves as a transition into the one that follows.

111. Wolfe again shifts to the present tense for immediacy.

ing—and he *pushes it down* instead . . . and zips right through Mach 1 as smooth as a bird, regaining full control![112]

Breaking the Sound Barrier happened to be one of the most engrossing movies about flying ever made. It seemed superbly realistic, and people came away from it sure of two things: it was an Englishman who had broken the sound barrier, and he had done it by reversing the controls in the transonic zone.

Well, after the showing they bring out Yeager to meet the press, and he doesn't know where in the hell to start. To him the whole goddamned picture is outrageous. He doesn't want to get mad, because this thing has been set up by Air Force P.R. But he is not happy. In as calm a way as he can word it on the spur of the moment, he informs one and all that the picture is an utter shuck from start to finish. The promoters respond, a bit huffily, that this picture is not, after all, a documentary. Yeager figures, well, anyway, that settles that. But as the weeks go by, he discovers an incredible thing happening. He keeps running into people who think he's the first *American* to break the sound barrier . . . and that he learned how to *reverse the controls* and zip through from the Englishman who did it first. The last straw comes when he gets a call from the Secretary of the Air Force.[113]

"Chuck," he says, "do you mind if I ask you something? Is it true that you broke the sound barrier by reversing the controls?"

Yeager is stunned by this. The Secretary—*the Secretary!*—of the U.S. Air Force!

"No, sir," he says, "that is . . . not correct. Anyone who reversed the controls going transonic would be dead."

Yeager and the rocket pilots who soon joined him at Muroc had a hard time dealing with publicity. On the one hand, they hated the process. It meant talking to reporters and other fruit flies[114] who always hovered, eager for the juice . . . and invariably got the facts screwed up . . . *But that wasn't really the problem, was it!*[115] The real problem was that reporters violated the invisible walls of the fraternity. They blurted out questions and spoke boorish words about . . . all the unspoken things!—about fear and bravery (they would say the words!) and how you *felt* at such-and-such a moment! It was obscene! They presumed a knowledge and an intimacy they did not have and had no right to. Some aviation writer would sidle up and say, "I hear Jenkins augered in. That's too bad." *Augered in!*—a phrase that belonged exclusively to the fraternity!—coming from the lips of this *ant* who was *left behind* the moment Jenkins made his first step up the pyramid long, long ago.[116] It was repulsive! But on the other hand . . . one's healthy pilot ego loved the glory—wallowed in it!—lapped it up!—no doubt about it! The Pilot Ego—ego didn't come any bigger![117] The boys wouldn't have minded the following. They wouldn't have minded appearing once a year on a balcony over a huge square in which half the world is assembled. They wave. The world roars its approval, its applause, and breaks into a sustained thirty-minute storm of cheers and tears (moved by my righteous stuff!). And then it's over. All that remains is for the wife to paste the clippings in the scrapbook.

---

112. Because of the earlier account, Wolfe does not need to explain here that de Havilland did not break the sound barrier.

113. This has the flavor of Yeager relating the story to Wolfe, and thus to the readers ("Well," "they bring out . . . ," "the whole goddamned picture," "the last straw").

114. The voice of Yeager and the other test pilots.

115. The voice and point of view of the downstage observer.

116. The voice of Yeager and the other test pilots in the fraternity.

117. The downstage observer. The capitalization of Pilot Ego underscores just how big those egos are.

A little adulation on the order of the Pope's; that's all the True Brothers at the top of the pyramid really wanted.

* * *

Yeager received just about every major decoration and trophy that was available to test pilots, but the Yeager legend grew not in the press, not in public,[118] but within the fraternity. As of 1948, after Yeager's flight was made public, every hot pilot in the country knew that Muroc was what you aimed for if you wanted to reach the top. In 1947 the National Security Act, Title 10, turned the Army Air Force into the U.S. Air Force, and three years later Muroc Army Air Base became Edwards Air Force Base, named for a test pilot, Glenn Edwards, who had died testing a ship with no tail called the Flying Wing. So now the magic word became *Edwards.* You couldn't keep a really hot, competitive pilot away from Edwards. Civilian pilots (almost all of whom had been trained in the military)[119] could fly for the National Advisory Committee for Aeronautics (NACA) High Speed Center[120] at Edwards, and some of the rocket pilots did that: Scott Crossfield, Joe Walker, Howard Lilly, Herb Hoover, and Bill Bridgeman, among them. Pete Everest, Kit Murray, Iven Kincheloe, and Mel Apt joined Yeager as Air Force rocket pilots. There was a constant rivalry between NACA and the Air Force to push the rocket planes to their outer limits. On November 20, 1953, Crossfield, in the D–558–2, raised the speed to Mach 2. Three weeks later Yeager flew the X–1A to Mach 2.4. The rocket program was quickly running out of frontiers within the atmosphere; so NACA and the Air Force began planning a new project, with a new rocket plane, the X–15, to probe altitudes as high as fifty miles, which was well beyond anything that could still be called "air."

My God!—to be a part of Edwards in the late forties and early fifties![121]—even to be on the ground and hear one of those incredible explosions from 35,000 feet somewhere up there in the blue over the desert and know that some True Brother had commenced his rocket launch . . . in the X–1, the X–1A, the X–2, the D–558–1, the horrible XF–92A, the beautiful D–558–2 . . . and to know that he would soon be at an altitude, in the thin air at the edge of space, where the stars and the moon came out at noon, in an atmosphere so thin that the ordinary laws of aerodynamics no longer applied and a plane could skid into a flat spin like a cereal bowl on a waxed Formica counter and then start tumbling, not spinning and not diving, but tumbling, end over end like a brick . . . In those planes, which were like chimneys with little razor-blade wings on them, you had to be "afraid to panic," and that phrase was no joke. In the skids, the tumbles, the spins, there was, truly, as Saint-Exupéry had said, only one thing you could let yourself think about:[122] *What do I do next?* Sometimes at Edwards they used to play the tapes of pilots going into the final dive, the one that killed them, and the man would be tumbling, going end over end in a fifteen-ton length of pipe, with all aerodynamics long gone, and not one prayer left, and he knew it, and he would be screaming into the microphone, but not for Mother or for God or the nameless spirit of Ahor, but for one last hopeless crumb of information about the loop: "I've tried A! I've tried B! I've tried C! I've tried D! Tell me what else I can try!" And then that truly spooky click on the machine. *What do I do*

---

118. The repetition of "not" emphasizes the secrecy and lack of publicity.
119. Parentheses used to insert information.
120. On first reference, always spell out the entire name of an agency that is commonly called by its initials.
121. The voice of the downstage observer.
122. The narrator's voice and point of view.

next?[123] (In this moment when the Halusian Gulp is opening?) And everybody around the table would look at one another and nod ever so slightly, and the unspoken message was:[124] Too bad! There was a man with the right stuff.[125] There was no national mourning in such cases, of course. Nobody outside of Edwards knew the man's name. If he were well liked, he might get one of those dusty stretches of road named for him on the base. He was probably a junior officer doing all this for four or five thousand a year. He owned perhaps two suits, only one of which he dared wear around people he didn't know.[126] But none of that mattered!—not at Edwards—not in the Brotherhood.[127]

What made it truly beautiful (for a True Brother!)[128] was that for a good five years Edwards remained primitive and Low Rent, with nothing out there but the bleached prehistoric shrimp terrain and the rat shacks and the blazing sun and the thin blue sky and the rockets sitting there moaning and squealing before dawn.[129] Not even Pancho's changed—except to become more gloriously Low Rent. By 1949 *the girls* had begun turning up at Pancho's in amazing numbers. They were young, lovely, juicy, frisky—and there were so many of them, at all hours, every day of the week! And they were not prostitutes, despite the accusations made later. They were just . . . well, just young juicy girls in their twenties with terrific young conformations and sweet cupcakes and loamy loins. They were sometimes described with a broad sweep as "stewardesses," but only a fraction of them really were. No, they were lovely young things who arrived as mysteriously as the sea gulls who sought the squirming shrimp. They were moist labial piping little birds who had somehow learned that at this strange place in the high Mojave lived the hottest young pilots in the world and that this was *where things were happening.* They came skipping and screaming in through the banging screen doors at Pancho's—and it completed the picture of Pilot Heaven. There was no other way to say it.[130] Flying & Drinking and Drinking & Driving and Driving & Balling.[131] The pilots began calling the old Fly Inn dude ranch "Pancho's Happy Bottom Riding Club," and there you had it.

All of this was fraternal bliss. No pilot was shut off from it because he was "in the public eye." Not even the rocket aces were isolated like stars. Most of them also performed the routine flight-test chores. Some of Yeager's legendary exploits came when he was merely a supporting player, flying "chase" in a fighter plane while another pilot flew the test aircraft. One day Yeager was flying chase for another test pilot at 20,000 feet when he noticed the man veering off in erratic maneuvers.[132] As soon as he reached him on the radio, he realized the man was suffering from hypoxia, probably because an oxygen hose connection had come loose. Some pilots in that state became like belligerent drunks— prior to losing consciousness. Yeager would tell the man to check his oxygen system, he'd tell him to go to a lower altitude, and the man kept suggesting quaint anatomical im-

---

123. The ill-fated pilot's voice.
124. The narrator.
125. The ground crew's voice and point of view.
126. The narrator.
127. The downstage observer.
128. The downstage observer.
129. Wolfe jogs our memory with enough detail to enable us to fill in the rest of his earlier description of Muroc Field.
130. The voice and point of view of the downstage observer.
131. Wolfe repeats the familiar refrain, this time with a new twist.
132. Wolfe follows the general statement with an anecdote that serves as an example of Yeager flying "chase."

possibilities[133] for Yeager to perform on himself. So Yeager hit upon a ruse that only he could have pulled off. "Hey," he said, "I got me a problem here, boy. I caint keep this thing running even on the emergency system. She just flamed out. Follow me down." He started descending, but his man stayed above him, still meandering. So Yeager did a very un-Yeager-like thing. He *yelled* into the microphone![134] He yelled: "Look, my dedicated young scientist—*follow me down!*" The change in tone—*Yeager yelling!*—penetrated the man's impacted hypoxic skull. *My God! The fabled Yeager! He's yelling—Yeager's yelling!—to me for help! Jesus H. Christ!*[135] And he started following him down. Yeager knew that if he could get the man down to 12,000 feet, the oxygen content of the air would bring him around, which it did. *Hey! What happened?*[136] After he landed, he realized he had been no more than a minute or two from passing out and punching a hole in the desert. As he got out of the cockpit, an F–86 flew overhead and did a slow roll sixty feet off the deck and then disappeared across Rogers Lake. That was Yeager's signature.

Yeager was flying chase one day for Bill Bridgeman, the prime pilot for one of the greatest rocket planes, the Douglas Skyrocket, when the ship went into a flat spin followed by a violent tumble.[137] Bridgeman fought his way out of it and regained stability, only to have his windows ice up. This was another common danger in rocket flights. He was out of fuel, so that he was now faced with the task of landing the ship both deadstick and blind. At this point Yeager drew alongside in his F–86 and became his eyes. He told Bridgeman every move to make every foot of the way down . . . as if he knew that ol' Skyrocket like the back of his hand . . . and this was jes a little ol' fishin' trip on the Mud River . . . and there was jes the two of 'em havin' a little poker-hollow fun in the sun . . . and that lazy lollygaggin' chucklin' driftin' voice was still purrin' away . . . the very moment Bridgeman touched down safely.[138] You could almost hear Yeager saying to Bridgeman, as he liked to do:

"How d'ye hold with rockets now, son?"

That was what you thought of when you saw the F–86 do a slow roll sixty feet off the deck and disappear across Rogers Lake.

Yeager had just turned thirty. Bridgeman was thirty-seven. It didn't dawn on him until later that Yeager always called him *son*. At the time it had seemed perfectly natural. Somehow Yeager was like the big daddy of the skies over the dome of the world. In keeping with the eternal code, of course, for anyone to have suggested any such thing would have been to invite hideous ridicule. There were even other pilots with enough Pilot Ego to believe that *they* were actually better than this drawlin' hot dog. But no one would contest the fact that as of that time, the 1950's, Chuck Yeager was at the top of the pyramid, number one among all the True Brothers.

And *that voice* . . .[139] started drifting down from on high. At first the tower at Edwards began to notice that all of a sudden there were an awful lot of test pilots up there with West Virginia drawls. And pretty soon there were an awful lot of fighter pilots up there with West Virginia drawls. The air space over Edwards was getting so caint-hardly

---

133. A delicate way of getting around an obscenity.
134. The downstage observer.
135. More of the downstage observer.
136. The downstage observer.
137. Wolfe provides still another anecdote to show Yeager flying "chase."
138. The beginning and end of this sentence is the voice of Wolfe, the narrator. He uses ellipses first for an insert that echoes Yeager's voice and then to emphasize each succeeding observation.
139. The story (in this case, chapter) comes full circle, returning to "the voice" that opened it.

super-cool day by day, it was terrible. And then that lollygaggin' poker-hollow air space began to spread, because the test pilots and fighter pilots from Edwards were considered the pick of the litter and had a cachet all their own, wherever they went, and other towers and other controllers began to notice that it was getting awfully drawly and down-home up there, although they didn't know exactly why. And then, because the military is the training ground for practically all airline pilots, it spread further, until airline passengers all over America began to hear that awshuckin' driftin' gone-fishin' Mud River voice coming from the cockpit . . . "Now, folks, uh . . . this is the captain . . . ummmm . . . We've got a little ol' red light up here on the control panel that's tryin' to tell us that the *lan*din' gears're not . . . uh . . . *lock*in' into position . . ."[140]

But so what! What could possibly go wrong! We've obviously got a man up there in the cockpit who doesn't have a nerve in his body! He's a block of ice! He's made of 100 percent righteous victory-rolling True Brotherly stuff.[141]

---

140. This time the voice moves in reverse, from the test pilots to the other air force pilots to the airline pilots to the particular voice and situation that opened the piece.
141. The excerpt ends with the downstage observer.

Acknowledgments

No book is ever the product of one person's efforts, and certainly this one was no different. It would never have become a reality without the help and suggestions of many supportive friends and colleagues. My biggest thanks goes to my editor, Anthony English, whose polite persistence nudged me into carrying through on an idea that had been incubating for years. Throughout the process of selecting, annotating, and securing permissions, Tony was always just an e-mail away, and usually responded with a delightful simile that made me think perhaps he should be the one writing the author introductions, and not me.

Special thanks go to Jim Conaway, Jon Franklin, Walt Harrington, and Norman Sims, whose wise counsel I have valued over the years and who were always ready with a thoughtful response whenever I e-mailed them for help and advice. All four have made tremendous contributions to the genre and our understanding of it.

Thanks to Elizabeth Bennett, Robert Cashdollar, and Iris Day for their comments on the manuscript. Thanks to Steve Satterfield for helping me track down the various stories and securing copies.

Thanks especially to the writers themselves for taking time to review my annotations and share their thoughts on reading and writing. I am grateful to them and the publications that originally published their stories for letting me reprint them here. I also want to thank the other writers who generously shared work that space prevented me from including.

My final word of appreciation is for my late father, who gave me a dictionary and my first typewriter and encouraged me to write.

About the Editor

*P*atsy Sims is the author of *The Klan, Cleveland Benjamin's Dead: A Struggle for Dignity in Louisiana's Cane Country,* and *Can Somebody Shout Amen! Inside the Tents and Tabernacles of American Revivalists,* which was named a noteworthy book of 1988 by the *New York Times Book Review.* She also co-authored the narration for the award-winning documentary "The Klan: A Legacy of Hate." Prior to writing books, she worked as a staff writer and editor for the New Orleans *States-Item,* the *San Francisco Chronicle,* and the *Philadelphia Inquirer.* Her work has appeared in the *New York Times Book Review,* the *Washington Post Magazine, Southern* magazine, the Discovery Channel's *TDC* magazine, and most major American newspapers. She has been a recipient of creative writing fellowships from the National Endowment for the Arts and the Washington, D.C., Commission on the Arts and Humanities and two Associated Press Awards for investigative-interpretive reporting. She directs the creative nonfiction writing programs at the University of Pittsburgh and Goucher College.

LaVergne, TN USA
12 April 2011
223825LV00004B/13/P